Nature's God

ALSO BY MATTHEW STEWART

The Management Myth
The Courtier and the Heretic
Monturiol's Dream
The Truth About Everything

NATURE'S GOD

*The Heretical Origins of
the American Republic*

MATTHEW STEWART

W. W. NORTON & COMPANY
New York London

For information about permission to reproduce selections from this book,
write to Permissions, W. W. Norton & Company, Inc.,
500 Fifth Avenue, New York, NY 10110

For information about special discounts for bulk purchases, please contact
W. W. Norton Special Sales at specialsales@wwnorton.com or 800-233-4830

Manufacturing by RR Donnelley Harrisonburg
Book design by Helene Berinsky
Production manager: Julia Druskin

ISBN 978-0-393-06454-4

W. W. Norton & Company, Inc.,
500 Fifth Avenue, New York, N.Y. 10110
www.wwnorton.com

W. W. Norton & Company Ltd.
Castle House, 75/76 Wells Street, London W1T 3QT

1 2 3 4 5 6 7 8 9 0

For Myo

Contents

Preface   1

1. The Dirty Little Screw of the American Revolution   9

2. Pathologies of Freedom   39

3. Epicurus's Dangerous Idea   77

4. On the Genealogy of Nature's God   130

5. Self-Evident Truths   201

6. The Pursuit of Happiness   263

7. The Empire of Reason   314

8. The Religion of Freedom   392

Acknowledgments   437

Notes   439

Index   535

Nature's God

Preface

ONCE IN A WHILE YOU FIND AN OLD BOOK THAT SPEAKS TO you in such a way that you feel as if you are the first person ever to have read it. You might come across it in a secondhand store, on a friend's bookshelf, or on the curb in certain parts of Brooklyn where the neighbors like to share their old finds. This project began many years ago when I discovered Ethan Allen's *Oracles of Reason* of 1784 in an electronic database at a public library. And it is distinctly possible that I *was* the first person to have read it in a very long time, if you don't count the half-dozen scholars who decided that the book was so bad that there was no point in reading it.

The *Oracles* isn't *that* bad, I found, though that isn't why it had such an impact on me. In my pixelated discovery I saw something oddly familiar and at the same time quite out of place with anything I remembered from schoolboy stories about the swashbuckling hero of the assault on Fort Ticonderoga. In fact, I saw something remote from anything I had ever learned about the American Revolution. The scholars also seemed to think that there was something strange about the work. Worse than bad, they said, it was stolen. Ethan Allen, according to the scholarly consensus to this day, had attempted to pass off another man's book as his own.

Sometimes, too, you come across an individual in history who makes you wonder why you have never heard of him before: the kind of person whose very existence stands like a riddle over the old stories. That was how I felt upon encountering Thomas Young—the man historians have fingered as the actual perpetrator of Ethan Allen's crime against literature. Every American deserves a "Forgotten Founding Father." Mine turned out to be Thomas Young. The more I learned about his life and ideas, the more I felt that I was awakening from a dogmatic slumber. Much of what I thought I knew about the people and the ideas that guided the American Revolution wasn't quite right. (And much of what the scholars thought they knew about Allen, Young, and their alleged literary conspiracy turned out to be wrong.)

Ethan Allen and Thomas Young were just two of the many individuals involved in the complicated event we call the American Revolution, and the book that lay between them represents just one among the many philosophical exercises put forward by America's founders, who were after all just about as eager to disagree with one another as to start a revolution. As I picked up the trail of clues that led from one book to another, I inevitably ended up very far from the point where the project began. Still, at every twist in this voyage of discovery, I found myself looking back to the story of these two men and their (supposed) collaboration. It's a small story in the scheme of things, yet I still imagine that it holds the key to the only question about the American Revolution that really matters. It tells us what we need to know about the revolutionary part of the Revolution: the part that changed the world for good.

I SHOULD SINGLE OUT one other text that nudged this project along at a critical moment. This one bore the curious title "Apple and Worm," and it came to me by regular mail. It, too, gave me a feeling of privilege, as if I were its only reader—and the feeling was, once again, disconcertingly close to the reality. In order to explain its impact, however, I should say something more about the nature of the mystery I saw in the work of Ethan Allen and Thomas Young.

The enigma that prodded me on this journey back into the past had to do with a certain set of alien presences, in a manner of speaking. That is, it was about the existence in revolutionary America of a set of ideas that, according to all sides in the usual debates, should not have been there. Perhaps the most troublesome of these philosophical specters could be summarized in a word (if I may substitute a name for an idea): Spinoza. There was—and is—no meaningful evidence of any direct influence at all in revolutionary America of the Dutch philosopher Benedict de Spinoza (1632–1677). To add to the conundrum, wherever I sensed the inexplicable presence of Spinoza, another philosopher was reliably to be found lurking in the vicinity: Locke. Now, it was not at all surprising to discover favorable mention of the English philosopher John Locke (1632–1704), who is widely and correctly regarded as the single most important philosophical influence on America's revolutionary leaders. But Locke and Spinoza are the chalk and cheese of the early Enlightenment, or so it has long been maintained. One was moderate in all things; the other a thoroughgoing radical. One was supposedly a devout follower of Jesus; the other was known in his own day as "the atheist Jew."

From the German philosopher Gottfried Wilhelm Leibniz (1646–1716), I had already absorbed the suggestion that there was something more to Locke than the usual stories allow, that he was much closer to Spinoza (and to certain ancient materialist philosophers) than he or his successors let on.[1] Could it be that Locke himself—perhaps indirectly, maybe even without intending it—was the original source of those alien presences in American thought? Still, as I waded back into Locke's treatises, I found myself getting lost in the morass of qualifications and circumlocutions that constitute so much of his work. With the modern, Anglo-American scholarship unanimously, even stridently opposed to any impeachment of Locke's Englishness or his piety, it seemed that Leibniz's hypothesis could never amount to more than a dubious conjecture.

It was at this point that "Apple and Worm" landed in my mailbox.

Its author, Wim Klever, is a professor emeritus at Erasmus University in Rotterdam and has devoted a lifetime to the study of the Dutch Enlightenment, early modern philosophy, and Spinoza in particular.[2] Having read my earlier book on Spinoza and Leibniz, in which I had mooted some of my vague suspicions about a radical Locke, he thought his unpublished manuscript might be of interest.[3] Indeed it was. Sometimes you can only be sure that you've seen something after someone else tells you what you saw. More than confirmation, Klever's work provided explanation and provocation. Here were not mere hunches or conjectures, but evidence, line by line and word for word, of a side of Locke last glimpsed only by his more perceptive contemporaries.

The strange partnership between two seventeenth-century philosophers may seem a long way from the American Revolution, never mind Ethan Allen and Thomas Young. For me, however, it was a necessary part of a wider reshuffling of the stories that have long made up the popular narratives in the history of philosophy. This rearrangement of the history was in turn a necessary part of a fresh look at the Enlightenment, which I take to be a much richer and more consequential body of thought than even its proponents today seem to allow. And this revision of the Enlightenment brought me back with renewed energy to those consummate men of ideas, America's founders, who rode the preceding thrust of the history of philosophy as if on the tip of a spear.

AS A FINAL PRELIMINARY, I should say something about the unusual sense in which I would like the title of this book to be understood. In their own time, Ethan Allen, Thomas Young, and a surprising number of their fellow founders were identified as "infidels" and "atheists." They were also called—more accurately, but mostly to the same effect—"deists." Allowing for the inevitable idiosyncrasies of personality and circumstances, we could describe them loosely as "heterodox." That is, they had some religion, but it wasn't by and large of the kind that the representatives of the mainstream religions of their time found acceptable. From the moment of creation to the present, there have been many attempts—most of them misinformed, some shamelessly deceitful—to deny or emend this basic fact of American history.[4] Yet the interesting question has never been about its truth but its interpretation. What exactly did it mean to be an "infidel," "atheist," or "deist"? And what does it tell us, if anything, that a reputedly godly country came to be founded by so many ungodly leaders?

In most versions of America's revolutionary history, the term "deism," if it appears at all, is taken to refer to a superficial theological doctrine about a "watchmaker God" who fashions a world of mechanical wonders and then walks away to the sound of ticking noises. Deism, according to this line of interpretation, was just a watery expression of the Christian religion, adulterated somewhat with the platitudes of the Enlightenment. It was the opposite of atheism, as the dictionary tells us, and it should count as thumpingly religious by modern standards. It arose in Britain around the turn of the eighteenth century and arrived in America in a moderate and conciliatory mood, quite different from the atheistic Enlightenment that took hold in France and elsewhere. The informed consensus today further supposes that deism was a detachable doctrine, present to some degree among the educated elites in revolutionary America, but only incidentally connected with the political ideology of its revolutionaries.

All of this, I now think, is not quite right. "Deism" in its own day referred not to a superficial theological doctrine but to a comprehensive intellectual tradition that ranged freely across the terrain we now associate with ethics, political theory, metaphysics, the philosophy of mind, and epistemology. It was an astonishingly coherent and systematic body of thought, closer to a way of being than any particular dogma, and it retained its essential elements over a span of centuries, not decades. In origin and substance, deism was neither British nor Christian, as the conventional view supposes, but largely ancient, pagan, and continental, and it spread in America far beyond the educated elite. Although America's revolutionary deists lavished many sincere expressions of adoration upon their deity, deism is in fact functionally indistinguishable from what we would now call "pantheism"; and pantheism is really just a pretty word for atheism. While deism could often be associated with moderation in politics, it served principally to advance a system of thought that was revolutionary in its essence and effects. This essentially atheistic and revolutionary aspect of deism, I further contend, is central to any credible explanation of the revolutionary dimension of the American Revolution. In a word, America's founders were philosophical radicals.

By "radical" I mean something more than that they aimed to change the order of society in a fundamental way or that they searched for the deepest roots of problems. The opposite of radical is not "moderate" or "conservative" but "common." Notwithstanding the many variations and exceptions that prove the rule, the common experience of human beings naturally gives rise to a certain shared set of ideas about what we are, how the world works, and how we ought to organize our moral and political existence, or so I will argue. This common consciousness is useful in a limited way for the purpose of making it through the everyday struggles of lives that, in the scheme of things, are not very long or broad. At least since Socrates began stirring up trouble in the Athenian marketplace, radical philosophers have maintained that there is something deeply flawed in these common ideas about things, something that induces us to betray ourselves and even participate in our own enslavement when those ideas are applied on any scale larger than that of daily life. Not coincidentally, the ideas of the common consciousness—though distinct from religion—are the same ones that make religion in all its popular and traditional forms credible. Which is why radical philosophers—though often endowed with a profound sense of piety and sometimes emerging from within religious traditions themselves—naturally tend toward heterodoxy.

The best illustration of the power and impact of America's original philosophical radicalism may be discovered in the first sentence of the nation's first founding document. Many historians today take for granted that the reference in the preamble of the Declaration of Independence to "the laws of Nature and of Nature's God" amounts to a gesture of conventional piety—and no doubt it was written partly in order to be read in this way. Religious conservatives today routinely celebrate it as proof that America was founded as a Christian nation.

These and similar interpretations serve mainly to express some deep and persistent assumptions about the nature of human experience: that we govern ourselves through acts of faith; that all authority must rest on the assertion of belief in some higher authority; and that all would be well if we could return to the simple faith of our fathers.

Yet "Nature's God" properly belongs to the radical philosophical religion of deism. It refers to nothing that we commonly mean by the term "God," but rather to something closer to "Nature." It tells us that we are and always have been the source of our own authority; that we govern ourselves not through acts of faith but through acts of understanding; and that if we should find ourselves beholden to some other imagined authority, this can only mean that we have constructed the conditions of our own servitude. The Declaration of Independence—precisely where it superficially seems to invoke the blessing of the established religion—really stands for an emancipation of the political order from God.

One might well ask why we should care about the paradoxical ideas of America's founders and their more exotic philosophical precursors. After all, nothing is true because a great philosopher said it was so, and no one is obligated to do anything just because an eighteenth-century rebel leader said it should be done. But I will argue that the radical philosophy of America's founders remains the best way to explain the persistence, the power, and the prosperity of the modern liberal order around the world to this day. Ever since Plato conceived of his republic, people have speculated about what might happen if philosophers should rule the world. We no longer need to wonder. "The present is an age of philosophy; and America, the empire of reason," said the American revolutionary Joel Barlow.[5] I aim to show that he was mostly right about that.

1

The Dirty Little Screw of
the American Revolution

W HAT DOES IT MEAN TO BE AN AMERICAN? ARE SOME
Americans more "real" than others? If so, then surely Ethan
Allen should have counted as one of the most real of all Americans.
He was raised on the roughest edge of the New England frontier, in
the kind of settlement where the cabins were hacked straight out of
the forest, where the people watered their rum with hard cider, and
where every tub was expected to stand on its own bottom.[1] He could
hoot like an owl with such skill, it was said, that the real owls would
hoot right back. He was free from the taint of schoolhouse learning. His mind, he defiantly proclaimed, was "nursed principally, in
the Mountainous wilds of America."[2] He achieved fame and fleeting
glimpses of wealth in the American way, by always keeping his eye on
the main chance. He almost made it as an iron-manufacturing mag-
nate before he almost made it as a real estate tycoon before he finally
found his place in history as the leader of a people's militia and the
spiritual founder of the state of Vermont. Like the nation he helped
to create, Ethan Allen was a rugged giant, enterprising and ambitious,
supremely confident in his own abilities, and convinced of the rightness of his cause, whatever it happened to be.

As uprisings go, the squatters' revolt in the Green Mountains that Allen led seems a distinctly American affair, a kind of prequel in miniature of the Revolution that followed. It featured hardy settlers, distant and oppressive overlords (in New York and New Hampshire in this case), an unimaginably fertile plot of land for the taking, and much talk about the unalienable rights of man and the consent of the governed. The talk may not have been as eloquent as what was soon to come from Philadelphia, but it was every bit as fierce in its demand for self-government. When the news about Lexington and Concord broke at the end of April 1775, the leader of the Green Mountain Boys raised his sights above the squabbling hills and, whatever other motives were at work in his busy mind, displayed something that his countrymen called patriotism and that we may describe simply as courage. It took courage to lead a pack of eighty-three hillbillies through the stony gates of Fort Ticonderoga on the dawn of May 10, 1775. It took courage of another sort when, face-to-face with the only woken officer of the King's garrison, still in his pajamas, Allen supposedly demanded the surrender of the mightiest fort in North America "in the name of the great Jehovah, and the Continental Congress"[3]—given that, as one historian noted, he had a commission from neither.[4] And it was courage all the same even if, as some later suggested, his actual words were more along the lines of "Come out of there you damned British sons of whores!"[5]

When the hero of Ticonderoga returned from thirty-two very hard months as America's first celebrity prisoner of war, George Washington himself was there to welcome him back with honors. "His fortitude and firmness seemed to have placed him out of the reach of misfortune. There is an original something about him that commands admiration, and his long captivity and sufferings have only served to increase, if possible, his enthusiastic Zeal," Washington told the Continental Congress.[6] The French consul and adventurer John Hector St. John de Crèvecoeur, too, thought that Allen was "one of the most interesting men in the United States, a wholly original being, like none other."[7] Herman Melville would later describe the hero of Green Mountains as "a wild beast; but of a royal sort."[8] "His spirit was essentially Western, and herein is his peculiar Americanism." And he lives on in the age of the shopping mall, in a certain way, as the archetypal hero of every spaghetti western and space adventure film. It seems only natural that in 1939 a pair of New York business-men, looking for a moniker as American as the colonial-style furniture they were selling, decided to name their company after Ethan Allen, thereby giving millions of Americans the false impression that the prophet of Ticonderoga was—in an irony that the man himself would surely have appreciated—some kind of revolutionary carpenter.

Yet Ethan Allen did something that real Americans don't custom-arily do. He wrote a book. Specifically, he wrote a *philosophy* book, a thoughtful, complicated, weirdly metaphysical, 477-page philoso-phy book. More to the point, the philosophy in his book involved a full-throttle assault on the Christian religion. Ethan being Ethan, the thing he finally stuffed between covers in 1784 was a lively affair. The full title gives some idea of the substance and the style: **REASON THE ONLY ORACLE OF MAN**, *or a* **Compenduous** [sic] **System** *of* **Natural RELIGION**. *Alternately ADORNED with Confu-tations of a variety of DOCTRINES incompatible to it; Deduced from the most exalted Ideas which we are able to form of the* **DIVINE and Human** CHARACTERS, AND FROM THE **Universe in General**. In the page headers and in his own correspondence, Allen chewed this mouth-ful down to *The Oracles of Reason*. Among the freethinking people of Vermont, it came to be known as "Ethan Allen's Bible."

Allen did not disguise the target of this philosophical pitchfork of a book. The pope hauls in "twenty Millions Sterling pr annum," and the Protestant holy men pull down another ten million, he explained to a friend. "In order to carry on this Priestcraft, the Clergy must invalidate the law of Nature, Reason is presented as Carnal, and depraved, and the natural State, a condition of mankind, to be damnable, to make way for their mysteries, insperations, and pious frauds, and thus most of the Human race, have been miserably Priest-ridden," he declaimed. "To remedy the human species, from this Ghostly Tyranny, (as far as in me lay,) was the Object of my writing, the Oracles of Reason, an object worthy of Gen'l Allen, whatever his success may be."[9]

Among the better sort of people in those times, there was a name for people like Ethan Allen: "infidel." He "denys the Being of a God and Denys that there is an Infernal Spirit existing," said one horrified Yorker.[10] Ethan and his equally obnoxious brothers were "notorious for blasphemous expressions in conversation, and ridiculing everything sacred," according to an advertiser in a Connecticut newspaper, who offered a hundred-dollar reward to anyone who could bring them in to face charges of blasphemy.[11] There was a more polite word for such wayward types at the time, too, and Allen himself used it in the preface of his book: "In the circle of my acquaintance (which has not been small) I have generally been denominated a Deist, the reality of which I never disputed, being conscious I am no Christian, except mere infant baptism makes me one."

Allen struck everybody, including himself, as a man of action, separated at birth from the printed word by miles of muddy trails. But in the years after the war he seemed to become a man of the book—his own book. In its pages, he confided to a friend, "you read my very soul."[12] He put everything on the line—and then borrowed some more. He mortgaged huge tracts of land along the shores of Lake Champlain to cover the cost of printing. Then he went to court and staved off creditors long enough to get the job done. Allen was a man who appreciated the value of a dollar; and yet there was something in him that demanded redemption through the printed word, something perhaps whose very existence might have seemed doubtful or unclear without the comforting reflection of reproducible type on paper. Even as he chased the grandest abstractions into a bewildering forest of arguments, dropping markers here and there in sentences that strayed far from their starting points, he never lost the conviction that "this method of scribbling" was the means to truth. No literary novelist ever suffered more from the vanity of writerly ambition, that longing to leave one's own time behind and enter into the conversation of the centuries. In his letters, just to make sure that the centuries got the point, he stopped calling himself a "General" and took to signing off instead as "Ethan Allen, The Philosopher."

He knew it wasn't going to happen without a fight—nothing good ever does. "However you may . . . censer my performance, I presume you will not impeach me with cowardice," he told his friend.[13] "I expect that the clergy, and their devotees, will proclaim war with me, in the name of the Lord . . . But I am a hardy mountaineer, and have been accustomed to the dangers and horrors of War, and captivity, and scorn to be intimidated by threats, if they fight me, they must absolutely produce some of their tremendous fire, and give me a sensitive scorching."

The clergy did not disappoint. The Reverend Josiah Sherman, a prominent minister in those parts, promptly assaulted the *Oracles* in a polemic that landed the first punch in its title: *A Sermon to Swine*.[14] The Reverend Timothy Dwight, the future president of Yale College, perhaps finding the comparison with pigs too favorable, perceived in Allen's work "the deformity, the venom, and the ill nature of the toad."[15] The so-called Philosopher of the Green Mountains, he sniffed, was "the great Clodhopping oracle of man."[16] The Reverend Nathan Perkins, rather less imaginatively, pilloried Allen as "an awful infidel, one of ye wickedest men yet ever walked this guilty globe."[17] When the offices of Allen's publisher in Bennington caught fire, sending all but a small number of the 1,500 expensively printed copies of the *Oracles* up in smoke, the defenders of the faith were quick to detect an interposition from on high. Others, more plausibly, suspected the publisher himself, who may have feared association with such a controversial work.

Allen's assault on the religion of Abraham proved to be a very bad career move. It crimped his political aspirations after the war, and the consequences proved much worse in the afterlife. In the hustling, self-absorbed aftermath of its successful Revolution, America wanted easy-to-love heroes of uncomplicated virtue and unremarkable religion. Allen was too popular to ignore, but too impious to celebrate. It didn't take long for the chroniclers of the new nation to understand that the situation called for surgery. So they lobotomized him, posthumously speaking. They excised "The Philosopher" and left behind a shell of tall tales about an up-country buffoon who could outrun deer, twist pennies with his teeth, and wrestle bears to the ground.[18] By the time the editor of one of the nation's first biographical dictionaries got his hands on Allen, he was reduced to "a man born for troublesome times." In a better age, it was said, "he might only have been distinguished for his great bodily strength, or rude, boisterous behavior."[19]

As for the book on which this bumptious hick squandered his fame, his fortune, and whatever there was of his very soul: informed opinion settled fast and furious. Jared Sparks—minister, historian, president of Harvard College, and one of Tocqueville's main informants— pronounced it "a crude and worthless performance, in which truth and error, reason and sophistry, knowledge and ignorance, ingenuity and presumption, are mingled together in a chaos, which the author denominates a system."[20] Allen's subsequent biographers repeated Sparks's judgment—and in many cases his exact words. (In 1902, for example, Charles Walter Brown described Allen's book as a "crude and worthless performance, in which truth and error" and so on are min- gled in a sentence lifted verbatim, but without acknowledgment, from Sparks.[21]) Even today, only a very few historians take note of the fact that Ethan Allen wrote a book, and almost all of them dispatch with the work in a few curt and familiar phrases. The combination of vitriol, imprecision, and borrowed contumelies strongly suggests that the crit- ics decided early on that there was little need to read a book that was so awful in every way.

That was too bad. Ethan Allen's Bible will never count as a Great Book, to be sure, though it does occasionally succeed in its deter- mined effort to bring back souvenirs of the sublime. Herman Mel- ville might well have been thinking of Allen, too, when he wrote, in a semi-autobiographical vein, "With the soul of an Atheist, he wrote down the godliest things."[22] Considered on its own, the *Oracles* is remarkable enough as the achievement of a man with Allen's evident lack of formal education. But what really makes it worthy of attention, strange as it may sound, is its lack of originality.

The way Allen told the story, the *Oracles* was a *solo* enterprise. It was about one man and his bottle of whiskey in a backwoods cabin, going *mano a mano* with the Great Jehovah and 1,800 years of civilization. "The Bible and a Dictionary have been the only books, which I have made use of," he declared in the book's preface. "As to being a Deist, I know not strictly speaking, whether I am one or not, for I have never read their writings." The pages that follow, however, are haunted by doctrines, arguments, and tropes that no one familiar with the preceding centuries of philosophy will suppose emerged spontaneously out of the forest floor of the Green Mountains. Even the informal title, as an early critic in the *Vermont Gazette* pointed out, appears to have been lifted from one of those books Allen never read—*The Oracles of Reason* of 1693 by the English deist Charles Blount.[23] Timothy Dwight thought it obvious that Allen's work was a "contemptible plagerism of every hackneyed, worn-out, half-rotten dogma of the English deistical writers," and accused its author of "meanness" in "denying the sources from whence they were so visibly borrowed."[24]

What is still more surprising, though, is that the philosophical specters that populate Ethan Allen's Bible hail from much farther and deeper into the history of philosophy than the narrow set of ideas now typically associated with the deist philosophers who flourished in Britain for a brief period around the turn of the eighteenth century. From the serenity of his mountain lair, Ethan Allen appears to have rediscovered an infinite, centerless, and eternal universe; a nearly pantheistic deity coeval, coeternal, and coextensive with this unending cosmos; a human body composed of the constant flux and reflux of material particles; a natural world of constant transformation in which nothing is ever truly created or destroyed; and a host of other speculative visions that seem both older and more profound than the best-of-all-possible-worlds of watchmaker Gods and providential blandishments with which deism has long been identified.

The inexplicably erudite character of Ethan Allen's homegrown opus certainly raises a question about his soul, or more exactly, how well he knew it. How could a mountain man know so much more about the history of philosophy than he seemed to think he knew? Did he find himself or did he lose himself in his own book? Generally speaking, is it possible to write a book without knowing what you are doing? However that may be, the book's oddly unconscious scholarship raises a more immediate question about how well we know the nation its author helped to create. Ethan Allen's unread book testifies to the presence in the remotest regions of revolutionary America of modes of thought that have almost universally been regarded as too old, too radical, and too continental to have played a role in the foundation of the American Republic. Opening its pages is like discovering an empty bottle of whisky on the moon. The fact that it is not a particularly well-argued bottle is beside the point. Its mere existence is enough to overturn all the usual stories.

For the nation's chroniclers, Ethan Allen's awful book was a problem that grew worse with age. Even those who said the work was too bad to read continued to suspect that it packed in much more learning than its brain-deficient author was entitled to claim. The solution to the problem this time took the form of a stunning allegation. In 1852—long after the last potential witnesses had been laid to rest—the historian and Reverend Zadock Thompson lifted the first eyebrow. "No person who is familiar with Allen's other writings can read the *Oracles of Reason* without suspicion that another person was concerned in its composition," he intoned.[25] Allen's biographers eagerly seconded Thompson's suspicion—in cases, word for word.[26]

In 1937, the historian George Pomeroy Anderson finally dropped the bombshell, or so it seemed to the hardy band of Vermont historians entrusted with consecrating the glory of their state.[27] Anderson took note of a number of passages in which the author of Ethan Allen's Bible evinced familiarity with the medicine and astronomy of his time. He then counted up the number of Latin-derived words per page. On the supposition that pages with a high number of such Latinate words could not have come from the mind of the hirsute, vaguely Teutonic leader of the Green Mountain Boys, he concluded that Ethan Allen was responsible for fewer than 100 of the 477 pages of his own Bible. "In putting himself forward as the sole author of the book," Anderson thundered, "Allen laid himself open to the charge of intellectual dishonesty, if not downright plagiarism." Recent scholars, with one notable exception,[28] have by and large accepted Anderson's verdict as final. It is now recorded among the facts of history that Ethan Allen's book was the scene of a crime.

HOW DO WE DECIDE who deserves a place in history? Generations of devoted American history buffs have spent countless hours reading and writing long books about the American Revolution without ever having come across the name of Dr. Thomas Young. Yet Young was, among other things, one of the people who brought us the original Tea Party. It was he who stood before the assembled people of Boston on November 29, 1773, and first articulated the transparently illegal proposition that the only way to get rid of the East India Company's loathsome cargo was to throw it into the harbor.[29] It was he who, on the evening of December 16, 1773, kept a crowd of thousands at the Old South Church shouting and clapping with a satirical speech on "the ill effects of tea on the constitution" while his best friends, dressed as Mohawks, quietly set off to turn the Boston harbor into a briny tea-pot.[30] And it turns out that kicking off the event that many years later came to be called the Boston Tea Party was not the most consequential of Thomas Young's many unsung contributions to the founding of the American Republic.

If it is true, as John Adams famously observed, that the American Revolution took place "in the minds of the people, and this was effected from 1760 to 1775 . . . before a drop of blood was shed at Lexington,"[31] then many of America's most celebrated founders should properly be counted as consequences rather than causes of the course of events. In his diary Adams himself described the Tea Party on the morning after as "an Epocha in History,"[32] and yet he wrote about it as an enthusiastic bystander, not a participant, much less an instigator. George Washington seems to have had few serious doubts about America's place in the Empire until the summer of 1774, when the ordeals of the people of Massachusetts forced him to reappraise the intentions of the King and his ministers.[33] Benjamin Franklin tarried in London until 1775, nurturing his dream of retiring to the life of a grand pooh-bah of the British Empire. Thomas Jefferson, born in 1743, "knew more of the eclipses of Jupiter's satellites than he did of what was passing in Boston," groused the envious Adams in later life.[34] James Madison (b. 1751) and Alexander Hamilton (b. 1755 or 1757) were mere schoolboys when the hard work of changing the American mind began. As America's busy hagiographers have been keen to observe, the men now exalted as America's founders and framers, taken on the whole, were revolutionaries by circumstance rather than by disposition. They were ambitious, upstanding citizens, generally happy with their lot in life, who at a singular moment in history were presented with a fateful choice.

Thomas Young, on the other hand, was no accidental revolutionary. He was present at the creation of the movement, and he never left. He was unhappy, brilliant, resentful, and heroically optimistic. He was a plotter, a conspirer, an ideologue, and a provocateur. He did not disguise his belief that in order to make a revolution you have to break some eggs. He vowed always—in his own words—"to fight the good fight."[35] Above all, he was a man with a message, so convinced of the merit of the ideas in his head that keeping his mouth shut would have seemed like a crime against humanity.

He published his first screed championing the natural rights of Englishmen against the injustices of imperial rule in 1764, when he was thirty-three. In the following year, he found himself at the head of a mob on the streets of Albany, leading the protests against the Stamp Act. He rose to the leadership of the local chapter of the Sons of Liberty and soon made contact with like-minded activists across the colonies. In 1766, he moved to Boston to join with the radical faction gathering around James Otis and Samuel Adams. As Boston struggled with occupation, he rapidly established himself as the most militant voice in the local newspapers and the go-to man whenever a rabble stood in need of rousing. Governor Thomas Hutchinson regularly named him as one of the four most dangerous men in town. In 1772, together with his fellow radicals, he founded the Boston Committee of Correspondence—a momentous breakthrough in propaganda technology that served to spread both rebellious sentiments and democratic practices throughout Massachusetts and the rest of the colonies.[36]

"What an engine!" John Adams exclaimed in 1815. "The history of the United States can never be written" until one had inquired into the activities of the Boston Committee of Correspondence, he said. "France imitated it, and produced a revolution. England and Scotland were upon the point of imitating it, in order to produce another revolution . . . The history of the past thirty years is a sufficient commentary upon it."[37] And Young's handwriting was all over the project—quite literally. In the files now held in the archives of the New York Public Library, his distinctive script appears on dozens of unsigned pages of Committee papers—more than any other Committee member—including on parts of a draft of the 1772 declaration of the "rights of the colonists" that John Adams later suggested was one of the models for the Declaration of Independence.[38]

In 1775, Young tumbled into Philadelphia, the scene of his greatest contributions to the revolutionary cause, and instantly fell in with Thomas Paine. In his political polemics, Young anticipated many of the ideas and even some of the language that figured in the pamphlet that changed the world: Paine's *Common Sense* of January 1776.[39] At the time, the government of Pennsylvania was mostly under the control of conservatives who favored reconciliation with Great Britain. In the decisive month of May 1776, Young, Paine, and a handful of their fellow radicals engineered a Bolshevik-style coup d'état that replaced the legitimately elected government of the province with a pro-independence faction. The new government of the colony in turn tilted the balance of the Continental Congress in favor of permanent separation from Britain, and within six weeks the Congress declared independence.

In the summer and fall of 1776, Young and his comrades organized a convention and produced a constitution for the newly independent state of Pennsylvania. It was "the most radically democratic organic law in the world at the time of its creation," one historian has observed.[40] It vested almost all power in a popularly elected legislature, stipulated a variety of measures to ensure that their representatives would remain answerable to the people, and included a declaration of rights along the lines of those that are familiar to us now from the Bill of Rights of the U.S. Constitution. Franklin handed out copies in Paris, and the people of the salons assumed that such a revolutionary document could only have been the great scientist's work. "In truth," John Adams sniffed, it was Young, Paine, and a pair of their radical friends "who were the authors of it."[41] And when Young finished with the job in Philadelphia, he sent a copy along with an open letter to the people of Vermont—a state whose name Young himself coined from the French for "Green Mountain"[42]—where, with some further modification, it served as the basis for the first state constitution to ban slavery.

It is the unapologetically democratic character of Young's revolution that makes him seem such a striking figure today. By birth, by reputation, and by conviction, Young was a man of the people. In Boston he saved his highest praise for the "common tradesmen" who at town meetings displayed "the wisdom and eloquence of Athenian Senators."[43] As a member of the Boston Committee, he demanded the overthrow of all the governments that put "the most powerful men in every county and every town" over "the common people."[44] In Philadelphia he invited the hatred of the ruling classes with his bold proposal that all men should be entitled to vote without regard to their property qualifications. As early as 1770, he had predicted, "A very little time will show you Great Britain reduced into absolute monarchy, or exalted into a Republic!"[45] In the years preceding the Revolutionary War, it should not be forgotten, only a tiny fraction of the American colonials desired independence, and only a much smaller fraction thought in terms of a democratic transformation of society and government. Young belonged to a numerically insignificant sliver who, long before their fellow colonials dared to imagine the possibility of a break from the mother country, dreamed of independence as a means to launch a democratic revolution that would sweep through the British Empire and then around the world.

Among his contemporaries, Young shone in a memorable light, electrifying some, shocking others. Ethan's brother Ira said Young was "highly distinguished as a philosopher, philanthropist, and patriot, and for his erudition and brilliancy of imagination."[46] Samuel Adams, defending his friend's prominent position in the Boston Committee of Correspondence, said that "Doctor Young (I dare you to contradict me) has ever been an unwearied assertor of the rights of his countrymen: has taken the post of hazard, and acted vigorously in the cause of American freedom. Such endeavors and exertions, have justly entitled him to the notice, to the confidence of the people."[47]

According to his detractors, on the other hand—of whom there were plenty—Young was a purveyor of "inaccuracy, malevolence, bad grammar, and nonsense"; a perfect specimen of "self-conceit, vain-baiting, and invincible impudence"; a "firebrand" and an "incendiary of the lower order"; a man "of noisy fame"; the last word in "boorishness and impertinent loquacity"; "the great Apollo of the ignorant"; and, most memorably, "an eternal Fisher in Troubled Waters."[48] Thomas Young had no family pedigree, no formal educational credentials, and no money in a society that placed enormous value on all three—and his enemies never let him forget that.

Even among those of his contemporaries who exuded a palpable distaste for the man and the vulgar forces he represented, however, one may find grudging acknowledgment of his remarkable impact on the affairs of the day. A condescending Bostonian, in words recorded by John Adams, described Young's place in the political world of the time with a beguiling metaphor:

> The watch would not go. The Artist at length with his Thumb and forefinger groping in the Dust upon his shopboard, took up a little dirty Pin, scarcely visible to my naked sight, blew off the Dust and screwed it into a particular Part of the Wheelwork, The watch then clicked in an instant, and went very well. This little dirty Screw . . . [is] Dr. Young in the Town of Boston.[49]

Yet Thomas Young remains, in the words of historian David Freeman Hawke, "unquestionably the most unwritten about man of distinction of the American Revolution." Hawke made that claim in 1970—and it is still mostly true. Apart from a few worthy pieces of scholarship, the "dirty little screw" of the American Revolution continues to languish on the shop floor of history.[50]

Part of the problem is that Young died too early for his own good, succumbing in July 1777 to a sudden fever contracted while serving as a surgeon for the Continental Army. Having done his best work on the streets and in the backrooms of revolutionary committees, he left no one with any great stake in fighting for his posthumous reputation—no one, that is, except the ever-loyal Ethan Allen, who was soon busy immolating his own legacy.

The biggest obstacle that stood between Thomas Young and the history books, however, was his unabashed deism. In a fistful of bracing newspaper columns, not-so-anonymous pamphlets, and private letters, Young left few of his contemporaries in doubt about the extreme heterodoxy of his religious views. "Could we raise up the spirit of one of the murderers of St. Stephen, to tell us what a figure Paul cut, when he breathed out threatening and slaughter against his *Savior*, then we might form an idea of Dr. Y——g," said one outraged Tory.[51] "Suffice it to say, this man stands accused of rebellion, not only against his Sovereign, but against *his God*."

Young's fellow citizens regularly accused him of being "a man of no morals," an "infamous character," and, of course, an "infidel."[52] And Young—this is perhaps the most unusual thing about him—regularly responded with daring public confessions in which he let it be known, in so many words, that if with such terms his antagonists meant to identify him a deist, then they were right. Rushing to his defense after one assault on the doctor's unacceptable creed, his fellow members of the Boston Committee of Correspondence marveled that on his journey through life he had accumulated many friends of high character, notwithstanding the fact that "uniform throughout, he appears in all places to have declared his sentiments on all subjects, natural, civil, and religious." The thing about Young, everyone agreed, was that he could not keep his mouth shut. When he died, the nation he served found it convenient to forget such a troublesome individual. Let him now face the consequences in the afterlife whose reality he so blasphemously denied, they said, and they moved on.

Young's philosophical oeuvre is not large or systematic, and it is sometimes obtuse, as one might expect from a self-taught medicine man moonlighting as a global revolutionary. Yet its neglect turns out to be the most damaging of the many unfortunate consequences of his omission from the history books. In the uncomfortably personal confessions he committed to print, Young tells us what it was like to come of age as a deist in prerevolutionary America. In his sundry philosophical treatises, he articulates a form of deism that is substantially more radical than that which has traditionally figured in the stories America tells itself about its philosophical heritage. And he makes clear that, at least in his own mind, this radical philosophy was the axis on which the Revolution turned. For him, the project to free the American people from the yoke of King George was part of a grander project to liberate the world from the ghostly tyranny of supernatural religion.

From Young's writings it is also evident that he was a man of the book—or, in his case, of many books. He piles reference upon reference in clumsy stacks that totter under the weight of an autodidact's vanity and insecurity. From his admiring brother we know that he amassed one of the finest personal libraries in New England—"a very valuable library . . . collected with great care and cost"—though it was never enough to impress the learned people.[53] When he died, however, he left his wife and six children destitute, and to the dismay of future historians, they were compelled to sell off the books to make ends meet. What we can infer from his own writings is that Young's lost library was lined with all those deist books that Allen claimed never to have read—including, for example, the work from which Allen possibly purloined his title, Charles Blount's *Oracles of Reason*.

The theory first mooted by Zadock Thompson, that Thomas Young was the real author of Ethan Allen's *Oracles of Reason*, takes its departure from at least one ascertainable fact. In 1764, while Young was living on the eastern border of New York in the village of Amenia—a name he coined from the Latin for "pleasing to the eye"—he took it as his duty to impart the secrets of philosophy to twenty-six-year-old Ethan Allen, a not-very-gentlemanly farmer then residing on the rough edge of western Connecticut. "After an Acquantance with Doctr. Thomas Young's a Deist, my brother embrased the same Centiments," said Ira Allen.[54] One of Vermont's first settlers, in a recollection committed to paper in1840, offered a backhanded confirmation of the relationship: Allen "studied Deism with Doctor Thomas Young until he thought himself a conjuror."[55] There is, however, no direct evidence that links Young with the composition of the work that Ethan Allen unrepentantly presented to the world as "My Theology"—no manuscript in the doctor's handwriting, no letter from outraged widows or heirs, indeed, no suggestion of any kind on the subject until Thompson raised the first eyebrow in 1852.

The plagiarism thesis really turns on two curious assumptions. The first, as we know, is that Ethan Allen lacked the cranial capacity to have written a book of philosophy. The second is that philosophers of the kind who might have produced such a work as Allen's *Oracles* were very sparse on the ground. Who but the outlandish Thomas Young could have done such a thing? This assumption reveals quite a lot about the view Americans began to take on their own history as they settled into their comfortable new way of life in the decades after the Revolution. But it, too, turns out to be entirely without foundation. The remarkable fact is that Thomas Young and Ethan Allen were not at all alone in their heterodoxy. They were distinguished chiefly by their willingness to shout their beliefs from the hilltops in the loudest possible way.

DO BOOKS MATTER? Do they change minds—or do we just read into them whatever we want to know? We live in the most literate age in human history, yet many people today find few things less useful than books, and no books as useless as those of the philosophers. Many scholars today take for granted that philosophy is a technical discipline concerned with questions that can make sense only to a cadre of professionals trained to a perfection of irrelevance. The wider public, meanwhile, tends to think of philosophy as a place to stash all the questions that well up wherever our knowledge runs completely dry: the meaning of life, why there is something rather than nothing, the existence of the supernatural, and all that. Of the many attributes that seem to mark America's founders as residents of a foreign time and place, probably none is more astonishing today than their unapologetic confidence in the power of books—and in particular the books of the philosophers.

At the age of five, according to family lore, Thomas Jefferson had already read through his father's entire library. At boarding school he developed a reputation as a bookish lad, devoting many of the daylight hours to mastering his lessons before joining his classmates in play. "To read the Latin and Greek authors in their original is a sublime luxury," he wrote in later life. "I would not exchange it for anything that I could have learned then or have not acquired since."[56] At the age of seventeen, he began to transcribe excerpts from his reading in his *Literary Commonplace Book*. Rearranged several times and later bound up into a cloth volume, the notebook served throughout his life as a prized source of quotes and phrases from philosophers past. At the same time, he began to amass the immense personal collection that eventually formed the literary cornerstone of the Library of Congress. "I cannot live without books," he acknowledged.[57] "I labor grievously under the malady of Bibliomania."[58]

Jefferson turned 6,487 books over to Congress, and most of them can be made available today to visitors to the Jefferson Building of the Library of Congress, opposite the U.S. Capitol. He catalogued about 150 of these volumes under the label of "moral philosophy." On that bookshelf of moral philosophy sits one of the few original editions of Ethan Allen's Bible.[59] Not long after acquiring Allen's *Reason the Only Oracle of Man*, as it happens, Jefferson counseled his nephew Peter Carr that "reason is the only oracle given you by heaven."[60] But there is no need to suppose that the author of the Declaration of Independence cribbed the line from The Philosopher of the Green Mountains. Oracles of reason are as common in deist literature as church steeples in New England.

Filling up the rest of Jefferson's shelf of moral philosophy are the books that Ethan Allen claimed never to have read—the spine and binding of the deist movement, the same books that bounced across the colonies in Thomas Young's lost library. Jefferson liked to say that he was "of a sect by myself, as far as I know."[61] And he was in many ways an extraordinary individual, at times unconstrained by self-contradictions, in certain lights verging on the hypocritical. But the philosophical ideas with which he made sense of the Revolution are by and large the ones that filled his bookshelf on moral philosophy. In his own time, the forces of righteousness certainly had little doubt about where to locate him on the spectrum of acceptable belief. He was a "confirmed infidel" and a "howling atheist," they said.

More than just the books themselves, men like Jefferson and Young shared a certain attitude toward them, one that could sometimes seem to reverse the usual order of life and literature.[62] Consider, for example, Jefferson's essay, penned in 1764 at the age of twenty-one, on the question, "Whether Christianity is part of the Common Law?"[63] His answer was confident and unequivocal: "We may safely affirm (though contradicted by all the judges and writers on earth) that Christianity neither is, nor ever was, a part of the common law." His reasoning was straightforward. The common law along with all the best and most democratic institutions of British government and life could be traced to the period before the Norman Conquest (or so said a group of Saxon-loving historians that both Jefferson and Young admired). Since "the common law existed while the Anglo-Saxons were yet Pagans, at a time when they had never yet heard the name of Christ pronounced, or knew that such a character had ever existed," it was absurd to think that the common law was based on Christianity. The mistaken idea that Christianity has something to do with common law, Jefferson argued, could be traced to a willful error in the translation of a key text in 1458, in which the French "*ancien scripture*" was incorrectly rendered as "holy scripture." Legal authorities have gone along with this false conflation of Christianity with the law in order to curry favor with the priests, Jefferson asserted, for "the alliance between church and state in England, has ever made their judges accomplices in the frauds of the clergy."[64]

At the age of twenty-one, then, Jefferson believed he had placed his literary scalpel on the carotid artery of a vast theocratic conspiracy. He alone got it right where all the philologists in history had it wrong. Here he evinced the instincts of a genuine radical, a cast of mind characteristic alike of cranks, Jacobins, hermits, and revolutionaries like Thomas Young. The most curious feature of Jefferson's Saxon narrative, though, is its strangely literary quality. The innocent state of Anglo-Saxon nature, he tells us, may be deduced from the inspection of some dusty medieval writings. The injustices of the present go back to a single, textual error—a fatal typo. And the future depends on reading the story aright. Jefferson, no less than Young, inhabited a tale of justice and injustice, of the righting of wrongs that endured across the centuries and that made sense only within books. Their lives, their careers, and above all their revolutionary ambition became coherent only when placed in the context of their erudition.

Benjamin Franklin took a less exalted attitude toward books, or so it would appear. He peddled thousands of them along the road to riches. It seems safe to say that he would have been more likely to use a spare volume to prop open the bathroom window than to memorialize it in a sacred hoard. "What Comfort can the Vortices of Descartes give to a Man who has Whirlwinds in his Bowels?"[65] he wanted to know. Yet in his *Autobiography*—a book itself remarkable for both the originality of its tone and the extent of its influence—Franklin provides ample testimony to the power of the written word. He describes himself as a "bookish lad" in childhood: "All the little Money that came into my Hands was ever laid out in Books."[66] One book converted him to vegetarianism (for a time). Another book taught him "the Socratic Method" (which he took to be the art of obtaining rhetorical victories "that neither my self nor my Cause always deserved"). Mainly, by his own account, his stash of printed luxuries took him away from the religion in which he was raised.

Upon reading a collection of many of the very same authors whose works would later appear on Jefferson's bookshelf of moral philosophy, Ben became "a real Doubter in many Points of our Religious Doctrine." He was "scarce 15" when, "after doubting by turns of several Points as I found them disputed in the different Books I read, I began to doubt of Revelation it self." In a decisive confession, he announces that his books had made him into a deist:

> Some Books against Deism fell into my Hands; they were said to be the Substance of Sermons preached at Boyle's Lectures. It happened that they wrought an Effect on me quite contrary to what was intended by them: For the arguments of the Deists which were quoted to be refuted, appeared to me much Stronger than the Refutations. In short I soon became a thorough Deist.[67]

It is an apt reflection of Franklin's subversively insouciant personality that he claimed to have formed his opinion *against* the authorities he read. The sermons that unintentionally converted Ben, in any case, were hard-hitting affairs, intended to beat into their readers' minds the conviction that deism is just a dishonest name for atheism. The sermons had specific targets for their theological odium, moreover, and the chief target of the first and most influential of the Boyle Lectures was Charles Blount—the author of the first *Oracles of Reason*.[68]

Though Franklin modulated the expression of his philosophical and religious views considerably as he matured, he never gave reason to think that he ever departed from the convictions acquired as youthful bibliophile. He was "an unbeliever in Christianity" who by his example did much "to make others unbelievers," said fellow philosopher (and notorious heretic in his own right) Joseph Priestley.[69] He was a man "of whom the infidels plume themselves much," complained the firebrand preacher Jonathan Edwards (the younger).[70] In a letter to Ezra Stiles in the last year of his life, Franklin confessed to a simple list of deist doctrines that could have been inserted without notice into Ethan Allen's Bible.[71]

By the time Franklin attained the wisdom of age, the books that he scrimped to buy as a young man were spilling out of the backpacks of the nation's university students. A typical product of Yale's class of 1778 was Joel Barlow: a friend of Paine, supporter of the French Revolution, and the author of the Treaty of Tripoli of 1797, in which it is announced, "The Government of the United States of America is not, in any sense, founded on the Christian religion." According to Lyman Beecher, class of 1793, Yale was indeed "in a most ungodly state" before Timothy Dwight arrived in 1795 to straighten things out. "That was the day of the infidelity of the Tom Paine school . . . most of the class before me were infidels, and called each other Voltaire, Rousseau, D'Alembert, etc. etc."[72] Philip Freneau—Madison's friend at Princeton, Jefferson's propagandist, famous in his own right as "the poet of the American Revolution"—owed essentially all of the philosophy in his radical verses to the books that lined Jefferson's shelf of "moral philosophy." Gouverneur Morris—the "penman of the Constitution," author of its sonorous preamble, and in the words of Roger Sherman, a "profane and irreligious man"—was a refined graduate of King's College (now Columbia University). At the College of William & Mary, one student wrote home to say, "There is not a man among us who would not enlist himself under the banner of a Paine or a Volney."[73] The only school worse than Jefferson's alma mater, the defenders of piety eventually concluded, was Jefferson's own University of Virginia.

Paradoxical as it may sound to modern ears, many of the ideas in the books on Jefferson's shelf also passed through the doors of America's churches. As Ezra Stiles explained, deism spread "very fast" in America, much of it through the Church of England, for "strange as it may seem . . . [a] man may be an excellent Ch[urc]hman & yet a profound Deist."[74] Indeed, deists like Franklin and Washington thought that serving local churches could be a useful way to contribute to the community. The more important fact is that much of the preaching they heard in church was philosophically very close to deism. There are of course fine distinctions to be drawn between infidels like Thomas Young and the proto-Unitarians who gathered around the likes of Jonathan Mayhew in Boston, for example. But the defenders of orthodoxy should be forgiven for not always being able to see that they mattered. "It must be owned, that the labor of the Deists in assaulting the Christian scheme, has been made very easy . . . by many treacherous professors of the religion of Jesus," explained one infuriated prelate. "Deists have had little to do, but to stand still and smile, whilst others were doing their work for them, perhaps without knowing it."[75]

Where official sources and methods failed to do the job, America's revolutionary deists added to the literature of "moral philosophy" with their own anonymous tracts. Perhaps the first systematic avowal of the deist position in America may be found in the bracing *Sermon on Natural Religion*, published anonymously by "a Natural Man" in Boston in 1771, which sets out to show that the New Testament is, well, wrong. In 1779 appeared another profoundly subversive tract, published by "The Author" in "New England," under the title *A Dialogue between A____ and B____ on a Subject of the Last Importance*—the subject of last importance being the falsity of the established religion.

Today the influence of heterodox writing in early America is easy to underestimate because we no longer know how to read it. To the untrained eye, for example, Robert Beverley's *History of Virginia* of 1722 is a straightforward travel narrative from an early explorer. To the sophisticated readers of the time, on the other hand, it would have been clear that the religious teachings about a Nature-God that Beverley put into the mouths of Native Americans, like their criticisms of "the white man's religion," were the same that could be found in the works of Jefferson's moral philosophers. In 1752, James Parker of New York published another deistic speech supposedly delivered by an Indian chief—the kind of speech that today would be viewed as a shopping-mall version of Christianity—but the theological police, wise to the strategy of ventriloquism, charged him with blasphemy. (Franklin stepped in to get his friend Parker off the hook.)[76]

By book, sermon, and anti-sermon, the ideas tucked between the covers of Jefferson's books ultimately spread across all geographic boundaries in revolutionary America. In Boston, Thomas Young found both a political and a philosophical ally in William Molineux—the suspected chief of the "Mohawks" responsible for throwing the tea into the harbor. Indeed, the Committee of Correspondence on which Young and Molineux sat was regularly pilloried in the press at the time as "a set of Atheists or Deists, men of profligate manners and profane tongues." Ezra Ripley—the same minister who later oversaw the spiritual development of Ralph Waldo Emerson—concluded that roughly the same could be said of the bulk of the educated population in Boston, excepting (most of) the clergy.[77] Vermont was no better, according to the Reverend Nathan Perkins, who reported with dismay in 1789 that "about one quarter of the inhabitants and almost all of the men of learning [are] deists."[78] A Gospel ministry would receive support from no more than half the population, he estimated; "the rest would choose to have no Sabbath—no ministers—no religion—no heaven—no hell—no morality." In New York, there were few professional men who were not infidels, recorded James Kent, eventual chancellor of the state, and literary societies such as "the Friendly Club" were widely suspected of freethinking tendencies.[79] In Philadelphia, the clergy routinely complained that "reasoning unbelievers" were everywhere and that the "conversations at taverns and coffee houses" overflowed with "ridicule for the gospels and the idea of an afterlife."[80] In Virginia, the Baptists circulated a petition in 1785 lamenting, "Deism with its banefull Influence is spreading itself over the state."[81] According to John Randolph, an alcoholic aristocrat who atoned for his own youthful lapses with a late-life conversion experience, Virginia during the revolutionary period was "the most ungodly country on the face of the earth . . . The last was a generation of free thinkers, disciples of Hume & Voltaire & Bolingbroke, & there are very few persons . . . of our years who have not received their first impressions from the same die."[82]

Often—and not just in the case of Ethan Allen—the ideas of those same, dangerous authors could be detected among those who cannot plausibly be suspected of having read very many of them at all. George Washington, for example, was no one's idea of a philosopher, and it seems doubtful that he would have made it through a tenth of Jefferson's books on moral philosophy. Washington's religion was never really separable from his character, yet many of his better-informed contemporaries read into that character, too, the heterodox philosophy of the age. Jefferson, Dr. Benjamin Rush, Gouverneur Morris, and possibly the Reverend Ashbel Green, Washington's own minister for many years in Philadelphia, were somehow convinced that the taciturn, book-shy Father of Our Country was a deist, not a Christian.[83] Allowing for all the imprecision of such labels and the inevitable personal variations, the same could be said for every U.S. president down to the sixth, James Monroe—another friend of Paine in Paris.

As for Paine himself, Jefferson was probably correct to point out that he was a man who thought more than he read. Yet—to a degree not widely appreciated today—every crucial step of logic and even many specific twists of language in Paine's *Age of Reason* can be traced to the library that Jefferson compiled. Paine's work is sometimes mistakenly supposed to have been the first public expression of American deism. But many observers at the time saw that it had so much in common with Ethan Allen's earlier work that they accused Paine of being ungracious in failing to acknowledge the debt. They could just as easily—and unfairly—have charged him with plagiarizing his great friend and ally in Philadelphia, Thomas Young.

Paine was the target of every insult that John Adams could gather from his richly choleric imagination: "a mongrel between pig and puppy, begotten by a wild boar on a bitch wolf." Yet Adams, who developed love-hate relationships with most things in life, turned around and conceded, "I know not whether any man in the world has had more influence on its inhabitants or affairs . . . Call it then the Age of Paine."[84] Adams's troubles, too, really began with books: he no less than Jefferson and Franklin was a founding introvert. As a boy, "I soon perceived . . . a Love of Books and a fondness for Study, which dissipated all my Inclination for Sports," said Adams. "I read forever."[85] He always considered himself a Christian of a sort, but the contradictions of this eminently self-contradictory man were situated exactly at the intersection of the philosophy in which he was so well versed and the religion he did not wish to dishonor. Adams—like the bulk of Jefferson's "moral philosophers"—maintained that the Christian religion as it had been handed down through the centuries amounted to so many impious "fables" and "corruptions"; that the story of Jesus's crucifixion and resurrection was an "absurdity"; that the doctrine of salvation through faith was "detestable," "invidious," and "hurtful"; and that the belief in original sin "damned the whole human Race, without any actual Crimes committed by any of them."[86]

If we step back from the multifarious individuals and conversations within the history and take in the broad scene of literary heterodoxy in revolutionary America, three striking facts emerge. The first is its very strong (though far from perfect) correlation with revolutionary activism.[87] Notwithstanding the loud laments of the defenders of orthodoxy about the corruptions of the age, the broad plurality of people in America remained active and observant within some variety or other of relatively orthodox religion. The leadership of the Revolution, however, was simply not representative of its people in this respect. Of course, it certainly was possible to participate in the Revolution without being an infidel. Samuel Adams, Roger Sherman, Elias Boudinot, and John

Jay come to mind as examples of conventionally pious founders. It was equally possible to be both a loyalist and a paid-up subscriber to the deistic Enlightenment. Cadwallader Colden, for example, was a member of Franklin's circle for a time and produced private treatises evincing a kind of pantheistic materialism, though as governor of New York he was naturally aligned with the Tory cause.[88] Even so, few observers of the time failed to notice a distinct and even scandalous connection between revolutionary politics and revolutionary philosophy.[89]

The second, striking feature of American deism is its international character. America's revolutionary deists saw themselves as—and they were—participants in an international movement that drew on most of the same literary sources across the civilized world. Their enemies, too, saw them as part of the same global republic of letters, and routinely directed their counterrevolutionary screeds against "deistical republicans" charged with promoting "deisms and democracies" around the world.[90] In 1789, when the notoriously irreligious French Enlightenment turned to revolution, America's revolutionary deists immediately and enthusiastically embraced it as a continuation of their work. "From that bright spark which first illumed these lands / See Europe kindling, as the blaze expands," exulted Philip Freneau in 1790.[91] Five years later, his friend and patron Jefferson was still enthusiastic: "This ball of liberty . . . will roll around the globe, at least the enlightened part of it, for light and liberty go together. It is our glory that we first put it into motion."[92] There were differences between the two revolutions, of course, but these had more to do with circumstances than principles.[93] The biggest difference was simply that the French Revolution, having failed, had its history written by its enemies, who had plenty of reason to emphasize its deviance from the past; whereas the American Revolution had its history written by its successors, who had equally good reason to stress the continuities. It was only after the situation in France descended into tyranny and its interpretation in America fell casualty to domestic political conflict that politicians and historians attempted to build a wall of separation between French atheism and American deism.

The third and most curious feature of revolutionary deism, in

America and elsewhere, is perhaps the easiest to overlook: the remarkable contrast between the heterogeneity of the people involved and the uniformity of their ideas. In personality, social status, circumstances, and convictions on a wide range of other matters, America's revolutionary infidels were as diverse as the people they led. They included slave owners and abolitionists, northerners and southerners, rich men and paupers, dyspeptic pessimists and serene optimists, refined products of the best universities and graduates of the school of mountain living. Yet their heterodoxy was everywhere the same. From the forests of New England to the plantations of Virginia, the ideas, tropes, and references that belong to the philosophical religion of deism repeated themselves in the same language, word for word, sometimes cited, more often tacitly referenced, from the same collection of works. Closing in on the end of the eighteenth century, Jonathan Edwards Jr. observed that deists were all "avowed infidels"; but it is perhaps more interesting to note that the important infidels at the time were all avowed deists.

So the strange fact about Ethan Allen's Bible is that a whole generation of otherwise exotically diverse American leaders could have written it. Whence came this unity amid diversity, this hypothetical partnership in a hypothetical crime? Where if not from the books—the books that Ethan Allen perhaps inadvertently plagiarized, the books that Thomas Young stuffed in his suitcases as he moved from one colony to another, that Franklin devoured as a lad, that Jefferson couldn't live without—books that were, everywhere and on the whole, the same books?

IF A GROUP of people hear a tree fall in a forest and nobody talks about it afterward, how do we know that anyone heard it? Discussions of a topic as fraught as the philosophical religion of America's founders often end before they start, with trees falling silently in faraway forests, if not insipid assurances that everyone is entitled to find in America's founders whatever they want to find.

The trouble really began with the founders themselves, who—setting aside the uncouth ones like Allen, Young, and Paine—seemed resolved to say as little as possible about the fallen tree. Franklin attributed his diffidence to a lesson learned as a teenager. On a visit to the home of Cotton Mather, Boston's most powerful preacher at the time, young Ben entered a narrow passage crossed by a beam overhead. The talkative lad, walking in front of the minister, had his head turned back and his mouth in its usual open position. "Stoop! Stoop!" Mather called out. Ben grasped the reverend's meaning only after his head smacked against the beam. The insufferable Mather, incapable of passing up an opportunity for moral instruction, laid his hand on Ben's shoulder and intoned, *"Let this be a caution to you not always to hold your Head so high. Stoop, young man, stoop—as you go through the world—and you will miss many hard Thumps!"*[94] One can easily imagine that Ethan Allen might have swung his ax at the offending beam. Thomas Young might have penned a screed about the injustices of home construction. Ben learned to stoop. Indeed, he stooped all the way to his last year of life. After revealing something of his creed to Ezra Stiles in his letter of 1790, he was quick to plead for discretion: "I confide that you will not expose me to Criticism and censure by publishing any part of this communication to you."[95]

Jefferson learned the same lesson later in life—around the time he was getting whacked as a "howling atheist." He made the point implicitly in a poignant letter to his grandson, Francis Eppes, who had asked his opinion of Paine as well as Lord Bolingbroke, the controversial English deist whose works figured prominently in Jefferson's own library of moral philosophy.[96] "They were alike in making bitter enemies of the priests and Pharisees of their day," said Jefferson. "Both were honest men; both advocates for human liberty. Paine wrote for a country which permitted him to push his reasoning to whatever length it would go. Lord Bolingbroke in one restrained by a constitution, and by public opinion." Yet in closing his letter, Jefferson seemed to tacitly revise his judgment about the country for which he and Paine wrote. "You have asked my opinion of these persons, and *to you* I have given it freely," he said to Eppes. "But, remember, that I am old, that I wish not to make new enemies." In a letter to John Adams, he was more direct: "Say nothing of my religion. It is known to my god and myself alone."[97]

George Washington, too, was skilled in the art of saying nothing about his religion. Toward the end of his presidency, a group of clerics, frustrated by his silence, resolved to do something about it. They approached him with a list of queries, one of which was specifically designed to elicit from him a profession of faith in the Lord Jesus Christ. As Jefferson observed with glee in his diary, however, "the old fox was too cunning for them" and simply skipped over the offending question without so much as a nod.[98]

When the founders did break their silence about religion, it was often only to dissimulate. The conservative nineteenth-century historian Cornelis de Witt understood the dynamic well. "Jefferson, Franklin, Gouverneur Morris, John Adams, were free-thinkers, but without intolerance or display, without ostentatious irony, quietly, and almost privily; for the masses remained believers," he observed. "Not to offend them, it was necessary to speak with respect of sacred things; to produce a deep impression upon them, it was requisite to appeal to their religious feelings; and prayers and public fasts continued to be instruments resorted to whenever it was found desirable."[99] Even today, religious conservatives trot out the Thanksgiving proclamations and similar edicts put out by America's early leaders as evidence of what they are not, namely, confessions of faith.

As the successes of America's revolutionary deism consolidated, the silence about it grew still more deafening. Perhaps because they began to suspect that God was on America's side after all, the nation's spiritual leaders stopped attacking the founders for their infidelity and settled on an enduring strategy for coping with their gross heterodoxy. As in the case of Ethan Allen's brain and Thomas Young's fame, they decided that the best thing to do was to remove the offending material from the history. Franklin—hailed in the early days as the "father of our country"—was humiliated in his last years and beaten to near oblivion after death, then brought back to life, against his own better judgment, as a homely parody of workaday Puritanism. Paine was condemned to the footnotes of history—quite literally—in the first editions of the nation's history books.[100] As for Jefferson—the less he was permitted to say on religious matters, the better. It was worth engraving in stone that he had "sworn upon the altar of God eternal hostility over all forms of tyranny over the mind of man." It was better to leave out the part where he made clear that the particular tyranny with which he was then concerned was that which the Protestant clergy exercised over the minds of his fellow Americans.[101]

With the passage of the years, denial yielded in its hapless way to farce. The founders were not merely to be absolved of impiety; they had to become paragons of piety, even miniature deities in their own right, for a godly country had to have godlike creators. Washington was compelled to kneel in paintings (a posture he resolutely refused to assume in church), to ascend into heaven (questionable, given that he also refused to take communion), to chop down cherry trees (didn't do it), and to utter a long list of declarations of faith in the Lord Jesus Christ that for some reason he couldn't bring himself to express while still alive. All too soon, the cult of the founders began to acquire a political edge that cut against the spirit of the Revolution itself. The founders may have maintained that legitimate government derives its power from the consent of the governed, but many Americans came to believe that legitimate government is possible only with the consent of the founders.

In the contemporary scholarship, to be sure, there are a number of scrupulous and worthwhile efforts to survey the unusual philosophical and religious opinions of America's revolutionaries.[102] Even so, America's revolutionary deism remains an uncomfortable and underreported topic. Some of the neglect stems from the general lack of respect for ideas in the writing of history, or the vogue for popular and social history, which tends to suppose that deism can be dismissed as a speculative bauble of the elite. Often the resistance to the topic takes refuge in various methodological concerns. It is very, very difficult to establish what dead people really believed, one line of argument goes; in the case of religious belief, it is all but impossible; and in the case of a religion whose adherents often sought to disguise their beliefs, it is wrong even to try. Yet another line of defense says that religious and philosophical beliefs have nothing to do with political beliefs, so we don't need to know about the founders' religion or philosophy. Like Thomas Young in Boston, deism is the "dirty little screw" of the American Revolution. It is the piece of the machine that polite society would rather not discuss but that somehow made the whole thing work. Yet the reasons given for the silence, now as in the beginning, don't withstand much scrutiny. Where they are more than mere prejudice, they amount to political reservations about broaching a question of fact.

To return to the case of the tree falling in the forest: Clearly, we may know that the people heard the tree fall if some of them come back and spill the beans. We may also know if we detect telltale clues in their conversations after the event, say, detailed descriptions of the kinds of sounds that only those who have heard a falling tree can offer. Mainly, we can know as much as we ever need to know if the people grab their hacksaws and head back into the forest with their fellow citizens to build a house out of the freshly fallen wood. In the case of the radical ideas of America's founders, the same rules apply. We know because some of them blabbed. We know because others left behind a pile of clues. Mostly, we know because they went back into the forest and built a republic out of those very same ideas.

2

Pathologies of Freedom

THE OFFENSE TOOK PLACE IN PLAIN VIEW, ON A SUMMER Sunday in 1764, in the muddy square in front of the meetinghouse that passed for the center of Salisbury, Connecticut. Ethan Allen was presumably stripped to the waist, loudly drunk, and hurling profanities for the amusement of the gathering crowd. Dr. Thomas Young, of nearby Amenia, New York, was brandishing his well-worn lancet. The incision, in accordance with the medical practice of the time, probably took place on Allen's arm. Into the bleeding wound, the doctor inserted a thread bathed in the festering pustule of an individual suffering from smallpox. Then he bandaged the cut. The patient, one may suppose, in accordance with another of the medical practices of the time, downed another shot of rum—several shots, more likely, to judge from the subsequent court records.

Smallpox was deadly—far deadlier to soldiers and civilians than all the muskets and bayonets of enemy armies of the time. Inoculation, as it was then practiced, amounted to the deliberate infection of one individual with whatever brew of virus bits and antibodies happened to be present in the sores of another individual. The medicine was rude, but it was known to work—at least most of the time. In one or two out of a hundred cases, inoculation led to full-blown infection followed by the complication of death. Given that one out of three who caught smallpox in the normal way died, the rough justice of statistics generally favored inoculation.

Yet smallpox inoculation was the object of passions that far outran the limited science involved. In the eyes of some religious conservatives, "the dangerous and sinfull practice of inoculation"[1] represented an arrogation of God's unalienable right to deal death to sinners. The Reverend Timothy Dwight allegedly sermonized that if death by disease was in the cards for any certain person, "it would be a frightful sin to avoid and annul that decree by the trick of vaccination."[2] The arguments for controlling (as opposed to prohibiting) smallpox inoculation, it should be noted, were not all unreasonable. If only some inhabitants of a town received the inoculation, the others might then be exposed to an increased risk of the disease; and inoculating everyone was expensive. From a legal perspective, it was a matter of authority. In many jurisdictions, the right to decide about inoculation—which for the most part meant the right to ban it—rested with the "selectmen," or board of three or five men, who ran each town.

In the eyes of progressive thinkers up and down the colonies, the authorities were usually in the wrong, and the restrictions on inoculation amounted to a crime against science and humanity. Many therefore went to considerable lengths to evade the controls. Jefferson, at the age of twenty-three, embarked on a solemn journey to Philadelphia for the purpose of securing his immunity there. In Boston, where the practice was more acceptable, John Adams holed himself up for an inoculation by Dr. Joseph Warren, and made use of his quarantine period to exchange lovelorn letters with fiancée Abigail. (Warren, the tragic hero of Bunker Hill, was soon to become a professional rival, then a friend and close political ally of Thomas Young in Boston.)

The good citizens of Salisbury cannot have been surprised to see Ethan Allen committing the crime in broad daylight. By the age of twenty-six, Allen had already accumulated quite a rap sheet. He regularly shows up in the courthouse records of the time "in a tumultuous and offensive manner," "with threatening words and angry looks," "his fist lifted up," and stripping himself "even to his naked body."[3] Thomas Young's involvement in the affair was no big surprise either. Now thirty-three, he, too, had already acquired a reputation as a man of "daring profaneness" and a "professed infidel"—and had a conviction for blasphemy from a New York court to prove it.

The selectmen of Salisbury had already expressly denied Allen permission to be inoculated—which is probably why he and his rogue doctor chose to make sure that everybody in town knew what they were doing. One of the selectmen was the Reverend Jonathan Lee, a cousin of Allen who had previously suffered the misfortune of serving briefly as his tutor. He knew all about Ethan's problem with authority. The other important selectman happened to be a Stoddard and thus a representative of the powerful New England clan that numbered among its members the late Reverend Jonathan Edwards, his grandson Timothy Dwight, and the occupants of a very large number of high offices throughout Connecticut and Massachusetts.

News of the spectacularly public act of inoculation soon reached the ears of Stoddard and Lee. By the time the town bosses caught up with the inoculators, the party seems to have moved into a local tavern. Young disappears from the record at this point, indicating that he perhaps wisely accepted a request for a house call in some faraway town. Allen, on the other hand, was present and accounted for, and making sure that everyone within shouting distance would know of his act of medicinal defiance.

Words were exchanged. Lee and Stoddard cannot have found the words from Allen's side pleasant to hear. Allen cannot have liked what Lee and Stoddard had to say either. Allen's state of mind survives in a convoluted oath he made at the time, duly recorded by the court:

By Jesus Christ, I wish I may be Bound Down in Hell with old Belzabub a Thousand years in the Lowest Pitt in Hell and that Every Little Insippid Devil should come along by and ask the Reason of Allens lying there, [if] it should be said [that] he made a promise . . . that he would have satisfaction of Lee and Stoddard and Did Not fulfill it.

In the end, the town overlords didn't charge Allen for the inoculation infraction. Instead they brought him in for blasphemy. The laws against blasphemy at the time were fierce—though the enforcement was lax except in instances, like this one, where it might be supposed to serve some socially useful purpose. Demonstrating a talent for courtroom sophistry that would serve him well in his future career as the leader of a squatters' revolt, Allen defended himself by arguing that his oath was merely a hypothetical one. Its blasphemous clauses, he pointed out, only kicked in if he failed to keep his own promise to himself. He won a surprise acquittal, though the damage to his reputation, such as it was, cannot have been negligible.[4]

Perhaps the most startling thing about the smallpox iconoclasts of Salisbury is that they got away with it—or at least enough of it so that the record survives for us to see. In an earlier time, society would surely have found a way to correct the deviance of men like Allen and Young. Indeed, the accepted method in the New England of yore would have called for the cropping of an ear, driving a hot iron nail driven through the tongue, or spending an afternoon in the stocks, to be followed by eternal banishment from the history books. Why did these two men not disappear, as such miscreants customarily did, into the endless void of unrecorded history as just another pair of village atheists, transmuting the injustices of superstitious religion into their own private rationalism? The other question to which the smallpox episode must give rise has to do with the degree of passion that erupted around the event. Clearly, these were the kind of men who didn't need much of an excuse to break things. Where did all that anger come from?

With the kind of wisdom that only historians can have, one could speculate that the conflict that played itself out on the steps of the Salisbury meetinghouse was the harbinger of a significant cultural and perhaps political revolution in North America. It could be seen as one among many collisions between religion and science, between authority and the common man, between the old and the new that would eventually add up to an overthrow of the existing order of things. What we may know for sure is that it points backward to a political and cultural transformation that had been a long time in building. The story really begins with the extraordinary events that took place several decades previously, around the time when the smallpox rebels of Salisbury first opened their eyes.

THE CONNECTICUT RIVER, New England's longest waterway, drains the eastern faces of the Green Mountains and carries the silt through a fertile basin down to Long Island Sound, tracing a plume of brown that extends far into the Atlantic Ocean. The town of Northampton lies on a misty stretch of the river that winds through the muddy lowlands of central Massachusetts.[5] Owing to the fertility of the land, the two hundred or so families who inhabited the town in the first decades of the eighteenth century lived in closer proximity than most other people in New England, and this density of contact, it was suggested at the time, explained something of the precarious intensity of the town's religious life. Yet nothing that came before or after was quite like the spiritual earthquake that rocked Northampton in the winter of 1734, when its thirty-one-year-old minister turned his icy gaze on his flock of farming folk and discovered only sinners in dire need of a renewal of faith.

Jonathan Edwards was born high on the stepladder of life, the pride of an established clan, destined for Yale and a life devoted to higher service.[6] He inherited his ministry at Northampton from his distinguished grandfather, and he relied in his office on the patronage of a rich uncle. His grandchildren rose to great fame (Timothy Dwight) and infamy (Aaron Burr). Perhaps conveniently, Jonathan believed in the rightness of the order of things, an order that cascaded from God down to the lowliest arachnid, in which all "have their appointed office . . . and everyone keeps his place."[7] But he wasn't what one could call a happy man.

He was tall, gaunt, and hollow around the cheekbones, owing to a troubled relationship with food; a brilliant student; a formidable theologian; and a writhing nest of the anxieties that typically beset Puritans as they fretted over the quality of their own belief and their uncertain prospects for salvation. The diary he kept as a young man shows that he could be as hard on himself as he would later be on his congregation. He was, in his own words, "base," "vile," "dull," "miserably negligent," "indulging in horrid laziness," "decaying," "dead," and often fantasizing about the circumstances of his own death. Fortunately, there was a way out. "I find myself much more sprightly . . . for my self-denial in eating, drinking, and sleeping," he observed. "After the greatest mortifications, I always find the greatest comfort."[8] In keeping with the custom of his time and place, he lashed himself down to an itemized list of seventy resolutions, and then he kept track of his progress by the number. Even his ministerial colleagues tended to find him "withal pretty recluse, austere and rigid."[9]

When we look back on the New England of the historical imagination, we sometimes like to see a city upon a hill, where everyone prayed to the same God and all were united under the cope of the same heaven. When Jonathan Edwards looked around, he saw a people slouching toward Gomorrah.[10] The young men and women of Northampton, he recorded with dismay, were given to "licentiousness," "night-walking," "frequenting the tavern," and holding "conventions of both sexes, for mirth and jollity, which they called frolics."[11] Worst of all, these modern ways were infecting everyone, Edwards was sure, even those who commanded the pulpits of the nation's churches. The entire region was slithering down the slippery liberal slopes of Arminianism—the infinitely conceited belief, associated with the controversial Dutch theologian Jacobus Arminius (1560–1609), that individuals have a meaningful role to play in bringing about their own salvation. "Whatever scheme is inconsistent with our *entire* dependence on God for all is repugnant to the design and tenor of the gospel," he announced on a visit to Boston—that fetid urban swamp of decayed theology.[12]

Toward the end of 1733, Edwards detected the first signs that perhaps God had greater things in store for the homely town of Northampton. The young people, he noted, had adopted a more serious mien and seemed newly open to the message that was just then being passed down from God through the office of his minister. In April 1734, two young people died unexpectedly, adding still more to the solemnity of the moment. In December 1734, "there were, very suddenly, one after another, five or six persons who were to all appearances savingly converted."[13] Around the dawn of the New Year, the lightning from above burst into a bright flame on the ground, and hundreds of Northamptonites found themselves engulfed by the message that Edwards had taken upon himself to deliver.

In the kindling pages of Edwards's narrative of the revival, the news of the surprising works of God spread like wildfire around New England and then leapt across the ocean to mother England. There the tidings moved a charismatic preacher named George Whitefield to awaken as many sinners as might fit into a large cow pasture. Whitefield was not the brightest bulb in the evangelical firmament, but he was unquestionably the loudest. Endowed with exceptional thespian talents—as a child he had shown great interest in theater—he broadcast Edwards's message with a booming voice and an entrepreneurial flair that its original exponent sorely lacked. His star quality was such that he could bring audiences to tears merely by pronouncing the word "Mesopotamia," or so it was said.[14]

In 1739, the sound and the fury sailed back to America, on the boat with Whitefield, touching off the spiritual conflagration known today as the First Great Awakening. Over the next two years, crowds numbering as many as thirty thousand gathered in fields and town squares up and down the colonies for the privilege of hearing that Almighty God had already decided their destination for them, between the brimstone furnaces of hell and the pearly gates of heaven. At one of his events, the revival brought forth such a stampede that the event was compared with "the time of the general earthquake."[15] Somewhere in that shaking mass of North American humanity, inflamed with the spiritual anguish of the moment, one might have found a little boy named Thomas Young.

JOHN YOUNG, his cousin Mary, and seventy or so of their kin sailed from Dublin in the spring of 1728, leaving astern an Ireland mired in "Poverty, Wretchedness, Misery, and Want."[16] The ship remained at sea for twenty-one weeks and three days, at the mercy of a psychotic captain who smashed the skull of one crewmember with a pipe and demanded a ransom from the passengers before bringing them ashore. Many of the older members of the clan died of starvation before the ship finally landed on Cape Cod. The survivors wintered in Massachusetts and then sailed around Long Island and up the Hudson River to Ulster County, coming to rest in the loamy foothills of the Catskill Mountains. There twenty-seven-year-old John bought three plots of cheap farmland, built a log cabin, and proposed marriage to Mary. In that cabin, on February 19, 1731, was born Thomas, the first of John and Mary's seven children.

According to his admiring younger brother Joseph, Thomas showed early "signs of a fertile genius and surprising memory."[17] As there were no schools in their remote settlement, Thomas relied on his grandmother for his education. By the age of six, he could read any English book correctly and fluently. Soon he cracked the hardest book on arithmetic that his father could find. When a new school at last opened several miles away, the villagers solemnly informed the new schoolmaster that he would earn great fame by educating such a prodigy. "If his other talents are equal to his invention of means to excite laughter and merriment," the schoolmaster soon reported back, "he is surely a most surprising lad."

One day at school the son of a local grandee told Thomas to quit disturbing the class with his pranks. "I shall have a great estate to manage, which will require all the knowledge I can gain to manage it, and support my rank," the pompous boy informed his wayward classmate. "But if you can gain a knowledge of pounds, shillings, and pence, it is all you will ever have occasion for." Thomas looked at the boy "with the most sovereign contempt" and announced that he would soon know enough to become his teacher. He stopped the horseplay and dedicated himself to becoming the school's star student. Even as he grew up to become a respected physician and prominent man of public affairs, Young still carried a sore spot of resentment that flared into rage whenever it rubbed up against pretensions to social superiority.

Thomas's formal education came to an abrupt and permanent end when, after a brief stint in the backwoods, the local schoolmaster was called away to start a new school in faraway New York City. The villagers agreed that it would be "almost criminal" to leave their homegrown genius without the benefit of higher learning. When business took them to the big city, they returned with stacks of books for their unschooled scholar. Out on the edge of the family farm, Thomas built himself an arbor out of grape vines, and there he retreated with his stash and taught himself everything he knew. His parents, alarmed by his bookish behavior, tried to get him to play ball with the other children, but Tommy just wanted to read. To the end of his days he spoke of his favorite authors with the enthusiasm of one convinced that the treasures of life are to be found between the covers of a good book.

We often think of America's revolutionary deists as an educated elite, the products of fine universities; and many of them—Jefferson, Madison, Adams, Freneau, Morris—were just that. But a surprising number, like Young, were compelled to make their own way in the world of letters. Paine's brief encounter with formal education came to an end at the age of thirteen. Franklin's schooling ended at the age of ten. And no one could outdo Ethan Allen in the annals of self-improvement. There was only one book readily available in the settlement of his birth—the Bible—and so it was the Bible Ethan read, over and over again, until its parables took up residence in every foxhole of his mind, always ready to sally forth to defend a friend or threaten a foe.[18] In later life, he developed a uniquely bombastic style of expression—"that sonorous pomposity so peculiar to him," said one critic—that made him sound like the King James's version of Moses after a long day in the desert.

Like Young, America's homegrown deists emerged from their self-directed educations with that gnawing combination of pride and insecurity that is the usual lot of those compelled to assume responsibility for their own advancement. The author of *The Oracles of Reason* was a man who claimed to have learned everything worth knowing from "the air we breathe in, the light of the sun, the waters of the murmuring hills," a man with a keen sense for the rhythm of the "rainy and fair seasons, monsoons and refreshing breezes, feed time and harvest, day and night."[19] Yet in his private letters as in the frank preface to his book, Allen never stopped apologizing for his lack of formal education; and although his apologies sometimes smack of an autodidact's backhanded self-congratulation, for the most part they read like the genuine laments of a proud man mortified by his deficiencies. Franklin, too, spoke of higher learning as one raised in the hard knowledge of just how easy things might have been. As a teenager, writing newspaper columns under the cover of a fictional woman called Silence Dogood, he lampooned Harvard College as a place where boys with more money than brains dally with "Madam *Idleness* and her Maid *Ignorance*."[20] Then he turned around and complained that denying "the Advantages of Learning to Women" is "one of the most barbarous Customs of the World."

Perhaps the curious thing about America's lowborn deists is that, for one reason or another, they all seem to have decided early that they didn't have to play the hand that life had dealt them. As a boy, Ben was so fed up with his lot as the thirteenth son of a soap-maker that he threatened to run out to sea. Tom Paine actually did ship out to sea, at the age of nineteen, aboard a privateer. The runaway experience gave him, as it did Ben, the sense that he was "the carver of my own fortune."[21]

Thomas Young, too, was a natural born rebel. He must have known that his natural intelligence would surely have guaranteed an easy path through college and then to a ministry or dignified profession, had he been born just a little closer to the sun. Some historians posthumously granted him a diploma from Yale, on the mistaken theory that every well-read man in the Revolution must have had such a degree. But Tommy was everything Jonathan Edwards was not. He was born to the class of children destined to listen to sermons, not to deliver them. It was from some of those sermons that the lively little boy first learned that he deserved to die.

THE MESSAGE THAT Edwards sought to convey to the sinners of Northampton had a bright side. To those who acknowledged their own depravity and impotence before the Almighty, Edwards promised a beauty beyond any beauty we know, a joy beyond joy. Nature itself gives us at least an inkling of the happiness that awaits us. "The beauty of trees, Plants, and flowers with which God has bespangled the earth is Delightsome, the beautiful frame of the body of Man . . . is Astonishing, the beauty of the moon and stars is wonderfull," Edwards exulted. "But"—and it was all about the "but"—"it is all Deformity and Darkness in Comparison with the higher Glories and beauties of the Creator of all."[22]

It was the dark side of Edwards's message that people tended to remember. He communicated it well in his most famous sermon, *Sinners in the Hands of an Angry God*, first delivered in 1741 a few miles downriver from Northampton in the town of Enfield, Connecticut.[23] In that instance, according to later eyewitness reports, the town's farming families arrived at the meetinghouse in a carefree, even insouciant mood. Edwards soon put an end to that. In his weirdly monotonic voice, he laid out in detail the torments that awaited them down beneath the brown earth on the banks of the Connecticut River. He told them of the lions that devoured the wicked, of serpents that swallowed sinners whole, and of much mischief with fire. He told them that God "holds you over the pit of hell, much as one holds a spider or some loathsome insect, over the fire, abhors you and is dreadfully provoked; his wrath toward you burns like fire . . . you are ten thousand times so abominable in his eyes as the most hateful venomous serpent." He told them it was no good trying to be good: damnation is the destiny of every soul "that has not been born again, however moral and strict, sober and religious, they may otherwise be." He let them know that the more they suffered, the more joy they would bring to the saved, who would delight in their pain for all eternity.

The printed text of *Sinners in the Hands of an Angry God* approaches its finale with a rhetorical masterstroke, in which Edwards makes it all seem as real as tomorrow morning's bacon and eggs:

> And it would be a wonder, if some that are now present should not be in hell in a very short time, even before this year is out. And it would be no wonder, if some persons that sit here now, in this

meetinghouse, in health, quiet and secure, should be there before tomorrow morning.

According to a witness, however, the preacher never made it to the end of the sermon, for he could not make his somber voice heard above the din. As the crowd fell under the sway of his quietly hypnotic delivery, a "great moaning and crying out" arose "throughout the whole house." "What shall I do to be saved," the people screamed. "Oh I am going to Hell."[24]

Edwards's preaching delivered an astonishing rush of converts of all ages in Northampton, but there was always something definitive about its impact on young children. In *Sinners*, Edwards himself directly warned the children that they, too, were doomed, and the little ones evidently got the message. According to one newspaper report, "The *terrible language* . . . frequently frights the *little children*, and sets them a Screaming: and that frights their *tender Mothers*, and sets them to Screaming, and by degrees spreads over a great part of the Congregation."[25]

Phebe Bartlet, for example, was a normal and sprightly four-year-old, according to Edwards's own narrative of the revival—until the day her eleven-year-old brother, who had already experienced a saving conversion, told her about hell. Terrified that she might suffer an eternity in the flames, Phebe took to shutting herself in her closet, five or six times every day, where she might contemplate her innate turpitude and pray to God for forgiveness. She fretted to her parents that she "could not find God." One day she was heard making loud noises in the closet. She emerged and began writhing on the floor before her mother. "I am afraid I am going to hell," she cried. Mother gathered up the tears in her soft arms. Then a smile burst through the clouds on the little girl's face, and she said, "Mother, the kingdom of heaven is come to me." Phebe returned to the closet for further contemplation and, upon emerging for a second time, announced, "I can find God!" Mother believed that her daughter had been savingly converted, and upon close examination of the evidence, Edwards concurred. That evening, there was much rejoicing in the Bartlet household. Phebe went on to become a devoted follower of her minister and an exceptionally good girl—the kind of girl who would adamantly refuse to eat the plums that her sisters plucked from a generous neighbor's tree, a girl whose great joy was bounded only by the knowledge that her unredeemed siblings were doomed to an eternity in hell.

The key to the joy beyond joy available to the savingly converted, as Phebe perhaps intuitively grasped, was absolute submission. Happiness is obedience itself, obedience without sense or purpose. In this respect Edwards's own wife Sarah served as a model of piety. Prone since childhood to depression—she had "many ups and downs," Jonathan observed—Sarah developed an invincible conviction of her own worthlessness. It was not just God's apparent indifference, she explained; it was also the "ill will" of her husband that made her hate herself so. But she soon came to understand that her sense of worthlessness was direct evidence that God had plans for her. Release, she understood, comes with submission; and submission brings a kind of power. Soon she rejoiced in the humiliation, for the more she suffered, the more she knew God cared, and the harder it hit her, the more she was sure that she could withstand anything for him. Impatient to become one with Jesus, she ecstatically declared herself prepared to die "on the rack or at the stake." Like a number of Edwards's other converts, she began to feel "impatient at the thought of living." In a passage that her great-grandson edited out of the first edition of her writings and that perhaps offers a glimpse of life in the Edwards household, Sarah makes clear that she was willing to make enslavement a way of life in the home:

> I . . . thought that if [my husband] should turn to be most cruel to me and should horsewhip me every day I would so rest in God that it would not touch [my heart] or diminish my happiness. I could still go on in the performance of all acts of duty to my husband.[26]

For the lucky few, such as Phebe and Sarah perhaps, Edwards's formula promised an incomparable bliss. For others, however, it posed considerable psychological risks. Some of those who remained mired in the first stage of conversion, wandering in the dark night of the soul and convinced of their unfathomable guilt, came to suspect that suicide might offer a more sure form of release than rebirth. The Northampton euphoria crashed to earth in the same year it began when a well-respected local merchant named Joseph Hawley, unable to find God in his heart, slit his own throat. Edwards acknowledged that many in the congregation seemed to hear a voice in their heads, whispering urgently, "Cut your own throat, now is good opportunity: *now! NOW!*" He had a ready explanation for the macabre end of his revival: "Satan seemed to be more let loose, and raged in a dreadful manner."[27]

THOMAS YOUNG was an exact contemporary of Phebe Bartlet. He was four years old when the revival exploded in Northampton, eight in the year that Whitefield turned the summer air thick with brimstone, and ten when Edwards fired off his famous sermon on the fate of sinners in the hands of an angry God. Whether the bookish immigrant child received the message from Edwards or Whitefield in person or from one of the other revivalists who fished for souls along the frontiers of New England is not known. That the idea of hell hit him hard is certain. Edwards and Young agreed on one point: that religious experience even at a very tender age can determine the course of a life.

"Before I was eight years old," Young informed the startled readers of the *Massachusetts Spy* in the fall of 1772, "[I] became a very serious enquirer of what I should do to be saved."[28] He, too, experienced "the blackness of darkness, misery, and despair" as he contemplated his own worthlessness and the reality that "God's glory required the eternal damnation of the sinner." There was no mistaking the terms of the transaction with Edwards's God: only "entire acquiescence" was evidence of "receiving grace." So Thomas yearned to submit: "God knows how much I prayed and labored for such a temper of soul, and how heavily I walked for some years, from a certain consciousness I had not yet obtained, and might therefore more probably have fallen among the many consigned to destruction, than the few whom sovereign grace was pleased to distinguish from the croud."

At the same time, Thomas could hardly suppress the instinctive horror he felt for the bargain that God appeared to be driving: "Doing, fasting, and praying were all abomination, while performed by me, confessedly a natural man; and yet these very abominations were pressed upon me as duties, for the neglect of which I must expect God's vengeance." He just wasn't the kind of kid who could lock himself in a closet and achieve a thrilling release through submission or take a knife and cut his own throat.

So Thomas rebelled. He rejected the very idea of an angry God who demands absolute humiliation upon pain of eternal damnation. The whole story, from the original sin of Adam to the Day of Judgment, he decided, was one big fraud. Worse, it was a form of blasphemy. "I never could reconcile these positions with the idea of an all-wise and powerful Being," he confessed in 1772. One does not have to read very hard into Young's confession to sense that what he really couldn't wrap his mind around as a boy, even more than the impeachment of God's goodness, was the idea of his own wickedness. He didn't think he was a sinner. He was, in his own curious phrase, "confessedly a natural man."

The very young age at which Thomas experienced his reverse-trip to Damascus, as it were, may strike us as precocious. But in fact it was par for the course for many of America's revolutionary deists. Thomas Paine, too, was "about seven or eight years" old, he later confessed, when he first doubted "the truth of the Christian religion." After attending a sermon on the subject of *Redemption by the Death of the Son of God,*" he writes, "I went into the garden, and as I was going down the garden steps (for I perfectly recollect the spot) I revolted at the recollection of what I had heard, and thought to myself that it was making God Almighty act like a passionate man that killed his son when he could not revenge himself any other way; and as I was sure a man would be hanged that did such a thing, I could not see for what purpose they preached such sermons."[29]

Franklin was twelve years old, according to family legend, when he urged his father to say his prayers over a barrel of beef rather than waste time saying grace before meals. He was fifteen when he "began to doubt of Revelation it self."[30] He was sixteen when Cotton Mather denounced the newspaper he was running with his brother as "a Wickedness never parallel'd any where upon the Face of the Earth."[31] He was seventeen when "my indiscreet Disputations about Religion began to make me pointed at with Horror by good People, as an Infidel or Atheist."[32] He was nineteen when he went to London, where he cavorted with the freethinkers who gathered in the city's coffeehouses like so many grounds at the bottom of a cup. And he was not yet twenty when he produced *A Dissertation on Liberty and Necessity*, a metaphysical treatise in which he made plain that he was not just a well-read freethinker but a radical one, sailing on the extreme edge of the atheistic materialism blowing in from Holland and sweeping across the English intellectual landscape.

Ethan Allen, too, "began early in life to dispute and argue on religious matters," according to brother Ira.[33] His parents, taking note of his "youthful disposition to contemplation," packed him off to Salisbury at the age of seventeen for a taste of formal education under his respected cousin, the Reverend Jonathan Lee. In the *Oracles*, Allen—and it can only be Allen in this instance—gives an idea of the uncomfortable scene that followed.[34] Upon sitting down with a reverend who was his instructor, the author reports, he informed his teacher that the doctrine of original sin is repugnant to reason. How could the careless behavior of Adam and Eve in the Garden of Eden, he demanded to know, be so unjustly imputed on their "un-offending offspring"? The reverend replied that it was essential to believe in the fall of man, for without original sin, there would be no need for redemption, and therefore no need for our Redeemer. The pupil mulled over the problem for some days and came back with an answer. The reverend was right: no original sin means no Jesus. And no Christian religion or Christian preachers, for that matter.

The author of Ethan Allen's Bible goes on to renew Thomas Young's assault on the theology of the revival religion with the repetitive fury of a lumberjack swinging an axe on deadwood. The God of Edwards, he declares, is "some inhuman, cruel and destructive being, who delighted in wo, and pungent grief."[35] The doctrine that God predestines only a small number of souls for salvation is "unworthy of

God."[36] The belief that the beneficiaries of God's selective largess are a handful of people who happen to attend the right church is "narrow and bigoted." The only conceivable proof of the depravity of man is the depravity of the priests who promote that pernicious doctrine in order to manipulate their gullible victims. The idea that God stokes the eternal flames of hell in order to sweeten the honey of salvation for the elect renders the author of the *Oracles* apoplectic in disgust: "*O horrible* most *horrible impeachment* of DIVINE GOODNESS!"

The sense of outrage that fires up the author of the *Oracles*, the same that leaps from the pages of Thomas Young's confessions, is just as present, and just as incandescent, in the works of a much more controlled man like Jefferson. "It would be more pardonable to believe in no God at all, than to blaspheme him by the atrocious attributes of Calvin," Jefferson fumes in one diatribe to Adams.[37] "Howl, snarl, bite, ye Calvinistick!" Adams replies to Jefferson. "Ye will say I am no Christian: I say Ye are no Christians."[38] It is often suggested that a cool skepticism pulled the heroes of the Enlightenment away from orthodox religion, as if their theological conclusions followed from a quiet deliberation on the evidence presented in scientific study. But they were as certain as could be that the revival deity they confronted was the hideous consequence not of logical error or factual mistake but of gross turpitude. They were cool only in the sense that fury can be icy.

The kind of anti-conversion that Thomas Young and his fellows experienced was in fact a definitive one for thinking people not just in America but also throughout the European world at the time. It was axiomatic among sophisticated observers that "freethinking" was a direct consequence of religious "enthusiasm," as the religion of the revivals was then called. "As the late enthusiasm is much abated, free thinking, as it is called, which is worse, takes the place of it," lamented New York's Samuel Johnson in 1753.[39] Over in Britain, David Hume took note of the same tendency. After "the first fire of enthusiasm is spent, men naturally, in all fanatical sects, sink into the greatest remissness and coolness in sacred matters," and thus "our sectaries, who were formerly such dangerous bigots, are now become very free reasoners."[40] The same might as well have been said about the situation in France.

Denis Diderot was a complacent student of theology until, in the same years that Northampton was being revived, he encountered a frenzied mob of *convulsionnaires* in the streets of Paris.[41] The *convulsionnaires* experienced divinely inspired seizures for hours at a time, believed in faith-based cures, and, though nominally Catholic, preached a theology striking in its similarity to Jonathan Edwards's Calvinism. These frenzied enthusiasts soon came to serve Diderot, Voltaire, and their fellow *philosophes* as the defining example of everything that their philosophy was not.

No doubt some of the prospective philosophers of the early modern world moved on from their early revulsion before the despotic deity that everywhere loomed over the religion of the revivals, settling into some uneasy coexistence with the popular religion of their time. Thomas Young was among those who did not. The first place he shows up in the historical record after leaving home is the Dutchess County Courthouse, where he was arraigned at the age of twenty-five. "Not having the fear of God before his eyes but being seduced by the instigation of the devil," reads the charge, Young "did . . . speak and publish these Wicked false and Blasphemous Words concerning the said Christian Religion (to wit) Jesus Christ was a knave and a fool." Young allegedly went on to clarify helpfully that "the said Jesus Christ of whom he then and there spoke was born of the Virgin Mary."[42] Young disputed the phrasing—but not the fact—of his blasphemy, and he was found guilty as charged. Two years later, perhaps hoping to scrub the dark spot on his curriculum vitae, Young returned to offer a belated apology, in which he did "own and acknowledge myself to have abused the person and character of Jesus Christ" and humbly begged the pardon "of God Almighty, the world of Mankind and the present Court of Sessions."

The apology did nothing to stop him from spitting into the wind. Later, upon his arrival in Boston, the following advertisement in one of the city's newspapers gives a sense of the kind of impression he created there: "*From Socrates to the Athenians*. Wherever you see a *Young* fellow, especially one that is a stranger among you, take upon him to censure of ridicule the established Religion of the country; whatever wisdom or knowledge he may pretend to, you may set him down for a contemptible coxcomb and an arrant FOOL."[43] Young promptly returned fire with his own advertisement, in which he explained to "the Athenians" that his intent was not to challenge true religion, but only "*Superstitions*."[44]

Though Young eventually learned to wrap the worst of his heterodoxies in deistic pieties, there remained something flinty, uncompromising, and willfully outspoken about his infidelity. He was a man for whom silence was guilt and moderation a vice. Even as a medicine man he proved to be something of an extremist. Case after case required the doctor to act, without cavils, before it was too late. Given the state of medical science at the time, it remains an open question whether with this heroic approach he killed more people than he saved. In his political career, the same all-or-nothing attitude made him a man to be watched—and to be watched out for. On the great dilemmas of the day, the irreligious doctor was usually the first to propose excision, amputation, or some other radical intervention in the body politic.

WITH AN AMBIGUITY that would prove more fatal than most, Jonathan Edwards always left it a little unclear as to whether the principal beneficiary of the theory of joy was to be the individual or the community. On the one hand, it seemed obvious that the thing to be revived was the group: the congregation, the town, the colony, perhaps the nation. "The true, spiritual, original beauty," said Edwards, is that of a people "united in benevolent agreement of the heart."[45] Indeed, the scriptures foretold that a people united in "extraordinary prayer" might one day experience an "unspeakably happy and glorious"[46] moment, "the glorious day of religious revival,"[47] in which "holiness" would be "inscribed on every thing, on all men's common business and employments, on the common utensils of life," and even the children would behave like hundred-year-old saints. The recent, extraordinary events in Northampton, Edwards went on to insinuate, gave cause to hope that Jesus might very well choose to establish his new kingdom in a neighborhood very near by. And thus his followers, like zealots throughout history, set about converting others so that they might believe in themselves.

This rapturous cry for unity, it should go without saying, arose from the unnerving experience of disunity that afflicted places like Northampton. The waves of settlers crowding in on the muddy flatlands, the frustrations of young people forced to postpone marriage and remain in their parents' homes, the constant shuffling of the order of things that placed young ministers in charge of aging settlers—these and other stresses of the moment inevitably produced a sense of dislocation and disorientation.[48] The confidence in a spiritual cure to these very material anxieties really rested on two very deep assumptions. The first was a kind of belief in belief: that only a shared act of faith, or a passion that stirs every heart together, can make us whole. The other assumption, usually left unstated, was the one that human beings invariably make about the groups to which they so anxiously wish to belong: that it is only worth being a member of a group if someone else isn't included. The strikingly cruel doctrines of election and predestination could be hedged and trimmed yet never quite extirpated from the religion of the revivals because they remained rooted in the very deep intuition that there is no "us" without a "them."

On the other hand, Edwards pushed to its extreme the other, individualistic side of Protestantism, the part that begins with the conviction that no clerical authority need or should stand in between the individual and the word of God. Indeed, he sometimes seemed to go even farther, to a place where God didn't need words at all. A pure act of faith uncorrupted by a single thought—the sheer will and affection of the believer—was sufficient, he seemed to suggest. His obsessive focus on the conversion experience had the effect of rendering the salvific magic of religion contingent upon something entirely personal and individual—something that you feel, on your own, deep inside the heart, something that you and you alone can know. Paradoxically, the religion of the revivals began to embody the same Arminian tendencies that Edwards thought the "utmost danger" to God's reign on earth.[49] It encouraged individuals to discover the sacred through the interpretation of the most particular elements of their personal experience. A colorful leaf falling at one's feet or a serendipitous encounter on the street might count as a more reliable communication with the Maker than a year in the pews. Edwards himself always demanded that the Bible should remain the foundation of worship. But in the minds of his followers—whose certainty about the truth of the scriptures often widely exceeded their knowledge of them—the texts that really mattered were the autobiographies of their own conversions.

Sovereignty over religion was passing from the pulpit to the pews, in a manner of speaking, and Americans soon discovered that democracy is a messy business. The kind of people that in an earlier time might have bowed to the spiritual instruction of their ministers now imagined that they had the power and the freedom to take salvation into their own hands. One Connecticut layman, capturing the mood of the times in an apt physical metaphor, marched on his old meetinghouse with an axe, chopped out the pew on which his family had prayed, and dragged it back to his own house. As the revival swept across the colonies, it tore apart souls and then it tore apart towns, with one side sneering at the crazed enthusiasts and the other side denouncing the agents of Satan. Then it tore them in half again, as groups within groups sought to remake the religious order according to the ideas that had been personally vouchsafed to them from God.

And so it came to pass that the revival, while pretending to unite the nation, in reality unified it only in the belief that there are aliens in our midst. These unbelievers—and the logic of the circumstances demanded that they would exist in great numbers—could only seem the very embodiment of evil and a living refutation of the nation's religious destiny. They came to be called witches, in the first instance, then Arminians, then freethinkers and infidels, and later communists and atheists; but they were always in some sense "un-American." Then as now, the believers who were most convinced of the exceptional place of their nation in the eyes of God were not coincidentally the ones who were most convinced of its depravity in the present moment. With respect to this dynamic of righteousness and paranoia, moreover, America was anything but exceptional. Thomas Hobbes had seen the same thing in Britain more than a century earlier. In 1640, "an amazing plague swept through our land, and countless learned men perished," he recalled in later life. "Whoever was infested by this plague thought that he alone had discovered divine and human right."[50]

In America, on the other hand, a new factor was in play, one that came down to a simple matter of geography. The travails of the Allen family illustrate the point well. In 1739 in Litchfield, Connecticut, when the Awakening ripped a line of fire between saints and sinners, it fell to Ethan Allen's father, Joseph, to stand up for the damned. Joseph was a liberal spirit, an Arminian or worse, and the local minister, a zealous acolyte of Jonathan Edwards, took it as a mission from on high to make his life in Litchfield unbearable. Joseph's solution to the problem would eventually become part of the American way: he picked up sticks and moved out to the frontier—which is why his one-year-old son grew up to know only the wilderness. The relief valve of geography made possible in America a degree of pluralism perhaps not attainable in any of the old countries of Europe, and so the Great Awakening really served as a kind of awakening to the multiplying divisions within a new and expanding modern state.

The most visible and consequential fractures at the time, it should be stressed, were not those between what today we might crudely file under the categories of the "religious" and the "secular," but among those who still called themselves Christians. The good old days of Christian America were deeply, angrily divided. In Boston, the Reverend Charles Chauncy collected the money and the loathing of the ruling elites of his city and set off to gather much of the information we have now about the practices of the revivalists. Chauncy's great protégé, the Reverend Jonathan Mayhew—the man credited with inventing the slogan "no taxation without representation"—was sure that the religion of Edwards was "puerile"[51] and "dishonorable to God and a libel on human nature."[52] Salvation, Mayhew pointedly inveighed, is to be found in "practical religion, the love of God, and a life a righteousness and charity" and "not any *enthusiastic fervors* of spirit . . . not a *firm persuasion* that we are elected of God."[53] Mayhew pushed so far in the opposite direction that he came down well beyond the Arminianism Edwards dreaded, landing in a territory that was then labeled Socinianism and is now generally called Unitarianism and that his many theological enemies branded simply as "atheism in the pulpit."[54] The controversy that raged around figures like Mayhew had the effect of pushing others—such as John Adams—into still more heterodox conclusions.[55]

As a bright Harvard-bound boy from a prosperous, religiously active family—his father was a deacon—John had inevitably grown up with the prospect of a ministry hovering over his future. All of that changed around his fifteenth birthday, in 1749, when the pastor at his local church in the Boston suburb of Braintree delivered a sermon titled *The Absurdity and Blasphemy of Depreciating Moral Virtue*. The Reverend Lemuel Briant was a "jolly, jocular, and liberal scholar," as Adams later recalled,[56] and a follower of Jonathan Mayhew. He, too, repudiated the doctrines of predestination and original sin that played such a prominent role in the religion of the revivals, and his convivial personality only made suspicions worse. Although nominally Arminian, he was sailing toward a carefree version of Christianity, if it can be called that, stripped of any belief in the divinity of Christ and in the Trinity.[57]

The scandalized clerics of Boston fired back with sermons like *The Absurdity and Blasphemy of Rev. Briant*. Jonathan Edwards himself lobbed in theological bombshells from a distance, violently depreciating all those who, like Briant and Mayhew, appreciated moral virtue at the expense of God's grace. Soon the city was on fire with "the exquisite rancor of theological hate," as one contemporary put it.[58] The controversy—some of which took place in the Adams family living room—"broke out like the eruption of a volcano and blazed with portentious aspect for many years," John later recalled.[59] After fighting back with more sermons and pamphlets of his own, sporting not altogether accurate titles like *Some Friendly Remarks* and *Some More Friendly Remarks*, Briant lost his job. He was saved from further theological opprobrium by premature death at the age of thirty-two.

John Adams was no Thomas Young; yet the secondary and tertiary consequences of the Awakening radicalized him in a certain way, too. Half a century later he could still recall his horror at the "spirit of dogmatism and bigotry in clergy and laity."[60] At the time, he made a life-altering decision to study for a career in law rather than the ministry. As he explained to his brother-in-law, "The frightful engines of Ecclesiastical Councils, of Diabolical Malice and Calvinistic good nature never ceased to terrify me exceedingly when I thought of Preaching. But the Point is now determined, and I shall have the Liberty to think for myself."[61] The example of moderation in religion that proto-Unitarians such as Briant and Mayhew set ultimately served to keep people like Adams (and his wife Abigail) within the loose folds of the religious tradition of their forebears even as they rejected every doctrine that nominally defines the Christian religion.

In 1750, the contradictions of the Awakening finally came home to roost in the place where it all began. Edwards's grip on the spiritual life of Northampton began to slip. Some of the trouble can be traced to causes of the ordinary variety: Uncle John Stoddard unhelpfully died, depriving Edwards of his chief patron; Edwards's insistent demands for a higher salary from the congregation were beginning to grate; they grated more when Sarah was caught one too many times compensating for her troubles by splurging on the kind of trinkets usually reserved for the fancy ladies; and Edwards's unduly harsh response when a few sexually frustrated young men were discovered doing bad things with midwifery books rubbed many people the wrong way. But the straw that broke the minister's career was his announcement that membership in the church henceforth would be available only to those who satisfied the church—meaning Edwards himself—that they had experienced a saving conversion. The source of the trouble, that is, went all the way down to the paradox at the bottom of Edwards's practice concerning who really had the power over salvation: the church or the people? The people decided that the power was theirs. So they fired Jonathan Edwards from the very pulpit from which he had delivered to them their religion.

In the aftermath of the insurrection of the Northamptonites, Edwards found himself wandering in a wilderness, quite literally. He moved to the Massachusetts frontier and performed missionary work among the Native Americans there. His name and his family eventually rescued him with an offer of the presidency of Princeton. He lived just long enough to watch his grand vision of a re-purified city on a hill dissolve amid the noise and the hate. His revulsion before the corruption of the times, true to his reactionary instincts, grew only more rancorous with age. "Things are going downhill so fast," he wrote to a friend a few years before his death in 1756. "A crisis is not very far off."[62]

THOMAS YOUNG'S youthful rejection of the established religion left him with much explaining to do; and he was convinced—to a degree that may be difficult to imagine today—that the answers were to be found in books. His journey of self-discovery really began in his backyard reading room. There he taught himself German to a high degree of fluency, as we know from his later efforts to foment revolution in Pennsylvania. His Latin and Dutch must have been serviceable, given his familiarity with the medical sources in those languages. As for French—he could read it, according to his brother, but he had no clue how to pronounce its mysterious *mots*, having found no one in the wilderness with whom he could converse. He also taught himself to play the violin, and in later life he carried his fiddle on his many travels.

Like many revolutionaries, Young had a taste for history, for he was certain that the key to a better future could be found somewhere in a forsaken past. He was particularly attracted to popular books of the time that retailed what has come to be called "the Saxon Myth": the saga of a noble race, blessed with democratic forms of government, that lost its freedom when William the French Bastard and his kleptocratic banditti befouled the British Isles with their foreign monarchy and foreign religion.[63] One important conduit for the legends of ancient Saxony was Algernon Sidney, whose *Discourses* enjoyed a very wide readership in America. Another key source was Thomas Gordon, whose translation of works by the ancient Roman historian Tacitus— the ultimate font of all representations of the Saxon lifestyle—came with a lengthy commentary in which Gordon hammered home the message of Saxon liberty. Together with his partner John Trenchard,

Gordon promoted the same message in a series of polemical writings assembled under the pseudonym of "Cato," in honor of the ancient Roman hero of republican virtue. Their work, gathered in *Cato's Letters*, has been widely cited as among the most important influences on revolutionary political thought in America,[64] and their impact on Young in particular is readily discernible.

Somewhere along the way Young became an avid reader of philosophy, and in particular of the kind of philosophy that, on account of its intellectual raciness, was widely suspected at the time of corrupting the youth. He later happily acknowledged his debt to Charles Blount, the author of the first *Oracles of Reason*. Like many in his time—though, curiously, unlike many scholars today—Young threw John Locke, the most famous English philosopher of the preceding century, in the same bucket with controversial deists like Blount. "Add to your libraries Locke's essay on human understanding," he urged the newspaper public of Boston.[65] Locke's "Essay on Government," he said, was "an invaluable little piece."

If one were to choose a representative source of philosophical inspiration for Young, a quiver for the growing bundle of maxims and arrows with which he fought back against the world's relentless demands for unquestioning obedience, the most apposite would have to be Alexander Pope's lengthy and controversial poem, the *Essay on Man* of 1734. Standing just four and a half feet tall and suffering from humiliating afflictions of the spine and bladder, Alexander Pope was unlucky in life and positively blighted after death.[66] The theologians heaped vituperation on his work, and his defenders didn't help by suggesting that he was too dim to detect the heresies that seeped like poison from his verses. Then he was revived as an English saint, and the controversy shut away in the cabinet of unwelcome memories. To this day, the *Essay on Man* is often brushed off as a confused exercise in happy-go-lucky classical deism, according to which God's stupendous wisdom bubbles beneath the crust of every well-baked apple pie. Yet Pope's talent was such that the phrases he minted have never stopped circulating: "to err is human"; "hope springs eternal"; "fools rush in"; "a little learning is a dangerous thing." At least in his own century, he won the admiration of great philosophers—Kant, Rousseau, Boling-broke, and Voltaire[67]—and Thomas Young, too, must be counted a member of this long-disbanded fan club. "Get Pope's *Essay on Man* and read it till [you] get him every word by heart," he wrote to a friend.[68] "The more you read and contemplate him, the more you'll love and admire him."

Many of Pope's contemporaries—Voltaire, for example—thought that the *Essay* owed everything to the work of the most famous deist of the age, and another of Thomas Young's heroes: Anthony Ashley Cooper, the third Earl of Shaftesbury. Few philosophers have suffered such cruelty as Shaftesbury at the hands of the historians of philosophy. In the first decades of the eighteenth century, his name shone with the luster of an Aristotle or a Plato, yet by the end of the same century it lay crumpled at the bottom of the trashcan of history. Shaftesbury blossomed as a philosopher while still in his youth, producing his first great work in his twenties, then faded fast from a respiratory ailment that brought his life to an early end in the finest continental hospices. He was an extraordinary philosophical stylist, ensconcing his insights in prose as comfortable as the drawing room furniture on which he languished, which gave many people the impression that his ideas were as benign as the aesthetic deity he celebrated. Yale president Ezra Stiles called him the "amiable Confucius of Deism."[69] But there was a subversive edge to Shaftesbury's thinking, and Young's later writings show that he found it.

Many readers at the time—including Young himself—subscribed to the theory that Pope's *Essay on Man* was just the verse translation of a prose message dictated by the notorious Henry St. John, Viscount Bolingbroke (1678–1751), a philosopher whose combination of worldliness and intellectual ambition few thinkers have ever matched. As a young man, Bolingbroke was famous mainly for keeping the most expensive prostitute in London (a Miss Gumley) and for his alleged ability to consume large volumes of wine without losing any of his celebrated dinner-table wit. Then he trained his formidable talents on politics and rose to become the most powerful minister in the Tory government. In 1715, when the succession of King George I scrambled the English power elite, it was suddenly all over, and Bolingbroke was forced to flee to France in mid-career. He settled in a country estate, married a rich widow (his second), scribbled down his philosophical musings, and impressed visitors such as Voltaire with his extraordinary ideas and even better table manners.

It takes some effort to imagine the sensation and alarm that surrounded the name of Bolingbroke when the four volumes of his rambling and sometimes tedious *Philosophical Works* were released posthumously in 1754, per the deceased's instructions. Samuel Johnson denounced him as "a scoundrel for charging a blunderbuss against religion and morality; a coward because he had not resolution to fire it off himself."[70] (Not coincidentally, Johnson was just as unkind about Pope.) The historian John Leland devoted the largest part of his polemical history of deism to Bolingbroke, accusing him of "extreme insolence," "virulence and contempt," and of engaging in "open attacks" on the Christian religion.[71] According to Jonathan Edwards's grandson, Timothy Dwight, "a great part of [Bolingbroke's] Works, particularly of his Philosophical Works, was written for no other end but to destroy Christianity."[72]

The aspects of Bolingbroke's works that the theologians most detested, of course, were the parts that appealed to readers like Young. Consider, for example:

> If redemption be the main fundamental article of the Christian faith, sure I am, that the account of the fall of man is the foundation of this fundamental article, and this account is, in all it's circumstances, absolutely irreconcilable to every idea we can frame of wisdom, justness, and goodness, to say nothing of the dignity of the supreme being.[73]

It is something more than coincidence that this passage from Bolingbroke, which so aptly condenses the reasoning behind Young's childhood anti-conversion, is among those that the young Thomas Jefferson copied into his *Literary Commonplace Book*.[74] In that student notebook, Bolingbroke alone accounts for an astonishing 40 percent of the words Jefferson deemed worthy of excerpting. (By contrast, the next most-cited source, the ancient Greek tragedian Euripides, registers a mere 5 percent.)

Indeed, the most representative aspect of Young's coming-of-age as a revolutionary deist was simply his reading list. Philip Freneau, the "poet of the American Revolution," all but plagiarized the *Essay on Man*, and hailed its author as "the heav'nly Pope." Ezra Stiles, the future president of Yale, whose learning and religion were in constant struggle, joyfully memorized every line of the *Essay on Man*, just as he thrilled over every mellifluous paragraph in Lord Shaftesbury's *Characteristicks*—until it dawned on him that these inspiring paeans to the deity were actually the filthy treasuries of the infidel philosophy of the age.[75] Franklin named Shaftesbury as one of the two philosophical guides of his youth. The other one was the deist Anthony Collins, a radicalized disciple of Locke. Locke of course was ubiquitous in America, as were Sidney and "Cato," whose columns were put to great use by Franklin, among many others.

Even the not-so-well-read Paine was connected within this relatively compact world of radical letters. When he returned to London from his teenage adventure as a privateer, sporting a tan, his trademark ponytail, a bundle of cash, and no duty beyond his own self-improvement, young Tom bought himself a couple of globes and attended the lectures of James Ferguson and Benjamin Martin, a pair of renowned astronomers and instrument-makers who took it upon themselves to disseminate Newtonian science along with helpings of deist philosophy to the common people.[76] Ferguson—whose work shows up in the anonymous *Sermon on Natural Religion* published in Boston in 1771—later put Paine in touch with Franklin, then in London, who in turn packed him off to America with a fine letter of recommendation.

When modern philosophers glance back at the authors that mattered for Young and his fellows, they tend to read into their work a number of modern philosophical preoccupations about the theory of knowledge, the philosophy of mind, and the various abstruse debates that go into converting the troublesome search for wisdom into a respectable academic discipline. All of those things were there, too, but to observers at the time there was a much more obvious thread that bound together writers such as Pope, Shaftesbury, Bolingbroke, Collins, Trenchard, Gordon, Sidney, and even (by some lights) Locke. They were all to some degree or other beyond the pale of religion. The only people these philosophers detested more than the priests were the tyrants who colluded with them for political gain. And they were unanimous in despising the religion of enthusiasm. One could even say that for those philosophers the problem of popular religion—how to understand this sudden effulgence of the new and increasingly empowered masses, how to contain the damage from it, how to reconcile it with the possibility of free self-government—was the problem of modernity itself.

IN THE LAST QUARTER of the eighteenth century, the conflict that flared on the front steps of the Salisbury meetinghouse in 1764 concluded with a decisive victory for the forces represented by Thomas Young and Ethan Allen over those of Jonathan Edwards, or so many observers at the time believed. In 1782, Allen's friend Hector St. John de Crèvecoeur noted with approval that "religious indifference" was one of the defining characteristics of the new America. "The strict modes of Christianity as practiced in Europe are lost," he observed. "The foolish vanity, or rather the fury of making Proselytes, is unknown here."[77] Edwards's self-anointed grandson Timothy Dwight, surveying the scene from the other side of the culture war, announced the same result in the title of his 1788 jeremiad: *The Triumph of Infidelity*.[78]

Crèvecoeur and Dwight were right, in an important sense, though in a more complicated way than can be conveyed by any linear narrative—whether of progress toward enlightenment or descent into godlessness. Even while infidelity captured the leadership of the Revolution, enthusiastic religious sects continued to proliferate and spread among the population. A half century after Crèvecoeur took note of America's religious indifference, another traveling Frenchman witnessed America in the throes of its Second Great Awakening. In

1831, according to Alexis de Tocqueville's report, the fury of making proselytes, far from being unknown, was something of a national pastime. By the middle of the nineteenth century, those denominations that had in an earlier time occupied the lunatic fringes of the revival came to dominate America's religious scene, especially on the frontier.

Enthusiasm and infidelity, moreover, were far from absolute contraries or mortal enemies during the revolutionary period. On the contrary, to a degree that seems surprising today, they established a crucial, if uneasy partnership in the course of the Revolution. The Awakening after all was a claim for popular sovereignty in matters of religion, and this democratization of church life naturally tended to ally itself with a democratization of political life. Even as they strived to impose an impossible spiritual unity on the land, the heirs of Jonathan Edwards therefore joined with Young and his rationalist friends in support of independence, revolution, and toleration. Both sides were expressions of the same pluralistic, individualistic, inherently "heterodox" reality. Young could hardly have emerged as an itinerant preacher of reason had he not been born to the same, inherently pluralistic, individualistic, and democratic land that spawned the traveling evangelists whose message he so adamantly rejected. Wandering infidels flourished alongside itinerant preachers because both were a species of infidelity—and this inherent, inescapable pluralism was and remains America's greatest strength, its genuine exception to the rule of history.

This alliance between infidels and enthusiasts, it is worth adding, was not in itself an American invention; it had its global antecedents. As Hume observed, religious enthusiasm (which he meant to contrast with the "superstition" of the Catholic Church) is generally a "friend to civil liberty." It was on this account, he noted, that during the gruesome religious-civil war in seventeenth-century England, "the Independents and the Deists, though most opposed in their religious principles, were united in their political ones, and were alike passionate for a commonwealth."[79] In America, the religious enthusiasts played an especially critical role in the establishment of a secular republic. When the time came to give force of law to the demands for religious freedom, infidels like Jefferson drafted the crucial bills while the members of dissenting sects provided the necessary votes for their passage.

Yet there remains an unbridgeable gap between the religious enthusiasts and the philosophical infidels, and it is readily visible in the matter where their tactical alliance mattered most: on religious freedom. In America as in England, religious dissenters rallied in support of religious freedom, but they rarely conceived of it as anything more than a means to the end of securing freedom for their own religion. The freedom to seek salvation through the personal interpretation of the Holy Scriptures was, in the final analysis, just the freedom to be a Protestant Christian, usually of one's own particular variety. In their practice, they were pluralists; in their theology, the enthusiasts were anything but. "Where they have not the power to carry on Persecution, and to become Masters, there they desire to live upon fair terms, and preach up Toleration," Locke observed about dissident religious sects. But as soon as "court-favor has given them the better end of the staff, and they begin to feel themselves the stronger, then presently peace and charity are to be laid aside."[80] John Adams made clear that Protestantism was no exception to the rule on religious "toleration": "Even since the Reformation, when or where has existed a Protestant or dissenting sect who would tolerate A FREE INQUIRY? Touch a solemn truth in collision with the dogma of a sect, though capable of clearest proof, and you will soon find you have disturbed a nest, and the hornets will swarm about your legs and hands, and fly into your face and eyes."[81]

Jefferson perhaps approached closest to the core of the issue in a passionate aside that interrupts his *Notes on the State of Virginia*:

Is uniformity attainable? Millions of innocent men, women, and children, since the introduction of Christianity, have been burnt, tortured, fined, imprisoned; yet we have not advanced one inch toward uniformity. What has been the effect of coercion? To make one half of the world fools, and the other half hypocrites. To support roguery and error all over the earth. Let us reflect that it is inhabited by a thousand millions of people. That these profess probably a thousand different systems of religion. That ours is but one of that thousand.[82]

The eternal, implacable demand for unity of belief, Jefferson intimates, is worse than just impracticable; it misconceives fundamentally the nature of human experience and the foundation of human community. Our problems don't arise from our failure to live up to the sure and simple creed of our forefathers; they stem from the delusion that the good old days ever really were.

America's founding radicals sought something more than freedom *for* this or that religion.[83] The Virginian Edmund Randolph detected the difference when he observed that Jefferson's "opinions against restraint on conscience ingratiated him with the enemies of the establishment, who did not stop to inquire how far those opinions might border on skepticism or infidelity."[84] Thomas Young, a man seemingly born with the insatiable desire to exercise the natural freedom of his own mind, hinted at the difference in his public answer to one of many charges of religious infidelity:

> Nothing has distinguished me more than my constant defence of the Magna Charta of Heaven, in matters of faith, *entire liberty of conscience.* We have no business . . . with any man's creed, further than its peculiar articles plainly threaten the peace of society. Whoever cannot be contented to worship the author of his being and giver of all his enjoyments, in the manner most agreeable to his own understanding and conscience, and quietly suffer his neighbor to enjoy the same privilege, . . . his temper is as opposed to the spirit of true religion as that which would countenance robbery and murder.[85]

To modern ears, Young's use of deistic tropes ("author of his being") and Protestant language ("conscience") might appear to align his position with that of the religious enthusiasts. But there is a critical difference between favoring the freedom of religion and saying that this freedom is itself "the spirit of true religion." In the eyes of Young and his fellow natural-born rebels, the questioning, the challenging, the rejection of all acts of faith—in short, the freedom *from* religion that makes possible the improvement of human understanding—was *all* of religion. Everything else that called itself religion was no better than "robbery and murder." They aimed not just for the freedom of religion but for a religion of freedom itself.

The differences between the enthusiasts and the infidels spring from a deeper set of differences having to do with ideas about ideas themselves. The religion of the revivals, like most popular religions, floats its doctrines on a wide ocean of unspoken ideas, a hidden religion before all religion whose tenets have to do with the very idea of moral agency, the difference between mind and matter, the nature of "nature" itself, the sources of social unity, and the foundation of political authority. All of these ideas deserve to be considered in more detail, though they revolve around a certain belief about belief. Only through an unthinking act of faith, a pure expression of the heart without mind, says the common religious consciousness, can we make ourselves whole as individuals and as a community. The radical philosophy that passed from the early modern philosophers through the hands of men like Thomas Young challenges the religion that precedes popular religion on every front, and the most fundamental disagreement falls on just this one point: that we realize our freedom and govern ourselves, individually and collectively, not through acts of faith but through acts of understanding.

When discussion turns to the history of ideas, there is a natural tendency to suppose that the ideas that matter in history are those that garner the largest number of votes. According to this line of thought, the theology of the revivalists, who undoubtedly outnumbered the infidels, must explain much more of the Revolution than the philosophy of its rationalist leaders. Indeed, probably the most popular narrative concerning the very idea of America—one that unites Christian nationalists with a large number of sober historians—has it that the American Republic owes its independence and its individual freedoms to its Protestant Christian legacy.[86] This narrative often comes with a distinguished lineage that traces the ideas of individual rights and freedom of conscience to seminal Protestant thinkers such as John Milton (1608–1674), and it characteristically represents Jefferson, Madison, and precursors like Locke as latitudinarian Protestants or (to use a label that at the time would have sounded like a gross oxymoron) "Christian Deists."[87]

But this gets the history of ideas almost exactly wrong. It is to confuse mere precedence in time with causality. It is to suppose, falsely, that the ideas that best explain the actions of a collective are those that a majority of people within it pretend to carry around in their heads. Reformed religion brought carnage to Britain and Germany in the seventeenth century and madness to America in the eighteenth because it was a symptom of modernity, not a cause—a pathology, not a theory. Like the theology of Jonathan Edwards, with its burning lakes of sulfur, its girls who won't eat plums, its exaltation of belief, and its primitive celebration of "us" the "elect," it expressed much but explained little. It revealed more about the constitution of the minds of its adherents than about the nature of the new world emerging around them. Although it was and remains particularly suited to flourish under American conditions, it is not therefore necessarily a way to understand them. It is modernity seen through premodern eyes.

The Enlightenment, not the Reformation, was the axis on which human history turned. The alliance between the infidels and the enthusiasts in America and elsewhere was therefore not in the final analysis a partnership of equals, still less a meeting of the minds. The enthusiasts supplied much of the labor of the Revolution, but the infidels provided the ideas. The latter ultimately got what they thought they wanted; while the former got taken for a ride. Which is not to say that America's revolutionary infidels got *everything* they thought they wanted. Ideas are acts of understanding; they involve clearing away old delusions, not erecting new ones; they are inherently open, not closed, and their effects are always to some degree surprising. No doubt from a suitably grand perspective, the record of the founders' activity, too, might one day be reduced to delusions and all of human civilization represented as something like an ant colony, which expresses in the totality of its operations an understanding that none of its members may be said to possess. But they grasped enough that our explanation of the course of events most reasonably passes through theirs. Here, then, is one instance where ideas have a chance of explaining history—a case in which philosophers happened to rule.

THE YEAR 1764 marks the low point in the careers of the two small-pox agitators of Salisbury. Out of money and rapidly losing friends, Allen moved north to—of all places—Northampton, Massachusetts. A cousin there pressed upon him a copy of the sermons of Jonathan Edwards. The results were predictably unhappy: Allen managed to chastise the citizens of Northampton for dumping their preacher even as he insulted their religion. After more scenes involving inappropriate speech and threats of physical violence, he once again found himself on the road out of town. As he pushed northward and outward from the civilized world, lurching toward the oblivion that is the statistical destiny of those who take too many chances in life, the traces of his existence gradually vanish from the historical record like a trail disappearing into the wilderness. By 1768, we are no longer certain of his precise whereabouts, except to say that in later life he carried around a bundle of yarns about chasing deer and conversing with Indians in the forest.

In 1764, Young put his money where his mouth was and promptly lost it all. Convinced that the future belonged to those who worked the land, and further convinced that the best land to work was in the patch of green mountains to the north that had recently opened up with the successful conclusion of the French and Indian War, he invested in titles sold by one Colonel John Henry Lydius. Some years previously, Lydius had struck a deal with local Indian tribes and was offering what he claimed was ownership to the land at a discount to those who promised to settle it. The colonial governments of New York and New Hampshire had their own designs on the land, however, and their courts soon rendered the Lydius titles worthless.

From Young's first bitter taste of the politics of land emerged his first political pamphlet, *Some Reflections on the Disputes between New-York*,

New-Hampshire, and Col. John Henry Lydius of Albany, in which he presented a spirited defense of Lydius's claims and of Indian-given titles in general against the land-jobbers of rapacious imperial governments. He also weighed in on the question that has dogged humanity since the domestication of wheat: Who owns the land? The answer he provided was the fiery one that has burned in the hearts of revolutionaries for millennia: the land belongs by natural right to those who make it bear fruit. He expressed this conviction in wrenching, quasi-Lockean language:

> Liberty and Property (the *Household Gods* of Englishmen) have called loudly for our *blood* and *treasure*. We, the common people, have freely lavished both; we are impoverish'd in war, and now want lands to exercise the arts of peace upon, at such rates as we can promise ourselves some recompence to our labours thereon . . . All we ask, request, and implore is, that we may enjoy our undoubted rights, and not have them so cruelly rent out of our hands.[88]

The same language about the two household gods of Englishmen would spill out from Ethan Allen's brain a decade later, in the continuing struggles over the land in the mountains. The most consequential aspect of Young's real estate fiasco was that it planted in the mind of his smallpox accomplice the seed of an idea for a new order in the Green Mountains.

In the final lines of his first pamphlet, Young warned that "the least intimation of an arbitrary, over-bearing, or partial disposition, will speedily raise the indignation and just resentment of a free and noble-spirited people, unused to the chains of abject slavery, and therefore infinitely irreconcileable to them." He urged the authorities not to push the common people to the point where they may be "drove to complain of injuries from them to whom we ought naturally to look for protection." The words were respectful, yet the insinuations were not. Young was hinting at something close to treasonous resistance against the King's representatives in the colonies and perhaps even against the King himself. His youthful rebellion against the religious authority of his time had already begun to acquire a sharp, distinctly political edge.

By the end of 1764, however, Young had nothing to take to the bank but his private treasury of injustices. At his brother's suggestion, he had moved from Amenia to Albany in search of steady work in the big city, bringing with him his growing family, his fiddle, his heterodox ideas, and a carefully tended flame of hatred that gathered more fuel from every encounter with wrongful power. Within two years, he was on the road again, leaving behind a cloud of accusations about his bad beliefs, and he never really stopped moving. While the vast majority of human beings in his time passed their entire lives within a few miles of the place of their birth, Young seemed almost eager to set up house in the next colony over. There is some evidence that he even tried fishing for a new life in the West Indies. He was a restless man, like his future friend Thomas Paine, a permanent misfit. Possibly it was just because life offered him no reasonable alternatives that he eventually came to imagine that his home was the earth itself and his cause the cause of all humankind.

3

Epicurus's Dangerous Idea

When in the course of human events . . .

IT TURNS OUT THAT SPACE ALIENS WERE EVERYWHERE IN the American Revolution. They could be found in the drawing rooms of Boston, in the taverns of Philadelphia, and even all the way up in the wilds of the Green Mountains. Probably the best indicator of revolutionary heterodoxy at the time was the belief in extraterrestrial life. And probably the best illustration of this connection can be found in what appears to be the first American publication overtly directed against the Christian religion.[1]

The *Sermon on Natural Religion*, published in Boston in 1771 by a writer who identified himself only as "a Natural Man," opens with a passage from 1 Corinthians whose interpretation it takes to be its business:

> The natural man receiveth not the things of the Spirit of God, for they are foolishness unto him; neither can he know them, because they are spiritually discerned.[2]

Readers of the time were undoubtedly shocked to discover that the point of the *Sermon* is not to explicate this morsel of New Testament wisdom but to refute it. Readers today will probably find the theological argument of the *Sermon* less surprising than the way it ends. After taking a battering ram to the Holy Scriptures, the author turns his gaze skyward and lifts his sermon to a rhetorical crescendo with a good couple of pages celebrating the reality of extraterrestrial life.

Where on earth did these aliens come from? And who was the Natural Man anyway? The first question brings us to the least-known chapter of greatest consequence in the history of ideas. It is a story that turns up some unexpected connections between a sixteenth-century genius, a president of the United States, and a long-lost ancient poem. It has something to say about the role of philosophy—as opposed to mere science—in the creation of the modern world. It also happens to lead a plausible answer to the second question, about the identity of America's first "natural man."

HE WAS A SKINNY, brilliant, wandering monk who couldn't keep his mouth shut. He styled himself "the Nolan"—ostensibly to honor the village outside of Naples where he was born in 1548, but just as likely to insinuate that Aristotle "the Stagirite" had finally met his match. Chased out of one center of learning after another—Geneva, Toulouse, Paris, Oxford, Frankfurt, Prague, Venice—he spread his ideas like a bad case of the flu. The mischievous Pierre Bayle dubbed him "the knight-errant of philosophy." At dawn on February 17, 1600, the people who took themselves to be responsible for the moral order of the world finally stopped his tongue with a leather gag. They hauled him out of his cell in the papal prison, loaded him onto a mule, and carried him like a bundle of roses to the Campo dei Fiori, the square that still serves Rome as a marketplace for flowers. Through the final minutes, they urged him to recant. They brought a crucifix up to his eyes, but he turned his head away with a fierce look. They stripped him naked, tied him to the stake, and lowered their torches on the pile of kindling wood and tar at his feet. While the flames incinerated his flesh, a squadron of monks chanted litanies for his soul.

There are a number of reasons why Giordano Bruno's life ended so badly, but all of the important ones point to the book that he was said to have carried in his pocket on all of his travels: *De rerum natura* [*On the Nature of Things*] by Titus Lucretius Carus (ca. 99–55 BCE), a didactic poem, all but lost to civilization for a millennium and a half, that consecrates each of its 7,400 or so lines to the philosophy of the ancient Greek thinker Epicurus (341–270 BCE). In Lucretius's poem, Bruno discovered the extraordinary vision of an infinite universe—a universe without beginning, end, center, or edge, everywhere abounding in extraterrestrial life. And to Bruno this vision of a limitless, eternal, wildly fecund cosmos served as the metaphorical, historically contingent representation of the simple but devastating idea that lies at the core of the Epicurean philosophy: that nature always explains itself. Epicurus's dangerous idea, as Bruno understood, is a kind of universal acid. It dissolves every pretension of religion in its popular and traditional forms to represent the meaning of existence. Epicurus was "that glorious religion tamer," as Bayle put it. Cardinal (later Saint) Robert Bellarmine—the "hammer of the heretics," who sixteen years later initiated proceedings against Galileo—had good reason to suppose that Bruno was a dangerous character.

Thomas Jefferson, too, must have walked around with a copy of Lucretius's poem in his pocket at times.[3] The library Jefferson turned over to Congress in 1815 included eight editions of *De rerum natura*. He diligently collected translations—in English, French, and Italian. Among the small number of books that he could not bring himself to surrender to Congress was a three-volume set on the philosophy of Epicurus by the French philosopher Pierre Gassendi (1592–1655). In his last years at Monticello, he studied Gassendi and Lucretius intensively in hopes of synthesizing their views within a comprehensive moral philosophy of his own. In a letter of 1819 to William Short, Jefferson made it official. "I too am an Epicurean," he announced.[4]

It should go without saying that the fates of these two ardent readers of an ancient Roman text differed so dramatically because in the two centuries that separated them the world had changed in an equally dramatic way. It is less well known today that the world had changed so much partly on account of the book that Bruno and Jefferson read so ardently. Although Jefferson was among a very few of America's revolutionary deists (his friend Philip Freneau was another) to trace his intellectual pedigree directly back to Epicurus, his judgment on this score was characteristically acute. The revival of the Epicurean philosophy that followed upon the rediscovery of Lucretius in early modern Europe was the decisive episode in the history of modern thought. It was more important than what we now call the scientific revolution, which was really its consequence rather than its cause. And it descended upon the European world as a shock from without, like an invasion from an alien planet, not a development from within. By the time Epicurus's dangerous idea reached America, it had come to be refracted through a variety of intermediaries and dissociated from its scandalous original source, and not many people understood whence those extraterrestrials originated. But their revolutionary force persisted undiminished.

In a useful history, dimensions matter. But the stage on which we usually set the story of the American Revolution is too small. In the laudable effort to accumulate knowledge about the past, America's historians have divided the history into periods, regions, and social groups, and so we trace chains of causality through the cramped confines of a handful of individual careers, a few battlefield triumphs, and intellectual fashions and political resentments that span just a few decades. Sometimes, as David Hume pointed out, the only way to get a clear view of things is to move up higher. The real story of America's philosophical origins properly begins in ancient Greece, and its first protagonist is the most famous atheist in the history.

ABOUT EPICURUS the man, we know little. He was born on the island of Samos, off the coast of what is now Turkey. At the age of thirty-five, he moved to Athens for good and purchased a home in the suburbs. In his leafy backyard he established an amiable philosophical commune that came to be known as "the garden." He ate simple foods, mostly vegetables, and collected a great many friends. He wrote a great many books. He died in his seventy-second year of a urinary tract complaint, reportedly greeting his final days of suffering with the equanimity his philosophy demanded.

The movement Epicurus launched became hugely popular in the Roman Empire. It stood for one side in a culture war whose other side was manned tentatively by the Stoic philosophers, then decisively by the emerging Christian religion. The other side won, which may explain something about why the Roman Empire failed to modernize. The victors crushed their old enemy ruthlessly. None of Epicurus's books survived intact. Our knowledge of his philosophy today is limited to a handful of letters, collections of sayings and fragments of texts, and the reports of others: Cicero, who was rather unfriendly; Seneca, who labored to conceal his sympathies; Diogenes Laërtius, a chatty philosophical-biographer; and, above all, Lucretius.

In antiquity, Lucretius enjoyed the kind of literary fame for which poets risk all the humiliations of their calling. Virgil (70–19 BCE) pilfered from his predecessor some of his most brilliant lines and many of his gemlike philosophical aperçus.[5] Ovid (43 BCE–17/18 CE), the laurel-bearer of the next generation of Roman poets, enthused that the sublime verses of *De rerum natura* would not perish until the day the earth died. He was very nearly wrong about that. The authorities of the rising Christian church saw only ugliness in the verses of Lucretius. Saint Jerome (347–420 CE) retailed some scurrilous stories about the poet involving love potions and a self-destructive exit, but these were just the tackier parts of a program to discredit the Epicurean philosophy by fair means or foul. Over the subsequent millennium, while the manuscript copies of his poem crumbled and disappeared, the name of Lucretius dissolved into obscurity. Today, we know almost nothing about the man beyond what can be inferred from his one surviving poem. Even his dates are uncertain. But with the benefit of hindsight, we can say that the pivotal link in the long chain of events that ended in the American Revolution was forged in 1417, when the indefatigable humanist scholar and part-time manuscript hunter Poggio Bracciolini laid his hand on the one surviving copy of *De rerum natura* from which all subsequent editions derive. Even in the history of philosophy, accidents can sometimes decide the course of human events.[6]

The signal flares of the Epicurean revival appeared in scattered bursts like colorful supernovae in the eclectic philosophical skies of the Renaissance. To the adventurous thinkers of early modern Europe, the scandal of Lucretius began with the beauty of his verses. For more than a millennium and a half, it had been taken for granted that the philosophy of Epicurus was as hideous as the debauchery that it advocated. But in *De rerum natura* the finer minds of Europe discovered "the creed of Epicurus set to music," as John Adams grumbled.[7] It wasn't long before a number of the new thinkers decided that anything that sounded so good must be true.

The Italian Neoplatonist philosopher Marsilio Ficino (1433–1499) wrote a careful commentary on Lucretius—and then, recognizing the danger to which he had exposed himself, committed it to the flames.[8] Niccolò Machiavelli (1469–1527) copied out all 7,400 lines of *De rerum natura* before going on to invent modern political theory. In Holland, Desiderius Erasmus (1467?–1536) took it as a personal mission to demonstrate that "there are no people more Epicurean than godly Christians";[9] though he had better luck with his prediction that "the theologians . . . will proclaim me a heretic."[10] The French skeptic and essayist of mental interiors Michel de Montaigne (1533–1592)—famous for his advice to forget much of what you read—read and annotated his copy of Lucretius so assiduously over the last twenty years of his life that his marginalia exceed the text in size.[11] In England, Lord Francis Bacon (1561–1626)—regularly named by Jefferson as the first of the great modern philosophers—promoted important elements of the Epicurean philosophy, though in most cases he took care to assign credit for them to less controversial names from the ancient world.[12] Shakespeare, too, may have crossed paths with the new philosophy: a (necessarily speculative) case can be made that Hamlet's troubles stem from a reading of the books that Bruno published on a controversial sojourn in England.[13]

Bruno should count as the first of the moderns to read Lucretius's work down to the bottom and discover in that ancient poem the foundations for a new and comprehensive philosophical system.[14] Bruno was so taken by *De rerum natura* that he palpably longed to become a new, better, perhaps more Italian version of its philosophical hero. Here, for example, is Lucretius on his chosen guru: Epicurus was "a God, a God indeed," who "burst open the cloistered gates of Nature," "marched far beyond the blazing battlements of the world," journeyed "through all the measureless universe," brought "light where there was darkness," and unveiled "the true nature of things."[15] And here is Bruno, writing about himself in the exalted third person, as was his wont: "Now behold, the man [me, Bruno] who has surmounted the air, penetrated the sky, wandered among the stars, passed beyond the borders of the world, effaced the imaginary walls of the first, eighth, ninth, tenth spheres, and the many more you could add . . . by the light of his senses and reason, he opened those cloisters of truth . . . he laid bare covered and veiled nature, gave eyes to the moles and light to the blind."[16]

Bruno converted two disciples that mattered. One, whose story is as famous today as it is misunderstood, was Galileo. The other, infamous in his own day and mostly forgotten now, was a wandering Italian priest and free spirit, Lucilio Vanini. Darting around licentious Paris in the 1610s, the extraordinarily curious and learned Vanini made a name for himself as "that ringleader of the atheists"[17] with his book *On the Wonderful Secrets of Nature, the Queen and Goddess of Mortal Beings*, in which, after hundreds of pages of semi-scientific, quasi-Epicurean descriptions of natural phenomena, from stars and planets to the origin of man and the nature of eyesight, hearing, and smell, he proved the existence of a God that many people said could not be distinguished from Nature. "The libertines are multiplying in France. They haven't reflected sufficiently on the example of Giordano Bruno, but they have adopted and acclaimed Vanini as their leader," wrote Paris's priest-about-town, Marin Mersenne—who was in a position to know, since many of those undesirables seemed to show up at his dinner table.[18]

The authorities finally caught up with Vanini in Toulouse in 1618. He was tried for atheism and convicted. On the dawn of February 9,

1619, they cut his tongue out. According to some reports, they did him the favor of strangling him before burning his body at the stake. Bayle, in his ironic way, glorified the memory of Vanini by passing along the story that he embraced his impending immolation as an opportunity "to die as a philosopher."[19] Jefferson thought enough of him to include his works in the compact section on "moral philosophy" in his library.

On at least one occasion in 1647, Father Mersenne played dinner host to the three philosophers who would carry the Epicurean revival forward into the second half of the seventeenth century.[20] The elder in the philosophical trio was Jefferson's favorite, Pierre Gassendi, a Catholic priest who began his professional life as a teenage prodigy and then inexplicably dedicated his career to systematizing and disseminating a putatively sanitized version of the Epicurean philosophy. Gassendi's friends and his enemies were mostly convinced that he, too, was a "libertine" and would have gone the way of Bruno and Vanini had his charming presence at all the good soirees not been so greatly esteemed. Thomas Hobbes was an English courtier, raised from obscurity by Lord Bacon, now huddling in Paris with aristocratic exiles from the turmoil of the English Civil War. Upon encountering Gassendi's Epicurean system for the first time, Hobbes reportedly declared that "it is as big as Aristotle's philosophie, but much truer."[21] The most famous philosopher of the three was René Descartes. A prickly and complicated man, Descartes was much more stingy than his fellows in revealing the sources and implications of his ideas—which may explain why, apart from his obtuse personal style, dinner parties involving him tended to end with sullen grimaces and unexplained disappearances. Notwithstanding the many fine points of disagreements among themselves and with their ancient mentor, the chief accomplishment of the three philosophers, and of Descartes in particular, was to have protected Epicurus's dangerous idea within a sheath of metaphysical rhetoric that allowed for its dissemination across the very hostile terrain of seventeenth-century Europe.

As the new philosophy spread, and especially after it crossed the channel on the boat with Hobbes, it learned to detach itself from the name of Epicurus and from the cruder formulations of its defining idea.[22] It appealed to other, more respectable ancient sources, notably the Stoics.[23] Sometimes—as in the cases of Montaigne and Bayle—it hid behind an extreme skepticism that pretended to justify faith by pretending to doubt everything else. Mostly, it wrapped itself in a theological rhetoric that could be made to resemble that of the established religion.

The defenders of orthodoxy in the seventeenth and eighteenth centuries, at least, weren't fooled. In his 1692 sermon *The Folly of Atheism, or what is now called Deism*—one of the Boyle Lectures against deism that converted Franklin to deism—Newton ally Richard Bentley named Epicurus as the "ancient master" of the atheistic deists. In the preface to a 1712 poem, Richard Blackmore claimed that the modern philosophers have simply "revived the absolute and exploded system of Epicurus." "Has [Hobbes] said anything new?" he sneers. "Does he bring any stronger forces into the field than the Epicureans did before him?"[24] Some of the attacks were merely polemical, intended to weigh down philosophical antagonists with the most heinous of ancient names. Some were merely symptomatic of the paranoia that seeped from every pore in such an anxious age. But the assaults on Epicureanism were so furious because they had in them much truth.

The Epicurean revival was not the first such challenge to the hegemony of the Christian religion over European culture. Aristotle, Plato, and the Stoics were pagans too, and in their work they sounded many of the themes that would make the Epicurean philosophy so dangerous, as did a number of the more radical theologians of the late medieval period. One could further complicate the narrative by pointing out that for some of the people some of the time, the Epicurean revolution passed for a renovation of the established religion from within. In Epicurus, however, there was nothing of that compromising, dialectical spirit that pervaded Aristotle and the others and allowed them to be wrestled to the ground and marked with the sign of the cross. "Among all the ancient obdurate atheists, and inveterate enemies of religion, no one seems more sincere and more implacable than Epicurus,"[25] observed Blackmore.

Among the influential philosophers of early-eighteenth-century Britain, the more radical they were—which is to say, the more likely they were to be of interest to individuals like Franklin and Young—the more likely they were to acknowledge in an explicit way their allegiance to Epicurus.[26] John Toland, an Anglo-Irish deist who had a substantial personal and philosophical influence on the Whig writers whose works populated American bookshelves, was as close to Lucretius as he was to his first modern disciple.[27] Indeed, he did for Bruno what Bruno did for Lucretius, carrying on his many travels the former's exuberantly titled *The Expulsion of the Triumphant Beast* and pressing it upon everyone who would take it. (The beast to be expelled was the superstition that burdened all religion before Bruno rediscovered Lucretius.) Among the writers who shared Toland's fascination with Lucretius and his epigones was Thomas Young's favorite poet, Alexander Pope. The *Essay on Man* borrows so many tropes and metaphors from *De rerum natura* that in places it reads like an homage to Lucretius. Thomas Young's favorite deist, Charles Blount, an avowed admirer of Hobbes, was even more open about his reliance on the bad boy of ancient philosophy. The subtitle of the first *Oracles of Reason* is *Lucretius Redivivus*— "Lucretius Revived."

For more than a century after the Epicurean doctrines washed onto British shores, it was not possible to admit in polite society to the unsavory origins of the doctrines that had been cemented into the foundations of the philosophy of the age. Toward the end of the eighteenth century, however, a moment arrived when it all seemed clear enough in retrospect and even uncontroversial. Adam Smith, after rehearsing a quintessentially Epicurean version of the theory of knowledge, frankly acknowledged that his own doctrine was "as old as Leucippus, Democritus, and Epicurus," and that it "was revived in the last century by Gassendi, and has since been adopted by Newton and the far greater part of his followers." It is now "the established system," "the system that is most in fashion, and most approved of by the greater part of the philosophers of Europe," he added, and it is opposed to "that species of metaphysics which confounds every thing and explains nothing."[28] When Smith went on to repeat the familiar charge that Rousseau swiped his natural history of society from Lucretius, he at least meant it as a compliment.[29]

IN ITS POPULAR FORM—not inaccurate but narrow—the teaching of Epicurus is easy enough to state. Happiness in this life, it says, is everything. The highest form of happiness is freedom from pain in the body and tranquility of mind. The surest path to happiness is a life of ordinary virtue. The greatest sources of needless unhappiness are the misunderstandings that give rise to unquenchable desires and baseless fears. The worst of our misunderstandings involve the fear of inscrutable deities and the fear of death. Religion exploits these fears for the benefit of priests and kings. Calm attention to the true nature of things allows us to cast aside harmful fears and superstitions and thereby to achieve happiness. Science—by which is meant the quiet pursuit of the understanding that brings happiness—is the only form of piety worth the name.

To modern nonspecialist readers, Epicurus's teaching might come across at first as a sensibility more than a philosophy—a choice in lifestyle rather than a matter of principle. Among modern academic philosophers and theologians, his philosophy is usually reduced to a label such as "materialism." But both approaches fail to grasp the deeper meaning of the Epicurean philosophy and the basis for its historical impact. The popular lifestyle-teaching and the metaphysical labels are really just incomplete ways of expressing a principle that speaks through all elements of the Epicurean philosophy. That guiding principle—which is to some extent the guiding principle of all radical philosophy—can be stated in a variety of ways and is much older than the Epicurean philosophy. Like all good philosophical ideas, it isn't a "first" principle, an arbitrary stipulation, or an act of faith, but something more like a reminder, a generalization over our reflections that keeps them from straying too far off course. It seems banal and even trivial until its implications are honored even at the logical extreme, at which point it suddenly begins to make some astonishing demands.

The most widely cited version of the guiding principle in the early modern world appears in the context of Lucretius's exposition of Epicurus's physical doctrines, and it takes the form of a seemingly innocuous proposition: "Nothing is ever produced supernaturally out of nothing."[30] Lucretius also presents, as equivalent, the converse: "Nature never annihilates anything."[31] In the Epicurean universe, there is change—indeed, things never cease coming to be and perishing—but all change is transformation. There is no such thing as "creation ex nihilo"—the creation of something out of nothing—nor can there be such a thing as total destruction.

The same guiding principle can be expressed in a richer form once we grasp that it involves a claim about the inherent lawfulness of nature. The most fundamental feature of the Epicurean universe—and the very thing that renders it a cognate of "nature"—is that like causes produce like effects. The contrary hypothesis—that like causes might produce unlike effects—involves the creation of anything out of anything, which entails the possibility of the creation of something out of nothing, which we know to be impossible.[32] In a phrase that repeats itself like a tic in Lucretius's poem, everything has within itself "a deep-set boundary stone"—that is, a law or reason or explanation (the word is "*ratio*")—"by which its power is limited."[33] The driving ambition of Epicurean philosophy—and the ultimate source of happiness for Epicurean man—is to understand *naturae species ratioque*, that is, to grasp the form and reason, or outward aspect and inner law, of nature.

To say that nature is inherently lawful is also to say what it is not: namely, arbitrary, or subject to the fiat or whims of any agent, however divine. "Nature is her own mistress and is exempt from the oppression of arrogant despots," says Lucretius, "accomplishing everything by herself spontaneously and independently and free from the jurisdiction of the gods."[34] According to Epicurus, there is no god or any other agent standing outside of nature that can explain why the things within it are one way and not another. Nature acts according to causes, not purposes.

In much of the Epicurean imagery, incidentally, the guiding intuition takes on a female form. For Lucretius, Nature is a "goddess," Venus, a "creatress," "the fruitful earth," a ceaselessly fertile substance, responsible for the "conception" of all things and rightly called "mother." Bruno embraces the same sensibility. "Matter," he says, "unfolds what it holds folded up," it is "a thing divine, the best parent, generator, and mother of all natural things," and so it is "called woman (to gather everything into a single term) by those who have most effectively evaluated its reality."[35] Vanini, too, evinces his fealty to the Epicurean "creatress" divinity when he describes Nature as "the Queen and Goddess of the Mortal Ones."

The same guiding principle of the Epicurean philosophy may also be expressed as a claim about the uniformity or homogeneity of nature. To suppose that nature acts everywhere according to laws, says Epicurus, is to suppose that it operates everywhere according to the same, universal laws. Bruno once again articulates the insight well. In his exuberant and immensely long poem *On the Immense and the Numberless*—not coincidentally composed in the same meter as Lucretius's poem—he tells us that "forces of similar nature are similar everywhere."[36]

The guiding principle of the Epicurean philosophy also involves a certain kind of "monism," to use the jargon of metaphysics—that is, the notion that nature is the activity of a single thing or substance. For, if the operations of universal natural laws neither create nor annihilate but only transform, then the underlying subject of all transformations can neither come into being nor perish. The "eternal corporeal substance," says Bruno, "is not producible *ex nihilo*, nor reducible *ad nihilum*, but rarefiable, condensable, formable, arrangeable, and 'fashionable.' "[37] Ultimate reality is thus "one, infinite, and immobile"; in brief, "all is one."[38] The crucial feature of this monism—and where we may perhaps begin to glimpse the difference between it and that shallow materialism with which the Epicurean philosophy is often associated—is that it refers to a substance that is essentially active. That is, the eternal substance of the world expresses itself not as a collection of inert material things whose properties we understand perfectly but as an endless series of lawful transformations of a singular thing that we understand only imperfectly.[39]

Hobbes takes this intuition about the material principle, or the singular substance of all moving things, to one extreme. In a curious autobiographical poem in which he ruminates on his continental travels and the epiphany that changed his philosophical career, he recalls, "I began to think perpetually about the nature of things, whether I was moving by boat, by coach, or by horse. I saw that there is only one thing in the whole world that is real, although it is undoubtedly falsified in many ways."[40] In his magnum opus, *Leviathan*, he condenses this monism into dogma: "Every part of the Universe, is Body, and that which is not Body, is no part of the Universe."[41]

Embedded in Epicurus's intuition about the monism or unitary lawfulness of nature lies a still deeper claim about the lawfulness of those laws themselves. At first glance, one might suppose that the laws through which we explain things have an arbitrary character. We have apples and planets, for example, and any number of possible laws of gravity that may connect one with the other. And if the laws of nature are arbitrary, then our explanations would seem to run out once we find them. In a manner that requires much further elaboration from Epicurus's successors in early modern Europe, however, the guiding principle says that the seemingly arbitrary character of the laws is the consequence not of any arbitrariness in nature itself but of the incompleteness of our explanations of it. There are no stipulated "first principles," no arbitrary "parameters" in nature, no explanations that hit bedrock with a "because it is so." Our explanations themselves always remain explicable, for the same reason that the laws of nature are themselves lawful.

Although often represented as a principle of physics (e.g., nothing comes from nothing) or theology (even the gods cannot create anything ex nihilo) or metaphysics (all is one substance; or, nature is a "woman"), the guiding principle of the Epicurean philosophy may also be expressed as a still more universal claim about the nature of intelligibility. The guiding principle says not just that like things produce like things, but that a thing is like *itself* only to the extent that it can be like other things. "Nothing in creation is one of a kind, nothing is born or grows by itself, alone," says Lucretius.[42] Every bird is special, one could say; yet if anything in the world is a bird, then it must be possible that there should be more than one of them—and the same is true of the sun, the moon, and the ocean. More abstractly, the point is that the laws of nature and the objects of those laws do not pertain to separate ontological categories; apples and planets do not exist before the laws that make them what they are. The laws are within the objects in a certain sense, and the objects are the artifacts of the laws through which we explain them. "Nature" is not outside of things, as Bruno puts it; rather, it "is nothing if not the force implanted in things and the law by which every being moves along its proper course."[43]

From this intuition about the nature of intelligibility follows a still more powerful claim about the intelligibility of nature. If things can be what they are only insofar as they are already part of the lawful, explicable pattern of nature, then it follows that there is nothing in nature—no object, no law, no property, no event—that is not intelligible as a matter of principle.[44] In practice, as Lucretius represents it, the Epicurean philosophy is all about explanation. Thunderstorms, earthquakes, waterspouts, and even the human mind—everything can be explained. The emphasis here is on the "can"—for Lucretius rests content with the demonstration *that* phenomena are explicable, rather than *how*. He typically offers a choice among several possible theories for any given phenomena, since his intent is limited to showing only that such an explanation is always possible. He further insists, in appropriately scientific fashion, that we should avoid getting too attached to any one explanation of specific phenomena. Our knowledge of nature is extremely limited as a matter of fact, even as it remains entirely unlimited as a matter of principle.

Another way to represent the claim concerning the intelligibility of nature is to say that there is nothing outside the world that may explain anything within it. Explanations are always only refractions from within. There are plenty of truths in the universe, one could say, but there is no truth about everything. Probably the best general statement of the guiding principle is this: nature always explains itself. And an appropriate modifier for the Epicurean philosophy, if that is what we want, is "immanent" or "this-worldly."[45] In the universe as Lucretius found it, there is no heaven but the one we project on the stars overhead. There is no hell but what our imagination can conjure out of our fears of this world. And there is nothing at all outside of experience that can bring us any more happiness, misery, good, or evil than we can find within the limits of the world we inhabit.

There is a still deeper label that applies to any philosophy that submits to the guiding principle, one that connects Epicurus with his ancient Greek predecessors, not least Socrates (much as that might have offended Epicurus's vanity). In pursuing explanations for all things, philosophy necessarily confronts the common ideas that human beings form through everyday experience and then deploy as tokens in their efforts to find a basis for collaboration. This divergence between "radical" philosophy and the common religious consciousness begins with the guiding principle itself.

Nothing is more common in human experience than the encounter with that which we do not understand. The question—Why are things one way and not another?—haunts us from the smallest matters to our ultimate concerns. Why was I born with a freckle on my chin? Why is the hotel wallpaper always so tacky? Why is there something rather than nothing? Everywhere, we succumb to the illusion that the things come first, and the explanations come later, or maybe not at all. From this experience, even many of those sophisticated individuals who style themselves philosophers develop a tenacious conviction that the world is teeming with permanent mysteries, such as the existence of this gnarly tree over here, or the puzzling fact of human consciousness, or the thankfully hospitable character of our planet. And so the common religious consciousness, confronting its own lack of answers, takes refuge in the illusory certainty of the questions, as if they were a fixed set of holes in the universe to be filled in only through acts of faith. But the guiding principle tells us that although life is full of riddles, none of them are permanent. Our questions describe the contours of our ignorance, not the shape of the world. The real mystery about the universe is that it is everywhere and without exception intelligible. Albert Einstein—who supplied a preface for an edition of Lucretius's *De rerum natura* in 1924[46]—was a radical philosopher in this sense: "The eternal mystery of the world is its comprehensibility."[47]

Today the basic imperative behind the guiding principle is sometimes represented, not altogether inaccurately, as a commitment to "the scientific method" or a "naturalistic worldview." But a better label for it is "the scientific spirit." At the core of the philosophy that expresses itself in the writings of Bruno and his successors is not a particular method but a commitment to method as such; nor is it properly characterized as a particular worldview, grounded on some arbitrary act of faith, since its primordial commitment involves the rejection of faith as a form of explanation at all. The scientific aspect of the guiding principle has an element of "spirit" in the sense that it is deeply connected with the idea of the pursuit of happiness and of true religion. This trinity of science, happiness, and true piety, together with the rejection of all particular methods in the name of method as such, remained at the center of early modern philosophy long after the name of Epicurus settled into disuse.

The bare outlines of the Epicurean philosophy are first discernible among America's revolutionary deists at this level, where the pursuit of happiness and true piety merge with the scientific spirit. Philip Freneau—who spent his first years after graduating from Princeton admiring nature in the West Indies—writes movingly of his adoration for "creatress nature" in verses that track Lucretius in an intimate way.[48] In a poem dedicated to Jefferson upon his retirement from the presidency in 1809, Freneau speculates that his friend and former boss will find happiness in his golden years through scientific pursuits, where he might "trace through nature the creating power."[49] (Epicurus himself says, "It is not possible to gain unmixed happiness without natural science."[50]) Indeed, Jefferson devoted much of his retirement to horticulture, and in what could be read as an oblique homage to Epicurus, he declared, "There is no culture comparable to that of the garden."[51] Paine, too, believed in the connection between science and the pursuit of happiness: "Those who knew Benjamin Franklin will recollect that his mind was ever young, his temper serene. Science, that never grows grey, was always his mistress."[52]

In their natural investigations, America's founders stayed true to the spirit of Epicurus's guiding principle by leaving most of his specific doctrines behind. In this respect, they followed the models of Montaigne, Bacon, Bruno, and Locke—thinkers who systematically avoided the excesses of system. Epicurus, after all, was a philosopher in the ancient manner. He was a dogmatist—a lawgiver for his community in the model of Pythagoras, who entombed his insights within inflexible doctrines. In style if not in substance, Epicurus was far from the cheerful and sometimes insouciant skepticism of America's founders. Jefferson understood well the importance of a lightness of touch in philosophy. "He is less remote from the truth who believes nothing than he who believes what is wrong," he declared.[53] "I never submitted the whole system of my opinions to the creed of any party of men whatever, in religion, in philosophy, in politics or in anything else . . . If I could not go to heaven but with a party, I would not go there at all."[54] Franklin, the most this-worldly of the Americans, was earthiness itself in his approach to philosophy. "Are there twenty Men in Europe at this Day, the happier, or even the easier, for any Knowledge they have pick'd out of Aristotle?" he wanted to know. "The Pleasure arising to a few Philosophers . . . can it be compared with the Ease and Comfort every Man living might feel seven times a day, by discharging freely the Wind from his Bowels? Especially if it be converted into a Perfume."[55]

THE DOCTRINE with which the name Epicurus has been most closely associated is his "atomism," or what today is sometimes called more generally his "materialism." Yet atomism is at bottom just a beguiling and somewhat problematic metaphor through which the guiding principle may be expressed. The world, says Epicurus, consists of nothing but atoms and the void through which they move. These atoms are invisibly small, colorless, odorless, indivisible, and indestructible. They have existed and will continue to exist for all eternity. They are also weighty, and "fall" through the void, constantly bumping into one another, entangling themselves in innumerable configurations. All of the things that we see coming into being and perishing—including ourselves—are simply varying configurations of these atoms. It is on account of this doctrine of atomism that the Epicurean philosophy is typically (though not altogether accurately) classified under the label of "materialism."

Epicurus borrowed his atoms more or less wholesale (and without any indications of gratitude) from his predecessors, mostly Leucippus and Democritus, who coined the term "atom" from the Greek for "uncuttable." He endorsed atomism not because he had discovered additional observational evidence to confirm the truth of the dogma, but because, within the conceptual limitations of ancient Greek science, atomism more than adequately expressed his fundamental intuition about the self-sufficiency of nature. Atomism is a way of visualizing how, in accordance with the underlying principle that nothing comes from nothing, unceasing transformation can be a permanent feature of a world where nothing is actually created or annihilated. The atoms stand for that which remains unchanged and indestructible in any transformation, while their many configurations represent the results of change. Perhaps the hardest thing to grasp about these atoms is that they are not "things" in the way we usually think of things, such as this apple or that book. They are, in a paradoxical sense, the things behind all things, or what it is that makes "thingness" possible. Lucretius captures a hint of this insight by translating "atoms" as *semina rerum*—"the seeds of things"—and Bruno passes along the message in the early modern world by adopting Lucretius's language and doctrine concerning the seeds of things.

The metaphor works, it has to be stressed, only to the extent that these seeds of things remain both indestructible and out of range of experience—invisible, odorless, and without specific properties. Properties (such as smell, for example) according to Epicurus and his atomist predecessors, are actually properties of the interactions between certain configurations of atoms (say, the nose) and other configurations (a rose). If atoms possessed such properties in their own right, they would themselves be composites, which would make them the changeable elements of some other, unchangeable substrate. "Whatever color bodies are," Lucretius therefore argues, seconding Democritus, "do not believe that the elements of their substance are tinged with this color . . . the atoms are all colorless."[56] The distinction between primary and secondary properties would prove of great consequence for Epicurus's philosophical successors in early modern Europe, and the individual perhaps most responsible for disseminating it was Galileo. Indeed, Galileo's role in propagating this aspect of the Epicurean philosophy may have been more consequential than the astronomical efforts for which he was once persecuted and is now celebrated.[57]

The doctrine of "materialism," by way of contrast, is usually associated with the idea that all events in the world may be explained entirely as the operation of certain kinds of objects whose properties are universally given (what are vaguely called "material" objects), and not some other kinds of things (the equally vague "immaterial" or "spiritual" objects). This idea naturally leads to the deterministic supposition that if only we knew the starting positions and attributes of every such object, we could map the entire future of the universe with the application of a few simple and fixed laws. The scientific revolution, it is often incorrectly suggested, rests on some such theory, or what is called a "materialistic" or "mechanistic" worldview. But materialism in this conventional sense violates the guiding principle: it requires that all explanations come to an end on arbitrary features of experience (such as properties, laws, or parameters) for which we can find no explanation. The Epicurean philosophy, along with the scientific revolution to which it gave rise, would prove far more robust than "materialism" ever could have been, because it comes to rest on the claim not that everything is explicable in just one way, but that everything is explicable. (It is for roughly the same reason that Epicurus's atoms are not at all the atoms of modern physics—for the latter *are* assigned "secondary" properties, and so whenever they are considered "fundamental" at the same time they invite all the paradoxes associated with reductive or deterministic materialism.)

Atomism also helps to express the intuition, deeply embedded in the guiding principle, that everything we encounter is in some respect irreducibly particular. That is, everything in experience is some combination of atoms, similar to any number of other things in any number of ways, yet always different in some way from everything else. "We see in this world an infinite difference and variety," as Montaigne puts it. "Everything is diverse."[58] There is "nothing in the world universal but names," Hobbes adds, "for the things named are, every one of them individual and singular."[59] To put it conversely, we never actually meet in reality the kinds of things that Plato would have called "Forms" or that the Aristotelian scholastics called "universals." (As a matter of fact, Plato so loathed atomism that, according to ancient legend, he wished to burn all of Democritus's writings.)[60] To suppose that certain universals are fixed or simply given in nature—that "Man" exists apart from all the many men in the world—is to suppose that there are some explanations for things that transcend all of nature and are established in an arbitrary way, as if by divine stipulation—and this is to violate the guiding principle, which tells us that no such explanations can actually explain anything.[61]

At bottom, atomism is a way of dramatizing one of the most remarkable—and unnerving—implications of the guiding principle. The atomistic universe is intrinsically lawful—and yet by virtue of this very lawfulness, it admits of no universal explanation. In an atomistic universe, every universalizing scheme we may devise for comprehending the interactions of composites must always fall short of the perfect lawfulness of the atoms themselves, and our consciousness is therefore always only an effort to approximate a set of explanations that in their totality must exceed our grasp. As a consequence, every attempt to relate any individual thing to the universe as a whole, to show that a thing must under all circumstances or in all conceivable universes be one way rather than another, is doomed to failure. All things—and all laws that appear to govern things—must appear to us as essentially contingent or random. Epicurus wraps up this insight in his doctrine concerning the "swerve" of the atoms (about which more later). Edmund Waller, a correspondent of Hobbes and a disseminator of Epicureanism in England, expresses the general sense of the Epicurean philosophy on this point in a poetical commentary on Lucretius—one that incidentally offers a first hint at how the doctrine of atomism will ultimately connect with a radical political philosophy:

> *No Monarch Rules the Universe;*
> *But chance and Atomes make this ALL.*

In order democratical;
Where bodies freely run their course,
Without design, or fate, or force.[62]

The randomness of all things in the world is a tough pill to swallow for the religious consciousness; and the toughest part of all is the randomness of our very own beings. The most psychologically fraught consequence of atomism is that it seems to reduce human beings and the human mind itself to so many putatively senseless configurations of atoms. All our hopes and deeds, all our flights of fancy and feelings of pain, our choices and our very existence may be explained through their causal interactions with other things, just like everything else, and these causes are not different in kind from those that move the things around us. We and everything we cherish are merely evanescent forms of something eternal, the temporary hallucinations of an indifferent reality.[63] Shakespeare crushes the insight into a pair of lines. "What have you done, my lord, with the dead body?" Rosencrantz asks. "Compounded it with dust, whereto 'tis kin," Hamlet replies.[64]

During the course of the scientific and philosophical revolution of the seventeenth century, the doctrine of atomism underwent a number of technical changes that need not detain us here.[65] The modified atomism that came to dominate early modern physics was (at least superficially) cleansed of its infamous association with Epicurus and thus deemed suitable for use even by theologically compliant scientists—such as, above all, Newton. Even so, the radical element of the doctrine could never be suppressed. In his *Essay on Man*, for example, Pope officially embraces Newtonian science, with its theologically correct version of atomism; and then he turns around and conjures a vision that sends us straight back to Lucretius:

All forms that perish other forms supply,
(By turns we catch the vital breath, and die)
Like bubbles on the sea of Matter born,
They rise, they break, and to that sea return.[66]

Freneau's admiration for Lucretius was second only to his attachment to Pope; and sometimes he manages to combine allusions to both, as he does in these characteristically melancholy lines:

> *The Trees that are around rise, fall, and rot*
> *And mouldering into ashes, are forgot . . .*
> *All Body shall return to native dust,*
> *And yet a single atom not be lost—*[67]

In his more metaphysical moments, Freneau all but explicitly follows Epicurus: "In endless circles all things move / Below, about, far off, above."[68]

One of the better summaries of Epicurean physics up to this point may be found in the letter in which Jefferson declares himself an Epicurean. In that letter Jefferson provides a *Syllabus of the Doctrines of Epicurus*, which includes this telegraphic version of his chosen philosopher's central physical doctrines:

The Universe eternal.
Its parts, great and small, interchangeable.
Matter and Void alone.
Motion inherent in matter which is weighty and declining.
Eternal circulation of the elements of bodies.

In a vital letter to John Adams, Jefferson makes clear that these Epicurean doctrines are essentially his own. "I feel therefore I exist. I feel bodies which are not myself: there are other existencies then. I call them *matter*," he writes.[69] Here he quietly paraphrases Lucretius, who says, "The common sensation of all men proves the existence of matter." Jefferson continues: "I feel them changing place. This gives me *motion*. Where there is an absence of matter, I call it *void*, or *nothing*, or *immaterial space*." Here he is all but quoting Lucretius: "There is, then, intangible space, void, and vacuity. Otherwise, movement would be absolutely impossible."[70] Jefferson's conclusion is definitive, even militant: "To talk of *immaterial* existences is to talk of *nothings*. To say that the human soul, angels, god, are immaterial is to say that they are *nothings*." And here is Epicurus himself: "Those who say that the soul is incorporeal are talking nonsense."[71] On the sources that inspired his views, Jefferson adds, "I believe I am supported in my creed of materialism by Locke, Tracy, and Stewart." But the manner in which he lapses into the language of Lucretius to articulate his ideas suggests that these later philosophers, whether consciously or not, served mainly as conduits for an ancient doctrine.

Jefferson did not balk at drawing out the radical implications of atomism on our understanding of the human condition. "The dead are not even things," he wrote two years before his own death.[72] "The particles of matter which composed their bodies, make part now of the bodies of other animals, vegetables, or minerals, of a thousand forms." The floral imagery echoes Pope, who urged his readers to "See dying vegetables life sustain / See life dissolving vegetate again."[73] It is possibly a more cheerful paraphrase of Hamlet: "We fat all creatures else to fat us, and we fat ourselves for maggots."[74] But the particles are unmistakably those of Epicurus and his ancient predecessors.

Jefferson borrowed from Epicurus not just the doctrines and metaphors but a certain tone: a mixture of scorn, indignation, and horror—the same sensitivity that Lucretius evokes in his harrowing descriptions of human sacrifice, and that Bolingbroke musters in his sometimes reckless tirades against all those who exalt the immaterial nothings of religious superstition. In Jefferson's writings, as in Bolingbroke's, "spiritualism" is a term of extreme abuse—a "charlatanerie of the mind." It is associated above all with Plato—a philosopher whose "whimsies, puerilities, and unintelligible jargon" Jefferson ruthlessly mocks. In endorsing its antithesis, his own "creed of materialism," Jefferson well knows, he has set himself on a collision course with the established religion. Of Jesus he says, "I am a Materialist; he takes the side of Spiritualism."[75] It was because Plato dealt in "mysticisms incomprehensible to the human mind," he adds, that he was "therefore all but adopted as a Christian saint." But Jefferson offers Jesus a possible escape from the spiritualizing shackles of the Christian religion: perhaps Jesus could be interpreted as an Epicurean after all. The early or "primitive" Christians, unlike their corrupt successors, says Jefferson, "generally, if not universally, were materialists, extending it even to the creator himself."—and this is obviously a point in their favor.[76]

By the time Epicurus's atomism reached America, there was no need to read either Epicurus or Lucretius in order to absorb its basic teachings. This is part of what makes Ethan Allen's Bible such a curious artifact. The author of the *Oracles of Reason* may be absolved of all acquaintance with ancient philosophy. Yet he was an Epicurean atomist in all but name. "The particles of matter which compose my body," he tells us, existed in "millions of different forms."[77] In what could be taken as a mountain man's rough translation of Lucretius, he manages to articulate the essential metaphysical point of atomism: "All the productions of nature, animate or inanimate, are no more than the production of forms, and their decay and dissolution is no more, than the dissolution of forms, and neither adds to nor diminishes from creation."[78] Crucially, he adds, all of these transformations follow universal "laws of cause and effect." This lawfulness of the universe inevitably leads the author of the *Oracles* back to a resounding endorsement of the guiding principle of the Epicurean philosophy: something from nothing is "contradictory" and "impossible."[79]

THE GUIDING PRINCIPLE of philosophy, pressed to the limits of the common consciousness, must always stumble over this seemingly innate objection, that life—especially intelligent, human life—is simply too complicated to be explained without supposing the intervention of some conscious and designing agent. How could a blind concourse of atoms produce a throbbing heart, or a poem about lost love, or the glories of the Roman Republic? Epicurus makes a number of efforts to push past this all-too-human sticking point, many of which are not particularly successful and belong to the antiquarian part of the history of philosophy. In his better moments, however, he relies upon a remarkably prescient suggestion, one that bids us to revise some common assumptions about the respective contributions of science and philosophy to the creation of the modern world. The complexity and diversity of life, says Epicurus, has arisen through a process of evolution by natural selection.

The Epicurean concept of evolution is deeply rooted in the vision of an atomistic world without forms: "Time transforms the nature of the entire world, and everything inevitably passes on from one phase to another. There is no thing that stays the same, everything is in flux; everything is altered by nature and compelled to change," says Lucretius.[80] The evolution of the world, crucially, is directed not from above but from below. New configurations of atoms arise in a random fashion, and these configurations are then tested against the pressures of survival. While the "badly made objects perish," according to Leibniz's summary of the Epicurean doctrine, the "well made ones are preserved."[81]

In Lucretius's presentation, the principle of natural selection applies in the first instance at the level of worlds, such as our earth-world. Mesmerizing passages of De rerum natura offer a speculative natural history of the earth-world, according to which the creation of the earth and sun are shown to result from a process of evolution by selection. The sun does not shine because it was designed to do so, the argument effectively suggests, but because it happens *not* to be one of the suns that failed to shine and so were never seen.[82]

The same, Epicurean version of the principle of natural selection next applies to the evolution of living creatures. In prehistoric times, says Lucretius, many "monsters" and "misshapen beasts" were born.[83] But the unfit were selected out: "Many species of animals must have . . . failed to propagate and perpetuate their race. Every species that you now see drawing the breath of life has been protected and preserved from the beginning of its existence either by cunning or by prowess or by speed."[84] Thus, the marvelous capacities of the species we now observe emerge not from any divine or preordained plan, but from the same natural processes that sustain us in our daily life. "The species of mortal creatures were not lowered from the heights of heaven to the fields by a golden rope," Lucretius insists. "They were generated by the same earth that now nourishes them from her own substance."[85]

Lucretius extends this principle even to the quasi-sacred territory of the human body: "No part of our bodies was created in order that we might be able to use it; the thing born creates the use. There was no seeing before eyes were born, no talking before the tongue was created."[86] In Leibniz's excellent paraphrase, "Feet are not made for walking, but people walk because they have feet."[87] The body, in short, is not an artifact of design but the outcome of a fortuitous natural process. Like everything else in the Epicurean universe, it is a kind of beautiful accident, the output of an algorithm that generates astounding complexity from the operation of a few simple rules.

In a twist that would prove crucial for early modern political theory (and not just Rousseau's), the Epicurean version of natural selection also applies to human societies. In the beginning, as Lucretius relates the history, human beings lived like animals, scavenging for food in a rather solitary way and procreating like apes in shady glens. Shortly after the invention of fire and basic weapons technology, men and women discovered the evolutionary benefits of a "stable union . . . to watch over their joint progeny."[88] Next they came to appreciate the survival value of group cooperation. "Neighbors began to form mutual pacts of friendship" in order to advance their common interests and agreed "with gestures and inarticulate cries that everyone ought to have compassion for the weak."[89] "Although it was not possible to achieve a universal concord, the substantial majority kept their compacts loyally" in those first days of civilization, according to Lucretius; "otherwise the human race would have been entirely extinguished at that early stage and could not have propagated and preserved itself to the present day."[90] After many failed experiments with anarchy and tyranny, human beings finally learned "how to constitute a government and establish rights, so that the people would want to obey the laws."[91] According to Lucretius's natural history of justice, in brief, better and more just arrangements of society have arisen not by the grace of any transcendent authority, nor as the result of a movement directed toward a preestablished or divinely ordained end, but through a process of evolution that pits human collectivities against the pressures of survival.

At the bottom of the Epicurean version of evolution by natural selection is a resolute insistence that everything in the universe, however marvelous and complex, can be explained only through causes, not purposes, and an equally resolute denial that the universe as a whole answers to the interests or purposes of one particular species of creature within it. "To assert that . . . the gods purposely prepared the world and its wonders for the sake of human beings . . . that it is sinful to use any means at any time to displace what was established by ancient design of the gods for the perpetual use of the human race . . . is *preposterous*," Lucretius asserts.[92] Bolingbroke gets the same point across in a passage that Jefferson thought worthy of putting in his *Literary Commonplace Book*: "I combat the pride and presumption of the metaphysicians in a most flagrant instance, in the assumption by which man is made the final cause of the whole creation."[93]

It has become a commonplace in the culture wars of today to represent Charles Darwin as a solitary scientific hero bursting through the millennia of darkness. The theory of evolution, together with the destruction of the foundations of supernatural religion, is said to have appeared with a bang with the publication of *On the Origin of the Species* in 1859. In his 1995 book *Darwin's Dangerous Idea*, for example, Daniel Dennett suggests that Darwin changed everything with the idea that nature operates according to a mechanical or non-teleological algorithm that is capable of generating complexity and diversity from a few simple rules in the absence of any guiding purpose. But at this level of abstraction, Darwin's dangerous idea was not Darwin's at all; and its dangers were evident to a great many people long before Darwin was born. David Hume, Denis Diderot, and the French astronomer Pierre-Louis Maupertuis (1698–1759)—to name three of Lucretius's radicalized admirers in the early modern world—offered speculative theories of evolution along the lines of Epicurus.[94] So, too, did Erasmus Darwin (1731–1802). A doctor, inventor, scientist, deist, world-famous poet, vocal supporter of the American and French Revolutions, friend of Franklin, and close associate of Jefferson's college tutor, Erasmus was as passionate about Lucretius as he was about the idea that all life on earth descended from a single "living filament" that emerged from the earth's oceans and evolved under the pressure of natural selection over untold millions of years.[95] He was also, not coincidentally, Charles's grandfather.

Now, Charles certainly did add to this dangerous idea the crucial concepts of speciation, heritability, and variability that make its application to biological phenomena much clearer and amenable to further research. He also deserves more credit than any other human being for ensconcing this refined version of the idea in a range of scientific observations that render it much more credible than anything that came before. So if our concern lies with the history of science, Darwin would win any priority dispute without breaking a sweat. If our concern is with the history of ideas, on the other hand, the story is different. Jefferson, to cite one case in point, was not at all Darwinian on biological questions (like many at the time, he didn't think that species went extinct); yet the part of his political philosophy that matters today deserves to be called (in the best sense, which will have to be disentangled from the many abuses to which the term has been put) Darwinian.

The proper dating of Epicurus's dangerous idea matters because it tells us something about the nature of that idea. Today's Darwinians agree with yesterday's Epicureans that the religious consciousness suffers from a deficit of knowledge, but they do not agree about how to understand that deficit. Darwin's epigones presume that the kind of knowledge that is missing is of the scientific sort—the kind that has been available only very recently, through the grand collaborative effort of the scientific community, and that rests on the rigorous application of what is vaguely called the scientific method. Epicurus tells us by his very existence, on the other hand, that the knowledge lacking to the religious consciousness is of the kind that was freely available to a man born on an island off the coast of what is now Turkey 2,300 years ago; and that this knowledge is needed to overcome a kind of ignorance that persists to the present. This knowledge is really just a kind of awareness that we should call wisdom. It deserves the name of philosophy. And as Epicurus's contribution to America's revolutionary political project shows, it had the power to change the world well before it achieved the luxury of scientific support.

TODAY THE HISTORIANS of philosophy tend to remember Epicurus by his atomism (or his "materialism"), and contemporary scientists will probably think that it was his proto-Darwinism that ought to be of greatest interest. In the revival of Epicurus's philosophy that began with Bruno, however, what really mattered was his cosmology. When Epicurus turned from atoms to the stars, projecting his intuition about the intelligibility of all things up into the night sky, he produced the spectacular vision of the infinite universe.[96]

In order to appreciate the impact of that vision, one must first call to mind the picture of the universe as it seemed to exist in the Middle Ages and as it continues to exist in the common religious consciousness. The medieval universe, which is mostly the universe of the common imagination, has a definite beginning and end. It has a center and an edge. It exhibits clear and all-important divisions of kind: between the fiery pits of hell, the putrefying surface of the earth, and the unchanging perfection of the heavens. It shelters only one earth and only one species whose redemption could be of interest to a creator. The universe of the human imagination, in short, is precisely limited, ordered, internally differentiated, and invested with meaning, like a jeweled egg that, in accordance with the assumptions of the primitive religion, could have been created in a moment by some supernatural agent and manipulated according to the rules of some other, higher form of world perhaps vaguely discernible to humankind through the words of the prophets or some other supernatural source. It is this delicate construction in make-believe that Epicurus, with the help of Lucretius's glittering verses, shatters into uncountable pieces.

The first of Epicurus's cosmological conclusions is that the universe must be eternal. Since nothing can come from nothing, he reasons, then all of our somethings must have come from some other things in the past and they must turn into other things in the future, which in turn must have come from still other things and must turn into still other things, and so on backward and forward in time forever. Though the doctrine is expressed in adventurously cosmological language, it is

in essence an imaginative restatement of the guiding principle of philosophy, for it says that the things of this world can only be explained
by other things within the world (and simply adds the unstated premise that some necessary subset of our explanations refer to causes that
precede their effects in time).

Through similar reasoning, Epicurus infers that the universe is
infinite in extension. Once again, the argument assumes a cosmological form: If you reach the edge of the universe and then toss a spear,
Epicurus asks, where does it land? At its deepest level, however, the
argument remains an elaboration of the guiding principle, for the
underlying point is that if the universe has an extremity—if there is
an "inside" and an "outside"—then the things within it cannot remain
fully explicable or intelligible. Spears will disappear mysteriously, for
example; or maybe they will bounce back in a weird way under the
influence of some extra-universal power.

From the infinite extension of the universe, Epicurus goes on to
infer that the universe has no center. Wherever you stand within the
universe, he says, it goes off into infinity in all directions. Everything
looks pretty much the same wherever you happen to be. Therefore,
just as the universe has no edge, it also has no center. The argument
here, too, is fundamentally an extension of the guiding principle, for
it is really just a way of saying that nature's laws respect no particular
spatial location as the beneficiary of arbitrary privilege.

Closely linked to the notion that the universe is centerless is the
idea that the universe is everywhere made of the same kind of stuff.
In the Epicurean universe, there are no fundamental divisions of kind,
such as that between the undying flames of the celestial spheres and
the moribund mud of the earth. Everywhere there can only be the
same sort of stuff. We are stardust—and the stars differ from campfires
in size but not in kind. Here again, the inference follows in a reasonable way from the insistence that the laws of nature are genuinely universal, and operate everywhere and always in the same way.

Epicurus rounds out this picture of the universe with one last,
provocative conclusion: we are not alone. "Under no circumstances
must we think it likely that this one earth and sky is the only one to

have been created," Lucretius announces.[97] "The earth, the son, the moon, the ocean, and all that exists, are not one of a kind, but rather of innumerable number."[98] Our earth-world, he explains, arose from a particular "entanglement" of atoms in one part of space, and it will undoubtedly perish. In an eternal, self-generative, and quasi-female universe, however, other worlds are being created and destroyed all the time, for nothing in being, save being itself, can be entirely unique in its kind. Life, in all its possible forms, including intelligent life, is everywhere.

Epicurus's cosmology was not grounded in any observations about the stars or planets, and it has little to add to our scientific knowledge about particle physics and the origins of the observable universe. Yet it still has philosophical teeth. Even if we suppose that the expansion of the observable universe points backward to an initial moment or a big bang, Epicurus would surely argue, that fact itself does not entitle us to any claims about a cause preceding the bang that might explain the existence and structure of things in this world, as some theologians today like to imagine. If we were to find evidence in the universe of such a prior cause and its consequent effects, then that would only mean that we have discovered a previously unknown part of the universe. In whatever way we modify our concepts of space and time to account for observation, Epicurus would surely conclude, the universe remains infinite and eternal in the sense that our explanations of it may never depart from it.

The glittering, haunting image of an eternal, infinitely extended, centerless, homogenous, and wildly fecund universe—the infinite universe for short—caused an almost unimaginable thrill, a delicious vertigo of freedom, among those who rediscovered Lucretius's long-lost poem in early modern Europe. No one was more exhilarated than the irrepressible Bruno. "Never shall you see the face of immense and starry Olympus Come to an end," he exulted. The universe endlessly produces "stars without number," he claimed, and not "a single one is less fertile than earth."[99] Indeed, he assured his readers, the "inhabitants" of these other worlds are "quite as good and even better" than those of our own.[100] In Bruno's mind—as in the view of all his alien-obsessed successors down through the American Revolution— extraterrestrials weren't little, green, or three-eyed, and they certainly weren't a saucer-flying menace to our way of life. They were just like us, maybe a little better: our brothers and sisters in the contemplation of nature's endless bounty.

From Bruno the infinite fever spread directly to England, its symptoms unchanged. Toland opened his *Pantheisticon*—a pamphlet intended to serve as a kind of liturgy for the Masons—with a euphoric "dissertation on the infinite and eternal universe" that reads as if lifted from Bruno.[101] He also left behind a manuscript on Bruno's life and a translation of Bruno's summary of his book "on the infinite universe and innumerable worlds."[102] Trenchard and Gordon offered lyrical descriptions of an infinite universe in which everything everywhere is in eternal motion.[103] Bolingbroke wrote—and Jefferson transcribed— the sentiment: "That noble scene of the universe, which modern philosophy has opened, gives ample room for all the planetary inhabitants."[104] Alexander Pope, too, succumbed to the ecstasy of the infinite:

> *Observe how system into system runs*
> *What other planets circle other suns,*
> *What varied being peoples every star*[105]

The astronomical revolution of the early modern period is often said to have "dethroned" or "humbled" humankind by depriving our planet of its central place in the cosmos. But this is hardly how Bruno and his radicalized followers saw the matter. In the medieval worldview, as Galileo memorably summarizes it, the earth is "the dump heap of the filth and dregs of the universe."[106] At the center of the universe, indeed, is hell. Depriving the universe of a center had the effect of raising the earth into the heavens, into the arms of a cosmic brotherhood without end, which is probably why it lifted Bruno's spirits so manically.

The liberation of the earth, it was clear from the start, involved a liberation from the established religion. Bolingbroke put his finger on the source of the trouble in yet another passage that Jefferson thought worthy of inscribing in his notebook:

Where the spirits of the other system reside was a question easily answered, when superstition and hypothesis made up the sum of religion and philosophy. But it is not so easily answered now. Are the good and pure spirits in heaven? But where is heaven? Is it beyond all the solar systems of the universe? . . . Where is hell? Is it in the center of any one planet for every system?[107]

To get to the point: Where in the infinite universe could one even pretend to find God? And what would Jesus do, confronted with so many planets to save?

No branch of the Epicurean family was more keenly aware of the thrill and the agony of the infinite universe than the American one. Paine endorsed the same vision of an infinite universe in a passage striking for both its elegance and its fidelity to the logic first offered by Epicurus:

It is difficult beyond description to conceive that space can have no end; but it is more difficult to conceive an end. It is difficult beyond the power of man to conceive an eternal duration of what we call time; but it is more impossible to conceive a time when there shall be no time.[108]

From these familiar premises concerning the eternity of the universe, Paine deduces all the expected doctrines concerning "the infinity of space,"[109] the "plurality of worlds,"[110] and the hyper-abundance of extra-terrestrials. Inevitably, he lunges for the theological jugular. Given the uncountable number of inhabited planets, he says, "the person who is irreverently called the Son of God, and sometimes God himself, would have nothing else to do than to travel from world to world, in an endless succession of death, with scarcely a momentary interval of life."[111]

Paine cites no sources, as is his custom, and yet it is reasonable to suppose that he did not re-invent the Epicurean cosmology from scratch. The likely story is that he gleaned the essentials from the lectures of Martin and Ferguson—the astronomer friends of Franklin who, shielding themselves under the saintly name of Newton, passed down the wisdom from Toland and Bruno. He might also have picked it up from David Rittenhouse, the famous Philadelphia inventor and astronomer and member of Franklin's circle. "The doctrine of the plurality of worlds is inseparable from the principles of astronomy," Rittenhouse declared in a lecture before the American Philosophical Society in February 1775.[112]

John Adams may have detested Paine's flamboyant deism, yet he directly confronted the challenge represented by the infinite universe in terms nearly identical to those of his bête noir. In a letter to Jefferson in 1813, he reminisced on a debate on the issue he had in 1758 in Boston with a freethinking doctor. "I drove him up, as I thought, into a Corner, from which he could not escape," Adams recalls. "Sir, it will follow from what you have now advanced, that the Universe, as distinct from God, is both infinite and eternal." To which the doctor replied, "Very true . . . Your inference is just; and I believe the Universe to be, both eternal and infinite." Adams was stunned: "Here I was brought up! I was defeated. I was not prepared for this Answer." But if we inspect his diary from the period, it seems that young John had already been struggling with the infinite universe for some time. An entry from 1756, written in his religiously tumultuous twenty-first year, makes exactly the point that Paine would drive home four decades later: "Astronomers tell us with good reason that . . . all the unnumbered worlds that revolve around the fixed stars are inhabited . . . If so, I ask a Calvinist whether he will subscribe to this alternative, 'Either God Almighty must assume the respective shapes of all these different species and suffer the penalties of their crimes in their stead, or else all these beings must be consigned to everlasting perdition."[113]

Adams goes on to tell Jefferson that when he was in England from 1785 to 1788 he had many conversations with Dr. Richard Price, the famous Unitarian philosopher and supporter of the American and French Revolutions. In their "most unreserved Conversations," alone at Price's house, says Adams, the radical preacher confided that he, too, believed the universe to be eternal and infinite.[114] On his travels through England, as it happens, Adams also met with the famous astronomer William Herschel (1738–1822). A principal champion of the infinite universe at the time, Herschel was so convinced of the reality of aliens that he was sure that he'd seen their houses and farms on the surface of the moon though his telescope. According to the astronomer's recollections, Adams pressed him on the theological implications of "the plurality of worlds."[115] In his ninetieth year, in one of his last missives to Jefferson, Adams at last seemed to confess just where he stood on the question of the cosmos. While lauding Jefferson for his plan to establish the University of Virginia, he urged his fellow revolutionary to staff the new school with professors from America, not Europe, for the Europeans "are all infected with Episcopal and Presbyterian creeds": "They all believe that [that] great principle, which has produced this boundless Universe, Newton's Universe, and Hershells universe, came down to this little Ball, to be spit-upon by Jews; and until this awful blasphemy is got rid of, there will never be any liberal science in the world."[116]

The best evidence for Epicureanism in the absence of Epicurus in America comes once again from Ethan Allen's Bible. With almost eerie precision, and yet without once placing foot in anyone else's book, the author of that work rehearses the key steps in the argument for the infinite universe. Since there can be no genuine creation, but only lawful transformations of things, he reasons, there can be no doubt but that the universe is eternal. Thus he blithely aligns himself with the radicals in the hottest part of the theological war of the preceding century.[117] Relentlessly pursuing the familiar chain of inferences, he goes on to assert that the universe must likewise be centerless, uniform, and infinite: "If it were possible that any of us could be transported to the farthest extended star . . . we should from thence survey worlds as distant from that as that is from this, and so on *ad infinitum*." And so, in conclusion, we are not alone. The innumerable worlds of the universe, says the sage of the Green Mountains, "are each and every of them possessed or inhabited by some intelligent agents or other."[118] Naturally, Ethan Allen's Bible does not stop short of the theological kicker. Those religions that presume to limit God's concern to the inhabitants of the planet on which their adherents happen to live are "degrading to a rational nature."

ON THE ONE HAND, it seems as obvious now as it did in the early modern period that the great champion of the guiding principle and its infinite universe was an atheist.[119] "There is but one compleat Antient *System of Atheism* (viz. EPICURUS's System, written by LUCRETIUS)," said Anthony Collins—who really should be understood to have meant it as a compliment.[120] On the other hand, Epicurus quite unambiguously affirms a certain, strange kind of belief in God and gods; and especially in the poetry of Lucretius this belief comes wrapped in detailed arguments and suffused with a genuine air of piety. And his heirs in early modern Europe and America were, to judge by their rhetoric, even holier in their sensibilities. Indeed, the theology of the infinite universe proved more puzzling than at first appeared. It took the great philosophical geniuses of the seventeenth century some time to figure out how atheism could be made so pious. At least in retrospect, however, the bare outlines of a solution are detectible in Epicurus.

The official theory, as put forward by Lucretius, is that the gods are a species that exist in the vast, empty stretches of space in between the earth-worlds of the infinite universe. We can just barely catch glimpses of these "intermundial" gods in our minds, and they can't hear our prayers. As a matter of fact, the gods don't want to hear our prayers. They lead ideal lives of unalloyed (and unemployed) bliss. These rock-star deities are surely superior to humankind, but they are not as grand as the universe itself, which they inhabit rather than control. Bruno, in his exuberant fashion, identifies the deities with the stars themselves, and suggests that they number "many hundreds of thousands." Jefferson sums up the doctrine well in the *Syllabus* included in his "I-am-an-Epicurean" letter: "Gods, an order of beings next superior to man, enjoying in their sphere, their own felicities; but not meddling with the concerns of the scale of beings below them."[121]

This official theology, it must be said, is so bizarre, not to say incoherent, that one might question whether a philosopher as remorselessly logical as Epicurus could have intended it seriously. The theory stipulates, for example, that the gods are made of atoms, just like everything else in the universe; but in that case, as the ancient critics pointed out, the Epicurean gods can't be immortal. Epicurus seems to leave the question dangling—mortal gods, immortal gods, who cares? Much more egregious is the remoteness of the Epicurean gods. If the gods have tuned out our prayers and won't lift a finger for us, are they gods at all? And why should we care about them?

Alongside his official theology, Epicurus offers an intriguing, arguably deeper theory concerning the gods. The intuition expressed in the deeper theory involves a kind of reversal of the traditional relationship between gods and humans: the gods do not cause us to exist, but rather we cause them to exist. Cicero hints at this theory when he reports that, according to Epicurus, the gods exist "because nature herself had imprinted the conception of them in all men's minds."[122] The basic point is that the gods serve as a kind of collection point for a specific set of impressions—namely, our impressions concerning ideal existence. So they reflect a truth not about the world but about the constitution of our own minds.

Implicit in this polytheistic vision of gods-as-ideals is a version of monotheism, or a singular ideal of all ideals. "Think of God as an imperishable and blessed creature, as the common idea of God is in outline, and attach to him nothing alien to imperishability or inappropriate to blessedness," Epicurus advises a friend.[123] In a sense, there is a top God in the Epicurean universe, and it stands for the highest ideal, namely, imperishability and tranquility. The B-list gods—the semi-mortal beings who are arguably not gods at all—stand for specific ideals, such as friendship, love, and maybe good food.

The projection-theory of the God and gods, perhaps surprisingly, rescues a certain space for prayer in the Epicurean universe. Of course, ideals will never grant wishes, and so prayer remains as useless as fan mail is to rock stars. Yet we have a natural inclination to pray, Epicurus suggests, and we should indulge this inclination because it can make us feel good and it may help guide us toward our ideals. The point of the strange theology of intermundial gods, in fact, may be just to give earthlings fitting objects toward which to direct their non-instrumental yet therapeutic prayers.

In the "Articles of Belief" that he composed upon his return to America in 1728 at the age of twenty-two, Franklin provides a lyrical example of just what it means to be an intermundial mono-polytheist of the Epicurean variety. He begins by accepting that the universe "is every Way infinite" and "fill'd with Suns like ours, each with a Chorus of Worlds for ever moving around him."[124] There are "many Beings or Gods, vastly superior to man," he goes on to say, and each god makes for itself a sun and beautiful system of planets (pretty much as Bruno suggests). There is at the same time a top God, the ultimate A-lister, tranquil and imperishable—the "Infinite Father"—but he is so remote and so self-satisfied that he can have no interest even in the lesser gods, let alone the pathetic race of earthlings. As for the B-list gods, "it may be that the lesser, created Gods, are immortal, or it may be that after many Ages, they are changed." Mortal gods, immortal gods—who cares? It may also be that the lesser gods don't actually exist. They come into being in Franklin's narrative because, he concedes, he feels the urge to pray and he needs "SOMETHING" at which to direct this urge. But no matter: it feels good to pray, so Franklin resolves to conjure into existence a race of semi-mortal, semi-fictional deities, one of whom presides in a humane way over our particular solar system, so that he may have a suitable object for his therapeutic prayer rituals.

Franklin's later writings include a number of equally startling and implausible professions of faith in a weird polytheism. The gods in question, just like those of Epicurus, are marvelous to behold but not expected to do much aside from making us feel good about ourselves. None of which proves that Franklin actually believed in their existence. Indeed, there is little reason to suppose that he took his polytheism any more seriously than his monotheism. He wore his theology lightly, like a collection of colorful raincoats. This lack of seriousness is itself perhaps the more profound mark of the influence of Epicurean theology on Franklin.[125]

The layers of irony that envelop the gods of both Franklin and Epicurus are in a sense a kind of protective coating that shields them from the requirements of the common religious consciousness. At the bottom of the strange theology that Epicurus supplies and Franklin embraces is the understanding that the gods of the philosophers—to the extent that they exist—are very different from the gods of the people. "The impious man is not he who denies the gods of the many," Epicurus writes to a friend, "but he who attaches to the gods the beliefs of the many about them."[126] Lord Bacon repeats the message for the benefit of readers like Jefferson: "There is no profanity in refusing to believe in the gods of the vulgar: the profanity is in believing of the gods what the vulgar believe."[127] The beliefs of the many, Bacon makes clear, are that the gods care a whit about us; that they respond to prayers and sacrificial offerings; and that they suffer, get angry, and, in general, behave like ornery human beings. Lucretius, as usual, says it better:

> This is not piety, this show of bowing a veiled head before a stone; this bustling to every altar; this prostration on the ground with palms outstretched before the shrines of gods; this drowning of altars with the blood of brutes; this binding of vow upon vow. True piety lies rather in the power to contemplate the universe with a tranquil mind.[128]

This last remark about the true nature of piety is perhaps the most stimulating, vexing, and influential aspect of the (anti-)theological vista that opened up for European civilization upon the recovery of Lucretius's lost poem. If "true piety" is just the contemplation of the universe, then there is no difference between the study of nature and the worship of God. And in fact, the longer the followers of Epicurus dwelt on the perfection and imperishability of their top God, the more they tended toward the conclusion that the only truly imperishable and absolutely blessed thing in the eternal, infinite, and self-moving universe is the universe itself.

IN MOST OF THE popular narratives of the history, the great spur of the scientific revolution and the primary source of friction between the new natural philosophers and the church is said to have been the discovery of a new fact: the earth orbits the sun, and not the other way around. Or, to put names on the story, Copernicus came up with the relevant theory, Galileo gathered everything that mattered through his telescope, and Bruno was just one of history's oddballs, a magician of sorts who can only be of antiquarian interest. But the real source of both the ecstasy and the despair was the doctrine of the infinite universe and the anti-theology that came with it. The controversy over Copernican theory was just the most prominent of several ways in which this deeper tension expressed itself. Heliocentrism, after all, contradicted only a minor biblical story about Joshua and the day God made the sun stand still over the sky; the doctrine of the infinite universe reduced the very idea of a biblical religion to farce.

Bruno, as it happens, was one of the first vocal advocates of Copernican theory. But in his attempts to promote that theory he articulated it so poorly that he had difficulty repeating it without introducing errors. He embraced its thesis that the earth is not the center of the universe, but he paid little heed to the implication that the sun is. Rather, following Lucretius, he cast the sun and earth together into the dizzy void of a centerless universe. At his inquisition, Cardinal Bellarmine charged him with, among other things, disbelief in the doctrine of transubstantiation, disbelief in the doctrine of the Trinity, and belief in "infinite worlds." Faced with teams of confessors—Dominicans, Franciscans, and Augustinians—who crammed into his cell and urged him to recant, Bruno denied that he had spoken out against transubstantiation and attempted to argue his way around the accusations that he had shown disrespect for Christian rites. But he never gave up on the infinite universe.

Galileo's ultimate significance in the history of ideas, too, may have more to do with the infinite universe than with the controversial stand in favor of the Copernican theory that brought him notoriety.[129] In the 1632 book that landed him before the Inquisition, the *Dialogue concerning the Two Chief World Systems*, he devotes fewer lines to elaborating the Copernican theory than to proving the claim that the earth and the heavens are made up of the same kind of stuff obeying the same universal laws. He also takes the extraordinary risk of dismissing Aristotle's proofs concerning the finite extension of the universe and posing, in the guise of a hypothesis, the infinite alternative.[130] From there he goes on to note that, like denizens of a forest who have never seen the ocean, we "terreni"—terrestrials—remain in ignorance of what forms of life might exist out in the unseen reaches of space.[131] Summarizing the *Dialogue* for the benefit of a Paris friend, he expresses his hope that it will "open the door for speculative minds to lose themselves in the immense"—a choice of words bound to warm the heart of any follower of Bruno.[132] Indeed, Galileo's words quite possibly *did* come from a follower of Bruno. Gassendi had written to Galileo some years previously to say that his work made him feel "unchained and free, wandering through the immensity of space, once the barriers represented by the popular theory of the cosmos have been broken down"—or pretty much what Lucretius said about Epicurus, and what Bruno said about himself.[133] The great astronomer Johannes Kepler (1571–1630) gently advised Galileo to acknowledge the true source of his inspiration: "Do not . . . begrudge our predecessors their proper credit . . . You refine a doctrine borrowed from Bruno."[134]

In the mind of the reaction, too, not heliocentrism but the infinite universe loomed as the seemingly invincible flagship of atheism. John Donne (1572–1631) expressed the anxiety of the moment well in his famous poem "An Anatomie of the World," penned on "the First Anniversarie" of the publication of Galileo's provocative book of 1610, *The Starry Messenger*:

> *And new philosophy calls all in doubt*
> *The element of fire is quite put out*

The new philosophers, Donne means to say, have poured cold water on the hallowed notion that the heavens are composed of a flaming substance ontologically superior to that of the earth. Hamlet, incidentally, made the same point a few years earlier on the English stage: "This brave o'erhanging firmament, this majestical roof fretted with golden fire, why, it appears to me no other thing than a foul and pestilential congregation of vapors."[135] In his next lines, Donne shows plainly that the focus of his concern is not that the earth moves—indeed, he else-where *endorses* the Copernican theory—but that the entire solar system has disappeared in the new infinity:

> *The sun is lost, and th'earth, and no man's wit*
> *Can well direct him where to look for it.*
> *And freely men confess that this world's spent,*
> *When in the planets and the firmament*
> *They seek so many new . . .*

In the concluding lines of the section, Donne leaves us with little doubt that his ultimate target is the atomistic philosophy that at the time was still unmistakably tied to Epicurus:

> *. . . they see that this*
> *Is crumbled out again to his atomies*
> *'Tis all in pieces, all coherence gone,*
> *All just supply, and all relation*

Today we like to suppose that science came first, and that the quarrel with religion was the consequence. But the facts reveal a very different history. The infinite universe and its alien residents were dis-covered in books long before they appeared (if they ever did) in the night sky. Those books included many speculations about the compo-sition of the moon and the stars, to be sure, yet they were concerned mainly to expose the ways in which human beings on this earth misun-derstand themselves and so bring upon themselves their own unhap-piness. Though the truths they discovered were what we now tend to call moral truths, they were no less certain on that account. When the revolutionaries of the early modern world peered through their tele-scopes into the night sky, the first thing they saw was injustice on earth.

THE INQUISITORIAL TRIALS of the first part of the seventeenth century had a dramatic impact on the subsequent history of Epicurus's dangerous idea—not on its substance, but on the manner in which it was disseminated. Descartes, for example, had nearly completed a work modestly titled *The World* when Galileo was put on trial. Upon learning of the verdict, he decided that *The World* could wait. "It is not my temperament to set sail against the wind," he later explained to a friend.[136] The wind was evidently blowing very much away from Epicurean cosmologies, and Descartes sailed with it in the direction of a new metaphysical program—one that he hoped would satisfy the religious authorities while still serving as a foundation for his own essentially Epicurean investigations of physical nature. When the text of *The World* made its posthumous appearance a few decades later, its author's reticence seemed justified.[137] Locke, in the travel journal he kept while in France in the 1670s, said that Descartes had quite obviously stolen his "vortices" from Bruno,[138] and Toland, too, suggested that Descartes was grossly in debt to Bruno.[139] Leibniz was convinced that Descartes, worse than Bruno, was a dishonest atheist.[140]

Possibly the most important fact about the philosophy of the Epicurean revival—and the ultimate source of the most significant differences between it and its ancient original—is that it was produced in a time when writers felt compelled to express their ideas indirectly.[141] "I have read . . . that *philosophers say plenty of things that they do not believe*," said Vanini—who was accused in his own time, not without reason, of saying many things that he did not believe.[142] A full century after Vanini's execution, John Toland observed, "Daily experience sufficiently evinces, that there is no discovering, at least no declaring of TRUTH in most places, but at the hazard of men's reputation, employment, or life." He said this in a handbook titled *Clidophorus*—meaning "key-bearer"—in which he explained the difference between the "esoteric" and the "exoteric" (or "internal" and "external") methods of writing.[143]

In the aftermath of its democratic revolution, America has tended to think of itself as the land where people say what they mean. Yet America's revolutionaries lived long enough ago to appreciate that the dissemination of dangerous philosophical ideas often advances through indirection. Paine forgave Montesquieu, Quesnay, and Turgot their shortcomings,[144] for example, because he understood that they lived in a time and place where open expression would have carried grave personal risks. Jefferson pardoned Bolingbroke his lapses on the same account.[145] The American revolutionary most keenly aware of the art of esoteric writing, not surprisingly, was the oldest—Franklin. In an issue of his *Pennsylvania Gazette* from 1730, under the cover of an anonymous letter, he supplies a raffishly American example of the practice:

> I know well that the Age in which we live, abounds in *Spinosists*, *Hobbists*, and *most impious Free-Thinkers*, who despise *Revelation*, and treat the *most sacred Truths* with *Ridicule* and *Contempt*: Nay, to such a Height of Iniquity are they arrived, that they not only deny the *Existence* of the *Devil*, and of *Spirits* in general, but would also persuade the World, that the Story of *Saul* and the *Witch of Endor* is an Imposture; and which is still worse, that no Credit is given to the so well attested One of the *Drummer* of *Tedsworth*.[146]

The anonymous writer follows this exercise in protesting too much with a transparently ridiculous story about a ghostly drummer-spirit.[147] The effect of the performance is quite obviously to make the stories of scripture seem just as absurd as the tale of the drummer boy, and thus to align the writer with the Spinozists and Hobbists he feigns to despise. To multiply the ironies, in a subsequent issue Franklin publishes a second letter whose pseudonymous author—"Philoclerus," that is, "priest-lover"—indignantly calls out the perpetrator of the first letter.[148] "Notwithstanding his seeming Reflection on *Spinosists*, *Hobbists*, *and most impious Freethinkers*, his Design is apparent, To bring the Dispensers of Religion among us into Contempt," complains Philoclerus. So now Franklin is taking a stand against the noxious, hidden message of his first letter—except that in doing so, he brings the hidden message out into the public, in case anybody missed it. It doesn't help that Philoclerus's arguments are feeble (he concludes that the testimony of two Reverend Fathers is quite sufficient to make the drummer story credible) and even counterproductive (he says that we should treat religious fables as true because the people cannot be governed well without them).

The esoteric writing of the period, however, was not all or even mostly about escaping persecution or avoiding opprobrium from religious and political hierarchies. It had much more to do with the distinctively modern problem of communicating a true and useful message to large numbers of people in the rapidly emerging public sphere. With the invention of the printing press and the spread of literacy, sophisticated writers at the time converged on two premises crucial to the understanding of their own craft. The first is that the public is inherently limited in its ability to understand things. The second is that this ignorance is the basis of all persecution: persecution not just of writers, but of the public itself. From these premises it follows that the point of writing is not just to slip a coded truth past the authorities but to adjust it to the limitations of the public understanding. The writer must present a truth that is useful to the public without at the same time provoking the persecutory reaction that is bound to follow upon release of the whole truth. Toland builds the program of his *Pantheisticon* around this purpose: "We must talk with the People, and think with the Philosophers."[149] Locke agreed that God has not delivered "Oracles by the Multitude" nor has Nature revealed "Truths by the Herd." "Vulgar opinions are suited to vulgar capacities . . . The Multitude reason but ill." At the same time, Locke was careful to distance himself from those who rejected the common opinions just because they are common. We do not "refuse to breath the air" because "the rabble" does so too, he noted.[150]

The greater challenge of esoteric writing, then, was not to escape the censors but to penetrate the internal defenses of its very own readers. Lucretius himself had pointed out that a spoonful of sugar helps the philosophical medicine go down (honey and wormwood were the metaphors he had to hand).[151] Locke was well aware of the medicinal strategy, though in typically convoluted fashion he projected its use on his philosophical nemesis, the divine rights theorist Robert Filmer: "Like a wary physician, when he would have his Patient swallow some harsh or corrosive Liquor, he mingles it with a large quantity of that, which may dilute; that the scatter'd Parts may go down with less feeling, and cause less aversion."[152]

Which may or may not serve to illustrate perhaps the most profound truth uncovered by the esoteric writers of the early modern world: that philosophers are no exception to the rule that authors are never in complete control of their own work. The "doctrines" that philosophers supply never amount to anything more than the reasons they offer for believing in them; and the fact that all of those reasons come out of a single philosopher or a single text is never any guarantee that they do in fact cohere or that they answer to some ultimate authorial intention. Possibly Locke believed in the religion of the cross and intended his philosophical exercises to support that belief. But that doesn't mean that they did. More than a few readers, then and now, quite reasonably detected in his arguments precisely the kind of "harsh liquors" that he claimed to detect in others. Indeed, as would become clear in the case of Isaac Newton—the man who perhaps inadvertently gave the infinite universe of Epicurus its biggest boost when he adopted it as the basis for his hugely credible system of physics—the most effective of the "hidden" messages of the time came from authors who almost certainly had no intention of putting them there at all.

Ultimately, the Epicurean revival succeeded because it was able to spread its core message in a range of fragments and constructs whose implications and interconnections were often not fully grasped by those who embraced and disseminated them. A new and subversive vocabulary emerged, bound together with secret chains of inference, under the partial control of some who glimpsed the general direction of things, yet cheerfully parroted even by those who imagined that they have nothing to hide. With the benefit of that new language, the revolutionary philosophers of early modern Europe were able to preserve and extend the reach of Epicurus's dangerous idea, presenting the public with a safe and graded path toward greater understanding even while evading the efforts of the theological police. The ultimate beneficiaries of this multi-sided form of discourse were the American people, whose revolutionaries used it to meld a large and diverse republic into a radical new force in history.

Although most of the new Epicureans labored hard to adapt their writings to the limitations of the moment, there were always a few who disdained all such artifices. On occasion, radical philosophy rose with implacable hostility to the surface of the texts, as if to destroy the pretense that it was not dictating terms from below. In most of the accepted narratives, these eruptions of radical philosophy are mapped into the chronology and thereby confined to a particular period in time, which usually turns out to be the heyday of the atheistic French Enlightenment in the final three decades of the eighteenth century. But the truth is that the conflict was logical, not chronological, and it was never far from the front pages throughout the early modern period. It was present in the time of Bruno in the late sixteenth century, it was abundantly evident in the life-stories that swirled around Spinoza in the late seventeenth century, and it was rendered explicit in a variety of semi-clandestine texts in the early eighteenth century. One of the most important and widely circulated texts of the entire period was the anonymous *Treatise of the Three Impostors* of 1720, which brazenly impugned Mohammed and Moses as well as Jesus. Whether or not it was the work of John Toland—as some scholars suspect—the treatise was just as central as he was to the underground philosophical dialectics of the age. Though radical philosophy was and still is routinely dismissed as the work of a fringe, it resurfaced every time it was suppressed not because it spoke for so few but because it spoke for so many.

IN THE YEARS before Allen and Paine trotted them out in public, America's space aliens mostly remained in disguise, hiding within private conversations and student notebooks. Yet, just as in Britain, Holland, France, and Italy over the preceding centuries, long before a handful of Parisian *philosophes* made such gestures seem fashionable, radical philosophy from time to time tore off its mask. A case in point is the bracing *Dialogue between A___ and B____*, published anonymously in 1779. Its author, too, believed in the infinite universe and its extraterrestrial inhabitants; and he made no effort to spare his readers the radical theological implications: "Can you believe that an unlimited Being . . . could be confined to one small spot of earth?" The most remarkable eruption of radical philosophy in prerevolutionary America, however, was arguably the first: the *Sermon on Natural Religion* of 1771 by the mysterious "Natural Man" of Boston.[153]

It is fitting that the Natural Man directs his anti-sermon at the words of Paul. The conflict between radical philosophy and the common religious consciousness begins even before Christianity, and Paul—who had contact with Epicureans and was evidently familiar with some of their doctrines—makes this conflict all but explicit in Romans:

> Those who live according to the flesh set their minds on the things of the flesh, but those who live according to the Spirit set their minds on the things of the Spirit. To set the mind on the flesh is death, but to set the mind on the Spirit is life and peace . . . I consider that the sufferings of this present time are not worth comparing with the glory about to be revealed to us . . . [T]he creation will be set free from its bondage to decay . . . We know that the whole creation has been groaning in labor pains until now; and not only the creation, but we ourselves, who have the first fruits of the Spirit, groan inwardly while we wait for adoption, the redemption of our bodies.[154]

The contrast with Epicurus could hardly be starker. Paul believes in the life of "Spirit"; whereas Epicurus and his followers are surely among "those who live according to the flesh." Paul eagerly awaits the "redemption" of his body; Epicurus says that without the body there is nothing to experience or enjoy. Paul envisions a kind of life free from decay and death; Epicurus maintains that decay and death are necessarily a part of anything that bears the name of life. Paul thinks that human reason is useless in attaining the highest good, that without faith we have no capacity to do anything but sin and be damned. Epicurus says that reason is the key to happiness, and faith in spiritual mysteries just a measure of our infidelity to ourselves. Paul's story of sin and redemption, in brief, makes no sense without belief in the reality of some other world, a world of "Spirit," a "world to come." Epicurus says that this world is the only one that ever was or can be.

The Natural Man makes no effort to split the difference. Paul is wrong: the natural man *does* set his mind on the things of the "Spirit"— if by "Spirit" one means "the perpetual motion and the universal direction of things," which is to say, the infinite universe. But of course that isn't at all what Paul means by "Spirit." In which case, Paul is quite right to suppose that the natural man fails to live according to the Spirit, but dead wrong to think that this is a bad thing. To be a man of "Spirit" is to profess belief in "incomprehensible, supernatural, and mysterious doctrines, acquired by inspiration, faith, and extraordinary divine instruction," all of which the natural man abhors as a kind of blasphemy against the plenitude of the infinite universe. In short, according to the Natural Man, Paul's religion, worse than false, is impious. It is an attempt to place our hopes and fears in some other world, a world that according to the guiding principle of philosophy cannot exist except as the illusory and nihilistic projection of our fears in this world.

The Natural Man makes clear enough on which sources he relies for support in his extraordinarily barefaced assault on the religion of Paul. He explicitly praises the incomparable John Locke. He alludes to signature phrases from Alexander Pope's *Essay on Man*. He borrows without acknowledgment a discussion of the nature of deism from Shaftesbury. He describes "Nature" in language that would fit easily into the works of Charles Blount. Though he indicates no direct familiarity with Epicurus, he invokes the physical doctrines of ancient materialism with his claims about "every atom in the universe," and he takes for granted the eternity of the universe. Appropriately enough, he closes his sermon not by returning to the discredited passage from Paul but with a lengthy citation from a contemporary work of popular science concerning the infinity of the universe and the reality of extraterrestrial life. The source of the citation happens to be Paine's teacher in London, James Ferguson.

So who was the Natural Man? There was, of course, some number of deists living in Boston at the time who would have sympathized with the Natural Man's views. There was a smaller, though still appreciable number who had the means and the motive to publish those views.

There is however a smoking gun in the case and it is to be found in the public profession of deist faith that Thomas Young offered in the *Boston Evening Post* of November 19, 1772, one year after the appearance of the *Sermon*. The moniker "a Natural Man" is a strange one, and a search through Boston periodicals in the decades preceding the Revolution yields exactly one relevant instance of the phrase. It is to be found in that part of Young's 1772 article in which he describes himself as "confessedly a natural man."

There is one additional piece of internal evidence. At a certain point, the Natural Man declares, "The clergy will perhaps object to me in regard of what I have advanced before." The proposition that he has apparently advanced previously is expressed in a rhetorical question: "And how can a Naturalist deny a revelation, when God reveals himself every day to him, in the contemplation of those immense and enormous bodies, which revolve in such regular order with the boundless space of the universe?" The provocative claim that nature is God's revelation—a claim that features centrally in Paine's *Age of Reason* of 1794—was a staple of deism, but it was hardly a commonplace in Boston publications at the time. In the *Boston Gazette* of August 27, 1770, a year before the *Sermon* appeared, however, Thomas Young wrote under his own name: "I invariably maintain that our beneficent Creator has imprinted this Revelation of his eternal wisdom, unlimited power, and unspeakable goodness upon every atom of the universe!"

That Young had the motive to write the *Sermon* is certain. No one in Boston in 1771 was more determined to spread the word of deism. That Young also had the means is easy to establish. The Natural Man's publisher—the freethinking Isaiah Thomas of the *Massachusetts Spy*—was the publisher of a number of newspaper pieces by Young. The specific contours of Young's intellectual profile—his devotion to Locke, Pope, Shaftesbury, and Blount—are also a close match for those of the Natural Man.

If Young is indeed the Natural Man, as he appears to confess in his 1772 article, this fact may begin to illuminate something about both the connections and the differences between him and his rogue pupil up in the Green Mountains. We already know that the author of

Ethan Allen's Bible, like the Natural Man and the rest of the deists of the time, champions the infinite universe and its extraterrestrials over the otherworldly spiritualism of Paul. More than that, he makes reference to exactly the same passage from Corinthians that is the object of instruction in the *Sermon*. So it seems reasonable to speculate that the author of the *Oracles* was acquainted with either the earlier pamphlet or its author. At the same time, he greets Paul's words with a rebuke that seems mild in comparison with that of the Natural Man. He agrees with the Natural Man on the substance of the critique, but not in the passion with which he approaches this particular passage of scripture. In short, the author of the *Oracles* was a "natural man," too; but it seems psychologically implausible that he was *the* Natural Man. If we suppose that Young was the Natural Man, then we will have reason to suspect that he was *not* the author of Ethan Allen's Bible.

THE COPY OF *De rerum natura* that Bruno slipped into his pocket would have looked and felt different from any of the several copies that Jefferson held in his hands. Bruno, who owned the 1566 edition by Obertus Gifanius, lived in a time when the paper was handmade, clumpy, knotted, tough, rich in texture, and inked in black or not at all, without a shade of gray.[155] The oldest of Jefferson's eight editions of the poem dated from 1675, though he more likely made use of an English edition of 1773, or perhaps on occasion the French translation by La Grange from 1799. The paper was thinner, smoother, whiter, machine-pressed.

There is every reason to suppose that the words on the paper, though composed of the same sequence of the same characters in the Latin alphabet, would have looked and felt just a little different, too. Probably most books are symptoms, not causes, of a chain of events that extends far beyond any facts to which we may be privy, and their direct influence is something that we never can or should attempt to prove to any very high degree of certainty. Even so, once in a while we come across a text and an individual that seem impossible to separate from one another. Who was Bruno if not the hero of Lucretius's poem, the man who blasted through the blazing battlements of the universe? And what is true of individuals is just as true of those equally complex actors we identify as states.

The fair copy of the Declaration of Independence was transcribed by a man named Timothy Matlack (1730–1829), a merchant, architect, penman, and, as it happens, a close political ally of Thomas Young in Philadelphia. It came out on a large piece of parchment, the expensive kind of paper made from animal skin, though it was promptly reprinted in newspapers around the new nation, where it was undoubtedly read in many different ways by many different people. The Declaration was never more than an approximation of whatever reality it pretended to unify. Yet it remains somehow central to the identity of the republic whose existence it announced. What the United States *is* may be impossible to establish with any great precision; what it is *supposed to be* is less disputable. It is the republic dedicated to the proposition that all people are created equal.

The first sentence of the Declaration of Independence offers little that is overtly philosophical, and the mellifluous string of words can easily pass between the ears, as it has for many generations, like little more than a symphony of truisms. Even so, that first line quietly but firmly situates the new republic within the universe opened up by the philosophical rebirth of the preceding centuries. The introductory phrase—"when in the course of human events"—alerts us that the event to be announced does not arise from any divine intercourse. Indeed, the story begins when "it becomes necessary for one people to dissolve the political bands which have connected them with another." The setting is unmistakably our own planet, for these people have now taken it upon themselves "to assume" their position not among "the powers that be," as Paul might have said, but "among the powers of the earth." Above all, the document promises an explanation of the "causes" that have brought about the action. This explanation is for the benefit of neither gods nor priests but answers only to "the laws of nature." In its graceful opening sentence, the Declaration makes clear that the event to unfold and the reasons with which it will be explained are entirely circumscribed within the experience of this world.

4

On the Genealogy
of Nature's God

. . . the Laws of Nature and of Nature's God . . .

W HAT EXACTLY DOES IT MEAN TO BELIEVE IN GOD?
According to a fairly common view, this is not a complicated
question. God is an agent, above and beyond any power we may find
in nature, that makes sure that things will turn out right for those
who do the right thing. Either you believe that such an agent exists;
or you do not (or you beg off from answering). But what happens if
we say, for example, that "God" is just a way of describing a certain
state of mind, like the experience of a beautiful sunset? What if "God"
exists to make sure that miracles *don't* happen? And if we add that
"God" is as self-evident as the air we breathe—would our belief count
as belief at all?

Today we tend to assume that the only interesting question of theology concerns the *existence* of God. For the overwhelming majority of
philosophers of the Enlightenment and for essentially all of the founders of the American Republic, however, the existence of God was never
in doubt. The important questions were all about the *nature* of God.
And the answers they provided were just as far from the common reli-

gious consciousness as anything that today we would call atheism. It is only with such questions and answers in mind, in any case, that one can begin to make sense of the theological opprobrium that greeted Ethan Allen after he published a book in which he *proved* the existence of what he called "the God of Nature," or the thunderstorm of denunciations that rained upon Thomas Young when in 1770 he became the first of America's future revolutionaries to declare in print his firm belief in what he called "the religion of Nature's God."

ON A FINE SUMMER DAY in 1770, Ethan Allen came down from the hills at the head of a mob. He leapt back onto the stage of history—or, at least, onto the floor of a New York courtroom, where his words and deeds might be recorded. He showed up in proud buckskin, the calm eye in a storm of thunderous pamphlets and torrid declamations concerning the rights of the settlers in the Green Mountains to own the land they tilled in accordance with the laws of nature.

He didn't stand a chance. With respect to the laws of humankind, the settlers' rights to the land they farmed rested on titles issued by Benning Wentworth, the disgraced former governor of New Hampshire. The grants were part of a project to sustain Wentworth in a lifestyle to which he had grown all too accustomed by selling land his colony didn't own in the first place. The New York court—which could not be reliably distinguished from the New York real estate industry—refused even to allow Allen's well-traveled bundle of hastily scribbled titles as evidence. On his way out of town, the new leader of the mountain people invited his citified antagonists to continue the discussion over in his neck of the woods. "The gods of the hills are not the gods of the valley," he intoned.

Up in the hills, Allen and his several hundred friends organized themselves into a force worth reckoning with. Headquarters was the Catamount Tavern in Bennington—named for the stuffed wildcat at the top of a pole, bearing its fangs in the direction of New York. The civilized world called them "the Bennington Mob." One Yorker, aiming to belittle, dubbed them "the Green Mountain Boys." The Boys decided they liked the name, and so it stuck. Now that he had an army, Allen thought it only natural that he should be accorded some rank. So, with pints raised high, he arranged to be appointed "Colonel Commandant" of the Green Mountain Boys. Pretty soon he'd found a colorful jacket and a massive sword commensurate with the dignity of his new office.

Thus began the campaign that to Allen and his Boys seemed like constructive citizenship, and to their opponents looked more like organized crime. When settlers bearing New York–based titles put down stakes and threw up fences, the Green Mountain Boys tore them down and burned them up. Sometimes the Boys made their appearance late at night, charcoal on their faces, dressed like Indians, aiming to scare. At other times, a polite word to the wise sufficed. On one occasion, it proved necessary to tie up a certain uncooperative individual and hoist him up a pole over the Catamount Tavern, so that the people of the hills could see justice in action.

Although Allen strained to cast himself throughout as a warrior, his greatest contribution to the cause of Vermont was always more about theater than military operations, and the most spectacular of his productions were his pamphlets. When a fellow mountaineer lost a thumb in a skirmish with villainous Yorkers, Allen splattered the snowy faces of his pamphlets with buckets of blood. Perhaps his real talent as a rebel was for a style that in its comically self-conscious failure to achieve literary elegance gave readers the sensation that the writer was laughing as he wrote, which in turn gave them confidence that he meant what he said.

Even as he rose high in the ranks of mountain life, Allen—like Young before him—did little to disguise his contempt for all things holy. When one Yorker demanded respect for the divinely ordained laws of the land, Allen retorted, "God damn your Governor, Laws, King, Council, and Assembly."[1] After torching a new subdivision of Yorker homes, Allen announced with a kind of pagan grandiosity that this act of arson was "a burnt sacrifice to the Gods of the World." When Allen and his equally feral brothers were formally charged with blasphemy, they had a ready response. "Though we uttered some words that might be construed satirical against doctrines that some sectaries of Christians" teach, wrote little brother Zimri in a 1773 newspaper article, "yet we are rationally certain that any of the pulpit thumpers . . . much more blaspheme the perfection of the God of Nature, than we did."[2]

The God of the Green Mountains soon began to make its presence felt in the battle-pamphlets that the Allen brothers issued in connection with their struggles over the land in the hills. As brother Ira put it in a typical exercise, the people of the New Hampshire Grants would never "be free and happy" until they threw off bondage to the "litigious government of New York" and claimed the "natural rights and liberties that was given them by the God of nature."[3] In the *Oracles* of 1784, Ethan (presuming it was he) at last made an effort to explain just what this "God of Nature" was. As would prove to be the case throughout his loud and busy life, however, the origins, significance, and interconnections of Ethan Allen's unusual theology and his insurrectionary politics became clear only when considered in light of the curiously parallel—yet perhaps somewhat more self-conscious—career of the man who sent him up into the hills in the first place.

THOMAS YOUNG, too, found his calling in life at the head of a mob. Young's friends actually called themselves "the Mob"—until they prudently changed their name to "the Sons of Liberty of Albany." It was a youthful mob (its members were mostly the sons of well-off, sometimes mortified parents); it drank freely (the likely story is that it was born of a night in an Albany tavern); and it was angry. The Sons of Liberty of Albany came together in response to the Stamp Act of 1765, in which the British Parliament imposed a tax on all transactions involving paper. The Sons took the view that any decision to impose a tax in which they or their direct representatives were not party to amounted to tyranny. To make their point clear, they rounded up seven suspected would-be tax collectors and thrust them before homegrown "tribunals."[4] The victims, not without some cause, called them "the Sons of Tyranny." In February 1766, these Sons of whatever put their names on a "Constitution" that really reads more like a blood oath among men concerned to make sure that, if they ever get caught, they will all go down together. The first of its ninety-four signatories was Thomas Young.[5]

Some years later, writing back to Albany on behalf of the Boston Committee of Correspondence, Young gave credit to his fellow Sons for making a bold first move in the patriotic cause: "The Spirit manifested in Albany in their vigorous opposition to the ruinous Stamp Act had undoubtedly a happy influence on the City of New York, and was of consequence efficacious toward its repeal."[6] Something else happened in Albany, too, though what it was wasn't exactly clear. The Albany aristocrat William Johnson wrote to a friend that Young had left town after some matter "not so pretty." Rumors that he had defamed the holy religion in Albany trailed him to Boston. According to his brother Joseph, however, his passion for social justice was the deciding factor in the move. Thomas settled in Boston because there the "energies of numbers of American patriots were in full operation."[7]

In Boston, Young, too, immediately took up a dual-track career, making waves as a religious scoffer even as he ascended to prominence as a political activist. When Parliament passed the Townsend Acts in 1767—a series of laws imposing various duties on imports to the colonies—Young joined loudly with James Otis, Samuel Adams, and Patrick Henry of Virginia in the chorus of patriotic protest against this outrageous program of taxation without representation. Young's contributions to the debate were notable for the stridency of their rhetoric and their unsubtle threats of violence. In an article from 1767, for example, he followed the example of Otis by citing John Locke on the natural rights of man, and then rather bombastically elaborated that the actions of the British government had left the American colonists "bastardized and alienated from the common wealth of human nature."[8] He closed on a menacing note: "Consider if mischief befall us, our blood will be required at your hands, as we can by no means recede one atom." When the British decided to occupy Boston with military force in the following year, Young declared that the colonists and the mother country were in "a state of nature"—by which he appeared to mean "a state of war."

Young's militancy didn't make him any friends in high places, but it was a hit with the ordinary people of Boston. " 'The Body' as they are called," recorded one eyewitness in July 1770, "proceeded through the streets with Dr. Young at their head with Three Flags Flying, Drums Beating & a French Horn."[9] Young became "the new Hero for Liberty" in Boston, sniffed the New York aristocrat William Johnson, and in this capacity replaced James Otis, who was beginning to show signs of the mental illness that ultimately took him away from public life. Thomas Hutchinson, the governor of Bay Colony from 1758 to 1774, regularly listed Young as one of the four principal leaders of "the mob," alongside Samuel Adams, Joseph Warren, and William Molineux. When the last known survivor of the Tea Party was interviewed in 1832, the leaders whose names he recalled were Molineux and Young. Young himself evidently adored "the Body" as much as it adored him. Indeed, he seemed to find in its affection the balm for that heavy chip he carried on his shoulder, the only sure measure of his worth. "On this part of the Stage believe I will be active!" he exulted. "I have nearly got the hearts of my brethren and can be attended to on the most arduous occasions."[10]

The most consequential of the political projects in which Young participated, the creation of the Boston Committee of Correspondence in 1772, was formally intended to serve as a communications point with other towns; yet it was at bottom an expression of Young's longing to connect with "the Body" and lead it to freedom. In his letters to Samuel Adams, Young laments the undue influence of "the most powerful men in every county and every town" and declares that the purpose of their labors on the Committee must be to create a form of government that will empower "the common people."[11] He also makes clear that the Committee was to transmit its democratic message not just in the substance of its communications but in its practice. By issuing declarations concerning the rights of the colonists to the inhabitants of hundreds of towns around Massachusetts and in other colonies, the Committee implicitly invited its correspondents to form committees of their own, where they might deliberate on the matter of the colonists' rights and then repeat them back to Boston in the name of the people of their own towns. For Young, it was all a grand educational exercise, an awakening of the common people of America to their own interest and rightful power. When his friend Hugh Hughes of New York complained of the difficulty of mobilizing the masses in his own colony, Young forcefully admonished him: "You complain of the ignorance of the common people; you may as well complain of the roughness of the desart [sic]! Our people would have known as little as yours had we taken as little pains to instruct them."[12] Ever the optimist about the power that comes from the improvement of human understanding, Young avowed, "We can reduce them to reason and make them our friends."

Even as he leapt to the vanguard of the people, Thomas Young continued to trail religious controversy like a dog tracking mud into the house. Every year or so from his arrival in 1766 until his sudden departure in September 1774, the city's newspapers blossomed in dark columns of anger over the newcomer's insults to the religion of the land. Most of the episodes in the culture war followed roughly the same sequence. A political enemy would accuse Young of being, for example, a "loose, profane, and irreligious man."[13] Young would rise in print to his own defense with confessions of his "creed." And his accusers would generally respond with all the more outrage. "If you think by giving us your CREED to deceive the vulgar; and palm yourself off on them for a *Christian*, let me tell you, you are much mistaken," bellowed one critic in answer to one of Young's confessions. "There is nothing in your Creed to distinguish you from the most thorough paced infidels, and virulent opposers of our holy Religion."[14]

In the summer of 1770, on the other hand, it seems that it was Young who picked the fight. In early August, while Boston sweltered under the hostile occupation of British forces, seething in memory of the event that came to be known as "the Boston Massacre," the aging revivalist George Whitefield came to town and delivered what would prove to be one of his final sermons. The topic of the sermon was evil, and Whitefield chose as the abject example of evil the noxious but ever-growing "sect of Deists." The founder of the deists, the reverend declaimed, was none other than Cain. It all came down to a passage in

Genesis, he obscurely alleged, where it was stated that Cain's sacrifice to God, which was vegetarian in nature, was not so gratifying to God as Abel's sacrifice, which involved tasty animal fats.

Perhaps because he took an attack in a personal way, or perhaps just because he had a score to settle with the arch-revivalist, Young took it upon himself to defend deists (and Cain for that matter) from such calumny. The religion of deism, he defiantly proclaimed in an article of August 18, 1770, is just as true and conducive to virtue as the religion of Christianity.[15] To prove his point, he cited the example of the ancient Persians. "The excellent system of true religion among the ancient Persians," he said, was not Christianity but "refined Deism, or the pure unallayed [sic] religion of nature," and it turned out to be a "blessing" for "that vast empire for many centuries." No less a theologian than Samuel Clarke, he added, acknowledged that deists can have fine family values. The main difference between the excellent natural religion of deism and the religion of Christianity, he concluded, is that the latter requires belief in certain allegedly revealed doctrines, such as those involving animal sacrifice. He made no bones about where he stood on that matter: "We must remain with good King David and the ancient Persians, doubters of the absolute necessity of embruing our hands in blood in order to please our Maker."

Whitefield had an answer. The founder of deism was not Cain after all—but the devil himself. It was Satan who first discarded revelation in favor of reason, said Whitefield, and who was therefore directly responsible for the cancer of deism in Boston.

Unbowed, Young hit the Boston public in two different newspapers in that hot summer of 1770 with even more vigorous professions of his faith in deism.[16] The furor, Young confided to a New York friend, "made a prodigious noise at first, and half the town thought I had ruined myself outright by daring publicly to call in question anything advanced by the infallible Mr. Whitefield against so abhorred a set of men as the Deists."[17] Still, the Cain affair "kept two presses steadily going a few weeks," he boasted, "and I defended my honor amazingly."

It was in one of the last two of his missives, published in the *Boston Evening Post* on August 27, 1770, that Young offered perhaps the

138 ★ Nature's God

most forthright public profession of deist faith in the colonial period of American history:

> That the religion of Nature, more properly stiled the Religion of Nature's God, in latin call'd *Deus*, hence *Deism*, is *truth*, I now boldly defy thee to contest.[18]

For the further clarification of the meaning of this "Religion of Nature's God," he referred his readers to "[Alexander] Pope's little *Essay on Man*, confessedly deduced from the inspiration of Lord Bolingbroke, and perhaps every sentence adopted by me."

In some alternate universe—such as perhaps the one constructed from the nationalist myths that have long gripped American historiography—Young's peculiar "Religion of Nature's God" might have amounted to little more than a historical oddity. It was just the cloudy reflection of a disturbing individual who was always fishing in troubled waters. To judge from the hate that filled the newspapers of the time, it was a quite unpopular form of belief, deeply at odds with all the accepted varieties of the Christian religion. Yet the curious fact is that Young, like Allen, manifestly saw his unusual religion as an intimate component of the revolutionary political struggle in which he was engaged. The rights he claimed on behalf of his countrymen against the British Parliament and even against the Crown itself were not the rights guaranteed to Englishmen by their constitution, nor the rights due to Christians, but the rights deriving from the laws of nature and of "Nature's God."

And Young and Allen were far from alone in their revolutionary theology. Indeed, "Nature's God" was the presiding deity of the American Revolution. Franklin invoked it in his newspaper articles as early as 1747. Philip Livingston, Joel Barlow, and Philip Freneau expressed their adoration for it in ecstatic verses.[19] James Madison included it in one of the very few theological speculations he allowed to slip into paper. The famous botanist William Bartram placed it over the entrance to his garden in Philadelphia. And Jefferson inserted it into history in the first sentence of the Declaration of Independence, which announces that it has become necessary for the people of the United States "to assume among the powers of the earth the separate and equal station to which they are entitled by the laws of Nature and of Nature's God."

Young was quite right to suggest that one could learn much about Nature's God from the works of Pope and Bolingbroke. But the history of America's revolutionary deity goes back farther than those heroes of the eighteenth-century Anglo-American Enlightenment. Though it may be traced all the way to Epicurus and his infinite universe, the genealogy of Nature's God properly begins in the late seventeenth century. The strange new vision first emerged in the work of the two greatest philosophers of the early modern world, one of whom became infamous by making it impossible for his contemporaries not to see it, the other of whom achieved fame by showing them how to pretend not to see it.

IT WAS TYPICAL of John Locke that when they came looking for him he was nowhere to be found.[20] By August 1683 the King's agents had already rounded up an alarming number of his friends and philosophical allies, all prime suspects in the Rye House Plot, an alleged conspiracy to assassinate the pro-Catholic Charles II and his brother James at a planned stop in a country mansion upon their return from the horse races. They found Algernon Sidney, for example, easily enough—they merely had to crash one of his fancy dinner parties. But then Sidney was an aristocrat in the old style, a man who left a tangible record of destruction on the battlefield and in the bedroom, a man who not merely organized assassination attempts but also was the intended target of them, the kind given to signing guest books in foreign capitals with grand proclamations like "this hand to tyrants ever sworn the foe." Locke was Sidney without the sex life. A better writer and a clearer thinker, Locke was able to frame in abstract argument the kind of points Sidney could make only through tiresomely elegant quotations and digressions. Mainly, Locke was better at keeping his nose clean. There was always in him something of the scholarship boy from the provinces made good, the watchful, distant bachelor, saved from the obscure fate of an Oxford don by the powerful men of his day, always much smarter than his masters but knowing well enough when to pretend otherwise. There was no certain evidence to prove that Locke was guilty of conspiring to kill the King (or even that there was a conspiracy). But that didn't stop many people from believing that he was involved in the plot. And it didn't stop Locke from behaving like a man who had something to fear from the long arm of the law. Even before Sidney handed off to friends a written copy of his final soliloquy and, disdaining blindfolds, placed his own neck beneath the executioner's ax, Locke had slipped across the channel to the safety of Holland.

Today we tend to think of the Dutch Republic of the seventeenth century as an atelier for the art museums of the future. At the time, it was a land of exhilarating freedom, the kind of place where love is all around and the people wear flowers in their hair. Amsterdam was the first city in world trade, and it was also, not coincidentally, the first city in religious toleration. "The devil is entirely banished in the United Provinces," enthused Anthony Collins.[21] For Englishmen in fear of political persecution at home, like Collins and Locke, Holland was the asylum of choice. Locke's great mentor, the first Earl of Shaftesbury, the leader of the Whigs and the mastermind of any number of plots against the King, preceded him in exile there by two years, and Locke was followed by his philosophical frenemy John Toland, among many others. More than a refuge, Holland was the hothouse of English designs and ambitions. Sidney had been there in 1666, hoping to persuade the Dutch to finance an invasion of his homeland, with himself in command.

Above all, the English came in search of intellectual contraband, for by virtue of its trading power and tolerant ways Holland had become the global hub in the commerce of ideas. The third Earl of Shaftesbury, grandson of the first, came over as a sixteen-year-old in 1687, stopping in on his exiled tutor, Locke himself, and acquiring in Holland much of his philosophical sophistication. He returned to the Low Countries a decade later to converse with its great thinkers, such as Pierre Bayle and the brothers de la Court. America's philosophical revolutionaries may have been "guided by English stars," as Garry Wills[22] puts it, but England's thinkers believed that the brightest lights in the republic of letters lay on the other side of the channel.

In the fall of 1688, the increasingly Catholic James II lost the confidence of his people and fled England. On the invitation of English leaders, William of Orange, the head of the Dutch royal house, sailed across the channel with an invading army and seized the throne with relative ease. In January 1689 Locke returned to his homeland in triumph, on the same boat with Mary, William's other half. He brought with him the manuscripts of the two works that would shortly make him the most famous and influential philosopher in Europe—his magnum opus, *An Essay concerning Human Understanding*, and his seminal work on political theory, *Two Treatises of Government*. He also shipped over twenty boxes crammed with books acquired in Holland.

In the most widely accepted versions of America's philosophical history, Locke receives the award as the single greatest intellectual influence on America's revolutionaries. Carl Becker articulates the consensus in his important 1922 study of the Declaration of Independence: "The lineage is direct: Jefferson copied Locke."[23] Becker's judgment remains essentially correct. In order to understand the genesis and structure of the political thought of revolutionary leaders as diverse as Jefferson, Madison, Young, Otis, Henry, and Dickinson, to name only a few, the indispensable philosopher is Locke. Where Becker goes wrong, however, is in his very next clause: "and Locke quoted Hooker." In the second draft of his essay on government, Locke pasted in some citations from the English theologian Richard Hooker (1554–1600), but he did so largely to provide respectable cover for ideas that otherwise might have linked him with a philosopher with whom he very much did not wish to be associated.

The Dutch Republic boasted a range of thinkers, all engaged in lively conversation and correspondence among themselves and with their British counterparts. But there was one philosopher who by all accounts mattered most. To be involved in the late-seventeenth-century republic of letters was to be for—or more likely ostentatiously against—Benedict de Spinoza, the Amsterdam-born philosopher of Portuguese extraction who came to be called, with a certain degree of imprecision on both counts, "the atheist Jew." Much has been written about the life of Spinoza, as if the biography of a man who mostly meditated in rented rooms and got along well enough with a small circle of friends and neighbors might reveal something essential about his thought. But it is mostly beside the point. He was a man of ideas, and perhaps his great accomplishment was that all that matters about his life can be discovered in his ideas.

Among sophisticated contemporaries, the decisive influence of Spinoza on the thinkers who rose to the vanguard of the deist movement in Britain was well attested. Charles Blount, the man who taught Thomas Young half of what he knew, was widely recognized as the first of Spinoza's disciples in England. In a work of 1683 under his own name, he reproduced in English most of a chapter of Spinoza's *Tractatus Theologico-Politicus* without acknowledgment.[24] One critic, responding to Blount with a booklet of his own, immediately detected the plagiarism and announced that "Spinoza" was the author's "Great Patron."[25] Blount was also the likely suspect in the anonymous publication in 1689 of the first complete English translation of Spinoza's extraordinarily controversial book.[26]

"I am told by those, who are very capable of informing me, that the modern Atheist has given up the system of *Epicurus* as absurd and indefensible, and adheres to that of the Fatalists," reported the poet Richard Blackmore in the preface to his 1712 jeremiad against the philosophy of the age. Blackmore named Hobbes, Vanini, and Spinoza as the fatalists in question, though he and the other serious critics had little doubt about which one counted as the fatalist-in-chief.[27] Bernard Mandeville (1670–1733)—one of nineteen-year-old Franklin's drinking buddies in London, author of the first thoroughly secular interpretation of human society, and a committed follower of Spinoza himself—detected the same shift in radical chic: "This doctrine, which is Spinosisme in epitome . . . begins to prevail again, and the atoms [of Epicurus] lose ground," he announced in *The Fable of the Bees* of 1714.[28] The first historian of deism, John Leland, named Spinoza "the most applauded Doctor of modern atheism"—by which he meant "deism"—

and added that Spinoza "has taken the most pains to form it into a system."[29] Anthony Collins agreed—perhaps too enthusiastically—that it was Spinoza who reduced atheism to a system. In the nineteenth century, long after the deists had succeeded in concealing their debt to the atheist Jew of Holland, the historian of philosophy Leslie Stephen was still able to see that "the whole essence of the deist position may be found in Spinoza's *Tractatus Theologico-Politicus*."[30] In recent years, Jonathan Israel has done an immense service for the history of ideas by recovering the story in extensive detail.[31]

One of the curious facts about England's forgotten Spinozists is that so many of them had intimate intellectual and personal bonds with Locke. Collins, for example, was to Locke what every old philosopher dreams of finding in a younger one. In Locke's senescence, Collins showed up daily at his door with fresh books, groceries, conversation, and boundless adulation. The two became so close that when Collins asked for a portrait of his teacher, Locke wished that it might be a "speaking picture" so that "it should tell you every day how much I love and esteem you."[32] Collins went on to establish a reputation as a man of phenomenal intelligence, learning, and sophistication, drinking wine shipped from Montepulciano, communicating with the leading lights of the continent, and amassing a collection of nearly seven thousand books that was said to be one of the largest personal libraries in England. Yet many of his contemporaries were sure that he was a Spinozist, and his own writings include an otherwise improbable number of arguments and phrases that read as if lifted directly from Spinoza's works.

Locke's other ward, even more famous, was the third Earl of Shaftesbury. By command of Locke's patron, the first earl, the younger Shaftesbury was "bred under his immediate care, Mr. Locke having the absolute direction of my education."[33] Yet from his writings many surmised that Shaftesbury had a certain diffidence toward his tutor and perhaps owed a still greater debt to another mentor. As a matter of fact, his borrowing from the philosophical anti-hero of the Dutch Enlightenment was so blatant that even a commentator as late as 1900 was able to detect that "his philosophy, as regards its bases, is drawn more or less directly from Spinoza."[34]

The most troublesome of Locke's successors was undoubtedly John Toland. An Irishman who seemed always to be just one step ahead of the theological police, Toland was the dynamo of the early modern republic of letters. A confidant of princesses, a veteran traveler, a self-promoter, sometimes a victim of his own uncontrollable jealousies, and an intellectual entrepreneur, Toland had a stake in an astonishing number of the philosophical projects that changed the landscape of modern thought. It was he who orchestrated the publication of a purloined edition of Shaftesbury's first work in 1699, against its author's perhaps too-loud protestations; who raised Giordano Bruno from the ashes to make him famous in England all over again; who restored the reputation of the republican theorist James Harrington with a posthumous publication of his works; who organized the publication of a hugely successful edition of Bayle's works; and who served as a kind of philosophical puppet-master for those polemicists of the Whig movement who had such a profound effect on America's revolutionaries— Robert Molesworth, Trenchard, Gordon, and the rest of the so-called Commonwealthmen. In his own writings, Toland exuded a kind of subversive erudition, trailing footnotes on footnotes to tie every thread of learning into elaborate tapestries whose messages were always more unsettling than they at first seemed. His direct influence, largely forgotten today, was felt all the way down to the leaders of the radical side of the French Enlightenment.

Toland first met Locke in 1693 through mutual friends from Holland, and his work rapidly assumed a very curious relationship with that of the most famous English philosopher of the day. Beginning with *Christianity Not Mysterious* in 1696, Toland seemed to make a game out of starting his works with respectably Lockean premises and ending with scandalously Spinozistic conclusions. "All the difference we see is, that [Toland] applies that to *Propositions in Scripture*, which [Locke] affirm'd of *Propositions in general*," complained Lord Edward Stillingfleet, the bishop of Worcester, in a 1697 book that found its way onto Jefferson's bookshelf on moral philosophy.[35] Locke himself, sensing the danger in his association with this wayward acolyte, did his best to pretend that they had never met. Not everyone bought it.

Alexander Pope condensed the common wisdom in a telling couplet that ultimately proved too sensitive to include in the published version of his *Essay on Man*:

> *What partly pleases, totally will shock:*
> *I question much if Toland would be Locke.*[36]

Among the learned, Toland's role as Spinoza's avatar in England was as obvious as his status as Locke's evil twin. Contemporaries mocked him as "Spinoza in abstract," and "a genuine Spinoza chick,"[37] and Mr. "*Tractatus Theologico-Politicus.*"

As for Locke himself, the godfather of this unruly brood—almost everyone insisted on his innocence, yet almost everyone suspected him of something. Within the history of deism, Locke occupies a peculiar position—peculiar because there is a seemingly irreconcilable disagreement about whether he is the most important of the deists or not a deist at all.[38] Many of his righteous contemporaries took Locke at his word that he was a defender of some version of orthodox Christianity, and indeed quite a few marched into the culture wars under the banner of his glorious name. In the nineteenth century, the historian of philosophy Leslie Stephen unequivocally exonerated Locke for the sins of his successors, saying that the great philosopher "was unmistakably free of any complicity, direct or indirect, in any attack upon the authenticity of Christian revelation."[39] Many modern scholars not unreasonably tend to classify Locke as a Socinian—that is, a member of the ultra-liberal Christian sect that ultimately morphed into Unitarianism. (This is perhaps less helpful than it sounds: the conservative theologians of the period were unanimous in their conviction that, as one put it, "a Socinian is an Atheist, or lest that should seem harsh, one that favours the cause of atheism.")[40] A vocal minority of modern scholars goes further, insisting on the primacy of what they call the "theistic" Locke. England's most famous philosopher, they say, was a "distinctively Biblical Christian"[41] whose philosophy answers to his "religious preoccupations" and "theological commitments"[42] and is ultimately grounded in his belief in a Christian God.[43]

Yet other interpreters have maintained that Locke is not at all what he appears to be. The suspicions, it should be acknowledged, come from serious people, acting independently over many years in many different settings, and not merely polemicists seeking to make insults by association. Bolingbroke, Hume, Dugald Stewart, Joseph de Maistre, and Newton (for a time, before taking it back), among others, accused Locke of covert "Hobbism" (the moral if not philosophical equivalent of Spinozism). Stillingfleet and Leibniz—who by virtue of his own youthful infatuations was surely in a position to know—were among the heavyweights to level the explicit charge of Spinozism, and they were joined in that extreme accusation by a chorus of less well-known professors, clerics, and writers of the period.[44] In a book published shortly after Locke's death, the prelate William Carroll argued that Locke had pursued a "double View, double Design, intended to fool the pious while promoting Spinozism."[45] Carroll dedicated three hundred angry pages, bristling with citations, to the proposition that in the tenth chapter of the fourth book of the *Essay concerning Human Understanding*, "Of Our Knowledge of the Existence of a God," Locke had set about with nefarious purpose to prove the existence of Spinoza's God.

Even those who perhaps too loudly proclaimed Locke's religious bona fides suspected that something was amiss in his philosophy. "Sir, you are highly considered and much quoted etc. by the Socinians, deists, Atheists, and the bold spirits of this Country," wrote Francis Gastrell, a high-ranking churchman, demanding an explanation.[46] The American theologian Samuel Johnson, too, believed that the road to hell was paved with Locke's good intentions: "the gradual but deplorable progress of infidelity and apostasy in this age of mighty pretense and reasoning" began with "the well-meaning but too conceited Mr. Locke."[47] In modern times, the view that Locke is not what he appears to be has been taken up by Leo Strauss and further pursued by Michael Zuckert and others.[48] For reasons that have to do with contemporary preoccupations and disciplinary boundaries rather than the actual history, Hobbes does most of the work that should be assigned to Spinoza—which then raises difficulties in crucial places where Spinoza (followed by Locke) differs from Hobbes. The Dutch scholar Wim Klever remains alone today in pursuing the suggestion first advanced in Locke's own day by Leibniz, Stillingfleet, and Carroll.

That Locke had the means and ability to do the deed is certain. Locke began early to assemble a complete collection of Spinoza's works, starting with the *Principles of the Cartesian Philosophy* of 1663. Notes in his own hand confirm that he did indeed read that work and its sequels with great interest. At Oxford in the 1660s, he also happened to be part of the circle gathered around Spinoza's correspondent Henry Oldenburg, the first leader of the Royal Society, who circulated Spinoza's letters among his English friends and sent back queries that sometimes look to have been written by committee. Locke began work on his *Essay concerning Human Understanding* after a conversation with his Oxford friends about religion and philosophy that took place in December 1670—the same year that Spinoza detonated explosive discussions on religion and philosophy throughout the republic of letters with the publication of his *Tractatus Theologico-Politicus*. Locke was in France from 1675 to 1679, when Spinoza was everywhere in the air, and then of course in Holland from 1683 to 1689, where Spinoza was in the water, too.

So, was Locke a model of orthodox piety or did he intend to communicate a secret and heterodox doctrine cribbed from Spinoza's books lying open on his desk? The truth is we don't know and probably never will. But the important questions about Locke have to do not with his inscrutable innermost convictions or private reading habits but with the structure of his thought and above all its systematically divisive effect on his contemporaries and successors. Indeed, the strange double effect of Locke may well be the most important feature of the history of the philosophy of the early modern period and perhaps of any period. The Enlightenment (and perhaps all philosophy) is sometimes divided between radical and moderate schools, and Spinoza and Locke are not unreasonably cast as paradigmatic representatives of these opposing points of view. The duality of Locke's legacy, however, serves to illustrate that the radical and moderate Enlightenments are really just two sides of a single body of thought. Spinoza is the prin-

cipal architect of the radical political philosophy that achieves its ultimate expression in the American Republic, and Locke is its acceptable
face. So-called Lockean liberalism is really just Spinozistic radicalism
adapted to the limitations of the common understanding of things.

HOW DO WE KNOW that there is a God? According to Locke, it's
as plain as the nose on your face. "It is beyond question that man has
a clear perception of his own being," he writes in his proof "of our
knowledge of the existence of a God" in the tenth chapter of the fourth
book of his *Essay*.[49] We further know, he says, "that nothing cannot
produce a being." Therefore it is evident "that from eternity there has
been something; since what was not from eternity had a beginning;
and what had a beginning must be produced by something else."[50] This
eternal thing, "which whether any one will please to call 'God,' it matters not," says Locke. "The thing is evident; and from this idea, duly
considered, will easily be deduced all those other attributes which we
ought to ascribe to this Eternal Being."[51]

That a God steps forth from Locke's proof might at first seem gratifying to an orthodox audience, and that is surely how Locke intends
his proof to be received and how modern scholars in general read it.
True, Locke's use of the indefinite "*a* God"—a phrase that appears in
earlier chapters of his *Essay*, too[52]—could (and did)[53] grate on orthodox ears. But at least he seems to believe in this "a God," unlike the
dreaded atheists. This God also appears suited to perform the role
classically associated with a deity, as the "first cause" of all things. It
is, loosely speaking, omnipotent (in the sense of being responsible for
everything), omnipresent (it is somehow involved in making every
individual thing what it is at every moment), and immutable (for it is
the unchangeable thing behind all that changes).

Yet all is not as kosher as it seems. A first hint that we are on dangerous ground is that Locke's proof derives all of its power from an
unwavering commitment to the guiding principle of Epicurean philosophy: that nothing comes from nothing.[54] A still more alarming fact
is that his proof that we know of a God sounds strikingly similar to

Epicurus's proof that the universe is infinite. Indeed, it *is* the proof of the infinite universe with the added premise that whatever is eternal must be God. Most damning of all—as sophisticated readers of the time such as a Collins or a Toland would have known—Locke's proof is an exact copy of one that Spinoza offers in his major work, *Ethics*. "The human mind has ideas from which it perceives itself, its own body, and external bodies as actually existing," says Spinoza. Yet we know that nothing can come from nothing, he reasons. Everything about us, including ourselves, must have come into being from some other thing, and must turn into some other thing, and so on forward and backward for eternity. Therefore, we may know that there is an eternal, infinite something, and this eternal something is what we mean by God. Ergo, "the mind . . . has an adequate knowledge of the eternal and infinite essence of God."[55]

At a certain level of abstraction, the Locke-Spinoza proof looks like any of the numberless banalities of natural theology, or the effort to prove the existence of God through the evidence of reason and the senses.[56] And it is that in a certain way—except that Locke and Spinoza swiftly push natural theology to the point where it becomes explicitly what it always was in practice, namely, an exercise in exposing the contradictions in the common conception of God. The common view supposes that we may know of God through miracles and signs; but Spinoza and Locke insist that we may know of God precisely because there are no miracles or signs that might disrupt the lawful chain of natural causes that leads from one thing to another through all eternity. The common view supposes that God acts *against* the laws of nature; but Spinoza and Locke take for granted that God can only work *through* the laws of nature. The common view says that belief in God requires a leap of faith; Spinoza and Locke say the existence of God is as self-evident as the existence of our own body parts. The God of the philosophers, as Spinoza puts it, bears as much resemblance to the common understanding of God as the constellation Dog does to a dog—and the same has always been true of the God of natural theology.

We can say something more about the strangeness of this "a God" of Locke and Spinoza by noting something important about the way in which it may be conceived as a "cause" of things. We usually think of causes as "external" to whatever they bring about, in the way that a chef is external to the meal she creates, or that the power of a motor refers to a different aspect of reality than the vehicular motion it makes possible. But God, or the eternal first cause, cannot be external to the world in this sense. An external God would be reduced to just another member of an infinite series in which something always follows from something else. In a sense, an external God would beg the question with which children routinely embarrass their parents: So who created God? David Hume and Bertrand Russell put their satirical fingers on this same paradox with various shopworn philosophical jokes about the world resting on elephants resting on turtles all the way down. Thus it seems to follow, from a rigorous insistence on the guiding principle, that the first cause must be "internal" to all things, which is to say, internal to all of our explanations of things as things.

Bruno anticipates the point when he suggests that God must be the "intrinsic" principle of things, and Spinoza formalizes Bruno's insight with his proposal that God is the "immanent," not "transitive" cause of things.[57] A transitive cause explains the existence of something through something else; an immanent cause explains something through itself. "Although each particular thing is determined by another particular thing to exist in a certain way," Spinoza explains, "the force by which each perseveres in existing follows from the eternal necessity of God's Nature."[58] Spinoza borrows from Hobbes and Descartes (and before them the Stoics) the term "conatus" to describe this drive to persist in being, and he asserts that the conatus of each individual thing is nothing other than the power of God. In the infinite universe, one could say, everything comes and goes according to external causes obeying inviolable laws, and yet everything has a kind of "this-ness" that stands for the infinite nexus of causes that makes it what it is and impels it to persist in being what it is. God, according to this conception, is the eternal this-ness of all things. It is the being-ness of beings, or the eternal being of all beings.

The other, very strange aspect of the God that emerges from the Locke-Spinoza proof is that it must act in a way that is somehow necessary. That is, God or the first cause must have some nature or essence, and the things of the world must follow ineluctably from this nature. Here again, the conclusion follows from the relentless application of the guiding principle and is really just an extension of a key insight embedded in the Epicurean philosophy: that the laws of nature must themselves be lawful. The general point is that if we were to allow that God might have produced any number of possible worlds, each with a distinctive set of laws, then we would have no explanation whence these possibilities arose. But this in turn would mean that the guiding principle has broken down, which would in turn destroy our proof of the knowledge of God. Bruno captures this intuition when he remarks that "the will of God is not only necessary, but also necessity itself; and its opposite is not only impossible, but impossibility itself."[59] Spinoza articulates the conclusion in an emphatic way: "Things could not have been produced by God in any other way or in any other order than is the case."[60] This is the "fatalism" for which his early modern critics lambasted him, or what we may call "necessitarianism" (not to be confused with its weak sister, "determinism").[61]

Spinoza (borrowing heavily from his essential predecessor Descartes)[62] summarizes what he knows of the strange nature of the philosophers' God in a doctrine formulated in the now somewhat arcane-sounding language of medieval theology: God, and God alone, is "substance," he asserts, and all the things we find in nature are "modes" of this substance. A "substance" is that which may be conceived or explained through itself alone, while a "mode" is always explained through something else. Now, if one substance could be conceived through another substance, Spinoza argues, then it would not be substance, and so it follows that there can be only one substance in the world. It also follows that this substance must be eternal, immutable, and indivisible. This substance, of course, is nothing other than God.[63] "Modes," then, are just necessary expressions of God, or "ways of being" of God. Bruno once again anticipates it all: "Nature is none other than God in things,"[64] and "God . . . is everywhere in all things, not above, not outside, but present, not a being not outside or above being, not a nature outside of nature, not a goodness outside of good."[65]

Although Locke, like the English people in general, wisely avoids the jargon of substance and modes, he is unable to disentangle himself from the underlying logic of the proof he borrows from Spinoza. And at certain critical junctures, despite his best efforts to resist, he also slips into the jargon. In an early chapter of the *Essay*, Locke offers a definition of substance as "an uncertain supposition of we know not what . . . which we take to be the *substratum*, or support of those ideas we do know."[66] In later sections, he argues that all our ideas of things in the world—every notion we have of particular material things, and even of our particular selves—refer not to any real substances but to combinations of modifications of some substance. In yet another section, he explicitly entertains the notion that there might be only one such substance, and that all things—from pebbles and trees to people and angels—might be modifications of this one substance. He calls this a "very harsh doctrine."[67] So he considers the alternative, that substance might mean different things when applied to trees, pebbles, and people. This idea he dismisses as absurd. Having backed himself into a corner where he must choose between a "harsh" Spinozistic monism and the absurd alternative, he proposes to ditch all talk of substance. Yet this substance that dare not speak its name continues to shadow Locke.[68] Indeed, the "eternal being," our knowledge of whose existence he proves in the tenth chapter of the fourth book of his *Essay*, is very simply this substance or substratum of all particular existence.

While Locke avoids direct contact with the paradoxical Substance-God that emerges from his proof, tellingly, his successors in the deist movement walk right up to it and shake its hand. A case in point is Locke's greatest pupil, the third Earl of Shaftesbury. "Is there any difficulty in fancying the universe to be one thing?" Shaftesbury asks in his celebrated *Characteristicks*.[69] "All things cohere and conspire; all things are in one, and are comprehended in the nature of the universe," he adds in his posthumously published work.[70] His defense of a Spinozan necessitarianism is almost strident: "Everything that happens is from the same nature (the nature of the whole), and, therefore, to be dissatisfied with what happens, is to be dissatisfied with nature."[71] "If any one cause be removed . . . the whole (which is one concatenation) must necessarily be rendered imperfect, and hence totally perish," he continues.[72] Of every thing and event in the world, he insists, "this was necessary, from causes necessary, and (whether Providence or atoms) could be thus only, and could not have been otherwise."

Locke's other wayward pupil, Anthony Collins, was so committed to a Spinozistic substance monism that he resorted to transcribing pieces of it from Spinoza himself. Here is Collins in his geometrically organized *Dissertation on Liberty and Necessity* on the deconstruction of "free will" (about which more later) that inevitably follows from necessitarianism: "The vulgar, who are bred up to believe Liberty or Freedom . . . feel themselves free on a thousand occasions. And the source of their mistake seems to be as follows. They either attend not to, or see not the causes of their actions."[73] Here is Spinoza on the same subject in his geometrically organized *Ethics*: "The mass of men believe they are free on this account only, that they are conscious of their actions and ignorant of the causes by which they are determined."[74]

Bolingbroke, like Collins, heaped praise on "that great man," John Locke.[75] Then, in the first of the letters to Alexander Pope that are thought to have shaped the *Essay on Man*, he offered a proof of our knowledge of an eternal being that follows Shaftesbury following Spinoza.[76] John Toland was still more outspoken in his commitment to the reality of an "eternally active," "eternally divisible," and necessary substance.[77] By the time the ideas reached Toland's protégés, the authors of *Cato's Letters*, the commitment to the substance monism underlying Locke's proof is almost casual. "There cannot be two or more such beings as are necessary and self-existing," says Trenchard. Thus, the one substance "must be the cause of all the rest; or, which is the same thing, must produce all the rest."[78]

AT A CERTAIN POINT in his double-sided proof of "a God," Locke launches into a discussion about our general ignorance of the ways of God. "If you do not understand the operations of your own finite mind," he shrugs, "do not deem it strange that you cannot comprehend the operations of that eternal, infinite Mind who made and governs all things."[79] To orthodox readers, once again, his words will sound reas-suringly pious. He appears to call for submission to a willful, cogitating deity that acts in mysterious ways and so can create something out of nothing every day of the week, if it so pleases him, without ever having to tell us why. And yet this declaration of ignorance points to one of the most profound points of contact between Locke and Spinoza and a fundamental feature of their deeply atheistic proof of a God.

The necessitarianism that follows from the Locke-Spinoza proof has always seemed so counterintuitive that superficial interpreters are wont to overlook the fact that it applies only to the totality of things, or "God," and not to any particular thing at all. That is, it extends only to claim *that* all things in the world are interconnected in a necessary way; it does not involve a claim that we may know *how* things are thus inter-connected when we consider them as they are in nature. Indeed, the most important claim Spinoza makes on the point is that our knowl-edge *that* all things are necessary is possible only on the condition that we will never know exactly *how* any particular thing is necessary.

Spinoza clarifies this claim with a beguiling analogy that he offers in a 1665 letter to Locke's friend and neighbor, Henry Oldenburg.[80] Imagine a worm in the blood, he says, surrounded by particles of lymph and other objects of various types floating by and interacting with one another. The worm—obviously a clever worm—will develop a set of laws with which to understand these particles. If the blood were a self-contained system, then our worm might aspire to an absolutely perspicuous understanding of the ways in which all the bodies it per-ceives behave. But in fact the blood is part of a larger system with which it interacts, and so no purely internal explanation of the activities of its parts can be complete. Therefore, the laws through which the worm interprets events in its sanguinary corner of the universe are always partial and fail to demonstrate the absolute necessity of any particular thing in the vascular system. Now, we are in nature just as the worm is in blood. The only difference is that the nature in which we find ourselves is infinite. The conclusion is blunt. We remain "completely ignorant" about *how* the actual, infinite series of causes and effects in Nature are linked together.[81]

In the jargon of substance and modes, Spinoza expresses the conclusion this way: "When we have regard only to the essence of Modes and not to the order of Nature as a whole, we cannot deduce from their present existence that they will or will not exist in the future or that they did or did not exist in the past."[82] In a letter to an acquaintance, he sums it up with a phrase borrowed from Aquinas: "Between finite and infinite there is no proportion."[83] Hume would later get credit for the point by articulating it in a language that the English could understand, as a distinction between causal and logical necessity. We could update it to twentieth-century philosophical vocabulary by saying that the laws through which we understand nature are always corrigible. Or, we could say that in their inherent falsifiability they bear within themselves a certain mark of our ignorance of infinite nature. Spinoza's necessitarianism, or alleged "fatalism," in sum, is best understood as one perspective on a universe in which, regarded from another perspective, everything is radically contingent. This kind of perspectival necessitarianism is incompatible with determinism as that term is usually understood (which is to say, as reductive determinism, or the thesis that all explanations reduce to explanations involving a limited and perfectly knowable subset of natural laws).[84]

Here we may also dissolve an apparent tension between Spinoza and Epicurus (or between Epicurus and his predecessor Democritus). Committed to the intuition that there is something radically contingent about the universe, but unable to reconcile this intuition with the intrinsically necessitarian doctrine of atomism he purloined from Democritus, Epicurus cooked up his most problematic doctrine, the dogma of the swerve, or *clinamen*. The atoms, he announced, occasionally swerve from their straight-line courses, and it is on this account that they get entangled in unpredictable ways and produce a contingent universe of phenomena. Spinoza effectively converts the seemingly arbitrary physical concept of the *clinamen* into a perspectival distinction. He certainly rejects the idea that anything in nature, adequately conceived, might swerve in a random way, since that would render the universe intrinsically unintelligible. But he does argue that from our limited perspective, as worms in the blood, everything that might appear to us to be an atom will have an intrinsic, inherently unpredictable swerve. Thus, far from overturning Epicurus's intuition about the randomness of life, Spinoza explains how the perception of chance is in fact an unavoidable feature of finite experience in an infinite, lawlike, "necessitarian" system. The crucial upshot is that we may have a God that "acts in mysterious ways," as it were, and yet does not for that reason violate any of its necessary laws. Human ignorance is here both recognized and "naturalized," and the atheism that first appeared with Epicurus is made much more formidable through the conversion of a seemingly arbitrary doctrine into a doctrine about the seeming arbitrariness of the world.

Now, it turns out that this "naturalization" of ignorance is precisely what Locke attempts to supply in his proof of our knowledge of God. The first clue comes from an earlier section in the *Essay*, in which Locke compares our knowledge of "the immensity of this fabric" that our "Maker" has produced with that of "a worm shut up in one drawer of a cabinet" in one among many "mansions."[85] (To be fair, there are other worms in early modern thought. The Italian philosopher and heretic Tommaso Campanella, for example, compares humankind to a worm inside a round of cheese.) Elsewhere, Locke summarizes the message with the words from Aquinas that can be found in Spinoza: "Finite of any magnitude holds not any proportion to infinite."[86] In yet another, much more forceful passage, situated in the crucial sections that lead up to his proof of our knowledge of a God, Locke drops any reference to the "Maker" or his worms and, in a stunningly brilliant move, opts to rephrase the argument in the language of the infinite universe:

How much the being and operation of particular substances in this our globe depend on causes utterly beyond our view, is impossible for us to determine . . . [T]he great parts and wheels, as I may so say, of this stupendous structure of the universe, may, for aught we know, have such a connexion and dependence of their influences and operations one upon another, that perhaps things in this our mansion would put on quite another face, and cease to be what they are, if some one of the stars or great bodies incomprehensibly remote from us should cease to be or move as it does. This is certain, things, however absolute and entire they seem in themselves, are but retainers to other parts of nature for that which they are most taken notice of by us.[87]

By placing the argument in the context of the infinite universe, Locke here allows for a radical application of the guiding principle of philosophy to the common human intuition that there can be no action at a distance. His point is not to show that there is action at a distance, but that the very idea of "distance"—or what distinguishes "near" from "far" and constitutes our "locality"—is always subject to revision. Those things that we imagine to be remotely far away may in fact be standing right beside us; and when we say that they act on us from a distance, what we really mean is that things are neither where nor what we think they are in every respect. More generally, the guiding principle tells us that no piece, part, or region of the universe may be thought to be entirely self-contained. There are no neighborhoods without neighbors in the universe; everything bears within itself some trace of an unknowable infinity.

Locke stashed it all away at the bottom of the pile of pages of his *Essay concerning Human Understanding*, but his successors once again dragged it into the light. Here is Alexander Pope, communicating Spinoza's parable of the worm in the interstellar translation supplied by Locke:

> *So man, who here seems principal alone,*
> *Perhaps acts second to some sphere unknown*
> *Touches some wheel, or verges some goal;*
> *Tis but a part we see, and not a whole.*[88]

Pope then goes on to articulate quite clearly the underlying dialectic of necessitarianism and ignorance:[89]

> *All nature is but art, unknown to thee*
> *All chance, direction, which thou canst not see*

All discord, harmony not understood
All partial evil, universal good[90]

It is worth citing Spinoza's *Tractatus* to show how closely the (ostensibly Catholic) Pope tracks him: "When something appears to us as ridiculous, absurd, or evil, this is due to the fact that our knowledge is only partial, that we are largely ignorant of the order and coherence of the whole of Nature."[91]

The idea that we may know of the necessity of the totality and yet remain deeply ignorant of the workings of all the particulars is one that appears in a vague way in many religious traditions, and in particular in the Christian tradition. Indeed, all religion may be said to take its start from the conviction that there are certain things in the world that we do not understand and that must therefore be attributed to some higher power. God's "greatness is unsearchable," says the psalmist.[92] God is he whom "no one has seen or can see," adds Timothy.[93] The idea of human ignorance of God's ways appears in extreme form in the *Deus absconditus* of Isaiah,[94] where God's actions are such as to defy any comprehension whatsoever. It is also part of the theology of Martin Luther and Jonathan Edwards—both of whom combine a rigorously necessitarian vision with a declaration of our absolute ignorance of God's purposes. Perhaps Paul expresses the intuition most poetically: "For we know only in part, and we prophesy only in part."[95]

Though it begins with a similar intuition, however, the religious conception of human ignorance ultimately falls into something very different from the deist position. While Spinoza and his successors ultimately ascribe our ignorance to the very lawfulness of nature itself, the common religious consciousness attributes it to the inscrutability of God's purposes and intentions, which is to say, the arbitrary or unlawful aspect of God's agency. The first, crucial implication of this difference has to do with how we may relieve our ignorance. According to the traditional religious conception, all we lack is a revelation through which God may advise us directly about the content of his otherwise unknowably arbitrary decisions. According to the philosophers, any putative revelation of the deity's arbitrary intentions would explain nothing at all; rather, we relieve our ignorance only through the continuous labor of finding explanations within the world for the connections among things in this world. The other crucial difference is that, according to the common religious consciousness, there is in a sense a single mystery, and it can be resolved at a stroke. When "the Word became flesh and lived among us," as John puts it, we got The Answer.[96] Paul assures us that, notwithstanding the partiality of our present lives, absolute knowledge is indeed possible in real time: "When the complete comes, the partial will come to an end . . . Now I know only in part; then I will know fully, even as I have been fully known." Radical philosophy rejects the very possibility of such an epistemic closure.[97] There are plenty of riddles left by the gaps in our knowledge, but, as Wittgenstein would put it, "*the riddle* does not exist."[98]

HAVING PROVED that we may know of an "eternal being" that "acts in mysterious ways," Locke understands that he must endow this mysterious being with a capacity for thought if he is to make it look anything like the God that inhabits the narratives of traditional religion. According to the popular view, after all, God must tug on his beard before actually rustling up the world. Locke begins the task by proposing that there are two classes of beings in the world. One consists of beings that are "purely material, without sense, perception, or thought"; the other is made up of "thinking perceiving beings, such as we find ourselves to be."[99] The first group he calls "incogitative"; the second, "cogitative." Locke next asserts, "It is as impossible to conceive that ever bare incogitative matter should produce a thinking intelligent being, as that nothing should of itself produce matter."[100] Divide matter into large or tiny pieces, he says, and "they knock, impel, and resist one another . . . and that is all they can do."[101] Thinking things, in sum, can only come from and be explained through other thinking things. Since we already know, in virtue of the principle that nothing comes from nothing, that all things come from other things all the way back to God, it follows that all thinking things could have come only from other thinking things all the way back to God. Ergo, God is a thinking thing.

The conclusion that God "is a thinking thing" has powerful resonance in essentially every religious tradition, and it is of particular
consequence for deism and its idea of Nature's God. It gives a certain
license—a license that many deists grandly abuse—to represent God
as a "Mind" or "Supreme Intelligence" or cosmic "Soul" and so on. At
the same time, the real meaning of this step in Locke's proof is very
different from what it might at first appear. That meaning becomes
obvious to alert readers (a Toland, a Trenchard, or a Collins) as soon
as it is noticed that Locke's argument that "God is a thinking thing"
once again would not look any different if he had simply translated
Spinoza into plain English. Indeed, he didn't have to work very hard,
since Spinoza proves, in plain Latin, that "God is a thinking thing."[102]

Spinoza's argument, like Locke's, begins with a fundamental distinction between ways of being. When we think of things as physical objects, says Spinoza, we necessarily think of them as existing and
interacting within space, or what philosophers then called "extension."
Throughout the infinite series of physical causes and effects that reach
backward and forward through eternity, he adds, we find them all situated within extension. Therefore, there pertains to substance an essential feature or "attribute" called extension. That is, God is an extended
thing—a conclusion that theologians of the time thought the epitome
of atheism. But extension is not the only attribute of substance, Spinoza hastens to add. Indeed, substance must have an infinite number
of attributes, since otherwise it would possess some set of arbitrary
features, in violation of the guiding principle. For reasons that have to
do mainly with the influence of Descartes, Spinoza identifies only one
other of the infinite attributes of substance: namely, "thought."

Crucially, Spinoza goes on to clarify that in whatever way thoughts
and minds are explicable, they are not explicable through the attribute
of extension. So much follows from the very definition of an attribute
and indeed from the guiding principle of philosophy. In his austere
vocabulary, a mode of substance conceived through one attribute may
be conceived to interact with or explain only other modes conceived
through the same attribute, since after all it is their common participation in that attribute that makes their connection possible and

intelligible. "So long as things are considered as modes of thinking, we must explain the order of the whole of nature, or the connection of causes, through the attribute of thought alone," Spinoza concludes. "And insofar as they are considered as modes of extension, the order of the whole of nature must be explained through the attribute of extension alone."[103]

If we step back from the scholastic terminology, it becomes clear that Spinoza's conclusion—"God is a thinking thing"—is both much more and much less than it first appears. In Spinoza's conception (about which more in the next chapter), thought pertains to substance not in the way that individual thoughts flit across the imaginary theater of our minds but in the way that thoughtfulness pertains to thoughts, or that spatiality pertains to spatial objects. Substance is thus not so much a thinking thing as a "thoughtful" thing, and we know of this thoughtfulness only in virtue of our very own thoughts, insofar as they necessarily involve the attribute of thoughtfulness. In simple terms, we may say this is a thinking universe for the reason that we know ourselves to be thinking within it. In grander terms, our thoughts, understood in a certain way, are God's very own thoughts. Still more alarmingly, while our thoughts often seem to focus on things that do not exist, God's thoughts, insofar as they are independent of us, express the essence of substance and so are always only of necessarily existing things. The general idea, Spinoza says, was intuited by those ancient philosophers who grasped that "God, God's intellect, and the things understood by God are one and the same thing."[104] But this means that God does not and indeed cannot think in some hypothetical place before or beyond the universe about this or any alternative, uncreated universes. Rather, this universe, the only universe, *is* the thinking of God.

If we return to Locke's version of this step of the proof of a God, it should be obvious that he is merely summarizing the word from Spinoza. The distinction between cogitative and incogitative things is functionally identical to Spinoza's claim that extension and thought are two of the infinite attributes of substance. Locke's assertion that particular material things cannot produce thought simply repeats Spinoza's point that modes of thought cannot be conceived as modes of the attribute of extension and vice versa. Indeed, by insisting that he is talking about "bare" matter, or "particles," Locke seems to go out of his way to assure the informed reader that he is here concerned with matter as matter, which is to say, matter as modes conceived through the attribute of extension, and not whatever real substance expresses itself through the attribute of materiality.[105] Thus, his grand conclusion that God is a thinking thing can only be meant in the same sense that Spinoza first proposes it. The universe itself is the thinking of God, just as the universe is the extension of God.

In what may count as the first of several efforts to feign some difference between his own position and that of Spinoza, Locke ostentatiously repudiates those "men of matter" who allegedly reduce God to mere extension. (Hobbes would have been one such man, and to the uninformed public, Hobbes and Spinoza were two peas in a very rotten pod.) Yet Locke's argument does not rule out the possibility that God, whatever else it is, is also an extended thing. Indeed, in making his case, Locke repeats the guiding conviction that it is impossible "that nothing of itself should produce matter," and so it follows by the same logic that says that God is a thinking thing, that God is also a material or extended thing. "Let it be so," Locke grandly allows, magnanimously yielding on a doctrine that to the theologians of the era was the height of abomination; "it equally still follows that there is a God."[106] His real target, it turns out, is not those who believe that God is an extended thing, but those who believe that God is *only* an extended thing. The nefarious but unnamed "men devoted to matter," he warns, attempt to reduce God to this one attribute of materiality; but "they will have as hard a task to make out of their own reasons a cogitative being out of incogitative particles as an extended being out of unextended parts."[107] Indeed, Locke is logically committed to reject the thesis that God is *only* a thinking thing: clearly, God must be both, if God is to account for both cogitative and incogitative beings. For the alert reader, Locke's attack on "men of matter" amounts to a *defense* of Spinoza against the charge of reductive materialism (or what could be called "Hobbism").

On this vital point, the decisive pattern among Locke's most intimate successors persists. "For what else is it you naturalists make of the world than a mere machine?" Shaftesbury has one of his antagonists ask in a pivotal dialogue. "Nothing else," comes the reply, "if to the machine you allow a mind." Shaftesbury has few qualms about absorbing the thinking of the deity into the universe itself: "The imaginations, sensations, apprehensions of men are included in this body [of Nature] and inherent in it, produced out of it and resumed again into it," he says.[108] "How are you then a self and nature not so?"

In an astonishing column included in *Cato's Letters*, Trenchard, too, rehearses the radical side of Locke's seemingly moderate proof. Certain philosophers, says Trenchard, "not being able to conceive that anything can be made of nothing, and seeing nothing real in the world but matter, conclude that matter has been in eternal motion." These philosophers—the target here is clearly Epicurus, Hobbes, and the nameless evildoers Locke identifies as "men of matter"—appear unable to explain the common intuition that we are thinking beings, and that there must be something responsible for the creation of thought and thinking things. But then a second set of philosophers comes along, says Trenchard, and proposes that thought and thinking beings, too, may be conceived as modes of a single essential nature. These new philosophers—obviously Spinoza, Shaftesbury, and the side of Locke's split personality that agrees with them—are heretics, too. "The contrary is much the more orthodox and religious opinion," Trenchard allows, in what seems a moment of hesitation. But then, caution to the wind, he throws his lot in with the Spinozists: "How much more modest and reasonable would it be to argue . . . that all causes must first or last center in the supreme cause; who from the essence of his own nature, must always do what is best, and all his actions must be instantaneous emanations of himself?"[109]

In the hands of Toland, Spinoza's reduction of the thinking of God to the thinking of the universal substance becomes putty in the fabrication of a new, surprisingly modern-sounding kind of religion. In his faux liturgy for the Masons, Toland asks his brothers to sing with him in praising "GOD, whom you may call the *Mind*, if you please, and the *Soul* of the Universe," and bids all to chant with him: "*The Sun is my*

Father, the Earth my Mother, the World's my Country, and all Men are my Relations."[110] As in numerous other instances, Toland here unites his Spinozism with an eclectic mix of hermeticism, Neoplatonic visions of a radiating cosmic intelligence, ancient Egyptian sun-worship, and Stoic rhetoric about a universal brotherhood—a cocktail that served as a powerful elixir of radical ideas across Europe and in America.

TOWARD THE END of his proof of "a God," Locke suddenly appears to acknowledge the heterodox drift of his argument. In the eyes of alert readers, he seems to declare his intention to break with his secret mentor at last. Yet in his seeming eagerness to rescue himself from infamous associations, he supplies perhaps the most damning evidence yet to those who would question the sincerity of his expressed convictions.

The rub has to do with the possibility of creation of something out of nothing, or creation ex nihilo as it is known in the theological trade. In particular, it has to do with the creation of *matter* out of nothing, since few people are as bothered as they should be by the hypothetical creation of a thinking God out of nothing. Locke knows that he has to prove the creation of matter out of nothing if he is to maintain his bona fides with the orthodox; yet he knows that this is a fiendishly difficult step to take, since it contradicts the first premise with which his proof begins, namely, that nothing comes from nothing.[111] So, how does Locke finesse this crucial moment in the argument? In an extraordinary move, he punts the whole bowl of spaghetti into obscurity:

> Nay, possibly, if we would emancipate ourselves from vulgar notions, and raise our thoughts, as far as they would reach, to a closer contemplation of things, we might be able to aim at some dim, and seeming conception how matter might at first be made, and begin to exist, by the power of that eternal first Being . . . But this being what would, perhaps, lead us too far from the notions on which the philosophy now in the world is built, it would not be pardonable to deviate so far from them.[112]

This is just astonishing. It is philosophical evasion raised to a performance art. Locke cannot bring himself to endorse the creation of matter ex nihilo; so he projects its rejection onto "the philosophy now in the world" and blames it on others if he must forego the counter-proof that he has just said is of the greatest consequence for the future of religion. Here as at so many other critical junctures in his work, he writes in such a slippery way that no two lawyers could ever reach agreement on who "Locke" is and what he "really" believes. It is this kind of writing that prompted Hume to sneer that his illustrious predecessor was a master of "ambiguity and circumlocution."[113] And yet at the end of the meal the fact remains that Locke has left on the table the one doctrine that in his own account must be swallowed if one is to ward off the dreaded evil of Spinozism.

Locke's successors in Britain did not hesitate to dot the i's and cross the t's. "As for what is said of 'a material thinking substance being never able to have produced an immaterial thinking one,' I readily grant it, but on the condition that this great maxim of 'nothing being ever made from nothing' may hold as well," Shaftesbury writes in a key passage in his *Characteristicks*.[114] The first clause alludes unmistakably to Locke's proof of "a God," and puts Shaftesbury firmly on board with the Spinozistic thrust of that proof, according to which thought and extension are eternal and independent attributes of substance. The second clause, however, makes clear that Shaftesbury does not follow Locke in his feigned attempt at a proof of creation of matter ex nihilo.

The most poignant example of this pattern of breaking with the great man in order to remain faithful to him comes from Locke's late-life amanuensis, Anthony Collins. In a debate with Boyle lecturer and Newton acolyte Samuel Clarke, Collins prepares to offer a proof of the existence of God by insisting repeatedly and emphatically that, if we are to avoid a disastrous collapse into the irreligious materialism of certain ancient and modern philosophers, it is absolutely imperative to prove the possibility of the creation of matter ex nihilo.[115] So, what does Collins offer to sustain this bulwark of orthodoxy against the unmentionable horror of Spinozism? Just as he arrives at the moment of truth, he abruptly stops and defers to his august tutor. He presents the reader with precisely the passage cited above, in which Locke egregiously showers his readers with pasta.

If Locke found it "not pardonable" to carry on with this crucial task, Collins declares with an all but visible smirk, then that "must make it more pardonable in me (who own myself to be infinitely below him in Abilities) if I omit for the present so useful a Design, or should leave it intirely to some of those Gentlemen that are appointed annually to Preach at the Lecture founded by the Honorable Robert Boyle." Since Collins has just devoted dozens of pages to exposing the incompetence of one such gentleman lecturer, this last line can hardly have been expected to give much comfort to the reader in search of a secure foundation for the true religion. Nor can there be much doubt that Collins categorically rejects the very idea of creation ex nihilo that he so ceremoniously sets out to prove. The idea that "nothing might produce something," he writes elsewhere, is "a real absurdity in itself."[116] A reviewer of the time not surprisingly described Collins's performance in the Clarke debate as "bare-faced Atheism."[117]

The gap between Collins and his mentor, one often senses, is emotional rather than logical. Collins is impatient, sometimes contemptuous of Locke for his timidity, and yet remains faithful to the underlying thrust of the older man's arguments. This same feeling of frustration appears in other readers of Locke, such as, notably, Jefferson: "Where [Locke] stopped short, we may go on."[118]

ACCORDING TO THE HISTORY of ideas as it has been narrated for the past two centuries or so, "pantheism" is the idea that all things are imbued with the animating spirit of a mysterious cosmic being, and in this form it has been generally construed either as an example of the magical thinking that preceded the Enlightenment or as artifact of the Romantic imagination that followed it. But pantheism is better understood as the idea that God and Nature are two ways of talking about the same thing, and in this sense it is the core religious sensibility of the Enlightenment, from its beginning with Bruno's rediscovery of

Lucretius through Locke's proof of a God to the American Revolution. Spinoza did not invent this movement; he epitomized it.

That Bruno felt this pantheistic intuition deeply is indisputable. There is a "principle of being, wellspring of every species," said the Nolan, and this principle is, in no particular order, "Mind, God, Being, One, Truth, Fate, Reason, Order."[119] Vanini ended his first book—composed when he still had hopes of getting along with the theologians—with a poem in which he, too, finds a "deep well-spring of wisdom" that may be described as, in no particular order, "Number . . . Order . . . Love . . . Reason . . . Truth . . . One . . . the Same."[120] "According to what internal religion did the ancient philosophers truly and piously honor God?" Vanini's foil asks in his second, more daring book. "According to the law of nature only," Vanini's alter ego replies, "for nature, which is God (for she is the principle of movement), has engraved this law in the heart of all men."[121] Gassendi was much more careful than Bruno and Vanini in insisting on a separation of God and Nature, yet he seemed unable to prevent himself from making all the wrong insinuations. "Nature cannot be without God, nor God without Nature; . . . God and Nature are the same thing, the very same Being; for these different Names are only different Titles of the same God," he wrote—and then dutifully hid those words in a fabricated citation from Seneca.[122]

The same message—still more carefully guarded—appears in the *Dialogue* that landed Galileo before the Inquisition. In one sentence, the astronomer speaks in pious tones of the magnificent work of "Divine omnipotence." And in the next sentence, he refers to those same productions as "the work of the most wise Nature."[123] He goes on to identify the providential agent ruling the world, with seemingly casual ambivalence, as "God and Nature."[124] In some of his private correspondence, he drops curious hints of his belief in a weird, quasi-Egyptian, quasi-Neoplatonic "world soul"—a "very spiritual, tenuous, and extremely rapid substance that, diffusing itself throughout the universe, penetrates everything without effort, brings warmth, enlivens, and renders fecund all living things" and whose "principal receptacle" is "the body of the Sun."[125] Among the successors of Galileo who picked up on something of this pantheistic intuition was Descartes. "By nature considered in general," Descartes notes almost as an aside in his *Meditations on First Philosophy*, "I understand . . . nothing else but God himself, or the order and arrangement that God has established among created things."[126]

The defenders of orthodoxy were well aware of the theological drift of the Enlightenment long before it was called the Enlightenment. In Paris in 1623, François Garasse (1585–1631), a Jesuit priest seething with learned rage, fired off a thousand-page polemic at the liberal crowd that had gathered around Vanini. The "new Epicureans," said Garasse, believe that "all things . . . are governed by Fate, which is irrevocable, infallible, immutable, necessary, eternal, and inevitable"; that "there is no other divinity or sovereign power in the world except NATURE"; and, in brief, that "God is Nature, and Nature is God."[127] In Holland, the rigorously Calvinist theologian Gisbertus Voetius, a sworn foe of all things Arminian, built a career out of defaming Descartes, whom he charged with emulating the example of Vanini in proving the existence of a universal deity who was no God at all.[128] Half a century later in England, Richard Bentley, the first and most accomplished of the Boyle lecturers who inadvertently converted Franklin to deism, complained that "the modern disguised Deists . . . do cover the most arrant atheism under the mask and shadow of a deity, by which they understand no more than some eternal inanimate matter, some universal nature, and soul of the world."[129]

Locke, like Gassendi, could be counted on to be as unyielding in his professions of orthodox faith as he was reliable in making all the wrong insinuations. At one point in his *Essay*, for example, he writes in pious tones that the connection between pleasures and pains on the one hand and our survival needs on the other "gives us new occasion of admiring the wisdom and goodness of our Maker"[130] and of our "Sovereign Disposer."[131] Rehearsing the claim a few pages later, he writes, "The great business of the senses being so as to make us take notice of what hurts or advantages the body, it is wisely ordered *by nature (as has been shown)* that pain should accompany the reception of several ideas [emphasis added]."[132] In a draft of an essay on miracles that he withheld from publication, he suggests that the ancient Hebrews ascribed "to the Spirit of God some things that were brought about in the ordinary course of providence. Such a way of speaking is not only not unusual but very consistent with the notions of a deity in whom we live move & have our being."[133] Spinoza, as it happens, makes pretty much the same point about the Hebrews in his *Tractatus Theologico-Politicus*, where he suggests that writers of the Bible routinely ascribed to "the Spirit" or "God" perfectly natural events that were contrary only to their limited understanding of the way things work in the world.[134]

What distinguishes Locke's successors in England from his predecessors is that their commitment to Spinozistic pantheism steps out of the shadows. Indeed, the very term "pantheism" is generally thought to have been the invention of Locke's evil twin, John Toland, who presented the doctrine in, among other places, his aptly titled *Pantheisticon*. Toland did little to disguise his awareness of the chief expositor of that doctrine in the modern world. In a characteristically outlandish effort to tar Moses with the brush of the ancient materialism, for example, he alleged that the putative author of the Pentateuch was "unequivocally . . . a pantheist, or as we in these modern times, would style him, a Spinozist."[135] Since the author of *Pantheisticon* was avowedly a pantheist, it follows that Toland would have styled himself a Spinozist, too. From Toland's language it is evident that he did not suppose that he was alone in England in his convictions—and indeed he was not. The preface to Charles Blount's *Oracles of Reason* of 1693—penned by his friend and executor Charles Gildon—opens with a triumphant salutation to "Nature, or that Sacred and Supream CAUSE of all Things, which we term GOD." Shaftesbury was even more direct. "O mighty nature! Wise substitute of Providence! Empowered creatress!" he exults.[136] Shaftesbury "made a God out of Nature, a God immanent in the world," Leslie Stephen aptly observed.[137] Trenchard tended to favor the strategy of quiet substitution pursued by Galileo and Locke. Shortly after uttering the seeming piety that "Almighty God" works in mysterious ways, he added, "Nature (as is said in print elsewhere) works by infinite ways; which are impenetrable to our vain and fruitless inquiries."[138]

The intuition that God is present in all things at all times and is embodied in the universe features in a certain way in many religions and in particular in the Christian religion. The psalmist expresses the idea in a particularly lyrical passage:

> *Whither shall I go from Thy spirit? Or whither shall I flee*
> *from Thy presence?*
> *If I ascend up into heaven, Thou art there; if I make my bed*
> *in hell, behold, Thou art there.*[139]

In Acts, Paul himself draws the connection between this intuition and the ideas of the ancient philosophers. On a visit to Athens, seeking common ground with a group of Epicurean and Stoic philosophers, he describes for them a God in whom "we live, move, and have our being." "Some of your own poets," Paul tells the philosophers, "have said we are his offspring."[140] Locke alludes to this passage from Paul in the draft essay cited above—and so does Spinoza, in a letter to Henry Oldenburg of 1675.[141] Among the philosophers of the early modern period—not just Spinoza and Locke, but also Bruno, Toland, Franklin,[142] and Ethan Allen[143]—Paul's description of a God in whom "we live, move, and have our being" is by far the most favorably cited piece of scripture concerning the nature of God. As Spinoza makes clear, however, the ultimate implications of this intuition about God are dramatically different from anything Paul seems to have contemplated.

Spinoza's contribution to the pantheism of the Enlightenment does not rest on the assertion of the ancient intuition that there is a relationship of identity between God and Nature, but rather in making that assertion unavoidable to all who shared with him the basic vocabulary of early modern philosophy together with a commitment to the guiding principle. In supplying the ground for the intuition, moreover, he drew out its implications, and these extended all the way to an entirely new conception of the political order, as the efforts of America's revolutionaries would demonstrate. The essential beginnings of this project of clarification and extension can be represented in Spinoza's pantheistic reappropriation of three concepts that have always been central to theology: "providence," "piety," and the "laws" of God or Nature.

According to the common conception of things, God is necessarily providential, and a providential God is one that acts against the laws of nature in order to grant favors to some of its creatures (whether as individuals, nations, or species). The God of Locke and Spinoza obviously cannot be providential in this sense. Yet, according to Spinoza, there is a way that God or Nature relates to the ends of particular individuals, and it is nothing other than the conatus through which each individual strives to persist in being. "Providence," Spinoza concludes, consists of "nothing else than the *striving* which we find in the whole of Nature and in individual things to maintain and preserve their own existence."[144] In a formula, providence provides for those who provide for themselves.

Providence in this Spinozistic sense, to be clear, is always perfectly "general," never "particular" or "specific." "The whole is the final cause of every part," and "no one or more parts is the final cause of the whole," Bolingbroke writes—and Jefferson copies.[145] We may still speak of mercy, wisdom, or beneficence in the deity, according to this line of thought, but only insofar as we use those terms to refer to what Epicurus would have called "impressions" of the "ideal." That is, our claims about providence, if genuine, serve only to evoke an attitude toward a totality of things whose specific workings are necessarily beyond our comprehension. Spinoza adds that the idea of "special" (as opposed to general) providence is a precursor to atheism (or what today we might call "nihilism"), for it is only when we maintain that God rules directly over the affairs of humankind that we may legitimately begin to doubt that God exists at all or that he takes his duties seriously.[146]

Just as important as the deconstruction of "providence" is the accompanying revision of the idea of "piety," or the proper service and worship of God or Nature. Piety, according to the common religious consciousness, is generally taken to involve fealty to some set of unconfirmed beliefs in supernatural agents together with acts of sacrifice or prayer intended to evince that faith and gratify those agents by abasing oneself before them. Bruno, perhaps drawing on Lucretius's reflection on true piety, hints at the radical alternative: "To the extent that one communicates with Nature, so one ascends to divinity through Nature."[147] Spinoza formalizes the doctrine: "True piety," he says, is the "intellectual love of God." The intellectual love of God is, on the one hand, the pursuit of science, or the understanding of the universe in the most general sense. "The greater our knowledge of natural phenomena, the more perfect is our knowledge of God's essence," says Spinoza.[148] Which is to say, in a manner of speaking, that nature is God's revelation, and science is the true theology. The intellectual love of God is, on the other hand, the ethical life that, through the practice of virtue, permits the individual to realize itself. The imperatives to know and to do good, taken together, amount to an affirmation of being, of our own being and that of the universe, and so they constitute the proper "worship" of God or Nature.

A final conceptual transformation—one that will prove particularly central in understanding the development of America's revolutionary political ideology—involves the kind of "laws" for which God or Nature may be thought responsible. The common religious consciousness invariably construes God as a lawgiver in the model of a political legislator (or a paternal figure): he lays down rules that ought not—but can—be disobeyed, and that if disobeyed bring about some ordained punishment. But Spinoza draws the inference that is implicit in Locke's proof of a God, namely, that "God's laws are not of such a nature that they could be transgressed."[149] "A man . . . cannot act against the eternal decree of God, which is inscribed on Universal Nature and which takes into account the order of Nature in its entirety," he explains.[150] "As for the divine natural law whose chief commandment, as we have said, is to love God," he goes on to say, "I have called it a law in the same sense as philosophers apply the term 'law' to the universal rules of Nature according to which all things come to pass. For love of God is not obedience but a virtue necessarily present in a man who knows God aright, whereas obedience has regard to the will of him who commands, and not to necessity and truth."[151] In sum, "we cannot . . . conceive God as a ruler enacting laws."[152]

Bolingbroke condenses Spinoza's point to a line: "I say that the law of nature is the law of God," he writes—and Jefferson once again copies it into his student notebook.[153] "Increase and multiply is the law of nature," Bolingbroke adds elsewhere; and "the manner in which this precept shall be executed with the greatest advantage to society is the law of man."[154] The proto-Darwinian notion that the laws of nature command us only to survive and prosper—and that civil laws serve mainly to encode this imperative—is a commonplace of deist literature of the period, and, as with Bolingbroke, it is often expressed by co-opting the biblical language about increasing and multiplying.

Viewed from within the common religious consciousness, the pantheism of Spinoza and his fellow radicals is quite obviously a species of atheism. The theologians of the late seventeenth and early eighteenth centuries, at any rate, were under no illusions about the program. In order to incline "the unwary" to his side, lamented Richard Blackmore, Spinoza "Declares for God, while he that God betrays"; he "saves the name," and yet "subverts the thing."[155] Bishop Berkeley (1685–1753)—perhaps the most sophisticated of the philosophical reactionaries of the period—tossed Hobbes, Leibniz, Bayle, Vanini, Shaftesbury, and that nasty little Collins into a single bonfire of Spinozism: "That atheistical principles have taken deep root, and are farther spread than most people are apt to imagine, will be plain to whoever considers that pantheism, materialism, fatalism are nothing but atheism a little disguised."[156] According to Leslie Stephen, Spinoza's pantheism, though superficially attractive to liberal theologians, amounted to the "euthanasia of God." Perhaps the most perceptive observation comes from the early-eighteenth-century prelate William Carroll, who, taking note of the extraordinary convergence of Locke and Spinoza in their proof of our knowledge of a God, exclaims that the two philosophers together "undertake to confirm us in Atheism, by convincing us, that *there is a God.*"[157]

Even so, the aura of piety that seems to envelope the atheistic pantheism of early modern philosophy cannot be dismissed as mere posturing. And the reason for this is that the thrust of that philosophy is not so much to diminish God as to rescue nature from the importunities of the common religious consciousness. Radical philosophy really begins with the intuition that the great problem with the common religious consciousness is not that it thinks so highly of God but that it thinks so little of nature. The common consciousness conceives of nature as something inherently inert, passive, mechanical, and therefore unable to give life meaning, and it congeals its nihilism in the hallucination of an otherworldly God. Radical philosophy attempts to show that nature itself contains a principle of infinite activity; that it is the real source of the enigmas we falsely gather under the name of God; and that it is the font of everything that we may value.

Although the vocabulary of Spinoza's pantheism belongs to a particular period in history, long since consigned to obscure books on the history of ideas, the sensibility it invokes is confined to no time. It arises everywhere among those who find in the world more cause for wonder than fear. Albert Einstein offered about as pithy an exposition of Spinoza's God as one is likely to find anywhere:

> I cannot conceive of a God who rewards and punishes his creatures, or has a will of the type of which we are conscious in ourselves . . . Enough for me, the mystery of the eternity of life, and the inkling of the marvelous structure of reality, together with the single-hearted endeavor to comprehend a portion, be it ever so tiny, of the reason that manifests itself in nature.[158]

Today we have become used to a very different, hit-and-run kind of atheism: one that zeroes in on the question of the existence of God and leaves the scene once it has been shown that there is no credible evidence for such an existence. The atheism inherent in the Locke-Spinoza proof, on the other hand, concentrates on the nature of God and seeks to explain—and thereby explain away—God. It gathers up the meaningful and worthy intuitions that motivate the religious consciousness—the sense of humility before a power greater than ourselves, the awareness of the depths of our ignorance about the universe, the feeling that even in our innermost thoughts we are merely passing forms of something eternal—and it shows that they refer not to the fictitious, meddling deity of the religious imagination but to nature itself or the universe comprehended as a whole. It is a way of talking about God long after God is dead.

MEASURED IN NUMBERS—of citations, of admirers, of acres of adulatory prose—the most influential theologian of the early modern world was not Locke or Spinoza but Isaac Newton. Newton's unrivaled scientific achievements gave him an almost unimpeachable authority on theological questions, and that authority waxed to the extent that his scientific findings seemed to reinforce his theological pronouncements.[159] According to the most widely accepted narratives of early modern philosophy, consequently, Newton's version of deism—which differed vociferously from Spinoza's pantheism—is represented as the dominant theology of the period and the one that ultimately mattered in America's Revolution. Yet the philosophy of Newton—whose intentions, unlike Locke's, seem above suspicion—serves mainly to illustrate the power of the underlying ideas. The Newtonian philosophy is essentially a reactive one; and, like all such enterprises, it remains captive to that against which it reacts.

The Newtonian reaction is mostly a logical—as opposed to chronological—phenomenon, and it begins well before Newton. Gassendi, an early adept in playing on both sides of the debate, was among the first to attempt to offset the heretical tendency of his materialistic philosophy with a deistic reappraisal of God's role in the world. The universe is an infinite congeries of senseless atoms, Gassendi concedes, and yet it "was not created without the deliberation and providence of God, and if atoms were the instrument used, they coalesced into the magnificent work of the universe, not by a chance occurrence, but according to divine disposition."[160] Here then is the basic statement of what may be called "classical deism." The universe is a "machine," to use Gassendi's word, and God is the "Maker" of the machine. Later, for reasons that have to do with the advances in chronometry at the time, the preferred metaphor becomes the "clock" or "watch," and Gassendi's deity becomes "the watchmaker God."

The most obvious problem with the watchmaker deity is that it removes God from any ongoing involvement in the world (and of our precious human world in particular). Richard Bentley, in his Boyle Lecture of 1692, makes the point forcefully: "The Deists seclude [God] from directing the Affairs of the World, from observing and judging the Actions of Men"; and the journey that begins with this line of thinking "is terminated in downright Atheism. For the Divine Inspection into the Affairs of the World doth necessarily follow from the Nature and Being of God."[161]

By the time the debate over deism reached Newton, the theological pitfalls of classical deism were widely understood. So the great scientist, with the professional assistance of his theological consultants Richard Bentley and Samuel Clarke, took it upon himself to fill in the holes. Though Newton's belief system was idiosyncratic and bizarre and much of it lies forever buried with him, the one thing we may know he wished to believe for sure is that God is God. "There is a Being incorporeal, living, intelligent, omnipresent," he announced, and "this Being governs all things . . . as Lord over all."[162] God is eternal and infinite, Newton goes on to insist, but we must at all cost avoid the suggestion that he is "the Eternal" or "the Infinite." We must under no circumstances conceive of God "as the soul of the world." Also, "we are not to consider the world as the body of God." The essential feature of Newton's God is that he is distinct from the world and has real dominion over it. He is a master, and he must have servants.

It took Newton a while to settle on an explanation of exactly how God acts as commander in chief of the infinite universe. In his middle years, he appeared to find an answer in his law of gravity. Within the landscape of seventeenth-century physics—which generally conceived of physical action entirely as a contact sport among extended objects— Newton's law of gravity raised the paradox, not to say absurdity, of action at a distance. So the great scientist's first suggestion was, to put it roughly, that God is obliged to reach into the world and pull the apples off the trees and drag the planets around the sun. But he soon conceded that there must be some physical explanation for gravity (such as the existence of an invisible "ether" that communicates gravitational forces). His next theory, which follows closely that of Gassendi, was that God's purpose in life is to account for the beneficent design of the universal system revealed to us by Galileo's telescopes and Newton's own theories. We have God to thank for the fact that, for example, there is only one sun in the solar system, helpfully located at the center, not too close but not too far from our temperate earth. This line of reasoning, however, implicitly confined God's activity to the moment of creation and thereby invited back the demons associated with Gassendi's machine-maker idea.

Newton's enduring solution for the problem of classical deism seems to have arisen out of his discovery that the system of the universe, as modeled through his universal law of gravitation, is intrinsically unstable. Why have the stars not pulled themselves together and imploded? Why have the planets stayed in their orbits instead of straying under the complex influences of other planets and comets? The universe seemed to him like a forest of needles all standing on their points. Without constant regulation by a higher power, everything would topple over. "To compare and adjust all these things together in so great a variety of bodies," he reasons, requires the presence of a deity "very well skilled in Mechanics and Geometry."[163] God, in other words, is a lot like Newton, except that he is even better at math. "The most beautiful system of the sun, planets, and comets," the famous scientist concludes, "could only proceed from the counsel and dominion of an intelligent and powerful being."[164]

Newton's vision has always had appeal among those who like their deity to win awards for scientific achievement but also want him to have a day job. Yet it was no more difficult for Newton's contemporaries than it is for us to see through the artifice. As Collins acidly observed, the picture of God as an interstellar grease monkey bears no serious relationship to the God who allegedly died on the cross. Newton's God was and is quite obviously a "God of the gaps"—the mysterious being that looms on the other side of the ever-shifting boundaries of human ignorance. (The gaps that mattered then—the seeming instability of the planetary orbits—are hardly the gaps that matter now; and yet the God of the gaps endures.) The most interesting and problematic aspect of the Newtonian theology, however, is that it involves a commitment to the same radical premises—above all, the guiding principle of philosophy—that serve to undermine it from within. Indeed, the chief occupation of early modern radicals like Toland and Collins was simply to trace the many iterations of the dialectic through which Newton's Lord Over All unwinds into Spinoza's Nature.

The radicalization of Newton began, appropriately enough, in outer space. Newton's scientific vision committed him to the infinite extension of the universe, but the infinite extension of the universe led to the ancient theological paradox concerning just where God might be found in this unending space. In his first stab at the problem, in the first draft for the theological pronouncement contained in his *Opticks*, Newton speculated, "Is not infinite Space the sensorium of a Being incorporeal, living, and intelligent, who sees the things themselves intimately . . . ?" Upon sending the manuscript off to the printers, however, he feared that perhaps he had gone too far. And indeed, as his radical enemies would promptly point out, to make space an attribute of God is precisely what Spinoza proposes. Newton hastily rewrote the passage to say that God "in infinite space, *as it were* in his sensory, sees the things themselves intimately, and thoroughly perceives them." Sure that his *"tanquam"*—"as it were"—would rescue him from the disgraceful imputation of pantheism, Newton rushed to gather every copy of the edition and undertook a cut-and-paste operation of the literal variety. But it was too little too late.[165] Even before Newton's emended version reached the public, one of his mathematical sidekicks had already put forward the argument that, within the Newtonian universe, "space is an attribute . . . of the first cause."[166] Samuel Clarke, Newton's chosen theologian, compounded the heresy when, attempting to defend Newton against the false charge of having turned space into God's brain, he argued that space is not a "substance" but "the property of an incorporeal substance," namely, the "eternal" and "necessary" substance we call God.[167]

The Spinozists in England were quick to pounce, as was Leibniz from the other side in Germany. Toland mailed in his signal contribution from Holland, in his particularly mischievous *Letters to Serena.* "I am satisfied that most of those Gentlemen [Newton and his allies] did firmly believe in the Existence of a Deity, and I charitably hope it of 'em all," Toland concludes with impish delight. "But in my Opinion their unwary Zeal refin'd him into mere Nothing, or (what they would as little allow) they made Nature or the Universe to be the only God."[168] He cites some doggerel—apparently making the rounds in the coffeehouses—that mocks Newton and his acolytes for having turned God into an infinite vacuum.[169] He closes with a wink to alert readers by tossing in a reference to Spinoza's trademark phrase, "God or Nature." Collins, too, exulted over Newton's slip on the question of space. Now more than ever, he told his friend Trenchard, it will be possible to maintain "the infinity of matter"—the crucial pillar of the Epicurean philosophy now associated with Spinoza. Mocking the many liberal clerics who have injudiciously embraced Newton as their savior, he gloated that "a great many whereof know not upon [such] weak foundations the matters of the greatest consequence to them stand."[170] Those clerics known for having an ear to the philosophical ground, such as Bishop Berkeley, agreed with Collins that the space war ended disastrously for the Newtonians.[171]

The deconstruction of the Newtonian position promptly expanded beyond space. It is perhaps best expressed in a general form in the widely read epistolary debate that took place over the winter of 1715–16 between Newton's representative Samuel Clarke and Newton's nemesis in the dispute over the invention of the calculus, Leibniz. Already famous as the exponent of a version of classical deism, according to which God is a "supra-mundane intelligence" responsible for selecting and creating "the best of all possible worlds," Leibniz was also a world-class expert in sniffing out disguised Spinozism among his fellow philosophers. And this was precisely the stench he detected from the direction of England.

The debate between Leibniz and Clarke is particularly interesting inasmuch as it reveals something about the origins of the "clockmaker God" that is now commonly used as an abbreviation for deism and specifically pinned on Newton. Far from being a doctrine that the deists actually embraced, the "clockmaker God" first emerged as an insult that they hurled at one another.[172] Leibniz got off the first shot when he said that, according to Newton and his misguided supporters,

> God's watch—the universe—would stop working if he didn't *re-wind* it from time to time! He didn't have enough foresight to give it perpetual motion. The machine he has made is so imperfect, that from time to time he has to *clean* it, by a miraculous intervention, and even has to *mend* it, as a clockmaker mends his work.[173]

Clarke, speaking for Newton, threw the clockmaker slur right back in Leibniz's face:

> The notion of the world's being a great machine—like a clock ticking along without help from a clockmaker—is the notion of materialism and fate, and tends, (under pretence of making God a *supra-mundane intelligence*,) to exclude providence and God's government in the reality of the world. With the same reasoning . . . a skeptic will easily argue still farther backwards, and suppose that things have from eternity gone on without any true creation or author at all, but only what such arguers call all-wise and eternal nature.[174]

To be called an arguer for materialism, fate, and an eternal all-wise nature, as Leibniz knew very well, is to be accused of the highest philosophical crime, namely, to be a follower of the dreaded Spinoza. Well, two can play at that game. In his testy reply, Leibniz retorted that if, as Newton and Clarke maintain, God must intervene regularly in the world, then he must do so either supernaturally or naturally. If the first, God must undertake continual miracles, which amounts to "reducing an hypothesis *ad absurdum*." If the second, "God . . . will be comprehended under the nature of things; that is, he will be the soul of the world."[175] That is, either God is an incompetent clockmaker; or God the clockmaker is indistinguishable from God the clock. Thus, on the assumption that Newton is not absurdly charging God with shoddy clock-making, he is a follower of the dreaded Spinoza.[176]

Defenders of orthodoxy looked upon these mighty debates and despaired. "It is their Newtonian philosophy which hath Made . . . so many Arians but Theists," complained the high churchman George Hickes.[177] Newtonian mathematics, added Bishop Berkeley, was "one short way of making infidels."[178] No one doubted the existence of God, the wags added, until Samuel Clarke set out to prove it. Among the radicals who matter in explaining America's Revolution, on the other hand, the internal combustion of the Newtonian theology was a welcome development. The authors of *Cato's Letters*, undoubtedly following Toland's lead, implicitly declared the winner of the debate between Leibniz and Newton/Clarke to be Spinoza. It is far more pious to imagine that God "formed the system of nature . . . to produce all the effects and operations which we daily see" by means of "its own energy and intrinsic power" than it is to believe that God is "often interposing to alter and amend his own work," say America's favorite republican theorists, aiming squarely at the glass jaw of Newton's theology.[179]

Perhaps the unkindest cuts came from Alexander Pope. In many of the shallow narratives that pass for the history of the Enlightenment, the *Essay on Man* is represented as the cheerful statement of Newtonian deism, which is in turn taken to stand for a theology so naively optimistic that the saturnine Newton would surely have found it abhorrent. This conventional view seems amply justified in the gushing epitaph Pope composed for the great scientist:

> *Nature and Nature's laws lay hid in night:*
> *God said, "Let Newton be!" and all was light.*

Yet the attitude Pope evinces toward Newton in his *Essay*, like that of his underappreciated poem taken as a whole, has a kind of complexity and irony that is not always visible at first glance. "Superior beings" might show "a NEWTON as we show an ape," says Pope with a tinge of contempt. "Could he whose rules the rapid comet bind / Describe or fix one movement of his mind?"[180]

THE *ESSAY ON MAN* reaches its rhetorical climax in these extraordinary lines:

> *All are but parts of one stupendous Whole,*
> *Whose body Nature is, and God the soul;*
> *That, changed through all, and yet in all the same,*
> *Great in the earth, as in th'ethereal frame,*
> *Warms in the sun, refreshes in the breeze,*
> *Glows in the stars, and blossoms in the trees,*
> *Lives through all life, extends through all extent*
> *Spreads undivided, operates unspent*
> *Breathes in our soul, informs our mortal part,*
> *As full, as perfect, in a hair as heart.*[181]

Every major element in the anti-theology of the age is here compressed in exquisite code: the monism ("one stupendous whole"); the idea of substance as the self-moving principle of infinite action (that "operates unspent" and remains "in all the same"); the identification of two of Nature's infinite attributes (one that "extends through all extent," and another that "breathes through the soul"); and the pantheistic intuition that divinity is nothing but the warming sun, the glowing stars, the blossoming trees, and the immanent stance that says that all of life takes place within a world that admits no before or beyond. Pope's summation is also all but explicitly anti-Newtonian. His declaration that God is the "soul" and Nature the "body" of the world was published a mere seven years after Newton expressly forbade such usages. Voltaire thought the *Essay on Man* was pure Shaftesbury;[182] but a scandalized Swiss theologian, citing these very lines just a few years after their publication, was closer to the mark: "A Spinozist would express himself in this manner."[183]

"Nature's God" at long last enters the stage of English letters in the verses of the same profoundly Spinozistic poem:

Slave to no sect, who takes no private road
But looks through Nature up to Nature's God![184]

"True piety," in other words, consists in the scientific study of nature, not in adherence to any private, sectarian faith.[185]

The phrase "Nature's God" also appears in one of the letters that Bolingbroke sent to Pope, composed before the *Essay* was but published long after. Bolingbroke undoubtedly drew support for the intuition, if not the phrase itself, from his encounters with Shaftesbury and Locke among others. Whatever the actual and unrecoverable chain of direct and personal influences—and even allowing that they might well have drawn their inspiration directly from those glowing stars and blossoming trees without need of elaborate metaphysical treatises—those two philosophers and their many allies were simply decorating an idea that emerged in antiquity, was present in the work of Bruno and Vanini among others, and was most perspicuously articulated by Spinoza. To cut a long story short: "Nature's God," the God of Thomas Young and the presiding deity of the American Revolution, is another word for "Nature."

"NATURE'S GOD" appears in American print for possibly the first time in an issue of the *Maryland Gazette* from 1747. On trial at an undisclosed location in New England, the paper reported, was a hearty specimen of American womanhood named Polly Baker. She was before the court on charges of having given birth to her fifth "Bastard child." Her defense was masterpiece of theology. "'Tis the duty and first great command of Nature, and of Nature's God, increase and multiply," she testified. Though condemned to "eternal Fire" by the Calvinist God of her neighbors, Polly avowed that she was merely performing her "Duty" as set forth by her naturalistic divinity. With too many "Batchelors" recoiling from the expense of raising a family, she explained, she was forced to take matters into, ahem, her own hands. Polly presented her case so well, the *Gazette* records, that one of the judges overruled his own religious scruples and married her the next day.[186]

Polly was one of Franklin's jokes, of course. Franklin rarely talked theology without cracking a smile. But he was pretty serious about America's obligation to follow the one commandment of his late-night deity. In an essay written four years after Polly's fictional acquittal, Franklin forecasts—or rather demands—a doubling of the English population of North America every twenty-five years. "So vast is the Territory of *North-America*," he says, "that it will require many Ages to settle it fully." He predicts that within the following century the population of North America will exceed that of the mother country, increasing and multiplying from 1 million to 16 million.[187] Amazingly, this turned out to be an underestimate. In the most provocative section of his essay on the increase of American-kind, Franklin considers whether and how religion will spread in the newly peopled continent. Tellingly, it does not occur to him to suggest that success will reward those religious sects that worship the one true God. Instead, channeling Bolingbroke, he predicts that those sects whose members manage to increase and multiply fastest will inherit this vast stretch of the earth. The more babies a sect has, the better it will do; and the more babies from other sects that it can recruit, the better still. The logic of the heavens will follow from the logic of the soil; and the Gods of the various sects ultimately answer to the one commandment of Polly's God—Nature's God.

There cannot be much doubt that Franklin was well informed about the radical precincts from whence Nature's God emerged. His *Dissertation on Liberty and Necessity*, penned at the age of nineteen, begins with the obligatory nod to "that ingenious Artificer," the God of Newton: "Those who have study'd [the universe] demonstrate that nothing can be more harmonious and beautiful. All the heavenly Bodies, the Stars and Planets, are regulated with the utmost wisdom!"[188] Yet it promptly embraces a rigorous form of necessitarianism. The universe is "a great Machine," a "Clock" with "many "intricate Wheels"—the very metaphor that Samuel Clarke, on Newton's behalf, had vigorously condemned a few years previously. There is "no such Thing as Liberty," the author proves according to a geometrical method. If a stone falling through the air were conscious, it would believe itself to be free. The geometrical style, the basic thesis, the phrase "no such thing as Liberty," the metaphor of the falling stone, and the very title of the *Dissertation*, as it happens, may be found among the works of Anthony Collins. Though Collins was certainly capable of coming up with it all on his own, it seems worth pointing out that the same geometrical style, the same thesis, and the same metaphor of the stone also appear in the works of Spinoza.[189]

In later life, Franklin scrupulously avoided metaphysical ratiocinations of the sort he pursued as a young man. Indeed, he gathered up all the copies of his first treatise save one and burned them. A personal transformation is already in evidence in the "Articles of Belief" that he composed two years after the *Dissertation*, upon his return to Philadelphia. On closer inspection, however, it turns out that the "new" Ben is all the more radical in his sensibility for having shed the earlier dogmatism. The universe and its "Father," he says in his "Articles," are infinite, and it is "impossible for me to have any positive clear Idea of that which is infinite and incomprehensible." So he resolves to focus his energies and prayers not on this inaccessible deity, but on the B-list quasi-Epicurean God of our local solar system—the middle-management, semi-mortal demiurge whose existence depends on Franklin's urge to pray to it. This mock deity, it now becomes clear, is nothing other than Newton's astronomical repairman God. Thus the stern metaphysical critique of Newtonianism in the *Dissertation* yields to something much more deadly: mirth.

For the rest of his career, irony was the signature of Franklin's theology. In places—in his various declarations that the older he gets, the surer he is that everything is part of a grand plan—he almost succeeds in striking a note of humble sincerity.[190] Yet the mask quite drops from his theological pleasantries. In one letter he quips that Providence, having taken notice of the fact that French women do not nurse, has wisely endowed them with small breasts. In another letter he remarks that Providence, having callously resolved to sweep America clean of its obstinate native population, appears to have settled on rum as the means. In his announcement of the invention of the lightning rod, he notes that it has pleased the Almighty "at last" to show humankind how to prevent needless death and destruction from above—impishly begging the question: What took him so long? Franklin's *Autobiography*, as John Updike has observed, is an "elastically insouciant work, full of cheerful contradictions"[191]—not the least of which is the contradiction between his vague assurances at the outset that the hero of the story owes everything to a higher power and the tale it tells of a man who made his own luck through a combination of hard work and opportunistic scrambling. Facetious pieties aside, Franklin's Providence is of the kind that Polly understands: it provides for those who provide for themselves.

In the fall of 1769, Franklin articulated his own theory of Providence in a letter to—of all people—the Reverend George Whitefield, captain of the revivalists:

> I *see* with you that our affairs are not well managed by our rulers here below; I wish I could *believe* with you, that they are well attended to by those above: I rather suspect, from certain circumstances, that though the general government of the universe is well administered, our particular little affairs are perhaps below notice, and left to take the chance of human prudence or imprudence . . . It is, however, an uncomfortable thought, and I leave it.[192]

Whitefield knew very well what he was dealing with here. "*Uncomfortable* indeed!" he scribbled in the margins of Franklin's letter. "And, blessed be God, *unscriptural.*"[193] When, just a few months later, Whitefield told Thomas Young and his fellow Bostonians that the deists were spawn of Cain, he undoubtedly had people like Franklin in mind. And Franklin, just as surely, would have found the charge very amusing. Whitefield "us'd indeed sometimes to pray for my Conversion, but never had the satisfaction of believing that his prayers were heard," Franklin recalled in his *Autobiography*. There, in that stiletto of quiet sarcasm, one can see the kind of man that Thomas Young might have been, had he been as worldly as Franklin and a touch less hopeful about the prospects for liberating his fellow human beings from their delusions.

Franklin's theological ironies multiplied up to a kind of climactic absurdity at the Constitutional Convention of 1787.[194] At a particularly tense moment in the debates, he piously proposed that the delegates should join together in a prayer to "the Father of Lights" in order to heal the rift. The proposal went down much better with twenty-first-century religious conservatives (who have hijacked the event to serve as evidence of America's Christian founding) than it did with the Convention delegates, who, as Franklin noted, "except for three or four persons, thought prayer unnecessary." In arguing for the prayer proposal, Franklin reasoned that if the Convention failed, "Mankind may hereafter, from this unfortunate Instance, despair of establishing Government by human wisdom." Which is to say, we should pray for divine intervention now so that people in the future will realize that they don't have to.

Franklin's contemporaries mostly understood that they were facing a mask. When they tried to lift it, however, they discovered only their own hopes and fears. The American diplomat and spy Hezekiah Ford, for example, came to Paris in 1779 "with the highest opinion of Dr. F__ as a Philosopher, a Statesman, and even the Pater Patriae," or so John Adams recorded in his *Diary*. But Ford swiftly concluded that the aging Father of Our Country "has very moderate Abilities. He knows nothing of Philosophy . . . He is an atheist, he don't believe in any future state." Even more fascinating than the opinions about Franklin that Adams projects onto Ford are the opinions Adams searches for in himself: "I believe it is too much to say that he is an atheist and that he don't believe in any future state: tho I am not certain. His hints, and his Squibs, sometimes go so far as to raise Suspicions: —and he never tells anybody I fancy that he believes a G[od], P[urgatory], or [future state]." Later that same year, joking with the Marquis François de Barbé-Marbois about Franklin's flagrant lack of interest in chapel services, Adams still can't get himself to accept what he himself appears to be saying. " 'No,' said I laughing," recorded Adams, " 'because Mr. Franklin had no—' I was going to say what I did not say, and will not say here. I stopped short, and laughed. 'No,' said Mr. Marbois; 'Mr. Franklin adores only great Nature, which has interested a great many people of both sexes in his favor.' 'Yes,' said I, laughing, 'all the atheists, deists, and libertines, as well as the philosophers and ladies, are in his train, —another Voltaire and Hume.' "[195]

AMONG THE REST of America's revolutionary deists, the tone varied yet the pattern was remarkably consistent. On the surface, they were all Newtonians; in logic, they were Lockeans; and in their practical conclusions they were—for the most part implicitly—Spinozists. Ethan Allen's *Oracles* of 1784, for example, follows the example of Franklin's *Dissertation* of 1726 with its opening bow to the God of Newton:

> When we consider our solar system, attracted by its fiery center, and moving in its several orbits with regular, majestic, and periodical revolutions; we are charmed at the prospect and contemplation of those worlds of motion, and adore the wisdom and the power by which they are attracted, and their velocity regulated and perpetuated.[196]

The Natural Man of Boston, too, launches his theological speculations into Newtonian space. The mind boggles, he says, as it contemplates the "almighty regulator" and "perpetual motor of the universe," whose most marvelous feat is to send into orbit around the sun "these immense bodies which we daily see."[197] Washington likewise spoke of his deity in the almost endless variety of euphemisms that grew up around the Newtonian vision: "Governor of the Universe," "Great Author of the Universe," "Grand Architect of the Universe," "Sovereign Dispenser of Life and Health," "Supreme Disposer of All Events," and the ever-handy "Supreme Being."[198] Tellingly, he almost entirely avoided the use of the word "God,"[199] and he deliberately edited out references to "Jesus." The astronomer David Rittenhouse invoked the same cosmic deity in his lectures on the infinite universe for the benefit of the American Philosophical Society in Philadelphia.[200] Perhaps the most lyrical rendition of the Newtonian chorus comes from Jefferson, writing to Adams almost a century after Franklin composed his first treatise:

I hold (without appeal to revelation) that when we take a view of the universe, in its parts general or particular, it is impossible for the human mind not to perceive and feel a conviction of design, consummate skill, and indefinite power in every atom of its composition . . . We see, too, evident proofs of the necessity of a superintending power to maintain the Universe in its course and order.[201]

Wherever the Newtonian vision in America extended beyond bland pieties, the Lockean substructure came into view. Paine, whose celebrations of the universal order could rank with Jefferson's, offers a restatement of the first step of the Locke-Spinoza proof remarkable for both its style and its adherence to the original logic:

Every man is an evidence to himself, that he did not make himself; neither could his father make himself, nor his grandfather, nor any of his race; neither could any tree, plant, or animal make itself; and it is the conviction arising from this evidence, that carries us on, as it were, by necessity, to the belief of a first cause eternally existing, of a nature totally different to any material existence we know of, and by the power of which all things exist, and this first cause man calls God.[202]

In the *Age of Reason*, incidentally, Paine admits to having consulted Spinoza's *Tractatus Theologico-Politicus* on one particular point of scriptural interpretation; but in fact the criticisms he offers of the Bible match those of Spinoza, chapter and verse, on dozens of points.[203] He could just as easily have picked up his proof of our knowledge of a God from his teachers in London, Martin and Ferguson.

The author of Ethan Allen's Bible, too, discovers his deity at the very same moment that he proves the universe to be eternal: "Eternal creation is the necessary result of [God's] eternal existence and activity."[204] The luxury of an extended volume on the subject allows him to lose himself further in the radical implications of this first step in the Lockean proof. Here, for example, is the Green Mountain version of Spinoza's distinction between transitive and immanent causes: "It is not good sense . . . to say that [God] is the first cause of all things; for if it was true, there would have been second third, fourth and fifth causes in the series."[205] God must therefore be a "self-existent cause." And here is the mountain man's take on the necessitarianism that ineluctably follows from such a line of argument: "We are authorized from reason to conclude, that the vast system of causes and effects are thus necessarily connected (speaking of the natural world only) and the whole regularly and necessarily dependent on a self-existent cause," he says.[206] (The parenthetical limitation to "the natural world only" strikes an interesting contrary note, worth pursuing in a moment.) The Natural Man chimes in with an emphatic (and unqualified) endorsement of necessitarianism in language reminiscent of Pope: "The Naturalist knows, that all things by the all-powerful directions of the all-wise Being are regulated so as they happen; consequently that nothing can happen otherwise than it happens, and that all what is, is good and perfect in his kind."[207]

The next, crucial reversal in the logic—from necessitarianism to the wormlike ignorance of humanity—follows just as surely in America as it does in Locke's rendition of Spinoza. "Canst thou find out the Almighty to *perfection?*" Paine asks. "No," he replies emphatically. The part of the universe that presents itself to us "is probably but a small display of that immensity of power and wisdom, by which millions of other worlds, to me invisible by their distance, were created and continue to exist."[208] Jefferson makes the point in a laconic way. Having committed himself to the existence of a supreme being, he says, "Of the nature of this Being we know nothing."[209] The author of Ethan Allen's Bible expands on the underlying inferences. "Should we attempt to trace the succession of causes of our dependence, they would exceed our comprehension," he reasons.[210] Borrowing the formula handed down from Aquinas, Spinoza, and Locke, he adds, "There is no medium between infinite and finite."[211] Thomas Young, writing under his own signature, repeats the point in his confession from November 1772: "I believe in one eternal God, whose being, wisdom, power, holiness, justice and beneficence are altogether inconceivable to such atoms of animated nature as are yourself and I."[212] Whether through questionable grammar or conscious intent, Young manages to compress this defining dialectic of deism in one word, "inconceivable," which could be taken to mean either "infinitely greater than anything one can imagine" or, simply, inconceivable.

From the logic of the Americans' anti-theology, there naturally followed a certain kind of "Providence." Like Newton himself, Providence was everywhere held high in revolutionary America. It introduced Franklin's life-story, it was firmly relied upon in the final paragraph of the Declaration of Independence, and it still peers out at us from the eye at the top of the pyramid on the back of the Great Seal. But Providence wasn't what it used to be. It is easy to forget that in the early colonial period, long before anyone foresaw a revolution, Providence in America really was something special. An old school minister like Cotton Mather—the fire-breather in whose house Franklin bumped his head at the age of eighteen—saw in every deformed squash and anomalous weather event an intervention from on high intended to supply eminently identifiable benefits to the chosen people of New England. America's revolutionary deists, on the other hand, came to think it absurd to suppose that Providence would stoop so low as to meddle in the vegetable gardens of a particular tribe.

The author of Ethan Allen's Bible explains well enough the logic underlying the change in perspective: "God displays his providence in the series of nature's operations. It is the want of a right understanding of the divine agency, which makes us imagine that the series of nature's operations, that fall under our notice, is the immediate exercise of God."[213] Freneau makes the same point in a panegyric "On the Uniformity and Perfection of Nature":

> Could she descend from that great plan
> To work unusual things for man
> To suit the insect of an hour—
> This would betray a want of power.[214]

The same, critical transformation of Providence is evident even in the least philosophical of America's revolutionary deists. Washington, for example, frequently pointed to specific events as signs of some higher interest in the course of human events, and he often indulged the sentiment that there is in history some higher power or "Hand" at work. America's General, however, was no Moses, still less a Reformation-theocrat along the lines of Oliver Cromwell. The events he celebrated, on closer inspection, turn out to violate only the laws of probability, not the laws of nature. No rivers part supernaturally before the chosen people of North America, no voices speak out of bushes, no visions appear in the night sky to guide the troops forward. Rather, bullets following the relevant physical laws improbably fail to hit their target; a fog descends unseasonably early, providing lucky cover for tactical maneuvers; and, in general, highly unlikely "concatenations" of causes somehow do the right people some amazing favors—though they sometimes work against us, too.

Washington's Providence, in short, accomplishes only those miracles that stand for our ignorance of the grand scheme within which we are placed. It—and it is very often an "it," not a "he"—is characteristically "inscrutable," and its "Hand" is always "Invisible." Its emotional resonance goes far beyond the inert and indifferent thing modern readers have learned to associate with nature; and yet Washington's God functions chiefly as a synonym for what the ancients called variously "chance," "fate," and "fortune," and what Spinoza's successors conceived as the soul of infinite nature.

Although America's revolutionary deists by and large refrained from pantheistic rhetoric, the radical tendency embedded within their deism isn't hard to see. "If we form in our imagination a compendious idea of the harmony of the universe, it is the same as calling God by the name of harmony," says the author of the *Oracles*, sounding almost like the mystical kind of pantheist.[215] He then embraces a view that Jefferson attributes to some early Christian sects: "Nature must have been *co-eval* with the eternity of God, and must necessarily remain to all duration *co-extensive* and *co-existent* with the divine nature."[216] If God and Nature are two sides of the same eternal coin, it is a very short step to the conclusion that God and Nature are simply two ways of talking about one thing. Yet that is a step that the author of the *Oracles* does not take—and that Allen himself, quite interestingly, explicitly refuses to take.

The Natural Man, on the other hand, shows no reluctance to follow the path all the way to the top of the mountain. "Reasoning in this manner," he sermonizes, we "will find that there can be no more but only one single individual . . . that it is impossible, that an infinite God can have equals, or that any thing can exist without or besides himself, as an infinity comprehends the whole, and every atom in the universe." In a newspaper confession under his own signature, Thomas Young uses similar language to announce that God is "infinite, eternal, and unchangeable" and imprinted "upon every atom of the universe." Citing a definition from "Rider's *Dictionary*," the Natural Man finally plants his flag on the rocky summit of pantheism: "Nature . . . though held by the ancients to be a cause distinct from the deity, is no other than God, the first cause of all things and the preserver and ruler of all the phenomena of nature."[217] Young's loyalty to Locke was never in doubt; and yet—assuming he was the Natural Man—he was undoubtedly a follower of Spinoza and Pope.

The Natural Man wasn't the only American scaling the peak. Here, for example, is Jefferson's confidant Freneau, in a poem on "the Constitution, or Frame of Nature":

> *Thou, nature's self art nature's God*
> *Through all expansion spread abroad,*
> *Existing in the eternal scheme*
> *Vast, undivided, and supreme*[218]

Some commentators, taking note of Freneau's undisguised pantheism, have assumed that it reflects some Romantic inspiration from the turn of the nineteenth century. In view of the manifest convergence between Freneau and Pope in both the letter and the substance of their speculations, such a theory seems unnecessary. Freneau himself declared that Pope's *Universal Prayer* "comprises the principles of all real Religion."[219]

SO WHERE EXACTLY should we draw the line between deism and pantheism, or between pantheism and atheism? The leaders of the French Enlightenment were convinced that a deist is just a dishonest atheist.[220] With respect to men such as Washington and Jefferson, however, the suggestion that the difference has to do with a deficit of integrity doesn't sound right. It might also be conjectured that deism, insofar as it identifies the order of things in this world with the order of God, is inherently conservative, while atheism is politically radical. The idea that the distinction maps easily into a different political orientation, however, also seems simplistic. Newton's own deism may have arisen as a conservative reaction to revolutionary pantheism, yet some Newtonian deists were radical revolutionaries (think of Paine); and politically conservative atheists were not unknown either (think of Hume or Cadwallader Colden).

A good place to look for answers, it turns out, may be the long-neglected pastures of Vermontese philosophy. In an *Appendix* to the *Oracles*, written in his own hand and published posthumously in 1873, Ethan Allen entertains the suggestion of pantheism and then explicitly refuses to endorse it. We must conceive of God to be "the author of nature, but not nature itself," he cautions, for "to suppose God is all things, would be to exclude his creation."[221] Allen's position here aligns him almost exactly with Jefferson. "The disciples of Ocellus, Timaeus, Spinosa, Diderot, and D'Holbach," says Jefferson, insist on the "eternal pre-existence of something" and identify that "something" with "the world"; whereas Jefferson himself, having observed the marvels of astronomy revealed by Newton, holds that "it is impossible for the human mind not to believe that there is . . . an ultimate cause, a fabricator of all things."[222]

We are therefore seemingly entitled to draw a firm line between the Natural Man and Ethan Allen (and Jefferson, for that matter). The first approvingly cites the claim that "nature . . . is no other than God"; the second insists that God is "the author of nature, but not nature itself." The Natural Man is therefore a pantheist; while Allen is quite clearly a "deist"—and so, too, is the author of the *Oracles*, at least insofar as we may judge the intention of his arguments as opposed to their consequences. If our concern is to establish the authorship of the *Oracles of Reason*, then this distinction between deism and pantheism has some clear utility. On the assumption that Thomas Young is the pantheistic Natural Man, it seems implausible that he could have been the author of the mostly deistic book that Ethan Allen put out under his own name.

Yet, if we set aside the somewhat trivial matter of who wrote Ethan Allen's book, what exactly does this difference between the two iconoclasts of the Green Mountains tell us? Who can doubt that, however we split the philological hairs between deist and pantheist, Allen and Young were fighting on the same side of every important battle? It remains just as plausible—arguably more so—that Allen acquired essentially all of his philosophical learning from Young. The eternity of the universe, the doctrine of necessitarianism, the unstated substance monism, the attribution of extension to the God of Nature, the very title of the book—where did these concepts and phrases that furnish the world of Ethan Allen's Bible come from if not from the erudition of his friend Young? And it remains just as certain that their philosophical radicalism was the foundation of the same revolutionary political project.

Credos and labels like "atheism," "pantheism," and "deism" are at best the starting points of discussion. They mean almost nothing without the far-ranging reasons, evidence, and assumptions on account of which they are held true. Even the existence of God is no exception to the rule that few things in life or philosophy are worth less than a concept or doctrine taken in isolation. Bruno, Vanini, and Spinoza unequivocally and emphatically proved the existence of God—and it didn't matter then and doesn't matter now. The history of ideas matters because ideas make actors out of human beings, and they make actors out of us precisely insofar as they occupy this open, uncontrollable, and inherently unlimited universe of explanations, not the stultifying dogma of a supposed conceptual scheme, not the inert, always epiphenomenal utterances we call doctrines or first principles.

Jefferson touches on this constellation of issues in a revealing response to Adams, who had written to him complaining of the school of atheistic materialism that had grown up in France—Diderot, Baron d'Holbach, and the fast crowd that gathered around them. In his calm reply, Jefferson deflects Adams's invitation to join him in bashing the French radicals— for the sage of Monticello is broadly sympathetic to them personally and philosophically—and instead offers a telling observation:

> [Atheism] was a numerous school in the Catholic countries, while the infidelity of the Protestant took generally the form of Theism. The former always insisted that it was a mere question of definition between them, the hypostasis of which on both sides was "Nature" or "the Universe."[223]

At first glance, Jefferson appears to draw a line between atheism and theism (which here means deism), or French radicalism and English moderation. Upon closer inspection, however, there is little to indicate that Jefferson does not in fact agree with the radicals that the difference between the two is at bottom a matter of definition and context. Jefferson's suggestion is fruitful: The deeper category is the "infidelity" that makes a God out of nature or the universe. French atheism and English deism are merely the ways in which this infidelity expresses itself in different circumstances.

If we ask where this "infidelity" comes from, we most likely will fall back on intuitions that are as ancient as civilization. If we want to know how and why it rose to gain control of the modern world, however, we can find a clue in its seemingly irreducible multiplicity—maybe even in its ability to modulate between deism and atheism. What was new in the philosophy of the early modern world was the rich and varied patina of moderation with which it presented itself. In the bundle of metaphors and apothegms with which they brought Nature's God to life, the philosophers of the early modern period translated the insights of ancient philosophy into a language that made it possible even for those who did not comprehend the program in its entirety to become the agents of history. If there is such a thing as a conceptual scheme, it should probably be reserved for this kind of competence without comprehension, or a thinking without thought. The crucial development in the history of ideas, then, was not an idea but a new kind of writing, one made possible by the printing press and made necessary by the emergence of a public sphere. In this respect, it was Locke, not Spinoza, who was the pivotal figure of the period. It was the strange, perhaps irresolvable duality of his work that allowed for the widespread dissemination of ideas that, presented in the raw, might easily have died in the obscurity of a village in Holland.

The real significance of the difference between Allen and Young is just this: that the ideas that best explain Allen's actions were in some cases not the ones that came out of his head. At the highest level of abstraction, where the broadest connections between thought and action are forged, the ideas that mattered for Allen were the ones that Young articulated. In this respect, the partnership between these homegrown philosophers may serve as a model for the relationship between the moderate Enlightenment and its radical core, between Locke and Spinoza, and between America's religiously conventional population and its heterodox revolutionary leadership.

THE EMOTIONAL CORE of America's revolutionary deism always remained where Franklin first discovered it: in the study of nature. "That which is now called natural philosophy, embracing the whole circle of science, is the study of the works of God and . . . is the true theology," said Paine. "As to the theology that is now studied in its place, it is the study of human opinions and of human fancies *concerning* God."[224] In the words of the philosopher of the Green Mountains, "The knowledge of nature is the revelation of God."[225] James Madison made the same point when, in an 1825 response to a theologian who had favored him with the kind of a priori proofs about God that were then in fashion, he gently pushed back in the language of Pope: "Whatever effect may be produced on some minds by the more abstract train of ideas which you so strongly support, it will probably always be found that the course of reasoning, from the effect to the cause, 'from nature to nature's God,' will be the more universal and persuasive application."[226]

On occasion, America's deists perhaps got carried away in their identification of piety with science. Jefferson's insistence that the species never go extinct—a claim that he thought followed from the plenitude of Nature God's creation—seems a case in point. On the whole, however, Jefferson and his fellow revolutionaries understood that true piety involves a commitment to the methods of science, not to any of its specific results. In rebutting a suggestion from Voltaire that moisture is bad for animal growth, for example, Jefferson announced, "The truth of this is inscrutable to us by reasonings *a priori*. Nature has hidden from us her *modus agendi*. Our only appeal on such questions is experience."[227] Even in the unfortunate instance of his theory of non-extinction, he hewed to the scientific spirit at least in principle, gathering troves of data against which to test the theory (although in practice he exhibited more than a small degree of that characteristically human tendency to cast the evidence of observation in the light that happens to be most favorable to one's preconceptions).

In an extraordinary piece of advice to his nephew Peter Carr, Jefferson makes clear the order of things and the nature of his kind of piety:

> Fix reason firmly in her seat, and call to her tribunal every fact, every opinion. Question with boldness even the existence of a god; because, if there be one, he must more approve of the homage of reason than that of blindfolded fear.[228]

The reversal of reason and God—one on the bench, the other on the dock—is the signature feature of Jefferson's thought, just as it is of the Enlightenment as a whole, just as it is of philosophy in general as it pursues its ancient mission to render the world intelligible.

The lyrical celebrations of God's astonishing benevolence and incomparable skill that adorn the writings of Jefferson and his fellow American deists, to be sure, are too numerous and too impassioned not to be taken seriously. They are more than shields designed to protect their bearers against accusations of atheism. But their sincerity should not distract from the fact that these are evocative rather than declarative utterances. Indeed, they are invariably couched as representations of a state of mind rather than pronouncements of doctrine. They are concerned with what "the mind prefers," as Madison puts it, or with what it cannot but "perceive and feel," as Jefferson says. Their real effect is to communicate the attitude one ought properly to adopt before the totality of things. The effusive tributes to the stupendous solar system and the bounty of the earth are really just a long way of expressing gratitude for an existence that we can neither fully comprehend nor deny. The piety shown to the eternal being of all beings, in the end, is just another name for the affirmation of being itself.

In Jefferson's first draft of the Declaration, as it happens, there was no "Creator." "All men are created equal & independent," reads the manuscript, and "from that equal creation they derive rights inherent & unalienable."[229] So we may discover our rights not in the commandments of a revealed authority but by observing the fact of our equality in nature. The revised version of the Declaration, according to which all men "are endowed by their Creator with certain unalienable rights," has given much joy to the many actors in American history who have wished to credit communications personally vouchsafed to them from above for the demands they seek to impose on those around them. Jefferson undoubtedly anticipated that the change in wording would have such an effect on some of his contemporaries and posterity. For him and his fellow revolutionary deists, however, the substitution cannot have had any great significance. In the infinite universe of Nature's God, "creation" and "Creator" refer to the same thing.

SOME WEEKS AFTER the surprising victory at Ticonderoga in May 1775, the good people of Bennington filled the pews of First Church to hear the Reverend Jedediah Dewey explain what it all meant. The heroes of the day, Ethan Allen and a number of his Green Mountain Boys, were there too, undoubtedly stretching themselves out in the back rows. The point of Parson Dewey's sermon, it soon became clear, was to ensure that all present understood that credit for the battlefield triumph belonged solely and exclusively to Almighty God. After the reverend put it all down to Providence for the third time, Allen couldn't take it any longer.

"Don't forget, Parson, that I was there!" he stood up and called out. "Sit down, thou bold blasphemer!" the reverend shouted back.[230]

But Allen never really did sit down. After the war, upon returning from his long imprisonment, he told the weary inhabitants of Vermont that the time had come for them to stand up and assume the freedom for which they had struggled over the previous years. Appropriately enough, he expressed the sentiment in words borrowed from one of the last things his great philosophical friend wrote. "This is the happy aera," said Allen, "which our worthy and deceased friend, Doctor Thomas Young, beautifully expressed himself to the inhabitants of the state of Vermont, in these words":

As the Supreme Arbiter of Right has smiled on the just cause of North America at large, you, in a peculiar manner, have been highly favored. God has done by you the best thing commonly done for our species. He has put it fairly in your power to help yourselves.[231]

This is the God of the Green Mountains, and it is the only God that survives through the baroque abstractions and double-sided intellectual maneuvers that characterize its progress through two and a half centuries of Enlightenment. America's natural-born rebels, marked from their earliest days as no great prospects for submission to authority, demanded a God they could revere, but not obey; a God of publicly promulgated laws, not of private and inscrutable acts; a God who could stand as an ideal, but who would never stand in the way. They wanted—and, in Nature's God, they found—a God who helps those who help themselves. Had they been reared on one of the many other inhabited planets of which they wrote so ecstatically, and acquired a language very different from that which passed through the texts of early modern philosophy, there is every reason to suppose that they might still have lavished great praise on their deity and then acted for all practical purposes as if it was nothing more than the force that drove them to become what they already were.

5

Self-Evident Truths

We hold these truths to be self-evident . . .

WHAT KIND OF STUFF ARE WE MADE OF? WHAT DOES IT mean to think, to know, and to desire? What happens to us after we die? The big questions about the human condition must have been on seventeen-year-old Ethan's mind when, on the day of his father's funeral, he went missing. According to family legend, the Allens first noticed the eldest son's absence as they gathered in the house following the burial of Joseph. After a frantic search, they found Ethan in the backyard, flailing his arms over the freshly dug grave, beseeching his dead father to come back and tell him whether there is life after death. His brothers grabbed hold of the sobbing giant and wrestled him back to the house. Joseph's sudden collapse forced young Ethan to trade in the dream of attending Yale for the muddy reality of managing a pig farm and his seven younger siblings. It also left him with a question about death that shadowed him for the rest of his years, even as he set off on a career that was almost profligate in creating opportunities for a violent end.[1]

In his philosophical speculations, Allen answered that question without equivocation. "There can be no rational doubt or disbelief," writes the author of the *Oracles*, "but that the God who made us, has constituted our souls, so that they will survive their bodies, and exist in such a manner, as is of all others the best for them."[2] According to legend, Allen once suggested that perhaps God's plan involved transmigration; in which case, he announced, he would return to earth as a white stallion roaming freely across his beloved Green Mountains.[3] The legend probably isn't true, but it is worth repeating because it does reflect something about his theological insouciance and perhaps about his character, too.[4] In Ethan Allen's world, the hereafter was always a brighter, shinier version of the here and now.

Yet the exuberant conviction of Allen's theological pronouncements never completely masked a grim awareness of the reality of death. In his thirty-two months as a prisoner of war, when disease and malnutrition pushed him close to the precipice, Allen was both defiant and somber in his attempts to grapple with philosophy's hardest task. "If a cruel death must inevitably be my portion, I would face it undaunted," he writes in the bestselling *Narrative* of his captivity published in 1779. "As death was the natural consequence of animal life to which the laws of nature subject mankind, to be timorous and uneasy as to the event and manner of it was inconsistent with the character of a philosopher or a soldier."[5] In the *Oracles*, incidentally, the language of life and death reads very much as if it came from the same pen: "The laws of the world in which we live, and the constitution of the animal nature of man, are all but one uniform arrangement of causes and effects; and as by the course of those laws, animal life is propagated and sustained for a season, so by the operation of the same laws, decay and mortality are the necessary consequences." And then again: "The period of life is very uncertain, and at the longest is but short; a few years bring us from infancy to manhood, a few more to dissolution; pain, sickness and death are necessary consequences of animal life."[6]

Intimations of mortality are sprinkled like teardrops throughout Ethan Allen's Bible, but they reach a peculiar intensity in a number of weirdly medicinal passages of the book. Consider, for example, this vivisection of the human body:

The nutrition extracted from food by the secret aptitudes of the digesting powers (by which mysterious operation it becomes incorporated with the circulating juices, supplying the animal functions with a vital heat, strength, and vigour) demands a constant flux and reflux of the particles of matter, which is perpetually incorporating with the body, and supplying the place of the superfluous particles, that are constantly discharging themselves by insensible perspiration; supporting, and at the same time, in its ultimate tendency, destroying animal life.[7]

At times, the author of the *Oracles* appears to draw his philosophical insights from what sounds like the personal experience of a clinician. For example:

A blow on the head, or fracture of the perecranium [*sic*], as also palsies and many other casualties that await our sensorium; retard and in some cases wholly prevent the exercise of reason.[8]

The "pericranium" is the lining of the skull. That Ethan Allen had a talent for thumping people upside it is beyond dispute. A more curious tale hangs on the fact that such an obtuse word should apparently have emerged out of his own such organ.

IN EACH OF the four colonies where he settled with his family, Thomas Young pursued three strangely overlapping career goals. The first was to organize his fellow citizens to resist imperial tyranny, as we know, and the second was to liberate them from the religion of their birth. His third job—the only one that paid money—was to practice medicine. Over time, Young added some august names to the roster of his patients. In Philadelphia, for example, he serviced John Adams and at least one other member of the Continental Congress.[9] But the bread and butter of his practice was always the mass of ordinary people, the same "Body" that he sought to free from political and religious oppression. Thomas Young was "the great Apollo of the ignorant."

On a typical working day, he would lug his bag of leeches and lancets from bedside to aching bedside. He would douse his fevered people with crushed millipedes served in wine to flush their kidneys, sal ammoniac (ammonium chloride) mixed in gruel to flush out everything else, and, as the circumstances demanded, horseradish. In properly indicated situations, he might drain his patients of a few ounces of their blood. Some of the cures he favored—such as calomel, that is, mercurous chloride, a neurotoxin now used as an insecticide—may today be judged unhelpful. Others—such as chamomile tea—are now thought to be mildly beneficial. What is certain is that in keeping with the cruelty of statistics and the realities about the medical practices of his time, Young watched a lot of people die.

For all his experience on the subject, Young did not take the death of his patients easily. In one instance, he insisted on accompanying one of his wards on a trip to the countryside for what proved to be a final journey. At the time, Young was at the hectic height of his involvement on the Boston Committee of Correspondence. But he was so distraught over the condition of his patient that he stuffed in his desk one of the many incoming letters to which he was assigned to respond, and forgot about it for several weeks. Of the many surviving outgoing letters from the Committee in Young's handwriting, the only one that bears his signature is the personal apology he belatedly wrote to the senders of the forgotten letter. On the other hand, there is no suggestion in that letter or any of Young's other writings that he harbored anything like the hope that Ethan Allen had for a free-ranging afterlife, equestrian or otherwise.

Young was serious about his medicine. A substantial part of his surviving writings consists in medical tracts published in various Boston and Philadelphia periodicals. Though the writings were undoubtedly intended in part as advertisements for his own services, they also show that he was a staunch advocate of what one could call health care reform. His ambitious agenda was to make a science out of the theory of medicine and to make a profession out of its practice. At the time, it should be remembered, medical remedies were routinely tested only against what was written in ancient textbooks, and barbers could make themselves surgeons with the simple expedient of cutting off their clients' limbs. Young proposed the establishment of a "College of Physicians" in Boston, where the doctors of the future might receive formal training and professional credentials. He also advocated the creation of a public library for "Anatomy, Surgery, Midwifery, and Medicine," where the knowledge of medicine might accumulate and be made available to all.

In the theoretical part of his medical oeuvre, Young presents a bracingly physico-mechanical vision of the human body. The human being, he says, is a "pneumatico-hydraulic engine," "a material system . . . subject to the laws of nature." It is a complex of "hard, soft, and liquid elements," and its chief business is to engage in a constant flux and reflux of "particles of matter."[10] Fever is a great "foe to human happiness," and its conquest involves gaining control over the ingestion and expurgation of these particle flows. In agreement with many of the medical authorities of the time, Young seems to have supposed that the cure to what ails us has to do mostly with the exit strategy. So, in his practice, he relied heavily on the prescription of emetics, diuretics, laxatives, and anything else that might return particles from within the body to the outside.

The fluxes and refluxes of particles in Young's medicinal writings are pretty much the same as those that feature in Ethan Allen's Bible. And so it was perhaps unavoidable that, in his inflammatory article of 1937, the scholar George Pomeroy Anderson should have cited the medicinal passages in Allen's work as conclusive evidence that Thomas Young was its principal author.[11] As a matter of fact, it is eminently plausible to suppose that the medical knowledge reproduced in Allen's book originated in Young's pericranium. But that is not quite the same as claiming that Allen did not write his own book.

THOMAS YOUNG'S combination of medicine with political radicalism and religious heterodoxy may seem like just another idiosyncrasy of biography, and the presence of the same trifecta of agendas in Ethan Allen's Bible must therefore appear, as it did to Anderson, like a bright red flag over the question of its authorship. But the interesting fact is that Young and Allen were not at all alone in this triple treat of revolutionary enthusiasms. On the contrary, their medico-politico-theological activism marks them as members of a multifaceted movement that swept across the civilized world over the course of several centuries.

Today, thanks to the thrilling exploits of Galileo and Newton, we tend to think of the scientific revolution as an astronomical event. But in the eyes of many observers at the time, the story of science had at least as much to do with a new approach to the body. And there was always something religiously suspect about those people who sought to probe the sacred territory of the human frame. Hippocrates himself was a notoriously vocal challenger of the religious superstitions of his time. In the Middle Ages, a common saying had it that "where there are three doctors, there are two atheists."[12] In early modern times, the proportions may have seemed even more alarming.[13]

Descartes, for example, thought of himself as a "natural philosopher," but he probably spent less time meditating on metaphysics than he did dissecting animal cadavers sent over from the local butcher. "The spirit [is] so thoroughly dependent on the temperament and disposition of the organs of the body," he explained, "that, if it is possible to find some means which will in general render men wiser and more skillful than they have hitherto been . . . it is in medicine that one must seek it out."[14] Descartes was hardly the only doctor residing in Holland in its century of philosophical glory. The most unwritten-about man of distinction of the Dutch Enlightenment must surely be the part-time medicine man Franciscus van den Enden (1602–1674)—the freethinking, free-loving buccaneer of early modern philosophy who took on the young Spinoza as a pupil and quite possibly taught him much of what he knew about God and Nature.[15] Another philosophico-medical Dutchman was Lodewijk Meyer (1629–1681), the author of an anonymously published and promptly banned book arguing for a philosophical interpretation of the Bible, as well as author of an informative preface to Spinoza's first work, *Principles of the Cartesian Philosophy*. Perhaps the most famous of the Dutch doctors was Herman Boerhaave (1668–1738), whose immense contributions to medicine took second

place in the public eye only to the charges against him for philosophical and religious felonies.

English medicine, too, seemed compromised by the heresies
of the age. John Locke, for example, was in the first place a doctor.
Indeed, he won the first Earl of Shaftesbury's undying patronage not
by relieving him of philosophical misconceptions but by fitting him
with a pipe to drain an abscess in his liver. Franklin's philosophical
coming-of-age in London involved enough irreligious doctors to staff
a small clinic in hell. Ben's crypto-Spinozist *Dissertation* won him the
favor of a Dr. Lyons, who was himself the author of some racy philosophical material. Lyons put his arm around the budding infidel and
marched him over to the Ale-House in Cheapside, where they joined
the medico-philosophical circle around Bernard Mandeville (1670–
1733), the Dutch-born physician and fellow student of Boerhaave at
Leiden who promoted a mechanico-Cartesian view of the body[16] and
achieved notoriety in England as the author of *The Fable of the Bees*, in
which he argued that "private vices" produce "publick benefits" and
established himself as a pioneer in the field of economics. Ben found
the much-decried champion of vice to be "a most facetious and entertaining companion." Lyons and his sidekick next sidled over to Batson's
Coffee House, where Ben made the acquaintance of Dr. Pemberton, a
friend of Isaac Newton.

The American homeland proved no exception to the rule about
forward-thinking doctors. At an inn outside Philadelphia, Ben fell
into the company of an "itinerant Doctor," a "sociable," "friendly," and
"ingenious" man, "but much of an Unbeliever" who later "undertook
. . . to travesty the Bible in doggerel verse."[17] The young John Adams
first learned of the heresy of the infinite universe, as we know, from a
freethinking doctor in Boston. The popular suspicion that the nation's
doctors were lacking in piety was so widespread that in 1824 a Dr.
Charles Caldwell thought it necessary to issue a *Defence of the Medical
Profession against the Charge of Infidelity and Irreligion*.[18]

It seemed equally obvious to observers at the time that the new
medicine men tended to be just as advanced in their politics as they
were in their religion. Van den Enden, for example, died on the scaf-

fold in Paris in 1674 after attempting to lead a rebellion that, had it succeeded in realizing the plan he had laid out for it, would have made the northern region of France the first liberal democracy in the modern world. A century later, when crowds at the Bastille finally picked up where Van den Enden left off, doctors such as Jean-Paul Marat played starring roles in their country's Revolution.[19] In America, Benjamin Rush maintained that the "physician who is not a Republican holds principles that call into question his knowledge of the principles of medicine." Historian Pauline Maier reports that twenty-two doctors served on the Massachusetts Provincial Congress of 1774–1775; eleven died at Bunker Hill; five signed the Declaration of Independence; and as many as twelve thousand were involved on the American side of the Revolutionary War. Doctors, adds Maier, "more than any other profession leaned toward Jeffersonian ideas."[20]

It isn't hard to see that at the bottom of the revolutionary medicine of the early modern world lay a new philosophy of the body. And it isn't much of a stretch to suppose that the troubling aspect of this new philosophy of the body was in reality its corresponding philosophy of the mind. Clearly, there was something in the new way of thinking about the human condition that challenged many of the ideas that human beings have long cherished about themselves and their special place in nature. This new and radical philosophy of mind was in fact the vehicle that turned radical medicine into a fellow traveler with revolutionary politics and heterodox religion. It eventually made possible dramatic improvements in health care, of which all human beings now alive are the beneficiaries. But the curious fact is that it changed the world long before it managed to cure any great number of people suffering from disease.

THE RELIGION that comes before every popular religion tells us that we humans are made of some very special stuff, something intangible, indivisible, immaterial, and alive, unlike anything else in nature. Only the idea that each and every one of us has a "soul" or something like it makes it possible to imagine that we persist over time as the responsible subjects of moral action; that we are all of equal worth; and that we may be the object of divine concern—or so the story goes. The common view further insists that the special thing about the human soul is that it has a mind. To have a conscious mind, the thinking goes, is to enjoy a certain kind of experience; it is what it feels like to be me, or you, or a bat, or a girl named Mary; it is the privilege of existing in a certain kind of space, unlike space, filled with objects, unlike objects, that we call thoughts or ideas. Above all, it means that we have a kind of absolute freedom, especially in matters of belief, for the mind is what we know best of all things. The article that precedes every article of faith is that we may choose what we wish to believe without reason or cause. To be a believer, according to the common sense of the matter, is nothing other than to take a leap of faith that Jesus is the Christ or that Allah is God.

A common view today says that this universal belief in human exceptionalism is also the foundation of modern liberal democracy. The "ego"—that is, the "subject" or "autonomous individual"—of liberal modernity was the invention of western philosophers such as Descartes and Locke, or maybe it was Immanuel Kant, say many erudite commentators today. Some go on to enthuse that this newly fabricated self-mind of modernity is a good thing, a necessary preliminary to respecting human rights in a liberal world.[21] Others inveigh that it is a bad thing, a selfish delusion of the selfish Enlightenment: modernity's very own original sin.[22] On either side of that debate, the reigning narrative takes for granted that the belief in the special nature of human existence is the foundation of civilization, while doubts about it are of recent origin and quite edgy, the result of late-breaking developments in twenty-first-century neurosciences.

Yet the common view gets the actual history of ideas almost exactly backward. In fact, the definitive teaching of the radical philosophy that revolutionized the early modern world is that the human being is a part of nature, no less subject to its laws than everything else in the infinite universe. This philosophy directly challenges the common ideas about ideas themselves, about the self, and about the nature of human freedom. It says that we often know our minds least of all things, that we have no choice but to believe what we understand, and that we are free only when we act with, not without, reason. Its greatest historical accomplishment was the "naturalization"—or, better, "euthanasia"—of the soul.[23]

America's founding philosophers, moreover, were functionally committed to this revolution of the mind not only in their medicine but also in the execution of their political project. Contrary to the conventional wisdom, the modern liberal order remains grounded in humanity's ability to overcome its all-too-human convictions about itself. Human beings have made themselves special by learning how to act on the understanding that they are not special at all. Though many people living within liberal societies persist in imagining otherwise (and quite a number of contemporary philosophers of mind appear to be determined to encourage them in their delusions), history has already resolved the big questions in the philosophy of mind. Modernity exists because the soul does not.

IDEAS

According to the common view, ideas are immaterial things, a species of mental images, like paintings in a ghostly art gallery. The mind, like a visitor to the gallery, has the power to choose which of these tenebrous visions it will regard as true. Consciousness, according to this picture-theory, is a feeling or a state of being, a generalized awareness that precedes the awareness of the immaterial representations with which it concerns itself. You either have it or you don't; you are in the gallery, or you are knocked out. This gallery of the mind, according to the common view, also happens to be a very private one. Our ideas come out of our heads only in the shape of words or signs; our words often fall short of our ideas; other people's words often fall even shorter of theirs, all too often with nefarious intent; and this common experience of misdirection and miscommunication confirms us in the view that ideas themselves are essentially secret things, spectral entities that subsist only in the moist interior of the pericranial gallery.

The picture-theory of consciousness is not without some insight and merit for the everyday purposes of human existence. We have all learned what it means to weigh the evidence in favor of one view of things or another, to keep our deliberations private, to withhold judgment where appropriate, and to take a "leap of faith" when necessary. We are all experts in the art of stepping back, as it were, and discovering the "I" that lurks behind every "I." At the same time, the common view, pushed beyond the bounds of its limited utility, gives rise to some obvious paradoxes. If consciousness is a binary, take-it-or-leave-it kind of thing, then how do we account for the borderline cases of animals, sleepers, dreamers, drunkards, children, the demented, and those suffering from brain injuries or afflictions? One can even question whether the picture-theory offers an account of consciousness at all. It explains the mind by positing a mind within the mind; but, in that case, the question goes begging, how do we explain the mind within the mind? In what does the consciousness of the visitor to the gallery of the mind consist?

The most important and paradoxical consequence of the picture-theory of mind is its (often unstated) theory of knowledge. If consciousness is a feeling, then knowledge, it seems natural to suppose, is something that happens after consciousness. It results from some operation of the will, according to which Mary attaches the qualifier of "true" to some subset of those representations that have already made their way into the gallery of the mind. So Mary can choose what she wishes to believe just as she may choose what she wants for breakfast. The picture-theory of consciousness is also, therefore, as a direct consequence of this implicit theory of knowledge, beset with a kind of absolute skepticism. How can Mary know that what she knows is true? Since she can never step outside the private gallery of her thoughts, her cherished claims to knowledge boil down to mere acts of faith. She could be wrong about everything. The common conception of religion really begins here, with an absolute skepticism that seems to beg for an unqualified leap of faith—and it is precisely for this reason that the radical philosophers of the early modern world set out to destroy the picture-theory of consciousness.

The radical philosophy of mind properly begins, as always, with the guiding principle of philosophy—the mind, whatever it is, must be explicable—and can be traced back to Epicurus. "Since we perceive that the eggs of birds change into live chicks . . . it is evident that the sensible can be produced from the insensible," says Lucretius.[24] Chicks continued to hatch from eggs in the work of every radical philosopher from Galileo to Anthony Collins, both as a quiet homage to Lucretius and as a reminder of an unmet challenge to the common conception of mind. Hobbes in particular offered an aggressive reprise of the Epicurean vision. "Spirit," if it means anything at all, he said, "is either a subtle, fluid, and invisible body, or a ghost, or other idol or phantasm of the imagination."[25] "Substance incorporeal" is therefore a contradiction in terms, akin to "incorporeal body." As many sensed at the time, however, Hobbes, like Epicurus before him, did not so much solve the problem of mind as decapitate it.[26]

The radical philosophy of mind turned in a dramatically new direction with an insight first glimpsed in the work of a philosopher who pretended very hard to be looking the other way (and who has since been grossly misinterpreted on the point): Descartes. The intuition that guides Descartes's philosophy of mind, expressed in the roughest terms, is that there is something odd about thought—something that makes it altogether different from images. This peculiarity of thought comes into view as we chase the position of the absolute skeptic to its terminus. I may doubt the veracity of anything I perceive; I may even imagine that a malign demon is manipulating my sensations to conjure an imaginary world outside; but I cannot doubt that all the while I am thinking. Hence the most repeated catchphrase in the history of philosophy: "I think therefore I am." Descartes immediately leaps to a set of implausible inferences from this proposition concerning the nature of the 'I' that thinks—about which more in a moment. But the most interesting implications of the thesis have to do not with the idea of the "ego" but with the idea of ideas Descartes proposes, for what Descartes discovered is not a feature of the mind but a feature of the world.

Phrased in general terms, Descartes's insight is that every thought of any particular thing, whether real or not, comes accompanied with the thought of that thought; or, every consciousness is attended by self-consciousness. A thought "counts as thought *because* we are aware of it," Descartes says.[27] It is this reflexive quality of thought that makes it different from the idea of matter in a very deep way. Beliefs, desires, intentions, and every other act that we associate with thought come with this strange thinking of thinking; whereas flowers and neurons do not. Nor, for that matter, do pictures or words—which are not thoughts but only extended things that we take to stand for thoughts. As Descartes puts it, the faculty of "imagination," whereby we picture objects to ourselves, is not the same thing as "the understanding," for "we can . . . make sense of *thought* without bringing in imagination."[28]

The other side of Descartes's intuition—the side that Descartes himself tries hard not to see—has to do with the converse of this claim about the inherently reflexive nature of thought. Just as there is no object of consciousness without consciousness, we could say there is no consciousness without an object. The common view supposes that consciousness is a jar and ideas are its marbles, and that the one may go on without the other. But the radical view says, in effect, that there is no jar at all: the mind is in the marbles. The intuition is an ancient one, and may be detected in the work of, among others, the Pre-Socratic philosopher Parmenides: "Thinking and the thought that it is are the same; for you will not find thought apart from what it is, in relation to which it is uttered."[29] In the potted histories of philosophy that fill the bookstores today, Hume is usually given credit for the insight. "When I enter most intimately into what I call myself, I always stumble upon some particular perception or other, of heat or cold, light or shade, love or hatred, pain or pleasure. I never can catch myself at any time without a perception," Hume famously observed.[30] But in the actual sequence of events, it was Descartes who revived the basic idea in the modern world, and Spinoza who first built a system around it.

Spinoza's philosophy of mind begins with Descartes's intuition about the reflexive nature of thought. In his *Principles of the Cartesian Philosophy*, Spinoza agrees with Descartes that every idea necessarily involves the "form" of the idea, "through the immediate perception of which I am conscious of that same thought."[31] An idea, Spinoza emphasizes, is not a "dumb picture on a tablet"—for indeed a picture, like any other extended object, lacks the crucial feature of reflexivity.[32] Truth and certainty, according to this view, are not states of mind but features intrinsic and specific to the ideas themselves.[33] Every idea, in other words, comes with its own internal measure of truth. Ideas are acts of understanding, one could also say, and our representations do not precede knowledge but presume it. In his radical moments, Descartes hints at this position when he argues that our ideas, insofar as they are clear and distinct, have a kind of "self-evident" character that makes them necessarily true. Spinoza formalizes the doctrine thus: "The way in which we become aware of the formal essence is certainty itself."[34]

It follows from the nature of ideas, Spinoza adds, that "he who has a true idea knows at the same time that he has a true idea, and cannot doubt its truth."[35] "A true idea involves the highest certainty," he continues; "nor can anyone doubt this unless he thinks that an idea is something mute, like a painting on a tablet, and not a mode of thought—not the understanding itself."[36] As if to soothe Mary's doubts, he concludes, "In order to know, I need not know that I know"; and, conversely, "in order to know that I know, it is necessary that I must first know."[37] More compactly, "truth is its own standard."[38] The underlying intuition here—that there is something primitive about truth; or that without truth our consciousness never gets off the ground—is again an ancient one, and it is already present in a certain form in Epicurus. "The concept of truth begins in the senses," Lucretius says. "The senses cannot be refuted."[39] Like Spinoza, he insists that it is necessary first to know something before we can doubt that we know it.

Locke often wobbles around the meaning of key terms, yet his contribution to humanity in this instance, as in his theology, is chiefly to have made the insights of his Franco-Dutch mentors available to the Anglo-American world. "I see no reason to believe, that the Soul thinks before the Senses have furnish'd it with Ideas to think on," he says, thus rejecting the common conception that consciousness precedes its objects.[40] Then he dutifully endorses the converse: it is "impossible for anyone to perceive, without perceiving that he does perceive."[41] Most importantly, Locke traces the origin of our knowledge to the reflexive feature of ideas: knowledge "consists in the perception of the agreement or disagreement of ideas"[42] and is thus "an internal perception of the mind."[43] The critical upshot is that Locke's theory of knowledge, like Spinoza's, is at bottom an epistemology of certainty, not of doubt. "With me," says Locke, "to know, and to be certain, is the same thing; what I know, that I am certain of; and what I am certain of, that I know."[44] This much follows, he says, from the claim that knowledge consists in an "internal perception" of the mind. "He that demands a greater certainty than this demands he knows not what."[45]

The radical philosophy of ideas that Spinoza and Locke share has some extraordinarily counterintuitive implications, most of which are drawn into the light in the work of the former just as they largely swept under the shaggy prose in the work of the latter. It implies, for example, that we cannot explain consciousness except in terms of what we are conscious of—for to be conscious is nothing other than to be conscious of the weather, the social dynamics in a classroom, trout-fishing, the history of art, and the objects of each and every scientific theory. It in turn implies that to explain consciousness fully it is necessary first to explain the world in its entirety, which in turn tells us why the attempt to supply a theory of consciousness per se is an errand for misguided philosophers. It leads to the seeming paradox that ideas are "in" the world—or "in Nature" or "in God," Spinoza would say—not in our minds;[46] which is to say, that our explanations of ourselves, all our cherished experiences of this or that time of day, our memories of last night's dinner, and our theories about the future of the universe and our place within it, all consist of ideas that explain one piece of the universe through another, while what we grandly call our conscious mind is just the string we tie around the bundle of ideas that makes each of us what we distinctly are.[47]

These radical ideas about ideas of the early modern philosophers enter into a seemingly speculative terrain where not many people then or since have ventured, and so our first inclination may well be to set them aside. And yet, as in the case of Nature's God, while peering through the gaps of the common consciousness of things, radical philosophy arrives at critical insights that could be and were formulated in such a manner as to preserve its revolutionary force even among those who did not necessarily grasp all of its implications. We can begin to glimpse the critical payoff for the founders of the American Republic by turning the radical spotlight on certain common misconceptions about the nature of "willing," "believing," and "doubting."

THE PICTURE-THEORY of consciousness confirms the notion that we possess a faculty of will that stands apart from consciousness and is involved in the affirmation or negation of ideas. "Those who confound a word with an idea, or with the affirmation which an idea involves, think they can oppose their will against that which they perceive," Spinoza observes.[48] The tendency is particularly acute with respect to abstract ideas, or ideas of ideas: "Those who think that ideas consist in images formed in us by the concurrence of bodies, persuade themselves that those ideas of things of which we can form no similar images are not ideas, but only fictions which we form to ourselves by the decision of a free will."

According to the radical view that begins with Descartes, on the other hand, affirmation and negation are intrinsic to ideas themselves.[49] The idea that the sun is hot affirms heat of the sun, says Spinoza; the idea of a winged biped affirms that some bipeds have wings; and the idea of anything in general affirms that the thing has a certain essence. Ideas are not merely propositional contents, one could say; they are judgments. In more general terms, the point is that ideas are intrinsically belief-like, and that consciousness necessarily takes the form of these belief-like ideas. Thus, concludes Spinoza, there is no faculty of will that roams the mind and pastes the label of truth on its favorite ideas. Rather, the will pertains to ideas in the way that stoniness belongs to stones: "In the mind there is no absolute faculty of willing and not willing, but only of particular volitions, namely, this or that affirmation, or this or that negation."[50] We do suspend our belief in some ideas, in a manner of speaking, Spinoza allows. But what this really means is that we affirm some other idea—namely, that the first idea is uncertain. Consciousness is not a neutral space. There are only thoughts against other thoughts. All consciousness is action.

From this radical position it follows that our beliefs are involuntary in an important sense. We no more choose to see what we know to be true than a mathematician chooses to make 2 + 2 equal 4, for to understand the idea is nothing other than to explain why it is true.[51] We can believe only what we may explain to ourselves to be true; and if we cannot explain it, we do not believe it, for the simple reason that there is nothing there to believe in the first place. All of which follows, at a certain level of abstraction, from the guiding principle of philosophy. Expressed in a formula, the crucial result is just this: belief is a matter of evidence, not choice.

In the conventional narratives of the history of philosophy, Hume is the name most commonly associated with the radical conception of the connection between willing and believing. Yet in the actual history, Spinoza was the first to articulate it clearly, and Locke is the one who deserves credit for making it public in an acceptable way.[52] "The power of choosing" does not operate over "the power of thinking," says Locke in his exegesis of the word from Spinoza.[53] "Our will hath no power to determine the knowledge of the mind one way or the other; that is done only by the objects themselves."[54] Thus, "to believe this or that to be true, does not depend on our will."[55]

America's revolutionary deists did not always follow the many twists and turns of the radical theory of consciousness of the preceding two centuries, but they gathered the essentials, including in particular the radical doctrine on the connection between willing and believing. "There is no such thing as voluntary error," Franklin informs the Philadelphia public in 1735.[56] William Livingston repeats the message for the benefit of New York readers in his *Independent Reflector* of 1752 (which hews closely to Trenchard and Gordon's *Independent Whig* on the point).[57] In 1784 Ethan Allen picks up the radical baton: "Faith necessarily results from reasoning, forcing itself upon our minds by the evidence of truth, or the mistaken apprehension of it."[58] The same insight informs the work of the forlorn Elihu Palmer, America's first and last formal preacher of deism, who avers in his 1801 classic, *The Principles of Nature*, "Faith is the assent of the mind to the truth of a proposition supported by evidence . . . if the evidence be insufficient, belief becomes impossible."[59] It features again in the verses of Philip Freneau, in an 1815 poem "Belief and Unbelief," which is "Humbly Recommended to the Serious Consideration of Creed Makers":

> *In evidence, belief is found;*
> *Without it, none are fairly bound.*[60]

Paine draws the conclusion with customary panache: "Infidelity does not consist in believing, or in disbelieving; it consists in professing to believe what [one] does not believe."[61]

THE OTHER, cutting edge of the radical philosophy of ideas has to do with the nature of the doubt or skepticism it invites, for there is a certain kind of skepticism that follows from the radical position—but it differs fundamentally from the absolute skepticism associated with the common, picture-theory of consciousness. Absolute skepticism begins with the worry that we may be conscious of something that is not there, like a hallucination conjured by some demon. The kind of healthy skepticism favored by radicals since Epicurus, on the other hand, says that our troubles arise from the fact that we are often *not* conscious of something that is there. We humans routinely overestimate our intellectual accomplishments, mistake chains of unconnected facts for wisdom, and demonstrate an eagerness to affirm a welter of inconsistent and contradictory views because we are simply not conscious of that which we don't understand.[62]

In more technical terms, according to the radicals, a false idea is not one without an object, as the picture-theory supposes; rather, it is at bottom one composed of two or more ideas that are not clearly distinguished from one another. It now turns out that a good deal of our knowledge is confused in this way. In order to explain why this is so, Spinoza in effect undertakes to reconstruct the sources of those ideas that are "in Nature" insofar as they are explicated through the nature of the mind—which is to say, in plainer language, all of *our* ideas about the world.

Here Spinoza makes (or rather repeats in the new, Cartesian language) the defining move of the radical empiricism inaugurated by the ancient atomists. He asserts that the ideas about the world to which the mind has access are just "the ideas of the affections of a particular body." That is, we feel a body, our particular body, to be modified in a certain way, and all of our ideas about the world (including our ideas about ourselves) begin with these ideas of the modifications of the body. Thus, in a manner of speaking, our knowledge of the world begins with experience, and this experience is sensory. We know of external objects,[63] of our very own bodies,[64] and even of the mind itself[65] only through these ideas of the affections of the body.

The essential twist, suggested by Descartes and developed by Spinoza, is that these Epicurean sensations belong to the understanding not as things but as ideas, that is, not as mere affections of the body (or what some philosophers today call "sense qualia") but as inherently reflexive ideas of those affections. To perceive something is already to perceive a cause for our experience in the world, which is to have an idea. (When we see a desk, for example, we don't see a collection of sense data but an explanation for such a collection.) Precisely because they are ideas, moreover, the ideas of perception come with an intrinsic duality. We can think of them as representing objects in space, or we can think of them as ideas of those objects. In the first instance we may call them ideas of "sensation," and in the second instance of "reflection." The first corresponds to the attribute of substance that Spinoza calls extension, the second to the attribute of thought. These two forms of perception, Spinoza adds, exhaust the means of access to knowledge of which we are aware. Thus, all of our knowledge of the world arises from sensation and reflection, which is to say, more generally, that it all arises from experience conceived through one or the other attribute of substance.

The catch is that, however far our reflections multiply our ideas about the world, they never quite free themselves from their beginnings in the ideas of the affections of the body. We can attempt to move closer to the world, in a manner of speaking, by considering the sense organs of our own bodies as external objects, thereby attempting to understand the causes through which they operate and the nature of their interaction with the thing that modifies them. But then the regress continues, for we know our sense organs in the same way we know everything else, through modifications of the body. From this it follows that our perceptions of external things always involve two ideas that we can never completely distinguish from one another—the idea of the thing and the idea of our own body. Therefore, our knowledge of particular things in the world—and by extension of our very own bodies and minds—is always confused to some degree. Spinoza's emphatic conclusion is worth reciting:

> I say expressly that the mind does not have an adequate knowledge but only a confused and fragmentary knowledge, of itself, its own body, and external bodies whenever it perceives things from the common order of nature, that is, whenever it is determined externally.[66]

Perhaps the most powerful and influential statement of Locke's fundamental purpose in his *Essay concerning Human Understanding* is to be found in an elegant passage that, in effect if not intention, amounts to a paraphrase of Spinoza's theory of knowledge to this point:

> How comes [the mind] to be furnished? Whence comes it by that vast store, which the busy and boundless fancy of man has painted on it with an almost endless variety? Whence has it all the materials of reason and knowledge? To this I answer, in one word, from Experience . . . Our observation, employed either about external sensible objects, or about the internal operations of our minds, perceived and reflected upon by ourselves, is that which supplies our understanding with all the materials of thinking.[67]

Probably the most famous slogan from Locke's *Essay* is: "All ideas come from sensation or reflection."[68] Though he tries to avoid the jargon of his continental mentor, at times Locke just can't help himself, as when he writes that "all our ideas stem from two originals, that of extension etc on the one hand and that of thought on the other."[69] The implications, in any case, are pure Spinoza: "We want perfect and adequate ideas of those very bodies which are nearest to us, and most under our command";[70] "We know not wherein thinking consists";[71] "Our ignorance is infinitely larger than our knowledge."[72]

Among America's revolutionary philosophers, Locke's paraphrase of Spinoza's doctrine about sensation and reflection became commonplace, as did the healthy skepticism with which it is associated. In his *Dissertation* of 1726, Franklin articulates the basic idea in a rough and ready way: "All our Ideas are first admitted by the Senses and imprinted on the Brain, increasing in Number by Observation and Experience; there they become the subjects of the Soul's Action."[73] Ethan Allen in 1784 repeats the point in clunkier terms: "Human nature is compounded of sensation and reflection."[74] Jefferson is so tilted in favor of a purely Epicurean (or Hobbesian) materialism that in an 1820 letter to Adams he drops reflection from the equation altogether, even as he arrives at a robust statement of healthy skepticism: "On the basis of sensation, of matter and motion, we may erect the fabric of all the certainties we can have or need . . . When once we quit the basis of sensation, all is in the wind."[75]

THE RADICAL IDEAS about ideas have an immediate target, and they hit it with devastating force. That target is the very idea of revealed religion. The conventional wisdom tells us that religious faith begins with certainty and that the Enlightenment undermines it through doubt. In reality, faith begins with doubt and the Enlightenment demolishes it through certainty. Among the first to grasp this fact were the theologians of the seventeenth century. In his fiery response to Locke's *Essay*, Lord Stillingfleet, the bishop of Worcester, warns darkly that the proposition that "certainty consists in the perception of the agreement or disagreement of two ideas . . . may be of dangerous consequence to that article of Christian faith which he [Locke] has endeavoured to defend." Indeed, Stillingfleet inveighs, "This new method of certainty" destroys "the certainty of faith."[76]

The problem goes back to the fact that the very notion of "revealed" knowledge rests on the picture-theory of consciousness. Choose to believe the picture handed down to the mind from a supernatural source, says the religious consciousness, and you will be saved. More abstractly, one could say that the very possibility of revealed knowledge depends on the supposition that the content of an idea is entirely separate from the reasons we supply for holding it true. But this is precisely what the radical philosophers deny. There is no ultimate distinction to be drawn between our representations on the one hand and our reasons for holding them true on the other, the radicals say. From this it follows that revelation—a species of representations that we have no reason to hold true apart from our desire to believe in their truth—is not a form of knowledge or consciousness or belief at all. It is simply the sign of a desire that must always be explicable through some other ideas. It belongs by its very nature to a mind that does not know itself and cannot be acting freely.

The critique of revelation that emerges from the epistemology of certainty acquires its sharpest edge when applied to miracles. Bruno, Galileo, and especially Vanini offer trenchant versions of the critique of miracles, and Spinoza's role is once again to formalize what came before:

> Whatever we clearly and distinctly understand must become known to us either through itself or through some other thing that is clearly and distinctly understood through itself. Therefore from a miracle, or an event that surpasses our understanding, we can understand nothing.[77]

Alleged stories about miracles, the radical philosophers maintain, are nonetheless intelligible in a certain way—namely, as expressions of the limitations of the understanding of the people who believe in them. Bruno, Vanini, and Hobbes all make this point, and Spinoza summarizes it in a pithy way. "Miracles can be understood only in relation to human opinions," he says, "and refer merely to events whose natural cause we (or at any rate the writer or narrator of the miracle) cannot understand by a reference to any ordinary occurrence."[78] Miracles, then, are not a distinct class of events in the world, with a distinct ontological status, but rather a class of stories, possibly useful for ulterior purposes, that are essentially defined by a particular perspective—namely, the perspective of the relatively ignorant people who believe in them. They reduce to a representation of some other truth—hopefully, an instructive moral truth—in a language suited to the incomplete understanding of their audience.

Locke's published comments on miracles are characteristically evasive.[79] In a revealing private essay, on the other hand, he copies out the essence of Spinoza's definition: "A miracle then I take to be a sensible operation, which being above the comprehension of the spectator, and in his opinion contrary to the establish'd course of Nature, is taken by him to be divine."[80] He offers this definition while drafting a refutation of the view advanced by his nemesis, Lord Stillingfleet, that miracles are an ontologically distinct class of events involving a supernatural operation. In reducing miracles to a class dependent on a perspective, and in particular on the perspective of ignorance, Locke exposes his deep commitment to the radical critique of revelation.

The claims of revelation, according to our philosophers, are still further circumscribed by the fact that the purported reasons for holding them true almost universally amount to indirect rather than direct revelation. A direct revelation is when God himself appears before you and declares, "I am Jehovah." An indirect revelation is when it happens to someone else, who then calls to tell you about the conversation. The indirect character of most revelation further undermines the certainty, such as it is, that would be required for it to count as knowledge. "No *Probability* can arise higher than its first Original,"[81] as Locke acidly points out. "In traditional Truths, each remove weakens the force of the proof: And the more hands the Tradition has successively passed through, the less strength and evidence does it receive from them."[82] The stories that are handed down through scripture, he suggests, are little more than "the Hear-Say of an Hear-Say."[83] The same line of argument, incidentally, appears earlier in Hobbes and later in Hume.

The bottom line is that revelation belongs to what both Spinoza and Locke call (not coincidentally) the "imagination"—not genuine knowledge.[84] To be sure, Locke has many kind words for revealed religion, and his orthodox successors took great comfort from his declared interest in searching for answers to the great questions of life in the Holy Scriptures. At one point in his *Essay* he reserves space for truths that he obscurely deems to lie neither with nor against but "above" reason,[85] and many of his moderate successors have been anxious to exonerate him of any intention of undermining Christian revelation. Yet the defense of Locke's personal piety once again serves mainly to illustrate how little a philosopher's intentions have to do with his influence. To an improbably large group of discerning readers, the underlying message of his philosophy might as well have been written in neon letters. Hume gave up on supernatural religion, he confessed near the end of his life, after reading Locke as a young man; and then he dragged his mentor into his own corner with an egregiously backhanded compliment: "LOCKE seems to have been the first Christian, who ventured openly to assert, that *faith* was nothing but a species of *reason*, that religion was only a branch of philosophy."[86] Toland implicitly credited Locke for demonstrating that all faith is "entirely built upon ratiocination";[87] and then he went on to offer a full-throated endorsement of the central proposition of Spinoza's epistemology of certainty: "Not the Bare Authority of him that speaks, but the clear Conception I form of what he says, is the *Ground of my Persuasion*."[88]

That Locke absorbed the lesson about the involuntary character of belief in a deep and personal way becomes evident toward the end of his debate with Stillingfleet concerning the allegedly dangerous consequences to the faith of his "method of certainty." Locke says that the bishop need not worry about the consequences of his dangerous method because people will believe his theory if it has the support of the evidence, and not if it does not. So, if the theory that belief follows evidence lacks evidence, the people will have no choice but to disbelieve it—which, of course, is to suppose that the theory is true.

Locke may have caviled his way around the implications of his philosophy on the claims of revelation, but his successors in America did not. "Nothing is more evident to the understanding part of mankind, than that in those parts of the world where learning and science has prevailed, miracles have ceased," says the sage of the Green Moun-tains.[89] The more interesting fact is that Allen's rejection of miracles rests on the epistemological grounds so clearly articulated by Spinoza and privately seconded by Locke. "Miracles cannot be edifying or instructive to us," he argues, precisely because they are "mysterious, and altogether unintelligible."[90] Paine, too, rehearses the radical line of attack on revelation that descends from Hobbes and Spinoza through Locke and Hume. "It is revelation to the first person only, and *hearsay* to every other," he writes. "Is it more probable that a man should have swallowed a whale, or told a lie?"[91]

THE HISTORY of the radical ideas about ideas comes together in a permanent way on the white stone walls of the Jefferson Memorial in Washington, D.C. "Almighty God hath created the mind free," reads engraved text. The words come from the Statute for Religious Freedom that emerged from the Virginia legislature, after rancorous debate, in 1786. The draft of the bill that Jefferson first presented in 1777, how-ever, precedes the clause on "Almighty God" with a prior one: "well aware that the opinions and beliefs of men follow involuntarily the evidence proposed to their minds . . ." The engraved text goes on to invoke "the plan of the Holy Author of our religion." The part of the original deemed unfit for the chisel explains that God chose "to extend [this plan] by its influence on reason alone."[92] Madison, among others, clearly grasped the philosophy underlying this radical piece of legisla-tion. Lending decisive support for Jefferson's bill, he wrote, "The opin-ions of men, depending only on the evidence contemplated by their own minds cannot follow the dictates of other men."[93]

The Virginia Statue for Religious Freedom ranked for Jefferson as one of the three achievements worthy of gracing his tombstone (the Declaration of Independence and the University of Virginia were the other two). Madison was no less exultant. The enactment of the bill, "I flatter myself," he said, has "in this country extinguished forever the ambitious hope of making laws for the human mind."[94] It is also the right place to locate the tremendous political impact of the radical philosophy of mind that first arose in antiquity and burst into the world through the work of the philosophers of the early modern period. Although the radical idea of freedom of thought passes through some additional conceptual innovations having to do principally with the nature of freedom and natural rights, it gets its start in the critical insight that human understanding realizes itself only to the extent that it is free to follow the evidence it discovers in the world. To demand a certain kind of belief or to impose any faith—to pass "laws for the human mind," as Madison so eloquently phrases it—is not to direct the understanding but to attempt to destroy it.

The words that made it (in part) onto the walls of the Jefferson Memorial also allow us to return with greater precision to the sharp distinction between the radical idea of freedom of thought that motivated America's revolutionary philosophers and the Protestant idea of "freedom of conscience" that undoubtedly motivated a large number of religious dissenters to side with them in the struggle for religious freedom. The Protestant idea concerning "conscience" begins with the notion that no earthly authority may stand between the individual and the word of God as revealed in the scriptures.[95] But this is to suppose precisely what the radicals deny: that truth may take the form of a revelation, and that the freedom of the mind consists in its ability to choose what it will believe without reason or cause. It further supposes that this freedom is grounded in the particular revelation of the Protestant Bible (which is one reason why the Protestant idea of the freedom of religion has always tended to collapse into the freedom to be Protestant). In Virginia, one side was proposing a freedom *from* religion, while the other came to the voting booths in hopes of securing a freedom *for* religion. In the long run of history, where intentions are mercilessly tested against their consequences, it would become clear that only one side knew what it was doing.

SELF

From the picture-theory of consciousness, there seems to follow a certain existential inference, namely, that the mind exists, as a thing, like a visitor to its own art gallery, apart from its picture-ideas. This preexisting thinking, acting, feeling thing, according to the common religious consciousness, is the sacred self. The self-thing, it is widely supposed, is the first thing about us; it makes us what we are. It is present in human infants and even, some would say, at the moment where sperm meets ovum. The radical philosophy of mind, on the other hand, says that the self is not a thing at all. It is an action. Specifically, it is one of those acts of understanding that we call ideas. It is not the first thing about us but the last thing, the icing on the cake of experience, made possible only through the slow and steady improvement of our explanations of the world.

In the jargon of late-seventeenth-century philosophy, the entire difference between the common and the radical conception of consciousness can be summarized in a doctrine concerning "substance." The common conception supposes that mind is one kind of substance and body is another. Philosophers today call this "dualism." The idea that mind is a species of action can be compressed into the claim that mind and body are modes of attributes of a single substance. This view is "monism." (In many superficial interpretations, "monism" is construed as the idea that the mind is a thing that happens to be composed of material stuff. But this overlooks the fundamental claim of monism, that the mind is not a thing at all, but an action of some other thing, namely, substance; whereas what we call "material stuff" can likewise only be the activity of substance conceived through one of many possible attributes.)

The historical point of entry into this radical conception of mind is once again to be found in the work of Descartes. At his own insistence, paradoxically, Descartes has been widely represented as a dualist. But in fact Descartes's texts are radically ambiguous on the point, and they are ambiguous on account of the deep tension in his own reasoning concerning the nature of ideas. At a crucial juncture in his metaphysical ratiocinations, Descartes defines substance as a "thing that exists in such a way that it doesn't depend on anything else for its existence," and then immediately arrives at the astonishing conclusion that "there is only one substance that can be understood to depend on nothing else, namely God."[96] Perhaps sensing that he is close to a radical monism here, he proposes that we may also use substance in a different sense—"things that don't depend for their existence on anything else but God"—and thereby distinguish "corporeal substance" from "thinking substance."[97] A substance, he adds, may be known to us only through its "attributes," and the attribute of corporeal substance is "extension," while the attribute of thinking substance is "thought."[98] But now a quiet dilemma arises: In what way do we know the first substance, the only real one, if not through its attributes? If the pseudo-substances of mind and body depend on God, what stops us from saying that their attributes are in fact those of one substance?

One individual who thought he had a bead on the real Descartes was Henricus Regius, a professor of medicine at the University of Utrecht—another Dutch doctor with a rap sheet for misdemeanors against the holy religion. After corresponding with Descartes, perusing a draft of his unpublished book titled *The World*, and possibly even chatting with the man himself in his dead-animal home laboratory, Regius came to think of himself as an apostle. In fact, he came to think he knew his teacher so well that he suspected the great man was hiding something in his famous (and famously accommodating) *Meditations*. In 1647, this self-confident disciple saw fit to publish what he took to be the secret essence of the master's teaching:

> So far as the nature of things is concerned, the possibility seems to be open that the mind can be either a substance or a mode of a corporeal substance. Or, if we are to follow some philosophers, who hold that thought and extension are attributes which are present in certain substances, as in subjects, then since the attributes are not opposites but merely different, there is no reason why the mind should not be a sort of attribute co-existing with extension in the same subject, although the one attribute is not included in the concept of the other.[99]

By "some philosophers" Regius meant Descartes, and he was here hinting that the great man was a genuinely radical philosopher. The very suggestion scared Descartes witless. He broke vehemently with Regius and fought back hard against the insinuation of substance monism, which after all would have exposed him as the manipulative atheist that people like Leibniz would later say that he was.

Spinoza, as was his wont, did not hesitate to take the Cartesian philosophy where Descartes didn't want to go. There can be only one substance, he argues, and "thinking substance and extended substance are one and the same substance, comprehended now under this attribute, now under that."[100] The claim that the one substance may be comprehended in two different but parallel ways stands for a version of monism that goes under the name of "parallelism." Spinoza sums up this doctrine of monistic parallelism in a conclusion that seems far ahead of its century in its view on the relation of mind and body:

> Mental decision on the one hand, and the appetite and physical state of the body on the other hand, are simultaneous in nature; or rather, they are one and the same thing which, when considered under the attribute of Thought and explicated through Thought, we call decision, and when considered under the attribute of Extension and deduced through the laws of motion and rest, we call a physical state.[101]

The most important and unsettling implications of monistic parallelism have to do with the mind and the way in which it may know itself. The picture-theory takes for granted that the mind, by virtue of being "inside" of the "gallery," has a perfect grasp of itself before it knows anything about anything else. According to Spinoza, on the other hand, the mind is not "inside" anything. It is just another idea, out there in the world, that happens to explain or represent the activity of a particular body. Technically, it is a "mode of thought." Less technically, we could say that the mind of any individual is simply the theory that explains the behavior of that individual's body. In Spinoza's formula, the mind is the idea of a particular, existing body.[102] This mind, moreover, is the mind insofar as it relates to nature as a whole; that is, it is the theory that genuinely explains the activity of a particular body. The mind insofar as it relates to the mind itself is just the idea that a mind has of itself. Our self-consciousness is just a theory within a theory, or whatever we piece together about ourselves from our prior knowledge of the world. And this theory within a theory isn't in principle different from any of the rest of our ideas about the world, which is to say that it is limited by our experience, necessarily confused to some degree, and sometimes flat wrong.

The idea that the mind is just an act of substance, or that the self is just a theory within a theory, may seem abstract and essentially destructive. And yet it opens a door between a broad set of intuitions about human experience and a range of deep and fruitful inquiries that have since been made into useful sciences. It explains, for example, how it is that children and animals may have a certain kind of consciousness yet lack the theory of self that constitutes what we think of as self-consciousness or personhood; and so it sets the stage for developmental psychology. It allows for the possibility—which will prove quite significant when it comes to political theory—that the theory of self we concoct for ourselves may draw on a range of facts that lie "outside" of ourselves, such as, for example, facts concerning our interactions with other people, institutions, and ideas. It also gives sense to the notion that we have many "unconscious" ideas, which is to say that our bodies involve ideas that explain our behavior but do not form part of our idea of ourselves.[103] It also serves as the basis for an explanation of the familiar fact that our ideas follow upon one another neither through inferences of logic nor through acts of will but through chains of association, conditioned by our particular experiences and understanding, which in turn renders them open to investigation through empirical psychology.

On the whole, this radical view of the self gives flesh to the intuition—obvious from experience yet previously withheld from science on the basis of common religious prejudice—that mind and body are deeply interconnected and that the consciousness and self-consciousness that come with them are always matters of degree. Consciousness according to this radical view may be found in animals, plants, and even frying pans and thermostats, as some modern writers have suggested; but not all consciousness is created equal.[104] "He who, like an infant or child, has a body capable of very few things, and very heavily dependent on external causes, has a mind which considered solely in itself is conscious of almost nothing," Spinoza observes. "On the other hand, he who has a body capable of a great many things, has a mind which considered only in itself is very much conscious of itself, and of God, and of things."[105]

Although monistic parallelism receives its canonical expression in Spinoza, and may be found in various versions in the work of predecessors such as Bruno, Gassendi, Hobbes, and the side of Descartes that Regius exposed, it reached America principally through the texts of an English philosopher who feigned indifference to the new development. In the speculative fourth book of his *Essay*, a few chapters before his proof of "a God," Locke floats the fundamental idea at the end of a typically convoluted hypothetical:

> We have the ideas of matter and thinking, but possibly shall never be able to know whether any mere material being thinks or no; it being impossible for us, by the contemplation of our own ideas without revelation, to discover whether Omnipotency has not given to some systems of matter, fitly disposed, a power to perceive and think, or else joined to matter, so disposed, a thinking immaterial substance: it being, in respect of our notions, not much more remote from our comprehension to conceive that God can, if he pleases, superadd to matter a faculty of thinking, than that he should superadd to it another substance with a faculty of thinking.[106]

In this passage, Locke is careful to place defensive barriers between himself and the thesis he wishes to insinuate in the minds of his readers. So, for example, he notionally presents his version of monistic parallelism (God can "superadd to matter a faculty of thinking") as a hypothetical alternative to the presumably equally valid option of a pseudo-Cartesian dualism (God can "superadd to [matter] another substance with a faculty of thinking").[107] He also takes care to lay the whole synthesis at the feet of a pious-sounding "Omnipotency." Thus, for example, later in the same chapter he writes that the "constant and regular connexion" between mind and body is best attributed to "the arbitrary determination of an all-wise Agent."[108] He is also ostentatiously casual in his use of the term "substance," thereby seeming to signal that "substance" could not possibly refer to "the all-wise Agent" who so considerately yet only hypothetically underwrites the exactly observed parallelism between mind and body.

Even Locke's latitudinarian allies saw through him this time. "If this hold, then it is impossible to prove a spiritual substance in us from the idea of thinking," fumes Lord Stillingfleet in the book that one may still check out of Jefferson's library on moral philosophy. The bishop contemptuously dismisses the fig leaf of Cartesian dualism that Locke pretends to offer as a viable alternative, and specifically alleges that Locke has purloined his heterodox theory of mind from Spinoza and Hobbes. Feigning horror at the mention of those "justly decried names," Locke hides behind a palpable falsehood: "I am not so well read in Hobbes or Spinoza."[109]

Locke's radical friends smelled the rat, too, but of course for them it was the delicate perfume of philosophical truth. Toland, miming Locke's own words, celebrated the fact that his mentor had demoted both body and soul to accidents of some unknowable substance.[110] Blount—who did not need Locke to supply him with Spinoza—actually preceded Locke in his commitment to the notion that the mind is a species of action or idea, and then rehearsed the point after Locke in distinctly Lockean language.[111] In *Cato's Letters*, Trenchard and Gordon followed suit with unmistakable endorsements of monistic parallelism.[112]

Perhaps the most influential exponent of the "real" Locke was his protégé, Anthony Collins. Beginning in 1706, Collins engaged in an extraordinary epistolary debate about the nature of mind and self with Samuel Clarke, Newton's spokes-philosopher. Clarke righteously defended all the old verities: that the self is composed of some indivisible, immaterial substance, entirely different from and independent of matter. Collins represented himself, as others immediately understood him to be, as a devoted follower of Locke. But there was little to distinguish his position from that of Spinoza. The Clarke-Collins debate was reprinted and reread many times in subsequent decades, and Clarke's rhetorical skills led many of his contemporaries to award him a technical victory on points. Yet in the grand scheme of the long eighteenth century there can be little doubt that Collins won the war.

Hume once again rose like the Owl of Minerva, summarizing the results of the brightest period in the history of the philosophy of mind just as the sun was setting on it. In an essay titled "Of the Immortality of the Soul," which he perhaps prudently withheld from publication, he explains, "Metaphysics teach us . . . that we have no other idea of substance, than as an aggregate of qualities inhering in an unknown something."[113] Matter and spirit are therefore "equally unknown," and "we cannot know . . . whether matter, by its structure or arrangement, may be the cause of thought," he adds, quietly paraphrasing Locke paraphrasing Spinoza on the nature of substance. He then offers what could be taken as a handy summary of Spinoza's parallelism. Alterations in the body, he notes, are invariably "attended with proportionable alterations" in the mind. "The weakness of the body and that of the mind in infancy are exactly proportioned; their vigour in manhood; their sympathetic disorder in sickness; their common gradual decay in old age."

Two of Locke's successors deserve attention for their particularly prominent role in conveying the message to America. The first was Bolingbroke, who ably communicates the word from Spinoza in the language of Locke:

> It is nonsense, and something worse than nonsense, to assert . . . that god cannot give the faculty of thinking, a faculty in the principle of it entirely unknown to you, to systems of matter whose essential properties are solidity, extension &c. not incogitativity.[114]

The only difference is that Bolingbroke reduces Locke's hypothetical, pseudo-Cartesian fig-leaf alternative to "something worse than nonsense" (elsewhere he calls it "blasphemy"). This crypto-Spinozist passage from Bolingbroke, naturally, appears in Jefferson's *Literary Commonplace Book*.

The other figure that mattered for the Americans was Joseph Priestley (1733–1804), the remarkable scientist, dissenting cleric, philosopher, early leader of the Unitarian movement, and author of an avalanche of books that eventually totaled in the hundreds. Priestley's role in disseminating the dialectic of monistic parallelism is itself a revealing marker of the transformation of the age. When Collins took the fight to Clarke, it should be remembered, no serious thinker doubted that the Christian thing to do was to oppose the radical philosophy of mind at every turn. Now Priestley, writing at the end of the century, offered a radical, materialist, and necessitarian philosophy according to which mind and matter are two modes of a single, self-moving substance and the brain is emphatically capable of hosting thought—yet he certainly represented himself as a Christian. Many at the time disputed vigorously the accuracy of this representation, but few could doubt its sincerity. The Scottish minister and philosopher Thomas Reid expressed his horror at the changes in the culture in a review of Priestley's work: "How would Epicurus? How would Hobbes? How would Collins have triumphed had they lived to see this point given up to them, even by a Christian divine?"[115] Priestley himself named Descartes and Locke as his predecessors—itself a curious selection, inasmuch as the two belong in the same room only to the extent that Spinoza stands between them.

Jefferson exulted over Priestley's works. If we inspect Jefferson's thinking on the matter of body and mind, however, it isn't hard to see that Priestley is really just a bridge that takes him back to the ideas he transcribed from Bolingbroke as a young man and from thence all the way back to the semi-hidden side of Locke. In an important letter to Adams, Jefferson hits the nail on the head in the language forged in the critical debates of the late seventeenth century: "Why may not the mode of action called thought, have been given to a material organ of peculiar structure?" Then he makes his own judgment clear. He informs Adams that he remains "partial to Locke's one incomprehensibility rather than two."[116] Jefferson, in short, subscribes to monistic parallelism, and he credits Locke for having brought him to that view. He does not mention that Locke never actually owned up to this doctrine of the "one incomprehensibility" or that he cribbed the whole caboodle from Spinoza. But that hardly matters, since the idea did not suffer any lasting damage in its passage through the black markets of early modern philosophy.

In his reply to Jefferson, Adams shows once again that despite his profoundly conservative disposition, his ideas are functionally indistinguishable from those of the radical philosophers. "The question between spirit and matter appears to me nugatory because we have neither evidence nor idea of either," he writes. "All that we certainly know is that some substance exists, which must be the cause of all the qualitys and Attributes which we perceive: Extension, Solidity, Perception, memory, Reason, for all these are Attributes, or adjectives, and not essences or substantives."[117]

MONISTIC PARALLELISM is as much a philosophy of the body as it is a philosophy of the mind, and in this respect it targets another piece of the common consciousness of things. There is in fact a common theory of the body that corresponds to the common picture-theory of the mind, and we may call it the "lump" theory. The body, according to the common sense of the matter, is intrinsically inert and passive, like a lump of clay, and it acquires motion only through the animating force of the soul or mind. As Descartes points out, "We have been confirmed in this error"—that the activity of the body is always the activity of the soul—"in judging that dead bodies have the same organs as living ones, for they lack nothing but the soul and yet there is no movement in them."[118] According to radical philosophy, on the other hand, the body is an act of substance no less than the mind. Its activity is nothing other than the activity of nature itself, understood and expressed in a certain way. Descartes himself made a first, strenuous effort to explain the human body in thoroughly mechanistic or "corporeal terms," though it fell to his successors to draw out the implications in full.[119]

The body is an extremely complex action of substance, Spinoza observes. It must be so, indeed, if it is to "embody" in a literal sense all of those acts we call "ideas," as the theory of parallelism requires. Given the state of medical science in the seventeenth century, when many people still thought that the brain was as about as structured as a bowl of oatmeal, this was a very bold claim. But Spinoza stands firm: "Nobody as yet knows the structure of the body so accurately as to explain all its functions, not to mention that in the animal world we find much that far surpasses human sagacity." Borrowing from Descartes's medicinal observations, Spinoza goes on to observe that the body is composed of many parts, some of which are hard, some soft, and others liquid. In order to sustain itself, it continuously requires "a great many other bodies, by which, as it were, it is continually regenerated."[120] The body, in short, is not a clodlike thing but a process. It is a metabolism that continuously transforms whatever lies outside of itself in a certain range of ways. Its identity does not inhere in the specific material elements of which it is composed at any moment, for these are constantly changing. Rather, the body is what it is as a result of the organization of those constituents, and that organization is what it is insofar as it explains its own persistence among all the other things of the world.[121] That organization, moreover, does not come to be in an instant, but emerges out of a process of growth or self-realization. Every self has a history. In a letter to Locke's friend in Oxford, Henry Oldenburg, Spinoza sums it up in a formula: "Men are not created, but generated."[122]

Locke rinses the doctrine of jargon and then repeats. "The identity of the same man," he concludes, "consists . . . in nothing but a participation of the same continued life by constantly fleeting particles of matter, in succession vitally united to the same organized body." The complexity of the body, he agrees with Spinoza, far exceeds our comprehension: "There is not so contemptible a plant or animal that does not confound the most enlarged understanding."[123] A "fitly organized body," he further supposes, does not come into being in an instant but rather realizes itself through a personal history of growth.[124] "When the thing is wholly made new . . . as when a new particle of matter doth begin to exist in *rerum natura* . . . this we call 'creation'," he elaborates. "When a thing is made up of particles which did all of them before exist, [this] we call 'generation'." His conclusion reads as if lifted from Spinoza: "A man is not created but generated."[125]

The Cartesian-Spinozist philosophy of the body was a hit among the radical doctors of the Dutch Enlightenment, and none was keener on the new way of thinking than the seminal figure of Herman Boerhaave. A botanist and the founder of a renowned teaching hospital in Leiden, Boerhaave rose to fame as the champion of a new, empirical approach to the treatment of disease. He scorned the traditional methods of medicine—whereby the diagnosis of patients tended to proceed through the reading of Galen and Hippocrates—and demanded that his students spend long hours at the clinic testing firsthand the efficacy of different kinds of therapies. He stressed the importance of "attaining to certainty in natural philosophy" through observation.[126] He insisted that the human body is not a symposium of mysterious spirits and humors, as many clinicians at the time supposed, but a dynamic, self-moving organization of hard, soft, and liquid components, a diverse collection of pumps and pulleys, filters and funnels, all engaged in a constant process of ingesting and expurgating particles of matter with the rest of the world. He also noted that there were many aspects of the body's behavior—such as the beating of the heart and reflex actions—that required no self-consciousness or any other spiritual forces at all. He famously suggested that the circulation of the blood obeys the same laws of physics as the solar system. The brain, he added, is the "seat of sensation," and the purpose of the nerves is to carry sensory signals between the muscles and the brain.

Boerhaave was a man in the mold of Hippocrates, not Socrates; he wished to heal the sick, not merely engage in philosophical speculation. Yet he understood that to cure the body, it was necessary first to destroy the soul, that is, to set aside the prejudices of the common religious consciousness about the nature of the self. And so, in his magisterial summary of his research, he made the radical, Spinozistic philosophy underlying his medicine all but explicit. He asserted that "man consists of mind and body united"; that these two are "of entirely different nature," one involving "extension," the other "perception"; that perceptions or sensations are not "in the Object, or in the Nerve" but rather "in a certain idea which God has assigned to each particular change" in the body; that whatever involves the body can be "understood, explained, and demonstrated" only through things that share the properties associated with extension, while ideas can be explained only through ideas; and yet nevertheless, that "such a reciprocal connection and consent between the particular Thoughts and Affections of the Mind and the Body, that a Change in one always produces a Change in the other, and the reverse."[127] As the Dutch scholar Wim Klever shows, every step in this chain of arguments corresponds directly (and in places verbatim) to a proposition in Spinoza's *Ethics*.[128] Boerhaave himself tried to pass it off as a version of Leibniz's doctrine concerning the "pre-established harmony" ordained by God between body and mind, though it isn't hard to see that the Leibnizian position, here as elsewhere, is just the Spinozist one garnished with extra helpings of God-talk.

In his own time, Boerhaave was accused of being a follower variously of Descartes (which was not so bad, except among the genuine reactionaries), Leibniz (more suspicious), Epicurus (very bad), and Spinoza (unforgivable). Boerhaave defended himself vigorously against these potentially career-ending charges, but if a teacher may be judged by his pupils, there must have been cause for concern.[129] Among the many freethinking graduates of Boerhaave's teaching hospital in Leiden, perhaps the most notorious would prove to be Julien Offray de La Mettrie—a young Frenchman who returned home to write *Man a Machine* and other works notable for their unapologetically mechanico-physical representation of the human body, their hugely ambitious health-care reform agenda, and their strident atheism.

Another of Boerhaave's troublesome heirs—or so the evidence would suggest—was Ethan Allen. Here, for example, is the author of the *Oracles* with an elegant statement of Boerhaave's doctrine concerning the circulatory (solar) system:

> The natural palpitation of the heart, the beating of the pulse and gravitation of our bodies, with the other laws of our animal nature, are as mechanical as the movements of our solar system.[130]

The author of the *Oracles* also takes the time to articulate a version of Boerhaave's theory concerning the brain and the nervous system:

> The brain is evidently the seat of sensation, which through the nervous system conveys the animal spirits to every part of the body, imparting to it sensation and motion, constituting it a living machine.[131]

The author goes on to illustrate one of his medicinal insights with a reference to the Hottentots of the Dutch colony of South Africa—just the kind of reference that features in Dutch medical writing of the time.

The author nowhere mentions Boerhaave or any other medical authority, but it isn't hard to guess how the ideas got into the text. Thomas Young cites "the celebrated Boerhaave" as the foremost of his various medical authorities,[132] and indeed the pneumatico-hydraulic vision of the body he offers in his own medical writings is pretty much that of Boerhaave. So it seems safe to conclude that somewhere along those walks through the Connecticut countryside, when Young was schooling the up-and-coming Allen in the religion of Nature's God—or perhaps around the time that the itinerant doctor was inoculating his boisterous patient-friend for smallpox—the conversation must have turned to the philosophy of medicine.

Young and Allen weren't the only Americans to absorb the teachings of Boerhaave and the revolutionary doctors that followed in his example. In his eighty-second year, Jefferson found himself reading "the most extraordinary of all books," as he informed Adams. The book in question was a research paper by Jean Pierre Flourens, a French physiologist who pioneered the study of the brain through experiments with animals. "Flourens proves that the cerebrum is the thinking organ," Jefferson crows. "I wish to see what the spiritualists will say to this."[133]

THE GREAT PRIZE of revealed religion—and the chief inference drawn from the picture-theory of consciousness and the corresponding lump-theory of the body—is the conviction that the self-mind part of us may continue to exist after the body is gone. The radical philosophy of mind quite obviously destroys this specific claim of revealed religion—though in a manner more complex than is usually imagined.

The rejection of the common conception of immortality is of course a marquee feature of the Epicurean philosophy from its inception. Nothing composed of parts can last forever, says Lucretius, and the human being is certainly composed of parts. In all of our experience, he further argues, the mind is intimately united with the body. So, even if a philosopher were to suppose that the mind could go on without the body, it wouldn't be her mind, and she couldn't care about it or it about her. In hopes of quieting our needless and harmful anxieties about death, Epicurus teaches, "Death is nothing to us."[134] When we cower before the prospect of our own death, according to Epicurus, we surreptitiously imagine that we are still alive to witness it. But in fact, when we die, we die, and we are no longer around to experience death.

In the violent spiritual landscape of the seventeenth century, no philosopher could have survived long while publicly maintaining a view on the mortality of the soul so manifestly in contradiction with the doctrines of the established religion. Hobbes, following Gassendi and the inexorable logic of his materialist premises, did go so far as to assert that the soul is naturally mortal. But then he prudently turned around and granted God the right to resurrect it by miracle if and when God so chooses. A more subtle treatment of the matter emerged from the radical philosophy of mind that got its start in the work of Descartes.

Descartes himself is loudly associated with a pious defense of the immortality of the soul. "Now on the one hand I have a clear and distinct idea of myself, in so far as I am simply a thinking, non-extended thing; and on the other hand I have a distinct idea of body, in so far as this is simply an extended, non-thinking thing," Descartes famously argues. "And accordingly, it is certain that I am really distinct from my body, and can exist without it." Although Descartes's defense of the immortality of the soul elicited some rejoicing in the bastions of orthodox belief, not every theologian went home happy.[135] Setting aside the many tough objections raised by Gassendi and Hobbes, the suspicions about Cartesian immortality begin with his own descriptions (or lack thereof) of the cherished sequel of human experience. What exactly does the thinking thing think about in its disembodied future life? And what does its future life have to do with sin, redemption, and salvation by the blood of the Lamb on the Day of Judgment? Immortality in its original conception in the Christian tradition, it must be remembered, is a meaty affair. It involves flesh and bones shuffling out of graves and reassembling themselves under the ferocious gaze of their Maker. Cartesian immortality, as his contemporaries noted, sounds more like the continuation of life as an armchair philosopher. Indeed, if understanding is distinct from imagination and sensation, as Descartes insists, then what, if anything, does the understanding that putatively survives the body imagine or sense?

The root of the problem has to do with the monism that Descartes seems unable to shake. In rendering the existence of the immortal soul a result of his clear and distinct perception of himself as both body and mind, Descartes seems to suggest that the existence of the soul is a function of differing perspectives on a single thing. It is just the idea of an idea, as it were. Spinoza characteristically pushes this line of thought to the bitter end. Mind and body are indeed just two perspectives on the same thing: they are complementary modes of a single substance. It follows that when the body does not exist, neither does the mind: "We do not assign duration to the mind except while the body endures."[136] Hume—perhaps not coincidentally—makes the same point in very similar language: "Everything is in common betwixt soul and body . . . The existence therefore of the one must be dependent on that of the other."[137]

Locke flatters every audience and fattens his work with pieties about eternal life. And yet, as Stillingfleet points out, his arguments for monism lead inexorably to the materiality and the mortality of the soul. We need not detain ourselves here with his various circumlocutions[138] for the simple reason that by the time his work reached American ears, only the radical interpretation mattered. In the debates of 1715, Leibniz—who knew the real story—felt obliged to couch the incendiary charge in politely equivocal terms: "Mr. Locke, and his followers, are uncertain at least whether the soul be not material, and naturally perishable."[139] In 1820, Jefferson saw no ambiguity at all: "Mr. Locke . . . openly maintained the materialism of the soul"—a statement that is true only on a very forgiving definition of "openly."[140]

Jefferson himself showed little hesitation in embracing the conclusions that everyone supposed would follow from Locke's premises. "Nature will not give you a second life wherein to atone for the omissions of this," he admonished a friend in later life.[141] (Epicurus himself says, "We have been born once, and there can be no second birth."[142]) Freneau, too, combined Epicurean leanings with a Lockean theory of personal identity in these melancholy lines:

> *Like atoms round the rapid wheel,*
> *We seem the same, though changing still,*
> *Mere reptiles of a year.*[143]

Freneau consoled himself in such moments with quintessentially Epicurean thoughts: "Death is no more than never-ceasing change"; and "death is nothing to us."

Among the most radical of the American productions on the topic of the immortal soul is the first, Franklin's *Dissertation* of 1726. After borrowing Locke's vocabulary of sensation and reflection and articulating a Lockean version of monistic parallelism, nineteen-year-old Ben knocks the immortal soul into permanent coma:

> Now upon *Death*, and the Destruction of the Body, the Ideas contain'd in the Brain (which alone are the Subjects of the Soul's Action) being then likewise necessarily destroy'd, the Soul, tho' incapable of Destruction itself, must then necessarily *cease to think* or *act*, having nothing left to think or act upon . . . And to cease to *think* is but little different from *ceasing to be*.[144]

To cease to think may be little different from ceasing to be, as Franklin points out; and yet a gap remains. From within that gap, perhaps surprisingly, the radical philosophers of the early modern period rescue a certain intuition bound up with the old idea of immortality.

The story really begins with Epicurus, who in a curious coda to his resolutely mortalist reflections cracks open the door ever so slightly to an oddly metaphorical notion of immortality. In a letter expounding the principles of the good life, he leaves a friend with this advice: "Exercise these precepts day and night, both by yourself and with those who are like you, and then . . . you will live like a God. For people lose all appearance of mortality by living in the midst of immortal blessings."[145] However long we may hope to live here or in some imaginary hereafter, he means to say, no form of happiness can exceed the happiness available to us here and now. We do not escape death; but once we learn to accept that death means nothing to us, we may "absolve" it and become, if not quite immortal, "deathless" in another sense.

Among the radical philosophers of the early modern world, a similarly tenuous, thoroughly "immanent" concept of immortality somehow survives the destruction of the immortal soul. In what may count as the closest thing to a surprise ending in a treatise composed in the geometric style, Spinoza's *Ethics* follows the seemingly cold-blooded termination of the soul in its final sections with this remarkable pronouncement: "The human mind cannot be absolutely destroyed along with the body, but something of it remains, which is eternal."[146] There is in nature an idea that expresses the essence of our individual body under a form of eternity, he explains. This is not the mind of which we are aware in our daily lives, not the self that struggles through a life of hope and fear, but the mind that we are always seeking to know, as it is in nature, the self that expresses the eternal laws of nature in a form unique to itself. To the extent that we understand this eternal idea of our own existence, Spinoza says, "we feel and experience that we are eternal." The way in which we participate in this eternal idea of ourselves is through "the intellectual love of God." "The mind's intellectual love toward God," he explains, "is the love of God wherewith God loves himself not insofar as he is finite, but insofar as he can be explicated through the essence of the human mind considered under a form of eternity."[147]

The kind of immortality Spinoza offers, to be clear, does not involve a future existence in time. It includes no memories, no passions, no personal experiences of any kind. It is not an escape from death into some other world. It is rather, in keeping with the this-worldly spirit of the Epicurean philosophy, more like the achievement of a deathless moment in the present. Eternal life means nothing other than this life, lived and understood in its most complete form. It is being itself. And we may approach this moment of being through the understanding of ourselves and of the world in which we live: "The free man thinks least of all of death, and his thinking is a meditation on life."[148]

The kind of immortality that Spinoza and Epicurus offer has been available wherever there is philosophy. It appears, for example, in the idea of eternal presence that Lao Tzu expresses in the *Tao Te Ching*:

> *To never leave what you are*
> *is to abide,*
> *and to die without getting lost—*
> *that is to live on and on.*[149]

The same intuition motivates the medieval Arab theologian Averroes (also known as Ibn Rushd), who, after acknowledging that the individual mind perishes upon death, allows that it may achieve immortality through its participation in the universal mind. A version of the idea may be found in the defining doctrine of the Upanishads, *tat tvam asi*— you (the self) are that (the *atman*, or plenitude of being of the universal spirit). The suggestion surfaces in Nietzsche's vision of the "eternal recurrence of the same"—the suggestion that to affirm life is to know that every moment in it will come back in exactly the same form an infinite number of times throughout eternity. Wittgenstein reaches for the same conclusion when he says, "Eternal life is given to those who live in the present." And Einstein evokes it in a letter to the Queen of Belgium as he consoles her for a loss in the family:

And yet, as always, the springtime sun brings forth new life . . . and Mozart remains as beautiful and tender as he always was and always will be. There is after all something eternal that lies beyond the hand of fate and of all human delusions and such eternals lie closer to an older person than to a younger one oscillating between fear and hope. For us there remains the privilege of experiencing beauty and truth in their purest forms.[150]

The immortality of the philosophers stands not for the annihilation but the transformation of the common religious conception of immortality. It is an attempt to preserve certain valid intuitions embedded within that traditional conception: that we know ourselves only in part; that no finite moral calculus can discover a necessary justice in this world; that the pursuit of knowledge of our true interest and the recognition of our common fate with our fellow human beings can bring us to a kind of salvation. It is to the old immortal soul what Nature's God is to the God of Abraham: a way of talking about the soul long after the soul is dead. At the same time, philosophical immortality remains radically distinct from the common conception.

The traditional conception of immortality, for example, generally involves purportedly factual claims about the nature of the other world as well as our own. It tells us about the relative temperature of the two worlds, for example, or the differing opportunities afforded in each for pleasure and pain. The philosophers, in accordance with the guiding principle, maintain to the contrary that we can claim no knowledge of any kind with respect to some other possible world. They insist on what one may call the "epistemological containment" of immortality. In the model of Spinoza and his idea of immortality as the "intellectual love of God," they direct us to participate in eternity through the deepening of our knowledge and enjoyment of this world, not another one.

The traditional conception of immortality also takes for granted that the purpose of the afterlife is to resolve ethical problems across time zones: actions in this life receive their just consequences in the next. In the philosophical conception, however, eternal life stands only for the incompleteness of moral equations in this life, not as a term within those equations. "All the great ends of morality and religion are well enough secured, without philosophical proofs of the soul's immateriality," Locke avers.[151] One way in which the deists practiced this kind of "ethical containment" of immortality, surprising as it may sound to modern ears, was to guarantee an afterlife—but then insist that it could be no more than a scene of rewards without punishment. William Knox, a loyalist critic of America's Sons of Liberty, illustrated the point with a revealing comparison between the rebels' view of royal power and the deists' view of God. In the rebels' view, said Knox, the King's "power is like that allowed by the deists to the Almighty over his creatures, he may reward them with eternal happiness if he pleases, but he must not punish them on any account."[152]

In a rhetorical gesture that would have much influence on the deist movement, Locke transmutes the idea of eternal rewards and punishments into the idea of "the eternal and unalterable nature of right and wrong."[153] To say that a certain action will be wrong for all eternity sounds reassuringly like—and yet is profoundly different from—the notion that certain actions will be met with eternal punishment. Shaftesbury makes the same move more vigorously, explicitly rejecting the idea that virtue results from a bargain with God about an eternal afterlife and endorsing instead "the eternal measures and immutable independent nature of worth and virtue."[154] Thomas Chubb—an English deist whose work had the dual honor of receiving direct attack from Jonathan Edwards and of being included in Jefferson's library of moral philosophy—suggested that our immortality consists in nothing more than the feeling of eternity that follows from doing the right thing in this life. According to Chubb, too, what lasts forever is just the "eternal and invariable rule of right and wrong."[155]

From the ethical and epistemological containment of immortality follows its political containment. According to the radical philosophers, no claims about an afterlife may carry any weight in the legitimation of any political order or policy in this world. The thesis is present in Lucretius and perhaps first revived in the modern world in Machiavelli, but it is most robustly formulated in Hobbes. "There are some," Hobbes warns, who would base their political theories on "attaining of an eternall felicity after death":

But because there is no naturall knowledge of mans estate after death; much less of the reward that is then to be given to the breach of Faith; but onely a beliefe grounded upon other mens saying, that they know it supernaturally, or that they know those, that knew them, that knew others, that knew it supernaturally; Breach of Faith cannot be called a Precept of Reason, or Nature.[156]

The deeply Hobbesian (and Machiavellian) authors of *Cato's Letters* passed along the message to the Americans. In its dark millennium, they say, Europe succumbed to "religious mad-men and godly pedants" who "by pretending to know the other world, cheated and confounded this."[157]

The immortality of America's revolutionary deists, such as it was, invariably took on a philosophical character. In his later writings, for example, Franklin appears to adopt a more lively view of the afterlife than that of his youthful *Dissertation*. "Having experienced the Goodness of that Being in conducting me prosperously thro' a long life, I have no doubt of its Continuance in the next, though without the smallest Conceit of meriting such Goodness," he writes to Stiles in his last year.[158] By modern standards, this must count as a ringing endorsement of the immortality of the soul. But Jonathan Edwards Jr., speaking for his theologically correct contemporaries, easily detects the heresy: "All this implies, that on the principles of infidelity, nothing better is to be expected in the future state than we enjoy in the present."[159]

Paine, like the older version of Franklin, offers thoughts on immortality that, to a modern reader, must also sound piously optimistic. "I believe in one God, and no more; and I hope for happiness beyond this life," he announces in *The Age of Reason*.[160] About the nature of this possible afterlife, however, he admits, "I trouble myself not about the manner of future existence."[161] In his "Private Thoughts," he makes clear that he is dealing only in conjectures, not certainties: "I presume not to go beyond the comfortable idea of hope, with respect to a future state."[162] Once again, Jonathan Edwards is quick to spot the heresy: "It seems then that he is *uncertain* about it; he barely *hopes* for it."[163]

Washington expresses the little he has to offer on the topic of immortality in the formulas of deism. "The propitious smiles of Heaven can never be expected on a nation that disregards the eternal rules of order and right, which Heaven itself has ordained," he announces in his first inaugural address. Modern interpreters no less than the religiously active population of the time may take solace in the seemingly pious drift of his sentiments about divine ordainments, but to the deists of the time the "eternal rules" that Washington cited would have been those of Chubb and Locke, and necessarily involved a radical reconception of the relationship between here and eternity.

The most important practical feature of philosophical immortality is its political containment, and here America's revolutionary deists are as one. In an important letter to Madison on the topic of land inheritance, Jefferson makes the limitation explicit:

> I set out on this ground which I suppose to be self-evident: "That the earth belongs in usufruct to the living;" that the dead have neither power nor rights over it. The portion occupied by an individual ceases to be his when himself ceases to be.[164]

The soul, as Jefferson understood, is just a way of burdening the future with the past and thereby justifying the rule of the few over the many. Liberalism became possible only after it was understood that souls do not have rights.

THE OVERGROWN PASTURES of Green Mountain philosophy offer perhaps the most helpful illustration of the dialectics of the preceding history of philosophy—and those dialectics in turn can supply us with a final set of clues concerning the authorship of Ethan Allen's Bible. The author of that work must certainly be numbered among those who wanted to live forever, and the proof whereby he satisfied this desire for eternal life follows the classic lines laid down by Descartes. "The essence of thinking beings, and their manner of acting is essentially distinct from all and every part of the universe besides, and every simile or comparison, which we draw from thence, serves only to confound or perplex a just arrangement of ideas of our exalted intelligent nature and the superlative manner of its exertions or operations, which we depreciate (ideally) by deducing its character of nature or action, from matter," says the author of the *Oracles*.[165] From this seemingly substantial distinction between mind and body, the author infers that the mind may exist after the body is gone. Even better, he insists, the mind must "retain a memory of consciousness of this world" in its afterlife.[166]

The deeper he goes into this forest of speculations about life and death, however, the farther the author seems to get from the happy afterlife of a white stallion. The Lockean epistemology of the *Oracles* lands its author in precisely the paradox that Franklin articulates in his youthful *Dissertation*. If the sensations of the body provide the material on which the mind acts, then the death of the body must involve a rather serious change, to say the least, in the mind's capacity to act. The author of the *Oracles* circles around the paradox for five pages or so before arriving at a clear statement of the epistemological containment of the afterlife: "As certain as our souls are immortal, the manner of our immortality, cannot be understood by us in this life."[167]

The promised afterlife of the *Oracles* turns out to be thoroughly contained in ethics as well. "Mankind in this life are not agents of trial for eternity, but . . . will eternally remain agents of trial," the author tells us in an uncharacteristic fit of eloquence.[168] The afterlife, as in Franklin's later musings, is merely an extension of this life, operating according to the same, internal moral calculus that rules on earth. It is always in all respects a good thing, a bonus, a reward without punishment. Above all, it offers no purchase for the exercise of priestly coercion in this world. "Priests have it in their power to amuse us, with a great variety of visionary apprehensions of things in the world to come," the author scoffs; but we should pay no heed to their grisly and glittering tales from beyond the grave.[169]

In his posthumously published "Appendix," Allen pulls into still closer orbit around the radical core of the early modern philosophy of mind. In his previously published "theology," Allen announces, he erred on the side of immaterialism. "Whatever specific or intrinsic differences there may be between incogitative and cogitative beings," he now says, "yet in both kind of natures and existences, there must be something, which is the same as substance, which must constitute all entity." The soul is "propagated by natural generation with the body," he continues, and it must be united with the body in one physical location. "Such a union of different sorts of substances, one cogitative, and the other material, implies no contradiction, and at the same time constitutes the property of place to the soul." Here Allen oscillates between the contrary poles that define the Cartesian philosophy. With his talk of a "substance" "which must constitute all entity," he comes within a shouting distance of a doctrine of parallelism. Yet his conviction that mind and body are "different sorts of substances" remains paramount. Even after his arguments strip the vaunted doctrine of immortality of any content other than the expression of his determined wish to live forever, Allen emphatically continues to maintain that the soul is immortal.

The surviving works of the man who apparently taught Allen all the philosophy and medicine he knew, on the other hand, reveal a markedly different sensibility. On the subject of immortality, Thomas Young's characteristic gesture is silence. He lets us know unambiguously what is not there—no hell, no eternal damnation—but he says nothing about what is there. There are no white stallions or white clouds in his letters and confessions. And the same is true of the Natural Man.

The silence breaks only for a moment, in the lengthy confession that Young offered to the people of Boston in the busy month of November 1772. He begins by insisting that the rewards and punishments for good and bad deeds are contained within the limits of this life—in the happiness and misery, or good and bad conscience, that virtue and vice invariably deliver to their owners. Having rendered any putative afterlife implicitly irrelevant to the moral law, he then appears to broach the topic of the afterlife directly:

> I, most explicitly believe that all men shall be rewarded for the
> deeds done in the body, whether they be good or evil, according

to the eternal rule of right, by which the sovereign judge of the universe squares all his decrees.[170]

One might have supposed that only an idiosyncratic command of English grammar prevents Young here from making a forthright declaration of his belief in the immortality of the soul. In view of the fact that this profession of faith took place in the theological red zone of colonial New England, however, and given that it follows a declaration that the reward for virtue is to be found within the confines of this life, such a supposition would be farfetched. Young's omission would have been noted—indeed, it was noted by those who accused him of atheism at the time. More telling still, Young's deployment of "the eternal rule of right" where the orthodox would have expected to hear about eternal damnation follows the deist playbook precisely. Like Chubb, Shaftesbury, and Locke, he shifts eternity from the life of the individual to the universal nature that expresses itself through the individual, and he gamely hopes that the defenders of faith will not detect the sleight. Young's rejection of the afterlife placed him far out on the limb of radical philosophy in his own time. Only Jefferson, Freneau, and the nineteen-year-old version of Franklin joined him there, and even then only in the privacy of personal letters, lyrical poems, and youthful dissertations hastily committed to the flames.

All of which serves to illustrate that, even as their philosophies converge on every point that actually matters, the formal doctrines of the two iconoclasts of the Green Mountains remain irreconcilable. The spirit was the same, but the letter was unmistakably different. And this difference—which boils down to a residue of passions rather than ideas— makes it very hard to imagine that the older man could have written the book that his pupil put out under his own name. It is easy enough to picture the author of *The Oracles of Reason* haranguing a freshly dug grave, demanding answers about the nature of an afterlife that, by his own reasoning, he could never know and would never matter. Thomas Young, on the other hand, was not the kind of man who troubled himself with thoughts about a life beyond the grave. He was evidently among those who believe that eternity is already with us here and now.

FREEDOM

On most days in life the sun shines and it seems perfectly unobjection-
able to suppose that freedom just means getting what you want. Sometimes, though, maybe on a cloudy day, you can't help but wonder: Do
I really know what I want? How can I know that what I think I want
is what I really want? On rainy days, you might even get the creeping
sense that all this chasing after one thing and then another doesn't feel
like freedom at all. This is where the radical philosophy of freedom
begins. Liberalism is commonly thought to be a fair-weather creed;
but it was in fact born on a rainy day.

Pieces of radical freedom are scattered in the works of the Stoics and
Pre-Socratics as well as in every major religious tradition, but for the
purposes of understanding the revolutions of the early modern world,
Epicurus arrives at the points that matter. In the *Syllabus* included in
his I-am-an-Epicurean letter, Jefferson bottles up the central intuition
in a concentrated formula: "Man is a free agent."[171] At the same time,
the philosophy of Epicurus and his successors is very much at odds
with the idea of "the freedom of the will" that characterizes the common conception of things. In a universe where every atom follows its
prescribed course, there can be no arbitrary capacity for action such as
that which is commonly attributed to the free will. Epicurus grapples
with this knotty paradox by means of his doctrine of the *clinamen*—
the notion that the atoms engage in occasional, unpredictable swerves
as they fall through space. Guiding Epicurus's thought on this point
is a profound insight about the mutual interdependence of freedom,
the apparent contingency of all things in an infinite universe, and the
inherent incompleteness of our understanding of it. But it takes quite
some effort to extract this pearl from the murky dogma of the swerv-
ing atoms.

Beginning with Hobbes, the heirs of Epicurus in the early modern
world approach the problem by separating the useful idea of freedom
from the confused idea of free will. Freedom in the abstract, says
Hobbes, means simply the "absence of opposition," that is, the absence
of any outside force that prevents a thing from pursuing what it

wants.[172] Freedom therefore describes only the circumstances or conditions in which a thing operates, not the faculty of the will itself: "No liberty can be inferred to the will, desire, or inclination." When we say that the will (or any particular inclination) has "freedom," Hobbes continues, the only thing we can really mean is that it has "power," that is, the ability to overcome whatever hindrances stand in its way. He points out that we acknowledge as much when the opposition to our actions comes not from without but from within. When we are too sick to get out of bed, for example, we say that we lack power, not freedom.

The common idea of free will, Hobbes further contends, assumes that our actions are free only insofar as they are not necessary, that is, insofar as they are not determined by some prior set of causes. But this seeming opposition of freedom and necessity is mistaken. The opposite of freedom is not necessity but compulsion. Thus, "*Liberty* and *Necessity* are Consistent: As in water, that hath not only *liberty*, but a *necessity* of descending by the Channel."[173] Bruno expresses the same intuition when he declares that "necessity and freedom are one . . . [I]t is not to be feared that what acts through the necessity of nature does not act freely . . . rather, that which acts otherwise than as necessity and the necessity of nature require does not act freely."[174] The argument is at bottom an appeal to the guiding principle of philosophy, for the point is that the common idea of free will supposes that the mind is an uncaused cause, or something whose activity cannot be explained in the same way as everything else in the world, according to its antecedent causes.

Supposing then that freedom and necessity are not contraries, Hobbes and his successors next go on to suggest that freedom, insofar as it really refers to the power of an agent, does not mean not acting without causes but acting from causes that originate from oneself. That is, to be free is not to be *un*-determined, but to be *self*-determined. Hobbes deploys the term "conatus" to express some of this sense of freedom. Every physical body has an intrinsic inclination to move in a certain way, and this impulse or "endeavour" is its conatus. So a thing is free when it is able to pursue its own endeavor; and it is unfree when it is determined to act in one way or another by some other thing.

Spinoza adopts wholesale the Hobbesian position on freedom to this point. The "will," he argues, is just an empty abstraction that we form over a collection of volitions, and to attribute freedom to it is as senseless as to say that the stoniness that we find in all stones is itself stony.[175] He insists that our volitions, like everything else in this world, can be explained and therefore answer to necessary causes. But this necessary nature of our activity does not in itself rule out freedom. "That 'necessary' and 'free' are contraries is . . . absurd," Spinoza says, repeating Hobbes; for the opposite of freedom is "constraint or force."[176] He also takes over the term "conatus," as we know, which he defines as the power "with which each thing endeavors to persist in its own being." In a pregnant definition of freedom that will ultimately take him somewhere beyond Hobbes, he adds that a thing is free insofar as it "exists and acts from the necessity of its own nature."

Locke, as is his custom, waffles around a variety of inconsistent positions, so that different interpreters come back from his texts with mutually inconsistent representations of his views.[177] Yet there is no question that, on the topic of freedom and the will, there is at least one Locke who is carrying water for Hobbes and Spinoza. This Locke clearly rejects the idea of free will: "Liberty is not an idea belonging to volition." Like Hobbes and Spinoza, he identifies freedom with power: "Our idea of liberty reaches as far as that power [of doing, or forbearing to do], and no farther."[178] He also signs up for a version of the identification of freedom and necessity: "Voluntary is not opposed to necessary, but to involuntary." He goes on to embrace the idea of freedom as self-determination. Indeed, in his relaxed vernacular he repeats Spinoza's important definition of freedom as acting from the necessity of one's own nature: "Every man is put under a necessity by his constitution, as an intelligent being, to be determined in willing, by his own thought and judgment, what is best for him to do: else he would be under the determination of some other than himself, which is want of liberty."[179]

Locke's successors in the deist movement stay true to his radical side. Collins, for example, pays ritual obeisance to Locke and then repeats Hobbes and Spinoza: "Though I deny Liberty, in a certain meaning of that word, yet I contend for Liberty as it signifies a power in man to do as he will."[180] Nineteen-year-old Franklin follows Collins in attributing necessity to human action: "As Man is a Part of this great Machine, the Universe, his regular Acting is requisite to the regular moving of the whole." Trenchard and Gordon adopt the radical position that our volitions answer to necessity: "The passions of men, which are only the motions raised within us by the motion of things without us, are soothed or animated by external causes."[181] Hume once again rehearses what came before in his exquisitely polished arguments "against Liberty" and "for Necessity."

It is at this point in the history of early modern philosophy that Hobbes steps off the bus, as it were, and Spinoza (with a leg up from Descartes) carries on. Locke parts with Hobbes at this crucial juncture only to stay with Spinoza and Descartes, and the rest of the British deists remain on board, too. The difference can be traced back to the difference between the "classical" materialism associated with Hobbes and the more sophisticated, second-order materialism that begins with Descartes and Spinoza. According to Hobbes, there is only one kind of thing that is real in his world, namely, "Body," and there is consequently only one kind of freedom. "Liberty in the proper sense" is just "corporall liberty," he says.[182] According to the successors of Descartes, there are infinite ways of conceiving of the activity of substance, at least two of which we know about, and there are consequently two ways of thinking of freedom. While there is a kind of freedom associated with the attribute of extension, or body, there is also one associated with thought. It is this kind of freedom, according to Spinoza and his allies, that matters above all to us.

The seismic shift that begins with Descartes is evident—still in a very abstract way—in Spinoza's modification of Hobbes's concept of the conatus. If we imagine the conatus in a purely physical sense, as Hobbes does, it appears to be an accident attached to some preexisting thing. It is an inclination to move in one direction or another assigned to a particular lump of matter that is what it is before it moves anywhere. If we imagine the conatus as a mode of thought, however, it becomes evident that the conatus is not distinguishable from the thing itself, for the idea of any thing is whatever makes it what it is, inasmuch as to represent something is to represent it through its causes. Now, the conatus, or that which causes a thing to persist in being itself, is also really the sum of everything that makes the thing what it is. In Spinoza's words, the conatus of a thing "is nothing but the actual essence of the thing itself."[183]

This abstract distinction begins to hit the road when we take on board its implications for the idea of the mind. As Hobbes would (and did) say, a body is determined to act in one way or another by inclinations or appetites or what we may think of in general as physical causes. As Spinoza recognized, on the other hand, a mind does not act through appetites considered as physical events but from representations of those appetites. Its causes we may call reasons, and these reasons we may call desires. All desires are ideas, according to this radical view, and so they come with representations. That is, they have an object, and they involve an explanation of the relation between the mind and the object. This explanation, moreover, necessarily comes with the possibility of further reflection and so brings with it an implicit understanding of the world that the self and the object of its desire inhabit. Now, the identity or essence of a body, as we know, is just the sum of the causes that make it what it is. But the same now applies to the idea of the mind: it is nothing but the collection of desires that make it what it is.

The upshot is that our desires are not just accidents attached to a preexisting self, in the way that the inclinations are appended to Hobbes's particles of matter; they are the way in which we conceive of ourselves. The idea of the mind is nothing but a reflection on the thing that loves certain other things; that harbors proud memories of various achievements; and that seeks to explore and understand a certain part of the universe in certain ways. Just as he allows no ontological distinctions between the laws of nature and the objects of those laws, or between the objects of knowledge and the representations that constitute those objects, Spinoza here allows no ontological order of priority between the drives that move a mind and the idea of the mind itself, or between desires and the agent of desire. "Desire," he says, "is the very essence of man."[184]

To recognize that the mind knows itself only through representations of itself and its own desires, however, is not at all to say that its representations are necessarily accurate. On the contrary, as we know, our ideas are always imperfect or confused insofar as they derive from the external experience of things—and our ideas of our own body, our desires, and our very minds are certainly external in this sense. So we fall in love with the wrong person, fly into impotent rage over events that are beyond our control, and indulge ourselves in habits that can only hasten our own destruction. Our very own actions, just because they come from us, are not always explained through our essence, or that which accounts for our persistence in being. Which is to say, we often don't know what we really want at all or who we really are. And when that happens, we are not free.

Spinoza captures most of the implications of these forbiddingly abstract and very counterintuitive ideas with a distinction between "active" and "passive" power. When a physical body acts in a manner that can be entirely explained through internal causes, it is active. When its actions are determined by outside forces (which is to say, when its actions are really reactions), it is passive. An active body is "free" in the sense of being determined to act through its own nature, while a passive body is not self-determined. (So far, so Hobbesian, one could say.) The next step in Spinoza's argument amounts to applying this same distinction between active and passive to minds as well as bodies. When the mind acts through ideas that adequately explain itself and its place in the world, it is active. When it acts through inadequate ideas, it is passive. Freedom in this sense is obviously not a binary, take-it-or-leave-it thing like the imaginary "free will"; it necessarily comes in degrees—degrees that match the adequacy of our ideas or range of our consciousness. Locke repeats the distinction between "active" and "passive" and then applies it to "actions of both motion and thinking" in language close enough to Spinoza to raise suspicions of direct borrowing.[185]

From the analysis that Locke and Spinoza share to this point, it follows that the freedom of the mind, properly understood, does not consist in the ability to affirm propositions without reason or cause, as the common view supposes. Rather, freedom is just the power of the understanding itself. To be free it is necessary first to know oneself; and to know oneself it is necessary first to know the world. The absence of freedom, conversely, is just the lack of understanding. There is no such thing as an unfree mind, according to this view; there are unfree individuals, but what they lack is a mind. In a formula, radical freedom is *rational* self-determination. Or, to use the phrase that Jefferson inserted into the Virginia Statute for Religious Freedom, the mind is "created . . . free."

Radical freedom involves a reconception of the freedom of the body, too. The freedom of the body, according to the common, lump-theory of the body, is just the ability to move in one way or another without any antecedent physical cause. According to radicals like Locke and Spinoza, however, the identity of any particular body does not derive from the specific lumps of matter that comprise it, and so its freedom cannot pertain to them. Rather, its freedom has to do with its ability to persist over time in its identity, and since its identity consists in the organization that sustains itself through a ceaseless process of metabolism, the measure of its freedom is simply its power to become the thing that explains the movement of matter in which it participates as its cause—as opposed to becoming that which is explained as the effect of the same movement. Only to the extent that it explains itself in this way does the body realize its essence. The radical freedom of the body, then, is coextensive with its power of appropriation (and "de-propriation") of that which it requires from its environment in order to perpetuate itself. In simplest terms, the body can eat (and be free) or be eaten.

Now, this radical freedom of the body is not something new or different from the radical freedom of thought. Rather, it is that same freedom expressed in a different way. The stuff that the body appropriates—its food—is what we call the object of its desires, insofar as it is considered as a thinking thing; and the organization of matter that persists and grows, considered as a mode of thought, is the idea of the body, which is to say, its mind. Thus, says Spinoza, "in proportion as the actions of a body depend more on itself alone, and as other bodies concur with it less in acting, so its mind is more capable of understanding distinctly."[186] Though explained in different ways, then, the freedom of the body and the freedom of the mind are ultimately coextensive. Thus, while the common conception supposes that the mind remains free even after every finger of the body is lashed down, the radical view says that neither body nor mind can have freedom without the other.[187]

At a high-enough level of abstraction, the rainy-day intuition behind radical freedom merges with the teachings of many varieties of religion. Most religious systems, after all, recommend against satisfying our self-destructive passions, and they go on to locate our true freedom in some kind of "higher" self that saints like Aquinas call our "rational nature." On the other hand, the popular religious systems generally suppose that the lower self and the higher one are hopeless contraries, and that the only thing to do with the former is to crush it without mercy. Whereas the point of radical philosophy is that the higher self is just the lower one more perspicuously understood, and that freedom comes from realizing this self through the understanding, not suppressing it. This difference in theory translates into an even bigger difference in practice. Religious systems by and large propose that a straightforward revelation of our true interest—usually requiring only a pamphlet, a knock on the door, and maybe an afternoon or two of your time to explain in detail—can free the individual from bondage to the passions. Radical philosophy supposes that the long and arduous path to freedom passes through the continuous improvement in our knowledge of ourselves and of the entire universe around us.

WHEN THE HALCYON DAYS of the philosophy of mind came to an end around the turn of the nineteenth century, a host of professors who called themselves "philosophers" arose in defense of the hallowed prejudices about mind and soul. First a number of reactionary Scottish sentimentalists and then Immanuel Kant in particular made it possible to talk once again about transcendental egos and other exotic variations on the immortal soul that might survive the depredations of the guiding principle of philosophy. The resurrected soul achieved a great degree of popularity, and yet it was in reality an idle thing, a balm for those suffering under the weight of too much contrary evidence. Medicine and the nascent field of psychology had already broken free from the dead hand of the common religious consciousness (and have since prospered in the absence of "philosophy," to the great embarrassment of its professors). So, too, had the political order—even while many people in the modern world persisted in thinking otherwise.

Although the radical philosophy of mind takes us into that speculative terrain where philosophers traditionally come only to disagree, its implications for the theory on which modern liberal states rest are sturdy and visible. We can begin to glimpse something of the impact of radical philosophy—and to distinguish the theory of liberalism to which it corresponds from that of the common consciousness—by turning to the concept of "property" that figures so centrally in any version of liberalism. In radical liberalism, property does not in the first instance refer to the titles, estates, or other papers that represent a claim by the individual on the protective powers of the state. It is instead the object of the radical freedom of the body—that is, the freedom of appropriation. It marks out those parts of the world—beginning with the materials of the body itself—that the individual can and must appropriate for the realization of the individual's own being. It is this kind of property—not our titles or estates—that eventually becomes the object of an unalienable right (about which more later). We breathe the air; therefore we own it.

The paramount freedom of original liberalism is that associated with the radical freedom of the mind, and here the contrast with common ideas about liberalism is greatest. The common view is that liberal systems exist in order to shield the preferences, opinions, and desires that are already cemented within the ostensibly self-contained, self-sufficient, pre-social, autonomous, inherently equal mind-souls of modern individuals. Indeed, the most common of the metaphysical critiques of liberalism is that it atomizes society into a collection of agents that need never give reasons for their desires. But the truth is that if any political system ever did succeed in scrupulously sheltering and then acting on the passions and prejudices of its constituent individuals, it would promptly become a dreamland of misery and horror. Most of the supposed metaphysical critiques of liberalism are in reality liberal criticisms of the misdescriptions of liberalism as it appears before the uncomprehending gaze of the common religious consciousness.

The crucial premise of radical, original liberalism is that we often do not know ourselves very well at all, and that the ideas that constitute our desires are often unworthy even of ourselves. We do however have a power of understanding that will seek reasons and evidence just as surely as rocks will fall and planets rotate, and to the extent that we make way for this power, we realize ourselves. Genuine liberalism seeks to make possible radical freedom: not a freedom to commit random acts of faith but the freedom to set aside every dogma that stands between ourselves and our rational self-realization. The obstacles this liberalism seeks to overcome are not whatever prevents us from clinging to what we wish to believe but those that would constrain the questioning, the criticism, the search for evidence, and the conversation with others that might compel us to change our minds.

A genuinely liberal political system likewise aims not to satisfy the existing impulses of the majority but to hold the actions of an entire collective accountable to reason. The distinctive institutional arrangements of liberalism in the large-scale republics of the modern world really function only insofar as they serve this purpose; and they deserve to be criticized insofar as they fail to live up to it. The protections for the rights of minorities, the limits on government power over the individual, the open and deliberative character of the legislative process, the separation of powers that prevents the different parts of government from uniting against the people they are supposed to represent, the critical role of a free press, and the guarantees of freedom of religion—all of these characteristic features of constitutional government enhance human power and freedom precisely to the extent that they check the desires of momentary majorities against the requirements of rational self-determination. Genuine liberalism is at bottom a system designed to ensure that self-government among naturally passionate individuals takes place, as it must, through acts of understanding. It is both a republic of learning and a learning republic. In its ideal form—never perfectly realized in any specific set of institutions—it is a truth machine, and the purpose of its truths is freedom.

IF TRUTHS ARE "self-evident," why do we need to "hold" them to be so? The famous second sentence of the Declaration of Independence might seem to scratch the surface of a contradiction. Are the truths that follow indeed able to stand on their own? Or are they merely true because we arbitrarily hold them to be so? If we translate that line from the language of the radical philosophy of mind in which it was written, however, the apparent contradiction dissolves, and we can glimpse how the insights recorded in that philosophy, far from representing an accident of history or the accumulation of metaphysical dogma, informed the revolutionary ambition of America's founders.

In Jefferson's original draft, the phrase was "sacred & undeniable." The change, which came at Franklin's suggestion, was in this case a fortunate one. It serves to alert us that there will be no appeal to truths handed down from scriptures or announced by prophets. There will be reasons for beliefs, not beliefs without reasons.[188] We "hold" these truths to be self-evident because the free understanding is an active power, not a passive one. It does not consist in the capricious affirmation of or negation of random propositions. Its job is to realize our freedom by rendering the unintelligible intelligible, and it succeeds when it holds things up in such a way as to make them self-evident. The opening of the Declaration does not guarantee that the claims that follow are true. It does assert that they will be performed through the power of understanding. From the same set of commitments follow the most important of these self-evident truths. We are equal and have certain unalienable rights not because we take on faith the idea that we represent an exception to the laws of nature but, on the contrary, precisely because we understand that we are a part of nature and subject to the same universal laws that make all things explicable.

6

The Pursuit of Happiness

. . . life, liberty, and the pursuit of happiness . . .

WAS THOMAS YOUNG A GOOD MAN? THE INTERIOR LIVES of dead people remain as inscrutable as ever, so perhaps historians should avoid such questions of character and motives. Young's own contemporaries, on the other hand, did not have the luxury to refrain from judgment. And he did leave them with quite a record to consider.

On March 5, 1770, in front of the Customs House on King Street, the "Body"—as the mass of people whose names seemed unimportant was called—lost control of itself. Facing off against a squadron of British troops, the surly crowd began to hurl insults, then snowballs, then a stone or two. In a confused panic, the troops fired their muskets point-blank into the mass of people, killing three instantly and mortally wounding two others. A group of men picked up one of the wounded, a seventeen-year-old sailor named James Caldwell, and rushed him in a trail of blood to Dr. Young. It was too late to save the young man. That evening, the Body filled the streets, seeking an outlet for its rage, while the thinking part of Boston cowered in fear of a destructive riot.

Young's political career hitherto had rested largely on his talent for rousing this same rabble. But he seems to have understood right away that further mayhem would not only damage the city but also undermine the patriotic cause. He sallied onto the streets "sword in hand" to urge the people to return to their homes. In the calm light of morning, the city was somber yet collectively satisfied that it had absorbed the violent affront with dignity and would respond through the arm of the law. On the anniversary of the event, Young was invited to give a speech before the Body commemorating the event on King Street, which some time later, in the course of increasingly histrionic displays of patriotic fervor, came to be called "the Boston Massacre."

Three and a half years after helping to head off a riot, Young took on the equal but opposite burden of persuading the people that the right thing to do involved the destruction of private property. In the last week of November 1773, three vessels bearing the tea of the East India Company took up moorings in Boston Harbor. By law they would have to be unloaded within twenty days. If the cargo made it to shore, the colonists would be compelled to acquiesce in the detested Tea Act, with its three-penny duty on tea, which by implication would involve submitting to government without representation, or what Young and his fellow agitators called "tyranny."

On November 29, thousands of Bostonians gathered at Faneuil Hall for a town meeting. The crowd grew so large that the event was moved to the Old South Meeting House. Samuel Adams took charge and pushed through a resolution demanding that the tea be returned to England with the duty unpaid. In essence, he was holding out the prospect for a nonviolent resolution to the crisis that, as he and his fellow radicals could well have anticipated, Governor Hutchinson would not accept. Then Thomas Young rose to speak. "The only way to get rid of the Tea was to throw it overboard and destroy it," he reportedly said. He was the first person to offer in public this felonious proposal, and the only speaker to do so at the meeting of November 29.[1] He was clearly playing the bad cop to Sam Adams's good cop. No one appeared ready to join him.

On the night of December 16, 1773, Young once again exposed

himself on the front lines of the struggle. Thousands had gathered at the Old South. When the news broke that the governor had rejected their demand to return the tea, reported one Tory witness, a "hideous Yelling . . . imitating the Powaws of Indians" arose from the street. Some people began to rush toward the wharf, but Adams, Young, John Hancock, and other leaders urged the people to stay put.[2] At Adams's suggestion, Young rose to deliver a final speech. "The substance of which," the Tory witness reported, "was (as near as I could collect, the People often shouting and clapping him) the ill Effects of Tea on the Constitution—the Confidence he reposed in the Virtue of his Countrymen in refraining from the Use of it, and also in standing by each other in Case any should be called to an Account for their Proceedings. He affected to be very merry and when he had done, the Audience paid him the usual Tribute of Bursts of Applause, Clapping, etc."[3]

. Young's contribution to the moment did not come without some personal risk. While his fellow radicals hid behind their disguises or quietly retreated to their homes to protect their alibis, Young's very public part in events, as he later confessed to a friend, left him unmasked before "the tools of power."[4] When the speech was over and the clapping subsided, the Body streamed over to the wharf. There it watched in silence as a hundred or so "Mohawks" clambered aboard the ships, smashed open chests, and hurled mounds of tea leaves into the salt water. The tea was piled so high in the shallow water that great wads of it poked above the surface, and boatloads of men were sent to beat it back into the brine to make sure that thirsty locals would not take any of it home and thereby convert a principled protest into a mere act of larceny.

To read Young's correspondence through 1774 is to witness the birth of a freedom fighter. Step by step he advances to the conviction that only violence will answer to the violence of the people's oppressors. In May, writing to his New York friend and future Continental Army general, John Lamb, he seems eager for a moment of truth: "At length the perfect crisis of American politics seems arrived; and a very few months must decide, whether we and our posterity shall be slaves or freemen."[5] In August 1774, he tells Samuel Adams, "Whatever the people now give up is lost forever, unless forced back by dint of arms." He then makes an astonishingly bold—and, in light of events in Pennsylvania in May 1776, remarkably prescient—proposal: "We should rather make advances towards reforming the Constitutions of those Colonies where the Councils are all the tools of administration."[6] By September 1774, his mind is made up. The time has now come, he tells Adams, "when ARMS seem the proper argument to hold up to our oppressors." Adams's reply indicates that he is on the same, violent page: "I have written to some of our friends to provide themselves without delay with arms and ammunition, to get well instructed in the military art . . . and prepare a complete set of rules, that they may be ready in case they are called to defend themselves against the violent acts of despotism."[7] Adams did indeed arrange for the accumulation of an arsenal in the outlying town of Concord, and by January 1775 someone had also evidently given him the idea that he should send an agent up north into the Green Mountains and Canada, to discuss with the settlers there what role they might play should hostilities break out with the mother country.

That the risks Young ran in adopting such a militant stance were real seems borne out by an event that took place in the summer of 1774. As he was walking home one day, according to the story passed along by his brother, two British soldiers rushed him. One of the soldiers swung a musket down on his head. By reflex, Young turned aside at the last instant. The weapon scraped his temple and smashed into his shoulder. He fell to the ground bleeding. The soldiers ran off, leaving him for dead. A couple of passersby picked him off the ground and carried him home, where his wife Mary nursed him back to health. Later in the same year, a Boston newspaper printed a letter ostensibly discovered among the British troops, in which a loyalist names fifteen individuals who should be "put to the sword" at "the instant rebellion happens." Number one on the hit list is Samuel Adams; number three is Thomas Young.[8] (Number two is James Bowdoin (1726–1790)—future governor of Massachusetts, friend of Franklin, amateur scientist, and avid partisan of the Enlightenment.) Young and his family were increasingly "apprehensive from the measures that are taking that he may be taken up." His wife, he told Adams, was suffering from "constant terrors."[9]

Young decided the time had come to make an escape. On September 13, 1774, he and his family hastily packed their belongings and set off for Newport, Rhode Island, where they arrived two days later. Young promptly signed up with the local militia and began to train himself in the use of firearms. He boasted to his friends in Boston and New York that the martial spirit was as strong in Rhode Island as it was in Massachusetts.

In April 1775, General Thomas Gage, acting on orders from London, decided to bring the hammer down. He dispatched seven hundred regular soldiers to seize the cache of arms that Samuel Adams had stashed away in the suburbs. At the same time, according to the story passed along by Young's brother Joseph, he sent a man-of-war down to Newport to abduct Young.

In one of Newport's loyalist households, a young sewing girl who had previously worked for Young's family overheard whispered conversations about the plot. Hiding her thread in her clothes, she told her mistress that she had to go off and buy some more. She hurried through the streets to alert a merchant whom she knew to be one of Young's allies. The merchant found Young and warned him that if he was not off the island by midnight, the British would take him prisoner. He offered to find Young passage aboard one of his ships. "What of my family?" Young asked. The merchant promised to send them along after him.

Arriving home to collect his things, Young found his wife and eldest daughter entertaining two ladies from a Tory family who had never visited before. Immediately suspecting that the plot was already under way, he feigned a sprightly air and played a few tunes for the ladies on his violin. Then he excused himself, beckoning his daughter to come with him on the pretense that he needed her help in preparing some medicine. In the back room of the house, he explained the situation. He told his daughter to detain the ladies as long as possible. Then he slipped away with a bundle of clothes. His merchant friend dressed him up as a sailor and hustled him aboard a boat bound for Philadelphia. His family joined him there a few days later.

So, was Thomas Young a good man? Those who worked most closely with him, wherever they recorded their sentiments, judged that he was a man of good character or "virtue." Samuel Adams was surprised by Young's sudden move to Rhode Island, yet he wrote to say, "I trust it will be to the publick Advantage—wherever you may be I am sure you will employ your Talents for the publick Good."[10] The Boston Committee of Correspondence, in response to charges concerning his religious infidelity, took considerable trouble to marshal together a list of testimonials on his behalf. It might also be counted as a point in Young's favor that he died poor. By and large, he seems to have held his contemporaries accountable to the same high standard of virtue he set for himself. Writing to his New York friend Lamb in praise of the Sons of Liberty there, he asked his correspondent to "give my regards to those worthy gentlemen, whose love of human happiness has inspired them to act as becomes men. Their characters will shine, while mercenary, self-seeking, and bespoke wretches will only be remembered with horror."[11]

If we are to judge according to the opinion of those who might have legitimately claimed to represent the largest number of people at the time, on the other hand, Thomas Young was a very bad man. He was "loose," "profligate," "an infamous character," "a man of no morals," a "fool," and a "coxcomb," they said. Though political motives were behind much of the vituperation, and professional medical rivalries accounted for some of the rest—and the general orneriness of the eighteenth-century press should never be underestimated—quite a few of the charges were clearly made in earnest as much as they were in spite. If we look to the substance of the allegations, however, we find no specific evidence of felonies, adulteries, betrayals, or other tangible examples of turpitude. Young's crimes were invariably crimes of belief. His accusers supposed it too obvious to need proving that someone of such bad religion was bad.

ETHAN ALLEN always rode much closer to the line that separates the freedom fighter from the outlaw. In the late 1760s and early 1770s, on his climb to the pinnacle of Green Mountain life, Allen did many a good turn. Helping a farmer clear a field here, bearing a marriage proposal across the hills over there, and rounding up the gang to terrorize Yorkers as the occasion demanded, he won many friends. He came to be regarded as the man who could be counted on to do the things that needed to be done.

Even while he was racking up so many good deeds, however, Allen was amassing an immense portfolio of titles to land in the New Hampshire Grants, one that might have made him lord over estates more vast than those of any ordinary English aristocrat—if only all the cards came up good. He was clearly aiming high, much higher than a tranquil life of subsistence farming in a rustic idyll. The hitch was that in the considered estimation of the neighboring colonial administrations, his titles had no value. The real problem he had with the Yorkers, his contemporaries sometimes suspected, was not that they were bent on erecting a system of mastery and serfdom in the guise of land tenancies and onerous credits, but that they proposed to make themselves the masters and him the serf.

By late 1774, in any case, the situation in the Green Mountains reached a crisis point, and it seemed only natural that Allen should have been the one to stand up for the rights of the settlers. In January 1775, he organized a convention among the settlers on the western side of the Grants, and cajoled his fellow residents to form a compact to defend their "liberty and property, the household gods of Englishmen" against the depredations of creditors and land-jobbers.[12] In the same month, he had a conversation with the agent representing Sam Adams's group, in which he put forward a breathtaking suggestion on what could be done, if need should arise, about a certain immense British fortress on the shores of Lake Champlain. On March 1, he wrote a letter to a friend declaring his astonishing intention to create an independent jurisdiction in the Grants. On March 13, the crisis in the mountains drew first blood.

In the village of Westminster, out on the eastern edge of the Grants, the dark forces of empire had recently established a so-called court of law—a court, the people believed, that would serve mainly to enforce a system of servitude to faraway creditors. Now a local mob occupied the courthouse and refused to allow its officers to begin their proceedings. A sheriff and a band of Tories, after soaking for several hours in the town tavern, chose to blast their way in. One man died on the courthouse floor and another was mortally wounded. Several hundred outraged settlers swiftly converged on the site of the "massacre." Allen pounded in on horseback, and soon it was another convention. At Allen's urging, the convention adopted a resolution proposing that their homeland "be taken out of so oppressive a jurisdiction, and either annexed to some other government or erected and incorporated into a new one."[13] Had history taken a slight turn to the left, Westminster might well have been Lexington and Allen's resolution might just have been celebrated for all eternity as the Declaration of Independence of the United Settlements of Vermont.

When the news about the battles in Lexington and Concord reached Westminster on April 21, 1775, Allen faced a moment of truth. He leapt on his horse and raced over to the Catamount Tavern in Bennington, where he might ponder "futurity" for a few days, as he later said, no doubt with the help of some liquid nourishment. In the hugely popular narrative of his adventures that he offered to the American public some years later, the moment had clean lines and high purpose:

> Ever since I arrived at the state of manhood and acquainted myself with the general history of mankind, I have felt a sincere passion for liberty. The history of nations, doomed to perpetual slavery, in consequence of yielding up to tyrants their natural born liberties, I read with a sort of philosophical horror; so that the first systematical and bloody attempt, at Lexington, to enslave America, thoroughly electrified my mind, and fully determined me to take part with my country.[14]

There was undoubtedly something sincere in the words, something that expressed a certain passion for freedom, and that impelled action on a grand scale. His contemporaries said there was something honorable in Allen, something magnanimous in the way that he never looked back or down, but it wasn't always easy for them to say exactly what it was. At the same time, it cannot be excluded that Allen, like the tail that wags the dog, was wily enough to have figured out that igniting a global revolution might be just the thing to do in order to hang on to a stake in the Green Mountains.

In the field of daily human endeavor, in any case, Allen's moral ratiocinations never seemed to get too far off the ground. One day, for example, an earnest young man who had recently been conscripted into the King's Army approached the leader of the Green Mountain Boys for advice. It was his moral duty to serve the King, the young man explained, but he opposed the King's policy and he was sure that enlisting in the army would mean an early death. Allen advised the young man that the first duty of morality, to which all others must answer, is to preserve oneself. So he should tell the King to go to hell.

The King's representatives in America, perhaps not surprisingly, tended to think that Allen himself was pure evil. The epithet most commonly associated with his name in New York was "wicked." Be that as it may, as the month of April 1775 came to a close, Allen had his sights set on the prize that would bring him a kind of glory and perhaps serve as the ultimate test of his intentions: Ticonderoga.

WHAT MAKES Allen and Young interesting as subjects of moral inquiry is that they both grapple explicitly with the questions of moral philosophy in their writings. The author of Ethan Allen's Bible, it so happens, is very much in favor of morality. "Morality, in the nature of the thing itself, is prerequisite to . . . happiness," he says. "It is the conscious exercise of moral goodness only, which is capable of happifying the rational mind." To a modern reader, Allen's insistence on the "ecstatic felicity of moral happiness" sounds high-toned, perhaps even prudish in its celebration of virtue.[15]

Thomas Young, too, offered a moral theory that seems high on morality, at least on first pass. In his "CREED" of November 1772, written in response to "infernal falsehoods" peddled by his accusers concerning his religion, he presents these reflections on the nature of good and evil:

> I believe that, in the order of nature and providence, the man who most assiduously endeavours to promote the will of God in the good of his fellow creatures, receives the most simple reward of his virtue, that peace of mind and silent applause of a good conscience, which administers more solid satisfaction than all the other enjoyments of life put together.
>
> On the other hand, I believe, that the man who endeavours to build up either his fortune or fame on the ruin of the estate or character of his neighbor, acts contrary to the rule of right, and in consequence must fall short of that approbation from God and his own conscience, which the performance of his known duty would have ensured him of.[16]

Not many people today would detect signs of depravity in this credo, which might easily slip past modern ears like so many pious platitudes about the goodness of being good. Indeed, the references to "conscience" and "the approbation from God" are likely to be invoked as evidence of the pious hankering for religious "virtue" that is widely thought to have suffused America in its years of revolutionary glory.

In the ears of his own contemporaries, however, Young's answers screeched of profanity. In his creed, Young finds no need for creeds at all—and no need for ideas of sin or redemption. He offers no incentive to virtue beyond his own "peace of mind" or personal "satisfaction." He acknowledges no restraint on vice beyond the pangs of his contemptible "conscience." (And he clearly conceives of "conscience" as just another font of pleasure and pain, not the anguished awareness of our unfathomable dependence on a Puritan God.) Sure, he makes a pious gesture toward "the order of . . . providence"; yet it is clearly "the order of nature" that carries the burden of his argument. His idea of virtue is a "nature's virtue," by analogy with "Nature's God," which is to say that, in the words of his contemporaries, it is "the virtue of infidelity." Not surprisingly, Young's "CREED," far from calming his antagonists, only lathered them to even greater heights of righteous indignation.

AT STAKE in the debate over the virtue of the iconoclasts of the Green Mountains was the future of a certain, very common conception of what it means to be moral. Our moral obligations, according to the common view of things, must originate from somewhere outside of us. Morality is not what we *want* to do, but what we *have* to do, and what we have to do is respect the duties, commands, and laws that emanate from some authority above us. Virtue and happiness are orthogonal, if not fundamentally at odds, according to this common conception, as are the public good and private pleasure. We have a free will that allows us to choose between one and the other, and belief alone— belief in God; belief in the soul; belief that our existence serves some higher purpose; at bottom, the belief that it is good to be good—gives us reason to choose the right thing. The alternative to such belief, or so it is said, is nihilism: the disenchanted state that accompanies the loss of all values.

This common or "transcendental" conception of morality, it should go without saying, is not without some insight and utility. There clearly is something about moral judgments that stands outside our fluctuating whims, something often at odds with the pleasures of the moment, something that requires the kind of reflection that we often codify in the form of principles from which we are unwise to depart upon light and transient causes, something on the basis of which it is possible to criticize the most entrenched conventions of a society and even to condemn whole societies. It is also a straightforward matter of observation that people do not act always from conscious calculation of self-interest, that they often feel good about doing good without regard to immediate advantages, and that they often explain their actions by referring to their belief in some transcendental good or higher authority.

This transcendental conception of morality is present as far as the eye can see on every side of history. It was highly popular at the time of the Revolution and remains so today. Many interpreters today go so far as to insist that America's founders—who everywhere celebrated the virtue of "virtue"—epitomized this common belief in the goodness of being good. Behind such historical judgments it isn't hard to detect the same, transcendental conception of morality writ large. Only righteous belief produces righteous leaders, the reasoning goes, and only righteous leaders can create a righteous system of government: ergo, the founders of this great nation must have been great believers. And if we have fallen on hard times, this can be only because we have lost our belief in the goodness of being good, our "religion."

Yet the fact of the matter is that the history of ideas moved in exactly the opposite direction. The transcendental conception of morality is deeply flawed, even self-contradictory, a kind of hallucination conjured out of common misconceptions about the nature of self, mind, and freedom. The radical philosophy from which America's founders drew their ideas of virtue therefore set about to demolish and replace the common idea of morality. Radical philosophy says, in a nutshell, that virtue is happiness; that acts of understanding, not acts of faith, are the foundation of morality; and that the public good is nothing but the private good perspicuously understood. Belief in God, the soul, and otherworldly authorities offers only a simulacrum of morality, often quite at odds with the thing itself. Otherworldly religion is not the cure for nihilism but a symptom of it. It has nothing to do with good government: virtuous people are the consequence, not the cause, of virtuous government.

Call this radical ethical philosophy the "immanent" conception of morality. It wasn't popular at the time of the Revolution and is far from universally accepted today. Yet it had influence enough at the time to make possible the creation of the American Republic, and it remains the best way to make sense of moral life.

Virtue is happiness in this world. The pursuit of happiness is the animating force of the Epicurean philosophy, just as it is the animating force of Epicurean humankind. Every other doctrine that Epicurus produced, from theology to the philosophy of mind, is provisional and in a way unserious, inasmuch as all ultimately answer to the teaching of his ethics, that happiness is the only point of life. Behind the lifestyle teaching that glosses its surface, nonetheless, Epicurean ethics is at bottom an attempt to apply the guiding principle of philosophy to the question of how one may live.

Epicurean ethics begins in a formal sense with the doctrine that pleasure is the only true good and pain is the only true evil. This claim generally goes under the name of "hedonism"—from the Greek word "*hedon*," meaning pleasure—though that label is often the source of more misunderstanding than insight. The common view, abetted by Epicurus's enemies in the early Christian church, falsely construes Epicurus's hedonism as the claim that we should gratify our immediate sensual desires at the expense of all other goods. It is on this account that the term "epicurean" remains even today a synonym for "sybaritic," "decadent," or just "scrumptious." Yet those who trouble themselves to look beyond his unearned reputation—as Diderot,[17] for example, did—soon discover that Epicurus's idea of the good life is one of moderate, sociable, and rather ascetic virtue. While Epicureanism is everywhere associated with fine wines and fatty foods, its founding philosopher lived on a diet of plain salads and fruits. "A man's great wealth is to live sparingly with a tranquil mind," says Lucretius; "for there is never a shortage of little."[18] While hedonism is usually thought to be a selfish creed, Epicurus was famous for the value he placed on friendship.[19] "You should be more concerned about whom you eat and drink with than what you eat and drink," says Epicurus.[20] It is "more pleasurable to confer a benefit than to receive one."[21]

The point of Epicurus's hedonism is not that pleasure is the highest or best good, but that it is the *only* conceivable good. The distinctive feature of Epicurean ethics is not that it rejects those dispositions of character that we typically unite in the idea of virtue—prudence, fortitude, charity, honesty, and so forth—but that it explains and defends them as expressions of pleasure and pain. In his reprise of the Epicurean philosophy, Gassendi states the underlying agenda in the language favored by the early modern philosophers: "Virtue alone is called inseparable from pleasure, because . . . it is the necessary cause of pleasure, that is, when virtue has been posited, pleasure and felicity follow."[22] Thus, according to Gassendi's paraphrase of Epicurus, "It is impossible to live pleasurably without living sensibly, nobly, and justly."[23]

When we oppose virtue to pleasure, according to Epicurus, we are not opposing an unpleasant duty against pleasure, nor are we opposing the passions with reason or will. Rather, we are simply pitting a more perspicuous understanding of our pleasure against a less perspicuous one. Abstaining from "lustful eating," for example, allows us to avoid the pain of a bloated belly and bad health. In the letter in which he identifies himself as an "Epicurian," Jefferson identifies the relevant "canon" of the Epicurean philosophy: "The indulgence which prevents a greater pleasure, or produces a greater pain, is to be avoided." When we champion the durability of virtue over the fleeting quality of immediate gratification, Epicurus adds, we are simply acknowledging that most pleasures consist chiefly in the temporary overcoming of specific pains. Eating is pleasurable as a means to removing hunger, for example, but once the belly is full there is no more pleasure to be had from filling it. When we turn away from the excesses of sensual dissipation, we wisely recognize that there is a limit to our sensual happiness, that pleasures cannot be stacked on top of one another like pancakes without end.

According to Epicurus, the wise man avoids stealing, cheating, and other vicious behavior not just because the calculus of costs and benefits rarely favors crime as much as we imagine it does, but because our conscience prevents us from enjoying our ill-gotten gains in peace. Our conscience, says Epicurus, is itself a passion; specifically, it is the feeling that follows naturally from our knowledge that we can never be certain that our acts of injustice will not be discovered.[24] "Let nothing be done in your life which will bring you fear if it should be known to your neighbor," Epicurus intones. "The tranquil man causes no stress to himself or anyone else."[25] The highest virtue for Epicurus is also the highest pleasure, namely, the tranquility or peace of mind that comes naturally with a life of modest virtue.

At the bottom of Epicurean ethics is the notion that virtue is a measure of our faithfulness to our own true nature, that is, of our authenticity. In the influential 1699 English translation of Bernier's French translation, Gassendi expresses this sentiment in a loose but vivid rendering of the Epicurean philosophy of life:

> Tis a strange thing, that considering we are born but once, that our days are to have an end, and that the morrow being out of our power, nevertheless we always put off till the next day to live. So that our life is spent miserably in these continual delays . . . for we occupy ourselves in everything else, but to Live.[26]

All virtue, according to this line of thought, is a matter of pursuing one's genuine interest or self-realization. It supposes an awareness of oneself, and of every aspect of one's actual life, in the present. It is not far from what in the Buddhist tradition is called "mindfulness." Conversely, all vice is a form of self-betrayal, and all crimes are at bottom crimes against oneself. They begin when we delude ourselves about our very own selves. The opposite of virtue, in Lucretius's memorable words, happens when we "run away from ourselves."[27]

Notwithstanding the glistening rhetoric of virtue in which it was delivered, the hedonistic ethics of the Epicureans represented a hugely controversial position in the early modern world. Those who adopted it at the time were regularly compared with "swine" and "vile beasts" and accused of doing many filthy things that they didn't actually do. Yet, to an astonishing degree, the most important philosophers of the period—and all of the ones that mattered for America's revolutionary deists—took the side of the pigs and monsters. More than simply taking over the Epicurean philosophy, in fact, they explained it in a way that deepened its meaning and impact. In effect, they framed it as not merely a "hedonistic" ethics, but an "immanent" one.

Setting aside Gassendi, whose principal contribution was that of an expositor, the first systematic proponent of the new Epicurean ethics was Hobbes. "Every man, for his own part, calleth that which *pleaseth* him and is delightful to himself, good," says the man who came to be known to the public as "the monster of Malmsbury."[28] Though often caricatured as a hedonist in the shallowest sense of the term, Hobbes makes clear that his concern is not to advocate a particular variety of good but to clarify the meaning of the terms "good" and "evil." Good and evil, Hobbes explains, "are ever used with relation to the person that useth them: There being nothing simply and absolutely so; nor any common Rule of Good and Evill, to be taken from the nature of the objects themselves."[29] To be good is always to be good *for* some one or some thing or some species,[30] he says; it is a perspective on things, not a property of them. (Or, as Hamlet puts it, "There is nothing good or bad but thinking makes it so.")[31]

Spinoza follows Hobbes (and Hamlet) on this essential point. "Good and bad," he says, "indicate nothing positive in things considered in themselves, and are nothing but modes of thinking."[32] Playing music, he observes, may be a good thing for the melancholy, a bad idea for those in mourning, and a matter of indifference to the deaf. The good, then, is "what we certainly know to be useful to us," and the bad is whatever gets in the way.[33] More dramatically, Spinoza tells us that we do not desire or detest things because we judge them to be good or evil; we judge them good or evil because we desire or detest them.

Locke—to the consternation of those interpreters bent on representing his philosophy as a conventionally religious one—fully embraces the hedonism of Epicurus, Hobbes, and Spinoza to this point, though without acknowledgment of any association. In a section of his *Essay* titled "Good and Evil What," he makes his position plain:

> That we call "good," which is apt to cause or increase pleasure . . .
> And, on the contrary, we name that "evil," which is apt to produce
> or increase any pain . . . Things are good or evil only in reference
> to pleasure or pain.[34]

It is in fact difficult to sound more Epicurean than Locke: "Every intelligent being really seeks happiness, which consists in the enjoyment of pleasure, without any considerable mixture of uneasiness."[35]

The radical philosophers of the early modern period also absorb and develop the quintessentially Epicurean intuition that achieving our genuine good, or happiness, involves pitting our pleasures against one another, rather than against an external or transcendental good. Reason, according to this line of thinking, may order the passions but it cannot overrule them; only other passions can stop the passions. Though Hobbes is the first of the moderns to articulate this position,[36] Spinoza makes the underlying point in a formula that will prove to have crucial further implications: "No emotion can be checked by the true knowledge of good and evil insofar as it is true, but only insofar as it is considered an emotion."[37] Like every moralist of the period from Bayle and Locke to Franklin, he underscores the point with a famous citation from Ovid: "I see the better course yet follow the worse."[38]

Locke repeats. The object of the will, he says, is "*not*, as is generally supposed, *the greater good in view*, but some (and for the most part the *most pressing*) uneasiness a man is at present under."[39] "Let a man be never so persuaded of the advantages of virtue," he emphasizes, ". . . yet till he 'hungers and thirsts after righteousness,' till he feels an uneasiness in the want of it, his will will not be determined to any action in pursuit of this confessed greater good."[40] Hume elegantly summarizes (and then perhaps overstates) the position in his famous claim: "Reason is, and ought only to be, the slave of the passions."[41]

Perhaps the most complex and fruitful aspect of the radical moral philosophy of Epicurus's early modern successors has to do with the development of the intuition that the ethical life is grounded in self-realization, that is, that virtue always involves a kind of authenticity or responsibility to oneself. Once again Hobbes is the first to revive the intuition in a systematic way, and he does so within the first-order materialist framework for which he is justly famous.[42] The essential or fundamental conatus of each individual, he stipulates, is to preserve itself. It is this drive of self-preservation, according to Hobbes, that is the fundamental motive for all those actions we call virtuous and for the disposition we call virtue. The "First Law of Nature," that "every man ought to endeavour peace," he maintains, is a "Precept, or general Rule, found out by Reason, by which a man is forbidden to do that, which is destructive of his life, or taketh away the means of preserving the same."[43] The obligation to be virtuous, in other words, arises in an immanent way from the drive of the conatus to pursue its own preservation and realization.

Spinoza, as we know, borrows Hobbes's conatus to this point: "No virtue can be conceived as prior to this one, namely the conatus to preserve oneself."[44] He then goes on to redefine what we mean by "pleasure" in order to make clear that it is part of an immanent—not merely hedonistic—account of ethics. Pleasure is not an oh-so-good sensation, nor is it fundamentally a distraction from our true purpose, says Spinoza; it is just the term that corresponds to an increase in our power to realize ourselves. Pain is a decrease in the same. That is, pleasure (or what might be better called "joy") is a transition from a lesser to a greater state of perfection of the conatus; and pain works the other way around. Thus, to be good is not just to be good *for* someone, as we already know, but to be good for the *essence* or identity of that someone, or whatever it is that makes it what it is. There is a concept of utility at work here—one that can be linked backward to Epicurus and forward to the utilitarian philosophers—but it is a richer and more sophisticated version than the one we normally use. For the moment it is worth pointing out that unlike the utility of the utilitarians—which involves units of pleasure that are thought to be commensurable across individuals and that always reduce to an indescribable good sensation—this is an intrinsically individual utility, and the sensations with which it is associated are not necessarily what we call pleasant (for what we mistakenly call pain may involve a gain).

From Spinoza's elaboration of the Hobbesian position follow a number of counterintuitive identities that prove central to any explanation of America's revolutionary political philosophy. It follows, first, that virtue necessarily involves the pursuit of advantage: "The more every man endeavors and is able to seek his own advantage, that is, to preserve his own being, the more he is endowed with virtue."[45] This view, Spinoza acknowledges, is the opposite of the common view, according to which "the principle that every man is bound to seek his own advantage is the basis, not of virtue and piety, but of impiety." It follows, next, that virtue is really a synonym for power: "By virtue and power I mean the same thing."[46] And it follows that a state of highest virtue is the state of highest pleasure—which is to say, happiness. "Virtue itself" is "happiness itself."

Locke characteristically avoids the metaphysical jargon, yet he offers an account that walks us calmly through the paces of Hobbes and Spinoza's conatus. "Uneasiness," says Locke, is "the chief, if not only spur to human industry" and "the spring of all action."[47] "This uneasiness," he adds, "we may call, as it is, desire."[48] Though Locke is careful to obscure the heterodox implications, he soon grants that this pursuit of happiness is essentially indistinguishable from the pursuit of virtue. God, he says, has "by an inseparable connexion, joined virtue and public happiness together, and made the practice thereof necessary to the preservation of human society, and visibly beneficial to all."[49] The theologians of his time immediately pounced upon the section in which Locke moots this claim, and Locke responded in the usual way, by retreating into a cloud of caveats. Yet the phrase Locke mints here—that there is an "inseparable connexion" between "virtue and . . . happiness"—is one of the most enduring formulae of deism. Sometimes, as in this instance with Locke, this connection is attributed to God; other times it is assigned to nature; but this is a distinction without a difference.

Turning to Locke's successors in the British Enlightenment, it is evident that the radical, Hobbesian-Spinozist side of Locke is the one that matters. Shaftesbury, to be sure, has many bad things to say about Hobbes (more on that in a moment), and he makes just enough noise about the eternal nature of virtue to have been cast as a Platonist or a Stoic of sorts. Yet the roots of his moral philosophy are firmly planted in the immanent conception of his Epicurean predecessors.[50] All of our moral actions must be explained through emotions or affections, the third Earl asserts, and from this it follows (to paraphrase Spinoza and anticipate Hume) that "there is no speculative opinion, persuasion or belief that is capable immediately or directly to exclude or destroy" our sense of right and wrong; "nothing beside contrary affection . . . can operate upon it."[51] Though Shaftesbury's conception passes through an idea concerning "the moral sense" that requires further discussion, the essential fact is that virtue, as he understands it, ultimately coincides with individual utility. "Virtue is the good and vice the ill of every-one,"[52] he says; "virtue and interest may be found at last to agree";[53] and "moral rectitude, or virtue must accordingly be the advantage, and vice the injury and disadvantage of every creature."[54]

In the course of the British Enlightenment, the term "self-love" assumed most of the functions of the conatus of Hobbes and Spinoza. This was somewhat unfortunate because, as Rousseau would later be forced to point out, there is a difference between self-love as *amour propre*—which has to do with the narcissistic pride we take in the opinions other people have about us—and self-love as *amour de soi*—which recovers some of the idea of the conatus. In any case, Bolingbroke writes—and Jefferson copies into his student notebook—the thesis: "There is in the whole animal kind one intellectual spring, common to every species, but vastly distinguished in its effects,"[55] and this "original spring of human actions" is "self-love."[56] In *Cato's Letters*, Trenchard and Gordon signal their unambiguous acceptance of the foundations of the immanent ethical program: "Of all the passions which belong to human nature, self-love is the strongest, and the root of all the rest, or, rather, all the different passions are only several names for the several operations of self-love."[57]

In his *Essay on Man*, Pope once again manages to condense the gist of the preceding century of radical philosophy in rhyming verses. First he states the basic premise of hedonism:

> *Self-love and Reason to one end aspire,*
> *Pain their aversion, Pleasure their desire;*[58]

In another couplet, he explains that this pursuit of pleasure and avoidance of pain form the natural foundation of virtue itself:

> *The surest virtues thus from passions shoot*
> *Wild nature's vigour working at the root*[59]

He then compresses into a single line Hobbes and Spinoza's doctrine concerning the conatus, in the language favored by Bolingbroke:

Self-love, the spring of motion, acts the soul.[60]

He concludes this poetic discourse on ethics with an emphatic endorsement of Spinoza's claim that virtue and happiness are together creatures of this world:

Virtue alone is happiness below.[61]

Although the immanent ethics that spans radical thought from Epicurus to Pope usually enters the historiography as just another dogma, lined up against any number of other arbitrary assertions of this or that value, it is in fact better understood as an effort to think through or clarify a certain set of confusions that hobble the common or transcendental conception of morality. The common view, say the radicals, begins with the valid intuition that the good cannot be something that fluctuates according to every change in fancy of an arbitrary will. It must come with reasons, and those reasons must be found in our understanding of things as they are, not as we wish them to be. However, the common view—misled by those common misconceptions about the self and mind with which we are already familiar—goes on to suppose falsely that because our idea of the good does not involve an arbitrary affirmation of the will, it must therefore be a fixed property of things in themselves. In effect it multiplies the errors of the common conception of mind, for it imagines that the good exists independently of all our reasons for thinking that it is good, in the same way that it imagines that our representations stand before consciousness independently of the reasons for which we hold them true. Yet in taking this extra step toward an imaginary certainty, the common view destroys the very insight with which it begins. In direct violation of the guiding principle of philosophy, it renders the good an arbitrary feature of the world, a motive independent of all motives, a cause that can move us without itself answering to any other cause, something that we are obliged to do for no other reason than that it is good to be good.

The immanent conception, on the other hand, stays longer with the insight at the core of the common conception. It, too, says that there are always reasons to be good; and then it further insists that we can always continue to reflect on these reasons, and ask why the good is good. In keeping with the guiding principle, it says that whatever moves us, like whatever moves anything in the infinite universe, must be explicable. So the good always comes with reasons for its goodness; those reasons must refer to those motives that we generically identify as pleasure and pain; and those reflections on the affections can always be the subject of further reflection, elaboration, and qualification. The inherent intelligibility of moral life, in other words, rules out the very possibility that arbitrary dogmas, creeds, or acts of faith can ever be more than provisional and revisable by-products of a moral life. Those who misguidedly maintain that there is some good independent of all our motives, according to this radical critique, do not in fact succeed in creating one. They simply read their own motives into the things themselves and confuse their limited perspective with a fixed fact about the world. In establishing some imaginary authority outside of themselves, they really only oppose themselves to themselves, and the vaunted certainty of their conviction serves chiefly to mark the tenacity of their ignorance.

Notwithstanding the usual variations of personality and circumstance, America's revolutionary deists are notable for the cheerfulness with which they embrace this first, crucial step in the ethical program of radical philosophy. A concise summary of Epicurean ethics to this point, as it happens, may be found in the *Syllabus* Jefferson offers in the letter in which he declares himself to be a follower of Epicurus:

> Pleasure active and In-do-lent.
>
> In-do-lence is the absence of pain, the true felicity.
>
> Active, consists in agreeable motion; it is not happiness, but the means to produce it.
>
> Thus the absence of hunger is an article of felicity; eating the means to obtain it.
>
> The *summum bonum* is to be not pained in body, nor troubled in mind.
>
> i.e. In-do-lence of body, tranquility of mind. [62]

In that same *Syllabus*, Jefferson distills the immanent essence of the Epicurean position into a mere three lines:

> Happiness the aim of life.
> Virtue the foundation of happiness.
> Utility the test of virtue.

That Jefferson adopted this trinity of happiness, virtue, and utility as his own is clear. "Nature has constituted *utility* to man the standard and test of virtue," he writes elsewhere. And "without virtue, happiness cannot be."[63] In the *Syllabus*, Jefferson goes on to list the four essential virtues of the Epicurean philosophy as "1. Prudence. 2. Temperance. 3. Fortitude. 4. Justice." From his use of this more or less classical list, incidentally, we may infer that Jefferson's Epicurus owes much to Gassendi; for it is Gassendi who, borrowing from Plato, gives this particular list a highly prominent position in early modern Epicureanism.

Franklin, too, is resolutely Epicurean in his ethical stance. Indeed, in his first *Dissertation*, he is more dogmatic even than Epicurus. Good and evil are merely "empty distinctions," he says; pleasure and pain are all there is. Not only that, but "*Pleasure* is caused wholly by *Pain*, and no other thing at all." He then represents the conatus in language that echoes that of Locke and Bolingbroke: "Uneasiness" is "the first Spring and Cause of all Action."[64] In his autobiography, Franklin offers an amusing anecdote from about the same period in his life that serves to elaborate the point made by Spinoza and later associated with Hume, that reason is the slave of the passions. Ben was a committed vegetarian, he tells us, until the day he smelled some fish frying deliciously over a fire. Just as the fish were coming out of the pan, he recollected that he had seen smaller fish inside the stomachs of bigger fish. "If you eat one another," he reasoned, "I don't see why we mayn't eat you." Whereupon he marveled, "So convenient a thing it is to be a reasonable Creature, since it enables one to find or make a Reason for everything one has a mind to do."[65]

In later writings, Franklin mellows into something closer to the true spirit of Epicurus. "A wise man will desire no more than what he may get justly, use soberly, distribute cheerfully and live upon content-edly," he says.[66] Following Epicurus, he takes for granted that utility is the standard of virtue: "Vicious actions are not hurtful because they are forbidden, but forbidden because they are hurtful, the Nature of man alone consider'd."[67] Conversely, "nothing is so likely to make a man's fortune as virtue."[68] As if to underscore the heterodox implications of this thoroughly immanent conception of virtue, he adds, "If rascals knew all the advantages of virtue, they would become honest out of rascality."[69] In a dialogue printed in the *Pennsylvania Gazette*, he celebrates the "SCIENCE OF VIRTUE," which, it turns out, amounts to developing "knowledge of our *true interest*" which is to "arrive at our main End in View, HAPPINESS." He wraps it up with a paraphrase of the line that Pope published in the same year: "Without virtue man can have no happiness in this world."[70]

Franklin was an epicurean in something close to the ordinary sense of the term, too. In Philadelphia, London, and perhaps most egregiously in Paris as an elderly ambassador, the great scientist made a point of living well—too well, according to the rather uptight John Adams, who groused about his colleague's all-play-and-no-work habits. In a characteristically irreverent parody published in the *Pennsylvania Gazette*, he puts a smile on this carefree philosophy of life.[71] A fictional clergyman named Joshua Smith moans, "All the few days we live are full of Vanity; and our choicest Pleasures are sprinkled with bitterness." Franklin's alter ego fires back: "All the few Cakes we have are puffed up with Yeast; and the nicest Gingerbread is spotted with Flyshits!" In his conclusion, Franklin announces the creed that seems to have guided his journey through the numberless lifestyle choices of daily existence: "I am for taking *Solomon's* advice, *eating Bread with Joy, and Drinking Wine with a merry Heart.*" When Franklin later proposed a society for moral reform in Philadelphia, he called it, with appropriately Epicurean flair, "the Society of *the Free and Easy*."[72]

The immanent conception ultimately ascended into the office of the presidency of the United States. In his first inaugural address, Washington delivers the ethical line from the Epicurean Enlightenment: "There exists in the economy and course of nature an indissoluble union between virtue and happiness; between duty and advantage." In his second inaugural address, Jefferson joins the chorus: "With nations as with individuals, our interests, soundly calculated, will ever be found inseparable from our moral duties."[73] In a private letter he adds, "The order of nature [is] that individual happiness shall be inseparable from the practice of virtue."[74] Both Washington and Jefferson seem to echo the words of Locke, cited earlier, concerning the "inseparable connexion" between virtue and happiness. The only difference—one of words, not substance—is that while Locke attributes this connection to God, the Americans are content to lay it at the feet of Nature.

Virtue is understanding (or, the cognitive turn in radical ethics). In its passage through the debates of early modern philosophy, the revived version of the Epicurean ethics underwent a substantial transformation. The dividing line falls directly between Hobbes and Spinoza and splits Descartes in two, as it were, and it has to do with the familiar shift from the first-order materialism associated with Hobbes to the second-order variety associated with Spinoza (and problematically with Descartes).

Hobbes does not systematically distinguish between pleasure and good on the one hand and pain and evil on the other; Spinoza does, and in a manner that follows from the elemental difference concerning the attributes of substance. The two pairs, says Spinoza, refer to the same reality but from different perspectives. We call them pleasure and pain when we consider them as dispositions of the body, or modes of extension; and we call them good and evil when we consider them as ideas, or modes of thought. "The knowledge of good and evil," he explains, "is nothing other than the emotion of pleasure or pain insofar as we are conscious of it."[75] Pleasure and pain may also be called "appetites," and as such they may be found in things and animals and ourselves insofar as we are not considering them as objects of conscious reflection. Good and evil, on the other hand, are the names we give to the objects of our desire, and they necessarily involve ideas.

In Spinoza's world, then, all desires involve representations. There are no longings without objects, no moods without reasons, no vague feelings of unease about one knows not what, no interests that have not already been mediated through some set of concepts. As representations, moreover, desires can themselves be represented, and subject to further, intrinsically emotional representations. By virtue of the independence of the attributes of substance, crucially, our explanations of our ideas of the good always pass through other modes of thought, which is to say other representations of pleasure and pain, but not through modes of extension, or our actual pleasure and pain. We know our own motives in the same way that we know everything else that moves in the infinite universe of Epicurus: through our explanations of them.

Spinoza goes on to define a variety of emotions—hatred, joy, despair, envy, and so forth—as ways of conceiving or representing pleasure and pain. Love, he explains by way of example, is "pleasure accompanied by the idea of an external cause."[76] Hatred is "pain accompanied by the idea of an external cause." Hope is "inconstant pleasure arising from the idea of a thing . . . of whose outcome we are in doubt." Fear is pain arising from similarly uncertain things. And so on.

Locke continues to track Spinoza. Although pleasure and pain are often thought to be of the mind or body, Locke says, in reality they are "only different constitutions of the mind." Love, he explains by way of example, is "the thought . . . of the delight which any present or absent thing is apt to produce."[77] He then goes on to copy out in a rather blatant way the same definitions of other emotions in the same format that Spinoza offers. Hatred is "the thought of pain" associated with an external object; hope is pleasure "at the thought of a probable future enjoyment"; fear is pain at "the thought of future evil likely to befall us"; and so on.[78]

This view, that all emotions are representational, is a fundamental component of the deep rationalism of Spinoza and his allies, and raises many questions that should be pursued elsewhere. In order to understand its implications for America's revolutionaries, however, the essential claims are straightforward. The obvious initial point is that this move makes it possible to understand the gap, often invisible to Hobbes, between what we want and what we *think* we want. Hobbes, implicitly adhering to the contours of the common conception of morality and mind, in effect takes for granted that since our pleasures and pains are "internal," we always know what we want, that is, that we have a perspicuous knowledge of our own appetites and interests. According to Spinoza and Locke, however, there is no reason to suppose that our inherently representational desires are not as confused as our representations of anything else. Because "things come to be presented to our desires under deceitful appearances," Locke elaborates, men often bring misery on themselves.[79] "The cause of our judging amiss when we compare our present pleasure or pain with future, seems to me to be the weak and narrow constitution of our minds."[80] So we fall in love with the wrong person; we react with futile rage to events that are beyond our control; we covet possessions that can only hasten our ruin; and in general we suffer from the "passions" that arise from our "passive" or inadequate ideas about the world. And yet, by virtue of this very same power of understanding, we have the ability to learn from our mistakes, to imagine new futures for ourselves, to abandon the past even as we pursue what we really always wanted.

A still deeper insight embedded in the radical conception is that our knowledge of good and evil, such as it is, cannot be replaced with a thoughtless calculation delivered by some moral theory on the basis of some fixed set of rules, for it must follow from our awareness of the interconnections of things in the universe as a whole, taken without limit. In other words, to explain good and evil per se—just as to explain consciousness—it would be necessary first to explain the world in its entirety. From this it follows that the hunt for universal laws that occupies moral philosophers to this day, that takes us for a ride through deontological, utilitarian, virtue-based, Kantian, and any number of exotic schools of thought in the perennial pursuit of the almost-but-not-quite-finished moral theory that will supposedly deliver to us an expert system capable of telling us once and for all what really matters, is an absurdity. It amounts to chasing after the horizon as if it were a fixed line in space. There is only one categorical imperative left standing in the forlorn discipline of moral philosophy, and that is the imperative to improve the understanding. "The mind, insofar as it exercises reason, judges nothing else to be to its advantage except what conduces to understanding,"[81] says Spinoza. Thus, "we know nothing to be certainly good . . . except what is really conducive to understanding."[82]

Locke brings it all together in a crucial chapter of his *Essay* appropriately titled "Power." The "greatest good" of man is to realize himself as an intelligent being, he tells us there, and this good, as it happens, is both "the foundation of our liberty" and "the utmost pleasure we are capable of."[83] He condenses a version of this immanent synthesis of freedom, understanding, virtue, power, and happiness in a passage that, not coincidentally, sheds much light on the origins and significance of the most popular phrase in the Declaration of Independence:

> As therefore the highest perfection of intellectual nature lies in a careful and constant ***pursuit of*** true and solid ***happiness***, so the care of ourselves, that we mistake not imaginary for real happiness, is the necessary foundation of our liberty. The stronger ties we have to an unalterable ***pursuit of happiness*** in general, which is our greatest good, and which, as such, our desires always follow, the more are we free from any necessary determination of our will.[84] [emphasis added]

There is more than a little historical irony in the fact that the "pursuit of happiness," long taken to stand for the thoughtless, selfish, amoral consumerism and materialism that splashes around at the shallow end of American culture, actually originated from a philosophy that identifies happiness with virtue and the improvement of the understanding.

From the Lockean-Spinozist claim that virtue is understanding—which is at bottom just a reprise of a tune from Socrates in the key of early modern philosophy—it follows conversely that vice is misunderstanding. Thus, contrary to the common conception, vice is not the pursuit of self-interest at the expense of virtue, but the dissolution of the self that occurs when we act through inadequate ideas, or what Spinoza and Locke identify as the passions, or passive emotions. And in fact, since most people operate with rather inadequate ideas of themselves and the world, according to both Spinoza and Locke, most people find themselves at the mercy of self-destructive passions. Which is to say, people are generally vicious and corrupt, not because they act as rational calculators of self-interest, but because they fail to do so.

The conception of virtue as understanding also returns us with greater insight to the mildly ascetic side of Epicureanism. The common view—often falsely associated with Epicurus, Hobbes, Spinoza, and their heirs—says that freedom consists in the unfettered ability to satisfy every impulse that surges into consciousness. But the radical view says that the random satisfaction of urges is the essence of unfreedom. The indulgence of the appetites, says Spinoza, reflects "a weakness of the mind" rather than "an instance of the mind's freedom." As we chase down the false objects of our passions, the first thing that we lose is ourselves. Conversely, "freedom is the greater as a man is more able to be guided by reason and control his appetites."[85]

Although the idea of virtue as understanding that emerges from the Epicurean revival involves a number of complexities and can be debated much further, its most important message can be summarized in three basic propositions. The first is that every person or thing necessarily pursues its own idea of the good.[86] This is the premise that motivates the rejection of the doctrine of free will and that expresses the deep rationalism of Epicurean hedonism: that all of our actions are explicable. Spinoza calls this proposition a "law of nature"—as does Paine. Pope articulates it in another one of his distinctly Spinozistic couplets:

> *Modes of Self-love the passions we may call*
> *Tis real good, or seeming, moves them all . . .*[87]

Pope's reference to a "seeming" good here introduces the second basic proposition: that the ideas of the good that motivate individuals do not necessarily represent their true good. When we act badly, it is not because we aim for the bad but because we are not conscious of our good. Seneca captures the idea in a line copied down by, among others, the young James Madison: "Why does no man confess his vices?

Because he yet continues in them; it is for a man who is awake to tell his dream."[88] The third and conclusive proposition is that understanding is the one and only virtue that stands by itself.

The most elegant summary of the three propositions that characterize the cognitive turn in Epicurean ethics, as it happens, is to be found in the work of Shaftesbury. "Grant but this, *that all vice is error; that all pursue their good and cannot but do so; that there is no good but a good mind, and no ill but an ill one*: immediately all is right."[89] It seems hardly a coincidence that Shaftesbury's three clauses here correspond almost verbatim (but without acknowledgement) to three specific propositions in Spinoza's *Ethics*.[90]

At some point in the eighteenth century, the new (or revived) concept of virtue as understanding was loaded aboard a merchant ship and carried across the Atlantic Ocean. In 1767, it appeared in, among other places, a newspaper article that Thomas Young authored. Those who preach the "depravity of reason," says Young, contradict themselves. Our faculty of reason, he declares, is a power "natural to man" that directs us "in the ways of wisdom and virtue to happiness" even as it cautions us with the understanding that our knowledge can always be improved.[91] Then he sings a paean to reason so defined: "It loves those who love it, and they who seek it early shall find it; its fruit is better than gold, and its revenue than choice silver; it leads in the way of righteousness . . . it renders the future present, and timely provideth for that which is yet afar off." Such celebrations of the virtue of reason might easily have been padded with references from the works of Spinoza or, more plausibly under the circumstances, Shaftesbury. Interestingly, Young invokes a more respectable authority whose links to those radicals has long been overlooked: "For your assistance herein, I recommend to you the method of Mr. Locke."

Self-love and social are the same. According to the hackneyed interpretations that gained currency with the Counter-Enlightenment and have since come to dominate the common view of the matter, the moral philosophy of the Enlightenment involves an unpleasant judgment about human nature: that we are particularly nasty creatures and care only about ourselves. But the radical core of the Enlightenment involves no such judgment. The common view also complains that the Enlightenment devalues the social values associated with community and tradition. But this, too, amounts to a falsification of the history of ideas.

The radical core of the Enlightenment is best understood neither as a judgment on human nature nor as the promotion of one moral value over another, but as a reflection on the nature of morality itself. It begins with the intuition that human beings come into the world with a common conception of morality that is close enough to the truth to lead us dangerously astray. This common conception may be the result of a process of evolution by natural selection, as some theorists now propose, or it may be the accidental by-product of the structure of human cognition. In either case, its defining premise is that we have no reason to be good to anyone other than ourselves—and therefore that only a blind faith in authority will keep us on the straight and narrow. Radical Enlightenment says that this premise is false. Public virtue and private happiness, far from opposites, are two perspectives on the same reality.

In Spinoza's version—one of many, to be sure—the argument takes its start from the claim that things may affect the power of other things to act only insofar as they share a common nature: "Our power to act, in whatever way it can be conceived, can be determined, and consequently assisted or checked, by the power of another individual thing which has something in common with us, and not by the power of a thing whose nature is entirely different from our own."[92] Food nourishes us because it is made of organic stuff like us; a knife can harm us because it shares with us a certain physical nature. At the bottom of Spinoza's claim is the intuition that everything—and especially every living thing—is a dynamic process, an organization of matter rather than an inert lump of matter. Power is therefore not a fixed attribute of any particular material thing, but an attribute of the relationships through which a complex body is continually regenerated and persists in being.

The highest degree of interaction among things, Spinoza goes on to argue, obtains among members of the same species: "Nothing can be more in harmony with the nature of anything than other individuals of the same species."[93] With respect to humankind, Spinoza continues, "Nothing is more advantageous to man than man."[94] In fact, if the human species has one noteworthy feature, it is the extremity of the gain in power it experiences through cooperation. In the absence of cooperation, Spinoza observes, human beings are notable for their weakness compared with other animals. Our skin is thin, our muscles feeble, our eyes unremarkable, our noses inept. Banded together in cooperative harmony, on the other hand, human beings achieve unequaled power, both individually and collectively. Paine puts the same point succinctly: "A thousand motives will excite" people to cooperate, "the strength of one man is so unequal to his wants."[95]

Shaftesbury played a starring role in disseminating the word of Spinoza: "If anything be natural in any creature or kind, it is that which is preservative of the kind itself and conducing to its welfare and support."[96] Alexander Pope then passed the message along, sexing it up a touch in his verses:

> *Each loves itself, but not itself alone,*
> *Each sex desires alike, till two are one.*
> *Nor ends the pleasure with the fierce embrace:*
> *They love themselves, a third time, in their race.*[97]

In this instance as in others, Pope follows his notoriously concupiscent mentor. "Self-love . . . made the union between man and woman," says Bolingbroke.[98] Pope next makes clear, in sumptuous metaphors drawn from the cosmopolitanism of the Stoic tradition, that this expanding sphere of self-love is what we mean by virtue itself:

> *Self-love but serves the virtuous mind to wake,*
> *As the small pebble stirs the peaceful lake;*
> *The centre moved, a circle straight succeeds,*
> *Another still, and still another spreads;*
> *Friend, parent, neighbor, first it will embrace,*
> *His country next, and next all the human race.*[99]

Bolingbroke once again anticipates sentiment: "We love ourselves, we love our families, we love the particular societies to which we belong; and our benevolence extends at last to the whole race of mankind. Like so many vortices, the center of all is self-love."[100]

To be clear, the cosmopolitan sociability that Spinoza describes and his English successors embrace is grounded not on any feature specific to our species (or any other). It is not of the kind associated with the Aristotelian philosophy and scholasticism, which says that human beings are sociable in the same way that bees are sociable: only with other members of our species and merely because we have a certain instinct to be so. Human beings may indeed have such instincts, but the possession of such instincts does not explain why they might be good to have. The moral life begins with the fact that we have a *common* nature, not a *specific* nature, and to some extent it must apply across species, inasmuch as we share some nature (though perhaps not much) with rocks and trees, too. The radical philosophy at the origin of liberal modernity, then, is not properly speaking (or exclusively) a humanism. It is closer to a naturalism that might one day be expected to embrace all species, a planet, and perhaps the universe itself.

Those who grasp the value of harmony with others for their own fulfillment, Spinoza next argues, necessarily desire this harmony. Spinoza is concerned enough about the point here to iterate it at length:

> Men, I repeat, can wish for nothing more excellent for preserving their own being than that they should all be in such harmony . . . that all together they should aim at the common advantage of all. From this it follows that men who are governed by reason, that is, men who aim at their own advantage under the guidance of reason, seek nothing for themselves that they would not desire for the rest of mankind; and so are just, faithful and honorable.[101]

The desire that the reasonable person feels for virtue, it is important to stress, is indeed a desire.[102] According to the common conception (which is also that of Hobbes in this case), our desires come to an end at our fingertips, in a manner of speaking, and everything else is a conscious matter of pretense. According to Spinoza, on the other hand, our desires are always modes of thought, and thus they represent causes outside of us (for the most part) such as, above all, our fellow human beings. Thus, to the extent that we are more perspicuously "selfish" in a metaphysical sense—pursuing our own advantage—we are less "selfish" in the ordinary sense of the term—we pursue instead universal friendship.

The difference between the common and the radical conceptions of morality here extends down to the very identity of the individual agent of desire. Insofar as desires involve intrinsically social representations, as Spinoza suggests, then the essence or identity of the agent is social, too. The power of the conatus, as Spinoza puts it, is not just enhanced through our relations with other things and in particular with other people; it is "conceived" and "determined" through them. Our relations to other people differ in degree but not in kind from our relations with the parts of our own bodies. It is for this reason that people will sometimes volunteer to give an arm or leg for a friend. We all need other people in order to become what we are. In a formula, the rational self-determination of the individual is coextensive with the rational self-determination of the collective.

Shaftesbury's restatement of Spinoza's position is probably the one that mattered most in getting the word to the English: *"To have the natural, kindly or generous affections strong and powerful towards the good of the public is to have the chief means and power of self-enjoyment and . . . to want them is certain misery and ill."*[103] "To be well affected towards the public interest and one's own is not only consistent but inseparable," he repeats.[104] The wise man therefore seeks "equal, just and universal friendship" with all humankind.[105]

In the catalogue of virtues that Spinoza analyzes in detail, "fortitude" occupies a position of prominence and offers a useful illustration of the link between private advantage and public good. Fortitude, according to Spinoza, means "strength of mind" or perhaps "constancy."[106] It is the "mindfulness" that we possess insofar as we exercise genuine understanding of ourselves and our world. This strength of mind, Spinoza continues, may be described as a composite of a private or internal virtue called "courage" and an external or public one called "nobility." Courage is "the desire whereby every individual endeavors to preserve his own being according to the dictates of reason alone." More specifically, it is a combination of the first virtue of survival—the "courage to be," as the theologian Paul Tillich[107] puts it—with the first virtue of understanding—the courage to see things as they are according to reason, and not as our passions wish they might be. Self-control, sobriety, resourcefulness, and other such virtues hailed in the classical tradition, according to Spinoza, are all species of courage. Nobility, on the other hand, is "the desire whereby every individual, according to the dictates of reason alone, endeavors to assist others and make friends of them."[108] Modesty, mercy, honesty, and good faith are forms of nobility. The important feature of Spinoza's analysis is that courage and nobility cohere not on the basis of mere compatibility or a negotiated truce. We are not noble at the expense of being courageous any more than our courage detracts from our nobility. We are both noble and courageous when we live under the guidance of reason. These are the two sides, on equal terms, of the one virtue of fortitude.

Vice no less than virtue, according to Spinoza and his successors, has a public face. "Insofar as men are assailed by emotions that are passive," Spinoza explains, they become "inconstant" and "variable" in themselves, and they also become "contrary to one another."[109] Corruption in a society is thus very much like—indeed it is the same thing as—vice in the individual. In a vicious person, individual passions fight one another for control and drive the person to self-destruction. In a corrupt society, factions fight one another for the right to exploit the other and thereby drive the society toward dissolution. As Shaftesbury observes, private vices and public corruption alike make us "miserable," "irregular," and unfit for society.

From this deeply rationalist conception of virtue and vice emerges a version of the idea of "conscience" or "moral sense" that reaches back to one of the core intuitions of the Epicurean philosophy. According to Epicurus, as we know, those who knowingly do wrong suffer misery at the hands of their very own conscience. And the reason for this, expressed in Spinoza's terms, is that their conscience is just the moral judgment embedded in their own emotional representations of the world. This judgment tells them that their actions have diminished their own power even as they have diminished the power of others, and so it involves sadness. In the eighteenth-century tradition that matters for the Americans, it is Shaftesbury who—ironically, given his professed disdain for all things Epicurus—best articulates this Neo-Epicurean idea of conscience: "No creature can maliciously and intentionally do ill without being sensible at the same time that he deserves ill. And in this respect, every sensible creature may be said to have conscience."[110] There is a bright side of conscience, too, as Epicurus was the first to point out, and it has to do with the fact that human beings often get more pleasure from doing favors than receiving them. "Virtue is its own reward," the authors of *Cato's Letters* explain, both on account of "the felicity which would accrue to every man, if all men would pursue virtue" and the fact that "pleasure attends the consciousness of doing well."[111]

In much of the modern historiography, the consciously antisocial or egoistic hedonism associated with Hobbes is taken to represent the core view of the Enlightenment in general and of liberalism in particular. But Enlightenment liberalism overthrows precisely this ethical delusion of the common religious consciousness. Its actual message is the cosmopolitan one that Pope, with characteristic precision, cements into a couplet that brings us back to Nature's God:

> *Thus God and Nature link'd the gen'ral frame,*
> *And bade Self-love and Social be the same.*[112]

What deist virtue is not. If our interest were to catalogue the entire range of ideas and traditions within the history of philosophy that intersected with the individuals who led the American Revolution, we would necessarily have to look much farther than the somewhat roguish band of thinkers who might narrowly be labeled Epicureans and deists. The ministers and theologians of the Christian religion, the writers of the Stoic tradition, and the "moral sense" philosophers of the Scottish Enlightenment, for example, would rank higher in any popularity contest among America's revolutionary generation. But the history of philosophy is not the same thing as the philosophy of history. To the extent that our concern is not to catalogue influences and reading lists but to explain the ideas that mattered in the creation of the modern world, those other traditions are useful mainly to illuminate by contrast what the "virtue" of the deists is not.

THE CHRISTIAN TRADITION, for example, converges in important ways with radical philosophy on the exaltation of virtue, and America's revolutionaries in particular were understandably eager to stress the parallels. Spinoza points to a large patch of common ground with Jesus when he declares, for example, "He who lives by the guidance of reason endeavors as far as he can to repay the hatred, anger, and contempt of others with love."[113] Yet a crucial gap remains. In the versions of Christianity available in the early modern period, the reward for virtue was generally supposed to come after the fact, as a dispensation from above. Spinoza is not shy to draw a sharp contrast:

> Hence we clearly understand how far astray from the true estimation of virtue are those who, failing to understand that virtue itself and true piety are happiness itself and utmost freedom, expect God to bestow upon them the highest rewards in return for their virtue and meritorious actions as if in return for the basest slavery.[114]

Shaftesbury, too, adamantly rejects the "bargain" conception of virtue: "If virtue not be estimable in itself, I can see nothing estimable in following it for the sake of a bargain," he writes to a friend.[115] "The cruel enemy opposed to virtue is religion itself," he adds.[116] In a passage that provoked a great outcry in his own time, he makes clear that the anti-virtuous religion he has in mind is Christianity:

> Private friendship and zeal for the public and our country are purely voluntary in a Christian. They are no essential parts of his charity. He is not so tied to the affairs of this life, nor is he obliged

to enter into such engagements with this lower world as are of no help to him in acquiring a better. His conversation is in heaven. Nor has he occasion for such supernumerary cares or embarrassments here on earth as may obstruct his way thither or retard him in the careful task of working out his own salvation.[117]

The same charge—that the Christian concern for otherworldly salvation results in a selfish and bigoted diminishment of virtue—features in the work of Trenchard, Gordon, and Hume, all of whom follow the lead of Machiavelli on the point.[118]

Deist virtue and Christian virtue are also quite obviously at odds over the question of self-denial. "I have no greater enemy than my body," said Francis of Assisi, speaking for that part of the Christian tradition that elevates asceticism to the commanding heights of an ideal.[119] The deists, on the other hand, though moderately ascetic in their counsels, are emphatically not so in principle. They decry, with Montaigne, the "inhuman wisdom that would have us disdain and despise the cultivation of the body."[120] Franklin, speaking for all deists, makes the difference plain: "None do more mistake the divine nature, and by consequence do greater mischief to religion, than those who would persuade us, that to be truly religious, is to renounce all the pleasures of human life." "Self-denial," he insists, is "not the essence of virtue."[121]

With respect to the opposite of virtue, there is likewise an important but superficial convergence between deism and the prevailing versions of Christianity. According to most versions of Christian doctrine, human beings are naturally and hopelessly depraved. In Adam's fall we sinned all, or so the story goes. Deists, too, frequently lament the corruption of their fellow humans. Most people most of the time suffer from inadequate ideas, they say, and these inadequate ideas correspond to passions that in turn produce misery and vice. There is a long tradition in the historiography of seizing upon the observations of the deists concerning the turpitude of their fellows and taking them as positive proof that they were actually dogmatic Calvinists.

Yet a profound gap remains between deist "corruption" and Christian "depravity." The Christian view says that we are so bad that our only hope for redemption lies with some otherworldly source; whereas the deist view says that we can redeem ourselves in this world. The Christian view identifies our depravity with pride and more generally with our selfishness; the deist view identifies corruption with a loss of self and weakness of nature. In its extreme form, as in the teaching of Jonathan Edwards, the Christian view says that the passage to virtue begins only after we learn to hate ourselves. The deist view says that virtue is always grounded in self-love. Perhaps the best indicator of the distance between Christian depravity and deist corruption may be found in the chasm that divides Milton's *Paradise Lost* from Pope's *Essay on Man*. Milton promises to "justify the ways of God to man," and for this purpose offers a sweeping retelling of the story of man's original sin.[122] Pope, writing seventy years later with the self-conscious intent of becoming the new Milton, similarly promises to "vindicate the ways of God to man." Yet his grand history takes us through the innumerable worlds of the infinite universe and deep into a natural history of the passions and the crooked timber of humanity without offering a single credible allusion to the doctrine of the Fall of Man.

THE VIRTUE of the deists is often, with better cause, identified with the virtue of the Stoics. Spinoza's ethics is often cast as a version of Stoicism, and Shaftesbury's is said to be nothing but Stoicism. If one were to keep score by number of citations and favorable mentions, then America's revolutionary deists, too, would have to be counted as Stoics rather than Epicureans. The first professionally produced play in the colonies, and by far the most popular, was Joseph Addison's *Cato*, a play all about Stoic "virtue"—a word that is hurled across the stage more than thirty times in the course of the drama.[123] In the final act, the insufferably virtuous Cato throws himself on his own sword rather than join in the corruption of Rome at the hands of the tyrant Julius Caesar. "A day, an hour, of virtuous liberty is worth a whole eternity in bondage," the suicidal Stoic proclaims. *Cato* inspired Patrick Henry to coin his famous slogan—"Give me liberty, or give me death"—and echoes of its virtuous bombast resound in the writings of Franklin, Otis, and the Adams cousins. Washington admired the play so much that he ordered a winter performance to buck up the troops at Valley Forge.[124]

The Stoic philosophy, too, finds virtue and happiness to coincide. It also identifies virtue with knowledge. Reason, it says, is the ultimate source of good and is sufficient to redeem human beings without recourse to faith or revelation. Indeed, Stoic virtue is close enough to deist virtue that the same rhetoric often served for both, and thus Stoic authors—always much more acceptable in polite society—were used to put a respectable face on radical ideas.[125] Yet Stoicism achieves the unity of virtue and happiness, rather notoriously, by defining happiness almost out of existence. It excludes from happiness just about everything that normal people imagine goes into it. Beauty, wealth, and health, it says, should be counted as merely "indifferent" (or, in moments of laxity, "preferred," other things being held strictly equal). As in the case of Cato, Stoicism sometimes goes so far as to put virtue above self-preservation, thereby fostering a cult of suicide that (Addison's overwrought hero notwithstanding) most people in the eighteenth century found just as unappealing as we do now. Stoicism also ultimately fails to capture the essence of early modern insights concerning reason, the will, and the passions. Indeed, its prescription for happiness and virtue, reduced to a credo, is for the will to round up all the passions and have them shot in the name of reason.

Deist virtue never reached the degree of austerity and self-denial of the Stoics because it simply wasn't the same thing. The Stoics "had many admirable and virtuous precepts," the authors of *Cato's Letters* allow, but "their philosophy was too rigid." "It is the highest stupidity to talk of subduing the passions," they argue, firmly distancing themselves from the doctrines of their namesake.[126] Bolingbroke is equally contemptuous of the Stoics: "Their theology and morality were alike absurd."[127] Pope makes clear what deist virtue is not:

> In lazy apathy let Stoics boast
> Their virtue fixed; tis fixed as in a frost.[128]

The deist critique of Stoic virtue ultimately converges with the critique of Christian virtue. When the self-flagellating Stoics "came into Christianity," Trenchard and Gordon explain, they "brought along with them the severe notions of their sect" and then augmented the power of those austere ideas about virtue by "tacking on to their opinions the rewards and terrors of the world to come." The horrifying result of this fusion of Christian and Stoic virtue, they add, was that the self-mortifying "dreams" of the Stoics, "added to some sayings and passages of the gospel, ill understood, were vehemently urged, as if they had been so many certain passports to paradise; and soon turned men's brains, and made them really fond of poverty, hardships, and misery, and even of death itself: Enthusiasm conquered reason, and inflamed nature; and men, to be devout, grew distracted."[129] Machiavelli could hardly have said it better.

Jefferson stakes out his position on the debate between deism and Stoicism in his memorable *Dialogue between my Head & my Heart*—composed in Paris in 1786 in the heat of an affair with a married woman named Maria Cosway. The "Head," it turns out, is something of a frosty Stoic. It supplies him with "frigid speculations" and "miserable arithmetic." The "Heart" sounds like Rousseau in one of his better-to-burn-out moments. It grants Jefferson a "generous spasm" of "solid pleasure." The *Dialogue* strives for a distinctly Epicurean balance between Head and Heart, one that measures virtue in degrees of happiness and friendship in this world. Franklin, appropriately enough, telegraphs the same sensibility in a twisted paraphrase of Addison's *Cato*. In his dying soliloquy, Cato explains that his self-destruction is all part of the Stoical pursuit of happiness, for the "power above us . . . must delight in virtue," and whatever makes God happy must make us happy.[130] Franklin flips it around: "I believe [God] is pleased and delights in the happiness of those he has created, and since without Virtue Man can have no happiness in this World, I firmly believe he delights to see me Virtuous, because he is pleas'd when he sees me Happy."[131] Thus, to complete the logic: if vice turned out to be a condition of happiness, then presumably God would clamor to see us vicious.

IN SCOTLAND in the early eighteenth century, the radical philosophy that passed from Spinoza through Shaftesbury experienced a kind of creative misunderstanding. Some of the insight was lost, but a certain ease of communication was gained in what came to be known as the "moral sense" school of philosophy. We human beings are so constructed, the Scots observed, that doing good things makes us feel good. Therefore, they inferred, we possess a moral instinct of sorts, and this instinct comes with a special faculty that allows us to touch and feel moral truths that exist out there in the world. Just as we perceive a stove to be hot and fresh fruit to be delicious, so we experience pleasure and pain upon contemplating good and bad deeds.

The seminal figure of the moral sense school was the Scottish philosopher and cleric Francis Hutcheson. Lord Kames (a significant influence on Jefferson), Hume (loathed by Jefferson), and Adam Smith (whose exaltation today bears little connection with his meager influence on America's revolutionaries) are also important representatives of the school (though in distinct ways). Shaftesbury, who often got carried away in his celebrations of the pleasure of virtue and misery of vice, has often been named the father of the movement, though this really amounts to judging a philosopher by his excesses.

The rhetoric of the moral sense school spread widely in America. Paine, for example, insists that "the knowledge of [morality] exists in every man's conscience."[132] Ethan Allen makes similar appeals to "human conscience" and claims somewhat obscurely that "the senses are well calculated to make discoveries of external objects . . . and to investigate the knowledge of moral good and evil."[133] The American leader with the deepest and most revealing connection with the moral sense school was Jefferson. "Every human mind feels pleasure in doing good to another," Jefferson tells Adams.[134] "But how happens it that [good acts] give us pleasure?" he asks another correspondent. "Because nature hath implanted in our breasts a love of others, a sense of duty to them, a moral instinct."[135] "The moral sense, or conscience," he tells his nephew, "is as much a part of man as his leg or arm."[136] This natural moral sense, moreover, is intrinsically aimed at the social virtues: "Man was destined for society. His morality therefore was to be formed to this object."[137]

The moral sense school, however, did not endure for long. As many of its critics quickly grasped, it rapidly crumbles under the weight of an internal contradiction. The basic intuition that good feelings accompany good deeds unto others and bad feelings bad deeds, as we know, is fundamental to the philosophy of Epicurus, Spinoza, and Shaftesbury alike—for good and evil are nothing but pleasure and pain insofar as we are conscious of them. The distinguishing feature of the moral sense school is neither the claim that such sociable or virtuous feelings exist, nor that they have a foundation in reason, but that they refer to properties of good and evil that inhere in actions or events entirely independent of those feelings and reasons. The moral sense school is at bottom an attempt to graft a claim about the transcendental status of good and evil onto a moral philosophy that is otherwise thoroughly immanent.[138]

But if our conscience delivers sensory knowledge of good and evil as properties that inhere in the things themselves, as Locke asks in a rebuttal of an earlier form of the doctrine,[139] then how come different people (and especially people in different cultures) disagree so completely and irreconcilably about the moral status of particular things? As a number of deists were quick to point out, the relatives of an Indian widow may feel good about burning her alive along with the remains of her deceased husband, but elsewhere the vaunted moral sense appears to deliver a rather different verdict on the practice. The radical conception does not deny that moral feelings exist; but it does insist that they may and often do involve deeply flawed—hence ultimately immoral—representations of the self and the objects it values. It may feel good to be loyal to kin, to exact revenge, to adopt a sanctimonious air in the face of social deviants. And it may well be the case that evolution through generations of village life has bred within humans an instinct to respond in these ways to commonly experienced stimuli. But that doesn't make the actions that evoke those feelings necessarily good for all time. Precisely because it opened up the possibility of a rational critique of our moral feelings, radical philosophy had a revolutionary character and played a prominent role in the creation of a new world order, while the moral sense idea tended to drift into a mindless conservatism, according to which the service provided by moral philosophy is simply to read the prejudices of the age back into the nature of things (which is more or less what happens now in some versions of evolutionary psychology).

David Hume, the most acute of the representatives of the moral sense school, laid his case to rest on the sensible, immanent foundations of the moral sense philosophy. "I wish from my Heart, I coud avoid concluding, that since Morality, according to your Opinion as well as mine, is determin'd by mere Sentiment, it regards only human Nature & human Life," he writes in a moving letter to Hutcheson. "This has been often urg'd against you, & the Consequences are very momentous."[140] Hutcheson was not ready to forgive Hume for exposing the impious premises of his project. When Hume's name came up for a professorship, Hutcheson slapped it down. Yet Hume did not alter his fundamentally Epicurean convictions. "All the philosophy, therefore, in the world, and all the religion, which is nothing but a species of philosophy, will never be able to carry us beyond the usual course of experience, or give us measures of conduct and behavior different from those which are furnished by reflections on common life," he says. "No new fact can ever be inferred from the religious hypothesis; no event foreseen or foretold; no reward or punishment expected or dreaded, beyond what is already known by practice and observation."[141]

Though Jefferson remained committed to the rhetoric of the moral sense school throughout his life and viscerally antagonistic to Hume for largely political reasons, the logic of his arguments concerning the moral sense generally returns to the pattern of Hume and his fellow Epicureans. Jefferson entertains the objection mooted by Locke that the moral sense appears to deliver contradictory results in different locations, for example, and then responds with the suggestion that virtue varies from place to place because the utility of particular virtues varies. It is at this point that he declares, "Nature has constituted *utility* to man the standard and test of virtue."[142] But this of course is just to say that the moral sense does not discover properties in the things themselves. It is simply a description of the feeling that accompanies useful action. Here Jefferson reduces the moral sense idea to what it is: a temporary detour on the road to an immanent, Epicurean conception of morality.

We can love God but not obey him. Does God love us? Will he do right by us if we do right by him? Having translated God as another word for Nature, Spinoza and his fellow deists would seem committed to answer with a firm no. Yet there is a certain sense in which the deists allow that we may say that God—or perhaps just the memory of a deceased God—remains part of the ethical equation. In this instance, just as with Nature's God and the naturalization of the soul, they seek to preserve a certain valuable intuition embedded in the common conception of things.

When we practice virtue or charity toward our fellow beings, according to the logic Spinoza articulates, we realize our own striving to persist in being. Now this practice of virtue extends just as far as our understanding of nature, as we know, and to understand nature is the same thing as to understand God. So, we could say, with Spinoza, that "the mind's highest virtue" is "to know God." And since our highest virtue is also our utmost pleasure and happiness, here accompanied with the idea of God as its object, we could also call this virtue, as Spinoza does, "the intellectual love of God."[143] Ergo, we do love God. At the same time, our own pursuit of happiness is nothing other than God as it expresses itself through us, for the striving within us is just the way in which nature realizes itself. It follows that "the mind's intellectual love toward God is the love of God wherewith God loves himself."[144] Ergo, God loves us! It also follows, inasmuch as the practice of virtue directs us to love our fellows, "that God, insofar as he loves himself, loves mankind, and, consequently, that the love of God toward men and the mind's intellectual love toward God are one and the same."[145] So love is all around! If we step back from the abstractions, it should be clear that we are not talking here about a supernatural entity dispensing favors and prizes for the needy human race in exchange for altruistic sacrifices or expressions of fealty. God's "love" is just a redescription of the good things that come back to us when we do good things. In the end, the love you take is equal to the love you make.

Another way to say it is just this: the true worship of God is nothing but the practice of virtue. "The desire to do good which derives from our living by the guidance of reason," says Spinoza, is "Piety."[146] The "Holy Spirit," he adds, "is nothing other than the peace of mind that results from good actions." Or, to put the point in the negative: *belief* in God is no part of piety or virtue. "We should reject the view that anything of piety or impiety attaches to beliefs taken simply in themselves without respect to works," Spinoza declares.[147] "Faith in itself is not salutary; it is so only in respect to the obedience it implies."[148]

From Bruno to Jefferson, this is the one truth that all deists take to the bank: that true religion is the practice of virtue—and absolutely nothing besides. Locke, as usual, repeats the message in bland terms: "The business of true religion is . . . the regulating of men's lives, according to the rules of virtue and piety."[149] Shaftesbury is more forceful, if abstract: "The religious conscience supposes the moral or natural conscience."[150] Pope, in a couplet cited by Thomas Young in one of his articles, makes the idea sing: "For modes of faith let graceless zealots fight / His can't be wrong whose life is in the right."[151] Franklin joins the chorus in his *Autobiography*: "The most acceptable service of God is doing good to man." Jefferson chimes in: "I must ever believe that religion substantially good which produces an honest life."[152] Ethan Allen repeats it in his clunky voice: "Moral rectitude, which is morality in the abstract, is the sum of all religion, that ever was or can be in the universe."[153] Thomas Young, writing to his devoutly orthodox friend Abigail Dwight, gets to the point when he says that "the last end of true religion, yours as well as mine," is "teaching peace and goodwill towards man."[154]

As Young suggests, the idea that charity is piety—that God is love—finds expression in all of the world's religious traditions and in particular within the Christian tradition. John famously says in his first Epistle, "Everyone who loves is born of God and knows God";[155] "whoever does not love does not know God; for God is love." James makes the point in the negative: "Faith without works is dead."[156] Many deists, from Spinoza to Jefferson, cite John and James favorably on precisely this account. Franklin in particular appeals to James regularly—especially in the course of his irate polemics against abuses of clerical power.[157]

Within the Christian tradition, as within all religions that flourish under the constraints of the common or transcendental conception of morality, however, such claims are inevitably surrounded with tensions, not to say contradictions. Unable to conceive how virtue can subsist without something above or beyond this life that authorizes and rewards it, the religious consciousness oscillates between the conviction that religion is virtue in this life and the opposing view that religion requires faith in some other life. After telling us that it is not the profession of belief that assures us of being "in" Jesus,[158] for example, John turns around and asks, "Who is the liar but the one who denies that Jesus is the Christ?"[159] Thus, God is love—but if you happen to love the wrong God, you are in for plenty of hate. James is more consistently committed to the importance of works over faith; but perhaps for that reason he has been overlooked or rejected by many of the most prominent Christian theologians. Martin Luther, for example, directly contradicts James when he announces, "Faith alone justifies us."[160]

In the philosophical world of the long eighteenth century, the cutting edge of the doctrine that virtue alone is piety was the paradox of the virtuous atheist, and the writer out in front of the paradox was the elusive Pierre Bayle.[161] In his first and extraordinarily subversive work, *Various Thoughts on the Occasion of a Comet*, Bayle opens with a hard-hitting critique of popular superstitions about heavenly signs such as comets, but he eventually swings around to his real point, which is to advance the incendiary proposition that atheists not only are potentially virtuous but also make for good or better citizens than the average believer. "Faith in a religion," Bayle tartly observes, "is not the rule of the conduct of man, except that it is often apt to excite in the soul anger against those who are of a different sentiment."[162] "A society of atheists would perform civil and moral actions as much as other societies do," he predicts.[163]

Bayle's arguments rest squarely on the immanent conception of morality. "Delight is the nerve of all human affairs," and "man loves delight more than he hates pain," he says.[164] "The inclination to act badly comes from the ground of man's nature and . . . is strengthened by the passions, which . . . are . . . modified in many ways according to the accidents of life," he adds. "Religion is useful . . . only in having fine declamations made from the pulpit and in showing us our duty, after which we absolutely conduct ourselves by the direction of our taste for pleasures," he concludes. "Whence it results that atheists are not necessarily more corrupt than idolaters."[165] "Thus we have no right to maintain that an atheist must necessarily be more unregulated in his morals than an idolater," he insists.[166] Bayle names Epicurus, "that glorious religion tamer," as one example of a virtuous atheist.[167] He goes on at considerable length about Spinoza, "the greatest atheist there ever was," whose "constancy" or strength of mind, Bayle mischievously proposes, reached almost absurd heights.

After Bayle, the paradox of virtuous atheist became an essential piece of the furniture of early modern philosophy.[168] Shaftesbury in particular had influence with a modified, more complex version of the argument. He suggested that deists and atheists can be more virtuous than polytheists (by which he meant Christians, inasmuch as they believe in the trinity) and demonists (by which he meant Calvinists, or those who believe in a capricious deity with sadistic tendencies).[169] At the same time, he proposed that theists, that is, classical deists, would have an advantage over outright atheists, inasmuch as they would enjoy a kind of aesthetic pleasure in contemplating themselves and the world and thus would have an extra incentive for virtue. Bolingbroke more or less copied Shaftesbury on the point, and Jefferson copied Bolingbroke.[170] The authors of *Cato's Letters*, following Shaftesbury, also classify Christianity as a form of polytheism, except where it has degenerated into a Calvinistic demonism. They go on to cite Bayle himself. "Multitudes of Christians believe well, and live ill, but Epicurus and his followers had, on the contrary, very ill opinions, and yet lived well," they say.[171] "Will the world never learn, that one man's corn grows not the worse, because another man uses different words in his devotion? That pride and anger, wealth and power, are of no religion? And that religion is inseparable from charity and peace?"[172] Hume elegantly summarizes what came before: "Probity and honour were no strangers to Epicurus and his sect."[173]

In America, the virtuous atheist makes a first appearance in the Franklin brothers' newspaper of 1722. "Virtuous hereticks," declares Silence Dogood, are better for public morals than "hypocritical pretenders" to religion. A decade later, Franklin champions virtuous heretics in his Philadelphia newspaper columns, and then again six decades later, when, ruminating on the controversy surrounding that frantic genius Joseph Priestley, he suggests that there is something about heretics that marks them as *more* virtuous than believers. Philip Livingston, too, alludes to the virtuous atheist in his magazine from the 1750s: "It is an Opinion too generally received, that Man is led into all the Crimes and Extravagancies he commits, thro' Unbelief. And no Wonder this Doctrine, false as it is, should be so vigorously inculcated by Men whose Interest consists in a Depression of rational Faculties."[174] Elihu Palmer repeats the claim in his deistic sermons: "If a thousand Gods existed, or if nature existed independent of any; the moral relation between man and man would remain exactly the same in either case."[175]

The most notorious eruption of virtuous atheism in revolutionary America is to be found in the work of Jefferson. "It does me no injury for my neighbor to say that there are twenty Gods or no God. It neither picks my pocket nor breaks my leg," he says in the most controversial passage in his *Notes on the State of Virginia*.[176] In the election campaign of 1800, these words were wielded against him with all the subtlety of pitch tar. "Ponder well this paragraph. Ten thousand impieties and mischiefs lurk in its womb," intoned one Federalist minister. "This is nothing less than representing civil society as founded on atheism."[177]

Yet Jefferson never wavered from the intuition that atheists could be virtuous. His most revealing comment on the matter is to be found in his letter of advice to Peter Carr.[178] There Jefferson counsels his nephew to enter into reflection on whether or not God even exists. Then he adds:

> If it ends in a belief that there is no god, you will find incitements
> to virtue in the comfort and pleasantness you feel in it's exercise,
> and the love of others which it will procure you. If you find reason
> to believe there is a god, a consciousness that you are acting under
> his eye, & that he approves you, will be a vast additional incitement.

Here as in his theology, Jefferson's view seems closest to that of
Shaftesbury. Belief in God is not necessary for a moral life. It may in
fact be quite harmful, if that God is a demon in the Calvinist manner
or the incomprehensible triune God of orthodox Christianity. Insofar
as it helps, it does so as an extra pleasure felt in the exercise of virtue, a
kind of reflected joy that follows from the awareness of our participation in eternity. If God is the name of a feeling, an affirmation of being
and a love of all things, he might well have added, it would seem that
even those who believe in God may be virtuous.

WHEN COMMENTATORS TODAY look around for culprits for our
descent into shopping-mall nihilism, they often point the finger at the
supposed philosophical foundations of liberalism. Liberal modernity,
they say, is the system that places no real value on anything at all. It
protects "rights," but it is entirely "neutral" with respect to "goods."
It cares about the selfish pursuit of consumer satisfaction, not about
community, religion, or tradition. It focuses only on the "form," not
the "substance" of ethical life, or so it is said.

There are indeed many valid critiques to be made about the shal-
lowness and absurdity of contemporary culture. But the sensible ones
are not critiques of liberalism at all. They are in reality liberal critiques
of certain betrayals of liberalism. In its original form as well as in its
actual foundations to the present, liberalism is not "neutral" about the
good. It says that there is one good that is always and everywhere good:
the improvement of the understanding. It does not seek to protect all
the shallow distractions that we name from time to time as our goods. It
says that they do not exist except as provisional markers of the horizon
of our ignorance. Nor does liberalism begin with the idea that the indi-

vidual is the sole source of value in the world. On the contrary, it starts with the insight that the rational self-determination of the individual is largely coextensive with the rational self-determination of the collective. What today is sometimes touted as "communitarianism"—which is really the celebration of the value of community without respect to the values of any particular community—has never been more than one way in which liberalism corrects itself.

If one were to rummage through the history of philosophy for the words that might express the moral wisdom at the core of American liberalism—the knowledge that we realize ourselves individually and collectively not by bemoaning our depravity and abasing ourselves before inscrutable deities but through the improvement of the understanding that brings with it both pleasure and virtue—it would be difficult to find a more apt phrase than the one that Jefferson placed at the heart of the Declaration of Independence: the pursuit of happiness. Precisely because they elevated this radical pursuit of happiness above the common conception of morality that makes religion in all its popular and traditional forms credible, America's founders were able to construct a system of government unlike anything that came before, a system that has permitted a certain, limited, and eminently reversible degree of moral progress. Once upon a time it may have seemed reasonable to fear that the loss of religion would destroy everything in a bonfire of nihilism. But today we don't really need to wonder what a society founded on the principles of atheism would look like. We just need to understand aright the history of the United States.

7

The Empire of Reason

"ALL HONOR TO JEFFERSON," SAID ABRAHAM LINCOLN, "TO the man who, in the concrete pressure of a struggle for national independence by a single people," was able to express in the Declaration of Independence "an abstract truth, applicable to all men and all times."[1] Thomas Paine—whose books Lincoln read avidly in his youth—anticipated the underlying point. "The independence of America, considered merely as a separation from England, would have been a matter but of little importance, had it not been accompanied by a revolution in the principles and practice of governments," said Paine in 1791.[2] The enduring question about the struggle for American independence has never been why it happened but why it was so revolutionary.

If we confine our focus to the personalities and circumstances immediately surrounding the War of Independence, to be sure, it is easy enough to cast the struggle as just another exercise in the consolidation of power by a rapacious, slave-driving elite. Even the deism of America's founders, one could plausibly argue, served some of the time in some places as a rearguard action—yet another vain attempt by those on top to justify the order of society as the order of God. If we expand the focus from the peculiarities of a past age and search out instead the ties that bind it with a later world, on the other hand, a startlingly different picture emerges. Of the many valid critiques that can and have been laid at the feet of America's founders, the most effective invoke the same principles with which they announced their revolution. The man who freed the slaves was a part of the same revolution announced by the man who owned slaves; and the story didn't end with him. Perhaps the most interesting question about the American Revolution, considered over the long run, is why it *remains* so revolutionary.

The revolutionary principles announced at the origin of the American experience are the water of modern political thought. They are as ubiquitous as they are invisible. But what do they really mean? Why do they seem so self-evident today? We say that all people are equal when they obviously aren't. We ascribe to individuals a set of rights that can be created only through the collective apparatus of government. We say government derives its power from the consent of the governed when in fact no one has ever given it. We say it is the right of the people to rebel and then we shoot them if they try. We use "democratic"—which for most of human history counted as an insult—as a synonym for all that is good in the political order. Why?

Probably most people today, if pressed, will say that the principles of liberalism are the elaboration of a certain moral intuition about treating other people with respect. Some might add that those principles are the arbitrary artifact of a particular culture, or of a certain social or economic system. Still others will point to a source from on high. In the abstract reaches of academic political theory, these common ideas about liberalism often take the form of a theory of justice, according to which the principles of liberalism are said to arise from a universal concept of justice as fairness or something like that. If we try to dig down further in search of a foundation for these claims, the explanation usually ends where it starts, in an act of faith, a moral intuition, or a reference to the arbitrary predilections of a particular culture. In the view of a representative modern philosopher, liberalism is "just the way we do things around here."[3]

All of these common ideas about liberalism, however, are not so much theories of liberalism as they are descriptions of what people living within modern liberal societies profess to believe. They rest on the assumption—so common as to be overlooked—that a political order is whatever the common beliefs of the people within it suppose it is, and that the purpose of a political theory is merely to articulate this consensus. In fact, these common ideas about liberalism describe a political order that probably could not exist and in any case would not last very long.

Liberalism in its original form is not the elaboration of some common moral intuition, the articulation of an arbitrary creed or cultural formation, or a theory of justice. It is a theory of power. Its principal claim is that the source of human power and freedom is the understanding. It rests in an essential way on the same radical philosophy that begins with Nature's God and passes through nature's virtue. And that radical philosophy remains the ultimate source of liberalism's revolutionary power to the present. How the uncommon ideas of radical philosophy came to structure—and then continuously restructure—the common experience of humanity is the real story of the American Revolution and of the modern world that emerged in its wake.

I
"... THAT ALL MEN ARE CREATED EQUAL ..."

With the benefit of hindsight, we can say that the awakening power of the people over the presumptions of their highborn masters might have been just barely discernible on the eastern shore of Lake Champlain in the morning light of May 9, 1775. In their makeshift encampment, Ethan Allen and 180 of his Boys were anxiously making preparations for their surprise attack on Fort Ticonderoga, when suddenly the ruling class of New England showed up in the person of Benedict Arnold.

A smallish man with a large, plumed hat, Arnold was thirty-four years old and fervently committed to the American side of the struggle at this point in his tumultuous career. He arrived in the Green Mountains with a hundred pounds in cash, ten horses, a personal valet, a big wad of gunpowder, and a bright new uniform that made Allen's own elaborately conceived costume feel just a little tatty. This was still the era when "no Mans imagination aspired to anything higher beneath the skies" than "to be worth ten thousand pounds Sterling, ride in a Chariot, [and] be Colonel of a Regiment of Militia," as John Adams later recalled.[4] And Arnold had just picked up his commission as a colonel of the Massachusetts militia six days previously. He was everything Ethan Allen wanted to be, if only wishes were as good as land deeds.

Arnold marched up to Allen and demanded to be put in charge of the expedition. His ace in the hole was a crisp letter from the Massachusetts Committee of Safety in Cambridge, which duly granted him the authority to mount a military operation in the area. It was a fine work of penmanship, and it made the grandly named Committee of War that Allen had recently rousted from the taverns look pretty shabby by comparison, too.

Allen knew just what to do. Confident in the power of the people, he called his men together and paraded the high-ranking visitor before them in his sparkling uniform. For all his grandstanding and grandiosities, Allen understood his men and remained one of them. "God gave mankind freedom by nature and made every man equal to his neighbor, and has virtually enjoined them to govern themselves by their own laws," said brother Ira in one of his pamphlets, ably articulating the Allen family's political philosophy.[5] Ethan made sure that the people got a load of Arnold's "valet"—probably the first such individual ever to set foot in the Green Mountains. Don't worry, he told the Boys, you will still get your two dollars a day, and the brilliantly conceived plan of battle won't change.

He cannot have been terribly surprised when the people took one look at "that fancy bastard" and refused. They stacked up their weapons, folded their arms, and announced that they would not serve until Allen agreed to take back the command. Aware that Arnold's involvement in the project would bring some benefits, and perhaps unwilling to buck the evident will of the Massachusetts Committee, Allen graciously proposed that Arnold might accompany the invasion force as a kind of extra commander—or so ran the version of the story that descended through one line of Vermont historians. Then he went off in search of boats to ferry the invading force across the water that night.

Around four o'clock on the morning of May 10, the rosy fingers of dawn pulled aside the curtain on Allen's date with destiny to reveal a screw-up of epic proportions. Allen had failed to find enough boats for the mission, and as a result only 83 of his 180 men stood with him on the western shore of Lake Champlain. His logistical skills, it seems, were no match for his charisma—he was always more of a showman than a general. A more cautious commander might have opted to postpone the attack for a day. Allen decided that the element of surprise mattered more than the number of beans in the wager. He lined up his 83 heroes in formation, three columns of fearsome buckskin, and, according to his own later account, delivered a mighty harangue. "We must this morning either quit our pretensions to valour, or possess ourselves of this fortress," he declaimed.[6] Given that the squadron was now within earshot of the enemy, historians have doubted whether all that much speechifying took place. Be that as it may, the Green Mountain Boys set off on the march with Allen front and center.

Where was Arnold? In his own narrative, Allen doesn't mention Arnold at this point at all. According to the later testimony of the young scout who served as Allen's local guide on the expedition, the freshly pressed colonel remained on the other side of the lake and would not make it across until after the mission had been accomplished.[7] According to the version passed down through another line of historians, on the other hand, Arnold was there at the moment of peril, standing to Allen's left, serving per their agreement as his wingman. The underlying assumption—not unlike the one that required Thomas Young to serve as the ghostwriter of Ethan Allen's Bible—was that a rough specimen like Allen surely could not have managed a serious military operation without the assistance of a properly bred individual of Arnold's standing.

Now, this side of the story continues, Arnold shinnied up beside Allen. If there was glory to be had, the colonel wanted some, too. Ethan, never known for any enthusiasm in sharing spotlights, broke out into a trot, moving out into the lead again. Arnold pulled up beside him, and then the two men were running without shame, each striving to be the first one through the unrepaired breach in the southern wall of the fort that was to be their point of entry. Whether Arnold got through first or it was a tie depended on just who was telling this version of the story.

Was Arnold really there? If so, did he slip into the lead? Or did these representatives of two very different kinds of American humanity establish a momentary partnership in glory? The very fact that imaginations have been exercised over a question for which the evidence is so thin and disputable tells us something important about the axis of internal struggle around which turned the complicated event that came to be known as the American Revolution. It was mostly men of Arnold's class who ascended into the leadership of the Revolution and the new republic. One way or another, they managed to get themselves written into the headlines. Yet they were often simply responding to forces beyond their control. For all their success in accumulating authority, they often showed up as supporting characters in a narrative that was mostly written by the kind of people who were staking out new lives in the Green Mountains. And so they often found themselves, as Arnold did, desperately chasing men like Allen, either on the field of battle or into the stories told about it after the fact.

"The sun seemed to rise that morning with a superior luster," Allen later recalled. It undoubtedly shone all the more after his men uncovered a stash of ninety gallons of rum in the fort's pantry. The victors "tossed about the flowing bowl and wished success to Congress and the liberty and freedom of America," he gushed.[8] The reporting British officer took a rather more sour view of the matter: "The plunder was most rigidly performed as to liquors." Allen, belatedly seeking to paper over the potential stain on his budding career as a gentleman-warrior, wrote out a receipt, duly authorizing the Connecticut Treasury to reimburse the British commander for his liquid "Property, which is greatly wanted for the Refreshment of the Fatigued Soldiary."[9] By late morning, the party included the hundred Green Mountain Boys who had spent the night on the other side of the lake plus another couple hundred settlers who emerged from the surrounding countryside to share in the good times.

Arnold, whose presence in the aftermath of the victory is well attested, could not contain his disgust. The Green Mountain Boys showed no great fondness for him, either. They ran up to him and released Indian-style war whoops into his ears. Then they accidentally-on-purpose fired weapons off over his head. Allen decided to give him the silent treatment. In the end, Arnold grudgingly acknowledged, "He is perhaps the proper man to head his own wild people."[10]

The seizure of Ticonderoga was no exercise of military genius. It was bold to the point of rashness, and the entire trick turned on total surprise. Even so, the effect of Allen's venture on the course of events to follow should not be underestimated. According to a British historian, the news that a band of self-starters had seized the mightiest fort in the Empire "caused an extraordinary outburst of pride and gratification throughout the entire Confederacy."[11] The strategic value of Ticonderoga lay mainly in what it denied the enemy. Had they controlled the waterway from the north, the British might well have been able to press to the south from Canada in the summer of 1776, rather than having to wait until the less favorable winter of the following year. The most tangible spoils of victory were the two hundred pieces of artillery that the fortress and its satellites yielded. Later in the year, Henry Knox and his men hauled the sixty tons' worth of fieldpieces over the hills and through the snow and deposited them on the outskirts of Boston, where George Washington used them with great effect to drive the British out of the city.

In the Second Continental Congress, which had convened in Philadelphia on the very same day that the assault on Ticonderoga took place, the concern was that Allen had kicked the ball far out in front of where it ought to have been. Many delegates feared the consequences of such a blatant act of rebellion. So the Congress voted to express its meek hope that the King's property might be "safely returned" to its rightful owner. Allen, almost bursting outside of himself with frustration, complained of the slow pace of developments in grandiloquent letters to the Congress. "I wish to God America would at this critical juncture exert herself agreeable to the indignity offered her by a tyrannical ministry," he wrote. "A vast continent must now sink into slavery and poverty, bondage and horror, or rise to unconquerable freedom, immense wealth, inexpressible felicity, and immortal fame."[12]

In early July 1775, when Allen was at the zenith of his glory, he swooped down to Philadelphia to present himself and his vision for America's future to the Congress. According to Allen, the delegates took favorable notice of his "zeal in the common cause."[13] Though the evidence has long been lost to time, it seems reasonable to suppose that in the course of the week or so he spent in the city of brotherly love, Allen might have been found in a tavern with an old friend who first urged him in the direction of the Green Mountains, perhaps raising a pint or two with him in honor of the new era of human equality.

Impatience getting the better of him, Allen returned to the mountains and maneuvered to take matters where he always intended them to be, into his own two hands. Four months after the triumph at Ticonderoga, he surfaced at the northern end of Lake Champlain as the head of an army of a hundred or so untrained French Canadians and Indians. This time, the plan was to storm Montreal, a fortified city with a population in the thousands. It wasn't a good idea. After a long firefight outside city gates in which no one was actually hit, Allen and the thirty or so of his men who had not deserted the battlefield were surrounded and taken in. For Allen, it was the beginning of an entirely unexpected and fiercely painful chapter in his life. He became a prisoner of war before there was a proper war, and he would remain one for nearly three years.

LOOKING BACK in 1784 on the extraordinary burst of constitution-making that characterized the heady first years of the Revolution, Jefferson ably articulated the principle on which turned the internal axis of struggle between men like Ethan Allen and Benedict Arnold. "The foundations on which all these [new constitutions] are built," Jefferson wrote to Washington, "is the natural equality of man, the denial of every pre-eminence but that annexed to legal office, and particularly the denial of a preeminence by birth."[14] Where exactly did this revolutionary idea of "natural equality" come from?

In every human collective throughout history, it has always been a matter of straightforward observation that the distribution of power, goods, talents, and abilities among people is quite unequal. No one has ever seriously supposed that parents, princes, CEOs, the rich, the famous, and colonels in the Massachusetts militia are "equal" to children, common laborers, serfs, slaves, the poor, and Green Mountain gangsters in the influence they exercise over others and the claims they lay against the resources of the earth. Throughout history, human beings by and large have tended toward the view that these differences among people arise from the nature of things. The lion is the king of the beasts; kings are like lions among men; and God is the lion king of them all—or so the common sense of the matter goes. In modern societies, the same intuition takes a different form, yet it is not so different in substance as is often imagined. Not many people today are inclined to say that the order of society is grounded in the order of nature; but quite a few assume that the order of society follows from the nature of individual human beings. The lions among us rise to become CEOs; the mice become something less than full-time workers.

Given this common intuition that people are naturally or inherently unequal, the common consciousness universally interprets the claim that "all men are created equal" as a moral imperative. Justice, the common conception supposes, involves treating people as equals *despite* the fact that they are not. It means granting them the power to rule themselves *despite* the fact that in the natural order of things they would have to submit to the rule of others. Since this imperative so obviously runs counter to the motives and the powers that are perceived to arise from the nature of things, the common conception further infers that it can have force only insofar as it arises from some transcendental authority. Only a commandment from God (or some uncontrollable feeling of empathy among human beings) can compel people to treat unequal people as equals.

The radical political philosophy that guided the American Revolution, on the other hand, begins not with this common assertion of the *moral* equality of human beings but with an explicit denial of the premise concerning the *natural* inequality of human beings. Human equality begins in nature, it says, not in moral imperatives. Although the history of the idea should properly be traced to Lucretius's natural history of justice, in the early modern world it was Thomas Hobbes—whose debt to Epicurus on the point was so obvious to his contemporaries that it hardly needed to be stated[15]—who made the first and sharpest claim for natural equality:

> Nature hath made men so equall, in the faculties of body, and mind; as that though there bee found one man sometimes manifestly stronger in body, or of quicker mind than another; yet when all is reckoned together, the difference between man, and man, is not so considerable, as that one man can thereupon claim to himselfe any benefit, to which another may not pretend, as well as he.[16]

This natural equality, it should be clear, is neither exact nor universal with respect to all human attributes. It is a rough equality between human beings considered in the abstract and has to do principally with one particular attribute: power. Take away our ability to command the resources of society, says Hobbes, and we are roughly equal in power. More graphically, he asserts, we are equal because, left to our own devices, we all have the power to kill one another. (Or perhaps more accurately: any two human beings, considered abstractly in terms of their basic faculties in maturity, can overcome any one individual.)[17] To find genuine natural inequalities, according to this line of thought, one would have to look across categories or species. Human beings and chickens, for example, are naturally unequal, since people can almost always defeat poultry in battle. (And indeed, a Hobbesian would point out, there is not much justice between people and chickens: we raise them in captivity, and then we eat them.)

The natural equality of human beings does not imply that we have a moral obligation to treat all people as equals in every context. Indeed, as a royalist, Hobbes comes to almost exactly the opposite conclusion. Its core meaning is just that the inequalities observable among individuals in any actual society are not attributable to the nature of people or things. That is, there is no natural order of subordination among human beings. Lucretius made the point first when he observed that "slavery and freedom, poverty and wealth, war and peace" are not properties of the atoms themselves, but only of human arrangements.[18] "Our actual inequality," Hobbes emphatically concludes, "has been introduced by civil law."[19] An indication of just how seriously Hobbes takes this claim concerning natural equality is his stance on paternal authority, which he maintains is also a product of civil and social arrangements—quite a radical position in the unthinkingly patriarchal world of the time.

The idea of natural equality figures centrally in the thought of Spinoza—who agrees with Hobbes and Gassendi that human beings "share in one and the same nature"[20]—but the most influential (and misunderstood) theorist on the subject is Locke. Locke's equality, too, is an "*equality* of Men by Nature."[21] Men are equal on account of their "being furnished with like Faculties, sharing all in one Community of Nature."[22] Locke goes on to offer an implicit version of Hobbes's argument, that the natural equality of men is evident in the fact that in the state of nature men are equally able to kill one another.[23] In a phrase that remains popular all the way down to Jefferson, he abbreviates the claim that there is no natural subordination among human beings into the slogan that all men are "equal and independent."[24]

In his writings about equality, Locke makes liberal use of Nature's God, and among some audiences then and now, his invocations of the deity have been taken to prove that his point is that we have the moral obligation to treat people equally in virtue of a commandment from God. Nothing could be farther from the meaning of Locke's actual arguments:

> Man has a *Natural Freedom* . . . since all that share in the same common Nature, Faculties, and Powers, are in Nature equal, and ought to partake in the same common Rights and Privileges, till the manifest appointment of God, who is *Lord over all, Blessed for ever*, can be produced to show any particular Persons Supremacy.[25]

The appearance of the "Lord over all" sounds vaguely pious, yet the fact is that God's presence here is made known only by his absence.

Human equality arises from the deity's failure to countermand the equality of humankind that we observe in nature. Thus, equality depends not on the word of God but on the silence of God. We can of course say—as Locke and countless successors do—that the equality we observe in nature has a divine source, inasmuch as all of nature is the work of God. But we can do so only by supposing that our equality is not distinct from anything else in nature on this point, which is in turn to imply that whatever obligation arises specifically from this equality does not depend on the claim that it is of divine origin. We would also have to acknowledge that divine revelation is entirely dispensable, since the observation of nature alone suffices to demonstrate our natural equality. In short, as happens repeatedly in Locke, we can keep God in the picture by rendering "God" functionally interchangeable with "Nature."

At the bottom of the conception of natural equality that characterizes the Epicurean tradition lies a still more profound commitment to a certain, thoroughly immanent or anti-transcendental conception of justice. "Justice does not exist in the abstract," Epicurus flatly asserts; it is just "a compact to not harm or be harmed"; and this contract varies in its details from place to place.[26] As Gassendi makes clear in his reprise of the Epicurean philosophy, this compact of justice begins with the natural, not moral, equality of human beings: we enter into it on account of the "similitude and mutual Resemblance of Bodies as well as Souls or Manners."[27] The basic form of the compact, Gassendi adds, is the Golden Rule: do not unto others what you would not have them do unto you. He goes on to make the anti-transcendentalism explicit: "There is nothing perfectly Just but what the Society by common Agreement or Approbation hath thought fit to be observed."[28] Spinoza agrees that, absent the compact, "there is nothing . . . which, by the agreement of all, is good or evil."[29] Locke (with some hems and haws) also agrees that, without a compact, "there wants an *establish'd*, settled, known *Law*, received and allowed by common consent to be the Standard of Right and Wrong."[30]

This compact, Epicurus makes clear, necessarily begins and ends with the expectation of some mutual benefit among naturally equal beings. Justice, he says, is "founded on utility."[31] Gassendi hammers the point home without apology: "Right or natural Equity is nothing else but what is mark'd out by Utility or Profit";[32] and that which is "truly Right and naturally Just" must necessarily be "effectively Useful and Good."[33] More abstractly, we could say that, in the same sense that the good is always good *for* someone, according to Epicurus and his followers, justice is always justice *with respect to* a specific relationship between two (or more) equal parties. (This is like utilitarianism, but it isn't the same thing: most modern versions of that doctrine are implicitly transcendental, in that they suppose that we have an inexplicable duty to treat all of the "utils" of individual human beings as equal.)

On the basis of these thoroughly naturalistic ideas of equality and justice, the heirs of Epicurus constructed a thoroughly naturalistic account of the rise of civil society. In what Hobbes calls "the natural condition" of humankind—and what his successors generally call "the state of nature"—there is no justice. By virtue of their roughly equal power, the scarcity of goods, and their finite understanding of things, people will come to disagreements, and the results will not be pretty. The natural condition, Hobbes famously says, is a "war of all against all," in which the typical life is "solitary, poor, nasty, brutish, and short."[34] Up to this point, Spinoza is fully on board: "Men are necessarily subject to passions," he argues; they "pity the unfortunate, envy the fortunate, and are more inclined to vengeance than compassion," and are "equally desirous of preeminence"; so they invariably "fall to quarreling" when left to their own devices.[35]

The civil state, according to Hobbes and his successors, is the natural answer to the troubles of the state of nature. In Hobbes's version, human societies establish the compact of justice by constructing a superior natural force among themselves: the terrifying "Leviathan" that wields the power of the "commonwealth" against those who would violate the compact. As Gassendi explains, legitimate government arises when the members of society transfer to some authority "the power of punishing" violations of commonly agreed standards of justice.[36] In Spinoza's words, the civil state arises when people create a common authority that "claims for itself the right that every man has of avenging himself and deciding what is good and what is evil."[37] This new authority, he says, has "the power to prescribe a common rule of life, to make laws, and to maintain them—not by reason, which cannot restrain the affects, but by threats."[38] Locke repeats what came before: "Therefore is the magistrate armed with the force and strength of all his subjects, in order to the punishment of those that violate any other man's rights."[39] Hobbes underscores the benefits of this naturalistic arrangement of power in the mesmerizing prose that to many of his contemporaries seemed dangerously unforgettable: "Outside the commonwealth is the empire of the passions, war, fear, poverty, nastiness, solitude, barbarity, ignorance, savagery; within the commonwealth is the empire of reason, peace, security, wealth, splendor, society, good taste, the sciences and good will."[40]

At bottom, the anti-transcendental social-contract theory that Hobbes picked up from Lucretius and passed down to his successors is an effort to apply the guiding principle of philosophy to the question of power within human society. The demand for equality among beings that are naturally equal is really just the demand that all power should explain itself. A justice that comes from nature is in essence a justice that comes with reasons and is therefore subject to explanation and revision. It is this insistence on explanation—not any moralistic imperative to be nice to other people, nor the appeal to arbitrary and unreliable feelings of empathy arising out of the human breast—that would make the Enlightenment such a revolutionary force in human history.

Today we tend to lose sight of the impiously anti-transcendental origins of the political theory that guided the American Revolution. But the defenders of orthodoxy in the early modern world certainly did not. The divine rights theorist Sir Robert Filmer (1588–1653) vehemently attacked Hobbes for saying—as in fact he did—that men "emerged from the earth like mushrooms . . . without any obligation to one another."[41] Pointing the finger at Hobbes, Grotius, and (*avant la lettre*) Locke,[42] he inveighed that the power of the King is a "donation of God," not "of the people,"[43] and that the "conceit of original freedom" is a "great scandal of Christianity" and the gateway to "atheism."[44] A century and a half later, Timothy Dwight pummeled his students at Yale with the same, furious insistence on the transcendental origins of the political order. *"The foundation of all government is, undoubtedly, the Will of God,"* he declaimed. "Government, since the days of Mr. Locke, has been extensively supposed *to be founded in the Social Compact.* No opinion is more groundless than this."[45] Filmer and Dwight undoubtedly had a solid part of scripture on their side. As Paul himself says, "The powers that be are ordained of God."[46]

Yet it was the inherently anti-transcendental, Lockean conception that held sway among the ungodly founders of the American Republic. Although Americans everywhere followed Locke in tracing their equality to Nature's God, it is a fairly straightforward matter to see through the glittering pieties to the Neo-Epicurean logic to which they committed themselves. In Jefferson's strident *Summary View of the Rights of British Colonists* of 1774, to name one of countless examples, the argument against parliamentary power rests on a theory of purely natural equality: "Can any one reason be assigned why 160,000 electors in the island of Great Britain should give law to four millions in the states of America, every individual of whom is equal to every individual of them in virtue, in understanding, and in bodily strength?"[47] Jefferson, too, begins by suggesting that our natural equality is the gift of God. But by the end of the *View*, God proves dispensable, and the colonists can claim their equal rights directly "from nature."

In Jefferson's first draft of the Declaration of Independence, interestingly, the relevant clause reads as follows: "all men are created equal & independent." The phrase "equal & independent" comes from Locke, and here it serves to remind us that neither God nor nature supplies any order of subordination among humans. In that first draft, Jefferson's derivation of our rights from "that equal creation"—rather than from the Creator—confirms that the equality of concern here is a fact of nature, not an imperative from on high. Because the self-evident truths that follow upon our equal creation involve certain unalienable rights, many readers who lose the grammatical thread at this point imagine that the thrust of the preamble is to assert some number of rights with no explanation for their existence other than their transcendental rightness. Yet if we trace the arc from the beginning to the end of that same sentence, we can catch a glimpse of the connection between rights and ends—or between justice and utility, or power and its explanations—that characterizes the immanent conception of radical philosophy. The transition begins about halfway over the rainbow, where, after listing our unalienable rights, the Declaration turns to consider governments that are "destructive of these *ends*." And the final clause finds its pot of gold in the conclusion that the ultimate purpose of government is "to effect [the] Safety and Happiness" of the people. The common or religious consciousness always resists this reduction of justice to utility; yet the neutralization of its transcendental delusions about the nature of justice forms the core of the radical political theory that explains the genesis and structure of the American Republic.

II

"... THAT THEY ARE ENDOWED BY THEIR CREATOR WITH CERTAIN
UNALIENABLE RIGHTS, THAT AMONG THESE ARE LIFE, LIBERTY,
AND THE PURSUIT OF HAPPINESS ..."

When the delegates of the Second Continental Congress converged on Philadelphia in that first week of May 1775, throngs of a greater number "than ever known" lined the roads to greet them, the press reported. "All the principal gentlemen" of the city came out in carriages and on horseback to greet the heroes from Massachusetts and Connecticut. Bands played, bells rang, and streets echoed with "demonstrations of joy."[48] The delegations from the south came in by boat and encountered similar effusions of patriotic spirit. The men whom history would one day anoint as the Founding Fathers—George Washington, John Adams, Benjamin Franklin, along with most of the future signers of the Declaration of Independence—gathered in Philadelphia almost as if ready for the sculptors to break out their chisels and the historians to commence the joyful labor of deification.

In that same week, Thomas Young, too, arrived in Philadelphia. He came by boat, and was soon joined by his wife and six children. His arrival merited a line in the *Pennsylvania Evening Post* of May 13, 1775, but otherwise passed without great notice.[49] Few could have doubted that the soon-to-be fathers rode in on the saddle of history, and people like Young were just stringing along in their outsized footsteps.

Within a couple weeks of his arrival, Young bumped into his old acquaintance John Adams, who was feeling low from various ailments. "After scolding at me, quantum sufficit for not taking his Advice," John wrote to Abigail, Young "pill'd and electuary'd me into pretty good Order."[50] About a month later, the readers of the Philadelphia press were treated to the following advertisement:

Having the world a sixth time to begin anew, and being advanced three years beyond the term, when a man is said to be either a fool or a physician, I have that confidence in the justice and generosity of the worthy citizens of this metropolis, as to presume, that from the peculiar circumstances of my condition, they will consider the following address to them as the open application of an honest man who wishes to maintain himself and numerous family, by serving them faithfully, rather than a puffing empiric, who has found out the secret to extract the gold from their pockets by Elixir Bardana or Essence of Waterdock.[51]

The author of the piece goes on to expound his familiar theory that "the human body is undoubtedly an hydraulic machine." Evidently, the people of Philadelphia were ready to be treated like water pumps, for the newly arrived medicine man was "getting into Business fast," reported Samuel Ward (1725–1776), the former governor of Rhode Island, now representing his colony in the Continental Congress. Young inoculated all six of Ward's children and his wife against smallpox. Ward unaccountably neglected to have himself inoculated and perished nine months later from the disease.[52] At night, in the taverns and at his desk, meanwhile, the radical doctor continued to pursue his plan for the liberation of the people. "His Pen is frequently employed in the common Cause," Ward recorded before expiring.[53] From that pen flowed much of the familiar language about the "state of nature" and the "state of war" (which now very clearly meant the same thing). That pen also appeared to reserve more than the usual volume of ink for the subject nearest to Young's heart: the "natural rights" of the "common people" above all of those who pretended to be their betters.

It was a message that many of those people were eager to hear. The province in which Young landed was one of the richest in America; it was also home to some of America's poorest citizens. With forty thousand or so inhabitants, Philadelphia was the largest metropolis in British America, and it offered just about everything money could buy. Yet half the population owned no taxable property, and the bottom 60 percent could claim a mere 8 percent of the total wealth.[54] The entire colony was in a very real sense the private property of an aristocratic family in England—the well-fed descendants of William Penn—and it was divided internally between an extremely wealthy oligarchy, concentrated in Philadelphia and the southeast, and a vast population of farmers, laborers, slaves, and immigrant hordes, many of them German, who read newspapers in their own language and washed down their pickled cabbage with the bitter ale of resentment. Within Philadelphia, a new class of white male artisans, mechanics, and tradespeople arose out of the economic turmoil and began to assert themselves against the established powers. These were Benjamin Franklin's people, and now they found a new hero in Thomas Young.

As in Boston and before that in Albany, Young almost instantly fell in with a group of like-minded agitators. This time it was a gang of six, all frustrated idealists versed in radical thought and cherishing visions of social transformation that in normal times might well have counted as signs of mental distress. Thomas Paine would become the most famous of the six, though at the time he was an obscure thirty-eight-year-old magazine editor freshly arrived from a failed life in England as a corset-maker, schoolteacher, excise tax collector, and tobacco salesman. James Cannon (1740–1782) was a Scotch immigrant and professor of mathematics who developed a reputation as "a fanatical school-master" and was known for his "scholastic predilection for the antique in liberty, which generally falls to the lot of the pedagogue."[55] Timothy Matlack was a merchant, architect, and handwriting expert with equally radical views. Dr. Benjamin Rush, who served alongside Young in a professional capacity, and Christopher Marshall, a devout Quaker, rounded out the gang, though their relative moderation eventually provoked a split from the other four.[56] A crucial ally for the gang of six was Thomas Young's old comrade from Boston, Samuel Adams, who came to Philadelphia as part of the Massachusetts delegation to the Congress and had considerable influence over his cousin John.

The gang swiftly left its mark on the indignant consciences of its political enemies. "Cato," also known as the Reverend William Smith (1727–1803), in the course of his attacks on Paine, named the key members of the gang in a poetical polemic intended to appeal to the better sort of readers:

> *Who would endure this Pain?*
> *This foul discharge of wrath from Adam's sons?*
> *Marshall'd in dread array, both old and Young*
> *Their pop-guns here, and there their heavy Cannon*
> *Our labor'd pages deem'd not worth a Rush*[57]

The striking fact about Young and his gang, as Cato quite clearly perceived, is that they aimed to start two revolutions. They wanted to settle the question not just of home rule but also of who should rule at home. They were, as John Adams said with scorn, "the democratic party," and in articles hurled from the Pennsylvania press like so many pitchforks, they seemed just as keen to invite the hatred of America's very own ruling classes as of their British overlords. If "the upper part of a nation . . . has the authority of government solely in their hands," explained "A Tradesman" in one piece, "[they] will always be for keeping the low people under." He held out the frightening vision—to the oligarchs, that is—of a future society in which "all ranks and conditions would come in for their just share of the wealth."[58] For perhaps the first time in America, a tone of righteous populism begins to fill the hitherto respectful pages of the local culture. It isn't hard to detect in this the hidden hand of the Great Awakening merging with radical politics, empowering the lowborn to stake their moral worth against the venal few who pretend to be their earthly masters. One writer railed against the "profane, obscene, trifling conversation so peculiar to high-life." Of the common people he said, "Vulgarity is seated only in their manners" not in their "minds."[59] Possibly the words came from Young himself.[60] If not, they expressed well enough another man's struggles with the rage that trailed Young out of the log cabin in which he was born on the banks of the Hudson River.

Although many historians and quite a few participants have sought to portray the American Revolution as an essentially conservative movement, intended to preserve an existing political culture, Young and his allies made abundantly clear that their target was the British Constitution and indeed the British way of life itself. "Once grant that a government by Kings, Lords, and Commons, is, without exception, in all states and circumstances, the best of all possible governments, and then, certainly we can have no rational objection to a convenient number of Lords being created in America; and that as naturally requires a *Royal Sovereign* to give beings to such *gods on earth*, whose *sacred person* shall be Lord Paramount, or God over them all," Young writes under the name of "Eudoxus." He takes note of the argument put forward by Cato, among others, that history affords no instance of a large-scale republic, and rejects it outright. "To season our palates the better for this transcendent mode of government," he sarcastically inveighs, "we are told the ancient republics were all feeble. But this is just to argue that we should hand over our property to a robber on the grounds that he would steal it from us anyway." He sticks resolutely to his democratic plan: "The effectual remedy for this intolerable evil is the *new experiment* Cato and his party so earnestly combat. This is the faction, sedition, agrarian law, leveling scheme, anarchy, democratical power, they so bitterly hate and oppose."[61]

Like revolutionaries throughout history, Young and his gang understood that in order to change the future it is necessary first to change the past. Following the lead of the radical Whigs in England, they concentrated their revisionist energies on the legends of ancient Saxony. The Saxons, Young maintained, "considered every man alike as he came out of the hands of his maker." Consequently, they practiced a form of representative democracy, according to which "no freeman shall be taxed, excised, burthened or charged in any shape or for any use without his own or representatives consent."[62] The trouble with the British Empire, said Young, started with William the Conqueror and his "infernal system of ruling by a *few dependent favorites*, who would readily agree to divide the spoils of the lower class between the supreme robber and his banditti of feudal lords." The lesson of the story, as Young tells it, is deeply subversive: the political order of Great Britain is hopelessly corrupt—and has been since 1066.

The radical faction achieved its breakthrough moment with the publication of Paine's *Common Sense* on January 9, 1776. The work "burst from the press with an effect which has rarely been produced by types and paper in any age or country," said Rush. Ten days after publication it was already making "a great noise" in Virginia. Within two weeks it had gone into its second printing, and it eventually sold 150,000 copies—one for every twenty people in the colonies.[63] As Paine's friend Joel Barlow observed, "The great American cause owed as much to the pen of Paine as to the sword of Washington."[64] That cause, at least as Paine understood it, was not merely independence but revolution—along the same lines that Thomas Young had been pushing since leaving Albany more than a decade previously.

In *Common Sense*, Paine ferociously attacks not just King George but the British Constitution and indeed the very idea of monarchy. He, too, picks up on the hoary thread of Saxon mythology and traces the corruption of the mother country all the way back to that "French Bastard landing with an armed Banditti" who took England private in 1066.[65] He ultimately rests his case for the rights of the colonists on nature itself. All "mankind," he insists, are "originally equals in the order of creation."[66] Government derives its power from the consent of the governed, and the only legitimate government is representative government. On the basis of these principles he proposes institutional arrangements more democratic than anything the modern world has known hitherto. The vision was limited by neither geography nor history: "The cause of America is . . . the cause of all mankind." "We have it in our power to begin the world over again."[67]

Paine's pamphlet was as revolutionary in its style as it was in its substance. Even today, the contrast with the other political literature of the period is startling. The earlier pamphlets in the American struggle are learned exercises, often written by lawyers, ornamented with erudite citations, diffusing their agendas in complex theories about the British Constitution and the nature of representation. Paine's work offered common sense for the common man. It was composed in a language that could be easily understood even by those who had to have it read out loud to them.

Though *Common Sense* avoids the overt theological critiques that Paine brought forth seventeen years later in his *Age of Reason*, it does contain important hints about the heterodox foundations of its political philosophy. In his assault on monarchy, for example, Paine cites an old and long discredited interpretation of a passage in 1 Samuel that purports to establish that the God of the Old Testament was a closeted republican. Defenders of orthodoxy, such as Cato, immediately suspected that Paine's preposterous and possibly impious reading of scripture was a theological spit-and-polish operation, intended to accommodate unwary religious folk by putting the shine of piety on an ungodly revolutionary project. John Adams confronted Paine on the subject, and was scandalized to hear him express "a Contempt of the Old Testament and indeed of the Bible at large." "I have some thoughts of publishing my Thoughts on Religion," Paine told Adams, "but I believe it will be best to postpone it to the latter part of Life."[68]

And then there is the bizarre ceremony that Paine proposes in *Common Sense* to mark the end of monarchy and the triumph of republicanism on earth. Take a crown and place it on "the charter" of the new political order, then place both on a copy of "the word of God," he recommends, and then throw a party around it in order to demonstrate "that in America THE LAW IS KING." Then, when the festivities end, "lest any ill use should afterwards arise, let the crown . . . be demolished, and scattered among the people whose right it is."[69] The ceremonial deconstruction of Law-King's crown on earth imitates precisely what comes to pass in Paine's deism with the Law-King who allegedly rules above. In the reign of Nature's God, too, the law is king—the law of nature—and yet its crown, too, is just a projection of the collective, to be smashed and parceled out to all those beings that express that same law through their very own nature.

It was the revolutionary aspect of *Common Sense* rather than its argument for independence that constituted its distinctive (and in many quarters unwelcome) contribution to the debate. Adams, a monarchist by instinct and a "monarchical republican" by virtue of his own convoluted theorizing on the subject, was as vigorous in his support of independence as he was militant in his disgust with the democratic aspect of Paine's pamphlet. "What a poor, ignorant, malicious, short-sighted, crapulous mass," he fumed.[70] "It is certain in theory that the only moral foundation of government is, the consent of the people. But to what an extent shall we carry this principle?" he wanted to know. "Women will demand a vote," he intoned with horror, as might "every man who has not a farthing."[71] Paine's radical ideas about government, Adams sniffed, were intended to please only "the democratic party in Philadelphia, at whose head were Mr. Matlack, Mr. Cannon, and Dr. Young."[72]

Through the winter and spring of 1776, debaters flamed one another in the newspapers of Philadelphia. Cato fired off his polemics against Paine; Paine shot back under the name of "Forrester"; Cannon rallied to Paine's side as "Cassandra"; and Young joined the fray as "Eudoxus" and "An Elector." Though the radicals appeared to be gaining traction, the power of the state in Pennsylvania remained firmly in the hands of the old oligarchy, which favored reconciliation with Great Britain and emphatically no change in the social order that had done them so many favors. The Pennsylvania delegation to the Continental Congress, led by the relatively conservative John Dickinson, resolutely opposed the movement toward independence, and the opinion of the Pennsylvanians was decisive for the representatives of the middle colonies of New Jersey, Delaware, and even New York. Although in retrospect the march from Lexington to the Fourth of July often strikes us as inevitable, it is worth remembering that at the time a substantial number of very powerful people thought the movement for independence could be stopped—and they were indeed stopping it.

The radicals chose not to wait for the much-studied lucubrations of the soon-to-be Founding Fathers in the Continental Congress to tell them what to do. Instead, they decided to tell the fathers what to do. They organized their plan around elections scheduled for May 1, 1776, in which Philadelphia's four seats in the Pennsylvania Assembly were in play. If they won those seats, they could take the Assembly, and then swing the colony and its neighbors behind the movement toward independence and revolution. The choice before the voters could not have been clearer. On one slate were the "Moderates," representing the old world of wealth and power and favoring reconciliation with mother England. On the other slate were the so-called Independents, the allies of Paine and Young, who demanded both independence and political transformation.

For the final preelection issue of the *Pennsylvania Packet* of April 29, Young sent in one of his most remarkable contributions to the revolutionary moment. Writing under the pseudonym "An Elector," he called for "a radical reformation" of the Pennsylvania government. Specifically, he proposed eliminating the fifty-pound property qualification for voters—a qualification that disenfranchised as many as half of the white male population. The right to vote, he said, properly belongs to "Every man who pays his shot and bears his lot." To prove the point, he wheeled in those paragons of democratic virtue, the ancient Saxons. Dickinson and other leaders of the Moderates promptly seized on Young's hotheaded calls for expanding the franchise. Here was proof positive, they retorted, that a vote for the Independents was a vote for the mob.

The first of May was a sunny Wednesday in Philadelphia. Young spent the morning getting out the vote. Using his language skills, he canvassed mostly among the Germans, who leaned strongly toward the Independents. At one o'clock, the gang met for a strategy lunch at the house of James Cannon. At two o'clock came the first sign of trouble. A Moderate had challenged the allegiance of the Germans to the colony and contested their right to vote. Now a large and rowdy group of Germans gathered in front of the State House in vigorous protest against these efforts at voter suppression. As the day wore on, the election got rougher. At six o'clock, the town sheriff inexplicably closed the polls. Many of the city's artisans and mechanics—overwhelmingly supporters of the Independents—had counted on voting in the evening, after normal working hours. Paine and friends marched on the State House in a high dudgeon. After many hot words, the sheriff acquiesced to their demands and reopened the polls. Many would-be voters did not get the message, however, and failed to vote.[73]

Early on the morning of May 2, the results were posted outside the State House. The Moderates claimed three of the four seats in the contest, and Pennsylvania and the Continental Congress remained in the hands of those who wished to pursue a policy of reconciliation with Great Britain. The margin of victory was incredibly narrow—a swing of merely eleven out of the two thousand or so votes cast would have produced a very different outcome—but the result was definitive. The movement for independence appeared to have been stopped cold.

Throughout the debates leading up to this point in the American struggle, everyone seemed to have certain "rights" on their side. Those who sought independence claimed their "rights" against their overseas masters; and those who sought revolution claimed many of the same "rights" against their masters at home. Often, the polemicists—among them Thomas Young—went out of their way to pretend that the rights in question were essentially English, or at least "Saxon." But in fact they weren't—and it was a fairly trivial matter for Tories to demonstrate that the British Constitution entailed few of the rights they claimed, least of all the right to resist their King and Parliament. More often the revolutionaries made loud efforts to derive their rights from God—from which fact some historians infer that the Revolution was a theological project designed to fulfill a mission ordained from on high. But this, too, is pretty much the opposite of the truth. Almost everybody on the revolutionary side of the struggle claimed that their rights were founded in nature—and on this point they were correct, though not always in the sense that they imagined, for the political theory from which America drew its rights was deeply at odds with the common conceptions of things.

THERE MAY BE no feeling more universal among human beings than that associated with the experience of power without right. Every child on a playground can bear witness to it, every teenager scowls in the face of it, every employee in every workplace and every citizen in every political system ever devised knows what it feels like. So it is probably inevitable that human beings should suppose that power and right are entirely separate things or even contraries; and indeed few claims strike the common consciousness as more preposterous than that "might is right." Power is what other people use to take what they don't deserve, or so we tend to think. And if there is any justice in the world—a point that every child and teenager learns to doubt—then it can only obtain on the inherently dubitable proposition that there is some higher power, above all the rest, that happens to value what is right and so can make up for all the crimes of the lesser powers.

In their pursuit of the foundations of justice and power, however, the heirs of Epicurus arrived at the insight that "right" is indeed nothing but "might" perspicuously understood. They wrapped this insight in a respectable language of "natural rights" and "laws of nature" purportedly ordained by God above. But in fact they found a way of explaining rights that reduces God to nothing more than the very principle that all rights may be explained in terms of power. Curiously, the process really began with a kind of unraveling from within of natural theology.

At least since Moses descended from Mount Sinai with his stone tablets, the common religious consciousness has identified God as the ultimate authority on all matters of justice. God, according to the common conception, is a lawgiver, and his laws are commands that we ought to (but don't always) obey. Moses's laws are the epitome of "revealed" laws—that's what the stone tablets were for—but the idea that God issues "natural" laws as well as revealed ones, too, is an ancient one, and also appears in the Bible. As Paul explains, "When Gentiles who do not possess the law [of Moses] carry out its precepts by the light of nature . . . they display the effect of the law inscribed on their hearts."[74] Theologians from Aquinas to the present drew upon Paul's inscribed hearts to construct a long and complex tradition of "Natural Law." "Engraved" hearts also happen to be a staple of deist literature, and are enthusiastically cited in the works of Spinoza and Locke, as well as Vanini, Tindal, Jefferson, and Allen, among others. But the laws of Nature's God are dramatically different from—indeed they are in a crucial way the opposite of—the "Natural Law" of the theologians.[75]

According to the theological view, which is also the common view, natural laws differ from ordinary moral and civil laws in their method of discovery but not in their structure or substance. That is, although they are made available to us through experience and reason as opposed to the revealed word of God, natural laws impose obligations, invoke the authority of a lawgiver, and can be violated. Indeed, they give rise to the concept of a "crime against nature." Modern Natural Law theorists tend to discover, for example, that gay sex, contraception, and other practices that disagree with their convictions or otherwise make them feel uncomfortable constitute violations of natural law. The "Laws of Nature" of the deist tradition, on the other hand, impose no obligations, cannot be violated, and reduce the idea of a "crime against nature" to a contradiction in terms.

Arguably the first and in any case the most influential expression of the deist conception of the laws of nature is to be found in the work of Hobbes.[76] A law of nature, according to Hobbes, is "a dictate of right reason about what should be done or not done for the longest possible preservation of life and limb."[77] So, for example, since drinking heavily is not conducive to long life, one should not drink heavily if one wishes to live long. Hobbes adumbrates a list of nineteen or twenty such laws, depending on the moment of writing. So far, so medieval, one could say. But then, in what marks a critical break from the Natural Law idea, Hobbes makes a startling yet eminently reasonable observation: "These dictates of Reason, men use to call by the name of Lawes; but improperly: for they are but Conclusions, or Theoremes concerning what conduceth to the conservation and defence of themselves; whereas Law, properly is the word of him, that by right hath command over others."[78]

Properly speaking, the theorems or dictates that Hobbes identifies as "Laws of Nature" cannot be disobeyed. One may drink heavily, to be sure; but one cannot drink heavily and live long. Nor may these laws be said to incur any punishment or involve any enforcement beyond the natural consequences of the acts they appear to proscribe. Thus, the "punishment" for intemperance is disease, and the punishment for deceit is loss of trust. "For seeing punishments are consequent to the breach of laws; natural punishments must be naturally consequent to the breach of the laws of nature; and therefore follow them as their natural, not arbitrary effects," says Hobbes.[79] Now, inasmuch as God is the alleged author of these "Laws of Nature," God is not a moral "lawgiver" in anything like the traditional sense. God is at most a "theorem-giver," and our duty is not to "obey" his theorems but simply to understand them. Hobbes's contemporary critics had little doubt about his agenda on this point. "If Atheistical persons could, as they would, exterminate the good God of heaven from having to do in this world, that, which they call reason and the law of reason, would be indeed a rule, but not truly and formally a law," wrote Matthew Hale, his polemical guns trained on the monster of Malmsbury.[80]

A parallel deconstruction of the concept of "natural right" can be traced from Hobbes through Spinoza. According to the common conception, a "right" is distinct from a "law" in that it prescribes not what one must or must not do, but only what one may do. A "right" may nonetheless be translated into a "law" for other people, inasmuch as a right for one person represents a duty for others not to infringe it. In the traditional conception associated with Natural Law, natural rights are indeed duties discovered in nature but nonetheless absolute in the demands they place on other people. It is this traditional concept of natural rights that Jeremy Bentham, speaking for a great number of modern philosophers, called "nonsense upon stilts"[81]— which, from the perspective of Epicurus's successors, is exactly what it is, inasmuch as it pretends to discover in nature what only a collective of human beings can impose on one another through a compact. As a consequence of his radical conception of the "Laws of Nature," however, Hobbes conceives of a "Natural Right" (which we will here distinguish with use of the uppercase singular form) that behaves very differently from "natural rights" as they have traditionally been understood.

Natural Right, says Hobbes, means "a liberty each man has of using his natural faculties in accordance with right reason."[82] What reason requires, as we know, is embedded in those "dictates of reason" that Hobbes calls "Laws of Nature." Since those laws are essentially theories about how to stay alive, it follows that our first and fundamental Natural Right is the freedom to do whatever is in our power within reason to stay alive. Now, as we know from the arguments concerning the natural equality of men, we all have the power to kill one another. So Hobbes goes out of his way to make clear that we have a Natural Right to kill and maim other people, perhaps even eat their babies, insofar as our self-preservation requires it. A right in this sense involves no duty implicitly imposed on other individuals; it is simply a duty to oneself.

Spinoza draws out the radical implication of Hobbes's logic. The Laws of Nature whose exercise is our Natural Right, he notes, include the law that everything seeks to preserve itself, for indeed "it is the supreme law of Nature that each thing endeavors to persist in its present being." But from this it follows that Natural Right is just another way of talking about the power through which everything strives to realize itself. Spinoza makes the point with memorable force:

> It is by sovereign natural right that fish inhabit water, and the big ones eat the smaller ones. For it is certain that Nature, taken in the absolute sense, has the sovereign right to do all that she can do; that is, Nature's right is co-extensive with her power. For Nature's power is the very power of God, who has sovereign right over all things. But since the universal power of Nature as a whole is nothing but the power of all individual things taken together, it follows that each individual thing has the sovereign right to do all that it can do; i.e. the right of the individual is co-extensive with its determinate power.[83]

Natural Right, understood in this sense, is what we might now call "Darwinian" in tooth and claw. It is as permissive as one can imagine and involves no "ought" or "commandment" to obey anyone or anything outside oneself. Spinoza makes no bones about it: "The right and law of nature, under which we all are born and for the most part live, forbids nothing save what nobody desires and nobody can do: it forbids neither strife, nor hatred, nor anger, nor deceit."[84] The critics are clear on the matter, too. Theorists like Hobbes and Spinoza, says the seventeenth-century theologian Richard Cumberland, "assign'd no larger Bounds to *Right* and the *Laws of Nature*, than the Preservation of this frail *Life*; as if Men, like Swine, had Souls given them only, instead of Salt, to preserve the Body from Putrefaction."[85]

At about this point in the argument, Spinoza splits with Hobbes, and the resulting difference between the two is in some ways the most important development in the history of political thought in the early modern period. At the same time, the break is more like an internal development of Hobbes's thought, and it ultimately makes Spinoza (and Locke) more Hobbesian than Hobbes, in a manner of speaking. In a letter to one of his correspondents, Spinoza offers a first take on the break in this way: "The difference between Hobbes and myself consists in this, that I always preserve the natural right in its entirety, and I hold that the sovereign power in a State has right over a subject only in proportion to the excess of its power over that of a subject."[86]

In Hobbes's somewhat idiosyncratic version of the social contract, human beings agree, each with every other, to authorize a sovereign to serve as their representative and to protect each from the other in all their mutual dealings. This act of "re-presentation," according to Hobbes, creates an "artificial person"—the state or the "Leviathan." Because the sovereign is a product of but not party to the social contract, as Hobbes sees it, the sovereign has no obligations to individuals or even to the people as a whole. Conversely, individuals have no right to resist the authority of the sovereign, for they represent themselves through it. Consequently, the social contract is something like a once-and-for-all exit from the state of nature into the civil state, from which there is no return. Once we contract to establish a sovereign, he concludes, we are "as absolutely subject to them, as is a child to the father, or a slave to as master."[87] In Hobbes's world, then, Natural Right is like a brief glimpse of freedom as we shuttle from the terror of the state of nature to a life of enslavement under our self-created (and self-identical) sovereign.

Spinoza's objection is that Hobbes has surreptitiously imported a transcendental claim into his otherwise anti-transcendental conception of the social contract. We enter into the Hobbesian contract through Natural Right, but then we are barred from leaving it by a juridical obligation to respect our contracts. In a thoroughly anti-transcendental philosophy, however, the social contract can have force not because we have a duty to follow it but because it is useful: "The validity of an agreement rests on its utility, without which the agreement automatically becomes null and void."[88] So, for example, according to Hobbes, if a "theefe" takes me hostage and extracts from me a promise that I will pay him a ransom after he releases me, I am bound to pay him: "For whatsoever I may lawfully do without Obligation, the same I may lawfully covenant to do through feare: and what I lawfully Covenant, I cannot lawfully break."[89] Our obligation to obey our sovereign, Hobbes indicates, answers to the same logic: a deal's a deal. Spinoza takes exactly the contrary view. If a robber demands with threats that we deliver to him goods at a later time, he says, we have the Natural Right to break our promise and even to deceive him.[90] Our obligation to our sovereign, he likewise infers, can never exceed the utility of that obligation perspicuously understood.

This is anti-transcendentalism taken to a radical extreme, a kind of Hobbism on steroids—and Hobbes himself appeared to agree. According to a friend, upon reading the *Tractatus* in his old age, Hobbes declared that Spinoza "had overthrown him a bar's length, for he durst not write so boldly."[91] The critics also tended to agree: "Spinosa is more fearless than Hobbes . . . In his treatise of Politics, especially in the broad assertion that good faith is only to be preserved so long as it is advantageous, [he] leaves Machiavel and Hobbes at some distance and may be reckoned the most phlegmatically impudent of the whole school."[92] It is precisely this deep coherence—which is to say, his fidelity to the agenda first articulated by Epicurus—that makes Spinoza's philosophy so powerful in understanding the revolutionary force in modern political thought.

In Spinoza's vision, it now becomes clear that the state of nature is not a historical state at all. It is something closer to an ongoing perspective on all social experience, and we never actually depart from it. It is our reality; though it is only one way of understanding or expressing that reality. The civil state, likewise, is not a historical state but a perspective on our reality. The social contract has force because it is a more useful and in a sense more accurate representation of the state of nature for all parties, and it fails when it ceases to represent the underlying state of nature. This claim—that the civil state is just the state of nature perspicuously understood or realized—helps make clear the link with a second way in which Spinoza distinguishes his position from that of Hobbes.

"Although Hobbes thinks otherwise," Spinoza writes in a note appended to his *Tractatus Theologico-Politicus*, "reason is entirely in favor of peace."[93] In his analysis of the natural condition of humankind, Hobbes gives the impression that the reasonable thing for human beings to do is to plunder and pillage and in general satisfy all of our lusts at the expense of our neighbors. At the same time, there is a difficult tension in Hobbes's own thought at this point, for his very first Law of Nature or "dictate of right reason" tells us that everybody should seek peace with one another. So reason in this instance would seem to be on the side of peace rather than war. Spinoza in effect stays on the sunny side of Hobbes. The conflict among individuals in the "empire of the passions," he points out, follows not from their rationality but from their irrationality, that is, from their passionate nature. It is not because human beings seek their advantage, but because they fail to seek it in a perspicuous way that they descend into the war of all against all. Indeed, inasmuch as human beings have a common nature, as we know from the ethical identity of "self-love and social," they can reasonably wish for nothing more useful than to live in harmony with one another and so to maximize the fruit of their cooperation. "If men lived by the guidance of reason, every man would possess this right of his [to act according to his perception of his own advantage] without any harm to another," Spinoza concludes.[94]

Here we can also see how the root source of the split between

Hobbes and Spinoza involves the same metaphysical differences that lie at the core of the deist philosophy in general and that emerge most strikingly in the philosophy of mind. As a first-order materialist, Hobbes conceives of freedom as nothing but the freedom of bodily motion. Consequently, he cannot but conceive of the natural condition of humankind as a state of pure freedom in which every individual is free because all can move their bodies in accordance with whatever strikes their fancy at any moment. The civil state, he inevitably infers, can represent only a severe restriction on freedom, and so he describes the civil laws as nothing more than "Artificiall Chains."[95] According to Spinoza, on the other hand, freedom as Hobbes imagines it—the unfettered ability to act out every impulse—is actually a form of slavery. As a second-order materialist, Spinoza maintains that we realize our freedom instead through rational self-determination, that is, by gaining control of ourselves and of our environment through the improvement of the understanding.

Inasmuch as the civil state is the state of nature made reasonable, according to Spinoza, it follows that "the man who is guided by reason is more free in a state where he lives under a system of law than in solitude where he obeys only himself."[96] Thus, "the more a man is guided by reason—that is . . . the more he is free—the more steadfast he will be in preserving the laws of the state."[97] The civil state is therefore more than an odious enslavement to which we submit in hopes of avoiding the Hobbesian nightmare of a war of all against all. "Peace is not the mere absence of war, but a virtue based on strength of mind," says Spinoza.[98] "The purpose of the state is, in reality, freedom."[99]

Spinoza's position involves modifying the binary opposition between the state of nature and the civil state with a third state, which we may call the "state of reason." A state of reason describes the hypothetical or ideal order that would obtain among people who live entirely under the guidance of reason in the absence of a civil state. A state of reason would need or want no civil laws, for the people within it will achieve harmony by acting as reason requires, and reason, as we know from radical ethics, requires only that we seek continuously to improve the understanding and never specifies any other particular good. The state of nature describes the order that would obtain among people as they are, passionate and unreasonable, in the absence of a civil state. It, too, has no civil laws, but the results are, as we know, very unpleasant. And the civil state is the actual state that results from the attempt to build a bridge from the state of nature to the state of reason. Its aim is to induce naturally rebarbative human beings to behave as if they were reasonable. A civil state that accurately represents the state of nature, which is to say, a civil state in which a people is able to realize itself according to reason, may be called, to borrow a term from the sunny side of Hobbes, the Empire of Reason.

The Empire of Reason, to be clear, does not contain or restrict nature but realizes it, and so it is also by definition the most powerful form of state. It maximizes the freedom or power of the individual, insofar as we understand freedom or power as rational self-determination (as opposed to the satisfaction of passions). But the rational self-determination or power of the individual, as we know from radical ethics, is in fact coextensive with the rational self-determination of the collective. Consequently, Spinoza concludes, "The commonwealth that is based on reason and directed by reason is most powerful and most in control of its own right."[100] And "the greater the number of men who thus unite in one body, the more right they will all collectively possess."[101] Thus, the application of the guiding principle of philosophy to the question of power—which is to say, the demand that all power must explain itself—is the way in which we maximize both power and right. There could hardly be a starker contrast with the political imagination of the common religious consciousness—which universally supposes that "power" grows in inverse relation to "reason" and "right."

All of these fine reflections about the rational mediation of nature through civil society might well have ended as a curiosity in an Amsterdam bookshop or gone up in smoke—as they did when Hobbes's books were burned in an Oxford quad by the King's men in the aftermath of the Rye House Plot in 1683—had it not been for the diligent public relations effort masterminded by John Locke. Considered in terms of its basic structure, Locke's enormously influential political theory follows Hobbes up to the point where Spinoza breaks off, and thereafter he follows Spinoza, with the usual savvy adornment of a rhetorical theology.

In the spirit of Hobbes, Locke grounds Natural Right on the "Fundamental Law of Nature," which he defines as "Man's being to be preserved."[102] He similarly deduces a series of "laws of nature" that are in fact "laws of reason" and that reduce to theorems concerning what an individual must do in order to survive. The most important of these laws, he says, picking up the thread that stretches back to Gassendi and Epicurus, is a version of the Golden Rule. In his analyses of the sources of justice, consequently, Locke inevitably slips into the identification of power and right so characteristic of Spinoza and Hobbes.[103]

As in theology, the philosophy of mind, and ethics, Locke's signal contribution to human history and to the American Revolution in particular has to do not with his originality but with his success in packaging the radical position to this point in a language that makes it seem more agreeable to orthodox convictions and that serves to emphasize the impulse toward true piety which it shares with all religion. To wit, Locke stresses that our Natural Right to preserve ourselves may be expressed as an obligation to God:

> For Men being all the Workmanship of one Omnipotent, and infinitely wise Maker; all the servants of one Sovereign Master, sent into the World by his order and about his business, they are his Property, whose Workmanship they are, made to last during his, not one anothers Pleasure.[104]

Man must rely on "the voice of God in him," says Locke; and this voice "tells us, that men, being once born, have a Right to their Preservation." Thus, Locke would have the faithful believe, our seemingly selfish and amoral pursuit of a proto-Darwinian Natural Right is really a selfless act of submission to the will of a God who demands that we defend ourselves in the name of his property rights.

As should be abundantly clear by now, this seemingly preposterous identification of obedience to God with the Darwinian pursuit of self-preservation makes perfect sense—provided one understands by "God" the same thing that Spinoza understands by "Nature." Locke's claim that our drive to preserve ourselves is the voice of God within us is merely an imaginative restatement of Spinoza's claim that the conatus through which each individual thing strives to preserve itself is nothing other than the conatus of God. (Or Bruno's claim that Nature is nothing but "God in things," for that matter.) From Locke's own premises, it follows that the will of God can never contradict the will of the individual nor impose a duty that isn't also a desire perspicuously understood. The supposed "commandment" of God to protect his "Property," stripped of its theological euphemisms, isn't a commandment at all but the statement of an inviolable law of nature.

When Spinoza moves past Hobbes to the ultra-Hobbesian position that the state of nature persists in civil society, Locke ditches his English mentor to follow the Dutch one. "The Obligations of the Law of Nature cease not in Society," says Locke.[105] (For comparison, here is Spinoza rejecting Hobbes: "The natural right of every man ceases not in the civil state.")[106] Tellingly, Locke brings up the case of the promise-demanding thief and emphatically sides with Spinoza.[107] "A rational creature cannot be supposed, when free, to put himself into subjection to another for his own harm," he reasons.[108]

Locke's Spinozism (or ultra-Hobbism) comes into clearer focus once we understand that he makes a somewhat confusing terminological shift, designed chiefly to obscure the heterodox drift of his thought. To Locke, "the State of Nature" refers not to the condition of human beings in their unreasonable humanity in the absence of a civil state, as it does to Hobbes and Spinoza, but to what Spinoza would call the state of reason. "Men living together *according to reason* [emphasis added], without a common Superior on earth, with Authority to judge between them, is properly the state of nature," says Locke. "The *State of Nature* [emphasis in the original] has a Law of Nature to govern it, which obliges everyone. And Reason, which is that Law, teaches all Mankind, who will but consult it, that being all equal and independent, no one ought to harm another in his Life, Health, Liberty, or Possessions."[109] If men lived according to reason, says Locke, miming

Spinoza, "there would be no need" of government. Thus, when Locke, targeting Hobbes, asserts that the state of nature and the state of war are "as far distant as a state of peace . . . and a state of enmity," he is essentially repeating the second claim with which Spinoza distances himself from Hobbes: that reason always favors peace.

Notwithstanding his conflation of the state of reason with the state of nature, Locke by no means rejects Hobbes and Spinoza's characterization of how human beings in their unreasonable humanity will behave in the absence of a civil state, or what most writers mean by the "state of nature." In the absence of civil government, he concludes, there would be "no peace, no security, no enjoyments, enmity with all men and safe possession of nothing, and those stinging swarms of miseries that attend anarchy and rebellion."[110] And the reason for this is "the corruption, and the vitiousness of degenerate Men."[111] Which of course is exactly what Hobbes and Spinoza said.

By identifying the state of nature with the state of reason, Locke is really just bringing alive Spinoza's underlying point: that the state of reason is simply the state of nature perspicuously understood. It is the way in which we understand and thereby realize the freedom that always begins and ends in nature. In perfect agreement with Spinoza against Hobbes, Locke therefore conceives of the civil state not as an abridgement of our natural freedom, but as its realization. The "law . . . is . . . the direction of a free and intelligent Agent to his proper interest," says Locke. "Where there is no Law, there is no freedom," he adds, directly inverting Hobbes.[112] Locke summarizes the case for the civil state in language that follows Spinoza in all but the quotation marks: "The end of the law . . . is to preserve and enlarge Freedom."[113]

The basic intuition that expresses itself in the political philosophy that Locke takes over from Spinoza—that within a reasonable state it is the law that sets us free—is of course an ancient one. Cicero himself was the first to say, "We are servants of the law in order to be free." In Cicero's version, moreover, natural law ultimately comes to rest on the understanding that all crime is at bottom a crime against oneself: "He who does not obey [the law of nature] flies from himself, and does violence to the very nature of man, and by doing so he will endure the severest penalties even if he avoid the other evils which are usually accounted punishments."[114] Though Cicero places a Stoic deity in charge of this law of nature, Gassendi shows how its intrinsic naturalism ultimately leads to a convergence with the Epicurean position. "True and natural Liberty is easier to be found in a Society," says Gassendi, walking along the bridge that connects Epicurus with Spinoza.[115] "As the wise man acts all things for himself, and for his own Good and Satisfaction, there is nothing that will contribute more to this purpose than in carefully observing the Rules of Justice."[116]

Republican ideas rose to great prominence in England in the course of the English Civil War, then again in the tumult surrounding the Glorious Revolution of 1688, and then again in the course of the American Revolution, and there cannot be much doubt that they did so because they helped theorists of the time explain a reality that was already taking shape on the ground. We shouldn't imagine that Hobbes, Spinoza, and Locke created this reality, or that they were the only writers who influenced elite or popular interpretation of it. Even so, allowing for the inevitable roughness and multiplicity of history, it remains the case that the other influential writers of the period and their many contributions to the history can be mapped into the structure of thought that emerges from the debate among these three giants of the seventeenth century.

The authors of *Cato's Letters*, for example, begin by flying the political flag of Hobbes. He was "a great philosopher" who called "the *State of Nature* a *State of War*."[117] "The first and fundamental Law of Nature" is "the great Principle of Self-Preservation," they tell us; and "the first elements, or knowledge of politicks, is the knowledge of the passions; and the art of governing is chiefly the art of applying to the passions."[118] The highly influential Sidney traces out the transition from Hobbes to Spinoza: the people "have not conferred upon [the sovereign] all, but only a part of their power."[119] In the civil state, "the people continue as free as the internal thought of man," he adds.[120] Alexander Pope condenses into a couplet the philosophical message passed down from Epicurus through Hobbes and Spinoza to Locke:

The same self-love, in all, becomes the cause
Of what restrains him, government and laws.[121]

America's revolutionary leaders naturally drew on a wide range of sources and experiences, and many of those leaders may be presumed to have been sincere in thinking that their assertions about natural right derived from God above were in conformity with the religion of their forefathers. But the success of the American Revolution turned largely on the fact that their intentions and beliefs on this point were irrelevant to the reality. The Boston Declaration of 1772 on which the impious Young, the orthodox Samuel Adams, and the unclassifiable Otis collaborated, to cite one among many examples, begins with the following proposition, derived from Locke yet traceable to Hobbes: "The duty of self-preservation . . . [is] commonly called the first law of nature." In yet another formulation from the Hobbes-Locke line, it adds, "In the state of nature every man is, under God, judge and sole judge of his own rights and of the injuries done to him." Then it tracks the shift from Hobbes to Spinoza/Locke: "It is the greatest absurdity to suppose in the power of one, or any number of men, at the entering into society, to renounce their essential natural rights, or the means of preserving those rights." All law, it concludes, must conform to "the law of natural reason."[122]

Jefferson in particular illustrates how fidelity to Locke—though sometimes also deployed for conservative ends—was a key to American radicalism. In his formal reflections on the state of nature, Jefferson unambiguously agrees with Locke against Hobbes that there is a "plain difference between the state of nature and the state of war" and that under the laws of nature "all men should live in peace."[123] Like Locke, however, Jefferson does not imagine that human beings without government would in fact live in peace. On the contrary, in contemplating the prospect of human society in the absence of a governing civil power, he falls back directly on the Hobbesian position, that the natural condition is a "war of all against all."[124] The real thrust of this position, as with Locke, is to insist that the state of reason is just the state of nature perspicuously understood, and that the point of the civil state is to guide human beings toward the realization of their own nature as reasonable beings.[125]

Ethan Allen, too, was fluent in the language of natural rights—though, in what may be taken as an indication of the double-edged nature of the doctrine, he applied it initially not against the British but against his fellow Americans. Acquiescence in the villainous policy of the land-jobbing Yorkers, he announced, was "inconsistant with the Law of Self-preservation; but this Law being natural as well as eternal, can never be abrogated by the Law of Men."[126] Ira Allen, too, invoked the "free and natural rights and liberties" of the great people of the New Hampshire Grants.[127] The claim that we possess a "natural right" to something—especially when it came from the mouth of one of the Allen brothers—was often interchangeable with the assertion that "you do not have the power to stop us from seizing it." Even so, Ira and Ethan were not anarchists but republicans in the mold of Locke, Spinoza, and Cicero: "Probably there are some in every state who are averse to any mode of government at all; and such, I fear, are out of the reach of argument and reason; such are untractable and barbarous souls, who enjoy no satisfaction in the happiness of their species, or in the effusion of domestic peace, order, and social virtue," said the notorious outlaw Ethan Allen. "But all good and wise men, will exert themselves in establishing and supporting good government and order, which are inseparably connected together.[128]

HOW DO WE get from a seemingly unlicensed Natural Right to a specific set of individual rights that may be encoded in civil law?[129] In the thought world of early modern philosophy, it is important to stress, Natural Right and civil rights, though deeply connected, are not the same thing. Generally speaking, civil rights are the ways in which Natural Right is interpreted and expressed through the civil law, while Natural Right is where we end up when we explain or justify civil rights in terms of their utility, that is, through the law of nature or reason. Civil rights take the form of imperatives; they derive their authority from the civil state; they pertain to individuals but impose duties on other people; they restrain the power of the collective; and they vary in their specific content substantially across time and place. Natural Right involves only the inviolable laws of nature; it imposes a duty only on oneself; it is coextensive with the power of the collective; and it is roughly constant, at least to the extent that the human condition does not change substantially across time and place. The most obvious feature of civil rights is that they can be granted and taken away. Natural Right, on the other hand, is not something that can be "granted." It is something with which we are "endowed," something "inherent." It cannot be eliminated except by destroying that in which it inheres in some essential way.

Now, Natural Right is singular in origin and infinitely variable in its specific applications, as a matter of principle, inasmuch as utility varies infinitely according to specific conditions and circumstances of the particular individual and social compact in question. Reason, as we know from radical moral philosophy, prescribes no specific goods. Consequently, there can be no regime of civil rights that is absolutely universal or unconditionally derived from Natural Right in every conceivable circumstance—one that might work on a moon colony, among intelligent plants, as well as in the context of a total war to the death among civilizations, for example. At the same time, life is not quite so variable as all that. Some aspects of human experience are so universal that they give rise to specific interpretations of Natural Right that remain the same in all circumstances relevant to the conception of a universal (human) political theory. These relatively stable perspectives on Natural Right are not themselves civil rights, but they do provide a direct foundation for a set of civil rights that are universal in all relevant circumstances, and so they may be associated in a loose sense with a set of civil rights. In Jefferson's first draft of the Declaration, these right-like perspectives on Natural Right are called "inherent." In the fair copy, he described them as "inalienable." In the published version, they are "unalienable."

Though they cannot be alienated by definition, unalienable rights can be recognized or criminalized. Indeed, this is what happens when they are specifically enumerated (or denied) in the civil state. To recognize unalienable rights is really just to recognize the elemental sources of individual and collective self-realization, and to criminalize them is just to impose punishment on those same sources. The recognition of unalienable rights, according to this radical view, necessarily advances the power of the individual and collective, while criminalization diminishes it. A state can criminalize the breathing of air or drinking of water, for example, but in doing so it either kills its citizens or turns them into outlaws and perhaps rebels. In either case, the power of the state itself ultimately collapses (if the individuals don't first). As always, the "punishment" of a violation of natural right is just a redescription of the "crime" itself. Unalienable rights, in a formula, are the most durable expressions of the utility of the social compact in any civil state involving ordinary human beings.

Hobbes is among the first theorists to offer a version of unalienable rights, though his position on the matter is deeply conflicted.[130] In places he allows that individuals cannot surrender to the sovereign his life and "all things else without which a man cannot live well." In other places, however, his absolutist instincts dominate, and he reduces this vestige of Natural Right in civil society to nothing more than the right to make a run for it as one is hustled blindfolded to the gallows. Spinoza, sticking to the firm conviction that the state of nature persists even in the civil state, is the first philosopher to plant the flag of unalienable rights in its radical form without equivocation.[131] In Anglo-American political thought, it is Locke (with an assist from Sidney) who is most closely associated with the doctrine.

Locke is generally thought to have divided his rights into three categories: life, liberty, and property. This triad appears everywhere in eighteenth-century American political thought, and especially where Locke's influence is palpable. The overtly Lockean declaration of "the rights of colonists" produced by the Boston Committee of Correspondence in 1772, to cite one of innumerable instances, asserts that we possess "First, a right to life; Secondly, to liberty; Thirdly, to property" and that these rights "are evident branches of, rather than deductions from, the duty of self-preservation, commonly called the first law of nature." Locke, however, is anything but a dogmatist, and he actually presents several different lists of unalienable rights. Sometimes he uses "estates" or "possessions" for "property," and sometimes he throws in "health" (or "health and indolency of body") to make it a foursome (or a four-and-a-half-some), and he even makes it up to five in one place ("Life, Liberty, Health, Limb or Goods").[132]

Unalienable rights can in fact be divided in any number of ways (just as laws of nature can be so divided, as Hobbes inadvertently reveals when he changes his lists of "immutable" laws from one book to the next), because all are ultimately perspectives on a singular Natural Right, the right to self-preservation, or the self-realization of the conatus, and the process of their division and enumeration involves the introduction of the specific conditions of experience. Among the radical philosophers of the early modern world, there is one distinction between different kinds of experience that is most fundamental, as we know, and it is the one associated with the distinction between mind and body. And it is on this account that unalienable rights divide most easily into the dyad favored by Young and Allen: "Liberty and Property . . . the household gods of Englishmen."

Property haunts the name of Locke as it does the legacy of the American Revolution. "I got mine," it is often suggested, was for good or ill the battle cry of the new republic. The United States, according to this common line of interpretation, was founded on the bizarre belief, latterly attributed to Englishmen, that the political order serves only to protect the land, houses, and toys that one would have accumulated without it. But this is to badly misread both English thought and the American Revolution.

In order to gain some clarity on the subject, it is essential to distinguish between two senses of "property" as that term appears in the works of Locke and his successors, and the two kinds of right to which they correspond, civil and natural. When he uses it as a synonym for "estates" or "possessions," Locke means by "property" more or less what we mean in ordinary language—namely, our land, houses, and furniture, together with the civil right, vested in titles, to call upon the state to defend them against any who propose to deprive us of them. But Locke also uses the term in another sense—which we may distinguish with the uppercase "Property"—according to which it refers to every external material thing that contributes in an essential way to the self-realization of the individual. The paradigmatic example of Property in this metaphysical sense is not a home or a car, but the human body itself. And indeed, according to Locke, "Every man has a *Property* in his own *Person*."[133] It is only with this second notion of "Property" distinct from "property" that one can make sense of Locke's otherwise illogical statement that "Lives, Liberties, and Estates" are actually one thing "which I call by the general name, *Property*."[134]

Locke elucidates the metaphysical idea here with his famous "labor theory" of Property. All claims to Property, he argues, originally and naturally derive from the labor that individuals put in to acquiring it. The apple belongs to us because we picked it; the plow belongs to us because we forged it. In order to realize ourselves as free beings, according to Locke's reasoning, we must be able to claim the fruit of our own labor. And we need to be able to do this because our bodies are not inert lumps but rather active organizations or processes that persist through metabolism—for example, the unceasing process of picking and eating apples. At the foundation of Locke's idea of an unalienable right of Property, as we know, is Spinoza's concept of the body.[135]

It is Property—not property—that is unalienable and thus an expression of Natural Right. To take away an individual's metabolism is to take away its life. More precisely, to use the Spinozist categories underlying Locke's argument, to take control of the process whereby a body reproduces itself and thereby realizes its conatus is to deprive that body of its essential nature. The compulsory transfer of property in the sense of titles and possessions, on the other hand, isn't necessarily deadly, nor is it always unjust. Indeed, if property were not alienable, taxation would always be tyranny. Not only *can* the ordinary civil right of property be alienated, according to Locke, but in cases it *should* be alienated from the individual in the name of Property. For Property involves a Natural Right to those things that we make and *use*, not to everything that gets tossed up in the attic. Things are for a person "to enjoy," says Locke. "As much as anyone can make use of to any advantage of life before it spoils; so much he may by his labour fix a Property in. Whatever is beyond this, is more than his share, and belongs to others."[136]

One thing that nobody can appropriate in the name of Property, according to the logic that Locke and Spinoza share, is the land itself. "As much land as a man tills . . . so much is his Property . . . he cannot appropriate, cannot inclose, without the Consent of all his Fellow Commoners, all Mankind," says Locke.[137] Spinoza is even more blunt about the kind of "property" that since the beginning of the agricultural revolution was everywhere the foundation of civil inequality: "In a state of Nature the one thing a man cannot appropriate to himself and make his own is land."[138] In short, while the fruits of the earth belong to those who work it, the earth itself belongs to us all.

More generally, the point is that Property, like Natural Right in general, is inherently collective in a way that property is not. A civil right necessarily comes with the possibility of conflict between the individual and the collective: my right to hoard, for example, may conceivably diminish the public good. But Property is intrinsically socialist, in a manner of speaking, inasmuch as it identifies a power that, when realized in the individual, necessarily enhances that of the collective.

Among Locke's successors in America, crucially, it is the commitment to the radical (and quasi-socialist) concept of Property—not the defense of property—that defines the revolutionary project. Jefferson expresses the underlying theory well: "A right to property is founded in our natural wants, in the means with which we are endowed to satisfy these wants, and the right to what we acquire by those means."[139] Starting from this basic understanding, Jefferson moves to a position on property as radical as anything Spinoza says. In confronting the great evil of primogeniture in Virginia, Jefferson draws on this same radical philosophy of the earth. Individuals own the land "not by any natural right" but "by a law of society," he writes to Madison. "No man can by *natural right* oblige the lands he occupied, or the persons who succeed in him in that occupation, to the payment of debts contracted by him."[140]

Jefferson was also quite explicit about the "socialist" implications of "Property." One day in 1785, while walking through the French countryside on his way to one of the King's levees, he fell in with an impoverished peasant woman. As they strolled past the luxuriously untilled estates reserved for game-hunting aristocrats, she described for him the miserable poverty in which she and the majority of French peasants lived. He handed her twenty-four sous, and she "burst into tears of gratitude." The encounter with the grotesque economic inequality of the *ancien regime* prompted him to write to Madison: "Whenever there is in any country, uncultivated lands and unemployed poor, it is clear that the laws of property have been so far extended as to violate natural right." In order to rescue the natural right of Property from the corruptions of civil property, he proposes a policy of taxation of "property in geometrical progression," or what we would call progressive taxation.[141]

In 1796, Thomas Paine came to a similar conclusion. Disgusted upon hearing a bishop one day deliver a sermon proclaiming "the wisdom and goodness of God, in having made both rich and poor," Paine returned home to draft what we might now call a first pass at Social Security. On the basis of a distinction between "Agrarian Justice" and "Agrarian Law" that faithfully tracks the radical distinction between Property and property, he makes the case for imposing a tax on the latter and using the proceeds to fund a universal pension scheme.[142] John Adams[143] and Ben Franklin,[144] too, favored efforts to reduce economic inequality on the clear understanding that the natural right of Property justifies the civil right of property up to a certain point, and then cuts the other way.

No one was more outspoken on the virtues of Property than Thomas Young. In the 1764 pamphlet about land-dealing in the Green Mountains that marked his first step toward revolutionary activism, Young staked his claims, too, on the radical philosophy of the earth. He demanded "lands to exercise the arts of peace upon, at such rates as we can promise ourselves some recompence to our labours thereon."[145] Indeed, had he attempted to rest his case on those titles that individuals wave high when they want the men in blue to come and rescue their possessions from the unwashed, he would have had no case at all. In Philadelphia in 1776, Young's demands for wealth redistribution quite transparently favored Property at the expense of property.

The American obsession with Property, in any case, should not distract from the fact that there is another variety of unalienable right, associated with the freedom mind. Young called it "Liberty." Setting aside the restrictions on government's powers of criminal prosecution it involves, the chief ingredient of Liberty is what we may call the "freedom of thought." It is this freedom of thought that approaches closest to the heart of liberalism. Property is really "an appendage to liberty," as Sidney says; for "it is impossible for a man to have a right to lands or goods, if he has no liberty."[146] "Without Freedom of Thought there can be no such thing as . . . publick Liberty," add the authors of *Cato's Letters*.[147]

The radical freedom of thought begins with the claim that the mind is not in fact free to affirm or deny ideas at will, but is rather constrained to follow the evidence and reasons presented to it. The mind achieves its freedom, according to this line of thought, by pursuing reasons and evidence toward a more perspicuous understanding of itself, its own body, and the world around it. The mind needs its ideas in the same sense that the body needs to appropriate pieces of the outside world: in order to generate itself. To deprive a mind of the material through which it understands itself and the world is to deprive it of its ability to persist in being, or of the activity that necessarily constitutes its essence. The freedom of thought, then, amounts to an unalienable or Natural Right.

Hampered by his classical, one-dimensional materialism, Hobbes was unable to make the case, and so Spinoza became the first to champion for the freedom of thought in a perspicuous way. "No one can surrender his faculty of judgment; for what rewards or threats can induce a man to believe that the whole is not greater than its parts, or that God does not exist, or that the body, which he sees to be finite, is an infinite being, in short, to believe something that is contrary to what he perceives or thinks?" he writes. "No one is able to transfer to another his natural right or faculty to reason freely and to form his own judgment on any matters whatsoever, nor can he be compelled to do so."[148] From this Natural Right to the freedom of thought, Spinoza derives a civil right to freedom of expression. "Utter failure will attend any attempt in a commonwealth to force men to speak only as prescribed by the sovereign despite their different and opposing opinions . . . The most tyrannical government is one where the individual is denied the freedom to express and to communicate to others what he thinks, and a moderate government is one where this freedom is granted to every man."[149]

The Natural Right of freedom of thought, too, has a "socialist" side. It can be helped and hindered—indeed it hardly exists without—the free exchange of ideas, the uninhibited scrutiny and critique of all points of view, and the unfettered collaboration with others in the pursuit of new truths. And this advance of the understanding in turn confers its greatest benefits on the human collective taken as a whole. Thus, while a civil right generally protects my right to express my views, the corresponding Natural Right extends also to your need to hear what I may have to say. "This freedom [of expression] is of the first importance in promoting the sciences and the arts, for only they succeed in those fields whose judgment is free and unbiased," say Trenchard and Gordon.[150] "Liberty produceth virtue, order, and stability; slavery is accompanied with vice, weakness, and misery," adds Sidney.[151] Jefferson is once again quite explicit about the convergence of individual and collective right. In his famous letter to the Baptists of Danbury, he writes, "I shall see with sincere satisfaction the progress of those sentiments which tend to restore to man all his natural rights, convinced that he has no natural right in opposition to his social duties."[152]

The Natural Right of thought obviously corresponds to a civil right of religious freedom. "Religious right, or the right to worship God, is something no one can transfer to another," Spinoza asserts.[153] "Religion . . . can be no more forced than Reason, Memory, or any Faculty of the Soul," Trenchard and Gordon agree.[154] Here, though, it is worth noting a couple of caveats that distinguish this radical idea of "religious right" from the most common ideas about "religious toleration" today (about which more later). According to radical philosophy, religion accrues an unalienable right insofar as it is part of the pursuit of understanding—and not insofar as it represents some species of mental activity, such as acts of conscience, that are imagined to be different from other forms of understanding. So there is no recognition of any special privilege or exemption given to religious thinking alone in this original and radical conception of religious right. A second point to note is that religious right is unalienable here insofar as it relates the individual power of understanding to the collective taken as a whole. It does not single out religious subgroups or professional clerical hierarchies for any privileges or exemptions that do not apply to other subgroups or associations within society.

In the Anglo-American world, Locke must count as the single most important conduit in the transmission of the basic idea concerning the freedom of thought and religious right (though a strong case can be made for the influence of Sidney).[155] Locke's specific proposals concerning civil rights associated with expression and religion, however, fall notoriously short of the universality of the freedoms of expression and religion that Spinoza proposes (and that Sidney seconds). According to Locke, Catholics and avowed atheists, for example, do not deserve freedom. On the other hand, the philosophical foundation from which Locke draws his specific proposals remains indistinguishable from that of Spinoza. "Such is the nature of the understanding, that it cannot be compelled to the belief of anything by outward force," he writes.[156] And again: "Every man . . . has the supreme and absolute authority of judging for himself."[157] And again: "It is vain for an unbeliever to take up the outward show of another man's profession."[158] In his notes on the first draft of the Virginia Bill for Religious Freedom, Jefferson makes clear the dynamic of the underlying intellectual genealogy: "Where Locke stopped short, we may go on."

In America's various founding documents, to be clear, the Protestant language concerning freedom of conscience often sits side by side with the philosophical language associated with the freedom of thought and religious right. The Boston Declaration of 1772, for example, stipulates, "As neither reason requires nor religion permits the contrary, every man living in or out of a state of civil society has a right peaceably and quietly to worship God according to the dictates of his conscience." The blend of vocabularies was present no doubt because it brought together two very different constituencies whose immediate political objectives overlapped to an important degree. Yet the differences remained. The liberty of conscience is a duty allegedly imposed by a deity upon believers, not an unalienable right. Indeed, its premise is that one may transfer all authority to affirm or deny the truth of a wide range of ideas to a sacred text or figure whose answers are taken as final before we even know what the questions are. The difference seems abstract, but it could lead to real conflict, as events surrounding the Pennsylvania Constitution of 1776 would show.

III

". . . THAT TO SECURE THESE RIGHTS, GOVERNMENTS ARE INSTITUTED AMONG MEN, DERIVING THEIR JUST POWERS FROM THE CONSENT OF THE GOVERNED . . ."

In the days immediately following the disastrous election of May 1, 1776, Philadelphia's radicals hatched a plan that should really be described as a coup d'état. The aim was nothing less than to disband the legitimately elected government of Pennsylvania and replace it with a new government dedicated to pursuing the twin goals of national independence and political revolution at home. Young and his fellows met with Samuel Adams over at his quarters, and Sam evidently persuaded cousin John to join the plot.

Even as the plot unfolded, events shifted the ground dramatically in favor of the radicals. On the heels of the election, rumors spread that the British were organizing a force of forty-five thousand foreign mercenaries—Hessians and Hanoverians—thirsty for the blood of colonists and salivating over the prospect of seizing American women and livestock.[159] Then a pair of British warships cruised into the river "for no good purpose." Alarm guns were fired, and for one terrifying afternoon many Philadelphians believed that their city was under bombardment. The mood was suddenly very different than it had been just a week before.

On May 10, John Adams offered a resolution in Congress recommending that those colonies "where no government sufficient to the exigencies of their affairs have been hitherto established" should adopt new governments. The immediate target was Pennsylvania, and the implicit intention was to annul the May 1 election. John Dickinson, the leader of the moderate faction in the province, permitted the resolution to pass, on the understanding that Pennsylvania *did* have a "government sufficient to the exigencies" and so would not be required to adopt a new government. It was a gross miscalculation. Confident that the movement for independence had once again been put to bed, Dickinson compounded his error by opting to take a vacation.

On May 15, while Dickinson relaxed in his country home, John Adams added a preamble to his resolution that effectively put Pennsylvania back on the firing line. "Every kind of authority under [the] crown [of Great Britain] should be totally suppressed," he wrote. Astonishingly, many moderates in Congress still did not quite grasp the implications. The resolution, with its pointed preamble, squeaked through by a vote of six colonies to four. John Adams described it at the time as "the most important resolution that was ever taken in America."[160] In later life he would suggest that it—and not the grandiloquent screed associated with that upstart Thomas Jefferson—was the true declaration of independence. And in fact the resolution effectively asserted the right of the Congress to exclude the King himself from government. It amounted to independence in all but name.

On May 19, the gang made their move. They put out a broadside, "The Alarm," also published immediately in German, in which they announced that, pursuant to the Congress's resolution, the existing government in Pennsylvania, which rested on the authority of the Crown, would have to be totally suppressed. A new government would have to be established "on *the authority of the people*." How to accomplish this? The Alarmist offered a bold proposal: "CONVENTIONS, my Fellow-Countrymen, are the only proper bodies to form a Constitution."[161]

On the following day, four thousand Philadelphians assembled under a raging downpour in front of the Liberty Bell and carried out a peaceful revolution. It was in effect Philadelphia's first town meeting, modeled on Boston's famous gatherings. By acclamation, the crowd assented to a resolution determining that the existing government of Pennsylvania was "not competent to the exigencies of our affairs." They voted to align themselves in a "happy union with other colonies"—by which was meant: to pursue separation from Britain.[162] They also called for the formation of a provincial conference, whose task would be to create a provincial convention for the purposes of producing a new constitution for Pennsylvania. With Pennsylvania now firmly in favor of separation from Britain, the path to a declaration of independence by the Continental Congress was free from obstruction. One attendee at the meeting described the event, appropriately enough, as "a *coup de grace*" against the King.[163] In retrospect, the speed, efficacy, and boldness with which the radicals engineered the overthrow of a government that had reigned in Pennsylvania for more than a century and a half is nothing short of astonishing. It perhaps deserves to be compared with achievement of Lenin and the Bolsheviks in October 1917.

The Provincial Conference met in June, and the Provincial Convention, under the chairmanship of Benjamin Franklin, ran from July 15 to September 28, 1776. It involved exactly the kind of people that Pennsylvania's ruling elites called "the wrong sort." One of Dickinson's friends wrote to him by way of reproach: "You have thrown the affairs of this state into the hands of men totally unequal to them."[164]

Pennsylvania's extraordinary exercise in constitution-writing was controversial from the beginning, and the trouble started, appropriately enough, over the question of religion. Large numbers of those who rallied in support of the effort came to the cause through the religion of the revivals. In an effort to fuse the evangelical fervor of these recruits with the new political movement, populist leaders from the dissenting countryside proposed to include in the new constitution a religious test for office. In its first iteration, the proposed oath called on prospective state officials to "profess faith in God the Father and in Jesus Christ his eternal Son, the true God, and in the Holy Spirit" and to "acknowledge the holy scriptures of the old and new testaments to be given by divine inspiration." Supporters of the proposed oath undoubtedly believed in the "freedom of conscience" guaranteed in the preamble of the very same constitution; but they evidently supposed that this freedom was really just the freedom to be a Protestant Christian.

Young, Matlack, and Cannon angrily opposed the oath. In their eyes it grossly contradicted the right to freedom of understanding enshrined in the same document. Rush opposed the oath, too, arguing that there were many men—surely he had the likes of Young in mind—"whose morals were good" but who could not take the oath. "I am not one of that Class," he added hastily. Of the gang of six, only the eldest, the fifty-something Christopher Marshall, favored the oath—indeed, he "strenuously supported" it. Cannon and Marshall apparently had a harsh confrontation on the subject. Cannon attacked supporters of the oath as "fools, blockheads, Selfrighteous, and zealous bigots" who acted with "a manifest view and tendency to keep Some of the most best and valuable men out of government."[165] Marshall never got over the shock of discovering that his younger revolutionary comrades were infidels or at the very least accomplices to infidelity. He was, he said, "maltreated by sundry of my friends, as I thought & who, I believed was really religious persons & loved our Lord Jesus Christ, but now declare that no such Belief or Confession is necessary in forming the New government."[166]

After wrenching debate, Jesus Christ and the Holy Spirit were left on the cutting floor of history along with any reference to the Trinity. But the requirement that officeholders should swear to "belief in one God" and the acceptance of "Divine Inspiration" of the scriptures remained. The compromise left the defenders of the faith more disgruntled. Marshall felt that the insult to Jesus was irredeemable. He flipped sides and campaigned aggressively against his old friends and their new constitution. "Farewell Christianity when Turks, Jews, infidels, & what is worse Deists & Atheists are to make laws for our State," he lamented.[167]

On October 21, 1776, the newly drafted and presumptively atheistic constitution of Pennsylvania was put before the people at a town meeting in front of the Philadelphia State House. The principal speakers in favor of the new order of things were Timothy Matlack and Thomas Young. Franklin, who had served as the lackadaisical chairman of the convention, took a copy with him when he shipped off to Paris that winter, charged with raising French money and arms for the

American cause. The French were sure that the ingenious constitution must have been the work of the great scientist; but, as John Adams groused, everyone in Philadelphia knew who the real authors were.

At least on paper, the new state constitution was a near-total triumph for the democratic political vision of Thomas Young and his radical gang. It called for a single legislature, elected annually, with strict term limits on representatives. It allowed for a president, but vested executive authority in a rotating committee with a dozen members, also limited in their terms. It established a judiciary, also with term limits. It mandated a number of measures to ensure that the legislative process would remain subject to public scrutiny from beginning to end. It extended suffrage to all male citizens who pay taxes of any sort, without respect to the amount of property they own—and also without respect to race, granting African-American males a right to vote in Pennsylvania that held until 1837.[168] It also included a declaration of the rights of the people, among which were the freedom of speech and assembly; the freedom of religious exercise; the right to bear arms; the right to trial by jury; and the right not to give evidence against oneself.[169]

"Government is, or ought to be, instituted for the benefit, protection, and security of the people, and not for the particular emolument or advantage of any single man, family, or set of men," the new constitution boldly announced. The language was not as polished as that which Gouverneur Morris inserted into the preamble to the U.S. Constitution eleven years later—but the message was the same. This was to be government of, by, and for the people.

THE UNITED STATES OF AMERICA is not a "democracy" in any formal sense, if by that term we mean a system of government in which the people rule in a direct and equal way on all matters of common interest. Yet, like every other self-respecting republic in the modern world, the United States is routinely described as "democratic" to some degree or other. And this description, insofar as it is not altogether inaccurate, universally comes with a favorable judgment. How it came to pass that republics like the American one are valued for something that they formally are not is the story of America's radical revolution.

That story begins with a new and radical theory of sovereignty. Generally speaking, the sovereign is and always has been understood to be that which has ultimate power in any human collective. For most of human history, it was taken for granted that the sovereign is the kind of thing that has a proper name: usually King So-and-so; sometimes, more exotically, the Senate or Parliament. At a certain point in the early modern history of political thought, a new concept emerged: that "the people" are the sovereign. By the time of the American Revolution, "the sovereignty of the people" had gone from being an incendiary thesis to a ubiquitous axiom, at least among sophisticated thinkers of the time, and indeed it was the cornerstone of both the Pennsylvania Constitution of 1776 and the U.S. Constitution of 1787. James Wilson, a key figure in the 1787 Convention, made the point explicitly when he wrote that in the new U.S. Constitution, "all authority is derived from THE PEOPLE."[170] James Madison, the so-called father of the Constitution, agreed that "the people are the only legitimate fountain of power."[171]

Many historians today interpret "the sovereignty of the people" as a collective act of make-believe.[172] It is a fiction that cleverly masks the fact that the people are anything but sovereign, or so they say. Probably most people today read "the sovereignty of the people" as an imperative. The people *ought* to be sovereign, they should be given a voice in government, even if they usually are not. Yet within the radical political theory that ultimately decided the course of the modern world, the sovereignty of the people is neither a fiction nor an imperative. It is a statement of fact. The sovereign simply *is* the people.

This fact of popular sovereignty follows in a primordial way from the axiom that human beings are natural equals. Insofar as human beings are naturally equal, according to the radical line of thought, the power through which rulers impose their will on others can come only from the people themselves. All the money, titles, rights, and influence that individuals wield as instruments of power within society are in reality nothing more than the power of other people in society appropriated according to certain ideas. If human beings were as naturally unequal as lions and lambs, to put it in the converse, the sovereign might be identified with a particular (leonine) subset of a human collective; but they aren't, so it isn't. In a formula, the Natural Right of the sovereign—under the condition of natural equality—can never be anything more than the extension of the Natural Right of its constituent individuals.[173]

Implicit in this new conception of sovereignty is a crucial distinction between "the government" and "the sovereign."[174] The government is that which wields the power of the sovereign at any particular moment: typically, a person or a set of political institutions. It has power only by proxy, insofar as it has the ability to appropriate the power of the sovereign. There may be more than one government at a time—in which case the situation is usually not healthy—and "government" in this general sense may include institutions of society that are not formally considered part of the political order (such as, for example, a priesthood).

Throughout history, political theorists and ordinary people alike have tended to conflate "the government" with "the sovereign," and the reason for this may be found in the defects of the common consciousness of things. Not grasping that power is nothing but the understanding itself, human beings naturally tend to anthropomorphize it. Power, they tend to think, always belongs to the kind of thing that has a proper name. So they confuse the political power of their own collective with that of the king or institution that happens to wield it, in the very same way that they confuse the collective power of all things in nature with that of a presiding deity, to which they give the name of God.

The common ideas about things make it especially difficult to see how it is that the sovereign, as distinct from government, may be identified with the people. Failing also to grasp that right is simply might perspicuously understood, the common view supposes that all authority—which is to say, all rightful power—must rest on some still higher authority. The authority of any individual in society must come from the authority of the ruler, which must come from the authority of the state, and so on in a infinite regress of authorities that can end only in God, or so the religious consciousness imagines. So the notion that authority might actually begin from the bottom—from the same people who are themselves subject to the sovereign—seems incomprehensible. The sovereignty of the people, in short, was really only conceivable as something other than a potentially useful fiction after radical philosophy had undermined some of the most fundamental premises of the common religious consciousness.

The undermining began with Hobbes. According to Hobbes, the sovereign is in reality "the common-wealth," and the king or government acquires its power from this sovereign through an act of representation. Spinoza makes clear the underlying inference: "The king's sword or right is in reality the will of the multitude itself";[175] "the right of the commonwealth is determined by the common power of the multitude."[176] Sidney repeats the claim in English: "The strength of a nation is not in the magistrate, but the strength of the magistrate is in the nation."[177] "Government therefore can have no power, but such as men can give," the authors of *Cato's Letters* conclude.[178] James Wilson traces out the same logic in his reflections on the foundations of the U.S. Constitution: "The only reason why a free and independent man was bound by human laws was this—that he bound himself."[179]

From the theory of popular sovereignty, it follows that all human collectives are "democratic" in a certain sense and always have been and always will be. The trouble is that some collectives do not realize it. When a government uses one part of the people to oppress another, for example, it is really turning the sovereign against itself, and in this sense is not fully democratic. Only insofar as it marshals the Natural Right of all individuals in service of the Natural Right of the collective—or the "general welfare"—does a government make it possible for the sovereign to realize itself and thus become a genuine democracy. The more democratic a government is, in this abstract sense, the more powerful and the more reasonable it is. It is on this account that, for Spinoza, the definitions of sovereignty and democracy converge: "A united body of men which corporately possesses sovereign right over everything within its power is called a democracy."[180]

The idea of democratic sovereignty in turn converges with reason, for the collective that organizes itself according to the guiding principle of philosophy is very simply the "Empire of Reason."

Democracy or the Empire of Reason here, to be clear, is not a particular form of government, but something more like a principle to which all collectives are obliged to answer insofar as they seek to maximize their power. The immense and concrete task of a political science, as Spinoza puts it, is to show "how men, even when led by passion, may still have fixed and stable laws."[181] The mark of a well-constituted state is that it makes it possible "to avoid the follies of appetite and to keep men within the bounds of reason, as far as possible, that they may live in peace and harmony."[182] Political theory, according to this radical line of thought, is not so much a theory of democracy as a theory of "democratization," as the French philosopher Balibar suggests.[183] Its purpose is to lay out the general principles through which one may discover under specific historical circumstances that form of government which will best lead a people to their rational, democratic self-realization.

The most obvious general principle of democracy is that it finds one way or another to give all individuals an equal voice in public affairs. In a democracy "all men remain equal, as they were before in a state of nature," says Spinoza.[184] Thus, "without any infringement of natural right, a community can be formed," and this democratic state approaches "most closely to that freedom which nature grants to every man." Democracy is therefore "the most natural form of state." Though Sidney mostly disdains democracy, understood as the institutional form that involves rule of the masses, he endorses a version of Spinoza's argument for democracy in this general sense: "Of all governments, democracy, in which every man's Liberty is least restrained, because every man hath an equal part, would certainly prove to be the most just, rational, and natural."[185] Thomas Young is probably rehearsing Sidney's version of Spinoza's argument when, amid his incendiary calls for universal suffrage in Pennsylvania, he declares that of all governments democracy is the "most consonant with nature."[186]

A related, general feature of democracy, according to Spinoza, is that it preserves a distinction between the beliefs of the individual and the necessarily provisional beliefs on which the government grounds its actions. In any collectivity of individuals, Spinoza notes, differences of opinion are bound to obtain, and in a state of nature these differences lead to conflict. Therefore, if one is to establish a powerful state capable of realizing the sovereignty of the people, "it is imperative to grant freedom of judgment and to govern men in such a way that the different and conflicting views they openly proclaim do not debar them from living together in peace."[187] And this is what democracy accomplishes: "In a democracy (which comes closest to the natural state) all the citizens undertake to act, but not to reason and to judge, by decision made in common. That is to say, since people disagree with one another and even with themselves over time, they come to agree that a proposal supported by a majority of votes shall have the force of a decree, meanwhile retaining the authority to repeal the same when they see a better alternative." Democracy in effect turns to its advantage the pluralism that characterizes all human collectives—and that the common religious consciousness tends to find abhorrent.

Elections or representative government may be a common feature of democracy, according to this line of thinking, but they are not the same thing as democracy. The people do not become sovereign by electing the members of their government—they are already sovereign, after all—but elections may be one mechanism through which the people keep their rulers in check and thereby ensure that government stays true to the sovereign. Jefferson grasps the point when he explains that "every other government is more or less republican, in proportion as it has in its composition more or less of this ingredient of the direct action of its citizens."[188] The key insight here is that direct action is an ingredient—perhaps better, a symptom—of democracy, not necessarily the same thing. It follows that limitations on direct action—a distinct characteristic of the U.S. Constitution—are not necessarily undemocratic (though they certainly may be).

The most important general principle of democracy is that it involves the rule of law. In a democracy, says Spinoza, "the welfare of the whole people, not the ruler, is the supreme law,"[189] and only through the law can a democracy "organize the state so that all its members, rulers as well as ruled, do what the common welfare requires."[190] Locke agrees that the "first and fundamental positive Law" in any legitimate government is the creation of the legislative power, or the power of making laws.[191] The Boston Declaration of 1772 follows Locke quite literally on the point: "The first fundamental, positive law of all commonwealths or states is the establishing of legislative power." In a collective of naturally equal individuals, moreover, there can be only one law for all that is in conformity with reason and aims for the common welfare. As Locke puts it, there must be only one set of rules "for Rich and Poor, for the Favourite at Court, and the Country Man at Plough,"[192] and all such rules must be "conformable" to the "Eternal Rule" of the law of nature or reason.[193] The Boston Declaration is once again Lockean to the letter: the law must apply equally "for rich and poor, for the favorite at court, and the countryman at the plough" and must conform to "natural reason."

The rule of law means more than the use of laws in order to rule—something that undemocratic tyrants can always do by decree. In the republican theory that Locke and Spinoza embrace, the rule of law is the state in which the law itself rules. As Jefferson has it, the "fundamental principle" of a "commonwealth" is that there shall be no "exercise of powers undefined by the laws."[194] In abstract terms, the underlying point is that there is an intrinsic rationality to the law, something against which the laws themselves may be tested. That is, the law of the reasonable commonwealth must itself be "lawful," in the same way that the "laws of Nature's God" are infinitely explicable, rather than arbitrary.

The more immediate and practical point is that even—especially— the lawmakers of the state cannot be above the law. Indeed, the purpose of the law must be in part to make sure that the naturally passionate people who rise to leadership are constrained to act within reason and the law. "When the safety of a state depends on any man's good faith, and its affairs cannot be administered properly unless its rulers choose to act from good faith, it will be very unstable," Spinoza notes. "If a state is to be capable of lasting, its administration [*res publicae*] must be so organized that it does not matter whether its rulers are led by reason or passion."[195] It is on the same account that republican theorists have universally insisted (with inevitable variations in the detail) on the separation of the executive and judicial functions of government from the legislative. Where the three become one, the rulers of the state are in a position to rule by decree and make whatever "legal" exceptions to the law that suit their passions.

Here it is possible to see how the radical philosophy of ethics paves the way for a radical revision of political theory that features centrally in American constitutional thought. The common religious consciousness supposes that right belief alone is the foundation for right action, and so it concludes that good religion is the necessary foundation of good government. The Reverend Timothy Dwight ably articulates the train of thought: "How soon would law and government lose that authority and energy which are now chiefly sustained by appeals to the presence, the will, and the agency, of a Ruler all present, all powerful, and unchangeable and infinitely opposed to every iniquity?"[196] The radical philosophers, on the other hand, say that understanding, not belief, is the source of all morality, and that the reasonable state embodies this understanding in its laws. Trenchard and Gordon make the contrast with the common religious conception as sharp as nails:

> Where human laws do not tie men's hands from wickedness, religion too seldom does; and the most certain security, which we have against violence, is the security of the laws. Hence it is, that the making of the laws supposes all men naturally wicked; and the surest mark of virtue is, the observation of laws that are virtuous. If therefore we would look for virtue in a nation, we must look for it in the nature of government; the name and model of their religion being no certain symptom of the cause of their virtue. The Italians profess the Christian religion, and the Turks are all infidels: are the Italians therefore more virtuous than the Turks? I believe no body will say that they are.[197]

Repeating the point passed down from Machiavelli through Spinoza, they insist that in a well-run state "checks and restraints" leave "nothing, or as little as may be" to "the humours of men in authority." "Those nations only who bridle their governors do not wear chains."[198] Sidney helpfully draws out the reversal of the common view on the link between good people and good government: "Man naturally follows that which is good, or seems to him to be so," he says. "Hence it is, that in well-governed states, where a value is put upon virtue . . . virtue itself becomes popular."[199]

America's founders were functionally unanimous in their conviction that good government starts with human beings as they are—mostly irrational and hence vicious—and produces virtue by relying not on acts of conscience but on acts of law. As Paine so eloquently puts it in *Common Sense*, "Society is produced by our wants and government by our wickedness . . . Were the impulses of conscience clear, uniform, and irresistibly obeyed, man would need no other lawgiver."[200] Madison makes the point in language that seems drawn directly from Hume in his Spinozistic moments: "As long as the reason of man continues fallible, and he is at liberty to exercise it, different opinions will be formed. As long as the connection subsists between his reason and his self-love, his opinions and his passions will have a reciprocal influence on each other; and the form will be objects to which the latter will attach themselves." Consequently, Madison goes on to insist, "conscience . . . is known to be inadequate in individuals" and "in large numbers little is to be expected from it."[201] Joel Barlow rehearses the argument in his critique of Montesquieu and the moral sense philosophers. "The common idea of virtue," by which is meant "those moral habits by which men are disposed to mutual benevolence and happiness," says Barlow, "cannot be the foundation of a republican government or of any government."[202] "It is the vices, not the virtues of men which are the object of restraint, and the foundation of government."

Thomas Young made the crucial link between this radical political theory and the new constitutional thinking to which he made such a distinctive contribution:

> I esteem the people at large the true proprietors of governmental power. They are the supreme power, and of course their immediate Representatives are the supreme Delegate power; and as soon as the delegate power gets too far out of the hands of the constituent power, a tyranny is in some degree established.[203]

The bristling array of checks and balances in the Pennsylvania Constitution of 1776—the term limits, impeachment procedures, divisions of power—arise from the idea that even the rulers of the state are passionate beings and that they and the people may be brought to virtue only through the law, not through conscience or belief. Eleven years later, Madison made clear that the same line of thought was central in the creation of the U.S. Constitution: "The genius of Republican liberty, seems to demand . . . not only that all power should be derived from the people; but, that those entrusted with it should be kept in dependence on the people."[204]

Just as interesting as the notional state that lies at the happy end of the process of democratization is the one that lies at the other end. In a general way, it may be said that the opposite of democracy is, as Young suggests, "tyranny." Tyranny happens when a society turns against itself, with one part usurping the power of whole and applying it to the exploitation of the rest. Corruption, or the misdirection of public effort for private gain, is one common feature of tyranny. A democratic government, Sidney notes, strives to rid itself of corruption; "on the other hand, the absolute monarch must endeavor to introduce it, because he cannot subsist without it."[205] Government through fear is another common feature of tyranny, since it is through fear that one part of the society can induce the other to betray its own interests.

Just as democracy is notionally the most powerful form of government, tyranny is the weakest. "He whom many fear, should stand in fear of many," says Spinoza, citing Machiavelli and Seneca on the point. Consequently, "tyrannical governments never last long."[206] The radical Whigs repeatedly draw from history the same lesson about the perils of fractured sovereignty. So long as the Roman people kept their magistrates "within due bounds," say Trenchard and

Gordon, the republic "could defend herself against all the world." Upon being "enslaved (that is, her magistrates having broke their bounds)," Rome fell.[207]

The defining feature of tyranny, however, is neither fear nor corruption. If sovereignty always belongs to the people, then under a tyrannical government it is the people who tyrannize themselves. So all tyranny involves a kind of misunderstanding of the people by the people. Among the radical philosophers, there is of course one form of self-deception that stands above the rest as the model and source of all the others, and that is religion in all its popular forms. The opposite of the Empire of Reason is in reality the Empire of Faith. Hobbes calls it "the Kingdom of the Fairies"; in more modern terms, we could say that the opposite of democracy is theocracy.[208]

Lucretius got there first, of course. In his natural history of justice, the sorriest part of the human story happens when priests or "fable-mongers," coveting control over other people's bodies, collude with kings to take advantage of the credulity of the people in order to satisfy their own unreasonable lust for power.[209] Thus, superstition permits individuals suffering from one set of passions to feed off individuals suffering from another according to a logic that neither side understands, and in this manner society lacerates itself in a fury of thoughtless self-destruction. Among the heirs of Epicurus, Spinoza provides the pithiest expression of the doctrine in the hard-hitting preface to his *Tractatus Theologico-Politicus*:

> The supreme mystery of tyranny, its prop and stay, is to keep men in a state of deception, and with the specious title of religion to cloak this fear by which they must be held in check, so that they will fight for their servitude as if for salvation.[210]

Alexander Pope helpfully condenses Spinoza's message in a stanza that could easily have been lifted from Lucretius:

> *Force first made conquest, and that conquest, law;*
> *Till superstition taught the tyrant awe,*

Then shared the tyranny, then lent it aid,
And gods of conquerors, slaves of subjects made[211]

No proposition could have elicited more support from the radical precursors to the American Revolution than that the priests are the chief instrument of tyrants. Harrington, having learned much from Hobbes, banned clergy from public office in his fictional utopia. Locke was no less obstreperous. "By flattering the ambition, and favouring the dominion of princes and men in authority," says Locke, the priests "endeavour with all their might to promote that tyranny in the commonwealth, which otherwise they should not be able to establish in the church . . . This is the unhappy agreement that we see between church and state."[212] Trenchard takes up the polemic with gusto in *The Independent Whig*. Thanks to "corrupt priests," he says, "virtues are made vices, and vices made virtues."[213] "The lowest Degeneracy Man can sink into, is knowingly and deliberately to inculcate Errours, or to Obstruct the Progress of Truth," he adds.[214]

In many of the Whig writings, the animus against the priesthood is overtly directed at the Catholic Church, and it naturally draws on the anti-papal enthusiasms of the English population at the time. The logic of the critique, however, is universal, and at least on occasion, to their peril, the Whigs let as much be known. In his highly controversial *Account of Denmark* of 1694, for example, Molesworth argues that "it has been a general mistake" to think "that the popish religion is the only one of all the Christian sects proper to introduce and establish slavery in a nation . . . Other religions, and particularly the Lutheran, has succeeded as effectually in this design as Popery every did . . . It is not popery as such but the doctrine of a blind obedience, in what religion soever it be found, that is the destruction of liberty and consequently of all the happiness of any nation."[215] By the time the critique reached Hume, it was in fact perfectly general and aimed at even that popular religion which opposed "Popery": "Is there any maxim in politics more certain and infallible, than that both the number and authority of priests should be confined within very narrow limits, and that the civil magistrate ought, for ever, to keep his fasces and axes from such dangerous hands? But if the spirit of popular religion were so salutary to society, a contrary maxim ought to prevail."[216]

The impact of such representations of the anti-ideal political system of theocratic tyranny on America's revolutionary leaders is so manifest that it hardly needs stating. James Otis complained in his early pamphlets that "every devil incarnate, who could enslave a people, acquired a title to divinity."[217] "Of all the nonsense and delusion which had ever passed through the mind of man," John Adams added, "none had ever been more extravagant than . . . those fantastical ideas . . . which had thrown such a glare of mystery, sanctity, reverence, and right reverend eminence and holiness, around the idea of a priest," ideas that left the human race "chained fast for ages in a cruel, shameful, and deplorable servitude."[218] Jefferson explored the possibility of banning clerics from public office—until Madison persuaded him that the constitutional prohibition on the establishment of religion was good enough. Madison himself wasn't soft on priests; he asserted in 1785 that "the legal establishment of Christianity" in the preceding fifteen centuries has everywhere involved "pride and indolence in the clergy; ignorance and servility in the laity; in both, superstition, bigotry, and persecution."[219] Freneau wrote up the common wisdom of the founders on the subject of the priesthood in an "Ode to the Americans" that makes transparent the line of descent from Lucretius through Pope to America:

> Religion brought her potent aid
> To kings, their subjects to degrade[220]

With characteristic economy, the gist of the preceding history of the theory of democratization is ably encapsulated in the preamble to the Declaration of Independence. Like that theory, the Declaration is surprisingly neutral on the questions of political science concerning the precise institutional arrangements of a new government. It attacks King George III but not the institution of monarchy per se, and it allows people a right to choose whatever form of government suits them. Even so, there can be little doubt where the document stands on the question of democratization. It tells us explicitly that governments derive their legitimate power from the consent of the governed. And it communicates the same message in its form. Had it been produced in another time, or by leaders lacking the same courage of their ideas, the Declaration most likely would have taken the form of a petition to a king, a plaint before one tribunal or another, or an appeal to the Almighty. But the handiwork of the Continental Congress speaks only out of a "decent respect to the opinions of mankind."

IV
". . . THAT WHENEVER ANY FORM OF GOVERNMENT BECOMES DESTRUCTIVE OF THESE ENDS, IT IS THE RIGHT OF THE PEOPLE TO ALTER OR TO ABOLISH IT . . ."

The operative clause in the Declaration of Independence is the one that announces the right of the people to rebel. We are equal and have unalienable rights precisely to the extent that we have the power to answer the power of our rulers when they attempt—as they invariably will—to deprive us of our rights and equality. Legitimate government exists only by virtue of the rebellions that don't happen. The genealogy of this radical idea, as should be evident by now, properly begins at the point where Spinoza diverges from Hobbes.

According to Hobbes, "No man in the commonwealth whatsoever hath right to resist him, or them, on whom they have transferred this power coercive, or (as men use to call it) the sword of justice." "The attempt [to rebel against the sovereign] is against reason," he insists.[221] According to Spinoza, Hobbes is correct insofar as he means that the rebellion against any government or representative of sovereignty can never be grounded in any civil law. But Hobbes is quite wrong to suppose that rebellion against a government is always against reason: "A commonwealth does wrong when it does, or suffers to be done, things that can cause its downfall; . . . it does wrong in the sense in which philosophers . . . say that Nature does wrong . . . [that is] it does something contrary to the dictates of reason."[222]

The account of rebellion Spinoza offers, like the rest of his political philosophy, is thoroughly naturalistic or anti-transcendental. It explains not what is right or wrong about rebellion but simply how power works. A government holds the power of the sovereign only "as long as he has the power of carrying into execution whatever he wills; otherwise his rule will be precarious."[223] A government loses its right to rule only in a natural way, too.[224] When rulers misrule, the fear of the majority turns into indignation, and the state loses its power.[225] There is no room for moralizing here, and Spinoza, following Machiavelli, dismisses out of hand the idea that rebellions may be attributed to "the wickedness of subjects." Just as the virtue of a virtuous state is a property of the system, not of individuals, so the rebellion of a rebellious state is due "to the faulty organization of the state."[226] The right of rebellion, according to this line of reasoning, can only be a natural right, not a civil one: "It is not by civil right but by right of war that a king can be deprived of his power to rule."[227]

Locke was unquestionably the preeminent theorist of the right of rebellion in Britain and America, the thinker to whom all looked who sought a blessing for their defiance of the ruling authorities. So it is especially interesting to note that on this point he parts with Hobbes in order to follow the language and logic of Spinoza with particular precision. "There remains still *in the people a supreme power* to remove or *alter the Legislative*, when they find the *Legislative* act contrary to the trust reposed in them," he announces. "For all power given with trust for the attaining an end being limited by that end, whenever that end is manifestly neglected or opposed, *the trust* must necessarily be *forfeited*, and the power devolve into the hands of those that gave it."[228]

Though Locke makes a greater effort to cloak his theory of rebellion in the language of rights, his treatment of the subject is just as anti-transcendental as Spinoza's. He does not say that the people *should* rebel when their natural right fails to be recognized; he simply predicts that they have the power to do so and will exercise that power under certain circumstances: "When the *People* are made *miserable*, and find themselves *exposed to the ill usage of Arbitrary Power*, cry up their Governours, as much as you will for Sons of *Jupiter*, let them be Sacred and

Divine, descended or authoriz'd from Heaven: give them out for whom or what you please, the same will happen. The People . . . will wish and seek for the opportunity, which, in the change, weakness, and accidents of humane affairs, seldom delays long to offer it self." Driving home Spinoza's point, he adds, "What else can be expected but that these men, growing weary of the evils under which they labor, should in the end think it lawful for them to resist force with force, and to defend the *natural* rights, which are not forfeitable upon account of religion, with arms as well as they can?"[229] Rebellion happens, according to Locke, not when some civil right is breached but when "a long train of Abuses, Prevarications, and Artifices" provokes a people to the realization that the entire civil system runs against their natural right.[230]

For Locke just as much for Spinoza, in brief, the right of rebellion is a Natural Right, not a civil right. "The true remedy of *Force* without authority, is to oppose *Force* to it,"[231] says Locke. (For comparison, Spinoza's words are: "it is by violence alone that [a ruler's] subjects may resist his violence.")[232] According to Locke, "using *Force* upon the people without Authority" puts a government into "a *state of War* with the people," who thereby have a "right to *reinstate* their *Legislative*."[233] According to Spinoza, "a civil order that has not removed the causes of rebellion and where the threat of war is never absent and the laws are frequently broken is little different from a state of Nature" and can be deprived of power only "by the law of war."[234] Locke, always more sensitive to the theological resonance, tactfully euphemizes this appeal to the law of nature as "an appeal to Heaven."[235]

Sidney agreed with Locke on the natural right of rebellion,[236] and the Whigs followed the logic of their seventeenth-century mentors, which is one reason why, as the flames of the Glorious Revolution cooled, the names of those illustrious philosophers lost much of their shine on the British Isles and even became disreputable.[237] Just as their star was falling in the homeland, however, it rose among colonists chafing under what they perceived as the shackles of imperial rule. The Declaration of Independence manifestly makes its case for rebellion in the court of the law of nature, not civil law. It makes no effort to litigate the British Constitution, as so many pamphlets in the years preceding the Revolution did. Rather, borrowing a phrase from Locke, it cites "a long train" of abuses and prevarications that have, in effect, destroyed the King's natural right to rule the colonies. In a hard nutshell, its signers understood that their Revolution would count as a crime unless it succeeded—a crime unquestionably punishable by death. Jefferson, even while serving as president of the United States, was well aware of the extralegal origins of the new republic: "Should we have ever gained our Revolution, if we had bound our hands by the manacles of the law?"[238]

V

"... AND TO INSTITUTE NEW GOVERNMENT, LAYING ITS FOUNDATION ON SUCH PRINCIPLES AND ORGANIZING ITS POWERS IN SUCH FORM, AS TO THEM SHALL SEEM MOST LIKELY TO EFFECT THEIR SAFETY AND HAPPINESS ..."

The most remarkable aspect of the Pennsylvania Constitution of 1776 was not the form of government it proposed but the form of the document itself. That form expresses something essential about the radical political theory first put forward by the great philosophers of the seventeenth century. If the law is to be king, as republican theory demands, then legitimate government is not properly speaking a set of institutions or officials but a certain kind of law. This law finds its expression in the constitution itself.

The authors of the Pennsylvania Constitution understood clearly that the law embodied in their document is distinct from ordinary legislation. Ordinary laws derive their authority from the institutions that promulgate them, that is, from the institutions of government. Constitutional law, on the other hand, derives its authority from the people. This authority serves not only to establish those institutions, but also to ensure their continuing accountability to the people. A notable pamphlet, *Four Letters on Interesting Subjects*, published in Philadelphia in 1776 by an anonymous writer who was clearly on the side of Young and his fellow radicals, may serve as a definitive marker of the novel turn in constitutional thought:

> A Constitution and a form of government, are frequently con-
> founded together, and spoken of as synonymous things; whereas
> they are not only different but established for different purposes:
> All countries have some form of government, but few, or perhaps
> none, have truly a Constitution . . . It is easy to perceive that indi-
> viduals by agreeing to erect forms of government, (for the better
> security of themselves) must give up some part of their liberty for
> that purpose; and it is the particular business of a Constitution to
> mark out *how much* they shall give up. In this sense it is easy to see
> that the English have no Constitution, for they have given up every
> thing; their legislative power being unlimited without either con-
> dition or control, except in the single instance of trial by juries.[239]

The Pennsylvania Constitution itself was to be the law to which the
institutions it created would answer. It was in a sense the first attempt
in human history to establish a genuine rule of law.

In the first, hopeful years of the American Revolution, the Pennsylvania idea spread to a number of the other newly independent colonies. "Matlack, Cannon, Young and Paine had influence enough to get
their plan adopted in substance in Georgia and Vermont, as well as
Pennsylvania," the viscerally anti-democratic Adams fumed.[240] Young
did indeed recommend the Pennsylvania Constitution to his friends in
the Green Mountains as "a model, which, with a very little alteration,
will, in my opinion, come as near perfection as anything yet concerted
by mankind." He also made clear that the revolutionary power of the
new constitution challenged the tyrannical power from within American borders as much as that from overseas: "This Constitution has
been sifted with all the criticism that a band of despots were masters of
and had bid defiance to their united power."[241]

History would soon show, however, that Young and his fellow radicals had moved too fast and too far ahead of their people. As much as
it excited the theoretical imagination, the Pennsylvania Constitution
of 1776 rapidly came to grief on the muddy shoals of Pennsylvania
politics. Benjamin Rush, belatedly realizing that he had thrown in his
lot with a group of genuine radicals, pulled out of the gang. He decried

the new order as a "mobocracy" and laid blame for it on the shoulders of Cannon, Matlack, Young, and Paine.[242] The Moderates regrouped amid the disarray, got themselves elected under the auspices of the new constitution, and then proceeded to undermine it from within.

Though the proposed arrangements of the 1776 constitution were not without their defects—some of which Madison highlighted in his *Federalist* essays, others of which James Wilson identified in his lectures—the root of the trouble was that the "haves" hated it and the "have-nots" didn't know what they had in it. A writer to the *Pennsylvania Evening Post* at the height of the struggle put his finger on the problem: "Although it be granted on all hands, that all power originates from the people; yet it is plain that in these colonies . . . the government has, from the beginning, been in the hands of a very few rich men . . . The rich, having been used to govern, seem to think it is their right; and the poorer commonalty, having hitherto had little or no hand in government, seem to think it does not belong to them to have any."[243] After the war, Pennsylvania's elites pushed through a constitution more to their liking—though they paid a price for it by provoking some damaging popular uprisings along the way.

WHEN THE DELEGATES met for the Constitutional Convention more than a decade after the chaotic start of the Revolution, the atmosphere and the political thinking had changed in important ways. Many of the leaders in the formation of the new U.S. Constitution had opposed the radically democratic state constitutions of the earlier period. Many of the leaders of the earlier radical movement now allied themselves with the anti-Federalists against the new Constitution.

The proposed Constitution of the United States of 1787, as the critics accurately pointed out, failed to include a declaration of the rights of individuals. It created in the Senate an unrepresentative, quasi-aristocratic body that would gather into its hands control over the other branches of government. It exalted a presidency that some feared would be, in Edmund Randolph's words, the "foetus of monarchy."[244] It failed to say much of anything at all about the judiciary, thus opening up "a wide ocean" of potential abuse.[245] It mixed the legislative, executive, and judicial powers in the new institutions in a manner that some said would allow interested factions to commandeer the government and steer it in the direction of their own gain. It proposed a continental government whose very size and scale would make impossible the direct participation required for true republican government. In one respect only did the new Constitution seem more radical than its predecessors. In sharp contrast with the Pennsylvania Constitution, it boldly declared that "no religious test shall ever be required as a qualification to any office or public trust under the United States."

Yet neither the noise of the debate nor the complex shifts in political sentiments over the tumultuous preceding decade should distract from the fundamental fact that the U.S. Constitution was part and product of the revolutionary process that began in 1776. Many of the anti-Federalist arguments, it should be remembered, were ultimately absorbed within the final result. The passage of the Bill of Rights answered the principal concern of many of the anti-Federalists, and the Judiciary Act of 1789 eliminated a large part of the uncertainty surrounding Article III of the Constitution. Defenders of the Constitution were at pains to argue, with good reason, that the proposed office of the presidency was different in critical respects from that of a monarch.[246] There was in fact universal agreement that the new government should be a republic; the disagreements were over whether this was possible or had been realized in the proposed design. There was also universal agreement on the basic idea that the people are "the supreme power" and that all government power derives from their consent. What Madison said of the earlier state constitutions—that the Americans "reared the fabrics of governments which have no model on the face of the globe"[247]—was just as true of the new federal Constitution.

At a delicate moment in the process of ratification of the new Federal Constitution, when rejection seemed a real possibility, James Wilson addressed the ratifying convention of the state of Pennsylvania with words that many credited with tipping public opinion in favor of the motion. Wilson was the living antithesis of Thomas Young: avaricious, socially ambitious, lavishly educated, and stridently opposed to the Pennsylvania Constitution of 1776. He was also the architect of the "three-fifths" compromise that embedded the institution of slavery within the new Constitution. He was the personification of the "conservative" side of the American Revolution. Yet in his reasoning at this pivotal moment, he neatly picked up the thread that tied the Constitution of the United States to the principles of Young and his radical democrats:

> Somewhere there is, and of necessity must be, a supreme, absolute, and uncontrollable authority. This, I believe, may justly be termed the sovereign power . . . Blackstone will tell you, that in Britain it is lodged in the British parliament . . . if the question was asked, some politician, who had not considered the subject with sufficient accuracy, where the supreme power resided in our governments, would answer, that it was vested in the State Constitutions. This opinion approaches nearer the truth, but does not reach it; for the truth is that the supreme, absolute, and uncontrollable authority, *remains* with the people . . . [T]he practical recognition of this truth was reserved for the honor of this country. I recollect no constitution founded on this principle; but we have witnessed the improvement, and enjoy the happiness, of seeing it carried into practice. The great and penetrating mind of Locke seems to be the only one that pointed towards even the theory of this great truth.[248]

In a later version of the argument, Wilson goes on to associate that which he means to oppose—"from time immemorial, the strong-hold of tyranny"— with Edmund Burke, the darling of political conservatives to the present. According to Burke, says Wilson, "society requires not only that the passions of individuals should be subjected, but that even in the mass and body as well as in the individuals, the inclinations of men should be frequently thwarted, their will controlled, their passions brought into subjection. This can only be done by *a power outside themselves.*"[249] What Wilson means to contrast with the new Constitution, in short, is nothing other than the intuitive political theory of the common religious consciousness, which has always and everywhere maintained that all authority must come from some higher authority. In order to articulate the American alternative to these ancient prejudices, Wilson recites from the Declaration of Independence the lengthy sentence that begins with "We hold these truths to be self-evident . . ."

Shortly after the ratification of the Constitution, Wilson rose to become an associate justice on the Supreme Court, thereby claiming his perch in the order of power consolidated by the document he helped to craft. In later life, he luxuriated on his political views in the kind of college lectures that Thomas Young was not fortunate enough to attend. It seems unlikely that the two men would have sat down for tea, if their paths ever crossed in Philadelphia in 1776. Yet in Wilson's defining moment on the stage of history, it is hard not to see in him a figure like the one cut by Benedict Arnold outside the gates of Fort Ticonderoga, racing to seize the King's property through an opening created by another, very different sort of man.

The Declaration is not an official or governing document of the United States in the sense that the Constitution is. Yet in Wilson's fusion of the two, we can glimpse the source of the revolutionary force embedded in the American system of government. The power of democracy in America does not derive from the institutions or practices the Constitution prescribes. It rests instead on the common trust that the United States is a country that is ruled by law, that the highest law of the land is the safety and welfare of the people, and that the Constitution adequately expresses that law. When that trust is withdrawn, the Constitution must change or be discarded. But the Declaration remains. In short, the document that Wilson did so much to draft must answer to the one whose principles Thomas Young so ably embodied. There is more than poetic justice in the fact that, with passage of the Fourteenth Amendment in 1868, the infamous compromise with which Wilson perpetuated the architecture of power in his time was removed, while a paraphrase of the Declaration itself was inserted into the Constitution.

Thomas Young did not live to see the end of the Revolution. In the spring of 1776, he enlisted in a company of Philadelphia riflemen. From there he went on to serve as a surgeon in a hospital for the

Continental Army. At the same, he was elected secretary of the Whig Society under the chairmanship of Charles Willson Peale, a republican activist and painter now famous for his portraits of the heroes of the Revolution. In the summer of 1777, while treating soldiers, Young caught what appears to have been a case of yellow fever. He died in a matter of days. He left no money for his wife and six children, and they were forced to plead for charity in the local newspapers. Soon they sold off the books through which the rebellious doctor had come to understand his own mind. According to a friend, he died as he lived, agnostic on the prospect of any afterlife, certain only that if there was one, it would be a good thing.

HUMAN BEINGS achieved self-government only after they learned how to discard the politically dangerous delusions that arise from the common religious consciousness. At least, that is more or less how America's founders saw the matter. Here is how George Washington told the story of America upon his first exit from public life in 1783, when he voluntarily relinquished the command that, in a more ambitious man's hands, might easily have been converted into just another tawdry military dictatorship:

> The foundation of our empire was not laid in the gloomy age of Ignorance and Superstition, but at an Epocha when the rights of mankind were better understood and more clearly defined than at any former period.[250]

Upon his return to public life in 1789, in the undelivered draft of his first inaugural address, Washington expressed the same certainty about the connection between the philosophical liberation of the human mind and the political liberation of humankind:

> Though I shall not survive to perceive with these bodily senses, but a small portion of the blessed effects which our Revolution will occasion in the rest of the world; yet I enjoy the progress of human

society & human happiness in anticipation. I rejoice in a belief that intellectual light will spring up in the dark corners of the earth; that our freedom of enquiry will produce liberality of conduct; that mankind will reverse the absurd position that *the many* were made for *the few*; and that they will not continue as slaves in one part of the globe, when they can become freemen in another.[251]

Joel Barlow, making the case to the Society of the Cincinnati in Connecticut, compressed the message of the American Revolution in accordance with the same logic: "Here, neither the pageantry of courts nor the glooms of superstition have dazzled or beclouded the mind. The present is an age of philosophy; and America, the empire of reason."[252]

The most compelling statement about the meaning of America's Declaration of Independence came from the man who drafted it. In the fiftieth year of the new order of the ages and the last of his own life, Jefferson had this to say about that document and the event it announced:

> May it be to the world, what I believe it will be, (to some parts sooner, to others later, but finally to all,) the signal of arousing men to burst the chains under which monkish ignorance and superstition had persuaded them to bind themselves, and to assume the blessings and security of self-government. That form which we have substituted, restores the free right to the unbounded exercise of reason and freedom of opinion. All eyes are opened, or opening, to the rights of man. The general spread of the light of science has already laid open to every view the palpable truth, that the mass of mankind has not been born with saddles on their backs, nor a favored few booted and spurred, ready to ride them legitimately, by the grace of God.[253]

The boots and saddles allude to the famous last words of Whig hero Colonel Richard Rumbold, a personal friend of Locke who was executed along with Sidney in the aftermath of the assassination attempt on the King in 1683. The "chains" of "monkish ignorance and superstition" and "the light of science" make clear that in 1776 America declared independence not from one imperial monarch but from the tyranny that the human mind imposes on itself through the artifice of supernatural religion. "The grace of God," says Jefferson, is precisely what America learned to do without.

Lincoln was right to find in Jefferson's Declaration a lasting source of revolutionary principle, and he wasn't wrong to locate this force somewhere in the vicinity of the proposition that all men are created equal. There are however many ways to make people equal without necessarily leaving them better off, and the moral sentiment of brotherly love has never been a very strong card to play against the other passions of the human race. Liberalism has produced the most powerful and prosperous states that the world has ever known because it is far more robust than any collection of fictions or fickle emotions ever could be. The equality that Jefferson announced and that Lincoln partially advanced is at bottom the demand that all power must explain itself. In reality, the revolutionary force in the Declaration of Independence is the guiding principle of philosophy.

8

The Religion of Freedom

ETHAN MET FANNY IN THE FIRST DAYS OF 1784. HE WAS famous, she was rich, and their courtship blew over the hills as fast and fierce as a winter storm. General Allen, as he was then known, was at last collecting on the gambles of a lifetime. He was low on cash but high on hopes for his real estate portfolio. He was the leading man in the tales with which Vermont's growing population of settlers entertained themselves during long nights around the fireplace. And the as-yet-unpublished sheaf of furiously corrected manuscript pages that he called "My Theology" lay in that happy stage where he could bask impatiently in the glory of its imagined reception, thankfully oblivious to the incomprehension and the reputational damage it would soon wreak.

Fanny Montresor Buchanan was everything that Mary Brownson Allen was not. Mary, who had died six months previously, was what was known at the time as a good wife. She bore five children, two of whom survived into adulthood, and she and her husband formed a loyal partnership over the twenty years of their marriage. She was also illiterate, a world-class scold, and conventional in her religion, or so it was said in the taverns. Which may or may not have been a little unfair, but it could explain why Ethan spent most of those twenty years very far from home. Fanny, on the other hand, was a twenty-four-year-old beauty, fluent in French, talented with the guitar, witty, fashionable, and, yes, rich—or at least planning to be rich, once the inheritance from her third stepfather cleared the courts. She also came with a past. She was born illegitimate, thrust at the age of six into the family of her scheming aunt, pressed at the age of sixteen into marriage with a British naval officer, now widowed with child. Fortunately, the great iconoclast of the hills was a man quite capable of casting aside the baggage of history.

"If you marry General Allen, you will be queen of a new state," one of the tavern-keepers joked with her, as rumors of the affair spread. "Yes, and if I married the Devil I would be queen of hell," she snapped back. The barman and his drinking friends, having surmised that Fanny was the kind of woman who likes to live dangerously, took that as a good sign.

In Westminster, Vermont, on the morning of February 9, 1784, Ethan pulled up in his sleigh at the residence of his good friend Judge Stephen Bradley, where Fanny happened to be lodging. In the drawing room Bradley and a gaggle of fellow eminences were enjoying a morning smoke over their newspapers. Allen burst past them and found Fanny on the other side of the house in her morning gown.

"If we are to be married, now is the time," he abruptly declared, explaining that he had to travel across the mountains to Bennington that day.

"Very well, but give me time to put on my Joseph," she replied (Joseph being a brand-name coat).

Within minutes, the pair appeared arm in arm before the startled judges in the drawing room. Allen asked his friend Moses Robinson to perform the ceremony. "When?" the judge asked.

"Now," replied Allen. "For myself, I have no great opinion of such formality, and from what I can discover, she thinks as little of it as I do. But as a decent respect for the opinions of mankind seems to require it, you will proceed."

Judge Robinson reminded his friend that this was serious business.

"Do you, Ethan, promise to live with Fanny agreeable to the laws of God?"

Now here was a possible sticking point. Ethan turned his gaze on the snowy winter scene outside the window. "Which God?" he thundered. "The law of God as written in the great book of nature? Then—yes."

So Ethan and Fanny were married in the eye of Nature's God. When the ceremony was over, the newlyweds bundled into Ethan's sleigh. With Fanny's guitar strapped to the back, they sped over the Green Mountains to Bennington.

ACCORDING TO A widely accepted view today, religion is an eminently useful thing. Religious belief gives meaning to our suffering, teaches respect for the moral law, transmits the wisdom of experience from generation to generation, inspires great art, and unites communities with bonds of shared trust and so enhances their prospects for survival. We need only contemplate the beauty of a medieval cathedral, or listen to the inspired words of civil rights leaders, or marvel at the charity and discipline of religious societies to know that faith is so very good for us. Indeed, religion is so useful, some theorists today argue, that natural selection has seen fit to endow all human beings with a religious instinct that predisposes them to believe in what they don't understand. The Enlightenment, according to this line of thought, overestimates the human capacity for reason just as it underestimates the value of tradition and belief for a needy human race, and so it bequeaths us stillborn gods, disenchanted souls, and cultures of license and nihilism. Utility, one could say, is the last refuge of religion.

As an aside, it's worth noting that the utility (or not) of religion is much harder to establish on empirical grounds than the anecdotal just-so stories usually called in its defense tend to suggest. One would have to weigh the beauty of those medieval cathedrals, for example, against the lives crushed under the feudal system out of which they arose. The civil rights heroes would have to be offset against the preachers who legitimized the institution of slavery in the first place. It would also be vital to distinguish the fact that religion tends to make its adherents *feel* more moral from the claim that they actually *are* so, just as it would be important to distinguish the *certainty* religion confers on the moral judgments people pass on their fellows from the *accuracy* of those judgments. Perhaps even more important, "religion" is such a broad and variable thing across time and place that the definitions and qualifications are bound to multiply well beyond any valid empirical generalizations. It is one thing to discuss the effects of religion within generally secular or pluralistic societies, for example, and it is another thing to discuss religion in societies organized along theocratic lines. So a strictly empirical approach has probably never been attempted and seems hardly likely to yield a clear-cut answer on the utility of religion.

The problems on the logical front are much worse. When we really do believe in something, we say we believe in it because it is true, not because it is useful (even if it happens to be useful, as the truth usually is). So, when we say that we ought to believe in religion *just because* it is useful, we are also saying that there is no reason to believe it is true. What we really mean to say is that it is useful for *other people*—or for some imaginary version of ourselves that does not believe what we in fact believe. And if we try to salvage religion by claiming that it is not a system of belief in the first place but a set of practices, as many liberal apologists for religion are wont to do, all we are really saying is that these (other) people who practice it don't know what they are doing. Utility never justifies belief; it can justify only deceit and delusion. Now, how can deceit or delusion be useful? Mostly, they are not. On occasion, they can be used for good ends—but only to the extent that they induce people to act in accordance with something else that we know to be true. In making such a judgment about the utility of a delusion, moreover, we necessarily presuppose that it would be better for everyone to do the right thing for the right reasons. Thus, once we begin to justify religion by utility alone, we have already committed ourselves to the view that the most useful thing to do with it is to diminish its use.

The biggest whopper in the argument from utility, however, is the historical claim that it represents a *critique* of the Enlightenment. As a matter of fact, no serious thinker of the Enlightenment proposed that human beings are thoroughly rational or perfectible—most thought exactly the opposite—and only a few proposed that the broad mass of people could make do with no assistance at all from the storehouse of religious tradition. Indeed, the utility of religion first became visible through the work of the radical philosophers of the early modern world. Traditional cultures value *their* traditions; only to the extent that they are enlightened do they value tradition *as such*. Precisely because the revolutionary philosophers of the early modern world grasped the utility of religion, however, they worked hard to reform and contain it. The very point of understanding the utility of religion was to undermine its political pretensions as thoroughly as possible. America's supposedly "religion-friendly" deists in particular—exactly insofar as they draped themselves in a veneer of moderation—were in reality among the most radical of the early modern revolutionaries.[1]

EVERY THING in the universe strives to persist in being, say the radical philosophers, and the power of nature through which the human mind strives to persist is the power of the understanding. The moral law that requires people to seek peace with one another, the political order that keeps them within the bounds of reason, the pursuit of happiness that brings true virtue—all of these expressions of human power are nothing but exercises of the understanding itself. Yet the common man, stumbling through the distorted landscape of human passions, is prone to believe that piety means attacking those who believe differently, that the law is nothing more than a hindrance to personal satisfaction, and that virtue and happiness are necessarily opposed. How can such unreasonable and rebarbative individuals be included in a project to seek their own self-realization and that of their fellows in a political order that is organized around the pursuit of understanding?

To many people today it seems distastefully condescending or elitist to suggest that there is something flawed in the common consciousness of things, something that induces people to fight for their own destruction as if for their freedom. But the common ideas of concern are not at all the exclusive property of the uneducated, the lower orders of society, or "the masses." Indeed, those ideas are often defined and defended with greatest vigor by priestly elites or their professorial successors, and they become oppressive precisely to the extent that they are deployed outside the world of everyday experience. The radical philosophers did not invent this condition. They were simply the first to theorize it, and the first to take it for what it is: a serious challenge to the very possibility of rational self-government. For them, the ignorance of humankind—not just of the masses but of some of its more exalted representatives—was a problem to be solved. Reactionaries throughout history, after all, had only to point to the credulity and turpitude of human beings to justify their authoritarian schemes. It was the radicals who placed the biggest bet on the human race, for they supposed that, notwithstanding the common deficit of understanding, human beings are capable of democratic self-realization.

If one were to seek to explain how the common religious consciousness became a "problem" in this sense, one could do worse than point to the invention of the printing press, which both greatly enabled the transmission of ignorance and brought the process itself out into the open, where it could be scrutinized, modified, and calibrated with much greater precision. It was only natural that Bruno, the first of the first radicals, who came of age in the springtime of the printed word, should have turned his attention to the world's first best seller (and still number one): the Bible. The Holy Scriptures are not to be read as a codex of esoteric truths, said the Nolan, but as a device for presenting simple truths to the general public. "Those divine books do not deal with demonstrations and speculations about natural matters," he wrote.[2] "Rather, the scriptures direct the practice of moral actions" and "speak to the common people according to their way of understanding."

Galileo, too, took the view that the Bible is a way of adapting certain truths to the limited understanding of the common people. In a private letter that, unfortunately for him, was promptly made public, he cited the case of Joshua and the day the sun stood still as an example of a passage that required some elaborate "re-interpretation" if it was to be understood as a truthful claim.[3] Spinoza picked up on the case of Joshua and drove the point home:[4]

> Now the process of deduction solely from intellectual axioms usu-
> ally demands the apprehension of a long series of connected prop-
> ositions, as well as the greatest caution, acuteness of intelligence,
> and restraint, all of which qualities are rarely to be found among
> men . . . Hence it follows that if anyone sets out to teach some doc-
> trine to an entire nation—not to say the whole of mankind—and
> wants it to be intelligible to all in every detail, he must . . . above all
> adapt his arguments and the definitions relevant to his doctrine to
> the understanding of the common people, who form the greatest
> part of mankind.[5]

The crucial premise that links Bruno with Spinoza is that the parables and prophecies of revealed religion are not entirely false but rather serve as ways of approximating the truth for those who lack the capacity to understand it properly. "God adapted his revelations to the understanding and beliefs of the prophets, who may well have been ignorant of matters that have no bearing on charity and moral conduct but concern philosophic speculation," Spinoza explains.[6] "Scripture teaches only very simple doctrines," he adds;[7] these doctrines are in fact "precepts or rules of life" and they are "in accordance with reason."[8] In an early work that we know Locke read with careful attention, Spinoza concludes, "Scripture teaches nothing that is opposed to the natural light."[9]

Spinoza's further, crucial assertion is that without such useful sim-plifications we cannot expect a nation, taken on the whole, to absorb and act in accordance with the truths of the understanding. A popu-lar religion, then, involves some degree of falsification; but, provided this falsification takes place at the limit of the people's capacity for understanding—which is to say, provided it does not mislead but rather guides them toward an approximation of the truth—it can be a good thing. "If by believing what is false" an individual "becomes obedient to the moral law," Spinoza concludes, "he has a faith which is pious."[10]

Such a popular religion, he adds, is more than a luxury; it is "in the highest degree necessary for the common people who lack the ability to perceive things clearly and distinctly."

The same message—in almost the same language—may be found in Locke's reasoning on the subject:

> Tis at least a surer and shorter way, to the Apprehensions of the vulgar, and mass of Mankind, that one manifestly sent from God, and coming with visible Authority from him, should as a King and Lawmaker tell them their Duties; and require their Obedience; than leave it to the long, and sometimes intricate deductions of Reason, to be made out over them. Such trains of reasonings the greatest part of Mankind have neither the leisure to weigh; nor, for want of Education and Use, skill to judge of.[11]

In *The Reasonableness of Christianity*, Locke seems almost obsessive in his insistence on the connection between popular religion and the mental incapacity of the masses. In the first pages of that work, he tells us that scripture is plainly intended as instruction "for the illiterate bulk of Mankind in the way to Salvation."[12] And he hammers it home in the very last sentence of his book, where he applauds Christianity for teaching a doctrine such "as the poor could understand, plain and intelligible."[13] In his unpublished *Discourse on Miracles*, he makes clear that the point of the incredible stories about miracles is just to make salvation available to "the simple and illiterate (which is the far greatest part)" of humankind.[14] In his general comments on the epistemological status of scripture, as a consequence, Locke veers close to plagiarizing Spinoza. The Bible, says Locke, offers "a full and sufficient rule for our direction" which is "conformable to that of reason."[15] "These holy writers, inspired from above, writ nothing but truth," he adds.[16] "Scripture speaks not nonsense."[17] (For comparison, here is Spinoza: "Scripture cannot teach the nonsense that is commonly supposed.")[18]

Popular religion can take a variety of forms, according to the radical philosophers. But if it is to be useful for individual salvation as well as collective well-being (which are ultimately the same thing), according to both Locke and Spinoza, it must stick to its basic purpose of teaching the same moral laws or precepts of life that are otherwise available to philosophers through reason. Consequently, all useful popular religion will have certain generic doctrines in common. In his *Tractatus Theologico-Politicus*, Spinoza describes these generic doctrines in more detail. In one place[19] he offers seven examples of such doctrines, but in another place[20] he condenses all popular religion to three simple teachings:

1. That "there is a God or Being who made all things and who directs and sustains the world with supreme wisdom."
2. That true piety is the practice of virtue; that is, "obedience to [God] consists solely in justice and charity, or love towards one's neighbor."
3. That God will dispense rewards and punishments according to virtue: "All who obey God by following this way of life, and only those, are saved"; but, to make sure no one despairs of getting a second chance, "God forgives repentant sinners."

Coming as they do in the context of a radical, crypto-atheist core philosophy that teaches that God is just another word for Nature, that God can be loved but not obeyed, and that there is no salvation outside of this life, these doctrines of popular religion may seem to contradict Spinoza's most fundamental claims and involve him in a plot to bamboozle the masses. But in fact these doctrines of popular religion are best understood for what they are, namely, translations of the core philosophy into the limited language through which most people interpret their own existence and action in the world. According to Spinoza's core philosophy, there is indeed "a Being" that "makes" all things what they are (even if the way that it makes any particular thing out of the whole must remain forever opaque to us); that "directs" and "provides for" all things (though it does so through the laws that impel all things to strive to provide for themselves); that possesses "supreme wisdom" (in the sense that it embodies every intelligible idea); that rewards virtue, punishes vice, and offers us a path to salvation (because all of those things pay for themselves in happiness and misery)—and this Being may be called "God" (even if it is really just another word for Nature).

If God reduces to Nature in philosophy, one could say, Nature may be metaphorically elevated to the status of God in the common consciousness. Provided the translation is done right, it produces simple dogmas that will induce those who are not capable of understanding the radical core philosophy into behaving as if they did. The upshot—to anticipate the critical result for the theory of modernity underlying the American Republic—is that there exists what we may call a kind of religious sensibility that, if not the highest expression of reason, is compatible with it, just as there is a kind of popular religious life that is consistent with—even an expression of—the principled atheism on which a modern state must be founded.

Conspicuous by its absence from Spinoza's popular religion is any doctrine that offers reward for mere belief. Even the common people, apparently, can be made to understand that one does not serve God merely by declaring belief in him, but by doing good to one's fellow creatures. Also absent is any reward for favoring fellow believers over members of other sects. A useful popular religion must be universal and esteem charity toward all people, else it will involve its adherents in destructive sectarian conflict. Thus, a functioning modern society asks only for *good* faith, not the *right* faith.

In much of the modern historiography, the religion that Spinoza offers for public consumption is often mistaken for "deism" itself. But in fact this popular religion is better understood as the moderate exterior of the radical and essentially atheistic philosophy from which it emerges. We should call it "popular deism" in order to distinguish it from its parent, "philosophical deism." The relationship between the two could properly be compared to that between a scientific theory and its successor—provided we dispense with some common misunderstandings about the nature of scientific advance. Scientific advance happens (for the most part) not when a new theory falsifies an old theory, but when the new one explains the conditions under which the old one is true. Einstein's theory of general relativity, for example, shows not that Newton's theory of gravity is false but why it is true in the limited case of experience on an everyday human scale. In the same way, the kind of atheistic pantheism associated with Einstein does not refute the kind of popular deism associated with Newton so much as explain why it is close enough to the truth to serve most (but not all) of the purposes of everyday life.

Among the radical English philosophers who were later (mis)classified as "deists"—Blount, Toland, Bolingbroke, and Tindal, among others—"popular deism" generally traveled under the name of "natural religion." So long as a people remains free from the corrupting influence of priestly hierarchies, these philosophers maintained, there is a religion that emerges among a people through nature and experience. Perhaps the largest part of deist literature consists of extended investigations in comparative religion, all intended to demonstrate that the religions of the world derive from an original, simple, pure, natural religion.[21] This natural religion, of course, is not just reasonable but desirable for the illiterate bulk of humankind. It is, as Toland puts it, based on the "plain and simple, or (as we commonly speak) the naked truth."[22] Should Britain adopt such a popular religion, Toland predicts, it will become "the most happy, flourishing, and potent Empire of the whole world, especially by the destruction of superstition and vice." At the same time, he hardly expects that his fellow philosophical sophisticates will believe literally the doctrines of this popular religion. In his *Pantheisticon*, the brethren chant, "We must talk with the people, and think with the philosophers."

Just as a philosophical deist may wish to encourage non-philosophers in the embrace of popular deism, she may even welcome the opportunity to participate in a church that worships a deity in which she does not believe. In his years at The Hague, Spinoza frequently attended church services and participated in friendly discussions there following the sermons. The large attendance at his funeral in 1677 suggests that the excommunicated Jew was a well-liked figure in a city where almost everyone practiced one or another version of the Christian religion. Shaftesbury, too, was a contented, even avid churchgoer. Notwithstanding his overt hostility to Christian doctrine, Shaftesbury maintained that the "established rites" of the English church are "enough to answer to the highest character of religion."[23] Bishop Berkeley, the self-appointed foe of deism in all its forms, observed with chagrin that the freethinkers of the age could be counted on to attend church for all the wrong reasons.

On the utility of popular religion, as on so many other subjects of philosophical interest, America's revolutionary deists owe pretty much everything of importance to the preceding generations of radical philosophers. By the time it reached America, the case of Joshua and the extra-long day, for example, had become an almost hackneyed abbreviation for the general point that revelation is necessarily adapted to the limitations of the common understanding of things. Paine brings up the case, as does Allen, as does Jefferson. More than merely putting revelation in its place, America's revolutionary deists by and large recognized and embraced the argument for the (necessarily limited) utility of religion. New York's philosophically sophisticated governor, Cadwallader Colden, for example, seems to borrow directly from Toland when he writes that the Egyptian priests "were wise men and great philosophers and explained the principles of their philosophy to the initiated only." Since "common people are not capable of these sublime conceptions in philosophy," he adds, the priests gave them religion. "The public religion is founded on the public utility, and where its principles truly serve this purpose they are true."[24] Practicing what he preached, Colden was careful to withhold such comments from the public.

Franklin, too, followed the radical program in all its essential details. In a 1731 set of notes titled "Doctrine to be Preached," for example, he outlines a three-point religion for popular consumption that will sound very familiar to Spinoza's readers.[25] The first point is to teach that there is one God, "infinitely good"; the second is that God "loves such of his Creatures as love and do good to others"; and the third is that he "will reward them either in this World or hereafter." In his habits with respect to church life, Franklin more or less followed the custom established by his early philosophical guide Shaftesbury. In the course of building his multimillion-dollar business empire, he discovered that he could make many more profitable contacts mingling at the local church than slinging ales at the local tavern. After he accumulated his fortune, he made it a habit to donate regularly to church groups of every denomination. Throughout his life, he enjoyed dropping in for services. On hot days, he liked the cool air; on rainy days, he dried off.

John Adams, too, judged popular religion principally by its utility. "Twenty times in the course of my late reading have I been on the point of breaking out, 'This would be the best of all possible worlds, if there were no religion in it!!!'" he exclaimed to Jefferson.[26] But then he brought himself back from this "fanatical" precipice with an appeal to utility: "Without religion this world would be something not fit to be mentioned in polite company, I mean hell."

Ethan Allen rehearsed the general point in his *Oracles*: "Natural religion is sufficient and complete to effect the ultimate best good of mankind."[27] Thomas Young, too, underscored the value of popular deism or natural religion. In his 1770 contretemps with the evangelist George Whitefield, he argued that deism had served the Persian Empire well over many centuries. The Natural Man of Boston, seemingly channeling Bruno and Spinoza, defines popular religion as "the worship of one or more deities, according to the ideas and tenets which have been imprinted in the minds of worshippers." In order to communicate with the masses, the Natural Man adds, Moses wrote "in a mystical, figurative, and hyperbolical style" and "was obliged to mix the real with the fabulous."

The most famous and influential assertion of the utility of public religion in early America is to be found in the *Farewell Address* that Washington delivered as he was stepping down from the presidency:

> And let us indulge with caution the supposition that morality can be maintained without religion. Whatever may be conceded to the influence of refined education on minds of peculiar structure, reason and experience both forbid us to expect that national morality can prevail in exclusion of religious principle.

"Peculiar" in Washington's time was closer to "extraordinary" than "weird." Thus, while "religious principle" may be useful for the "national morality," as far as those peculiar philosophers who grasp this fact are concerned, religion is useful principally for *other* people.

THE RADICAL PHILOSOPHERS of the early modern period had some very kind words for Jesus and the Christian religion. In fact, if cited with the same degree of attention to context characteristic of studies today that purport to discover in America's founders a band of evangelists bent on establishing a Christian nation, they could easily be used to prove that these notorious atheists, too, were actually committed Christian nationalists. Spinoza, for example, maintains that Jesus "perceived things truly and adequately."[28] Jesus, he adds, possessed "a mind whose excellence far surpasses the human mind. Therefore I do not believe that anyone has attained such a degree of perfection surpassing all others, except Christ."[29] "The voice of Christ can thus be called the voice of God," he concludes, and "in that sense it can also be said that the wisdom of God . . . took on human nature in Christ."[30] And: "Did we not have this testimony of Scripture, the salvation of nearly all men would be in doubt."[31] Locke enthusiastically seconds the emotion. Jesus had an "admirable wariness of his carriage, and extraordinary wisdom, visible in his whole conduct."[32] His voice is the voice of God, according to Locke, and shows for all humankind the "way to Salvation."

What makes Jesus great, says Spinoza, is that his religion "consists essentially in moral teachings." Whereas Moses, for example, proposes a set of arbitrary positive laws suitable for a particular people in a particular time and place, as Spinoza explains, Jesus appeals only "to those axioms that are universally true." Therefore, "his teaching took the form of eternal truths, not of prescribed laws,"[33] and "the whole of Christ's doctrine can be readily grasped by everyone by the natural light of reason."[34] These eternal truths of reason, represented in a manner that can be grasped by the masses, take the form of the three-point program in popular deism: that there is a God; that the proper way to worship God is to obey the moral law; and that God offers rewards, punishment, and forgiveness for sinners. When conversing with the ignorant, to be sure, Jesus was sometimes "obscure" and often spoke in "the form of parables"; but these lapses in good taste were nonetheless organized around an effort to inculcate his followers in the moral law.[35]

The problems with Christianity, in a nutshell, have nothing to do with Jesus's teachings and everything to do with the corruptions of the priesthood: "Piety and religion—O everlasting God—take the form of ridiculous mysteries, and men who utterly despise reason, who reject and turn away from the intellect as naturally corrupt—these are the men (and this of all things is the most iniquitous) who are believed to possess the divine light."[36] Among those who view "the intellect as naturally corrupt," Spinoza cannot but mean to include Paul, Augustine, Luther, Calvin, and other priestly representatives of Christianity who turn away from the reasonable, easy-to-grasp teachings of Jesus in favor of unintelligible doctrines and denunciations of reason.

Locke repeats both the substance and the syntax of Spinoza's analysis. Jesus's contribution was to instruct the masses in the "Moral Law" and imbue them with "a clear knowledge of their duty," says Locke. "There is not, I think, any of the Duties of Morality, which [Jesus] has not some where or other, by himself and his Apostles, inculcated over and over again to his Followers."[37] Thus, Christianity stands for the *"Belief of One God,"*[38] says Locke (so much for the Trinity, then); it says that God wants us to be good; and that God rewards, punishes, and forgives: in brief, the three-point program. Emphatically missing from Jesus's plan, according to Locke, is any reward for belief per se: "None are sentenced or punished for unbelief, but only for their misdeeds."[39] The moral law is knowable "without making any allowance for faith."[40] (Locke does luxuriate on the role of faith in helping ordinary, fallible people make up for their inevitable failures to live up to the moral law. But here the thrust of the argument is to belabor the third point of the program—that God forgives repentant sinners—and thereby to reinforce that aspect of the moral law that is the chief concern in the Sermon on the Mount: that we should forgive others their trespasses as God has forgiven us.)[41]

Locke demands assent to one—and exactly one—belief supplied by revelation, namely, that "Jesus is the Messiah."[42] In this respect he follows closely on Hobbes, who maintains that the sole tenet of the Christian religion that must be accepted on faith is that "Jesus is the Christ." To modern ears, this doctrine sounds relatively pious, and it is at least superficially closer to orthodoxy than Spinoza's position, which does not insist on this or any other specific doctrine of revelation as a necessary bridge to the moral life. But Locke is never what he first appears to be. Slippery as ever, he starts down the slope by redefining what it means to be the Messiah. Being the Messiah, it turns out, does not mean being the Son of God. Nor does it involve the redemption of humankind through the assumption of guilt in an act of sacrifice, as most Christians have imagined. (Indeed, Locke undertakes a fairly radical reinterpretation of the story of Adam in order to free the human race from its supposed guilt for Adam's fall.) Being the Messiah, according to Locke, means serving as a vehicle for delivering to the masses the simple truths of the moral law. But this means that for those who have access to moral truths through reason—philosophers such as Locke himself, who insists repeatedly in his theoretical works that morality can be reduced to self-evident truths—the claim that Jesus is the Messiah is not a revelation at all. It is just a restatement of the palpable fact that Jesus's teaching conforms to the moral law as determined by reason. Thus, the only people for whom "Jesus is the Messiah" counts as a revelation are the illiterate masses who fail to grasp that Jesus's teachings are the same as the teachings of reason.

"It will here possibly be asked . . . What need was there of a Saviour? What advantage have we by *Jesus Christ*?" Locke pauses to inquire as he approaches the end of his reflections on the reasonableness of Christianity.[43] It is a valid question, given that according to Locke Jesus delivers only what reason already teaches us. (Though it is a curious question for someone who pretends to be Christian, after all, since in most versions of that religion the belief in the Son of God ostensibly comes first, and the analysis of putative advantages of this belief only later.) Locke's answer, in a nutshell, is that Jesus offers humanity the best chance of defeating the corruptions of the clergy. Jesus freed the Moral Law "from the corrupt glosses of the Scribes and Pharisees."[44] "Though the Works of nature, in every part of them, sufficiently Evidence a Deity," says Locke, the "fearful apprehensions" and blind "Sense and Lust" of the people "gave them up into the hands of the Priests." And then "the Priests every where, to secure their empire . . . excluded *Reason* from having anything to do with religion."[45] These Priests "were diligent in . . . the tricks of religion," but they "made it not their business to teach . . . *Virtue*."[46] Locke makes clear, by the way, that it is not just the pre-Jesus priesthood that deserves opprobrium; the worst representatives of irrationalism and mystification are to be discovered in the annals of the Christian churches.

Locke's *Reasonableness of Christianity*, like the rest of his work, divided his readers into seemingly irreconcilable camps. The reactionaries in Locke's own time believed they could see right through the friendly mask to the drooling infidel inside. The conservative cleric John Edwards,[47] writing about *The Causes and Occasions of Atheism in the Present Age*, named Locke as the most influential of such causes and occasions. On the other hand, Locke's public defenders—moderate or latitudinarian theologians such as John Tillotson, Samuel Clarke, and John Leland—took Locke at his word and enlisted him as a promoter of a generous, reasonable, open-tent form of Christianity. In repeating Locke's message about the reasonableness of Christianity, however, these moderates tended to replicate his functional role, dividing their own readers between those who took them at their word (say, Abigail Adams, who adored Tillotson) and those who took their word to be a species of reasoned infidelity (say, George Whitefield, who wanted to burn Tillotson's books).

The radicals, typically, agreed with the reactionaries about Locke, except that they liked what the latter detested. Christianity is so reasonable, Toland argues in *Christianity Not Mysterious*, that it does not require one to believe much of anything at all: just like Locke says.[48] To the extent that Bolingbroke has kind words for the Christian religion—and it is not a very large extent—Bolingbroke represents Jesus as a worthy teacher of natural religion or popular deism, useful for the intellectually challenged masses of the world.[49] To the extent that he is critical of Christianity—and the extent is quite large—his ire is focused on the Christian priesthood, for which no amount of vilification is enough to tame Bolingbroke's rage. Even in his praise for Jesus, though, Bolingbroke is rather more stinting than Locke or Spinoza. In a piece the young Jefferson deemed worthy of inclusion in his notebook, Bolingbroke denies that Jesus's system of ethics was complete or sophisticated, and credits ancient philosophers such as Seneca and Epictetus with doing a better job in moral philosophy.[50]

Perhaps the most influential, and in any case the most prolific, of the philosophers to pursue the dissolution of Christianity along these lines was Joseph Priestley. In his monumental *History of the Corruptions of Christianity* of 1782, and then again in his *History of Early Opinions concerning Jesus Christ* of 1786, Priestley is as kind to Jesus as he is harsh on the priesthoods that flourished in his name. His denunciations of the corruptions of Christianity—which include most of what was and remains widely thought to be the defining doctrines, practices, and hierarchies of Christianity itself—brought forth the haters in great number. It didn't help that he was a profound sympathizer of the French Revolution, which he saw first as heralding an "empire of reason" and then—for Priestley had distinctly millenarian leanings—as a sure sign of the Second Coming. In 1791, a righteous mob torched his house. Later they burned him in effigy alongside Thomas Paine. He fled to America in 1794, where he made the acquaintance of, among others, John Adams and Thomas Jefferson.

As is so often the case, the drift of the preceding history of radical meditations on the meaning and truth of the Christian religion comes to shore on the long and constantly evolving coastline of Jefferson's erudition. In the first half of his career, Jefferson on Jesus sounds the somewhat harsh notes of Bolingbroke. In 1787, for example, the forty-four-year-old Jefferson coolly describes the New Testament to Peter Carr as "the history of a personage called Jesus" and then offers his nephew a choice between the theory that Jesus was "begotten by god, born of a virgin, suspended & reversed the laws of nature at will, & ascended bodily into heaven" and the theory that Jesus was "a man of illegitimate birth, of a benevolent heart, enthusiastic mind, who set out without pretensions of divinity, ended in believing them & was punished capitally."[51] It isn't hard to guess which theory Jefferson favors.

Around the turn of the century—very likely in response to his encounter with the works of Priestley—Jefferson changes the key, if not the tune, of his song about Jesus. To Priestley himself he writes in 1803 that Jesus is "the most innocent, the most benevolent, the most eloquent and sublime character that has ever been exhibited to man."[52] To Adams he explains that he has read Priestley's *Corruptions of Christianity* and *History of Early Opinions of Jesus Christ* "over and over again, and I rest on them . . . as the basis of my own faith. These writings have never been answered."[53] Priestley returned the love. He dedicated one of his last books, *A General History of the Christian Church*, to "Thomas Jefferson, President of the United States." In the preface of that work, he avers that his newly adopted country "has a constitution the most favorable to political liberty and private happiness, of any in the world," and praises Jefferson as a "strenuous and uniform advocate of *religious* as well as *civil* liberty."[54]

The Jesus that Jefferson saw through Priestley, however, was not quite Priestley's Jesus. Rather, it was manifestly the Jesus of the three-point program. What makes Jesus great, according to Jefferson, is that he sought to teach the Jewish people "the principles of a pure deism."[55] The first of these principles is the "belief of one only God." The second consists of "moral doctrines, relating to kindred & friends," that conform "to the standard of reason, justice & philanthropy." "It is in our lives, and not from our words, that our religion must be read," Jefferson explains.[56] The third is "the doctrine of a future state." Though Jefferson himself harbored no discernible hopes for an afterlife, as we know, he allows that Jesus wielded this last doctrine "with efficacy, as an important incentive, supplementary to the other motives to moral conduct."[57]

In Jefferson just as in Spinoza, the three-point plan serves to collapse the Christian religion into natural religion or popular deism, which in turn reduces it to an expression of morality. Jefferson himself accomplishes this last reduction in a letter to Ezra Stiles: Jesus "has told us that God is good and perfect, but has not defined him. I am therefore of his theology, believing that we have neither words nor ideas adequate to that definition. And if we could all, after this example, leave the subject as undefinable, we should all be of one sect, doers of good, and eschewers of evil."[58] As it happens, we can be confident that Jefferson was initially inspired to this essentially Spinozistic reading of Christianity through his encounter not with Priestley, but with Locke. In notes from 1776 connected with his bill for religious freedom in Virginia, Jefferson offers a roughly similar summary of the essential teachings of Jesus under the revealing (or perhaps damning) title "Locke's System of Christianity."[59]

The problems with Christianity, Jefferson says, all have to do with—surprise—those "mountebanks calling themselves the priests of Jesus."[60] "The Christian priesthood, finding the doctrines of Jesus leveled to every understanding, and too plain to need explanation, saw in the mysticisms of Plato, materials with which they might build an artificial system which might, from its indistinctness, admit everlasting controversy, give employment for their order, and introduce it to profit, power, and pre-eminence," he informs John Adams.[61] Rescuing Jesus "from the imputation of imposture, which has resulted from artificial systems, invented by ultra-Christian sects . . . is a most desirable object, and one to which Priestley has successfully devoted his labors and learning," he adds—in the very same letter in which he identifies himself as an Epicurean.[62]

Just to be clear on what counts as a corruption in his mind, he scratches down in a footnote the "artificial systems" of the Christian religion: "the immaculate conception of Jesus, his deification, the creation of the world by him, his miraculous powers, his resurrection and visible ascension, his corporeal presence in the Eucharist, the Trinity; original sin, atonement, regeneration, election, orders of Hierarchy, etc." The defining doctrines of pretty much every major denomination of Christianity, in other words, are inauthentic corruptions of Christianity. Surprisingly, even Priestley's form of Unitarianism should count as an imposture, since Priestley remained committed to the doctrines of resurrection and ascension that Jefferson tosses out with the rest of revelation. Jefferson is also beyond Hobbes and Locke, for he leaves no room for even the pseudo-revealed doctrine that Jesus was the Messiah. When Jefferson famously told Benjamin Rush, "I am a Christian, in the only sense [Jesus] wished any one to be," he might more accurately have said that he was a Christian in the only sense that Spinoza wished any one to be.[63]

In 1804, Jefferson wrote to Priestley of an extraordinary plan to separate the moral pearls from the superstitious dung of the Christian religion. He sent to Philadelphia for some fresh copies of the New Testament, he tells his philosopher-friend, "with a design to cut out the morsels of morality, and paste them in the leaves of a book."[64] The plan was far more radical than anything Priestley would have contemplated. Jefferson evidently failed to grasp that, in Priestley's view, the Gospels (not just the morsels of morality in them) were revealed truth, and the corruptions came only later, in the way that they were (mis)read. But Priestley died before he could return an opinion to Jefferson.

So the president of the United States first took a pair of scissors to the Holy Bible sometime in 1805, over "2 or 3 nights only at Washington, after getting thro' the evening task" of running the nation's business. Some fifteen years later, his interest revived by his readings in ancient moral philosophy, he returned to the project from the comfort of his retirement at Monticello. The result was *The Life and Morals of Jesus of Nazareth*, a cut-and-paste version of the Gospels in four languages that spares us the stories about bread turning to fish, cripples finding their feet, and human beings rising from the dead.[65] The new "good book" was part of a larger project that takes us back from Priestley, past Locke, to the Bolingbroke of Jefferson's youth. The idea this time was to combine the Gospel truth with the moral insights of ancient philosophers such as Epictetus and Epicurus into a systematic statement of the morality of pure deism.

IF POPULAR RELIGION is sometimes useful for the public good, and the state is that which makes the public good its supreme law, then should not the state concern itself with the regulation and promotion of public religion? This of course is the question of the utility of religion, and it brings us back to the principal concern that occupies radical philosophers and revolutionaries from the start of the Epicurean revival to the creation of the American Republic. It also points to an aspect of radical philosophy, particularly prominent in the work of Hobbes and Spinoza, that sits uncomfortably with common (but false) conceptions today of the nature of liberal political systems.

According to the most common understanding of the U.S. Constitution and in particular the First Amendment, the state has no proper role at all to play in matters of religion beyond protecting the right of individuals to exercise it. According to the early modern philosophers who inspired the liberal revolutions, on the other hand, the state, which lays claim to sovereignty over everything useful in society, has and ought to have sovereignty over the practice of popular religion, too. These two positions, however, are not nearly as far apart as they seem at first glance.

Among the various proposals that earned Hobbes the title of "the Devil's Secretary" and similarly slanderous epithets, one of the most controversial was his suggestion that the appointment of ministers of the church and the control of public rites should fall to the sovereign. At the time, it should be remembered, the priesthood exerted tremendous power over the lives of individuals in society through its monopoly on rites such as baptism and marriage, and this power was mostly answerable to the priesthood itself. The real point of turning these powers over to the government was to keep them out of the hands of the priests, who, in Hobbes's mind, tended to foment bloody civil wars, suppress learning, and otherwise oppress the people in their quest for dominion. His fiercest polemics were always trained against the ministers of the church who "pretend the kingdom of God to be of this world, and thereby to have a power therein distinct from that of the civil state."[66]

Spinoza adopted the Hobbesian position and, as was his tendency, injected it with steroids, as it were. "God has no special kingdom over men save through the medium of those who hold the sovereignty," he announces.[67] The sovereign is therefore "the interpreter of divine law."[68] This means, first, that there is no priesthood by natural right. That is to say, there is no natural order within society that may claim power over the rest by virtue of its special purchase on the interpretation of the laws of God or Nature. The priesthood only has (and only ever has had) whatever power the sovereign people (implicitly or explicitly) grant it. If church and state are sometimes represented as separate powers, according to this line of thought, this can only mean that sovereignty is expressing itself in a divided way, or that the priests are attempting to usurp the authority of the rulers of the state. The other crucial implication is that the application of the moral law (or the moral judgment of action in society) is always in the first instance a matter of civil law, not religious law. Here Spinoza relies on an inference from social contract theory: that there is no "sin" outside the categories of acceptable behavior established through the contract.

The view that the state should control ecclesiastical matters was known at the time as Erastianism, after the Swiss scholar Thomas Erastus (1524–1583), who proposed a version of it in a posthumously published work. Hugo Grotius, Henry Parker, James Harrington, David Hume, and many other prominent political theorists of the early modern period also offered versions of the same position. Indeed, radical philosophy in the early modern world by and large was Erastian, not "tolerant" on religion, if by toleration we mean a policy of privileges or exemptions from civil law for religious groups whose religion differs from that of the state. The principal promoters of religious toleration in the early modern world were the dissenting religious sectarians, not the philosophers, and policies of toleration came to be accepted in varying degrees (and quite incompletely, by modern standards) in states like Britain and Holland to the extent that dissenting sects acquired some degree of political power.

Although the Erastian program may seem to modern readers to involve an attempt to fuse religion with the state, in fact it merges only a certain aspect of religion with the state. The program actually gets its start by dividing religion between public and private aspects, and this reconception of religion is ultimately its most important contribution to the creation of modern religious right. Hobbes's attempt to reduce Christianity to a single, simple tenet of faith—that Jesus is the Christ—was part of the plan. It was in essence an attempt to reduce sovereign control over the private aspect of religion in a Christian commonwealth to this one doctrine, thus leaving the private side of religion otherwise free, while at the same time transferring control over all the public elements of the Christian religion to the sovereign.

It was Spinoza, however, who first made clear the distinction between the public and private aspects of religion and made the latter the object of a religious right. The public aspect of religion, as he saw it, consists in the public ceremonies and the rites that serve to recognize certain socially important transactions, such as births and marriages; the hierarchies tasked with organizing those functions; and, in general, all the actions or behaviors of the individual insofar as they serve to express piety in a public way and relate to objects of the public good. The private aspect of religion consists in the purely inward belief of individuals together with whatever private expressions they undertake in order to advance their personal piety. Now, the role of the sovereign is to interpret the laws of nature or God, not to change them, and the laws of nature leave no doubt about the unalienable power of every individual to think for himself. Consequently, Spinoza insists, no laws should be passed against religious beliefs (though he does allow for an exception in cases where beliefs are "seditious" or "subversive").[69] Thus, even while the state assumes a monopoly over public religion, it guarantees a complete freedom to individuals with respect to private religion.

Locke, playing his role as chief marketing officer to perfection, fashions the slogans needed to sell the critical transformation of religion effected by his predecessors. In his famous *Letter concerning Toleration*, Locke sets out to resolve the interminable disputes over religion in modern polities by insisting on a firm distinction between civil and religious matters. The civil commonwealth, says Locke, is "a society of men constituted only for . . . advancing their own civil interests," and these civil interests are embodied in the familiar list of three to four-and-a-half unalienable rights. Locke's rhetorical genius is evident in the word "only"; for in reality these "civil interests" are everything through which the individual and the collective realize themselves. They are the public aspect of true piety, according to the radical philosophy to which Locke subscribes. What Locke magnanimously leaves over for "religious matters," then, is "the inward persuasion of the mind," which he euphemizes as "the care of souls." A "church," Locke concludes, is "a voluntary association of men, joining themselves together of their own accord to the public worshipping of God, in such a manner as they judge acceptable to him, and effectual to the salvation of their souls." In short, Locke collapses all religion into private religion and thereby defines public religion out of existence.

In a brief but highly influential essay titled *Of the Conduct of the Human Understanding*—included on Jefferson's bookshelf of "moral philosophy"—Locke offers further (and, again, implicitly radical) detail on the content of the private aspect of religion. "There is indeed one science . . . incomparably above all the rest," he announces, and it is "theology," and all who wish to improve themselves and serve God must study it. Theology, Locke explains, contains "the knowledge of God and his creatures" and "our duty to him and our fellow creatures."[70] "Theology" in this sense, of course, is just a restatement of the familiar, radical doctrine of "true piety," and has little to do with theological instruction as conventionally understood—as Spinoza makes clear in, among other places, the essay whose title Locke appears to have borrowed: *Treatise on the Improvement of the Understanding*. The important point is that Locke's genius for conciliatory rhetoric here allows him to present a definition of religion—the relation between man and his Maker—that feels pious in an orthodox sense and yet reduces religion to an essentially private extension of the individual quest for self-understanding.

From the radical position that Locke and Spinoza share, it follows that religion is not a fundamental category of human experience for legal or political purposes in either its public or its private aspects. Here we can glimpse the point where the moderate advocates of "religious toleration" and the radical proponents of "religious right" diverge irreconcilably. When advocates of toleration demand state protection for religion, whether in public practices or in acts of conscience, they generally take for granted that the activities and thoughts they associate with religion belong to a distinct category of human activity and deserve protection by virtue of their inclusion in that special category.

The radicals, on the other hand, collapse the public aspect of religious activity into public activity in general, and consequently allow no special privileges or exemptions for it from the power of the sovereign. The radicals then collapse the private aspect of religion into thought in general, and recognize an unalienable right associated with it on the basis of the freedom and natural equality of human minds. Thus they redefine and contain religion at the very moment that they guarantee its freedom.

The separation of church and state that emerges from the early modern revolutions in philosophy and politics does not in fact imply that the modern secular state is or ought to be neutral with respect to religion in every sense of that term. Rather, this separation at least implicitly involves the creation of a certain kind of public religion. This new, public religion is indeed tolerant of every religious belief—but only insofar as that belief is understood to be intrinsically private. It does not and ought not tolerate any form of religion that attempts to hold the power of the sovereign answerable to its private religious belief.[71] It also does not and ought not tolerate any attempt to shield the doctrines and practices of any religion from critical scrutiny.

Spinoza was one of the first theorists to make explicit claims about the nature of the public religion that a modern, sovereign state may reasonably promote. A state can always try to impose on its citizens a uniform code of laws concerning religious practices that makes them absolutely distinct from any other people, says Spinoza. Indeed, that was pretty much the policy of the ancient Hebrews, among others. But such an arrangement "could only be expedient for men who wanted to live their own lives behind their own frontiers, with no foreign trade or contact with the rest of the world."[72] A state may also attempt to impose arbitrary tests of faith on its people, that is, to legislate (professions of) belief. But such efforts are doomed to fail, and in failing produce only sectarian strife and mob violence. "The safest way to protect a state," he concludes, "is to make piety and worship consist simply in works, i.e. simply in the practice of charity and justice, and otherwise leave the individual to his freedom of judgment."[73] In other words, the general form of public religion in a reasonable civil state is nothing other than popular deism. Thus, the state can name a deity, but only one that demands nothing more than obedience to the moral law; it may propose beliefs, but it can judge only actions; and it should always hold out second chances for all those who inevitably fall short. In short, the state may adopt as a part of its public religion only whatever may be safely dissolved back into reason.

In the civil state that we call the Empire of Reason, this reduction of the public religion to natural religion attains a unique kind of closure. To the extent that the civil state approximates the state of reason, then the practice of virtue is made the direct object of civil laws. In that case, the public aspect of true worship—the exercise of justice and charity—is nothing other than the practice of virtuous citizenship. Obedience to the divine law (or law of nature) converges with obedience to the civil law, and the intellectual love of God stands for the understanding or self-awareness that accompanies participation in civil life. Thus, the distinction between public religion and public activity—which according to the radicals has no permanent foundation in theory—disappears in practice, too.

The Empire of Reason brings about a further, essential transformation of public religion. Radical philosophy, as we know, says that the practice of virtue and the pursuit of knowledge are two sides of the same coin of true worship. In the Empire of Reason, where the progress of virtue is the notional object of all public laws, the improvement of the understanding, too, becomes an explicit part of the public religion. The cultivation of the sciences and the development of culture and the arts become not just the means to advancing the other interests of the state but the end of the state itself. The enlightenment of the people becomes their own true religion, while the shell of tradition vanishes into empty symbols of the life of individual and collective self-realization. True piety in a reasonable world is the pursuit of happiness through the improvement of the understanding. Call it the religion of freedom.

At the same time, it cannot be supposed that all individuals, even in a republic of learning, conform to the religion of freedom and are transformed into atheistic philosophers practicing virtue and pursuing wisdom through harmonious action in scientifically minded collectives. On the contrary, the civil state of the Empire of Reason exists precisely because human beings by and large are passionate creatures and will always remain so. Consequently, it takes for granted that endless varieties of false religion will persist among the population. The important point is that such false religion remains confined to the private sphere, as a purely inward matter, where it is rendered harmless by the same civil laws that forbid the state from attempting to interfere with it. As Shaftesbury explained, "The wisdom of some wise nations"—he meant the ancient republics of Greece and Rome—was "to let people be fools as much as they pleased, and never to punish seriously what deserved only to be laughed at."[74]

MADISON AND JEFFERSON, too, defined religion—and thereby contained it—at the very moment that they guaranteed its freedom. In his draft versions of the Bill of Rights, Madison leaned on the work of George Mason, whose draft amendments to the Constitution define religion as the essentially individualistic "duty we owe to our Creator," adding that it can be "directed only by Reason and Conviction."[75] Jefferson repeats the same definition of religion throughout his life: "I have ever thought religion a concern purely between our Gods and our consciences."[76] In his more formal reflections on the nature of "theology," Jefferson simply paraphrases Locke paraphrasing Spinoza: "The relations which exist between Man and his Maker, and the duties resulting from those relations, are most interesting and important to every human being, and the most incumbent on his study and investigation."[77] It is precisely because they identify religion with its purely private or inward aspect that Jefferson and Madison insist that government can neither restrict its exercise nor impose it through an establishment of religion. Jefferson ties the bundle together with characteristic eloquence in his famous letter of 1802 to the Danbury Baptists:

Believing with you that religion is a matter which lies solely between Man & his God, that he owes account to none other for his faith or his worship, that the legitimate powers of government reach actions only, & not opinions, I contemplate with sovereign reverence that act of the whole American people which declared that their legislature should "make no law respecting an establishment of religion, or prohibiting the free exercise thereof," thus building a wall of separation between Church & State.[78]

The "reverence" with which Jefferson here contemplates the wall of separation is the same as the "spirit of true religion" that Thomas Young invoked in 1772, when he demanded that every individual should have "*entire liberty of conscience . . .* to worship the author of his being and giver of all his enjoyments, in the manner most agreeable to his own understanding."[79] It alerts us to the fact that behind the definition of religion as a purely private affair there stands another religion, or a sense of piety, and the object of this ur-religion, or true piety, is not any particular deity or doctrine but the pursuit of understanding itself.

It is often suggested that in separating church and state, Jefferson and his fellow founders sought to promote religion. And there is a certain truth in this, though not the one that many people suppose. America's founders did wish to promote religion—but not any and every kind of it that might be drawn from the horrifying history of human religious practices. The revolutionary part of their Revolution was at bottom a project of reformation and containment of popular religion. The religion that they hoped to bring to America—which they slyly construed as *all* religion—was that which measures piety in terms of doing good rather than believing rightly; that which imposes a duty on oneself, as opposed to one's neighbors; and that which builds the bonds of community even while robbing the priesthood of its corrupting political influence. In short, they wanted to bestow upon America the blessings of popular deism, or that variety of religion that translates into lively metaphors and memorized rituals the radical and essentially atheistic philosophy on which the modern liberal state rests.

Jefferson's vision for the future of American religion, for example, was as bright and clear as the spacious skies to the west, and it featured nothing but Unitarian churches from sea to shining sea:

I rejoice that in this blessed country of free inquiry and belief, which has surrendered its creed and conscience to neither kings nor priests, the genuine doctrine of one only God is reviving, and I trust that there is not a *young man* now living in the United States who will not die an Unitarian.[80]

Jefferson was certain that priestcraft and its paraphernalia of mystifying dogma would wither under the disinfecting light of the new empire of reason. "And the day will come," he told Adams, "when the mystical generation of Jesus by the supreme being as his father in the womb of a virgin will be classed with the fable of the generation of Minerva in the brain of Jupiter. But we may hope that the dawn of reason and freedom of thought in these United States will do away with all this artificial scaffolding, and restore to us the primitive and genuine doctrines of this the most venerated reformer of human errors."[81]

Paine's religious forecast was no less sunny than Jefferson's future perfect. In the *Age of Reason*, Paine puts his finger on the vital link between true popular religion and the separation of church and state:

> Soon after I had published the pamphlet, *Common Sense*, in America, I saw the exceeding probability that a revolution in the system of government would be followed by a revolution in the system of religion. The adulterous connection of church and state, wherever it had taken place, whether Jewish, Christian, or Turkish, had so effectually prohibited, by pains and penalties, every discussion upon established creeds and upon first principles of religion, that until the system of government should be changed those subjects could not be brought fairly and openly before the world; but whenever this should be done, a revolution in the system of religion would follow. Human inventions and priestcraft would be detected, and man would return to the pure, unmixed, and unadulterated belief of one God, and no more.[82]

Paine and Jefferson, as it happens, were simply rehearsing an argument that Ethan Allen had aired in his *Oracles*. Writing just one year after the conclusion of the War of Independence, Allen announced that the liberation of America has:

> depreciated Priestcraft, on the scale of at least fifty per cent. per annum, and rendered it highly probable that the improvement of succeeding generations, in the knowledge of nature, and science, will exalt the reason of mankind, above the tricks and imposture of Priests, and bring them back to the religion of nature and truth; ennoble their minds, and be the means of cultivating concord, and mutual love in society, and of extending charity, and good will to all intelligent beings, throughout the universe.[83]

The popular deism or natural religion that America's revolutionaries hoped to promote was distinguished above all by its commitment to the defining value of the Empire of Reason: the improvement of the understanding. "Enlighten the people generally, and tyranny and oppressions of body and mind will vanish like evil spirits at the dawn of day," said Jefferson.[84] In Virginia he attempted to make good on the promise with proposals to create a publicly funded system of primary education. "By far the most important bill in our whole code is that for the diffusion of knowledge among the people," he explained to George Wythe. "No other sure foundation can be devised, for the preservation of freedom and happiness."[85] Aside from cultivating his garden, the establishment of the freethinking University of Virginia was the great project of his retirement years. "If a nation expects to be ignorant and free, in a state of civilisation, it expects what never was and never will be," he explained.[86]

The nation's first president made the program official. Just a few lines down from the passage in the *Farewell Address* that is so often misconstrued to suggest that he wished to impose programs of religious indoctrination on the population, Washington declares that the genuine foundation of free government is to be found in "institutions for the general diffusion of knowledge." If the American experiment in democracy is to flourish, he explains, it is "essential that public opinion should be enlightened."

_____

A COMMON LINE of interpretation today says that America's revolutionary deists got the religious future wrong. Jefferson's Unitarians didn't take over the country; Paine died drunk and despised; and few Americans today have ever heard of Ethan Allen's unusual book. A boy born up in Vermont, not long after Allen died, reportedly discovered golden tablets on a hill in western New York and soon established a new religion based on his alleged conversations with an angel named Moroni. The Second Great Awakening, says the conventional wisdom, demonstrated once again that Americans are religious by nature, and that they like their religion like their liquor, homebrewed and hard as stone. In the early twenty-first century, with religionists in America seemingly as loud and self-righteous as ever, few claims are as unfashionable as the prediction that religion must wither under the light of reason in a secular world. _God is Back_, screams the title of one recent book.

It is true that Americans became more religious in a certain sense after the Revolution. But to suppose that this reflects a failure of the founders' project to reform and contain popular religion is to assume falsely that two things are the same across history because they happened to share the same name. In fact, what we now call "religion" isn't in every respect what religion once was. Modern liberal democracy in America and around the world does not conform to some preexisting religious conception of things. On the contrary, modern religion has for the most part been made to conform to the liberal order. It is only to the degree that religion is not what it once was, moreover, that we can and ought to tolerate it, and may hope to find in it some limited utility for modern society.

The transformation of religion in America dates in significant part from the Revolution itself and bears a meaningful connection with the seemingly optimistic prognosis of America's founders. Alexis de Tocqueville—the source most often used to chide the secularists who are thought to have forgotten that America is a religious and specifically Christian country—was among the first to observe that there was something new in the religion that was being revived in the first decades of the new republic. In an enlightened, democratic country, Tocqueville observes, religions that make claims that conflict with science or contradict common experience cannot long survive. "Religions should be most careful to confine themselves to their proper sphere, for if they wish to extend their power beyond spiritual matters they run the risk of not being believed at all," he cautions.[87]

Tocqueville notes that Christianity has a special role in the new American democracy—but the kind of Christianity he sees taking root will be instantly recognizable to anyone familiar with the preceding history of radical philosophy. The Gospels, he claims, offer no positive civil, political, or scientific laws but "deal only with the general relations between man and God and between man and man. Beyond that, they teach nothing and do not oblige people to believe anything." The kind of Christianity Tocqueville expects to survive in America, in short, is the one that descends from Spinoza through Locke to Jefferson—a Christianity reduced to the moral law, without need for Jesus and indeed without obligation "to believe anything," as de Tocqueville rather hopefully puts it.

Even so, the transformation of religion in America proceeded much more slowly than Jefferson or Tocqueville anticipated. One reason for this may be traced to the founders themselves. Their deism was on its rhetorical surface a strident effort to accommodate radical philosophy to the needs of the popular religion of a particular period in history. And the truth is that they often got carried away in their moderation. The ultimate source of the trouble is that America's founders arrived on the scene so early in the history of the modern world. In carrying out a revolution ahead of its time, they burdened their modern republic with the legacies of an earlier time, the most important of which were the connected institutions of slavery and supernatural religion. In a sense, America paid a price for the genius of its founders. Still, their deism, though often read as a sign of how far behind us they were, should really be taken as an indication of how far ahead of their own time they were.

Yet another factor that slowed the progress of modern religion in

America was the same size, dispersion, and diversity that made pluralism and toleration inevitable in the first place. Its enormous geographic advantages have in a sense always given the United States a supernormal margin for error. So it has been able to tolerate religious extremism of the sort that would have ended the careers of states with less open space in which to tuck away their mistakes.

Among the many, complex factors that slowed the progress of Tocqueville's kind of Christianity in America, however, by far the most important was and remains the institution of race-based slavery. A huge and vocal branch of American Christianity today descends from a spiritual line that at one time deployed its sacred scriptures not merely to justify but to exalt the practice of slavery and to explicitly reject the equality of the Declaration as the "equality of infidelity."[88] Another large branch arose in an attempt to compensate for slavery and its aftermath, both to mimic and to resist the master class.[89] Yet another branch—a significant part of it leaning toward the Unitarian and deist side of the spectrum—coalesced around the effort to abolish slavery.[90] On the whole, slavery helped keep the old-time religion alive; and then the ghosts of slavery extended its life still more.

And yet, even after allowing for the delays, the complexity, and the wide variations in doctrine and the many contradictory impulses it expresses, religion in the American mainstream today is neither as diverse nor as extreme as its conflicting theologies and loudest champions would suggest, and most of it has belatedly converged along the path that begins with Spinoza and Jefferson. The majority of believers today of whatever faith can be found to agree with the proposition that believers in other faiths also have a chance of getting to heaven. A plurality even agrees with the proposition that landed Jefferson in so much trouble: that belief in God is not necessary for morality.[91] The majority also tends to agree that the true meaning of religion, theirs or any other, is to extend charity and goodwill to all other people. The majority also accepts that religion is a matter of individual choice—a kind of consumer preference—and in fact a plurality has exercised its right to choose by changing religious affiliation one or more times in their adult lives. In other words, the majority has at least implicitly embraced the definition of piety as whatever it is in the infinite variety of individual experience that, within the bounds of the civil law, conduces to the practice of virtue, or the improvement of self and community.

America's mainstream religion is at bottom one form or another of popular deism, and popular deism is just atheism adapted to the limitations of the common understanding of things. To say that the United States is "one nation under God" is to conceal behind a euphemism the fact that it is and always has been one nation under nature. Whatever else we pretend to believe, we are in practice mostly atheists now—and for that we should be grateful.

The suggestion that there is in the United States a single, dominant quasi-statal religion—and that it is in reality a form of pious atheism—may seem to violate the "separation of church and state" that is rightly thought to characterize the American constitutional system. But this is mainly because the redefinition of religion that began with the seventeenth-century philosophers has been so successful. We now take for granted that the civil state has and ought to have ultimate control over most of the practical matters historically associated with religion: the registration of births, the recognition of marriage, and other defining rites and ceremonies of life. We take for granted that the civil authorities, not the religious ones, have the power and the right to determine what will and will not be permitted within public life and so to establish the real basis for civil morality. We take for granted that there are numberless particular ways in which we can establish worthwhile relationships, build communities, and engage in useful projects that are all connected with our common society and yet have nothing to do with anybody else's religion conceived as their speculative inward beliefs.

The replacement of traditional religion with "secularism"—as the attitude that characterizes religious life in a world organized according to the ideas of radical philosophy now tends to be called—is sometimes treated as a cultural fashion, that is, as one arbitrary "paradigm" exchanged for another. A more credible theory supposes that secularism is the consequence of a series of scientific discoveries dating back to Galileo or maybe Darwin. This is closer to the truth but still falls short—for science never can nor should be expected to close all the gaps in knowledge through which the common religious consciousness might project its hallucinations of divine agency. The best account of the spread of secularism remains the one that Jefferson first suggested: that it is the natural consequence of the freedom of thought in a free society. Not the orbits of the planets or the origin of the species but the daily movement of social, moral, and political experience in the modern world has made secularism inevitable.

To attempt to explain the world today through the categories of the common religious consciousness is to live in a kind of moral chaos. It is to inhabit a house of fractured mirrors, where submission to inscrutable authorities counts as freedom, where that which is good for the health of the individual and the collective is called evil, and where all are expected to bear the lifelong burden of pretending to believe one thing while doing another. Once upon a time, it took a certain kind of genius to see that atheists could be virtuous. Today, only those blinded by bigotry can think otherwise. The revolutionaries of the early modern period needed their books to imagine a world free from the chains of the common religious consciousness. Today we need only our eyes.

The club of radical philosophers and their fellow travelers today is a much more open and variegated affair than it was in the claustrophobic intellectual world of the eighteenth century. Now they call themselves humanists, atheists, pantheists, freethinkers, Universalists, or any number of other names that conform in their endless idiosyncrasy to the spirit of an intrinsically heterodox age. They are invariably tagged as a fringe, and in recent years some number of them have organized themselves in a self-conscious way as an identity group, yet another tiny minority seeking recognition from the ruling majority. But these free radicals, long present in the history, can claim something more than just a seat at the table. The truth is that they made the history—and then invited everyone else to join them at the table.

One might well ask whether this essentially atheistic public religion of the modern liberal world should be called religion at all. If by "religion" is meant some set of unfounded beliefs in supernatural agents, or some collection of behaviors intended to evince submission to such agents, or some commitment to vague dogmas about "absolute" or "transcendental" verities, then it clearly is none of those things. Yet it can count as religion insofar as it does what traditional religion tried and failed to do. It shows us how to find meaning and purpose in our short lives, it teaches us the importance of doing right by our fellow human beings, and it relieves us of all those false religions through which the mind enslaves itself. As Jefferson and Spinoza understood, it comes with a kind of piety all its own.

IN THE LITTLE MORE than two centuries since America's revolutionaries announced their "new order of the ages," a new order has in fact emerged. In total population, average lifespan, general health, levels of literacy, technological capabilities, scientific knowledge, and almost every other meaningful index of power and well-being, the human species today is a world apart from the one that inhabited the earth before the year 1800 or so. That this swift and far-reaching change is all to the good, aims at some preordained end, or originates from any single cause may well be doubted. That it is the one big event in recorded history is certain. In light of the planetary consequences of human activity—and, who knows, the interplanetary consequences—it may well be the one fact about the earth that demands explanation. Did ideas really have anything to do with it? Can philosophy have mattered all that much?

Many modern historians appear to regard ideas as little more than self-congratulatory vapors emanating from the machine-like operation of material forces. Economic self-interest, technological innovation, and the accidents of geography determine the course of history, they say, and the rest is just so many excuses for the domination of one group by another. Another influential view holds that ideas are merely the rationalization of certain passions bred in human beings through evolution by natural selection. There isn't much point in debating what people think, according to this view, because we already know how they feel. Probably the balance of educated opinion today says that it is absurd to look to philosophers for the explanation of anything other than their own confusions, and preposterous to suggest that their ideas might have accounted for any kind of moral progress in the world.

There are those who present themselves as champions of ideas today, of course. But on closer inspection it usually turns out that by "ideas" they mean "bad ideas." According to one popular school, for example, a religiously inculcated feeling of guilt over having been born goaded large numbers of stern-faced northern European types to work harder than they should have and thereby to stumble into the creation of the capitalist system. But this is just to shift the burden of explaining history from the untethered ideas in question to whatever pathology compelled people to embrace them in the first place. Another school says that the ideas that changed history were a set of absolute moral precepts, a collection of platitudes discovered once and for all by this or that philosopher, prophet, or nation, and marked with an exclamation point for all time. Which is really just a way of saying that the preceding generations of humanity had no capacity for thought and subsequent generations have no need for it.

These common approaches to the history of ideas, however, have less to say about the value of ideas than about the poverty of our common ideas about ideas. They take for granted that ideas are imaginary pictures in the mind, eternal doctrines taken on faith, the "first principles" that are in reality the last thing that anyone cares about, and all those husks that, littered in its wake, are commonly mistaken for the moving force of thought. Mostly, they assume that the ideas that explain our actions are the ones that come out of our mouths, and that the ideas that matter in history are the ones that receive the loudest affirmations from the largest number of people. So they overlook the defining feature—and predicament—of the modern liberal order: that it rests as if by design on a system of ideas understood only incompletely by most of the individuals who comprise it.

Ideas are acts of understanding. They derive their power from their truth, not their acceptance. They involve clearing away old delusions, not erecting new ones. They don't settle the future; they only make sense of the past. They are the ground of our freedom, not an instance of it. And the history of the past several hundred years shows that ideas in this sense did change the world. Self-government became possible—however imperfectly—only after radical philosophy cleared the field of those common misconceptions through which human beings participate in their own enslavement. Ideas explain the revolution in the principles of government with which America's founders adorned an otherwise parochial struggle for national independence. They explain the extraordinary fact of modernity, the planetary impact of the human species, and even in a certain way the evolution of life on earth.

In our tolerant age, we like to say that everybody is entitled their own worldview, that every worldview comes with its own "narrative" of the history, and that all such narratives are created equal. So, according to the wisdom of polite society today, it's a matter of personal preference whether the modern world emerged out of humankind's emancipation from the shackles of religious superstition or whether instead it sprang directly from the head of Zeus, or was delivered in the form of a bountiful continent to this or that group of sectarian zealots. But the only choice we really have is whether to be conscious or to persist in destructive delusions. Of course, it remains just as fashionable now as it was in Jonathan Edwards's day to lament the nihilism that supposedly grips us when we shed the false certainty of ignorance, and to bemoan the doom that will surely befall us when we depart from the simple faith of our fathers. But the fact remains that the common power of humanity—the capability for cooperative action that is really just another word for our moral well-being—was never greater than after we lost our religion.

Some historians might conjecture that it was just an accident that one specific movement of thought and not some other one happened to be present at the creation of the modern world. But this is true only if we confuse the ideas that changed history with the parade of peculiar and contingent doctrines through which they happened to be expressed at various points in time (such as "atomism," "the infinite universe," "substance monism," and "secularism"). There is no alternative to radical philosophy, or at least none yet. The explanation of the power and prosperity of the modern liberal world is largely the same as the explanation of the limits of the common consciousness of things.

Every successful liberal state succeeds in the liberal arts. To be sure, when viewed from within the self-perpetuating guild in which they are mostly housed today, and given the seeming obsession with dead masters and tendency to slide into banal relativisms, the humanities today can be the source of some discouragement. Yet they are the dirty little screw of modern democracy. Their purpose is to curate the resources from which radical philosophy must be constantly refreshed. They can do for us what Thomas Young did for his friend Ethan Allen, what a bookshelf on moral philosophy did for Thomas Jefferson, and what deism did for the rest of America's revolutionaries.

It was the good fortune of the United States to have come into being with a generation of leaders whose collective intellect and wisdom have rarely been equaled. It was its even better fortune to have acquired from them a form of government and way of life not beholden to their many errors. The ideas of America's founders were always more radical than the individuals themselves, just as their effects were more extensive than their intentions, just as the revolutionary power of the republic they created has always been greater than that of the various traditions that are often mistakenly supposed to define it. "The American War is over: but this is far from being the case with the American Revolution," Benjamin Rush said not long after the guns fell silent—and he is still right about that.[92]

The founding of the American Republic did not bring freedom to the slaves. It did not give justice to Native Americans. It did nothing to liberate women. And it still hasn't prevented malefactors of great wealth from twisting the political process to their advantage. All of these struggles fell to subsequent generations, and the provisional victories obtained thus far have been the work of those who have understood in one way or another that the American Revolution remains an ongoing concern. The main thing we can learn now from the persistence in modern America of supernatural religion and the reactionary nationalism with which it is so regularly accompanied is that there is still work to be done. For too long we have relied on silence to speak a certain truth. The noise tells us the time has come for some candor. It points to a piece of unfinished business of the American Revolution.

FOR FIVE HAPPY YEARS Ethan lived with Fanny in a small house on a large plot of land overlooking the Winooski River in Burlington. In some ways he was just like the Ethan of old, the boisterous mountain man who romped into Ticonderoga with eighty-three of his closest friends and maybe Benedict Arnold. He spent his days reeling in more fish than he could fry, trafficking in land titles, and from time to time exercising his powers of persuasion on unruly settlers as the commander in chief of whatever militia he could roust from the hills.

Yet there was something different about the Ethan who came back from the war. Though he continued to dabble in public affairs with an energy that would have left most men exhausted, he remained in a relatively meditative mood. Maybe it was his health, which never quite recovered from thirty-two months of imprisonment, some of it under very harsh conditions. Maybe it was the grim news that greeted him in his final year of captivity: that his eldest son, Joseph, had died of smallpox at the age of eleven.[93] Maybe it was Fanny. In any case, the daily tasks of building the state of Vermont increasingly fell to Ira, the wiliest of the Allen brood.

One day in 1786, representatives of Daniel Shays came to offer Ethan command of their rebellion in western Massachusetts. It is hard to imagine that the younger version of Ethan would have thought twice before leaping at the chance to become the warlord of a revolutionary backwoods republic. But the old vet had his mind on other things, and he firmly rebuffed the proposal. Ethan had become "weary of war," observed a friend, and longed "to devote himself to his philosophic studies."[94]

The emotional center of Allen's life had shifted, and, Fanny apart, the new sun around which it revolved was his book. The old man seemed determined at last to acquire that diploma from the university of higher things of which he had been so cruelly deprived as a young man. So the facade of the warrior melted into the forest, and Ethan Allen became what in his mind he always was: a man of ideas.

The preface to the *Oracles*, which appears to have been written after the book, is dated July 2, 1782. He must have started work on the opus not long after his release from captivity in 1778. Not until 1784 did he find a printer willing to risk the wrath of the Almighty on the project. The publication process dragged on for another two years and afforded far more than the customary allotment of humiliations. The printer, beset with second thoughts, stopped work at every excuse and demanded payment for all costs in advance. Every morning when he woke up, and every evening after returning home from the tavern, Allen made sure to curse his printer, and by extension all publishers of the world.

At last the 1,500 copies were ready. Then the bulk of them perished unread in the flames that mysteriously engulfed the publisher's warehouse. But Allen was used to high casualty rates, and the important thing was that, even if in greatly diminished numbers, his book was at long last before the eye of history. He asked his French friend Crève-coeur to lay his book "before the academy of Arts & Sciences at Paris, by whose Sentence I expect to *Stand* or *fall*."[95] He had only one cross left to bear, and it was the burden of his own philosophical ambition.

The good people of New England did their best to make sure it hurt. In the *Vermont Gazette* over the summer of 1786 there appears a letter ostensibly addressed to Allen from Lord George Gordon, an eccentric, rabble-rousing London politician of the time. According to "Gordon," the *Oracles* is an "incomparable code of reasoning," and its author is "an exalted genius, unparalleled in our present age." Gordon shows an uncanny appreciation for just how high Allen had set his philosophical sights:

> At a future day, when the sons of men will gloriously emerge from the ignorance and credulity in which they have been too long involved, through the pious frauds and artifices of the interpreters of the scriptures . . . then I doubt not, my venerable Vermontese *Demi god*, but you will be admired as a miracle of holiness and, like a second Mahomet (your great antitype and pattern) be worshipped on the Green Mountains with the veneration due to so much wisdom and piety.[96]

Now this was certainly hitting close to home. For the truth is that Allen did imagine himself as something more than a mere scoffer or skeptic, something akin to a religious reformer, maybe even a certain kind of prophet.

"Gordon" clearly feels the pain of this "second Mahomet" as he encounters incomprehension and rejection from the blockheads of the world—and then he twists the knife again. "What is it to you, if you can make yourself immortal by overturning every kind of religious prejudice, however sanctified by custom, to make way for your system?" "Gordon" promises Allen that in time he may expect to have "as many proselytes as Luther, Calvin, or any other pious reformado." The mock reviewer concludes by promising to forward a copy of Allen's world-shattering book to the Grand Signior of Turkey, where he supposes there is a particularly great need for a new religion.

They weren't through with him yet. In the *Vermont Gazette* a few days later an anonymous writer calls attention to the previously published "letter" from Gordon to Allen. "Gentlemen," says the writer, "if you do not communicate to the public the following important intelligence, the world will suppose it to be Ethan Allen's own production." There follows a news item:

BOSTON, May 10. Yesterday arrived in this harbor the . . . Seraglio, a ship from Constantinople, sent by the Grand Signior for the purpose of conveying Saint Ethan Allen to that city, in order to take the lead of the Mufti in that Empire, who are all converted by the four copies of his ORACLE of REASON, sent by Lord George Gordon to Constantinople. In this ship came four of the Grand Signior's Concubines, a present to St. Ethan from the Grand Turk.[97]

It was easy enough to laugh off Allen and his theological pretensions. It was easier still to bury them with him.

Ethan Allen died on a bright winter day in 1789, at the age of fifty-one, most likely from a stroke, while crossing a frozen patch of Lake Champlain on his sleigh to pick up some hay from a friend.

The Green Mountain Boys, many of them now generals, gathered in Burlington to bury him with due military honors. He left Ira with clear instructions that there were to be no prayers or preachers at his funeral.[98] Not that the preachers intended to come. "Died in Vermont the profane and impious Deist Gen Ethan Allen," the eminent Congregationalist Ezra Stiles, president of Yale, noted in his diary. "And in Hell he lift up his eyes, being in torments."[99]

As Vermonters settled into a peaceful life in their new state, embarrassed apologies gathered in to cover the theological deviations of their founding hero. Apart from Samuel Williams, who remained loyal to the end, the state's historians were quick to distance themselves from Allen's "errors" and "lapses." The Protestant clergy, taking up their grim task of patrolling the boundaries of the new American identity, furiously suppressed any memory of the thinking part of the one-time hero of the Green Mountains. His strange religion, they inveighed, belonged to an earlier, feckless time. It wasn't the religion of America.

Yet time changes all things. The theological policemen who hounded Allen after his death have now faded into the forgotten precincts of history, while the philosopher of the Green Mountains seems ready at last for his second coming. If we could see just a little farther into the future, where the reputations of the prophets are always made, maybe we would catch a glimpse of what Ethan Allen and his friend Thomas Young thought they saw in the first place: a nation that will have liberated itself from all forms of tyranny over the human mind. Call it the land of the free.

Acknowledgments

I would like to express my thanks and appreciation to the staff and fellows of the Dorothy and Lewis B. Cullman Center for Scholars and Writers at the New York Public Library, where I was the Gilder Lehrman Fellow in American History for 2010–11. I am also grateful to the following individuals for their insightful comments on and discussions of the project: Howard Burton, Charles Gillispie, Joseph Harvey, David Hinton, Wim Klever, Daniel Lakhdhir, Laura Rasmussen, Katherine Stewart, and William Warner. I owe special thanks to my editor at Norton, Alane Mason, and my agent, Andrew Stuart.

Notes

A Note on Sources for Thomas Young

There is as of this writing no full-length biography of Thomas Young. Readers interested in learning more about "the most unwritten about man of distinction" of the American Revolution should consult the following sources:

Huntington Library, San Marino, California. Letters to Hugh Hughes: March 2, March 22, May 17, July 26, and September 15, 1770; December 21, 1772. (MSS 41548-56).

Massachusetts Historical Society, Boston. Letters to John Wendell, November 23 and December 15, 1766; to Abigail Dwight, February 13, 1767; to Hugh Hughes, Boston, August 21 and December 21 (2), 1772. (Sedgwick II Papers and Misc Bound MS).

National Archives of the United Kingdom, Kew, Richmond, Surrey. CO 5/763, ff.85, 89.

New-York Historical Society, New York City. Letters to John Lamb: March 18, June 19, June 26, October 4, and November 19, 1774 (Lamb Papers). See also H. van Schaak papers, January 7, 1766.

New York Public Library, New York City. Bancroft Collection. Papers of the Boston Committee of Correspondence [abbreviated NYPL BCC].

University of Vermont, Burlington. Allen Family Papers.

Vermont Historical Society. Vermont Historical Center, Barre. Special Collections.

Vermont State Archives, MIddlesex. Ethan Allen Papers and Ira Allen Papers and Levi Allen Papers, Henry Stevens Collection.

Young to Sam Adams, September 4, 1774, in William V. Wells, *The Life and Public Services of Sam Adams*. Little, Brown, 1865. 1.237–8.

Young to Friends in Boston, in Margaret Wheeler Willard, *Letters on the American Revolution, 1774–76*. Houghton Mifflin, 1925. P. 33.

Young to John Lamb, May 13, 1774, in Isaac Q. Leake, *Memoir of the Life and Times of Gen John Lamb*. Joel Munsell, 1850. P. 85.

Young to Ezra Stiles, December 5, 1762, in Edmund S. Morgan, *The Gentle Puritan: A Life of Ezra Stiles*. University of North Carolina Press, 1962. P. 158.

Young to Henry Ward, March 27, 1776, in *Correspondence of Governor Samuel Ward, May 1775–March 1776*. Rhode Island Historical Society, 1952. Pp. 201–4.

Young to John Wilkes, in *Proceedings of the Massachusetts Historical Society*, 47 (1913–14): 209–10.

The Boston Evening Post: April 20, 1767; "Socrates to the Athenians," May 18, 1767; "St. Paul to the Athenians," May 25, 1767; June 1, 1767; "Sobrius." September 14, 1767; "Philodemus," September 21, 1767; "Britano Americanus," September 23, 1767; "Libermoriturus," November 9, 1767; "Probus," May 9, 1768; "To Sir Francis Bernard," September 11, 1769; "Messirs Edes and Gill," December 25, 1769, January 1, 8, 15, and 22, 1770; February 26, 1770; "Messirs Fleet," May 17, 1770; "Messirs Fleet," August 27, 1770; "Messirs Fleet," March 18, 1771; "Messirs. Printers," June 3, 1771; November 30, 1772; "To Agricultor," March 28, 1774.

Dunlap's Pennsylvania Packet: "An Elector," April 29, 1775; "Eudoxus," April 22, 1776.

Massachusetts Spy: "To the Reverend George Whitefield," August 18, 1770; "To the Public," August 30, 1770; "For the Massachusetts Spy," November 19, 1772; "To Sir Aaron Davis," December 4, 1772.

Pennsylvania Evening Post: April 20, 1776; August 29, 1776.

Pennsylvania Gazette: "To Messirs Hall & Sellars," July 26 and August 16, 1775; "An Elector," April 29 and May 15, 1776.

The Pennsylvania Journal; and the Weekly Advertiser: "To the public," July 5, 1775.

The Royal American Magazine: February, March, April, and September 1774; March 1775.

Young, Thomas. "Philodicaios." In *Some Reflections on the Disputes between New-York, New-Hampshire, and Col. John Henry Lydius of Albany*. New Haven: Benjamin Mecom, 1764.

———. *A Poem Sacred to the Memory of James Wolfe*. New Haven, 1761.

———. *To The Inhabitants of VERMONT, a Free and Independent State, bounding on the River Connecticut and Lake Champlain.* Philadelphia, April 11, 1777.

———. "A Natural Man." In *A Sermon on Natural Religion.* Boston: I. Thomas, 1771.

Aldridge, A. Owen. "Natural Religion and Deism in America before Ethan Allen and Thomas Paine." *William and Mary Quarterly* 54(4) (October 1997): 835–48.

Anderson, George Pomeroy. "Who Wrote 'Ethan Allen's Bible'?" *New England Quarterly* 10(4) (December 1937): 685–96.

Bellesiles, Michael A. *Revolutionary Outlaws: Ethan Allen and the Struggle for Independence on the Early American Frontier.* University of Virginia Press, 1993.

———. "Works of Historical Faith: Or, Who Wrote *Reason the Only Oracle of Man?*" *Vermont History* 57 (1989): 69–83.

Caldwell, Renwick K. "The Man Who Named Vermont." *Vermont History* 26 (October 1958): 204–300.

Doten, Dana. "Ethan Allen's 'Original Something'." *New England Quarterly* 11(2) (June 1938): 361–66.

Edes, Henry H. "Memoir of Dr. Thomas Young, 1731–1777." *Colonial Society of Massachusetts, Transactions 1906–7,* 11 (1910): 2–54.

Hawke, David Freeman. "Dr. Thomas Young—'Eternal Fisher in Troubled Waters'." *New-York Historical Society Quarterly* 54 (1970): 6–29.

———. *In the Midst of a Revolution.* University of Pennsylvania Press, 1961.

Hogeland, William. *Declaration.* Simon & Schuster, 2010.

Maier, Pauline. *The Old Revolutionaries.* Alfred A. Knopf, 1980.

———. "Reason and Revolution: The Radicalism of Dr. Thomas Young." *American Quarterly* 28(2) (Special Issue, Summer 1976): 229–49.

McCracken, Henry Noble. *Old Dutchess Forever!* Hastings, 1956.

Frequently Cited Sources and Abbreviations

John Adams

Adams, Charles Francis, ed. *The Works of John Adams.* 10 vols. Little, Brown, 1856.

Butterfield, L. H., ed. *The Diary and Autobiography of John Adams.* 4 vols. Belknap Press, 1962.

Taylor, Robert J., et al., eds. *The Papers of John Adams.* 16+ vols. Harvard University Press, 1983–.

Ethan Allen

Allen, Ethan. "An Essay on the universal plenitude of Being, and on the nature and immortality of the human soul, and its agency, by Ethan Allen Esq . . . This appendix to be Published at a future day when it will not infringe on my fortune or present living." *The Historical Magazine* (Morrisania, New York: Henry Dawson), 1873.

———. *Reason the Only Oracle of Man.* Bennington, Vermont: Haswell & Russell, 1784.

Duffy, John J., et al., eds. *Ethan Allen and His Kin: Correspondence, 1772–1819.* 2 vols. University Press of New England, 1998. [Abbreviated *EAK.*]

Graffagnino, J. Kevin, ed. *Ethan and Ira Allen: Collected Works.* 3 vols. Benson, Vermont: Chalidze Publications, 1992. [Abbreviated *EIA.*]

Bolingbroke

Bolingbroke, Henry St. John Lord Viscount. *The Works of Lord Bolingbroke.* 4 vols. Cary & Hart, 1841.

Bruno

Bruno, Jordano. *Opera Latine conscripta.* 3 vols. Morano, 1891.

Edwards

Edwards, Jonathan. *The Works of Jonathan Edwards.* Jonathan Edwards Center at Yale University, edwards.yale.edu.

Epicurus

Usener, Hermann, ed. *Epicurea.* Cambridge University Press, 2010. Principal translation consulted: Russell M. Geer, *Epicurus: Letters, Principal Doctrines, and Vatican Sayings.* Bobbs-Merrill, 1964. [Abbreviated as *Principal Doctrines* and *Vatican Sayings.*]

Franklin

Franklin, Benjamin. *Papers.* American Philosophical Society and Yale University, franklinpapers.org.

Freneau

Freneau, Philip Morin. *A Freneau Sampler.* Philip M. Marsh, ed. Scarecrow Press, 1963.

———. *The Poems of Philip Freneau: Poet of the American Revolution.* Fred Lewis Pattee, ed. 3 vols. Princeton University Library, 1903.

Gassendi

———. *Three Discourses of Happiness, Virtue, and Liberty.* Francois Bernier, unreliable translator, translated from French by "M. D." London: Awnsham & Churchil, 1699.

Hobbes

Hobbes, Thomas. *Leviathan.* Noel Malcolm, ed. 3 vols. Oxford University Press, 2012.

Jefferson
Boyd, Julian Parks, ed. *The Papers of Thomas Jefferson.* 40+ vols. Princeton University Press, 1950–.
Cappon, Lester J., ed. *The Adams-Jefferson Letters.* University of North Carolina Press, 1959.
Ford, Paul Leicester, ed. *Works of Thomas Jefferson.* 12 vols. Putnam, 1905.
Jefferson, Thomas. *Notes on the State of Virginia.* Frank Shuffleton, ed. Penguin Classics, 1998.
Peterson, Merrill D., ed. *Thomas Jefferson: Writings.* Library of America, 1984.
Wilson, Douglas L., ed. *Jefferson's Literary Commonplace Book.* Princeton University Press, 1989. [Abbreviated *Jefferson's LCB.*]

Locke
Locke, John. *An Essay concerning Human Understanding.* Ward, Lock & Bowden, 1909.
———. *Letter concerning Toleration.* William Popple, trans. London: Awnsham & Churchil, 1689.
———. *Two Treatises of Government.* Peter Laslett, ed. Cambridge University Press, 1960. [Abbreviated 1TG, 2TG.]
Nuovo, Victor, ed. *John Locke: Writings on Religion.* Oxford University Press, 2002.

Lucretius
Lucretius. *Titi Lucreti Cari De rerum natura libri sex.* Cyril Bailey, ed. 3 vols. Oxford University Press, 1947; *T. Lucreti Cari De rerum natura libri sex.* H. A. J. Munro, ed. Deighton Bell, 1866. Translations consulted include Martin Ferguson Smith, *Lucretius: On the Nature of Things.* Hackett, 2001; and A. E. Stallings, *Lucretius: The Nature of Things.* Penguin, 2007. [Abbreviated *DRN.*]

Madison
Hamilton, Alexander, James Madison, and John Jay. *The Federalist Papers.* Terence Ball, ed. Cambridge University Press, 2003.
Rakove, Jack N., ed. *James Madison: Writings.* Library of America, 1999.

Paine
Foner, Eric, ed. *Thomas Paine: Collected Writings.* Library of America, 1995.

Pope
Pope, Alexander. *Essay on Man.* In Pat Rogers, ed., *The Major Works.* Oxford University Press, 2008. [Abbreviated *EM.*]

Shaftesbury
Shaftesbury, Anthony Ashley Cooper, Third Earl of. *Characteristics of Men, Manners, Opinions, Times.* Lawrence E. Klein, ed. Cambridge University Press, 1999.

———. *The Life, Unpublished Letters, and Philosophical Regimen of Anthony, Earl of Shaftesbury*. Benjamin Rand, ed. Swan Sonnenschien, 1900.

Sidney
Sidney, Algernon. *Discourses concerning Government*. 2 vols. Hamilton & Balfour, 1750.

Spinoza
Spinoza, Benedict de. *Ethics*; *Tractatus Theologico-Politicus* [abbreviated *TTP*]; *Principles of the Cartesian Philosophy* [abbreviated *PCP*]; *Treatise on the Emendation of the Intellect* [abbreviated *TEI*]; *Treatise on Politics* [*TP*]; *Short Treatise* [abbreviated *ST*]; *Letters*. Principal translation consulted: *Spinoza: The Complete Works*. Samuel Shirley, trans. Hackett, 2002.

Trenchard and Gordon
Trenchard, John, and Thomas Gordon. *Cato's Letters*. Ronald Hamowy, ed. 2 vols. Liberty Fund, 1995.
———. *The Independent Whig: Four Volumes in One*. Richard Marsh, 1816.

Washington
Fitzpatrick, John Clement, ed. *Writings of Washington*. Government Printing Office, 1936.

Preface

1 See Leibniz, *New Essays on Human Understanding*, Peter Remnant and Jonathan Bennett, eds. (Cambridge University Press, 1996), pp. 59, 71–73.
2 The latest version of Wim Klever's manuscript in my possession is titled "Locke's Disguised Spinozism." If it is not published soon, I will post what I have on my website with his permission.
3 Matthew Stewart, *The Courtier and the Heretic* (W. W. Norton, 2006), pp. 265–68.
4 I should mention here the literature of Christian nationalism. I refer in particular to a set of writings and performances that began around 1980, when Jerry Falwell declared, "Our great nation was founded by godly men upon godly principles to be a Christian nation." Among the claims commonly made by Christian nationalists are, for example, that "the words 'separation of church and state' are nowhere in the Constitution"; that the founders kept God and religion out of the U.S. Constitution because they expected the states would pick up the slack; and that the founders intended to build a "one-way" wall, to keep the government out of religion but not the other way around. (See David Barton, *The Jefferson Lies* (withdrawn

from publication, 2012), *The Myth of Separation* (WallBuilder Press, 1992), *Original Intent* (WallBuilder Press, 2000), and any of the dozens of pamphlets, books, and videos produced by Barton's organization, WallBuilders; Gary DeMar, *America's Christian Heritage* (Broadman & Holman, 2003); John Eidsmoe, *Christianity and the Constitution* (Baker Books, 1987); and Tim La Haye, *Faith of Our Founding Fathers* (Master Books, 1994).)

When I first encountered the literature of Christian nationalism, I was eager to see what I might learn from a perspective that promised to reveal an America very different from the one I remembered growing up in. The main thing I learned is that large numbers of Americans are wedded to a version of American history that has little foundation in the facts. The other thing I learned is that there exists an army of writers who appear eager to encourage the public in its misapprehensions. One part of the Christian nationalist program—the least offensive part (to my mind), as old as the republic itself—is an effort to validate certain religious doctrines by finding evidence for them in history (or maybe just conferring on them the authority of the Founding Fathers). The other part—distinctly modern and frankly quite disturbing—is an attempt to legitimize a reactionary and authoritarian political project to "take back" the nation and make it what it never in fact was. America's resurgent Christian nationalists do not merely misread the American Revolution, I think; they betray it.

A good start on exposing the deceitful historiography of Christian nationalism has been made by, among others, Michelle Goldberg, *Kingdom Coming* (W. W. Norton, 2007); Jeff Sharlet, *The Family* (Harpers, 2008); Chris Rodda, *Liars for Jesus* (BookSurge, 2006); and Rob Boston, *Why the Religious Right Is Wrong about the Separation of Church and State* (Prometheus, 2003).

The new Christian nationalists represent a powerful force within American history, but their success consists chiefly in creating the illusion of a debate where in substance there is none. In 1959, Princeton historian R. R. Palmer could still write, "As for the leaders of the American Revolution, it should be unnecessary to demonstrate that most of them were deists." (Palmer, *The Age of Democratic Revolution* (Princeton University Press, 1959), 1.194.) In the "fair-and-balanced" media of the twenty-first century, on the other hand, the issue is invariably presented as a "debate" with two sides, while scholars tout their "even-handedness" by giving equal credence to every "narrative" of the history, however fatuous. A version of this false equivalence can be found in Mark David Hall, Daniel Dreisbach, and Jeffery Morrison, eds., *The Forgotten Founders on Religion and Public Life* (University of Notre Dame, 2009). To enter into that manufactured controversy, I think, is to impoverish our knowledge of both the past and the present. I continue to believe that the ideas behind the American Revolution are much more remarkable than the many false things that have been said about them.

5 Joel Barlow, "At the Meeting of the Connecticut Society of the Cincinnati" (1787), in William Bottorf, ed., *The Works of Joel Barlow* (Scholars Facsimiles, 1970), 1.19.

Chapter 1: The Dirty Little Screw of the American Revolution

1 I follow a number of Ethan Allen biographies on these details. See Stewart H. Holbrook, *Ethan Allen* (Macmillan, 1940); Charles A. Jellison, *Ethan Allen: Frontier Rebel* (Syracuse University Press, 1969); Michael A. Bellesiles, *Revolutionary Outlaws: Ethan Allen and the Struggle for Independence on the Early American Frontier* (University of Virginia Press, 1993); Willard Sterne Randall, *Ethan Allen: His Life and Times* (W. W. Norton, 2011); as well as the Ira Allen monograph in J. Kevin Graffagnino, ed., *Ethan and Ira Allen: Collected Works* (Benson, Vermont: Calidze Publications, 1992) [hereafter *EIA*], 3.1.

2 Ethan Allen to St. John de Crèvecoeur, March 2, 1786, in John J. Duffy et al., eds., *Ethan Allen and His Kin: Correspondence, 1772–1819* (University Press of New England, 1998) [hereafter *EAK*], 1.191.

3 Ethan Allen, *A Narrative of Colonel Ethan Allen's Captivity*, in *EIA*, 2.4.

4 Jellison, *Ethan Allen*, p. 119.

5 Or "Come out of there you damned old rat!" There are variations on the tale.

6 Washington to the President of Congress, May 12, 1778, in John Clement Fitzpatrick, ed., *Writings of Washington* (Government Printing Press, 1936), 11.381.

7 Holbrooke, *Ethan Allen*, p. 216.

8 Herman Melville, *Israel Potter* (New York: Putnam, 1855), ch. 22, p. 244.

9 Ethan Allen to Stephen R. Bradley, September 7, 1785, in *EAK*, 1.182.

10 See Bellesiles, *Revolutionary Outlaws*, p. 97; James Duane, *A Narrative of the Proceedings subsequent to the Royal Adjudication . . .* (New York, 1773), p. 15.

11 *Connecticut Courant*, April 27 and June 1, 1773.

12 Ethan Allen to Benjamin Stiles, November 16, 1785, in *EAK*, 1.185.

13 Ibid.

14 Josiah Sherman, *A Sermon to Swine: From Luke XV.16, containing a concise but sufficient answer to General Allen's Oracles of Reason* (Thomas Collier, 1787).

15 Timothy Dwight, "On the Doctrine of Chance," *American Museum* 2 (Philadelphia: October 1787): 410; also in *Daily Advertiser*, May 14, 1787.

16 Timothy Dwight, *The Triumph of Infidelity: A Poem* (Printed in the World, 1788), p. 23.

17 Nathan Perkins, *Narrative of a Tour through the State of Vermont*, 1789 (Elm Tree Press, 1920), p. 24.

18 Compare Samuel Williams, *Natural and Civil History of Vermont* (Burlington: Samuel Mills, 1809), 2.21. In Williams's account, written while the embers of revolution were still hot, Allen was "bold, enterprising, ambitious, with great confidence in his own abilities."

19 John Eliot, *A Biographical Dictionary containing a brief account of the first settlers etc.* (Boston: Edward Oliver, 1809), p. 25.

20 Jared Sparks, *The Library of American Biography* (Harper Brothers, 1853), 1.350. Sparks's judgment is not entirely negative by the way. He allows that Allen's *Oracles* is more ambitious and more successful in literary terms than any of his previous works, and that some of his opinions, such as on the immortality of the soul, though unoriginal, border on the acceptable, even inspirational.

21 Charles Walter Brown, *Ethan Allen, of Green Mountain Fame* (M. A. Donohue, 1902), p. 227.

22 Herman Melville, *Pierre: Or, the Ambiguities* (New York: Harper & Brothers, 1852), p. 462.

23 The co-author of the *Oracles of Reason* of 1693 was Charles Gildon, who was responsible for its preface and some other items. According to Lechler, Gildon put the book together from letters and manuscripts left behind by Blount after his death, which took place in 1693. (Gotthard Victor Lechler, *Geschichte des Englischen Deismus* (Cotta'Scher Verlag, 1841), p. 117.) The facts however are difficult to ascertain, and Gildon was by his own reckoning a disciple of Blount's (until he abruptly switched sides and renounced his earlier atheism), so I will continue to refer to the original *Oracles* as Blount's work.

24 Dwight, "On the Doctrine of Chance," p. 410.

25 Lecture delivered at Burlington on March 16, 1852, reprinted in *Vermont Historical Gazetteer* 1 (1867): 563–74.

26 See Jellison, *Ethan Allen*, p. 308; Brown, *Ethan Allen*, p. 233.

27 George Pomeroy Anderson, "Who Wrote 'Ethan Allen's Bible'?" *New England Quarterly* 10(4) (December 1937): 685–96. See also Dana Doten, "Ethan Allen's 'Original Something'," *New England Quarterly* 11(2) (June 1938): 361–66.

28 I am here indebted to Michael A. Bellesiles, "Works of Historical Faith: Or, Who Wrote *Reason The Only Oracle of Man?*" *Vermont History* 57 (1989): 69–83, who concludes his survey with the excellent question, "It is time to ask why, if there is not a single piece of evidence to the contrary, should we believe that anyone other than Ethan Allen wrote *Reason the Only Oracle of Man?*"

29 In the Public Record Office of the National Archives of the United Kingdom there is good evidence in support of this claim. In recorded testimony to the Privy Council on February 19, 1774, a sailor named Andrew Mackenzie said that at the town meeting beginning November 29, 1773,

"Dr. Young moved, that the Teas should be destroyed, and proposed that it should be done in the same way as was done at last." Captain James Hall, testifying in the same setting, said that Young was one of several "principal speakers, and that Dr. Young said the only way to get rid of the Tea was to throw it overboard and destroy it." Nathan Frazier, a merchant returning from Boston, said, "Mr Samuel Adams, John Hancock, and Dr. Young were present and spoke in support of the resolutions that passed at that Meeting" and "that he thinks a certain person proposed at the Meeting that the Tea should be destroyed. That he understood it was Dr. Young who made this Proposition, but the Body of the people declared against it." (National Archives of the United Kingdom, CO 5/763, ff.85, 89.) An unsigned document from the period, "Proceedings of ye Body Respecting the Tea," also suggests that Young was the first and only speaker at that meeting to propose destruction of the tea. See L. F. S. Upton, "Proceedings of Ye Body Respecting the Tea," *William and Mary Quarterly* 22(2) (April 1965): 287–300. See also Benjamin Woods Labaree, *The Boston Tea Party* (Oxford University Press, 1968), pp. 100–4.

30 Upton, "Proceedings of Ye Body Respecting the Tea"; Alfred F. Young, *The Shoemaker and the Tea Party* (Beacon Press, 1999), p. 102; John K. Alexander, *Samuel Adams* (Rowman & Littlefield, 2002), p. 126; Benjamin L. Carp, *Defiance of the Patriots: The Boston Tea Party and the Making of America* (Yale University Press, 2010).

31 Adams to Jefferson, August 24, 1815, in Lester J. Cappon, ed., *The Adams-Jefferson Letters* (University of North Carolina Press, 1959), p. 455.

32 Butterfield, L. H., ed., *The Diary and Autobiography of John Adams* (Belknap Press, 1962), 2.86.

33 See Joseph J. Ellis, *His Excellency* (Random House, 2005), pp. 61–63, who notes a curious "hiatus" between Washington's grumblings in 1769 about unfair British policies and his more strident comments beginning in 1774.

34 John Adams to Benjamin Waterhouse, January 30, 1818, in Charles Francis Adams, ed., *The Works of John Adams* (Little, Brown, 1856), 10.279.

35 Thomas Young to Hugh Hughes, March 2, 1770, in Huntington Library. Though alluding to scripture here, Young does not make the reference explicit. He tells Hughes three days later, "I do not trouble my friends with many quotations from Scripture."

36 See William Warner, *The Boston Committee of Correspondence and the Invention of a Public Machine for Revolutionary E(motion)* (University of Chicago Press, forthcoming); and Richard D. Brown, *Revolutionary Politics in Massachusetts: The Boston Committee of Correspondence and the Towns, 1772–74* (W. W. Norton, 1970).

37 Adams to Jedidiah Morse, December 22, 1815, in Adams, ed., *Works*, 10.196–97.

38 The formal title of the pamphlet in which this declaration was included is

The Votes and Proceedings of the Freeholders and other Inhabitants of the Town of Boston, In Town Meeting assembled, According to Law (Boston: Edes & Gill, 1772). It is commonly referred to as "the Boston Pamphlet." The first section is a statement of "the rights of the colonists," and the second a statement of "infringements and violations" of those rights. The first section of the Boston Declaration of 1772, redolent with high Lockean political theory, appears to have been principally the work of either Samuel Adams or James Otis or some combination of them and their peers. The case for Adams rests on the fact that an eight-bullet-point set of preparatory notes in his hand is preserved. The case for Otis follows from the content— something that John Adams must have sensed, for he attributed the work to Otis. Young was named to the subcommittee charged with drafting the second section of the Declaration, concerning the infringements of the colonists' rights. His handwriting is evident in one complete paragraph of that section, inserted at the end, and also on edits made to the existing draft, which is in the hand of a young copyist. From Young's other writings around the same time, it is also evident that he was in complete agreement with the ideas and authors cited in the first section of the pamphlet.

39 "So probable is it that Rush's medical and political assistants knew each other, that it is tempting to look for some share by Young in the pamphlet *Common Sense*," says Henry Noble MacCracken, in *Old Dutchess Forever!* (Hastings, 1956), p. 323. Paine's writing style is distinctive and personal, and it seems implausible that anyone but he actually wrote the pamphlet. But his ideas—the absolute rejection of monarchy and of the British Constitution, the proposal for a new unicameral, legislative democracy, the characterization of Norman's conquerors as "banditti," the call for independence—are all the stuff of Young's earlier work, and so it seems reasonable to speculate that Paine (who after all had arrived in America only a year and a half previously) owed a substantial intellectual debt to his new friend.

40 Richard Alan Ryerson, *The Revolution Is Now Begun* (University of Pennsylvania Press, 1978), p. 206.

41 John Adams to Samuel Perley, June 19, 1809, in Adams, ed., *Works*, 9.623.

42 Ira Allen, "A Natural History of Vermont," in *EIA*, 3.47.

43 Thomas Young to Hugh Hughes, May 17, 1770, in Huntington Library.

44 Thomas Young to Samuel Adams, September 4, 1774, in William V. Wells, *The Life and Public Services of Sam Adams* (Little, Brown, 1865), and NYPL BCC.

45 Young to Hughes, May 17, 1770.

46 Ira Allen, "Natural History of Vermont."

47 "Vindex," *Boston Gazette*, November 30, 1772.

48 These and other epithets are collected in Pauline Maier, "Reason and Revolution: The Radicalism of Dr. Thomas Young," *American Quarterly*

28(2) (Special Issue, Summer 1976): 229–49; and David Freeman Hawke, "Dr. Thomas Young—'Eternal Fisher in Troubled Waters'," *New-York Historical Society Quarterly* 54 (1970): 6–29. The "eternal fisher in troubled waters" comes from John Adams to Benjamin Rush, February 8, 1789, in *Old Family Letters: Copied from the Originals for Alexander Biddle* (Philadelphia: Lippincott, 1892), p. 30. A number of other phrases ("Apollo of the ignorant") come from articles written by Joseph Warren and other rival doctors, such as in *Boston Gazette*, July 6, 1767. Warren intervened in a medical dispute against Young, but the pair made up and later Warren retracted the insults.

49 Adams to Rush, February 8, 1789.

50 See in particular Maier, "Reason and Revolution"; Maier, *The Old Revolutionaries* (Alfred A. Knopf, 1980); and William Hogeland, *Declaration* (Simon & Schuster, 2010).

51 Henry H. Edes, "Memoir of Dr. Thomas Young, 1731–1777," *Colonial Society of Massachusetts, Transactions 1906–7*, 11 (1910), p. 29.

52 Town of Barnstable to William Molineux, March 11–19, 1773, in NYPL BCC.

53 Edes, "Memoir of Dr. Thomas Young," p. 49.

54 Ira Allen to Samuel Williams, June 6, 1795, in *EAK*, 2.443.

55 Unsigned letter to George Benedict, May 29, 1840, cited in Bellesiles, "Works of Historical Faith," p. 73.

56 These biographical details from Jefferson, "Autobiography: 1743–1790," January 6, 1821, in Paul Leicester Ford, ed., *Works of Thomas Jefferson* (Putnam, 1905), 1.1–160.

57 Jefferson to John Adams, June 10, 1815, in Cappon, ed., *Adams-Jefferson Letters*, p. 443.

58 Jefferson to Lucy Ludwell Paradise, June 1, 1789, in Julian Parks Boyd, ed., *The Papers of Thomas Jefferson* (Princeton University Press, 1958), 15.163.

59 The copy bears no personal marks from Jefferson, so we cannot know if he read it, but most of Jefferson's books are devoid of marginalia.

60 Jefferson to Peter Carr, August 10, 1787, in Boyd, ed., *Papers* (1950), 2.215.

61 Jefferson to Ezra Stiles, June 25, 1819, in Albert Ellery Bergh, ed., *The Writings of Thomas Jefferson* (Jefferson Memorial Association, 1907), 15.202.

62 See Gustav Adolf Koch, *Religion of the American Enlightenment* (Crowell, 1933), who makes a similar point and to whom I am indebted for this insight.

63 Ford, ed., *Works*, 1.453–63.

64 A full half century after writing this essay, Jefferson repeated its arguments in precise detail for the benefit of one of his correspondents. After lining up a rogue's gallery of legal authorities who colluded in ignoring the inconvenient truth about the pre-Christian origins of British common law,

the elder Jefferson exclaimed, "What a conspiracy this, between Church and State!" (Jefferson to Maj. John Cartwright, June 5, 1824, in Merrill D. Peterson, ed., *Thomas Jefferson: Writings* (Library of America, 1984), p. 1490.)

65 Franklin to the Royal Academy of Brussels, May 19, 1780, in Benjamin Franklin, *Papers* (American Philosophical Society and Yale University, franklinpapers.org), 32.396.

66 Franklin, *Autobiography*, part 2, in *Papers*.

67 Ibid., part 6.

68 Richard Bentley, *The Folly of Atheism and (what is now called) Deism* (London: Mortlock, 1693).

69 Joseph Priestley, *Autobiography of Joseph Priestley* (Adams & Dart, 1775), p. 117.

70 Jonathan Edwards, *The Works of Jonathan Edwards, D.D.* (Boston: Doctrinal Tract Society, 1850), 2.524.

71 Franklin to Ezra Stiles, March 9, 1790, in Franklin, *Papers* (unpublished).

72 Lyman Beecher, *Autobiography, Correspondence, Etc.* (Harper Brothers, 1864), 1.43.

73 Cited in Henry May, *The Enlightenment in America* (Oxford University Press, 1976), p. 247.

74 See Woodbridge Riley, *American Philosophy: The Early Schools* (Dodd, Mead, 1907), p. 217; and Gustav Adolf Koch, *Religion of the American Enlightenment* (Crowell, 1933).

75 Abraham Taylor, "The insufficiency of natural religion," in *A Defense of Some Important Doctrines of the Gospel* (London: A. Ward, 1732).

76 Robert Beverley, *The History of Virginia in Four Parts* (London: B & S. Tooke, 1722). One Indian helpfully explained to Beverley why his people do not worship God directly: "God is the Giver of all good Things, but they flow naturally and promiscuously from him . . . [T]hey are shower'd down upon all Men indifferently without Distinction . . . God does not trouble himself with the impertinent Affairs of Men . . . but leaves them to make the most of their free Will . . . The Priests and Conjurers have a great Sway in every Nation." Compare also William Bartram, *Travels through North & South Carolina* (Philadelphia: James & Johnson, 1791). Crèvecoeur reports that over the door of his greenhouse, John Bartram had inscribed the couplet from Pope referring to "Nature's God." (Crèvecoeur, *Letters from an American Farmer* (Doubleday, 1782), p. 265.) In 1741, John Webbe repeated Beverley's feat, publishing a deistic speech allegedly delivered by an Indian chief in *American Magazine*. In 1752, James Parker republished the native philosopher's piece in the *New York Gazette*. See A. Owen Aldridge, "Natural Religion and Deism in America before Ethan Allen and Thomas Paine," *William and Mary Quarterly* 54(4) (October 1997): 835–48.

77 Cited in Woodbridge Riley, *American Philosophy: The Early Schools* (Dodd, Mead, 1907), pp. 213, 317.

78 Perkins, *Narrative of a Tour through the State of Vermont*, pp. 19, 26.

79 Cited in Gustav Adolf Koch, *Republican Religion* (Holt, 1933), p. 323; Bryan Waterman, *The Friendly Club of New York City* (Johns Hopkins University Press, 2007).

80 Cited in Eric Foner, *Tom Paine and Revolutionary America* (Oxford University Press, 1976), p. 118.

81 Cited in Thomas C. Thompson, "Perceptions of a Deist Church in Early National Virginia," in Garrett Ward Sheldon, ed., *Religion and Political Culture in Jefferson's Virginia* (Rowan & Littlefield, 2000), p. 44.

82 John Randolph to Henry Middleton Rutledge, July 24, 1815, in May, *Enlightenment in America*, p. 330.

83 What Washington really believed is famously impossible to establish with any great certainty. What Jefferson believed that Washington believed, on the other hand, can be established with reasonably high confidence. In a diary entry from February 1, 1800, Jefferson passed along intelligence from Benjamin Rush and Ashbel Green, Washington's minister, that Washington was not a Christian but a deist. Then he added, "I know that Gouverneur Morris, who pretended to be in his secrets & believed himself to be so, has often told me that Gen'l. Washington believed no more of that system [the Christian religion] than he himself did." Jefferson's tone makes clear that he thought this assessment was likely accurate and reflected well on Washington. Ashbel Green later denied having questioned Washington's religious orthodoxy; yet other sources appear to confirm that he put out the intelligence he wished to retract. (Ford, ed., *Works*, 1.352–53.)

84 Adams to Benjamin Waterhouse, October 29, 1805, in Worthington Chauncey Ford, ed., *Statesman and Friend: Correspondence of John Adams with Benjamin Waterhouse* (Little, Brown, 1927), p. 31.

85 Butterfield, ed., *Diary*, 3.261–62.

86 Steven Waldman, *Founding Faith* (Random House, 2008), p. 35.

87 "A strong correlation between the most extreme reformers and heterodoxy, is the more striking result of recent inquiry, both in England and colonial America," writes historian Jonathan Clark, in *English Society, 1660–1832* (Cambridge University Press, 2000). David Hume, looking back at the struggles emerging from England's Glorious Revolution of 1688, thought it self-evident that "the leaders of the Whigs have either been Deists or professed Latitudinarians in their principles; that is friends to toleration, and indifferent to any sect of Christians." (Hume, "Of Superstition and Enthusiasm," in *Essays and Treatises* (T. Cadell, 1788), 1.69.)

88 See Scott L. Pratt and John Ryder, eds., *The Philosophical Writings of Cadwallader Colden* (Humanity Books, 2002), esp. pp. 96–97.

89 "We formed our Constitution without any acknowledgment of God," declaimed Timothy Dwight from his perch at Yale; and we would soon pay in blood for the "sinful character of the nation." (Timothy Dwight, *A Discourse in Two Parts, delivered July 23, 1812* (New Haven: Howe & DeForest, 1812), p. 46.) "There is not only in the theory of our government no recognition of God's laws and sovereignty, but its practical operation, its administration, has been conformable to its theory," said Bird Wilson. (John Eleazer Remsburg, *Six Historic Americans* (Truth Seeker, 1906), p. 120.)

90 In at least one court case in Boston in the 1730s, the writings of the most influential British thinkers of the period were denounced as being in "direct contradiction to the Holy Scriptures" and as the work of "Deistical Republicans." David Hume specifically identified James Harrington and Algernon Sidney—two of the most prominent republican theorists, the latter particularly influential in the American colonies—as deists "who denied utterly the truth of revelation, and insinuated, that all the various sects, so heated against each other, were alike founded in folly and error." By the time Franklin returned from France in the 1780s, the link between radical politics and religious heterodoxy was so firm that his detractors could lambaste him in one breath on account of his "deisms and democracies." See Isabel Rivers, *Reason, Grace, and Sentiment* (Cambridge University Press, 2000), p. 319.

91 Philip Morin Freneau, "On the Prospect of a Revolution in France," 1790, in Fred Lewis Pattee, ed., *The Poems of Philip Freneau: Poet of the American Revolution* (Princeton University Library, 1903), 2.385.

92 Jefferson to Tench Coxe, January 1, 1795, in Boyd, ed., *Papers* (2000), 28.373.

93 There are acres within the world's libraries dedicated to this subject, which would take us outside the scope of this book. I will however sketch my view, which I think differs from that of much of the literature. In France, the revolutionaries confronted a king on his own soil; they faced a single, overwhelmingly powerful religious organization in the Catholic Church; they came from a people with little experience in self-government; and they were met with an army of counterrevolutionaries who, unlike America's loyalists, had no other outposts of empire to which they might flee. As a result of these very different circumstances, the French Revolution took a very different course than the American one, and its practice (especially with Robespierre) diverged dramatically from its original principles. If we look back to the Enlightenment that first generated those principles in the years preceding the French Revolution, however, the differences between the American and French philosophies become inconsequential, essentially stylistic rather than theoretical, having to do, as Jefferson himself noted, mainly with the overwhelming presence of Catholicism in France.

John Quincy Adams, on the other hand, was one of many who sought to rescue the American Revolution from "the disgraceful imputation" that its principles were those of the French.

94 Franklin to Samuel Mather, July 7, 1773, in Franklin, *Papers*, 20.286.

95 Franklin to Ezra Stiles, March 9, 1790, in Franklin, *Papers* (unpublished).

96 Jefferson to Francis Eppes, January 19, 1821, in Ford, ed., *Works*, 12.194.

97 Jefferson to John Adams, January 11, 1817, in Cappon, ed., *Adams-Jefferson Letters*, p. 506.

98 See Jefferson's diary entry from February 1, 1800, in Ford, ed., *Works*, 1.352–53.

99 Cornelis de Witt, *Jefferson and the American Democracy*, R. S. H. Church, trans. (London: Longman, Green, 1862), p. 17.

100 Jill Lepore, in *The Whites of Their Eyes* (Princeton University Press, 2010), p. 146, says Mercy Otis Warren relegated Paine to a footnote.

101 Jefferson to Benjamin Rush, September 23, 1800, in Boyd, ed., *Papers* (2005), 32.166.

102 See Frank Lambert, *The Founding Fathers and the Place of Religion in America* (Princeton University Press, 2003); Susan Jacoby, *Freethinkers* (Metropolitan Books, 2004); David L. Holmes, *The Faiths of the Founding Fathers* (Oxford University Press, 2006); Steven Waldman, *Founding Faiths* (Random House, 2008); Kerry S. Walters, *The American Deists* (University Press of Kansas, 1992), *Rational Infidels* (Longwood, 1992), and *Benjamin Franklin and His Gods*, (University of Illinois Press, 1999); Daniel J. Boorstin, *The Lost World of Thomas Jefferson* (University of Chicago Press, 1948); A. Owen Aldridge, *Benjamin Franklin and Nature's God* (Duke University Press, 1967); and Charles A. Miller, *Jefferson and Nature* (Johns Hopkins University Press, 1988).

Chapter 2: Pathologies of Freedom

1 Edmund Massey, *A Sermon against the dangerous and sinfull practice of inoculation* (London, 1722).

2 The allegation appears to come from Robert G. Ingersoll, *The Works of Robert G. Ingersoll* (Farrell, 1900), 1.289. Note that opinion on the subject of inoculation evolved over time and did not consistently divide along theological lines. In the early eighteenth century, the Boston prelate Cotton Mather was the first champion of inoculation, whereas the opposition came from doctors suspicious of the practice. James Franklin covered the controversy in his newspaper, siding more or less with the doctors, but mostly because he opposed pretty much anything that Mather supported. By the 1760s, the opposition in many areas, where it was not merely tactical, came mainly from religious conservatives, and support came from those who viewed themselves as partisans of the Enlightenment. In Bos-

ton, on the other hand, the practice was widely accepted, and John Adams was part of a large program of inoculation at the time.

3 Charles A. Jellison, *Ethan Allen: Frontier Rebel* (Syracuse University Press, 1969), p. 9; Willard Sterne Randall, *Ethan Allen: His Life and Times* (W. W. Norton, 2011), p. 121.

4 See Jellison, *Ethan Allen*; and Michael A. Bellesiles, *Revolutionary Outlaws: Ethan Allen and the Struggle for Independence on the Early American Frontier* (University of Virginia Press, 1993).

5 See *View from Mount Holyoke, Northampton, Massachusetts* (also known as *The Oxbow*), a painting by Thomas Cole, 1836, Metropolitan Museum of Art.

6 Two indispensable texts on Edwards are George M. Marsden, *Jonathan Edwards: A Life* (Yale University Press, 2004); and John E. Smith et al., *A Jonathan Edwards Reader* (Yale University Press, 1995). See also Nathan O. Hatch et al., *Jonathan Edwards and the American Experience* (Oxford University Press, 1989); and Alan Heimert, *Religion and the American Mind* (Harvard University Press, 1966).

7 Cited in Gordon Wood, *The Radicalism of the American Revolution* (Vintage, 1993), p. 19.

8 Jonathan Edwards, *Diary*, in *The Works of Jonathan Edwards* (Jonathan Edwards Center at Yale University, edwards.yale.edu), entries for January 10 and 14, February 23, and March 2, 1723.

9 Marsden, *Jonathan Edwards*, p. 193.

10 Edwards refers to the "city upon a hill" in some of his sermons—but usually as a way of contrasting the decadent reality of his own time with an ideal.

11 Jonathan Edwards, *A Faithful Narrative of the Surprising Works of God*, 1737, in *Works*, 4.99ff.

12 Jonathan Edwards, "God Glorified in Man's Dependence," in *Works*, 17.200ff.

13 Edwards, *Faithful Narrative of the Surprising Works of God*.

14 Richard Hofstadter, *America at 1750: A Social History* (Alfred A. Knopf, 1971), p. 236.

15 Ibid., p. 243.

16 Franklin, *Pennsylvania Gazette*, November 20, 1729.

17 These and other biographical details in Henry H. Edes, "Memoir of Dr. Thomas Young, 1731–1777," *Colonial Society of Massachusetts, Transactions 1906–7*, 11(1910): 10–14.

18 See Jellison, *Ethan Allen*,, pp. 11ff.

19 Ethan Allen, *Reason the Only Oracle of Man* (Bennington, Vermont: Haswell & Russell, 1784), p. 81.

20 Benjamin Franklin, *Papers* (American Philosophical Society and Yale University, franklinpapers.org), 1.14.

21 Paine, *Rights of Man*, part 2, in Eric Foner, ed., *Thomas Paine: Collected Writings* (Library of America, 1995), p. 604.

22 Jonathan Edwards, "God's Excellencies," in *Works*, 10.421.

23 Jonathan Edwards, "Sinners in the Hands of an Angry God," in *Works*, 22.405ff.

24 Quoted in Richard Hofstadter, *America at 1750: A Social History* (Alfred A. Knopf, 1971), p. 233.

25 Charles Chauncy, *Seasonable Thoughts on the State of Religion in New England* (Boston: Rogers & Fowle, 1743), p. 106; also note "groaning, crying out, falling down, and screaming." (Ibid., p. 78.)

26 Marsden, *Jonathan Edwards*, pp. 244–48; S. E. Dwight, *The Life of President Edwards* (New York: Carvill, 1830), pp. 171ff.

27 Jonathan Edwards, "A Faithful Narrative," in *Works*, 4.207.

28 Young, "For the Massachusetts Spy," *Massachusetts Spy*, November 19, 1772.

29 Paine, *The Age of Reason*, in Foner, ed., *Thomas Paine*, p. 702.

30 Franklin, *Autobiography*, part 6, in *Papers*.

31 Cited in Philip Dray, *Stealing God's Thunder* (Random House, 2005), p. 15.

32 Franklin, *Autobiography*, part 3, in *Papers*.

33 Ira Allen to Samuel Williams, June 6, 1795, in John J. Duffy et al., eds., *Ethan Allen and His Kin: Correspondence, 1772–1819* (University Press of New England, 1998) [hereafter *EAK*], 1.443.

34 Allen, *Reason the Only Oracle of Man*, p. 386.

35 Ibid., p. 301.

36 Ibid., p. 77.

37 Jefferson to John Adams, April 11, 1823, in Lester J. Cappon, ed., *The Adams-Jefferson Letters* (University of North Carolina Press, 1959), p. 591.

38 Adams to Jefferson, September 12, 1813, in ibid., p. 374.

39 Quoted in Stephen Lalor, *Matthew Tindal: Freethinker* (Continuum, 2006), p. 4. No doubt Samuel Johnson had his eye fixed on the likes of William Livingston and the scoffing crowd gathering around his new magazine, *The Independent Reflector*, which was consciously modeled on the work of the radical Whigs John Trenchard and Thomas Gordon, and whose purpose, Johnson thought, was to make of the new King's College (now Columbia University) something of a "free-thinking latitudinarian seminary." (Samuel Johnson, *Samuel Johnson: His Career and Writings* (Columbia University Press, 1929), p. 4; see Thomas Pangle, *The Spirit of Modern Republicanism* (University of Chicago Press, 1988), p. 23.)

40 David Hume, "Of Superstition and Enthusiasm," in *Essays and Treatises* (T. Cadell, 1788), 1.69.

41 Denis Diderot, *Pensees philosophiques*, sec. 53; see *Diderot's Early Philosophical Works*, Margaret Jourdain, trans. (Open Court, 1911), pp. 60–62.

42 Henry Noble MacCracken, *Old Dutchess Forever!* (Hastings, 1956), pp. 321ff.

43 "Socrates to the Athenians," *Boston Evening Post*, May 18, 1767.

44 "St. Paul to the Athenians," *Boston Evening Post*, May 25, 1767.

45 Jonathan Edwards, *A Dissertation concerning the Nature of True Virtue*, in *Works*, 1.128; see Alan Heimert, *Religion and the American Mind* (Harvard University Press, 1966), p. 52. Note that the more time elapsed after the revival, the more Edwards modified his millenarian tendencies, turning what at first read like definite predictions of an imminent end of the world to more general claims about a cyclical renewal of faith. The concern here, in any case, is with the communitarian aspect of Edwards's thought, which consistently led him to see the renewal of faith and the unity of the community as the same thing.

46 Ibid., 2.287.

47 Jonathan Edwards, "An Humble Attempt," in *Works*, 2.281.

48 As Gordon Wood has pointed out, the revivals of the first half of the eighteenth century "were often diverse, complicated, and local in origins, but in general they grew out of people's attempts to adjust to the disturbing changes in their social relationships caused by demographic and commercial developments." (Wood, *Radicalism of the American Revolution*, p. 144.)

49 Jonathan Edwards, letter of 1750, cited in Dwight, *Life of President Edwards*, p. 306.

50 Thomas Hobbes, "The Life of Thomas Hobbes," J. E. Parsons and Whitney Blair, trans., *Interpretation* 10 (January 1982): 1–3.

51 Cited in Bernard Bailyn, ed., *Pamphlets of the American Revolution, 1750–1776* (Harvard University Press, 1965), p. 204.

52 Jonathan Mayhew, *Two Sermons on . . . Divine Goodness* (Boston, 1762), p. 38.

53 Jonathan Mayhew, *Seven Sermons* (Boston, 1749), pp. 145–46.

54 "Shunned by the ministers" and "dreaded by the orthodox," Mayhew was ordained in 1747 in a ceremony notable for the absence of any member of the local clergy. For many years thereafter, no minister dared to exchange pulpits with him (a common practice of the time, to relieve congregations of the boredom of hearing the same pastor every week). (George Willis Cooke, *Unitarianism in America* (American Unitarian Association, 1910), p. 61.)

55 The French consul and explorer Crèvecoeur provided a useful theory to explain the process. In a growing, pluralistic, and inherently democratic country, he noted, new sects flare up regularly and spectacularly. Each one claims to have the answer to all human concerns and wins enthusiastic converts. But every answer is inevitably different. As sectarians move around in the expanding country, they naturally bump into other sectarians, not to mention lukewarm believers and unbelievers. Upon encountering reasonable fellow countrymen of very dissimilar persuasions, their ardor for their own sect either cools or turns inward. Children, seeing that no ill comes to their playmates by virtue of the sectarian differences among the

elders, "grow up less zealous and more indifferent in matters of religion than their parents." All of these effects, Crèvecoeur maintained, are more pronounced on the frontier, and so it happens that as one recedes farther from the sea in America, "religion seems to have still less influence." The end result is that "the Americans become as to religion, what they are as to country, allied to all." "The general indulgence," he added, "leaves every one to think for themselves in spiritual matters; the laws inspect our actions, our thoughts are left to God." (J. Hector St. John de Crèvecoeur, *Letters from an American Farmer* (Doubleday, 1782), pp. 58–62.)

56 Adams to Thomas Jefferson, April 19, 1817, in Cappon, ed., *Adams-Jefferson Letters*, p. 509.

57 Charles Francis Adams, *History of Braintree, Massachusetts* (Riverside Press, 1891), pp. 47–56.

58 Ibid., p. 51.

59 Adams to Aaron Bancroft, January 21, 1823, in *Proceedings of the Massachusetts Historical Society* (Massachusetts Historical Society, 1894), p. 91.

60 L. H. Butterfield, ed., *The Diary and Autobiography of John Adams* (Belknap Press, 1962), 3.262.

61 Adams to Richard Cranch, October 18, 1756, in Robert J. Taylor et al., ed., *The Papers of John Adams* (Harvard University Press, 1977), 1.21.

62 Marsden, *Jonathan Edwards*, p. 449.

63 In a typical newspaper essay, Young writes, "People of the lower ranks among the Saxons had actually great privileges and a very free spirit." (Libermoriturus, *Boston Evening Post*, November 9, 1767.) Whig historians who peddled this kind of story included Paul de Rapin Thoyras, *The History of England*, N. Tindal, trans. (London: Knapton, 1726); Sir John Dalrymple, *An Essay towards a General History of Feudal Property in Great Britain* (London: Millar, 1758); Obadiah Hulme, *An Historical Essay on the English Constitution* (London: Dilly, 1771); and Henry Care and William Nelson, *English Liberties* (London: Bettesworth, 1719).

64 "The writings of Trenchard and Gordon ranked with the treatises of Locke as the most authoritative statement of the nature of political liberty, and above Locke as an exposition of the social sources of the threats it faced." Bernard Bailyn, *The Ideological Origins of the American Revolution* (Harvard University Press, 1967), p. 36. See also Carline Robbins, *The Eighteenth Century Commonwealthman* (Harvard University Press, 1959); and Heather E. Barry, *A Dress Rehearsal for the Revolution: John Trenchard and Thomas Gordon's Works in Eighteenth Century America* (University Press of America, 2007).

65 Philodemus, *Boston Evening Post*, September 21, 1767.

66 Voltaire, *We Must Take Sides, or The Principle of Action*, 1755, sec. 16., in Joseph McCabe, trans., *Toleration and Other Essays by Voltaire* (Putnam, 1912).

67 The history of the reception of the *Essay on Man* is long and full of injustice. The interpretation of the poem has fallen victim to the perennial war between poetry and philosophy: poets detect in it the unwelcome odor of philosophy, while philosophers complain of the stench of poetry. See Harry M. Solomon, *The Rape of the Text: Reading and Misreading Pope's Essay on Man* (University of Alabama Press, 1993).

68 Thomas Young to Abigail Dwight, February 13, 1767, in Massachusetts Historical Society.

69 Ezra Stiles, *The United States Elevated to Glory and Honor* (New Haven, 1783), in John Wingate Thornton, ed., *The Pulpit of the American Revolution* (Lincoln & Gould, 1860), p. 498.

70 Cited in Douglas L. Wilson, ed., *Jefferson's Literary Commonplace Book* (Princeton University Press, 1989) [hereafter *Jefferson's LCB*], p. 156.

71 John Leland, *A View of the Principal Deistical Writers* (London: Charles Daly, 1754), p. 299.

72 Timothy Dwight, *The Nature and Danger of Infidel Philosophy*, Richard D. McCormack, ed. (RDMc Publishing, 2001), p. 47.

73 Henry St. John Lord Vincent Bolingbroke, *The Works of Lord Bolingbroke* (Carey & Hart, 1841), 4.263; *Jefferson's LCB*, sec. 42, also 14.

74 *Jefferson's LCB*, sec. 42.

75 Woodbridge Riley, *American Philosophy: The Early Schools* (Dodd, Mead, 1907), p. 213.

76 Paine, *Age of Reason*, in Foner, ed., *Thomas Paine*, p. 701. See Benjamin Martin, *The Philosophical Grammar* (London: John Noon, 1755); and James Ferguson, *The Idea of the Material Universe* (London, 1754).

77 Crèvecoeur, *Letters from an American Farmer*, p. 64.

78 Timothy Dwight, *A Discourse, in Two Parts, Delivered July 23, 1812, on the Public Fast*, (Howe & Defroest, 1812), p. 24.

79 Hume, "Of Superstition and Enthusiasm," in *Essays*, 1.69.

80 John Locke, *Letter concerning Toleration* (London: Awnsham & Churchil, 1689), p. 17.

81 Adams to John Taylor, April 15, 1814, in Charles Francis Adams, ed., *The Works of John Adams* (Little, Brown, 1856), 6.517.

82 Thomas Jefferson, *Notes on the State of Virginia*, Frank Shuffleton, ed. (Penguin Classics, 1998), Query 17.

83 Madison worked as hard as anybody to bring in the support of religious dissenters for the new religious freedoms; but in the debate over the Constitution, he specifically excluded the appeal to religion as the foundation of toleration: "Religion itself may become a motive to persecution & oppression." (Madison, "Speech" at Constitutional Convention, June 6, 1787, in Jack N. Rakove, ed., *James Madison: Writings* (Library of America, 1999), p. 93.) As he explained to Jefferson, "Enthusiasm is only a temporary state of religion, and whilst it lasts will hardly be seen with pleasure

at the helm. Even in its coolest state, it has been much oftener a motive to oppression than a restraint from it." (Madison to Jefferson, October 24, 1787, in ibid., p. 151.)

84 Edmund Randolph, *History of Virginia* (University of Virginia Press, 1970), pp. 182–83, cited in Paul Rahe, *Republics Ancient and Modern* (University of North Carolina Press, 1994), 3.53.

85 Young, "To Sir Aaron Davis," *Massachusetts Spy*, December 4, 1772.

86 Alan Heimert, *Religion and the American Mind* (Harvard University Press, 1966), is perhaps the *locus classicus* of this argument, though it has never gone away. See also Steven Waldman, *Founding Faiths* (Random House, 2008); and Patricia Bonomi, *Under the Cope of Heaven* (Oxford University Press, 2003). Historians who fall back on the "majority rule" equals "Protestant nation" trope include T. H. Breen, *American Insurgents, American Patriots: The Revolution of the People* (Farrar, Straus & Giroux, 2010); Jack Rakove, *Revolutionaries* (Houghton Mifflin, 2010); and to some extent Gordon Wood.

87 In the work of the English theologian and Christian apologist William Paley (1743–1805), one could claim to find a version of Christian deism. But Paley's work arrived late on the scene, and it wasn't deism at all in the sense associated here with America's founders.

88 Thomas Young, "Philodicaios," in *Some Reflections on the Disputes between New-York, New-Hampshire, and Col. John Henry Lydius of Albany* (New Haven: Benjamin Mecom, 1764), p. 16.

Chapter 3: Epicurus's Dangerous Idea

1 Timothy Dwight maintained that Ethan Allen's *Oracles* of 1784 was "the first formal publication in the United States openly directed against the Christian religion." (Timothy Dwight, *Travels in New England and New York* (Harvard University Press, 1969), 2.283.) I borrow this and the claim concerning the Natural Man's priority from A. Owen Aldridge, "Natural Religion and Deism in America before Ethan Allen and Thomas Paine," *William and Mary Quarterly* 54(4) (October 1997): 835–48.

2 1 Corinthians 2:14.

3 See Charles Miller, *Jefferson and Nature* (Johns Hopkins University Press, 1988), p. 23.

4 Jefferson to William Short, October 31, 1819, in Paul Leicester Ford, ed., *Works of Thomas Jefferson* (Putnam, 1905), 12.140.

5 See Virgil, *Eclogues*, VI, and *Georgics*, II. "Echoes of Lucretius's verse are heard in almost every page of his, and phrases of Lucretius's, vivid as a lightning flash, stand out from the more subdued coloring of Virgil's poetry." John Masson, *Lucretius: Epicurean and Poet* (London: Murray, 1907), 1.68.

6 See Stephen Greenblatt, *The Swerve* (W. W. Norton, 2011).

7 Adams to F. A. Van der Kemp, March 3, 1804, in Charles Adams, ed., *The Works of John Adams* (Little, Brown, 1856), 9.588.

8 I am greatly indebted in the following to Catherine Wilson, *Epicureanism at the Origins of Modernity* (Clarendon Press, 2008). On Ficino, Machiavelli, and the reception of Lucretius in Renaissance Italy, see Alison Brown, *The Return of Lucretius to Renaissance Florence* (Harvard University Press, 2010).

9 Desiderius Erasmus, "The Epicurean," in *The Colloquies* (London: Reeves & Turner, 1878), 2.326.

10 Desiderius Erasmus, *The Praise of Folly* (Hendricks House, 1959), p. 95.

11 See Jean-Charles Darmon, *Philosophie Epicurienne et literature au xviie siècle en France* (Presses Universitaires de France, 1998), for a good case that Epicurus is more fundamental to Montaigne than his occasional references and allusions might make it seem.

12 Though he rejected the infinite universe, Francis Bacon cited Lucretius's words in supporting the doctrine of atomism—attributing them to the somewhat less controversial Democritus. Francis Bacon, "Thoughts on the Nature of Things," in James Spedding and Robert Leslie Ellis, eds., *The Works of Francis Bacon* (Taggard & Thompson, 1864), 10.280, 291. Also, compare "Of Atheism" with "Of Superstition" in Bacon, *Essays or Counsels* (London: Whittaker, 1854), ch. 16–17, pp. 81–85.

13 The allusions are not precise, but curious: "infinite space . . . nutshell"; "words, words, words"; "more things in heaven and earth than are dreamt of in your philosophy"; "what is this quintessence of dust?"; "nothing good or bad but thinking make it so." Bruno temporarily resided in England in the 1580s and made a splash among the kind of people Shakespeare might have known.

14 Bruno himself credits Nicholas of Cusa (1401–1464), the German cardinal, scientist, and humanist, for having taught the doctrine of the infinite universe, and Cusa may have picked it up from Lucretius. But his treatment of the issue and his philosophy in general fall far short of Bruno's.

15 Lucretius, *De rerum natura* [hereafter *DRN*], 1.73, 5.8.

16 Bruno, *The Ash Wednesday Supper*, Edward A. Gosselin and Lawrence S. Lerner, trans. (University of Toronto Press, 1995), p. 90.

17 Voetius, cited by Pierre Bayle, *A General Dictionary, Historical and Critical* (London: J. Bettenham, 1739), 8.449.

18 Marin Mersenne, *L'Impiete des Deistes, et des plus subtils Libertins* (Paris: Pierre Billaine, 1624), p. 512; Emile Namer, *La vie et ouvrage de J.C. Vanini* (Vrin, 1980), p. 155; Richard Popkin, *The History of Scepticism*, 3rd ed. (Oxford University Press, 2003), pp. 85ff.

19 Matthew Tindal, among many others, repeats the version of the story passed along by Bayle, according to which Vanini's death shows the paradoxical commitment of the atheist to give his life to spread truth among the people.

20 There is some dispute among scholars about whether the dinner took place in 1647 or 1648, whether there was more than one dinner, and where it or they took place at all. There is also a story that Gassendi was too sick to make the dinner, but that the guests marched over to his house and embraced him in bed. There isn't much doubt that Gassendi and Hobbes were friends, in any case, and that they both had personal as well as philosophical disagreements with Descartes. See Lisa T. Sarasohn, *Gassendi's Ethics: Freedom in a Mechanistic Universe* (Cornell University Press, 1996), p. 122.

21 As reported by Charles Cavendish (brother of Hobbes's patron) and quoted by Sarasohn in ibid.

22 Newton was likely sincere in his horrified attempts to distance himself from ancient materialism, and yet in constructing his philosophico-scientific system he relied significantly on ideas that flowed through Gassendi and Descartes. Newton's physical doctrines owe much to Robert Boyle, who openly acknowledged his debt to Gassendi, and to Walter Charleton, a noted physician and friend of Hobbes, who in 1654 published *Physiologia Epicuro-Gassendo-Charletoniana*, in which he promised on the title page to supply a "fabrick of Science Natural upon the hypothesis of atoms, founded by Epicurus, Repaired by Petrus Gassendus, [and] Augmented" by himself. Charleton authored a book on *Epicurus's Morals* and wrote a polemic against atheists, both of which borrow directly from Gassendi. See G. A. John Rogers, "Charleton, Gassendi et la recepcion de l'atomisme en Angleterre," and Rainer Specht, "A propos des analogies entre les theories de la connaissance sensible chez Gassendi et Locke," in Sylvia Murr, ed., *Gassendi et l'Europe* (Vrin, 1997).

23 See Carl J. Richards, *The Founders and the Classics* (Harvard University Press, 1994). On Stoics, see also Christopher Brooke, *Philosophic Pride* (Princeton University Press, 2012).

24 Richard Blackmore, *Creation: A Philosophical Poem* (London: S. Buckley, 1712), p. 32.

25 Ibid., p. 3.

26 See also John Digby, *Epicurus's Morals* (Sam Briscoe, 1712), which includes an essay in defense of Epicurus by the noted free spirit and adventurer Charles de Saint-Évremond (1613–1703).

27 There is a modern myth that Bruno was entirely forgotten until freethinkers in the nineteenth century revived him from obscurity. In fact Toland revived him in the early eighteenth century and paid special attention to the doctrine of the infinite universe. For more on Toland, see Justin Champion, *Republican Learning: John Toland and the Crisis of Christian Culture, 1696–1722* (Manchester University Press, 2003).

28 Adam Smith, "Of the External Senses," in *The Glasgow Edition of the Works and Correspondence of Adam Smith* (Oxford University Press, 1980), 3.140.

29 Adam Smith, "A Letter to the Authors of the Edinburg Review," in ibid., 3.337. See also Christopher Brooke, "Rousseau's Second Discourse: Between Epicureanism and Stoicism," in Christie McDonald, ed., *Rousseau and Freedom* (Cambridge University Press, 2010), pp. 44ff.; and Thomas Kavanagh, *Enlightened Pleasures: Eighteenth Century France and the New Epicureanism* (Yale University Press, 2010).

30 *DRN*, 1.150.

31 Ibid., 1.215.

32 Descartes captures this aspect of the Epicurean analysis of change with an important definition: "The rules by which these changes take place I call the Laws of Nature." Descartes, *The World*, ch. 7, in Stephen Gaukroger, ed., *Descartes: The World and Other Writings* (Cambridge University Press, 1998), p. 25.

33 *DRN*, 1.76–77, 1.595–96, 2.1087, 5.89–90, 6.65–66.

34 Ibid., 2.1090–92.

35 Giordano Bruno, *Cause, Principle, and Unity*, Richard J. Blackwell et al., eds. (Cambridge University Press, 1998), pp. 61, 70–72, 86.

36 Jordano Bruno, "De immenso et innumerabilibus," 7.18, in *Opera Latine conscripta* (Morano, 1891), 1.2.282.

37 Giordano Bruno, *The Expulsion of the Triumphant Beast*, Arthur D. Imerti, trans. (University of Nebraska, 2004), p. 75.

38 Bruno, *Cause, Principle, and Unity*, p. 87.

39 John Toland, among others, would attempt to capture Bruno's insight by insisting that "Action" is a necessary feature of all substance, and that, contrary to the common view, we never really think of matter except as matter in motion. See Toland, *Letters to Serena* (Bernard Lintot, 1704).

40 Thomas Hobbes, *Opera Philosophica* (Bohn, 1839), 1.lxxxix; see for translation J. E. Parsons Jr. and Whitney Blair, "The Life of Thomas Hobbes of Malmesbury," *Interpretation* 10(1) (January 1982): 1–7. Compare also Hobbes's summary of his work in physics (Hobbes, *Opera Philosophica*, 1.xcvi) with Lucretius, *DRN*, 6.43ff.

41 Thomas Hobbes, *Leviathan*, Noel Malcolm, ed. (Oxford University Press, 2012), 4.46.

42 *DRN*, 2.1077–78.

43 Bruno, *On the Immense*, 8.9, in *Opera Latina conscripta*, 1.2.310. See Ernst Cassirer, *The Philosophy of the Enlightenment* (Princeton University Press, 1951), p. 44.

44 In a more modern philosophical idiom, the first part of this claim is sometimes called the principle of sufficient reason: that for every thing that exists there is an explanation of its existence. I want to avoid that terminology because it comes with so much historical baggage that introducing it would require too many digressions. In fact, it is often interpreted to mean its antithesis: that everything exists to serve some purpose; or, as Winnie

the Pooh says, it's all part of the Plan. Michael Della Rocca makes a stimulating case that the principle of sufficient reason (properly understood) is the guiding principle of Spinoza's philosophy, in *Spinoza* (Routledge, 2008). The eighteenth-century German philosopher Friedrich Heinrich Jacobi (1743–1819)—who accurately perceived that the philosophy of the modern age was at bottom the philosophy of Bruno and Spinoza—made essentially the same claim about both of those philosophers, and was so disturbed by the implications that he abandoned philosophy altogether rather than accede to its guiding principle. (Friedrich Heinrich Jacobi, *Ueber die Lehre des Spinoza in Briefen an Herrn Moses Mendelssohn* (Breslau, Loewe, 1789), pp. 260ff.)

45 Note that Lovejoy uses this term. Arthur O. Lovejoy, *The Great Chain of Being* (Harper, 1936).

46 Lucretius, *De rerum natura: lateinisch und deutsch* (Weidmann, 1924).

47 Albert Einstein, "Physics and Reality," *Journal of the Franklin Institute* 221(3) (March 1936), in *The Einstein Reader* (Citadel Press, 2006), p. 54.

48 See, for example, Philip Morin Freneau, "On the Religion of Nature," in Philip M. Marsh, ed., *A Freneau Sampler* (Scarecrow Press, 1963), p. 125.

49 Freneau, "Lines Addressed to Mr. Jefferson on his Retirement," in ibid., p. 131.

50 Epicurus, *Principle Doctrines*, XII.

51 Jefferson to Charles Peale, August 20, 1811, in J. Jefferson Looney, ed., *The Papers of Thomas Jefferson, Retirement Series* (Princeton University Press, 2007), 4.93.

52 Paine, *Age of Reason*, in Eric Foner, ed., *Thomas Paine: Collected Writings* (Library of America, 1995), p. 771.

53 Thomas Jefferson, *Notes on the State of Virginia*, Frank Shuffleton, ed. (Penguin Classics, 1998), Query 6.

54 Jefferson to Francis Hopkinson, March 13, 1789, in Julian Parks Boyd, ed., *The Papers of Thomas Jefferson* (Princeton University Press, 1950), 1.1167.

55 Franklin to the Royal Academy of Brussels, May 19, 1780, in Benjamin Franklin, *Papers* (American Philosophical Society and Yale University, franklinpapers.org), 32.396.

56 *DRN*, 2.730ff., 842ff.

57 In his 1623 book titled *The Assayer* [*Il Saggiatore*], Galileo makes the distinction between primary and secondary properties and goes on to argue that the secondary properties, such as color, do not inhere in the particles of matter but rather result from their interaction with the particles of our sensory organs. A feather may tickle us, he points out, but that does not mean that the feather itself has some ticklish property. Though Galileo is careful not to cite sources, it is obvious to any informed reader that his ideas take for granted the physical doctrines of Epicurus and his atomistic predecessors such as Democritus. And in fact the readers in the Vatican at the

time were quite well informed. "Having perused Signor Galileo Galilei's book entitled *The Assayer*," reported one cleric, "I have come to consider a doctrine already taught by certain ancient philosophers and effectively rejected by Aristotle, but renewed by the same Signor Galilei"—namely, the doctrine of "the atoms of Anaxagoras or Democritus." "This opinion of Galileo's exudes Democritus from all sides," wrote another. The wags at the time simply referred to *The Assayer* as Galileo's "Epicurean book." (For reasons that are difficult to appreciate unless one happens to be a medieval theologian, Epicurus's atomism was particularly unwelcome in Catholic circles, for it challenged the metaphysical assumptions used to rationalize the obtuse doctrine of transubstantiation—the belief that bread and wine turn into the body and blood of Christ at Catholic mass when the priest says, *Hoc est corpus meum*.) Descartes, who happened to pass through Rome in 1624, learned much from the great astronomer. In a manuscript that he eventually chose to withhold from publication, he articulates a theory of sensory perception that tracks Galileo's theory very closely—and that indeed borrows without acknowledgment the example of the tickling feather.

For these citations and further detail, see especially Pietro Redondi, *Galileo Heretic*, Raymond Rosenthal, trans. (Princeton University Press, 1987), pp. 157,160, 283, 342. Redondi's work excited much controversy among Galileo specialists, especially insofar as he offered an alternative explanation of the motivations for Galileo's inquisition. See Richard Westfall, "Problems with *Galileo Heretic*," in *Essays on the Trial of Galileo* (Vatican Observatory, 1989); and Vincenzo Ferrone, "From Inquisitors to Microhistorians: A Critique of Redondi's *Galileo Eretico*," *Journal of Modern History* 58(2) (June 1986). Here I do not need to take a stand on Redondi's thesis insofar as it represents an assessment of the causes and nature of Galileo's trial (though I am inclined to think that his theories have better support than the critics suggest). I do however find that Redondi offers much evidence to confirm that Galileo was an atomist, and that he was so in a way that would have become problematic had it been known.

See also Nicholas Davidson, "Unbelief and Atheism in Italy, 1500-1700," in Michael Hunter and David Wootten, eds., *Atheism from the Reformation to the Enlightenment* (Clarendon Press, 1992), pp. 61–62. In response to an earlier contact in which Galileo also hinted at his atomistic inclinations, a sympathetic Campanella—another Italian philosopher with distinctly heterodox leanings—writes, "I am very sorry that you have discovered everything to be atoms . . . so that you have given your enemies the opportunity to deny all the heavenly things that you have shown us." See David Wootton, *Galileo: Watcher of the Skies* (Yale University Press, 2010), p. 143.

58 Montaigne, "Apology for Raymond Sebonde," in *The Essays of Montaigne*, Charles Cotton, trans. (London: Reeves & Turner, 1877), 5.134.

59 Hobbes, *Leviathan*, 1.4. See also *De Natura Hominis*, 5.6, in William Molesworth, ed., *The English Works of Thomas Hobbes* (Bohn, 1840), 4.22.

60 Diogenes Laërtius, "Life of Democritus," in *Lives of Eminent Philosophers* (Harvard University Press, 2000).

61 In atomism, the irreducibly particular nature of all things in experience is rendered in a metaphorical way by making space—or more precisely the property of occupying space—the defining feature of atoms. The convenient fact about space (at least as we ordinarily think of it) is that it distinguishes one thing from another only by the intrinsically inessential feature of place. (That is, space is what allows us to separate two things that might otherwise be identical in every respect.) Thus, to make space the essential property of all things is to render all things intrinsically particular, and conversely, to reduce all other properties of things, or universals, to the status of interactions or syntheses among things as opposed to anything embedded directly in the things themselves. Descartes places this intuition on a systematic footing for early modern philosophers when he writes, "I conceive of [matter's] extension, or the property it has of occupying space, not as an accident, but as its true form and essence." (Descartes, *The World*, 6.) In identifying extension as a property of things, on the other hand, Descartes got himself into much trouble, which need not concern us here.

62 Edmund Waller, "To his worthy Friend Master Evelyn, upon his Translation of Lucretius," in *The Works of Edmund Waller* (J. & R. Tonson, 1758), p. 88.

63 *DRN*, 3.669.

64 *Hamlet*, 4.2. The seventeenth-century philosopher and theologian Ralph Cudworth slammed "that monstrous Dotage and Sottishness of *Epicurus* and some other spurious Pretenders" (he had Hobbes in mind) who "make not only the power of Sensation, but also of Intellection and Ratiocination, and therefore all human Souls, to arise from the mere Contexture of corporeal Atoms, and utterly explode all incorporeal Substances." (Cudworth, *A Treatise concerning Eternal and Immutable Morality* (Knapton, 1731), p. 302. See Thomas M. Lennon, *The Battle of the Gods and Giants* (Princeton University Press, 1993), p. 7.) Cudworth's position was complex, incidentally, in that he embraced a strict version of Descartes's dualism alongside a purified atomism. So he applauded Descartes for being a genuine or "good" atomist, in that he took atomism to show that the material world must be explained in terms of properties (extension, motion, etc.) that are utterly incommensurable with thought. In adopting this approach, however, Cudworth perhaps inadvertently opened himself up to the countermove from Spinoza, who agrees that thought and extension are distinct attributes but assigns them to the same substance.

65 Descartes, for example, attempted to modify the doctrine, chiefly by eliminating the concept of a "void" through which the atoms move, that is, by

insisting on the plenitude of the material universe, and Hobbes made some similar gestures.

66 Alexander Pope, *Essay on Man*, in Pat Rogers, ed., *The Major Works* (Oxford University Press, 2008) [hereafter *EM*], 3.17–20. Pope's lines here could also be read as an allusion to Ecclesiastes—but the latter was in turn used by Locke, Spinoza, and Hobbes to make the point associated here with Epicurus.

67 Cited in Nelson F. Adkins, *Philip Freneau and the Cosmic Enigma* (New York University, 1949), p. 67.

68 Freneau, "On the Vicissitude of Things," in Fred Lewis Pattee, ed., *The Poems of Philip Freneau: Poet of the American Revolution* (Princeton University Library, 1903), 2.284.

69 Jefferson to John Adams, August 15, 1820, in Lester J. Cappon, ed., *Adams-Jefferson Letters* (University of North Carolina Press, 1959), pp. 567–68.

70 *DRN*, 1.335. Note that in the Letter to Herodotus included in Diogenes Laërtius, Epicurus himself refers to the void as "place, room, and intangible substance."

71 Diogenes Laërtius, "Epicurus," in Hermann Usener, ed., *Epicurea* (Cambridge University Press, 2010); and *Lives of Eminent Philosophers*.

72 Jefferson to Maj. John Cartwright, June 5, 1824, in Merrill D. Peterson, ed., *Thomas Jefferson: Writings* (Library of America, 1984), p. 1490.

73 Pope, *EM*, 3.15.

74 *Hamlet*, 4.2

75 Jefferson to William Short, April 13, 1820, in Thomas Jefferson Randolph, ed., *Memoir, Correspondence, and Miscellanies from the Papers of Thomas Jefferson* (Charlottesville: F. Carr, 1829), 3.320.

76 See Jefferson to John Adams, July 5, 1814, and August 15, 1820 (in Cappon, ed., *Adams-Jefferson Letters*, pp. 433, 565); Jefferson to William Short, October 31, 1819, and August 4, 1820 (in Peterson, ed., *Thomas Jefferson*, pp. 1430, 1435); and Jefferson to Benjamin Waterhouse, October 13, 1815 (in Paul Leicester Ford, ed., *Works of Thomas Jefferson* (Putnam, 1905), 11.490).

77 Ethan Allen, *Reason the Only Oracle of Man* (Bennington, Vermont: Haswell & Russell, 1784), pp. 137–40.

78 Ibid., p. 253.

79 Ibid., p. 51.

80 *DRN*, 5.828–31.

81 Cited in Catherine Wilson, *Epicureanism at the Origins of Modernity* (Clarendon Press, 2008), p. 102.

82 See *DRN*, 2.1087–89, 5.326–31.

83 Ibid., 5.845.

84 Ibid., 5.857–59.

85 Ibid., 2.1153–56.

86 Ibid., 4.834–35.

87 See Wilson, *Epicureanism at the Origins of Modernity*, p. 102.

88 *DRN*, 5.1012–13. There is some disagreement among scholars about whether this line is part of the original text.

89 Ibid., 5.1019–23.

90 Ibid., 5.1024–27.

91 Ibid., 5.1143–44.

92 Ibid., 5.156–65.

93 Douglas L. Wilson, ed., *Jefferson's Literary Commonplace Book* (Princeton University Press, 1989) [hereafter *Jefferson's LCB*], sec. 16.

94 See Peter Bowler, *Evolution: The History of an Idea* (University of California Press, 1984).

95 See Desmond King-Hele, *Erasmus Darwin* (De la Mare, 1999); and Rebecca Stott, *Darwin's Ghosts: The Secret History of Evolution* (Random House, 2012), p. 163. In poems and other works that abound in phrases and tropes borrowed from his favorite Latin poet, Erasmus Darwin boldly speculates that "all warm blooded animals have arisen from one living filament . . . with the power of acquiring new parts attended with new propensities . . . and of delivering down those improvements by generation to its posterity." (Erasmus Darwin, *Zoonomia, or The Laws of Organic Life* (London: J. Johnson, 1794), vol. 1, sec. 39.4.8, p. 505.) The original living filament, he theorizes, emerged from a certain arrangement of matter in the primeval oceans: "Organic life beneath the shoreless waves / Was born, and nurs'd in Ocean's pearly caves; / First forms minute, unseen by spheric glass, / Move on mud, or pierce the watery mass; / These, as successive generations bloom, / New powers acquire, and larger limbs assume." (Erasmus Darwin, *The Temple of Nature* (London: J. Johnson, 1803), 5.295–300.) As forms of life adapted to their environments and competed with one another, they evolved over a span of millions of years. So taken was Erasmus with this evolutionary vision that he rode around his home county of Derbyshire on a carriage inscribed with the heterodox motto *e conchis omnia*—"everything from shells"—which in turn promoted the local defenders of orthodoxy to write satirical poems comparing him with the infamous Epicurus. Though the critics called his ideas "glaringly atheistical," Erasmus's son Robert, also a doctor, embraced them. (King-Hele, *Erasmus Darwin*, p. 353.) When his father passed away, Robert Darwin adopted the shellfish motto as his own.

96 See Alexandre Koyre, *From the Closed World to the Infinite Universe* (Johns Hopkins University Press, 1957). Note that Koyre recognizes the centrality of the infinite universe but does not attribute to Lucretius or Epicurus the central role that I give them here. He also draws attention to Nicholas of Cusa, a predecessor who influenced Bruno and conceived of the uni-

verse as in some sense infinite. Of course the story is complex and there were many sources, but I do not understand why Koyre diminishes the role of Lucretius in favor of Nicholas.

97 *DRN*, 2.1052–56.

98 Ibid., 2.1085–86.

99 Translation from Ingrid Rowland, *Giordano Bruno* (Farrar, Straus & Giroux, 2008), p. 218. Bruno, "De immenso," 1.7, in *Opera Latine conscripta*, 1.2.226.

100 Bruno, *Ash Wednesday Supper*, p. 91.

101 John Toland, *Pantheisticon: or, the Form of Celebrating the Socratic-Society* (London: Paterson, 1751), p. 15.

102 John Toland, "De genere, loco, & tempore mortis Jordano Bruni, Nolani," and "An Account of Jordano Bruno's Book on the infinite Universe and innumerable Worlds," in *A Collection of Several Pieces of Mr. John Toland* (London: J. Peel, 1726), 1.304–49. The debate over the infinite universe fired up the presses of Augustan England with scathing rejoinders from the defenders of orthodoxy. Joseph Addison notes in 1712 that a copy of Bruno's *Spaccio* sold at an exorbitant price, and he goes on to identify Bruno as an outrageous atheist. (*Spectator*, no. 389, Tues., May 27, 1712.)

103 According to John Trenchard and Thomas Gordon, "Everything in the Universe is in constant Motion." *Independent Whig*, no. 53 (1732), in Trenchard and Gordon, *Independent Whig: Four Volumes in One* (Richard Marsh, 1816), 2.447.

104 *Jefferson's LCB*, sec. 16.

105 Pope, *EM*, 1.25–27. See also Pope's *Universal Prayer*, at the end of the *Essay*, in which he declares that God is "not Lord alone of Man" but rather presides over a universe of a "thousand Worlds."

106 Galileo, *Sidereus Nuncius* [*Starry Messenger*] (Venice, 1610), p. 57.

107 *Jefferson's LCB*, sec. 16.

108 Paine, *Age of Reason*, in Foner, ed., *Thomas Paine*, pp. 687, 705.

109 Ibid., p. 703.

110 Ibid., p. 704.

111 Ibid., p. 710.

112 David Rittenhouse made a (not very effective) effort to reconcile the plurality of worlds with Christian doctrine. He also attempted to derive the rights of man from classical deism. Perhaps the most interesting of his applications of the theory of the infinite universe was to the question of slavery: he expected that aliens would not be so obtuse as to divide people into masters and slaves according to the way in which their skin reflects the light of the sun. William Barton, *Memoirs of the Life of David Rittenhouse* (Edward Parker, 1813), p. 565.

113 Adams, Sunday, April 25, 1756, in L. H. Butterfield, ed., *The Diary and Autobiography of John Adams* (Belknap Press, 1962), 2.13; see also Sunday,

December 23, 1756: "space is absolutely infinite and boundless." (Ibid., 2.18.)

114 Adams to Thomas Jefferson, September 14, 1813, in Cappon, ed., *Adams-Jefferson Letters*, pp. 374–75.

115 Richard Holmes, *The Age of Wonder* (Random House, 2010), p. 167.

116 Adams to Thomas Jefferson, January 22, 1825, in Cappon, ed., *Adams-Jefferson Letters*, p. 607.

117 Allen, *Reason the Only Oracle of Man*, p. 51.

118 Ibid., p. 76.

119 Atheism "was first nourished up in the stie of Epicurus," fumed Henry More, a late seventeenth-century Platonist at Cambridge. Cited in C. A. Patrides, *The Cambridge Platonists* (Cambridge University Press, 1980), p. 27.

120 Anthony Collins, *A Discourse of Free-Thinking* (London, 1713), p. 91. Though modern scholars are understandably loathe to draw conclusions about such a sophisticated and slippery figure as Collins, I see no good reason to question the judgment of Bishop Berkeley, who told his American acolyte Samuel Johnson that Collins was the modern archetype of the Epicurean atheist. (Samuel Johnson, *A Letter to Mr. Jonathan Dickenson* (Boston, 1747), in *Samuel Johnson: His Career and Writings* (Columbia University Press, 1929), 3.191.) On Collins's atheism, see David Berman, *A History of Atheism in Britain* (Routledge, 1988), pp. 71–74. For the opposing view of Collins as a twisted but true believer, see James O'Higgins, *Anthony Collins: The Man and His Works* (Springer, 1970).

121 Jefferson to William Short, October 31, 1819, in Ford, ed., *Works*, 12.140.

122 Cicero, *On the Nature of the Gods*, 1.43.

123 Epicurus, *Letter to Menoeceus*, 123.

124 Franklin, "Articles of Belief and Acts of Religion," in *Papers*, 1.101.

125 Alfred Owen Aldridge notes that Franklin's references to "gods" and "beings of a rank and nature far superior to ours" occur in the context of discussions with scientists. Epicurean atomism, as Franklin knew, supplied the philosophical foundation of early modern physics; it would seem only natural that he should have supposed that Epicurean theology, such as it was, would be of special interest to the scientifically inclined. Alfred Owen Aldridge, *Benjamin Franklin and Nature's God* (Duke University Press, 1967).

126 Epicurus, *Letter to Menoeceus*, 124.

127 Francis Bacon, "Of Atheism," in *Essays or Counsels* (London: Whittaker, 1854), pp. 16–17.

128 *DRN*, 5.1197–203.

129 Atomism was particularly bad in Catholic circles on account of its implications with respect to transubstantiation—and yet on this point Galileo seemed to court controversy. "I have never been able to understand fully

this transmutation of substance whereby matter has been so transformed that one must needs say it has been totally destroyed and nothing of its previous being remains in it and that another body, very different from it, is produced," he wrote. It is "not impossible," he argued, "for change to occur by a simple transposition of parts, without corruption or anything new being generated, because we see such metamorphoses every day." It didn't help his case that his discussion of everyday metamorphoses was a palpable allusion to a specific passage in Lucretius. On August 1, 1632, the Jesuits severely condemned the doctrine of atomism.

130 "I might very reasonably dispute whether there is in nature such a center [of the universe], seeing that neither you nor anyone else has so far proved whether the universe is finite and has a shape, or whether it is infinite and unbounded." Galileo, *Dialogue concerning the Two Chief World Systems*, Stillman Drake, trans. (University of California Press, 1967), p. 319.

131 Ibid., p. 60; see Wootton, *Galileo*, p. 211.

132 Galileo to Elia Diodati, December 6, 1636, in *Opere di Galileo Galilei* (Florence, 1905; www.gallica.fr), 16.523–24. See Wootton, *Galileo*, p. 252.

133 *Opere di Galileo*, 13.276, cited in Wootton, *Galileo*, p. 252.

134 Johannes Kepler, *Dissertatio cum Nuncio Sidereo* (Danielis Sedesani, 1610), pp. 24–25, cited in Rowland, *Giordano Bruno*, p. 281.

135 Hamlet, 2.2.

136 Descartes to Pollot, January 8, 1644. See also Descartes to Mersenne, November 1633. Charles Adam and Paul Tannery, eds., *Oeuvres de Descartes: Correspondence* (J. Vrin, 1975), 4.73, 1.270.

137 Descartes asserted, for example, that the extension of the universe was "indefinite"—a finesse that orthodox critics swiped aside in disgust. (Descartes, *Principles of Philosophy*, 2.22.) He then "proved" that there can be no plurality of worlds—but only after showing that the corpuscles or particles of matter dispersed throughout the universe naturally give rise to "vortices" that produce solar systems just like our own.

138 John Locke, Journal entry for August 11, 1677, in *Locke's Travels in France, 1675–1679* (University Press, 1953), p. 163. See S. Ricci, *La Fortuna del pensiero di Giordano Bruno* (Le Lettere, 1990), p. 172. I am indebted to Wim Klever for drawing my attention to this.

139 Toland, "De genere, loco, & tempore mortis Jordano Bruni, Nolani," 1.314.

140 According to Leibniz, Descartes's claim that "matter must successively assume all the forms of which it is capable" (*Principles of Philosophy*, 3.47) was the height of atheism. (See letter to Christian Philipp, January 1680, and also letter to Molanus, 1679, in O. Klopp, ed., *Die Werke von Leibniz* (Olms, 1970), 4.283.) Leibniz linked the doctrine forward to Spinoza, but Descartes's claim can also be read as a paraphrase of Lucretius's and Bruno's words. At around the same time that he was excoriating Descartes

and Spinoza in his letters, in fact, Leibniz composed a dialogue between a hermit and a self-declared Epicurean, in which he moots the same themes about the origin of the universe from chaos, though in a somewhat more sympathetic way. (*Conversation du Marquis de Pianese*, in *Vorausedition* (University of Muenster, 1989), 8.1808.) Descartes himself suggested that the laws of nature "are sufficient to cause the parts of this chaos to disentangle themselves and arrange themselves in such a good order that they will have the form of quite a perfect world"—which of course is exactly what Lucretius said about his universe. (Descartes, *Treatise of Light*, ch. 6, 9, in Stephen Gaukroger, ed., *Descartes: The World and Other Writings* (Cambridge University Press, 1998), pp. 23, 43. See Wilson, *Epicureanism at the Origins of Modernity*, pp. 98–99. Also, Descartes, *Principles of Philosophy*, 3.29.

141 This suggestion is most famously associated with Leo Strauss today, though his treatment is not unique. (Leo Strauss, *Persecution and the Art of Writing* (Free Press, 1952).) Critics have pointed out that a firm conviction in esoteric writing leads to the methodological problem that a text can be made to contain whatever internal message one wishes to find in it. Empirically speaking, there is some truth in the charge, though I don't think the criticism has a good theoretical foundation. One of my chief concerns with Strauss's idea of esoteric writing is that he seems to suggest that it always involves some conscious intent on the part of the author to convey a secret message; whereas I find that the most interesting cases of esoteric writing have little or nothing to do with conscious intentions to mislead.

142 Lucilio Vanini, *De admirandis naturae* (A. Perier, 1616), p. 441; also in Vanini, *Oeuvres philosophiques de Vanini* (Gosselin, 1842), p. 289.

143 John Toland, "Clidophorus," in *Tetradymus* (London, 1720), pp. 67, 94. See Berman, *History of Atheism in Britain from Hobbes to Russell*, p. 75. Francis Bacon also distinguished "the *Exoteric* method" from "the acroamatic or enigmatical method" whose intention is "by obscurity of delivery to exclude the vulgar . . . from the secrets of knowledge." "Of advancement of learning," in *Essays or Counsels* (London: Whittaker, 1854), 2.17.5.

144 "Montesquieu . . . went as far as a writer under a despotic government could well proceed: and being obliged to divide himself between principle and prudence, his mind often appears under a veil, and we ought to give him credit for more than he has expressed . . . Quesnay, Turgot, and the friends of those authors . . . labored under the same disadvantage." Paine, *Rights of Man*, in Foner, ed., *Thomas Paine*, p. 490.

145 Jefferson to Francis Eppes, January 19, 1821, in Peterson, ed., *Thomas Jefferson*, p. 1450.

146 *Pennsylvania Gazette*, April 21, 1730.

147 The story of the drummer ghost possibly derived from a tale from Restoration England that Addison turned into a play about a manor house haunted by a prankster-drummer.

148 "Philoclerus," *Pennsylvania Gazette*, May 7, 1730.

149 Toland, *Pantheisticon*, p. 16.

150 John Locke, *Of the Conduct of the Understanding* (Clarendon Press, 1881), p. 53.

151 *DRN*, 1.937–39.

152 John Locke, *Two Treatises of Government*, Peter Laslett, ed. (Cambridge University Press, 1960) [hereafter 1TG or 2TG], 1.7.

153 The citation within the *Sermon on Natural Religion* comes from James Ferguson, *Astronomy Explained upon Sir Isaac Newton's Principles*, 2nd ed. (London, 1757), pp. 24–25.

154 Romans 8:4–30.

155 See Rowland, *Giordano Bruno*, p. 93.

Chapter 4: On the Genealogy of Nature's God

1 See Michael A. Bellesiles, *Revolutionary Outlaws: Ethan Allen and the Struggle for Independence on the Early American Frontier* (University of Virginia Press, 1993), p. 97; James Duane, *A Narrative of the Proceedings* (New York, 1773), p. 15.

2 *Connecticut Courant*, June 1, 1773.

3 Ira Allen, *Some Miscellaneous Remarks* (Hartford: Ebenezer Watson, 1777), in J. Kevin Graffagnino, ed., *Ethan and Ira Allen: Collected Works* (Benson, Vermont: Chalidze Publications, 1992) [hereafter *EIA*], 1.129–30.

4 See A Note on Sources for Thomas Young for more information on his career in Albany. One of the beleaguered wannabe-taxers, H. Van Schaak, reported that Young and one of his fellows collected him at his home and escorted him to his "tribunal" before an angry crowd of "Sons of Tyranny" on January 7, 1766. (New-York Historical Society, Lamb Papers.) He recounted with some relief that Young and his companion "had influence enough to screen me from insult" from the other, presumably more surly Sons of whatever.

5 In May 1766, the Sons of Albany sent their regards to the Sons of New York, care of Young's new friend John Lamb; among the four to sign that letter on Albany's behalf was Young. New-York Historical Society, Lamb Papers.

6 Letter from Boston Committee of Correspondence to the Albany Committee, July 13, 1774, unsigned but identified by me as in the handwriting of Thomas Young, in New York Public Library, Bancroft Collection, Papers of the Boston Committee of Correspondence [hereafter NYPL BCC].

7 Henry H. Edes, "Memoir of Dr. Thomas Young, 1731–1777," *Colonial Society of Massachusetts, Transactions 1906–7*, 11(1910): 26.

8 Young writing as "Sobrius," *Boston Evening Post*, September 14, 1767.

9 John Rowe, *Letters and Diary of John Rowe*, cited in Edes, "Memoir of Dr. Thomas Young," p. 28.

10 Young to Hugh Hughes, July 26, 1770, in Huntington Library.

11 Young to Samuel Adams, September 4, 1774, in NYPL BCC.

12 Young to Hugh Hughes, December 21, 1772, in Huntington Library.

13 Or "very profligate and abandoned." See *Boston Evening Post*, September 11, 1769.

14 Aaron Davis, *Boston News-Letter*, November 26, 1772.

15 *Massachusetts Spy*, August 18, 1770.

16 *Massachusetts Spy*, August 30, 1770; *Boston Evening Post*, August 27, 1770.

17 Young to Hugh Hughes, September 15, 1770, in Huntington Library.

18 *Boston Evening Post*, August 27, 1770.

19 Joel Barlow, *The Vision of Columbus* (Hartford: Hudson & Goodwin, 1787), 8.325.

20 As with all attempts to discover the "real" Locke, controversy on his possible role in the political conspiracies of his time persists to the present. Richard Ashcraft, in *Revolutionary Politics and Locke's Two Treatises of Government* (Princeton University Press, 2006), puts forward a Locke intensely involved in the political machinations of the day. An example of the contrary view is Philip Milton, "John Locke and the Rye House Plot," *Historical Journal* 43(3) (2000), which rejects claims of Locke's involvement in the plot.

21 Cited in Leslie Stephen, *History of English Thought in the Eighteenth Century* (Smith, Elder, 1876), 1.206, 2.20.

22 Garry Wills, *Inventing America: Jefferson's Declaration of Independence* (Houghton Mifflin, 2002), p. 63.

23 Carl Becker, *The Declaration of Independence: A Study in the History of Political Ideas* (Harcourt, 1922), p. 79. The other classical source for the supremacy of Locke in American political thought is Louis Hartz, *The Liberal Tradition in America* (Harcourt, 1955). The influence of Locke on Jefferson and on America's revolutionary political thought has been the subject of massive debate, and the positions taken are generally correlated with one's views on the place of rights-based liberalism in America then and now. Beginning in the 1950s, a number of American historians sought to diminish Locke's standing in order to make room for "republican" theorists and other influences. Some important works from this school of thought are Caroline Robbins, *The Eighteenth-Century Commonwealthman* (Harvard University Press, 1959); and Bernard Bailyn, *The Ideological Origins of the American Revolution* (Harvard University Press, 1967). Garry Wills took perhaps the most extreme position in the debate in *Inventing America*, where he argued for an America founded on the Scottish (read socially sensitive) Enlightenment as against the (individualistic and hedonistic) Lockean one. The effort to deflate Locke received perhaps its biggest shot in the arm from

John Dunn. In a widely cited 1969 article, "The Politics of John Locke in England and America in the Eighteenth Century," Dunn went so far as to say that Locke's political philosophy was largely unknown in America before 1750, and his influence on the Revolution irrelevant except "in few possible cases." (Available in John Yolton, ed., *John Locke: Problems and Perspectives* (Cambridge University Press, 1969).) Also questioning the importance of Locke in America was J. G. A. Pocock, *The Machiavellian Moment* (Princeton University Press, 1975). A much-needed corrective to this line of interpretation came from among others Thomas Pangle, *The Spirit of Modern Republicanism* (University of Chicago Press, 1988). A useful survey and critique of the historiography can be found in Stephen Dworetz, *The Unvarnished Doctrine: Locke, Liberalism, and the American Revolution* (Duke University Press, 1990). See also Jerome Huyler, *Locke in America* (University Press of Kansas, 1995). Although I am reluctant to enter into the extended historiographical debate, I would like to say this much: The view associated with Dunn—that Locke was in essence irrelevant in colonial political thought—is preposterous, and I am baffled how it could have persisted among people who have any degree of familiarity with political thought in colonial America. The view associated with the "republican" interpretation has more merit as an interpretation of American political thought than it does as an interpretation of Locke and his influence. Locke was not a "Lockean liberal" in the sense in which that term is used in that literature. He was in fact the most important influence on those radicals now identified as "republicans." To the extent that there are differences between Locke and, for example, the authors of *Cato's Letters*, the latter are generally more radical—that is, closer to Hobbes and Spinoza, more atomistic and hedonistic, and therefore more "Lockean" as that term has been abused—than Locke could publicly allow himself to be.

24 Charles Blount, *Miracles No Violations of the Laws of Nature* (Luttmer, 1683).

25 Thomas Browne, *Miracles Works above and contrary to Nature* (Smith, 1683), p. 3.

26 See John Redwood, *Reason, Ridicule, and Religion* (Thames & Hudson, 1976), p. 99.

27 Richard Blackmore, *The Creation* (London, 1712).

28 Bernard Mandeville, *The Fable of the Bees* (1714; Indiana University Press, 1988), 2.312.

29 John Leland, *A View of the Principal Deistic Writers* (London: Charles Daly, 1754), 3.21.

30 Leslie Stephen, *History of English Thought in the Eighteenth Century* (Smith, Elder, 1876), p. 33.

31 See especially Jonathan Israel, *Radical Enlightenment* (Oxford University Press, 2001), pp. 515–28, 599–627, and *Enlightenment Contested* (Oxford University Press, 2006), pp. 344–56. Note, however, that Israel would dis-

agree entirely with the "radical" interpretation of Locke I offer here. Israel grasps that the radical side of the Enlightenment is the foundation for its revolutionary political impact and thus for the creation of the modern liberal world order, and he rightly castigates all those "Postmodernists" who speciously condemn the Enlightenment as just another "narrative," an individualistic, hedonistic, overconfident faith in reason that brought upon us the curse of nihilism and served as a cover for imperialism. However, Israel does not appear to see that the creation of moderate political exteriors was a necessary (if variable) part of the radical program—even (especially) in the case of Spinoza—but instead seems to think that radical philosophers are always revolutionary extremists and political moderates are always philosophical moderates. But this would force us to cast philosophical radicals like Hobbes and Hume as moderates on account of their politics, together with political radicals like Jefferson and Allen on account of their moderate theological positions, none of which makes much sense. If, as Spinoza maintains and I explain in chapter 8, there is a form of popular deism that amounts to philosophical radicalism translated for the benefit of the common understanding, then much of the so-called moderate Enlightenment becomes, whether intentionally or not, a part of the revolutionary project of modernity.

32 Roger Woolhouse, *Locke: A Biography* (Cambridge University Press, 2007), p. 456.

33 Shaftesbury to Jean Le Clerc, February 8, 1705, in *The Life, Unpublished Letters, and Philosophical Regimen of Anthony, Earl of Shaftesbury*, Benjamin Rand, ed. (Swan Sonnenschien, 1900), p. 328.

34 John M. Robertson in the "Introduction" to Anthony, Earl of Shaftesbury, *Characteristics of Men, Manners, Opinions, Times, etc.*, John M. Robertson, ed. (Grant, Richards, 1900): "His critics and commentators in general have rather oddly overlooked the fact that his philosophy, as regards its bases, is drawn more or less directly from Spinoza."

35 Edward Stillingfleet, *The Bishop of Worcester's Answer to Mr. Locke's Letter* (London, 1697), p. 43.

36 Cited in Stephen, *History of English Thought*, 1.92, among other sources.

37 See Justin Champion, *Republican Learning: John Toland and the Crisis of Christian Culture, 1696–1722* (Manchester University Press, 2003), p. 252.

38 A spokesperson for the view that Locke was, if anything, an anti-deist is John Yolton. "The most careful applications of the Lockean epistemology are to be found among the theologians who were seeking to undermine deism," says Yolton. The deists, by contrast, were "flashy and superficial" in their use of Locke's work. For reasons that I make clear in the rest of this book, Yolton's view is pretty much the inverse of the truth. See John Yolton, *John Locke and the Way of Ideas* (Oxford University Press, 1956), pp. 174ff. Gotthard Victor Lechler, on the other hand, includes a lengthy chap-

ter on Locke in his early history of deism, but notes that from the beginning there was debate about whether Locke was an ally of the deists or of their opponents. He also points out, correctly, that we should look to Toland to measure at least one way in which Locke's thought plays itself out. (Lechler, *Geschichte des Englischen Deismus* (Cotta'scher Verlag, 1841), p. 179.)

39 Stephen, *History of English Thought*, 1.94.

40 John Edwards, *Socianism Unmasked* (Robinson, 1696), p. 75, cited in Victor Nuovo, ed., *John Locke: Vindications of the Reasonableness of Christianity* (Oxford University Press, 2012), p. 9.

41 Dworetz, *Unvarnished Doctrine*, p. 118. Also George Santayana, *Some Turns of Thought in Modern Philosophy* (Scribner, 1933), p. 13.

42 John Dunn, *The Political Thought of John Locke* (Cambridge University Press, 1982), p. xi.

43 Jeremy Waldron, *God, Locke, Equality: Christian Foundations in Locke's Political Thought* (Cambridge University Press, 2002).

44 Ruard Andala, a Dutch professor, thought Locke's debt to Spinoza was so obvious and instructive that he required his students to defend in public the thesis that "Locke's philosophy is built on many Spinozistic foundations." (See Wim Klever manuscript, in my possession, as noted in note 2 in Preface.) John Witty, in *The First Principles of Modern Deism Confuted* (Wyat, 1707), writes, "What was the design of Mr. Locke . . . I won't examine: whether it was writ with an intention to establish Spinoza's material Deity."

45 The title of William Carroll's book lays it all on the table: *A dissertation upon the tenth chapter of the fourth book of Mr. Locke's Essay, concerning humane understanding. Wherein that author's endeavours to establish Spinoza's atheistical hypothesis, more especially in that tenth chapter, are discover'd and confuted. To which is subjoyn'd; a short account of the sense wherein the titles of, and the reasonings in the following pernicious books, are to be understood, viz. The reasonableness of Christianity [by John Locke] Christianity not mysterious [by John Toland] The rights of the Christian church, &c. [by Matthew Tindal] As also, how that sense and those reasonings are bottom'd, upon the hypothesis establish'd in the said Essay of humane understanding* (Matthews, 1706), p. 109. Carroll wrote a series of books accusing Samuel Clarke and Matthew Tindal of Spinozism. He was clearly obsessed. His expositions of Spinoza's doctrines are, however, thorough enough to raise the purely speculative suspicion that his aim was possibly (and perhaps in a self-loathing way) to disseminate them. Jonathan Israel dismisses Carroll as a "lightweight," and this may be accurate in a political sense, but it seems off the mark to me in comparing the quality of his arguments with those of his contemporaries. Carroll was a close and perceptive reader of Spinoza—and of Locke.

46 Cited in Margaret C. Jacobs, *The Radical Enlightenment* (Unwin, Hyman, 1981), p. 55.

47 Cited in Pangle, *Spirit of Modern Republicanism*, p. 23.

48   Leo Strauss, *Natural Right and History* (University of Chicago Press, 1953), pp. 201–51, and *What Is Political Philosophy?* (Free Press, 1959), pp. 197–220; Michael P. Zuckert, *Launching Liberalism* (University Press of Kansas, 2002), and *The Natural Rights Republic* (University of Notre Dame Press, 1996). Zuckert makes a very good case for rescuing Strauss's esoteric reading of Locke from his many (often excessively vituperative) critics, at least insofar as it concerns Locke's religious orientation. Zuckert disagrees with Strauss, however, on the question of Locke's alleged Hobbism. He argues (correctly) that Locke differs from Hobbes in crucial respects, and that it is Locke's rather more humane, civic-minded political theory rather than Hobbes's individualistic hedonism that is the true foundation of liberalism and the American political system. Setting aside the claims about natural rights (which, I argue in chapter 7, involve a thorough misunderstanding of deistic and Lockean conceptions of the law of nature and the immanent foundations of ethics), Zuckert's thesis has much merit. But his claim for Locke's originality appears to depend on a lack of awareness that the differences he finds between Hobbes and Locke are essentially (and I think not coincidentally) the same as those between Hobbes and Spinoza.

49   John Locke, *An Essay concerning Human Understanding* (Ward, Lock & Bowden, 1909), 4.10.2.

50   Ibid., 4.10.3.

51   Ibid., 4.10.6.

52   Ibid., 1.4.9, 1.3.6.

53   See Carroll, *Dissertation upon the tenth chapter*, among others.

54   "What distinguishes Spinoza's philosophy from all the others, what constitutes its soul, is that it maintains and applies with the strictest rigor the well known principle, *nothing comes from nothing, and nothing turns into nothing.*" Friedrich Heinrich Jacobi, *The Conversations between Lessing and Jacobi*, Gerard Vallee, ed. (University Press of America, 1988), pp. 102ff. See especially Michael Della Rocca, *Spinoza* (Routledge, 2008), passim.

55   Benedict de Spinoza, *Ethics* [hereafter just *Ethics*], IIP47Pr. This is not the formal proof Spinoza offers for God's existence, it should be noted, but the proof that the mind has possible knowledge of God's essence, which is also the proof with which Locke is concerned here.

56   Among the theologians who exhibited some of the relevant tendencies, one should mention Averroes (Ibn Rushd), whose work was cited in a significant way by Bruno and Vanini, among others. Pelagius, Aquinas, Maimonides, Llull, and Occam also deserve some credit. Even Jonathan Edwards, when he let his guard down, wound up identifying God with "being" and was as a consequence charged with pantheism by later theologians (though it would be far-fetched in the extreme to suppose that the crime was intentional).

57   Bruno uses the term "principle," as distinct from "cause," to express the

essence of Spinoza's distinction between immanent and transitive causes, and adds that the "universal intellect" is "the true efficient cause, not only extrinsic, but also intrinsic, in natural things." Giordano Bruno, *Cause, Principle, and Unity*, Richard J. Blackwell et al., eds. (Cambridge University Press, 1998), p. 37.

58 *Ethics*, IIP45Sch.

59 Bruno, *De immenso*, 1.11, in Jordano Bruno, *Opera Latina conscripta* (Morano, 1891), 1.1.243.

60 *Ethics*, IP33.

61 Ibid., IP16.

62 See Descartes, *Principles of Philosophy*, 1.51–65.

63 Benedict de Spinoza, *Short Treatise* [hereafter *ST*], 1.2: "Division never takes place in substance, but always and only in the mode of substance."

64 Bruno, *The Expulsion of the Triumphant Beast*, Arthur D. Imerti, trans. (University of Nebraska, 2004), p. 235.

65 Bruno, *De immenso*, 8.10, in *Opera Latine conscripta*, 2.312.

66 Locke, *Essay*, 1.4.18. For Locke's version of the doctrine of "modes," see *Essay*, 2.12.4: "Such complex ideas which, however compounded, contain not in them the supposition of subsisting by themselves, but are considered dependencies on or affections of substances."

67 Ibid., 2.13.18.

68 God first appears in the *Essay* in Locke's discussion of innate ideas. (Locke, *Essay*, 1.4.8.) The central, declared mission of the first book of Locke's *Essay* is to demonstrate that there are no innate ideas, and the idea of God turns out to be no exception to this rule. The idea of God, says Locke, must be acquired through experience, like every other idea. Following this provocative claim about God (which elicited instant howls from the orthodox theologians at the time), Locke pivots to a discussion of the idea of substance. Substance is not innate either, he says—but then he adds, in an astonishing yet characteristically Lockean obfuscation, it is also not acquired through experience. Since his avowed purpose is to demonstrate that all ideas come to us through experience, this unique exception for the idea of substance, even above the idea of God, is curious.

69 Anthony Ashley Cooper, Third Earl of Shaftesbury, *Characteristics of Men, Manners, Opinions, Times* (Cambridge University Press, 1999), p. 299.

70 Shaftesbury, *Life, Unpublished Letters*, p. 15.

71 Ibid., p. 10.

72 Ibid., p. 90.

73 Anthony Collins, *Dissertation on Liberty and Necessity* (Shuckburg, 1729), p. 26.

74 *Ethics*, I Ap.

75 Henry St. John Lord Viscount Bolingbroke, *The Works of Lord Bolingbroke* (Cary & Hart, 1841), 3.84.

76 Ibid., 3.67.

77 In the first of a pair of lengthy letters ostensibly aimed at a gentleman in Holland, Toland pretends that his purpose is to prove that Spinoza's philosophy is without foundation, for Spinoza allegedly fails to supply a principle of "Action" that would put inert matter in motion. Here Toland invokes a standard objection to materialism, associated with Newton (and raised obliquely by Locke, too): that it fails to supply a "prime mover" that gets all the billiard balls of the universe moving, as it were. By the end of his second letter, however, Toland has quietly slipped into the contrary conclusion: "Such as believe Matter created, may as well conceive that God at the beginning endu'd it with Action as well as Extension; and those who believe it eternal, may as well believe it eternally active, as eternally divisible." Since Toland elsewhere composes lyrical paeans to Bruno's eternal universe, there can be little doubt on which side of this divide he stands. His pretended attack turns out to be a defense of the Spinozistic doctrine of substance monism against a common misinterpretation. (John Toland, *Letters to Serena* (Bernard Lintot, 1704), p. 161.)

78 John Trenchard and Thomas Gordon, *Cato's Letters*, Ronald Hamowy, ed. (Liberty Fund, 1995), no. 111, 2.781.

79 Locke, *Essay*, 4.10.19.

80 Spinoza to Henry Oldenburg, November 20, 1665, Letter 32, in Benedict de Spinoza, *Letters*.

81 Benedict de Spinoza, *Tractatus Theologico-Politicus* [hereafter *TTP*], 4.4.

82 Spinoza to Meyer, April 20, 1663, Letter 12, in *Letters*.

83 Spinoza to Boxel, September 1674, Letter 54, in *Letters*; Aquinas, *Summa Theologica*, 1.2.2.

84 Determinists are generally taken to suppose that the universe, whether infinite or not, consists of a finite and perfectly knowable set of types of things and a finite and perfectly knowable set of laws those things obey; so that, given knowledge of the starting positions of all things, one should be able to know everything there is to know about the universe in all its past and future states to eternity. Spinoza's perspectival necessitarianism, however, rules out the possibility that any finite set of laws pertaining to the essence of any finite thing, or mode, can ever even conceivably make the existence of that thing necessary or in general reduce all of the particularities of the past and future to knowable necessities. Indeed, in one letter, Spinoza moots a version of the hypothesis of determinism only to dismiss it outright: "If anyone were to attempt to determine all the motions of matter that have ever been, reducing them and their duration to a definite number and time, he would surely be attempting to deprive corporeal Substance, which we cannot conceive as other than existing, of its affections, and to bring it about that Substance should not possess the nature which it does possess." (Spinoza to Meyer, April 20, 1663, Letter 12, in *Letters*.)

85 Locke, *Essay*, 2.2.3.

86 Ibid., 2.15.12.

87 Ibid., 4.6.11.

88 Alexander Pope, *Essay on Man*, in Pat Rogers, ed., *The Major Works* (Oxford University Press, 2008) [hereafter *EM*], 1.57–60.

89 See ibid., 3.21: "Nothing is foreign; parts relate to whole / One all-extending, all-preserving soul / Connects each being, the greatest with the least." In many of the conventional interpretations of Pope's words, such thoughts about the unity and order of the totality of things are often identified as expressions of the medieval idea that there is a great "chain of being" that places all things in an order of rank established by God. And it is quite plausible to suppose that Pope would have expected his work to be misread in this way. But in fact the order of being passed down from Bolingbroke to Pope is not something "established" by God, nor is it like a message from on high to be read out of experience. The order of the whole is God itself, which is to say, it is a way of describing the harmony and order of all things that Spinoza calls substance.

90 Ibid., 1.289–93.

91 *TTP*, 16.5.

92 Psalms 145:3.

93 1 Timothy 6:16.

94 Isaiah 45:15.

95 Romans 13:9.

96 John 1:14.

97 "Nature works by a thousand ways imperceptible to us." John Trenchard and Thomas Gordon, *Independent Whig: Four Volumes in One* (Richard Marsh, 1816), 2.448.

98 Ludwig Wittgenstein, *Tractatus Logico-Philosophicus*, 6.5.

99 Locke, *Essay*, 4.10.9.

100 Ibid., 4.10.10.

101 Ibid.

102 *Ethics*, IIP1Pr.

103 Ibid., IIP7Sch. Spinoza's premises commit him to a form of materialism, but this materialism is distinct from that which is usually comprehended under that label, or what one may call "classical materialism." According to classical materialism, the only things that are really real are those things that possess the basic features of matter (or what Hobbes calls "Body" and Epicurus identifies with his atoms), and everything in the world (such as thoughts and minds) is ultimately and exclusively explicable in terms of the behavior of particular things that possess these basic features. According to Spinoza's version—call it "second-order materialism"—existence in its fullest sense pertains not to what we conceive as particles of matter but only to substance, which has infinite attributes, only one of which is exten-

sion. Thus, while all things in the world may be conceived through the attribute we associate with materiality, they may also be conceived in an entirely independent way through other attributes—such as, for example, the attribute of thought. These other attributes, however, still behave in the essential, lawlike manner we observe in the world of extension, and so are something like additional perspectives on a single, lawlike essence. This "second-order materialism" is a higher or more abstract form of materialism, for it preserves the fundamental intuition of materialism— that all things in the world operate according to universal laws—but it dissociates this claim from any particular property or set of properties (such as extension or materiality) that are typically conflated with that intuition. Bruno, not surprisingly, anticipates this move. (In modern philosophical debates, the substitution of the term "naturalism" or "physicalism" for the unfashionable term "materialism" captures some, but not all, of the insight behind Spinoza's move away from classical materialism.)

104 Ibid., IIP7Sch.

105 In a separate chapter, Locke states the principle of exclusivity of attributes of substance quite directly: "How any thought should produce a motion in body is as remote from the nature of our ideas, as how any body should produce any thought in the mind." *Essay*, 4.3.28.

106 Ibid., 4.10.13.

107 Ibid., 4.10.14.

108 Ibid., p. 303; see also Shaftesbury, *Life, Unpublished Letters*, pp. 15–16: "Nothing is more certain than that what is intelligent cannot be produced out of what is not intelligent, and that what was never produced but eternal, must remain eternal." From this Lockean starting point, it follows that "there is one common principle of intelligence and wisdom—one eternal and infinite mind." And from this it follows that the universal mind is indistinguishable from its manifestation in "plant or animal body" of all things. But this of course is the point of Spinoza (and Averroes for that matter).

109 Trenchard and Gordon, *Cato's Letters*, no. 109, 2.771.

110 John Toland, *Pantheisticon: or, the Form of Celebrating the Socratic-Society* (London: Paterson, 1751), p. 8.

111 He takes a first swipe at the problem by noting that thinking things, like people, are created out of nothing all the time. We exist now, but we did not exist before we were born; therefore we came from nothing. Thus, making things (specifically thinking things) out of nothing is no big deal—it happens every day. "If, therefore, you can allow a thinking thing to be made out of nothing, (as all things that are not eternal must be)," Locke reasons, "why also can you not allow it possible for a material being to be made out of nothing?" (*Essay*, 4.10.18.) The first thing to note about Locke's argument here is how astonishingly bad it is. He sets out to show how matter as such may be created out of nothing, but in fact he shows only that both

material things and thinking things are constantly coming into existence (and presumably passing out of existence). He attempts to turn this truism into a claim about the possibility of creation ex nihilo through the pure sophistry of representing "coming into existence" as meaning the same thing as being "made out of nothing." Far from undermining his Spinozistic and Epicurean premises, his argument supports them; for it amounts to the assertion that modes of thought, no less than modes of extension, come into being and pass away even while neither one nor the other is ever truly created out of nothing. Presumably aware of just how bad his argument is, Locke moves on to the passage cited above.

112 Locke, *Essay*, 4.10.18.

113 David Hume, *Enquiry concerning Human Understanding* (1748), sec. 2, fn. 1.

114 Shaftesbury, *Characteristics*, p. 278.

115 Anthony Collins, *Answer to Mr. Clarke's Third Defence*, 2nd ed. (London, 1711), pp. 75–79. I am indebted for notice of this part of the debate to Berman, *History of Atheism in Britain*, pp. 78ff.

116 Anthony Collins, *A Dissertation on Liberty and Necessity* (Shuckburg, 1729), p. 47.

117 Cited by Berman, *History of Atheism in Britain*, p. 81.

118 Jefferson, "Notes on Locke," in Julian Parks Boyd, ed., *The Papers of Thomas Jefferson* (Princeton University Press, 1950), 1.548.

119 Bruno, *De immenso*, 8.10, in *Opera Latine conscripta*, 2.314. Firing a barb in the direction of the Stagirite, the Nolan says, "God is not an external intelligence who leads us around in circles. It is more worthy of God to be the internal principle of motion, which is his own nature, his own appearance." Cited in Ernst Cassirer, *The Philosophy of the Enlightenment* (Princeton University Press, 1951), p. 41.

120 Lucilio Vanini, *Amphiteatrum aeternae* (Antonii de Harsy, 1615), p. 336; also in *Oeuvres philosophiques de Vanini* (Gosselin, 1842), p. 207.

121 Lucilio Vanini, *De admirandis naturae* (A. Perier, 1616), p. 366; also in *Oeuvres philosophiques de Vanini*, p. 227.

122 Pierre Gassendi, *Three Discourses of Happiness, Virtue, and Liberty*, François Bernier, unreliable translator, translated from French by "M. D." (London, 1699), pp. 339–40; Seneca, *Letters*, 93, 95.

123 Galileo, *Dialogue concerning the Two Chief World Systems*, Stillman Drake, trans. (University of California Press, 1967), p. 102.

124 Ibid., p. 367.

125 Galileo to Piero Dini, March 23, 1614, in *Le Opere di Galileo Galilei* (Florence, 1890), 5.297. See David Wootton, *Galileo: Watcher of the Skies* (Yale University Press, 2010), p. 246.

126 Descartes, *Meditations*, part 6.

127 François Garasse, *La Doctrine curieuse des beaux esprits de ces temps* (Sebastian Chappelet, 1623), pp. 327, 675, 676.

128 Descartes, *Correspondence*, 3.545; see Jonathan Israel, *The Dutch Republic* (Clarendon Press, 1995), pp. 584–85.

129 John Leland makes the same point in his seminal history of deism: "To acknowledge a God that brought all things into existence, and yet to deny that he afterwards taketh care of the creatures he hath made" is "the same thing as not to acknowledge God at all." (John Leland, *A View of the Principal Deistical Writers* (London: Charles Daly, 1754), 2.204.) Hobbes boldly drew attention to the problem. Those who "take away from [God] the government of the world and of the human race by attributing inactivity to him" necessarily have "a poor opinion" of him, he noted. "For if, despite his omnipotence . . . he has no concern for things here below . . . he might as well not exist." (Thomas Hobbes, *De Cive*, 15.14, in Richard Tuck, ed., *On the Citizen* (Cambridge University Press, 1998), p. 178.) The naughty Hobbes went on to describe a God who can indeed have no concern for us or desire for our improvement.

130 Locke, *Essay*, 2.7.4.

131 Ibid., 2.7.6.

132 Ibid., 2.10.3. In another section, on the remarkable faculties with which animals are endowed, he enthuses that "the wisdom and goodness of the Maker plainly appears in all the parts of this stupendous fabric." But a few lines down he casually reminds us that these same faculties are "provided by nature." (Ibid., 2.9.12.) Elsewhere he moots the hypothesis that "God has designed things" in certain ways; but when he takes up the hypothesis the next time, it is phrased as "Nature has designed" them so. In his *Two Treatises on Government*, he likewise slides with casual ease between "the laws of God," "the laws of Nature," and "the laws of God or Nature."

133 John Locke, "Immediate Inspiration," in Victor Nuovo, ed., *John Locke: Writings on Religion*, (Oxford University Press, 2002), p. 38.

134 *TTP*, 6.4.

135 John Toland, *Origins Judaicae*, cited in Champion, *Republican Learning*, p. 175. Note that Toland's celebration of Moses as a great republican and the source of the first state religion is itself based on a reading of Spinoza's *Tractatus Theologico-Politicus*, especially chapters 18 and 19.

136 Shaftesbury, *Characteristics*, p. 298.

137 Stephen, *History of English Thought*, 2.17, 26.

138 Trenchard and Gordon, *Cato's Letters*, no. 77, 2.563.

139 Psalms 139:7–8.

140 Acts 17:28.

141 Spinoza to Oldenburg, December 1675, Letter 73.

142 See, for example, Franklin, "Letter to the Editor of the Federal Gazette, April 8, 1788, in Benjamin Franklin, *Papers* (American Philosophical Society and Yale University, franklinpapers.org) (unpublished).

143 Ethan Allen, *Reason the Only Oracle of Man* (Bennington, Vermont: Haswell & Russell, 1784), p. 151.

144 *ST*, 1.5.

145 Douglas L. Wilson, ed., *Jefferson's Literary Commonplace Book* (Princeton University Press, 1989) [hereafter *Jefferson's LCB*], sec. 46. Pope passes down the same message when he says, "the Universal Cause / Acts not by partial, but by general laws." *EM*, 4.35–36.

146 *TTP*, 19.

147 Bruno, *Expulsion of the Triumphant Beast*, p. 236. Bruno's thought here shows more than a trace of the influence of Neoplatonism, incidentally, which also played a substantial role in the intellectual history of early modern Europe. Plato's *Timaeus*, Plotinus, and Ficino were influential sources for this kind of thinking. Since the most enduring effects of this aspect of the tradition were simply to reinforce a kind of pantheism allied with the Epicurean tradition and very much at odds with the form-based, quasi-mystical pantheism that sometimes appears in Plato, however, we need not tarry with it here.

148 *TTP*, 4.5.

149 *ST*, 2.24.

150 *TP*, 2.22.

151 *TTP*, n34.

152 Ibid.

153 *Jefferson's LCB*, sec. 36.

154 Bolingbroke, *Works*, 4.230.

155 Richard Blackmore, *The Creation* (London, 1712), 3.742ff.

156 George Berkeley, *The Theory of Vision Vindicated*, sec. 6, in *The Works of George Berkeley* (Clarendon Press, 1901), 1.253. See also the dialogue *Alciphron*, where Berkeley directly contradicts the common view that the deists, on account of their name, must believe in God. Hobbes himself agreed, even while perhaps ostentatiously excepting himself: "Those who say that *the world is God*, are saying that *there is no cause of the world*, i.e. that *there is no God*." (Hobbes, *De Cive*, 15.14.) That Hobbes himself comes quite close to pantheism is evident: "That which I say necessitateth and determinateth every action . . . is the sum of all things, which now being existent, conduce and concur to the production of that action . . . This concourse of former causes, may well be called (in respect they were all set and ordered by the eternal cause of all things, God Almighty) the decree of God." Hobbes of course stridently maintained that he was not an atheist, and the almost limitless number of critics who accused him of atheism could never point to a single line where he explicitly declared himself one, none of which proves that they were wrong or he was right on the question of his beliefs.

157 Carroll, *Dissertation upon the tenth chapter*, p. 52.

158 Albert Einstein, *The World as I See It* (1946; Book Tree, 2007), p. 5.

159 To the extent that we are privy to Newton's religious motivations—and Newton was a very complicated man—it is plausible to suppose that he was an Arian—a believer that Jesus was the messiah but not divine or part of a triune God. At the same time, in his theological speculations, Newton often arrives at his heretical positions through the intense, even fanatical study of the scriptures. Unlike Spinoza, for example, he considers the Bible not just an exercise in moral philosophy but a factual report from God. (It just so happens, according to Newton, that other people—including the leaders of all the major denominations of Christianity for the previous millennium and a half—have failed to read that report correctly.) Even so, it should not be overlooked that Newton's evident aversion to superstition, his keen interest in comparative religion, and above all his view that Jesus came not to found a new religion but to restore an ancient one ally him in important ways with the deists and free spirits of his time. Over in the loud precincts of the hard right of the eighteenth century, in fact, Newton's Arianism implicated him along with the Unitarians and deists as just another face of infidelity.

160 Gassendi, *Selected Works* (1972), p. 408, cited in Catherine Wilson, *Epicureanism at the Origins of Modernity* (Clarendon Press, 2008), p. 27.

161 Richard Bentley, *The Folly and Unreasonableness of Atheism* (London: Mortlock, 1693), p. 5.

162 Newton, *Opticks*, 2nd ed. (Royal Society, 1718), p. 345.

163 Newton to Richard Bentley, December 30, 1692, in Andrew Janiak, ed., *Isaac Newton: Philosophical Writings* (Cambridge University Press, 2004), p. 96.

164 Newton, "General Scholium to Book Three," in *Principia*, 2nd ed. (Prometheus, 1995), p. 440.

165 For details on the space wars, see Alfred Rupert Hall, *Philosophers at War* (Cambridge University Press, 2002); Ezio Vailati, *Leibniz and Clarke* (Oxford University Press, 1997); Richard Westfall, *Never at Rest: A Biography of Isaac Newton* (Cambridge University Press, 1983), pp. 647–49; Alexandre Koyre and I. B. Cohen, "The Case of the Missing *Tanquam*," *Isis* 52 (1961): 555–66; and Edward Grant, *Much Ado about Nothing* (Cambridge University Press, 1981).

166 Joseph Raphson, *De spatio reale* (London, 1702), 5.13.

167 Samuel Clarke, *The Leibniz-Clarke Correspondence*, Fourth Reply (Manchester University Press, 1956), p. 47. Newton himself sought to correct Clarke.

168 Toland, *Letters to Serena*, p. 220.

169 Ibid., p. 161.

170 Cited in Margaret Jacob, *The Radical Enlightenment* (Oxford University Press, 1991), p. 54.

171 "It is certain that not a few divines, as well as philosophers of great note, have, from the difficulty they found in conceiving either limits or anni-hilation of space, concluded it must be divine. And some of late have set themselves particularly to shew that the incommunicable attributes of God agree to it. Which doctrine, how unworthy soever it may seem of the Divine Nature, yet I must confess I do not see how we can get clear of it, so long as we adhere to the received opinions." George Berkeley, *Of the Principles of Human Knowledge*, 1.117, in *Works*, 1.322.

172 The chief source for modern versions of the clockmaker God actually seems to be William Paley's 1809 treatise on *Natural Theology*, where Paley famously argues that if we were to encounter a watch on the beach, we would suppose it to be the work of a designer, ergo, etc. Paley, however, was not a deist but a Christian apologist, and his work lies far outside of the deist tradition as it is defined here.

173 Leibniz, *Leibniz-Clarke Correspondence*, First Letter.

174 Clarke, *Leibniz-Clarke Correspondence*, First Reply.

175 Leibniz, *Leibniz-Clarke Correspondence*, Second Letter.

176 In *Christianity as Old as the Creation* (London, 1730), Matthew Tindal tar-gets this same chink in the Newtonian armor from a different angle. He aims in particular at Samuel Clarke's claim that God acts only through eternal and immutable laws that emanate in an essential way from his character as an infinite and reasonable being. When Clarke then turns around and attacks the deists, arguing that their natural religion is super-seded "after the appearance of [Christian] revelation," Tindal has already set him up for a fall: "He can't differ with them, without differing from himself; & condemning in one part of his elaborate Treatise, what he has approv'd in the other." Either the laws remain immutable, in other words, or they were not so to begin with. The nineteenth-century historian Leslie Stephen, tracking Clarke's position in the debate with Tindal, brings the accusation into the open: Clarke "might be more accurately described as following the argument of Spinoza up to the point where its logic becomes irreconcilable with the ordinary theism." (Tindal, *Christianity as Old as the Creation*, p. 337; Stephen, *History of English Thought*, 2.11, 1.121.)

177 Cited in James E. Force, "Newtonians and Deism," in James E. Force and Richard H. Popkin, *Essays on the Context, Nature, and Influence of Isaac New-ton's Theology* (Springer, 1990), p. 53.

178 George Berkeley, "The Analyst: Addressed to an Infidel Mathematician," in *Works*, 3.17–60. Berkeley's pamphlet was one among dozens fired off at the time over the question whether mathematicians (especially Newtonian ones) were great teachers of infidelity.

179 Trenchard and Gordon, *Cato's Letters*, no. 77, 2.565.

180 Pope, *EM*, 2.35f.

181 Ibid., 1.267–78.

182 Voltaire, *Lettres sur les Anglais*, 22 (appendix), "On Pope," in John Morley, ed., *The Works of Voltaire* (DuMont, 1901), 19.132.

183 Jean-Pierre de Crousaz, *Examen de l'essay de Monsieur Pope sur l'homme* (Bousquet, 1737), p. 95. Some number of other readers leveled the charge of Spinozism against Pope, as is evident by the fact that the editors of two French translations of 1736 felt themselves obliged to defend him on the point. See Harry M. Solomon, *The Rape of the Text: Reading and Misreading Pope's Essay on Man* (University of Alabama Press, 1993), pp. 10ff. The controversy over Pope's *Essay* was immense and closely linked to the political and theological clouds hanging over Bolingbroke. Eventually William Warburton rose to defend the poet, who was fast becoming a national hero in England, chiefly by vigorously scrubbing the work of any provocative ideas at all, and Pope himself went along with the bowdlerization of his own work.

184 Pope, *EM*, 4.331–32.

185 Nature's God also shows up in at least one other work by Pope—a draft of the "Universal Prayer" appended to early editions of the *Essay on Man*, widely admired in America but derided earlier in England as the "Deist's Prayer": *Can sins of moments claim the rod / Of everlasting fires? / And that offend great Nature's God / which Nature's self inspires?* It is not clear whether Pope's successors in Britain and America read these not-very-Catholic sentiments, however, for Pope deleted the lines from his manuscript before publication, and they were only later recovered by a prelate who found this "licentious" stanza among his papers. (Joseph Warton, ed., *The Works of Alexander Pope* (London: J. F. Dove, 1822), 3.164.

186 "The SPEECH of Miss Polly Baker," *Maryland Gazette*, April 15, 1747, in Franklin, *Papers*, 3.120.

187 "Observations concerning the Increase of Mankind, Peopling of Countries, etc.," in ibid., 4.225.

188 Franklin, *Dissertation on Liberty and Necessity*, in ibid., 1.57.

189 The metaphor of the stone appears in Spinoza to Schuller, October 1674, Letter 58.

190 For the following anecdotes, see Alfred Owen Aldridge, *Benjamin Franklin and Nature's God* (Duke University Press, 1967), pp. 40ff.; and Kerry S. Walters, *Benjamin Franklin and his Gods* (University of Illinois Press, 1999).

191 John Updike, "Many Bens," in *Odd Jobs: Essays and Criticism* (Random House Reprint, 2012), p. 273.

192 Franklin to Whitefield, September 2, 1769, in *Papers*, 16.192.

193 Aldridge, *Benjamin Franklin and Nature's God*, p. 40.

194 "Convention Speech Proposing Prayers," June 28, 1787, in Franklin, *Papers* (unpublished).

195 L. H. Butterfield, ed., *The Diary and Autobiography of John Adams* (Belknap Press, 1962), May 10 and June 23, 1779.

196 Allen, *Reason the Only Oracle of Man*, p. 75.

197 Franklin, *Dissertation on Liberty and Necessity*, in *Papers*, 1.57.

198 Michael Novak provides a helpful list of one hundred or so names Washington uses for God, in *Washington's God* (Perseus, 2006), pp. 243–45. Although Novak seems to want to give comfort to those who would like to see the Father of Our Country as a pious Christian, the list makes plain that Washington owed pretty much his entire religious vocabulary to Enlightenment deism.

199 James Thomas Flexner, *The Forge of Experience* (Little, Brown, 1970), pp. 184, 244. See also Gordon Wood, *The American Revolution: A History* (Modern Library, 2003), pp. 129–30.

200 William Barton, *Memoirs of the Life of David Rittenhouse* (Edward Parker, 1813).

201 Jefferson to John Adams, April 11, 1823, in Lester J. Cappon, ed., *The Adams-Jefferson Letters* (University of North Carolina Press, 1959), p. 592.

202 Paine, *Age of Reason*, in Eric Foner, ed., *Thomas Paine: Collected Writings* (Library of America, 1995), p. 688.

203 Ibid., p. 733.

204 Ibid., p. 65.

205 Allen, *Reason the Only Oracle of Man*, p. 40.

206 Ibid., p. 29. As one of his first critics put it, "General Allen seems to deny that God is a free agent, but is under a fatal necessity to act without any wisdom or design." Josiah Sherman, *A Sermon to Swine: From Luke XV.16, containing a concise but sufficient answer to General Allen's Oracles of Reason* (Thomas Collier, 1787), p. 15.

207 Anonymous, *A Sermon on Natural Religion, by a Natural Man* (Boston: Isaiah Thomas, 1771).

208 Paine, *Age of Reason*, in Foner, ed., *Thomas Paine*, p. 690.

209 Jefferson to Adams, April 11, 1823, in Cappon, ed., *The Adams-Jefferson Letters*, p. 592.

210 Allen, *Reason the Only Oracle of Man*, p. 28.

211 Ibid., p. 43.

212 Thomas Young, "For the Massachusetts Spy," *Massachusetts Spy*, November 19, 1772.

213 Allen, *Reason the Only Oracle of Man*, p. 248.

214 Philip Morin Freneau, "On the Uniformity and Perfection of Nature," in Philip M. Marsh, ed., *A Freneau Sampler* (Scarecrow Press, 1963), p. 123.

215 Ibid., p. 275.

216 Ibid., p. 71.

217 William Rider's *Dictionary*, published in 1759, signals its theological orientation by citing Pope three times in its definition of "Nature," where its language also distinctly echoes the words of Young's favorite philosopher, Charles Blount, in the opening of the first *Oracles of Reason*. Rider's

definition of "God," just as scandalously, makes no mention of the Bible or Christianity. It proposes that God is a "self-existent, infinitely perfect and infinitely good being" whose name derives from the Saxon word for "Good," which serves to illustrate "the amiable and generous ideas which our ancestors had of the divine being." Note that Aldridge misidentifies the dictionary that the Natural Man cites, which is one way in which his interpretation of the *Sermon* is slightly off.

218 "Reflections on the Constitution, or Frame of Nature," in the 1809 edition of *The Poems of Philip Freneau* (Lydia Bailey, 1809), but inexplicably omitted from later editions. In "On the Universality, and Other Attributes of the God of Nature," Freneau again makes clear that Nature's God is just a pretty name for Nature: "*All that we see, about, abroad, / What is it all, but nature's God? . . . / He lives in all, and never stray'd / A moment from the works he made.*" (Marsh, ed., *Freneau Sampler*, p. 124.)

219 See Nelson Adkins, *Philip Freneau and the Cosmic Enigma* (New York University Press, 1949), p. 41.

220 In the final third of the eighteenth century, an explicitly atheistic version of the pantheism coursing through the Anglo-Dutch Enlightenment spilled into print in a spectacular fashion in France. Baron d'Holbach—whose works are included in Jefferson's library of moral philosophy—boldly represented God as another word for Nature, and did not stop short of announcing that the meddling, supernatural deity of the religious consciousness neither did nor could exist. Diderot and Volney, among others, followed suit in their own distinctive styles. Largely on account of the explicit and notorious nature of the French project, it has often been assumed that the radical or atheistic Enlightenment begins here. Yet all of the essential ideas in a work such as d'Holbach's hugely provocative and influential *System of Nature* are present in Spinoza and in the covert Spinozism of Locke's heirs. What d'Holbach does not crib from Toland (Jonathan Israel makes this point about d'Holbach and Toland in *A Revolution of the Mind* (Princeton University Press, 2010)), he borrows from Lucretius (whom the Baron translated with gusto). D'Holbach himself, looking back on the philosophy of the preceding century, suggests that deism ultimately serves to reduce "God" to a word that stands for nothing but "the energy of nature." "Le theisme etait fait pour se corrompre, et se degenerer," he says. (*Système de la Nature*, 2.87.) Volney, rejecting explicit atheism in favor of the language of deism, describes a "supreme agent" or "universal and identical mover" who is "designated by the appellation of God" but who turns out to be nothing other than the lawfulness of Nature itself. The "followers of the law of nature," explains Volney, "do not sully [God] with the foul ingredients of all the weaknesses and passions entailed on humanity." (*Volney's Ruins*, Count Daru, trans. (G. Vale, 1853), pp. 189–90.) The radicals among the *philosophes*, to be sure, are often

venomous in their assaults on classical deism. Diderot, for example, suggests that although deism cuts off a dozen heads of the Hydra of religion, in failing to cut the last one it opens the door for a return of all the old superstitions. (See Diderot, *Pensees philosophiques*, 22–24, 61.) Yet Diderot's complaint here is in essence tactical, not substantive. It is not the thrust of deism that he rejects but the unintended consequences of its unprincipled compromises with authority.

221 Ethan Allen, "An Essay on the universal plenitude of Being, and on the nature and immortality of the human soul, and its agency, by Ethan Allen Esq . . . This appendix to be Published at a future day when it will not infringe on my fortune or present living," *Historical Magazine* (Morrisania, New York: Henry Dawson), 1873.

222 Jefferson to John Adams, April 11, 1823, in Cappon, ed., *Adams-Jefferson Letters*, p. 591.

223 Jefferson to John Adams, April 8, 1816, in ibid., p. 467.

224 Paine, *Age of Reason*, in Foner, ed., *Thomas Paine*, p. 691.

225 Allen, *Reason the Only Oracle of Man*, p. 30.

226 Madison to Rev. F. Beasley, November 20, 1825. Available in Ralph Ketcham, ed., *Selected Writings of James Madison* (Hackett, 2006), p. 303.

227 Thomas Jefferson, *Notes on the State of Virginia*, Frank Shuffleton, ed. (Penguin Classics, 1998), Query 6.

228 Jefferson to Peter Carr, August 10, 1787, in Boyd, ed., *Papers* (1955), 12.14.

229 Boyd, ed., *Papers* (1950), 1.423.

230 See Willard Sterne Randall, *Ethan Allen: His Life and Times* (W. W. Norton, 2011), p. 355; and Charles Edward Crane, *Let Me Show You Vermont* (Alfred A. Knopf, 1937), p. 130.

231 J. Kevin Graffagnino, ed., *Ethan and Ira Allen: Collected Works* (Benson, Vermont: Chalidze Publications, 1992), 1.140.

Chapter 5: Self-Evident Truths

1 Michael A. Bellesiles, *Revolutionary Outlaws: Ethan Allen and the Struggle for Independence on the Early American Frontier* (University of Virginia Press, 1993), p. 7; Ira Allen to Samuel Williams, June 6, 1795, in John J. Duffy et al., eds., *Ethan Allen and His Kin: Correspondence, 1772–1819* (University Press of New England, 1998) [hereafter *EAK*], 2.442.

2 Ethan Allen, *Reason the Only Oracle of Man* (Bennington, Vermont: Haswell & Russell, 1784), pp. 157ff.

3 The legendary white horse rears its head in Jared Sparks, *The Library of American Biography* (New York: Harper Brothers, 1853), p. 351.

4 I am indebted to Michael A. Bellesiles, "Works of Historical Faith: Or, Who Wrote *Reason the Only Oracle of Man*?" *Vermont History* 57 (1989): 69–83, for this suggestion.

5 Ethan Allen, *A Narrative of Col. Ethan Allen's Captivity*, in J. Kevin Graffagno, ed., *Ethan and Ira Allen: Collected Works* (Benson, Vermont: Chalidze Publications, 1992) [hereafter *EIA*], 2.17.

6 Allen, *Reason the Only Oracle of Man*, p. 472.

7 Ibid., p. 140.

8 Ibid., p. 182.

9 John Adams to Abigail Adams, May 29, 1775, in Margaret Hogan et al., eds., *My Dearest Friend: Letters of Abigail and John Adams* (Massachusetts Historical Society, 2007), p. 58.

10 *Boston Evening Post*, series of articles beginning December 25, 1769. See also series in *Royal American Magazine* beginning January 1774, and Young's article in the *Pennsylvania Packet*, February 6, 1776.

11 George Pomeroy Anderson, "Who Wrote 'Ethan Allen's Bible'," *New England Quarterly*, 10(4) (December 1937): 685–96.

12 Cited in Ole Peter Grell and Andrew Cunningham, eds., *Medicine and Religion in Enlightenment Europe* (Ashgate, 2007), p. 1.

13 See especially Jonathan Israel, "Enlightenment, Radical Enlightenment, and the Medical Revolution of the Late Seventeenth and Eighteenth Centuries," in ibid., pp. 5ff.

14 Descartes, *Discourse on Method*, part 6.

15 Wim Klever, *Franciscus van den Enden: Free Political Propositions and Considerations of State*, trans. and commentary (Vrijstad, 2007); also Wim Klever, "Proto-Spinoza: Franciscus van den Enden," *Studia Spinozana* 6 (1990): 281–89.

16 See Mandeville, *De brutorum operationibus* (Leiden, 1689).

17 Benjamin Franklin, *Autobiography*, part 1, in *Papers* (American Philosophical Society and Yale University, franklinpapers.org).

18 Pauline Maier, "Reason and Revolution: The Radicalism of Dr. Thomas Young," *American Quarterly* 28(2) (Special Issue, Summer 1976), p. 241.

19 Even fictional doctors showed rebellious tendencies, as Maier points out. Beaumarchais's Figaro, the wily commoner who dares to consider himself the equal of counts in matters of love, is a student of pharmacy and makes a living as the barber-surgeon of Seville.

20 Pauline Maier, *The Old Revolutionaries* (Alfred A. Knopf, 1980), p. 135.

21 Juergen Habermas and Jaques Derrida, to name two of many, have suggested that the Christian ideas about the special and equal nature of all souls are the historical foundation of modern democracy.

22 John Gray is a spokesperson for this point of view. See, for example, *Straw Dogs* (Farrar, Straus & Giroux, 2007). Gray appears to grasp and accept something of the radical philosophy of mind, but fails to see that the liberal order he so vehemently attacks is grounded on precisely the deconstruction he appears to endorse. Which is doubly odd: as a professor and professional commentator he is the epitome of the liberalism he feigns to

despise, and the critique of the common conception that he carries out is the raison d'être of his position and of the order of which it is a part.

23 See Raymond Martin and John Barresi, *Naturalization of the Soul: Self and Personal Identity in the Eighteenth Century* (Routledge, 2003). See also Nietzsche, as cited by Paul Rahe, in *Republics Ancient and Modern* (University of North Carolina Press, 1994), 2.1: "What, then, is modern philosophy up to as a whole? Since Descartes—to be sure, more out of spite against him than on the basis of his precedent—all the philosophers have been making an assassination attempt on the old concept of the soul . . . which is to say, an assassination attempt against the fundamental assumption of the Christian teaching. Modern philosophy, as an epistemological skepticism, is covertly or openly anti-Christian."

24 Lucretius, *De rerum natura* [hereafter *DRN*], 2.927–30.

25 Thomas Hobbes, *Leviathan*, Noel Malcolm, ed. (Oxford University Press, 2012), 3.34.

26 In a kind of twisted version of the ancient intuition that the soul is like a breath of air, Lucretius proposed that the mind is composed of a species of exceptionally minute and flimsy particles that pervade the body and exit through the lungs in our last gasp. He also claimed that ultra-fine, film-like particles emanate from all objects, fly everywhere through space, and then intersect with our sense organs to produce impressions. Only Lucretius seemed to think that the theory was credible in its details.

27 Descartes, *Principles of Philosophy*, 1.9.

28 Descartes, *Meditations*, part 6, and *Principles of Philosophy*, 1.53.

29 John Manley Robinson, *An Introduction to Early Greek Philosophy* (Houghton Mifflin, 1968), p. 110; and G. S. Kirk et al., *The Presocratic Philosophers* (Cambridge University Press, 1983), p. 252. Here I prefer Robinson's translation, which captures the panpsychist tendency of Parmenides's philosophy.

30 David Hume, *A Treatise of Human Nature*, 1.4.6.

31 Benedict de Spinoza, *Principles of the Cartesian Philosophy* [hereafter *PCP*], I.Def.1. See also Spinoza's *Treatise on the Emendation of the Intellect* [hereafter *TEI*], on which Locke's *Essay concerning Human Understanding* is to some degree an extended commentary: "A true idea (for we do have a true idea) is something different from its object (ideatum). A circle is one thing, the idea of a circle another. For the idea of a circle is not something having a circumference and a centre, as is a circle, nor is the idea of a body itself a body. And since it is something different from its object, it will also be something intelligible through itself. That is, in respect of its formal essence the idea can be the object of another objective essence, which in turn, regarded in itself, will also be something real and intelligible, and so on indefinitely."

32 Spinoza, *Ethics* [hereafter just *Ethics*], IIP49CSch.

33 See: "The specific character of a true thought must be intrinsic to the thought itself." (*TEI*, 71.)

34 Ibid., 35.

35 *Ethics*, IIP43

36 Ibid., Scholium.

37 *TEI*, 35.

38 Ibid., 36.

39 *DRN*, 4.478–79.

40 John Locke, *An Essay concerning Human Understanding* (Ward, Lock & Bowden, 1909), 2.1.20.

41 Ibid., 2.27.9. See also 2.1.11.

42 Ibid., 4.7.2, 4.1.2.

43 Ibid., 4.1n.

44 Ibid., 4.1n.

45 Ibid., 4.2.1.

46 The intuition here is ancient (the ever-prescient Parmenides says, "Everything that exists has some measure of knowledge"), and it is sometimes called, disparagingly, "panpsychism," as if to suggest that it imputes a conscious mind to every particle in the universe. The thrust of the argument, however, is not to populate the world with an infinite number of talking heads but to disperse and thereby demolish the common conception of mind itself. Consciousness is everywhere because it isn't what we think it is.

47 According to Spinoza, the idea of something is just the idea of whatever set of causes makes the thing what it is (or the explanation for it), for "the idea of what is caused depends on the knowledge of the cause of which it is the effect." (*Ethics*, IIP7Pr.) Wherever we explain something through something else, we are in essence finding in those things in the world the feature of reflexivity, that is, something that reflects within itself an idea about the world and its place within it. From this it follows that there is an idea for every cup of wine and drop of ink, every leaf on every tree, and every molecule of every leaf, and that these ideas are interconnected and follow from one another in a rigorous way that is entirely independent of us, in the same way and with the same necessity that apples fall from trees. Perhaps most startling of all, it follows that the things in nature and the ideas of those things are in a certain sense the very same thing understood in two different ways. In Spinoza's technical jargon, "A mode of extension and the idea of that mode are one and the same thing, expressed in two ways." (*Ethics*, IIP7Sch.) It also follows that ideas precede the mind, and that the mind is explained through them: "When we say that the human mind perceives this or that, we are saying nothing else but that this: that God has this or that idea—not insofar as he is infinite but insofar as he is explicated through the nature of the human mind." (*Ethics*, IIP11C.)

48 *Ethics*, IIP49CSch.

49 Note that Descartes himself makes a determined effort to construe affirmation and negation as extrinsic to ideas and as exercises of an independent will. (*Principles of Philosophy*, 1.39-49.) Here however I think Descartes was trying to evade the fatalism inherent in his own system and was simply inconsistent with himself, and I am taking a view (not necessarily on any biographical grounds, more on the basis of his influence and where it genuinely mattered) on which side of the contradiction the "authentic" Descartes may be found.

50 *Ethics*, IIP49Pr.

51 "Our thinking is passive and determined by the nature of things." *PCP*, 2.10.8.

52 Locke's views on the subject were complex and went through several iterations, which are evident in his revisions of the relevant sections of the *Essay*. In one of his phases, he does insist that the will can suspend belief. In another phase, he takes positions inconsistent with that thesis.

53 Locke, *Essay*, 2.21.10.

54 Ibid., 4.13.2.

55 John Locke, *Letter concerning Toleration*, in *The Works of John Locke* (London: Rivington et al., 1824), 5.40.

56 Franklin, "Dialogue between Two Presbyterians," *Pennsylvania Gazette*, April 10, 1735.

57 John Trenchard and Thomas Gordon, *Independent Whig: Four Volumes in One* (Richard Marsh, 1816), 1.402.

58 Allen, *Reason the Only Oracle of Man*, pp. 341–42.

59 Kerry Walters, *The American Deists* (University Press of Kansas, 1992), p. 251.

60 Philip Freneau, "Belief and Unbelief," in Harry Hayden Clark, ed., *The Poems of Freneau*, (Harcourt, Brace, 1929), p. 424.

61 Paine, *Age of Reason*, in Eric Foner, ed., *Thomas Paine: Collected Writings* (Library of America, 1995), p. 666.

62 In the *Ethics*, Spinoza summarizes the radical position on the nature and limits of human knowledge by distinguishing three kinds of knowledge. This first kind of knowledge he calls opinion or imagination. The archetype of imagination is the perception of particular external objects, for in such perceptions the mind naturally construes its own act of representing the modifications of its own body as a real, existing object. In a sense, the imagining mind exchanges an idea for a picture. And the same potential source of misapprehension arises when the mind turns its attention to words and symbols like "man" or "horse" and treats them as pictures of things fully present to itself. Imagination, Spinoza cautions, necessarily involves inadequate ideas and is not properly speaking knowledge at all, for "imagination by itself . . . does not of its own nature carry certainty

with it." (*Tractatus Theologico-Politicus* [hereafter *TTP*], 2.) The second kind of knowledge Spinoza calls "reason," and it corresponds to reflection. Insofar as we limit ourselves to those properties that things have in common, says Spinoza, we can form adequate ideas. When we know things by reason, we know them to be true, and we know this for certain. The third kind of knowledge, "intuition," is really a special instance of the second. It begins not with common properties of things inferred from experience but with an adequate knowledge of the formal attributes of nature comprehended as a whole and arrives from thence to an adequate knowledge of the essence of things. Its claims are true in an immediate sense, for they suppose nothing but what is contained in their ideas themselves. Locke appears to have wished to avoid intellectual copyright issues by transcribing Spinoza's three kinds of knowledge in reverse order. Locke's third kind of knowledge—same as Spinoza's first, "imagination"—concerns "sensitive knowledge of particular existence." As with Spinoza, this kind falls short of genuine knowledge, for it boils down to opinion and picture-thoughts, and necessarily lacks the character of certainty. (*Essay*, 4.2.1–15.) Locke's second kind of knowledge (Spinoza's "reason") is "demonstrative knowledge." As with Spinoza, it involves the perception of necessary truths through the comparison of ideas. Locke's first kind of knowledge (Spinoza's third, "intuition") is "intuitive knowledge." It involves knowledge perceived immediately through the agreement or disagreement of ideas, without the intervention of other ideas. In a terminological gesture that would have wide influence all the way down to the Declaration of Independence, Locke says that "there our knowledge is self-evident." (*Essay*, 4.7.2.) Consistent with Spinoza, Locke indicates that the only self-evident truths we possess involving real existence concern our knowledge of the existence of God (or what we know to be the same as Nature or substance). Following his mentor, however, Locke allows for other kinds of self-evident truths that do not involve real existence. All "simple" ideas that represent themselves—for example, "white is white," "white is not red"—are self-evident. So, too, are the truths of mathematics. Most surprisingly—in a development that will call for much attention later—the truths of ethics belong to this happy category of self-evident truths: "I doubt not, but from self-evident Propositions, by necessary Consequences, as incontestable as those in Mathematicks, the measures of right and wrong might be made out." (*Essay*, 4.3.18, also 4.4.7.) The central point at the moment is that, for both Spinoza (and Locke), revealed religion belongs to the first (third) kind of knowledge, imagination, and thus it is not knowledge at all. It is worth adding that the concept of "imagination" is to be found in Descartes's works (especially *Meditations*, part 6, and *Principles*), and the tri-partite classification of knowledge is to be found in the work of Spinoza's teacher, Franciscus van den Enden.

63 *Ethics*, IIP25.

64 Ibid., IIP19.

65 Ibid., IIP23.

66 Ibid., IIP29Sch.

67 Locke, *Essay*, 2.1.2.

68 Ibid. Sensation, of course, is what Spinoza describes as the perception of external things through the attribute of extension. Reflection is when "the mind . . . observes its own actions about those ideas it has" and thus involves modes of thought. (Locke, *Essay*, 2.6.1.)

69 Ibid., 2.21.73.

70 Ibid., 4.3.26.

71 Ibid., 4.3.6.

72 Ibid., 4.3.22. Consider also: "The Dominion of Man, in this little world of his own Understanding, [is] much what the same as it is in the great world of visible things, wherein his Power, however managed by Art and Skill, works no farther, than to compound and divide the Materials, that are made to his Hand." (Locke, *Essay*, 2.2.2.)

73 Franklin, *Dissertation on Liberty and Necessity*, in *Papers*, 1.57.

74 Allen, *Reason the Only Oracle of Man*, pp. 79, 145ff.

75 Jefferson to John Adams, August 15, 1820, in Lester J. Cappon, ed., *The Adams-Jefferson Letters* (University of North Carolina Press, 1959), p. 567.

76 Cited in Locke, *Essay*, 4.1n.

77 *TTP*, 6. The same applies to allegedly divine "signs." In order to understand the sign "I am Jehovah," Spinoza reasons, one must already have a concept of God. If one already has the concept, the sign supplied through revelation adds nothing to our knowledge; and if one does not have the concept, the sign means nothing. "We consider it, therefore, impossible," Spinoza concludes in his *Short Treatise*, "that God should make himself known to men by means of external signs." (2.24.)

78 *TTP*, 6.

79 See Locke, *Essay*, 4.16, 4.18.

80 Locke, "A Discourse of Miracles," in Victor Nuovo, ed., *John Locke: Writings on Religion* (Oxford University Press, 2002), p. 44.

81 Locke, *Essay*, 4.16.11.

82 Ibid., 4.16.10.

83 Ibid.

84 Compare Spinoza: "The certainty afforded by prophecy was not a mathematical certainty" (*TTP*, 2); with Locke: "Whatsoever truth we come to the clear discovery of, from the knowledge and contemplation of our own ideas, will always be certainer to us than those which are conveyed to us by traditional revelation"(*Essay*, 4.18.4). Also note that in the first, unpublished draft of his *Essay*, Locke ruthlessly casts revelation into the dark well of pseudo-knowledge: "A strong and firm perswasion of any proposition

relation to religion for which a man hath either noe or not sufficient proofs from reason but receives them as truths wrought in the minde extraordinarily by god him self . . . seems to me to be Enthusiasme, which can be noe evidence or ground of assurance at all nor can by any meanes be taken for knowledge." (Richard Aaron and Jocelyn Gibb, eds., *An Early Draft of Locke's Essay* (Clarendon Press, 1936), p. 119.)

85 Locke, *Essay*, 4.18.7.

86 Hume, *Dialogues concerning Natural Religion*, part 1, in Dorothy Coleman, ed., *Dialogues concerning Natural Religion and Other Writings* (Cambridge University Press, 2007), p. 14.

87 John Toland, *Christianity Not Mysterious* (London: Sam Buckley, 1696), p. 127.

88 Ibid., p. 38. As Toland has it, testimony—by which he means to include scripture—can be a "means of information" but not a source of certain knowledge. Critics immediately held his feet to the fire, and Toland made an effort to modify his position somewhat. His sincerity in doing so may be questioned.

89 Allen, *Reason the Only Oracle of Man*, p. 265.

90 Ibid., p. 269.

91 Paine, *Age of Reason*, in Foner, ed., *Thomas Paine*, pp. 716, 668.

92 The engraved text comes from the Virginia Statute for Religious Freedom. The unengraved text comes from Jefferson's 1777 draft of the bill.

93 James Madison, *Memorial and Remonstrance Against Religious Assessments*, July 28, 1785, available in Jack N. Rakove, ed., *James Madison: Writings* (Library of America, 1999), p. 29.

94 Madison to Jefferson, January 22, 1786, available in Gaillard Hunt, ed., *The Writings of James Madison* (Putnam, 1901), 2.214.

95 There are of course varieties of Calvinism that insist that our choice of belief, like everything else, is already made for us by God. This has the virtue of being consistent with the doctrine of God's omnipotence, but comes at the expense of begging a question why we should worry at all about a choice that is out of our hands. It does not extract the theology from a commitment to revealed religion and its accompanying epistemology, since it supposes that the choice, whether made by us or God, involves the willful affirmation or negation of a revealed truth.

96 Descartes, *Principles of Philosophy*, 1.51.

97 Ibid., 1.52.

98 Ibid., 1.53.

99 Henricus Regius, *Corollaria* (Utrecht, 1647), in J. Cottingham et al., eds., *The Philosophical Writings of Descartes* (Cambridge University Press, 1985), 1.294–95.

100 *Ethics*, IIP7Sch.

101 Ibid., IIIP2Sch.

102 Ibid., IIP11–13.

103 In his proof of the point that the mind has only an inadequate idea of the body that is its object, interestingly, Spinoza makes use of, among other things, what may be called the argument from the detachability of body parts. The body consists of many interacting parts, he notes, and each one of these parts, considered in itself, must correspond to an idea in God that accounts for its place in the infinite causal network of nature. An adequate idea of the mind would therefore include all of these idea-parts. But some of these parts can be detached from the body without changing the mind's understanding of itself. Consequently, the mind does not have an adequate idea of the body as a whole. (*Ethics*, IIP24.) Curiously, Locke repeats the argument from the detachability of body parts in order to show that the mind has only imperfect knowledge of its object. (*Essay*, 4.3.11ff.)

104 Daniel Dennett makes a case for the consciousness of thermostats, and Michael Della Rocca explains why it is not so unreasonable to attribute to Spinoza the view that even a frying pan achieves a certain kind of consciousness. An electric frying pan with built-in thermostat would presumably be even more conscious. (Daniel Dennett, *The Intentional Stance* (MIT Press, 1989), p. 32, and numerous other publications; Michael Della Rocca, *Spinoza* (Routledge, 2008), p. 115.)

105 *Ethics*, VP39Sch., also IIP10C.

106 Locke, *Essay*, 4.3.6.

107 In an earlier section of the *Essay*, Locke likewise moots the possibility of monistic parallelism as a hypothetical: we are "in ignorance" of "the Nature of that Thinking thing, that is in us, which we look on as ourselves . . . whether it could, or could not perform its Operations of Thinking and Memory out of a Body organized as ours is." (Ibid., 2.27.27.)

108 Ibid., 4.3.28.

109 Ibid., 4.3n. Locke owned copies of all of Spinoza's works and had taken notes on them and in them. It is beyond far-fetched to suppose that he was unfamiliar with Hobbes. In his rebuttal to Stillingfleet, Locke goes on to recapitulate his position that, if anything, makes the connection with Spinoza all the more transparent: "The general idea of substance being the same everywhere, the modification of thinking, or the power of thinking joined to it, makes it a spirit, without considering what other modifications it has, as whether it has the modification of solidity or no. As on the other side, substance, that has the modification of solidity, is matter, whether it has the modification of thinking or no." Here no "all-wise Agent" is necessary to sustain the argument. "Substance" means simply substance in Spinoza's sense, as that which is conceived through itself; and minds and bodies are conjoined as modes of this single substance conceived through independent attributes of thinking and solidity. Insofar as Locke maintains that he is not a materialist, he means it only in the sense

that Spinoza is not one either—for in fact neither is a materialist in the classical or low-information meaning of that term, according to which modes of thought are supposed (incorrectly) to be explicable through the attribute of extension. In his clarification, Locke adds that his position on the mind-body problem "makes me the opposite only to the Cartesians." Evidently, he forgot that in the passage that provoked the entire controversy, Cartesian dualism is supposed to be the safe, hypothetical alternative to monistic parallelism. One could also point out that Locke's original presentation of Cartesian dualism as a hypothetical alternative to monism is disingenuous from the start, since Descartes's proof of dualism relies precisely on the claimed demonstration that there are no alternatives. Another reason to find Locke's "hypothetical" framing so much baloney is that Locke's theory of self is by and large constructed around the intuition that the self is an idea; but since Locke also says that our ideas stem from two originals, that is, are modes of two attributes of substance, he is obligated to consider the idea of mind as one or the other, and since he clearly doesn't think the mind is a mode of extension, it has to be a mode of thought, which is to say, an act of substance and not substance, and therefore perfectly attributable to a substance that also has modes of extension or matter. (*Essay*, 2.27.27.)

110 Locke fudges his way around the charge that he has undermined the existence of the soul by arguing that it is "as rational to affirm, there is no Body, because we have no clear and distinct *Idea of the Substance* of matter; as to say, there is no Spirit, because we have no clear and distinct *Idea of the Substance* of a Spirit." (*Essay*, 2.23.5.) Toland mischievously says the same thing with a different inflection: "We may as well deny the existence of the Body because we have not an idea of its real Essence, as call the Being of the Soul in question for the same reason." (*Christianity Not Mysterious* (London: Sam Buckley, 1696), ch. 2, p. 85.) While Locke means to insinuate that he does believe in the existence of the soul in the same way that we usually think that the body exists, Toland effectively points out that Locke's position entails that neither the body nor the soul exist in the way we think they do, as essences, but are instead modes of attributes of substance.

111 "If we confidently mark this inward perception of our knowledge, it may perhaps be nothing but the inward experience, which our imagination faculty gives us of what we know; and doth no more evince any separable faculty of the Soul, (as *Lucretius* observes) than the reflex and intrinsic perception of smart, which a Man's Foot gives him in a Fit of the Gout," Blount writes in an early work. In later work, Blount makes the case again, but this time in language distinctly reminiscent of Locke's paraphrase of Spinoza's parallelism: "And why the Intima Natura, that composes the Matter, which goes to the making up that definition of Body, as Extension,

Divisibility, Impenetrability, should be incapable of receiving the accident of Thought, I can find no Reason . . . how can we decide it magisterially against this Opinion, especially since Memory, Wit and Judgment . . . have so great a dependence on the Mechanism of the Brain." See David Berman, "Deism, Immortality, and the Art of Theological Lying," in J. A. L. Lemay, ed., *Deism, Masonry, and the Enlightenment* (University of Delaware Press, 1987), p. 68; and David Berman, "Disclaimers as Offense Mechanisms in Charles Blount and John Toland," in Michael Hunter and David Wootton, eds., *Atheism from the Reformation to the Enlightenment* (Oxford University Press, 1992), p. 255.

112 Consider, for example, this passage from *Cato's Letters*, which could be considered either Hobbist or Spinozist: "Every passion or affection of the mind produces visibly a suitable and correspondent disposition of the muscles and lineaments of the face, and consequently must affect and alter the whole mechanism of the body; and by like reason every thought or motion of the mind must do the same in a lesser degree."

113 Hume's essay "Of the Immortality of the Soul," like his *Dialogues concerning Natural Religion*, began to circulate in a clandestine way upon his death in 1776. An early edition, whose extended title gives some idea of the scandal caused by these posthumous works, is *Essays on Suicide and the Immortality of the Soul, Ascribed to the Late David Hume, Esq., Never Before Published, With Remarks Intended as an Antidote* (Smith, 1783). The essay is also available in *Essays and Treatises* (T. Cadell, 1788). See davidhume.org for texts.

114 *Jefferson's LCB*, sec. 11.

115 Cited in Raymond Martin and John Barresi, *Naturalization of the Soul: Self and Personal Identity in the Eighteenth Century* (Routledge, 2003), p. 128.

116 Jefferson to John Adams, March 14, 1820, in Cappon, ed., *Adams-Jefferson Letters*, p. 560.

117 Adams to Thomas Jefferson, May 12, 1820, in ibid., p. 563.

118 Descartes, "Description of the Human Body and All Its Functions," in Stephen Gaukroger, ed., *Descartes: The World and Other Writings* (Cambridge University Press, 1998), p. 170.

119 See in particular Descartes's "Treatise on Man" and "Description of the Human Body" in Gaukroger, ed., *Descartes*.

120 *Ethics*, IIPos.

121 Ibid., III.4-7.

122 Benedict de Spinoza, *Letters* [hereafter just *Letters*], 4.

123 Locke, *Essay*, 3.6.9.

124 Ibid., 2.27.6.

125 Ibid., 2.26.2.

126 Cited in Samuel Johnson, "Herman Boerhaave," *Gentlemen's Magazine*, January–April 1739, in *The Works of Samuel Johnson* (Pafraets, 1903), 14.154–84.

127 Herman Boerhaave, *Institutiones Medicae* (Van der Linden, 1720), sec. 27, pp. 8–10, and *Praelectiones Academicae* (Haller, 1738), 1.64–70.

128 Wim Klever, *Boerhaave 'sequiax Spinozae'* (Capelle aan den Ijssel, 2006), pp. 45–49. See also John P. Wright, "Metaphysics and Physiology," in M. A. Stewart, ed., *Oxford Studies in the History of Philosophy* (Oxford University Press, 1991), p. 259.

129 See Klever, *Boerhaave*; also "Herman Boerhaave oder Spinozismus als rein mecanische Wissenschaft des Menschen," in Hanna Delf, Julius Schoeps, and Manfred Walther, eds., *Spinoza in der europäischen Geistesgeschichte* (Ed. Hentrich, 1994), pp. 75–93.

130 Allen, *Reason the Only Oracle of Man*, p. 89.

131 Ibid., p. 140.

132 *Pennsylvania Gazette*, August 16, 1775; also *Pennsylvania Gazette*, July 26, 1775.

133 Jefferson to John Adams, January 8, 1825, in Cappon, ed., *Adams-Jefferson Letters*, p. 606.

134 Epicurus, *Principal Doctrines*, II; *DRN*, 3.830.

135 Henry More, the Cambridge Platonist who turned to Descartes early in his career in search of refuge from the atheistic drift of the age, eventually decried the Cartesian system as "the womb of impiety and godlessness." Leibniz and Voltaire agreed (for a change) that Descartes was just an atheist with a pretty face. The attacks and defenses of Descartes in his own age are notable for the vehemence with which they are expressed on both sides.

136 *Ethics*, VP23, IIP8; also: "The mind can exercise neither imagination nor memory save while the body endures." (Ibid., VP21.)

137 David Hume, "Of the Immortality of the Soul," in *Essays and Treatises*.

138 Locke's response is once again a model of the art of disseminating heterodox ideas while pretending to be (and, who knows, possibly believing oneself to be) a staunch defender of orthodoxy. Locke replies first that he does not deny that the soul might be immaterial; and second, just in case he does, that the materiality of the soul does not necessarily imply its mortality. To back up this second claim, he turns to scripture, and specifically to a passage in Ecclesiastes, which proves, he says, that the Hebrew term *ru'ah*, variously translated as "spirit" or "breath" and often used to mean the immortal "soul," at times refers to a material thing. Any reader familiar with the full text of the source Locke cites, however, knows that the passage comes with a twist: "For the fate of humans and the fate of animals is the same; as one dies, so dies the other. They all have the same breath [*ru'ah*], and humans have no advantage over the animals; for all is vanity. All go to one place; all are from the dust, and all turn to dust again. Who knows whether the human spirit [*ru'ah*] goes upward and the spirit [*ru'ah*] of animals goes downward to the earth?" So, the

scriptural passage Locke offers does support his point that *ru'ah* refers to something material—but only at the expense of undermining his declared aim, since Ecclesiastes clearly indicates that the materiality of the soul favors the presumption of its mortality. Making the reversal all the more delicious, Locke may be presumed to know, as high-information readers will be aware, that the decried Hobbes makes a similar point about *ru'ah* in his *Leviathan*, and that Spinoza offers a more detailed version of the same analysis of *ru'ah*, along with a reference to precisely the same lines from Ecclesiastes, in the first chapter of his *Tractatus Theologico-Politicus*. (Ecclesiastes 3:19; *TTP*, 1; Hobbes, *Leviathan*, 3.34.) Locke repeats the spectacle with a passage from Cicero's *Tusculan Disputations*. Once again, he turns to the citation purportedly only to show that great people in the past have conceived of the immortal soul as material; and yet the real impact of the citation is to suggest that the soul is both material and mortal: "For if the soul is the heart or blood or brain, then assuredly, since it is material, it will perish with the rest of the body; if it is breath it will perhaps be dispersed in space; if fire it will be quenched." This same citation, as it happens, makes it into the two-dozen or so quotes from Cicero that the young Jefferson includes in *Literary Commonplace Book*. (*Jefferson's LCB*, sec. 62, 1stR 439.)

139 Leibniz, *The Leibniz-Clarke Correspondence*, First Letter (Manchester University Press, 1956), p. 11.

140 Jefferson to Thomas Cooper, August 14, 1820, available in *The Thomas Jefferson Papers*, Series 1, at loc.gov: http://hdl.loc.gov/loc.mss/mtj.mtjbib 021115.

141 Jefferson to Cartwright, June 5, 1824, in Merrill D. Peterson, ed., *Thomas Jefferson: Writings* (Library of America, 1984), p. 1490.

142 Epicurus, *Vatican Sayings*, XIV.

143 Philip Freneau, "On the Vicissitudes of Things," in Fred Lewis Pattee, ed., *The Poems of Philip Freneau: Poet of the American Revolution* (Princeton University Library, 1903), 2.284.

144 Franklin, *Dissertation on Liberty and Necessity*, in *Papers*, 1.57.

145 Epicurus, *Letter to Menoeceus*.

146 *Ethics*, VP23.

147 Ibid., VP36; also *ST*, 2.23.

148 Ibid., IVP67.

149 Lao Tzu, *Tao Te Ching*, David Hinton, trans. (Counterpoint, 2002), p. 33.

150 Einstein to Queen Elisabeth of Belgium, March 30, 1936, cited in Krista Tippett, *Einstein's God* (Penguin, 2010).

151 Locke, *Essay*, 4.3.6.

152 William Knox, *The Controversy between Great-Britain and her Colonies Reviewed* (Boston: Mein & Fleeming, 1769), p. 10.

153 Locke, *Essay*, 2.28n.

154 Anthony Ashley Cooper, Third Earl of Shaftesbury, *Characteristics of Men, Manners, Opinions, Times* (Cambridge University Press, 1999), p. 175.

155 Thomas Chubb, *A Collection of Tracts on Various Subjects* (T. Cox, 1743), 2.2.5. As Leland points out in his scathing assault on Chubb and the other deists, they all labor to suggest that morality operates well enough "without the supposition and expectation of a future judgment." (John Leland, *A View of the Principal Deistic Writers* (London, 1754), 1.163.)

156 Hobbes, *Leviathan*, 1.15.

157 Trenchard and Gordon, *Cato's Letters*, no. 59, 1.410.

158 Franklin to Stiles, March 9, 1790, in *Papers*, (unpublished).

159 Jonathan Edwards, *The Works of Jonathan Edwards, D.D.* (Boston: Doctrinal Tract Society, 1850), 2.524.

160 Paine, *Age of Reason*, in Foner, ed., *Thomas Paine*, p. 666.

161 Ibid., p. 719.

162 Walters, *American Deists*, p. 238.

163 Edwards, *Works of Jonathan Edwards*, 2.524.

164 Jefferson to Madison, September 6, 1789, in Julian Parks Boyd, ed., *The Papers of Thomas Jefferson* (Princeton University Press, 1958), 15.392.

165 Allen, *Reason the Only Oracle of Man*, p. 95.

166 Ibid., p. 163.

167 Ibid., p. 164. "It is vain for us, while in this life, to expect to understand the manner of our future existence, or how mental beings (devoid of sensitive vehicles, or of such sort sensations as ours) exert thought and reflection on new subjects in a new world . . . These matters cannot be known to us, so long as we are dependent on our present senses for the predication of our knowledge. Our present organized sensations . . . were calculated for this world only . . . but are unequal to the task of giving our minds any images or representations of things beyond the grave." (Ibid., p. 159.)

168 Ibid., p. 130.

169 Ibid., p. 469.

170 Thomas Young, "For the Massachusetts Spy," *Massachusetts Spy*, November 19, 1772.

171 Jefferson to William Short, October 31, 1819, in Paul Leicester Ford, ed., *Works of Thomas Jefferson* (Putnam, 1905), 12.140.

172 This and following comments by Hobbes on freedom are to be found mostly in *Leviathan*, 2.21.

173 Ibid.

174 Jordano Bruno, *De immenso*, 1.11, in *Opera Latine conscripta* (Morano, 1891), 1.1.243.

175 See *ST*, 2.16–17.

176 *Letters*, 56.

177 Locke's chapter on power went through various painful iterations, and he ended up arguing for the ideas that freedom involves the ability to suspend judgment and that the will is determined.

178 Locke, *Essay*, 2.21.10, 11, 14, 20.

179 Ibid., 2.21.48.

180 Anthony Collins, *A Dissertation on Liberty and Necessity* (Shuckburgh, 1729), p. xix.

181 Trenchard and Gordon, *Cato's Letters*, no. 40, 1.280.

182 Hobbes, *Leviathan*, 2.21.

183 *Ethics*, IIIP6.

184 Ibid., IIID1.

185 "If I mistake not, there are instances of both kinds of action [i.e., actions of both motion and thinking] which, upon due consideration, will be found rather passions than actions . . . For in these instances the substance that hath motion or thought receives the impression, whereby it is put into that action, purely from without, and so acts merely by the capacity it has to receive such an impression from some external agent; and such a power is not properly an active power, but a mere passive capacity in the subject. Sometimes the substance or agent puts itself into action by its own power; and this is properly called active power." Locke, *Essay*, 2.21.72; also 2.21.2.

186 *Ethics*, 2P13Sch.

187 Rousseau perhaps made this point best when he observed that slavery of the body in most cases produces a kind of slavery of the mind.

188 As John Adams said, it tells us that the government to follow will be "contrived merely by the use of reason and the senses," not by "interviews with the gods" or "under the inspiration of heaven." See Adams's revealing letter to Jefferson, June 20, 1815, in Cappon, ed., *Adams-Jefferson Letters*, p. 445.

Chapter 6: The Pursuit of Happiness

1 See note 29 in chapter 1 for the evidence concerning Young's participation in the November 29 meeting.

2 L. F. S. Upton, "Proceedings of Ye Body Respecting the Tea," *William and Mary Quarterly* 22(2) (April 1965): 287–300.

3 Ibid.

4 Thomas Young to John Lamb, June 19, 1774, at the New-York Historical Society, Lamb Papers.

5 Thomas Young to John Lamb, May 13, 1774, in Isaac Q. Leake, *Memoir of the Life and Times of Gen John Lamb* (Joel Munsell, 1850), p. 85.

6 Thomas Young to Samuel Adams, August 21, 1774, at the New York Public Library, Bancroft Collection, Papers of the Boston Committee of Correspondence [hereafter NYPL BCC].

7 Correspondence between Thomas Young and Samuel Adams, September 1774, in NYPL BCC.

8 *Boston Evening Post*, September 19, 1774; Henry H. Edes, "Memoir of Dr. Thomas Young, 1731–1777," *Colonial Society of Massachusetts, Transactions 1906–7*, 11 (1910): 37.

9   Thomas Young to Samuel Adams, September 20, 1774, in NYPL BCC.

10 Samuel Adams to Thomas Young, October 17, 1774, in NYPL BCC.

11 Thomas Young to John Lamb, March 18, 1774, at the New-York Historical Society, Lamb Papers.

12 See *The Proceedings of the Convention of the New Hampshire Settlers; containing their Covenant, Compact, and Resolutions* (Hartford: Ebenezer, Watson, 1775).

13 Cited in Charles Walter Brown, *Ethan Allen of Green Mountain Fame* (Donohue, 1902), p. 81.

14 Ethan Allen, *A Narrative*, in J. Kevin Graffagnino, ed., *Ethan and Ira Allen: Collected Works* (Benson, Vermont: Chalidze Publications, 1992) [hereafter *EIA*], 2.3.

15 Ethan Allen, *Reason the Only Oracle of Man* (Bennington, Vermont: Haswell & Russell, 1784), p. 190. Also: "Moral good is the only source from whence a rational mind can be supplied with a happiness agreeable to the dignity of its nature." Ibid.

16 Thomas Young, "For the Massachusetts Spy," *Massachusetts Spy*, November 19, 1772.

17 "Epicureisme ou Epicurisme," *Encyclopedie* 5 (1755): 779ff.

18 Lucretius, *De rerum natura* [hereafter *DRN*], 5.1117–19.

19 "Of all the things wisdom acquires for the blessedness of life as a whole, by far the greatest is the possession of friendship." Epicurus, *Principal Doctrines*, XXVII.

20 Seneca, cited in among other places Pierre Gassendi, *Three Discourses of Happiness, Virtue, and Liberty*, François Bernier, unreliable translator, translated from French by "M. D." (London, 1699), p. 56.

21 Plutarch, *Against Epicurean Happiness*, 1097A.

22 Gassendi, *Syntagmatis philosophici (ethica)*, "De felictate," in *Opera omnia* (Anisson & Devenet, 1654; reprinted Friedrich Fromman, 1964), 2.678ff.; see Lisa T. Sarasohn, *Gassendi's Ethics* (Cornell University Press, 1996), p. 61; and Gassendi, *Three Discourses*, pp. 130, 69.

23 Epicurus himself, in the letter to Menoeceus cited by Diogenes Laërtius, says, "It is not possible to live pleasurably unless one also lives prudently, honorably, and justly."

24 *DRN*, 5.1151–60.

25 Epicurus, *Vatican Sayings*, LXX, LXXIX.

26 Gassendi, *Three Discourses*, p. 38; compare *DRN*, 3.1053ff.

27 *DRN*, 3.1067.

28 Thomas Hobbes, *De Natura Hominis*, 7.3, in William Molesworth, ed., *English Works of Thomas Hobbes* (Bohn, 1840), 4.32.

29 Thomas Hobbes, *Leviathan*, Noel Malcolm (Oxford University Press, 2012), 1.6; "Nor is there any such thing as absolute goodness, considered without relation." *De Natura Hominis*, 7.3

30 In modern debates on moral philosophy, it strikes me that an effort is made by Derek Parfit among others to evade this insight and return to the common conception by insisting on a distinction between "personal" and "impersonal" goods. The so-called impersonal goods, however, are not genuinely universal: they refer to goods that are good for a specific biological species (human beings) or a certain class of species (those that are optimistically deemed "rational" or possessed of "minds"). Not only are these impersonal goods obviously relational, but they are also quite obviously reinterpretable as systems of power with respect to all those beings that fall outside their putatively universal laws. Considered universally, they are agreements among one class of beings about how to organize themselves so as to make the best use of (i.e., exploit) all other beings—a point that would be obvious if pigs could talk.

31 *Hamlet*, 2.2.

32 Benedict de Spinoza, *Ethics* [hereafter just *Ethics*], IVPref.

33 Ibid., IVD1.

34 John Locke, *An Essay concerning Human Understanding* (Ward, Lock & Bowden, 1909), 2.20.2, 6.

35 Ibid., 2.21.62.

36 Hobbes, *Leviathan*, 1.11, 1.1–3, 8.

37 *Ethics*, IVP14.

38 Franklin mentions the phrase from Ovid in the voice of Silence Dogood, his female impersonation act as a sixteen-year-old. Bayle uses it in his *Various Thoughts* on a comet, and Locke uses it in the *Essay*.

39 Locke, *Essay*, 2.21.31.

40 Ibid., 2.21.35. In his youthful correspondence, Locke echoes the general sentiment: "Tis Phansye that rules us all under the title of reason . . . We are all Centaurs and tis the beast that carrys us," he says. "Truths . . . are entertained as they suite with our affections, and as they demeane themselves towards our imperious passions."

41 Hume more specifically writes, "The first virtuous motive that bestows a merit on any action can never be a regard to the virtue of that action, but must be some other natural motive or principle." (*A Treatise of Human Nature*, 2.1.) This is pretty exactly the point Spinoza makes in *Ethics*, IVP14.

42 Hobbes, *Leviathan*, 1.6.

43 Ibid., 1.14.

44 *Ethics*, IVP22.

45 Ibid., IVP20.

46 Ibid., IVD8.

47 Locke, *Essay*, 2.21.30.

48 Ibid., 2.21.31.

49 Ibid., 1.2.6.

50 "If philosophy be, as we take it, *the study of happiness*, must not everyone, in some manner or other, either skillfully of unskillfully philosophize?" he asks—which makes sense if one assumes, with the new Epicureans, that the essence of ethics is the pursuit of happiness. (Anthony Ashley Cooper, Third Earl of Shaftesbury, *Characteristics of Men, Manners, Opinions, Times* (Cambridge University Press, 1999), p. 336.)

51 Ibid., pp. 177–79.

52 Shaftesbury, *Characteristics*, p. 229.

53 Ibid., p. 167.

54 Ibid., p. 168.

55 Douglas L. Wilson, ed., *Jefferson's Literary Commonplace Book* (Princeton University Press, 1989) [hereafter *Jefferson's LCB*], sec. 12.

56 Henry St. John Lord Viscount Bolingbroke, *The Works of Lord Bolingbroke* (Carey & Hart, 1841), 5.79; see John Leland, *A View of the Principal Deistic Writers* (London, 1754), p. 368.

57 John Trenchard and Thomas Gordon, *Cato's Letters*, Ronald Hamowy, ed. (Liberty Fund, 1995), no. 31, 1.239.

58 Alexander Pope, *Essay on Man*, in Pat Rogers, ed., *The Major Works* (Oxford University Press, 2008) [hereafter *EM*], 2.87f.

59 Ibid., 2.183f.

60 Ibid., 2.59.

61 Ibid., 4.310.

62 Jefferson to William Short, October 31, 1819, in Paul Leicester Ford, ed., *Works of Thomas Jefferson* (Putnam, 1905), 12.140.

63 Jefferson to Amos J. Cook, January 21, 1816, available in *The Thomas Jefferson Papers: Series 1*, at http://hdl.loc.gov/loc.mss/mtj.mtjbib022285.

64 Franklin, *Dissertation on Liberty and Necessity*, in Benjamin Franklin, *Papers* (American Philosophical Society and Yale University, franklinpapers.org), 1.57.

65 Franklin, *Autobiography*, part 4, in ibid.

66 Franklin, *Poor Richard Improved*, 1756, in ibid., 6.315.

67 Franklin, *Autobiography*, part 10, in ibid.

68 This claim appears in a note that was dropped from many editions of the *Autobiography*. See Alfred Owen Aldridge, *Benjamin Franklin and Nature's God* (Duke University Press, 1967), p. 51.

69 Franklin to Cabanis, cited in Aldridge, *Benjamin Franklin and Nature's God*, p. 59.

70 *Pennsylvania Gazette*, February 11, 1734.

71 *Pennsylvania Gazette*, August 8, 1734.

72 Franklin, *Autobiography*, part 10, in *Papers*.

73 In an earlier letter, he writes that "nations like . . . individuals, stand toward each other only in the relations of natural right." (Jefferson to John Sinclair, March 23, 1798, in Julian Parks Boyd, ed., *The Papers of Thomas Jef-*

ferson (Princeton University Press, 2003), 30.197.) In this and elsewhere, Jefferson appears to follow Emer de Vattel, who offered an update on the Law of Nature doctrine in his 1758 work, *The Law of Nations.*

74 Jefferson to Jose Correa de Serra, April 19, 1814, in J. Jefferson Looney, ed., *The Papers of Thomas Jefferson, Retirement Series* (Princeton University Press, 2007), 7.301.

75 *Ethics,* IVP8.

76 Ibid., IIIP13Sch., III "Definitions of the Emotions."

77 Locke, *Essay,* 2.20.4.

78 Locke, *Essay,* 2.20 passim. Shaftesbury, incidentally, joins in this departure from the Hobbesian program—which is the ultimate source of his vocal disagreements with Hobbes. According to Shaftesbury's analysis—which follows that of Spinoza precisely—it is the representational character of our desires that makes them the subject of reflection, and it is this second-order reflection on desire that makes possible virtue.

79 Ibid., 2.21.61.

80 Ibid., 2.21.64.

81 *Ethics,* IVP26.

82 Ibid., IVP27.

83 Locke, *Essay,* 2.21.42.

84 Ibid., 2.21.51.

85 Benedict de Spinoza, *Treatise on Politics* [hereafter *TP*], 2.20.

86 On this point, Locke and Spinoza remain in agreement with Hobbes, who notoriously says: "of the voluntary acts of every man the object is some good to himself." (*Leviathan* 1.14.8; Locke, *Essay,* 2.21.48)

87 Pope, *EM,* 2.93f.

88 Seneca, *Letters,* 53, cited in Carl J. Richards, *The Founders and the Classics* (Harvard University Press, 1994), p. 186.

89 Anthony Ashley Cooper, Third Earl of Shaftesbury, *The Life, Unpublished Letters, and Philosophical Regimen of Anthony, Earl of Shaftesbury,* Benjamin Rand, ed. (Swan Sonnenschien, 1900), p. 30.

90 See *Ethics,* IVP23, EIVP19, EIVP27.

91 *Boston Evening Post,* September 21, 1767.

92 *Ethics,* IVP29.

93 Ibid., IVAp.

94 Ibid., IVP18Sch.

95 Paine, *Common Sense,* in Eric Foner, ed., *Thomas Paine: Collected Writings* (Library of America, 1995), p. 7.

96 Shaftesbury, *Characteristics,* pp. 51, 280.

97 Pope, *EM,* 3.121–24.

98 Bolingbroke, *Works,* 4.146–47.

99 Pope, *EM,* 4.363–68.

100 Bolingbroke, *Works,* 3.11. The leading figures of the Scottish Enlighten-

ment, too, insist on the deep identity between public virtues and the private pursuit of happiness. David Hume, for example, asks, "Why is it more doubtful that the enlarged virtues of humanity, generosity, beneficence are desirable, with a view of happiness and self-interest, than the limited endowments of ingenuity and politeness? Whatsoever contradiction may vulgarly be supposed between the selfish and the social sentiments or dispositions, they are really no more opposite than selfish and ambitious, selfish and revengeful, selfish and vain." (*An Enquiry concerning the Principles of Morals*, 9.2.)

101 *Ethics*, IVP18Sch.

102 Ibid., IVP37.

103 Shaftesbury, *Characteristics*, p. 200.

104 Ibid., p. 282.

105 Ibid., p. 256.

106 *Ethics*, IIIP59.

107 Paul Tillich, *The Courage to Be* (1952; Yale University Press, 2000).

108 *Ethics*, IVP59Sch.

109 Ibid., IVP34.

110 Shaftesbury, *Characteristics*, p. 306.

111 Trenchard and Gordon, *Cato's Letters*, no. 42, 1.291.

112 Pope, *EM*, 3.317–8.

113 *Ethics*, IVP46.

114 Ibid., IIApp.

115 Shaftesbury, *Characteristics*, p. 46.

116 Ibid., p. 262. Fear or hope of reward or punishment from this God cannot "consist in reality with virtue, if it either stands as essential to any moral performance, or as a considerable motive to any act, of which some better affection ought along to have been a sufficient cause." (Ibid., p. 268.) "Thank heaven I can do good and find heaven in [virtue]. I know nothing else that is heavenly. And if this disposition fits me not for heaven, I desire never to be fitted for it, nor come into the place. I ask no reward from heaven for that which is reward itself." (Shaftesbury, *Life, Unpublished Letters*, p. 344.)

117 Shaftesbury, *Characteristics*, p. 47.

118 Machiavelli, *Discourses*, II.1.

119 St. Francis, *The Little Flowers of St. Francis of Assisi* (Kegan, Paul, 1905), p. 177.

120 Montaigne, "Of Experience," in William Carew Hazlitt, ed., *Essays of Montaigne*, Charles Cotton, trans. (MobileReference, Digital edition), 3.13.

121 *Pennsylvania Gazette*, February 18, 1734.

122 Though some would say, not without cause, that the devil gets all the best lines in Milton's poem.

123 Written in 1713, *Cato* was first performed professionally in North Amer-

ica in Philadelphia in 1749. It was published in four American editions between 1767 and 1787. It included a poetical prologue by Alexander Pope, in which Cato is famously described as a great man falling greatly in a fallen state, or something like that. See Frederic M. Litto, "Addison's Cato in the Colonies," *William and Mary Quarterly* 23 (1966): 431–49.

124 See Garry Wills, *Cincinnatus: George Washington and the American Enlightenment* (Doubleday, 1984), pp. 10, 135–36; Forrest McDonald, *Novus Ordo Seclorum* (University Press of Kansas, 1985), p. 195.

125 In the ancient world—the thoroughly untrustworthy Seneca comes to mind—the convergence of Stoicism and Epicureanism was often, if warily, noted. In early modern debates over the infinite universe, the Stoics sometimes served as the source of a superficially safer version of that dangerous doctrine. Diderot went so far as to represent Stoicism and Epicureanism as two sides of the same story. In the debates over virtue, Stoicism often served to put a respectable face—the dignified visage of a Cicero, a Seneca, a Marcus Aurelius—on ideas that might otherwise have looked quite outré.

126 Trenchard and Gordon, *Cato's Letters*, no. 39, 1.273.

127 Bolingbroke, *Works*, 5.247, 317; see Leland, *View of the Principal Deistical Writers*, 1.304.

128 Pope, *EM*, 2.101–2.

129 Trenchard and Gordon, *Cato's Letters*, no. 39, 1.274.

130 Joseph Addison, *Cato*, act 5, scene 1.

131 Franklin, "Articles of Belief," in *Papers*, 1.101.

132 Paine, *Age of Reason*, in Foner, ed., *Thomas Paine*, p. 824.

133 Allen, *Reason the Only Oracle of Man*, p. 186.

134 Jefferson to Adams, October 14, 1816, in Lester J. Cappon, ed., *The Adams-Jefferson Letters* (University of North Carolina Press, 1959), p. 492.

135 Jefferson to Law, June 13, 1814, in Merrill D. Peterson, ed., *Thomas Jefferson: Writings* (Library of America, 1984), p. 1335.

136 Jefferson to Carr, August 10, 1787, in Boyd, ed., *Papers* (1955), 12.14.

137 Jefferson to Law, June 13, 1814, in Peterson, ed., *Thomas Jefferson*, p. 1335.

138 Those foundations are indeed immanent, even hedonistic in a shallow sense. Even as it posits that good deeds beget good feelings, the moral sense school takes for granted that the moral action of humans is explained through pleasure and pain. Hutcheson's humans act nobly, and yet their many noble deeds are simply the fruit of their efforts to seek the selfish pleasure of doing good and avoid the pain of doing bad. Having committed themselves to the hedonistic principle that all moral actions are explained through motives, or pleasure and pain, the moral sense philosophers inevitably render the transcendental properties of good and evil that they insist belong to the things themselves irrelevant to the explanation of moral action. As Leslie Stephen accurately points out, in Hutcheson's own "discussion of particular problems, the moral sense passes out of sight

altogether, and he becomes a pure utilitarian." (Leslie Stephen, *History of English Thought in the Eighteenth Century* (Smith, Elder, 1876), p. 51.) In fact, utilitarians owe to Hutcheson the catchphrase of their movement: "the greatest happiness of the greatest numbers." In order to rescue their claim that the moral sense must be sensing some real property in objects, the moral sense philosophers are forced to suppose that those real properties just happen to coincide with whatever the calculus of pleasure decides. Hutcheson goes so far as to propose a kind of divinely ordered harmony— much like Leibniz's preestablished harmony of mind and body—according to which our pleasures miraculously line up with a good that has nothing to do with our motives for pursuing it. But this is to explain morality as a miracle, which is to explain nothing at all.

139 Locke, *Essay*, 1.2.8.

140 David Hume to Hutcheson, in J. Y. T. Greig, ed., *The Letters of David Hume* (Garland, 1983), 1.40.

141 Hume, *Enquiry concerning Human Understanding*, 11.27. The critics were quick to see through to the foundations of his project. "There is no other difference, but that the Epicureans used the word pleasure, where our author adopts that of virtue," said one contemporary. (Isabel Rivers, *Reason, Grace, and Sentiment* (Cambridge University Press, 2000), 2.307.) Hume's evil intent, the theologian William Paley complains, is to devise a moral scheme that has no need of "uniting Ethics with Christian Theology." (Ibid.)

142 Jefferson to Law, June 13, 1814. Jefferson runs through the same argument in his letter to John Adams, October 14, 1816, in Cappon, ed., *Adams-Jefferson Letters*, p. 492.

143 *Ethics*, IVP28.

144 Ibid., VP36.

145 Ibid., VP36C; see also Spinoza, *Short Treatise* [hereafter *ST*], 2.24, "On God's Love of Man."

146 *Ethics*, IVP37Sch.

147 Spinoza, *Tractatus Theologico-Politicus* [hereafter *TTP*], 13.

148 Ibid., 14.

149 Locke, *Letter concerning Toleration* (London: Awnsham & Churchil, 1689), p. 6.

150 Shaftesbury, *Characteristics*, p. 305.

151 Pope, *EM*, 3.305–6.

152 Jefferson to Miles King, September 26, 1814, in J. Jefferson Looney, ed., *The Papers of Thomas Jefferson, Retirement Series* (Princeton University Press, 2010), 7.704.

153 Allen, *Reason the Only Oracle of Man*, p. 468.

154 Thomas Young to Abigail Dwight, February 13, 1767, in Massachusetts Historical Society.

155   1 John 4:7–8.

156   James 2:26.

157   See, for example, Franklin, "Dialogue between Two Presbyterians," *Pennsylvania Gazette*, April 10, 1735.

158   1 John 2:4–5.

159   1 John 2:22.

160   Martin Luther, *The Smalcald Articles*, Article 1.

161   The paradox was older than Bayle, of course. Among the first of the modern philosophers to probe it was Jefferson's idol, Lord Bacon. "Atheism leaves a man to sense, to philosophy, to natural piety, to laws, to reputation; all of which may be guides to an outward moral virtue; but superstition dismounts all these," he writes in an essay on superstition; "therefore atheism never did perturb states." (Francis Bacon, "Of Superstition," in *Essays or Counsels* (London: Whittaker, 1854), no. 17.)

162   Pierre Bayle, *Various Thoughts on the Occasion of a Comet*, Robert C. Bartlett, trans. (State University of New York, 2000), p. 178.

163   Ibid., p. 212.

164   Ibid., p. 205.

165   Ibid., p. 211.

166   Ibid., p. 180.

167   Ibid., p. 236.

168   Locke at least offered hints (mixed with furious back-pedaling): "If a Roman Catholic believe that to be really the body of Christ, which another man calls bread, he does no injury thereby to his neighbor." (Locke, *Essay*, 1.2.6.) Toland advanced the thesis—shocking at the time—that not just atheists but Jews, too, can be virtuous. In making the case for toleration of Jews, Toland takes more or less the same line that Spinoza articulates in his *Tractatus*. Jewish religious rites were "solely calculated for their own Nation and Republic" and so represent essentially secular and political as opposed to religious phenomena. (John Toland, *The Reasons for Naturalizing the Jews* (London, 1714); see Justin Champion, *Republican Learning: John Toland and the Crisis of Christian Culture, 1696–1722* (Manchester University Press, 2003), p. 143.)

169   Shaftesbury's discussion of the four types of religion (theism, atheism, polytheism, and demonism) occupies the opening sections of his *Inquiry concerning Virtue*.

170   The demonic Calvinist, worse even than the polytheistic Christian, is "as opposite to true theism as the atheist: nay, he is more injuriously so," Bolingbroke writes—and Jefferson dutifully copies. (*Jefferson's LCB*, sec. 17).

171   Trenchard and Gordon, *Cato's Letters*, no. 44, 1.298.

172   Ibid., no. 48, 1.321. In *The Independent Whig: Four Volumes in One*, 1.353, Trenchard and Gordon are more militant. There they make a distinc-

tion between speculative atheism and practical atheism, and argue that the former is of the business of philosophers and has no effect one way or the other on virtue. Practical atheism, on the other hand, is the special talent of priests. "Under the colour and name of religion, or the worship of God," they write, the modern priests labor to "have not only False-hood and Superstition put upon us, but the most detestable and wicked Practices introduced; such as tend to the Destruction of all Peace, both Publick and Private; all Virtue, Learning, and whatever is praiseworthy among men."

173 Hume, "Of Self-Love," appendix 2, in L. A. Selby-Bigge, ed., *Enquiry concerning the Principles of Morals* (Clarendon Press, 1975), p. 485. In his private writings, Hume makes clear that the virtuous atheist is for him not a paradox but a fact: "The worst speculative Sceptic ever I knew, was a much better man than the best superstitious Devotee & Bigot." (J. Greig, ed., *The Letters of David Hume* (Clarendon Press, 1932), 1.154.)

174 Philip Livingston, "Of Credulity," *Independent Reflector*, no. 47, October 18, 1753, in *The Independent Reflector* (Harvard University Press, 1963), p. 398.

175 Elihu Palmer, in Kerry Walters, *The American Deists* (University Press of Kansas, 1992), p. 264.

176 Thomas Jefferson, *Notes on the State of* Virginia, Frank Shuffleton, ed. (Penguin Classics, 1998), Query 17.

177 John Mitchel Madison, "The Voice of Warning to Christians," in Ellis Sandoz, *Political Sermons of the Founding Era* (Liberty Fund, 1998), 2.51.

178 Jefferson to Peter Carr, August 10, 1787, in Boyd, ed., *Papers* (1955), 12.14.

Chapter 7: The Empire of Reason

1 Abraham Lincoln, Letter to Henry L. Pierce and Others, April 6, 1859, in *Collected Works of Abraham Lincoln* (Rutgers University Press, 1953), 3.375. See Gordon Wood, *Empire of Liberty* (Oxford University Press, 2009), p. 7: American republicans believed that they had undertaken "a bold and perhaps world-shattering experiment in self-government."

2 Paine, *Rights of Man*, part 2, in Eric Foner, ed., *Thomas Paine: Collected Writings* (Library of America, 1995), p. 548.

3 Richard Rorty says something along these lines in *Contingency, Irony, Solidarity* (Cambridge University Press, 1989).

4 Cited by Joanne Freeman in an entertaining lecture on the American Revolution, History 116, Open Yale Courses, oyc.yale.edu.

5 J. Kevin Graffagnino, ed., *Ethan and Ira Allen: Collected Works* (Benson, Vermont: Chalidze Publications, 1992) [hereafter *EIA*], 2.117.

6 Ethan Allen, *"A Narrative of Colonel Ethan Allen's Captivity,"* in *EIA*, 2.3.

7 See Zadock Thompson, *Vermont Historical Gazetteer* 1 (1867): 567.

8 Ethan Allen, *A Narrative of Colonel Ethan Allen's Captivity*, in *EIA*, 2.4.

9 Ethan Allen to the Treasurer of Connecticut, May 12, 1775, in John J. Duffy et al., eds., *Ethan Allen and His Kin: Correspondence, 1772–1819* (University Press of New England, 1998) [hereafter *EAK*], 1.23.

10 Michael A. Bellesiles, *Revolutionary Outlaws: Ethan Allen and the Struggle for Independence on the Early American Frontier* (University of Virginia Press, 1993), p. 119.

11 Sir George Otto Trevelyan, *The American Revolution* (Longmans, Green, 1922), 4.98.

12 Ethan Allen to the New York Congress, June 2, 1775, in *EAK*, 1.34.

13 Ethan Allen to Jonathan Trumbull, July 6, 1775, in *EAK*, 1.43.

14 Jefferson to Washington, April 16, 1784 in Julian P. Boyd, ed., *The Papers of Thomas Jefferson* (Princeton University Press, 1953), 7.83.

15 "The admirers of Mr. Hobbes may easily discern that his Politics are but Lucretius enlarged," observes Thomas Creech in the preface to his translation of *De rerum natura* of 1683. "His State of Nature is sung by our Poet: the rise of Laws; the beginning of Societies; the Criterions of Just and Unjust exactly the same, and Natural Consequents of the Epicurean origin of Man; no new adventure." Cited in Catherine Wilson, *Epicureanism at the Origins of Modernity* (Oxford University Press, 2008), p. 180. See also Jon Parkin, *Taming the Leviathan* (Cambridge University Press, 2010).

16 Thomas Hobbes, *Leviathan*, Noel Malcolm, ed. (Oxford University Press, 2012), 1.13.

17 Hobbes, *De Cive*, 1.3, in Richard Tuck, ed., *On the Citizen* (Cambridge University Press, 1998), pp. 25–26.

18 Lucretius, *De rerum natura* [hereafter abbreviated *DRN*], 1.455–58.

19 Hobbes, *De Cive*, 1.3.

20 Benedict de Spinoza, *Treatise on Politics* [hereafter *TP*], 7.27.

21 John Locke, *Two Treatises on Government*, Peter Laslett, ed. (Cambridge University Press, 1960) [hereafter 1TG or 2TG], 2.5.

22 2TG, 2.6.

23 Ibid., 15.172. Locke says that the despot's power to take another man's life at whim is "a power which neither Nature gives, for it has made no such distinction between one man and another, nor compact can convey." But Locke here uses "power" in the sense of a right found in the state of nature conceived as a state of reason (see below). So the implicit assumption is that human beings do have the natural power to kill one another, a fact that confirms their equality and cannot be legislated away.

24 2TG, 2.6.

25 1TG, 6.67. Locke repeats the same argument at the start of the Second Treatise, where he asserts that nothing is "more evident, than that creatures of the same species and rank, born to all the same advantages of nature, and the use of the same faculties, should be equal amongst another without subordination or subjection, unless the Lord and Master of them

all, should by any manifest declaration of his will set one above another."
(2TG, 2.4.)

26 Epicurus, *Principal Doctrines*, XXXIII.

27 Pierre Gassendi, *Three Discourses of Happiness, Virtue, and Liberty*, François
Bernier, unreliable translator, translated from French by "M. D." (London,
1699), pp. 317–19, 325.

28 Ibid., p. 315. "Some are of the opinion, that what things are Just, are of
their own Nature and unchangeably so," he says, in Bernier's translation.
But " 'tis not so."

29 Benedict de Spinosa, *Ethics* [hereafter just *Ethics*], IVP37Sch.2. See also,
"Sin cannot be conceived except in a state, where what is good and bad is
decided by the common law." (*TP*, 2.19.)

30 2TG, 9.124. Locke, as discussed later, does insist that the state of nature
involves a law of reason that does prescribe what is good or bad. But, as
Locke knew very well, reason in this form never would or could take the
form of civil laws, for individuals living under the guidance of reason not
only would need no such laws, but would always find them unnecessarily
crude in the calculus of utility under all specific circumstances. Which is to
say, in reason there is no permanent good other than the improvement of
reason itself; whereas the laws that are required to make civil society function among unreasonable individuals do require the specification of classes
of good and bad actions and so forth.

31 Epicurus, *Principal Doctrines*, XXXI.

32 Gassendi, *Three Discourses*, p. 315.

33 Ibid.

34 Hobbes, *Leviathan*, 1.13.

35 *TP*, 1.5.

36 Gassendi, *Three Discourses*, p. 318.

37 *Ethics*, IVP37Sch.2.

38 Ibid..

39 Locke, *Letter concerning Toleration*, William Popple, trans. (London:
Awnsham & Churchil, 1689), p. 26. See also 2TG, 6–13.

40 Hobbes, *De Cive*, 10.1.

41 Ibid., 8.1; Robert Filmer, *Observations concerning the original of government*,
in Johann P. Sommerville, ed., *Patriarcha and Other Writings* (Cambridge
University Press, 1991), p. 183.

42 Tellingly, in his first treatise of government, Locke rushes to the defense
of those "philosophers and poets" who favor "natural freedom" against the
attacks from Filmer—thereby implicitly aligning himself with Hobbes and
the atheists to the "great scandal of Christianity." (1TG, 11.154; also 2.11.)

43 Robert Filmer, "Observations on Mr. Hobbes' Leviathan," in Sommerville, ed., *Patriarcha and Other Writings*, p. 87. See Algernon Sidney, *Discourses concerning Government* (Hamilton & Balfour, 1750), ch. 1, sec. 20.

44 Filmer, *Observations concerning the original of government*, p. 237.
45 Timothy Dwight, *Theology Explained*, Sereno Dwight, ed. (William Baynes, 1819), 4.141. See also Frederick Ross, *Slavery Ordained of God* (Philadelphia, 1857), p. 105. Of the self-evident truths, "each one is contrary to the Bible"; "all of this, every jot and tittle, is the liberty and equality claimed by infidelity." (Cited in Carl Becker, *The Declaration of Independence* (Harcourt, Brace, 1922), p. 246.)
46 Romans 13:1.
47 Jefferson, "A Summary View," in Merrill D. Peterson, ed., *Thomas Jefferson: Writings* (Library of America, 1984), p. 112.
48 *Pennsylvania Evening Post*, May 9, 1775; Christopher Marshall, *Passages from the Remembrancer of Christopher Marshall*, William Duane, ed. (J. Crissy, 1839), p. 28.
49 *Pennsylvania Evening Post*, May 13, 1775.
50 John Adams to Abigail Adams, May 29, 1775 in Lyman H. Butterfield, ed., *The Adams Papers* (Harvard University Press, 1963), 1.207.
51 *Pennsylvania Journal*, July 5, 1775, cited in David Freeman Hawke, "Dr. Thomas Young—'Eternal Fisher in Troubled Waters'," *New-York Historical Society Quarterly* 54 (1970): 23; see also Young's signed pieces in *Pennsylvania Gazette*, July 26 and August 16, 1775.
52 Hawke, "Dr. Thomas Young," p. 22.
53 Ibid.
54 Terry Bouton, *Taming Democracy* (Oxford University Press, 2007), p. 5.
55 Alexander Graydon, *Memoirs of His Own Time* (Lindsay & Blakiston, 1846), p. 288.
56 A number of sources also put George Bryan in the group and credit him with authorship of the Pennsylvania Constitution. The evidence permits us to identify the group but not really the roles of any of the individuals within it, apart from Paine's obvious inspirational contribution through *Common Sense*. Paine himself later suggested that he had no role in the actual writing of the constitution.
57 *Dunlap's Pennsylvania Packet*, March 25, 1776.
58 A Tradesman, *Pennsylvania Packet*, April 30, 1775, cited in Gary Nash, *The Unknown American Revolution* (Penguin, 2006), p. 185. Nash identifies the "Tradesman" as Thomas Young, but this seems doubtful, since the piece appeared the week before Young arrived in Philadelphia. For additional interesting analysis of radical populism in the Pennsylvania revolution, see also Sophia Rosenfeld, *Common Sense* (Harvard University Press, 2011); Bouton, *Taming Democracy*; and William Hogeland, *Declaration* (Simon & Schuster, 2010) and *Founding Finance* (University of Texas Press, 2012).
59 *Address of a Watchman to the Common People of Pennsylvania*, June 10, 1776 (pamphlet).
60 The identity of the author, "a Watchman," is not known, to my knowledge.

A case could be made for either James Cannon or Thomas Young. Cannon seems more likely, but in favor of Young is the fact that the Watchman's June 10 piece opens with observations on the behavior of Tories in Boston during the tea crisis and in New York during the Stamp Act crisis—matters on which Young in particular was uniquely positioned to comment.

61 Eudoxus, *Pennsylvania Packet*, April 22, 1776.

62 An Elector, *Pennsylvania Packet*, April 29, 1776.

63 Cited in Harvey J. Kaye, *Thomas Paine and the Promise of America* (Macmillan, 2007), p. 43.

64 John Eleazer Remsburg, *Thomas Paine* (Truth Seeker, 1917), p. 129.

65 Thomas Paine, *Common Sense*, in Foner, ed., *Thomas Paine*, p. 17.

66 Ibid., p. 12.

67 Ibid., pp. 5, 52.

68 L. H. Butterfield, ed., *The Diary and Autobiography of John Adams* (Belknap Press, 1962), 3.335.

69 Paine, *Common Sense*, in Foner, ed., *Thomas Paine*, p. 34.

70 Adams to Thomas Jefferson, June 22, 1819, in Lester J. Cappon, ed., *The Adams-Jefferson Letters* (University of North Carolina Press, 1959), p. 542. In letters to Abigail, Adams evinced sympathy with Paine's argument for independence and admiration for his vigorous prose.

71 Adams to James Sullivan, May 26, 1776, in Charles Francis Adams, ed., *The Works of John Adams* (Little, Brown, 1856), 9.375.

72 John Adams, *Autobiography*, in ibid., 2.507.

73 Marshall, *Passages from the Remembrancer*, p. 78.

74 Romans 2:14–15.

75 Some of the contemporary heirs of Leo Strauss appear to have resurrected a premodern conception of natural right, too, according to which America's founders discovered timeless moral precepts and laws embedded in nature itself. See, for example, pretty much anything written by Harry Jaffa, who repeats this claim several hundred times.

76 America's political theorists in the revolutionary period regularly cited the works of Pufendorf, Grotius, Beccaria, Blackstone, Montesquieu, Vattel, and a number of others whose impact on American legal theory would require an entirely separate investigation.

77 Hobbes, *De Cive*, 2.1; see also *Leviathan*, 1.14.

78 Hobbes, *Leviathan*, 1.15. Hobbes does allow that the dictates of reason can be converted to serve as the basis for genuine laws or commands: "But yet if we consider the same Theoremes, as delivered in the word of God, that by right commandeth all things; then they are properly called Lawes." Matthew Tindal perceptively interprets these two versions of "Lawes" as two perspectives on the same thing: one is "acting according to the reason of things considered in themselves; the other acting according to the same reason of things considered as the rule of God." Tindal's endorsement of

the Hobbesian position here should be taken as evidence that it is compatible with Spinoza's position. (Tindal, *Christianity as Old as the Creation* (London, 1730), p. 270.)

79 Hobbes, *Leviathan*, 3.31.

80 Matthew Hale, *Treatise on the Nature of Lawes*, cited in Richard Tuck, *Natural Rights Theories* (Cambridge University Press, 1981), p. 162.

81 Jeremy Bentham, "Anarchical Fallacies," in John Bowring, ed., *The Works of Jeremy Bentham* (Edinburgh: William Tait, 1843), 2.501.

82 Hobbes, *De Cive*, 1.7.

83 Benedict de Spinoza, *Tractatus Theologico-Politicus* [hereafter *TTP*], 16.2; see also *TP*, 2.4.

84 *TP*, 2.8.

85 Richard Cumberland, *Treatise of the Law of Nature* (1672; Liberty Fund, 2005), p. 345.

86 Benedict de Spinoza, *Letters* [hereafter just *Letters*], 50.

87 Hobbes, *Elements of Law Natural and Politic*, 2.20.16.

88 *TTP*, 16.

89 Hobbes, *Leviathan*, 1.14.

90 *TTP*, 16.

91 John Aubrey, *Brief Lives* (Clarendon Press, 1893), 1.357.

92 Henry Hallam, *Introduction to the Literature of Europe* (Armstrong, 1884), 3.188.

93 *TTP*, note 33.

94 *Ethics*, IVP37Sch.2.

95 Hobbes, *Leviathan*, 1.14, 21.

96 *Ethics*, IVP73.

97 *TP*, 3.6.

98 Ibid., 5.4, 6.4.

99 *TTP*, 20.

100 *TP*, 3.7.

101 Ibid., 2.15.

102 2TG, 3.16, 2.4.

103 Consider, for example: "Political power I take to be the Right of making Laws and Penalties." (2TG, 1.3.) In describing the force of Natural Right in history, in fact, Locke can't seem to stop himself from alluding to precisely the big-fish-little-fish metaphor deployed by Spinoza: "There are no Examples so frequent in history both Sacred and Prophane, as those of men withdrawing themselves, and their Obedience, from the Jurisdictions they were born under . . . and setting up new governments . . . which always multiplied . . . till the stronger, or more fortunate swallowed the weaker." (Ibid., 8.115.)

104 2TG, 2.6.

105 Ibid., 11.135.

106 *TP*, 3.3.

107 "Should a Robber break into my House, and with a Dagger at my Throat, make me seal Deeds to convey my Estate to him, would this give him any Title?" Locke asks. The answer is a firm no. (2TG, 16.176; also 18.202.)

108 Ibid., 14.164.

109 Ibid., 2.6; also 8.96, 3.19. Among modern commentators, Hans Aarsleff and Michael Zuckert recognize that Locke's state of nature is a "state of reason" or a "purely abstract state," though they don't seem to recognize that this makes Locke's position converge immediately upon Spinoza's.

110 Locke, "First Tract on Government," in Mark Goldie, ed., *Political Essays* (Cambridge University Press, 1997), p. 37.

111 2TG, 9.128. See also 2.11 on the inconveniences of the state of nature and the power of the magistrate.

112 Ibid., 6.57.

113 Ibid.

114 Cicero, as quoted by Lactantius and Augustine, *On the Commonwealth*, 3.22, in C. D. Yonge, ed., *Cicero's Tusculan Disputations* (Harper, 1890), p. 437.

115 Gassendi, *Three Discourses*, p. 225.

116 Ibid., p. 330.

117 John Trenchard and Thomas Gordon, *Cato's Letters*, Ronald Hamowy, ed. (Liberty Fund, 1995), no. 33, 1.236.

118 Ibid., no. 44, 1.276. The basic idea that politics is about governing people as they are, passionate creatures, rather than as we would wish them to be has its clear beginning point in Machiavelli, and is central to many other writers in the republican tradition: Harrington, Hobbes, and Hume, for example.

119 Sidney, *Discourses*, ch. 3, sec. 11, 28.

120 Ibid., 3.36. See also 3.33 ("Liberty subsists, as arising from the nature and the being of a man") and 2.20. One scholar recently suggested that Sidney created a kind of "Amsterdam-on-Thames": "His work shows the pervading influence of a number of Dutch thinkers, most particularly Benedict Spinoza." (Lee Ward, *The Politics of Liberty in England and Revolutionary America* (Cambridge University Press, 2004), p. 193.) See also John Toland: "Right Reason is the only true law, a law befitting Nature, extended to all, consistent with itself, and everlasting." (Toland, *Pantheisticon: or, the Form of Celebrating the Socratic-Society* (London: Paterson, 1751), p. 85.)

121 Alexander Pope, *Essay on Man*, in Pat Rogers, ed., *The Major Works* (Oxford University Press, 2008) [hereafter *EM*], 3.271–72.

122 Even a teenager like Alexander Hamilton was versed in the reigning theory of natural rights: "The sacred rights of mankind are not to be rummaged for among old parchments or musty records. They are written, as with a sunbeam, in the whole *volume* of human nature," says Hamilton in a pam-

phlet of 1775. (Alexander Hamilton, *The Farmer Refuted* (New York: James Rivington, 1775), p. 38.) In *Federalist* paper no. 43, Madison invokes the same version of Natural Right along with its corresponding nature-deity in a discussion of the possibility that the Constitution might be ratified by only nine states: "The first question is answered at once by recurring to the absolute necessity of the case; to the great principle of self-preservation; to the transcendent law of nature and of nature's God, which declares that the safety and happiness of society are the objects at which all political institutions aim, and to which all such institutions must be sacrificed."

123 2TG, 3.19. See Charles A. Miller, *Jefferson and Nature* (Johns Hopkins University Press, 1988), p. 189.

124 Thomas Jefferson, *Notes on the State of Virginia*, Frank Shuffleton, ed. (Penguin Classics, 1998), Query 13; see also Jefferson to James Madison, January 1, 1796; and Jefferson to John Adams, October 14, 1816, in Cappon, ed., *Adams-Jefferson Letters*, p. 492.

125 Among America's revolutionary deists, the native population sometimes served as a way of projecting Locke's reasonable State of Nature onto the world. Here is William Bartram on his travels through North and South Carolina, lauding the quasi-utopia achieved by natives operating free from the white man's religion: Their "constitution . . . seems to be nothing more than the dictates of natural reason, plain to every one, yet recommended to them by their wise and virtuous elders as divine, because necessary for securing mutual happiness." (Bartram, *Travels through North & South Carolina*, p. 494.)

126 Ethan Allen et al. to William Tryon, June 5, 1774, in, *EIA*, 2.30.

127 Ira Allen, *Some Miscellaneous Remarks* (Hartford: Ebenezer Watson, 1777), in *EIA*, 1.129–30.

128 *EIA*, 2.140.

129 Like all good intuitions, the idea that individuals have certain unalienable rights has many parents. The ancient historian Tacitus, for example, opened his most famous work by congratulating himself for living in a "happy era, where everybody is permitted to think what they will, and to say what they think." (Tacitus, *History*, 1.1.) The Dutch, German, and Swiss Natural Law theorists of the seventeenth century went further and recognized that some aspects of individual activity are beyond the ability of any other entity to control. According to Grotius, for example, "Inalienable things are things which belong so essentially to one man that they could not belong to another, as a man's life, body, freedom, and honor." (Grotius, *The Jurisprudence of Holland* (Clarendon Press, 1926), 1.42.) Radical thinkers of the English Civil War also advanced notions of individual right. "To every individual in nature, is given individual propriety by nature, not to be invaded or usurped by any . . . for every one as he is himself hath a selfe propriety," said Richard Overton. (Don Marion Wolfe, *Leveller Manifestoes*

of the Puritan Revolution (Humanities Press, 1967), p. 162.) According to many interpreters of the history then and now, the most important source for the idea that all individuals possess a right to the freedom of thought and expression is the Protestant doctrine of freedom of conscience, which receives passionate support in the works of John Milton and Thomas Hooker among others.

130 Hobbes, *Leviathan*, 1.14. In *Leviathan*, 2.21, for example, Hobbes says, "It is manifest, that every Subject has Liberty in all those things, the right whereof cannot by Covenant be transferred." Hobbes allows that individuals are under no obligation to obey laws that require them to act against the laws of nature, such as to kill themselves; but, having transferred absolute authority over all things to the sovereign, Hobbes by no means disallows the state from attempting to demand such actions. (*De Cive*, 2.18–19, 6.13.)

131 "Nobody can so completely transfer to another all his right, and consequently his power, as to cease to be a human being, nor will there ever be a sovereign power that can do all that it pleases." (*TTP*, 17.1.) Spinoza expands on the list of unalienable rights in his *Treatise on Politics*: "Likewise, what rewards or threats can induce a man to love one whom he hates, or to hate one whom he loves? And in this category must be included those things so abhorrent to human nature that it regards them as the worst of all evils, such as that a man should bear witness against himself, should torture himself, should kill his own parents, should not endeavor to avoid death, and the like. (3.8.)

132 2TG, 2.6.

133 Ibid., 5.27.

134 Ibid., 9.123.

135 Michael Zuckert gets the idea when he suggests that Lockean Property "involves an extension of rights from the spheres of one's own life, body, and actions to the external world. It proclaims the rightful power of human beings to make the external their own in the same way they can make their bodies their own." Zuckert, *The Natural Rights Republic* (University of Notre Dame Press, 1996), p. 221, and *Launching Liberalism* (University Press of Kansas, 2002).

136 2TG, 5.31.

137 Ibid., 5.32.

138 *TP*, 7.19.

139 Jefferson to Pierre Samuel Dupont de Nemours, April 24, 1816, in Peterson, ed., *Thomas Jefferson*, p. 1384.

140 Jefferson to Madison, September 6, 1789, in Boyd, ed., *Papers* (1958), 15.392.

141 Jefferson to Madison, October 28, 1785, in ibid. (1953), 8.681.

142 Thomas Paine, *Agrarian Justice*, in Foner, ed., *Thomas Paine*, p. 396.

143 "Property monopolized or in the possession of a few is a curse to mankind." John Adams, "Notes for a Dissertation on the Canon and Feudal Law," in Robert J. Taylor et al., eds., *The Papers of John Adams* (Harvard University Press, 1983), 1.106.

144 Franklin is supposed to have said, "No man ought to own more property than needed for his livelihood; the rest, by right, belonged to the state." I have not found the source for this quote.

145 Thomas Young, "Philodicaios," in *Some Reflections on the Disputes between New-York, New-Hampshire, and Col. John Henry Lydius of Albany* (New Haven: Benjamin Mecom, 1764), p. 16.

146 Sidney, *Discourses*, ch. 3, sec. 16.

147 "This sacred Privilege is so essential to free Governments, that the Security of Property, and the Freedom of Speech always go together, and in those wretched countries where a Man cannot call his Tongue his own, he can scarce call any Thing else his own." (Trenchard and Gordon, *Cato's Letters*, no. 15, 1.110.) Consider also Toland: "When men are once enslaved in their understandings (which of all things ought to be the most free), it's scarce possible to preserve any other liberty." (Cited in Justin Champion, *Republican Learning: John Toland and the Crisis of Christian Culture, 1696–1722* (Manchester University Press, 2003), p. 245.)

148 *TTP*, 20.

149 Ibid. Like all theorists on the subject, Spinoza recognizes that there are practical limits to freedom of expression, in particular where it involves sedition or agitation on behalf of hostile powers, and exactly how these limits are recognized within civil law is a difficult topic that could be debated much further and that in any case surely varies according to historical circumstances.

150 Trenchard and Gordon, *Cato's Letters*, no. 62, 1.432.

151 Sidney, *Discourses*, ch. 2, sec. 11.

152 Jefferson to Nehemiah Dodge et al., January 1, 1802, in Boyd, ed., *Papers* (2009), 36.258. Jefferson's language here, incidentally, follows that of the philosophers of the eighteenth-century Scottish Enlightenment (in this case most likely Lord Kames); but that serves mainly to demonstrate that those sources are most usefully seen as vehicles for the transmission of a message from the great philosophers of the seventeenth century.

153 *TP*, 3.8, 7.26.

154 John Trenchard and Thomas Gordon, *The Independent Whig: Four Volumes in One* (Richard Marsh, 1816), 1.282.

155 Sidney, *Discourses*, ch. 3, sec. 36.

156 Locke, *Letter concerning Toleration*, William Popple, trans. (London: Awnsham & Churchill, 1689), p. 131.

157 Ibid., p. 154.

158 Ibid., p. 144.

159 David Freeman Hawke, *In the Midst of a Revolution* (University of Pennsylvania Press, 1961), p. 116.

160 John Adams to James Warren, May 15, 1776, in Robert J. Taylor et al., ed., *Papers of John Adams* (Harvard University Press, 1979), 4.186.

161 Richard Alan Ryerson, *The Revolution Is Now Begun* (University of Pennsylvania Press, 1978), p. 235; Hawke, *In the Midst of a Revolution*, p. 135.

162 Ryerson, *Revolution Is Now Begun*, p. 214–15.

163 Ibid., p. 216.

164 Thomason to Dickinson, August 16, 1776, cited in Hawke, *In the Midst of a Revolution*, p. 178.

165 Hawke, *In the Midst of a Revolution*, p. 175.

166 Marshall, *Passages from the Remembrancer*, p. 90.

167 Hawke, *In the Midst of a Revolution*, p. 193.

168 Bouton, *Taming Democracy*, p. 43.

169 In language and substance, the Declaration of Rights in the Pennsylvania Constitution is very similar to the Declaration of Rights authored by George Mason and passed by the Virginia legislature in June 1776. "The bill of rights is taken almost verbatim from that of Virginia, which was made and published two or three months before that of Philadelphia was begun; it was made by Mr. Mason, as that of Pennsylvania was by Timothy Matlack, James Cannon and Thomas Young and Thomas Paine." (Adams, ed., *Works*, 3.220.)

170 James Wilson, *Speech to the Pennsylvania Convention*, November 24, 1787, in Mark David Hall, ed., *Collected Works of James Wilson* (Liberty Fund, 2007), 1.193.

171 Madison, *Federalist*, no. 49, in Alexander Hamilton, James Madison, and John Jay, *The Federalist Papers*, Terence Ball, ed. (Cambridge University Press, 2003).

172 See, for example, Edmund S. Morgan, *Inventing the People: The Rise of Popular Sovereignty in England and America* (W. W. Norton, 1988).

173 The relationship between the sovereign people and their government can be thought of as a contract of sorts—though a peculiar one in three respects. First, this is not a contract between two equal and opposite entities, for the government does not come to the party with any rights at all. The contract is something closer to an act of trust or assignment of fiduciary responsibility through which a people at one and the same time bring into being and authorize the government to represent them or act as their agent. As Locke aptly expresses it, the people turn power over to government "with this express or tacit Trust, That it shall be employed for their Good." (2TG, 15.171.) Second, this contract of trust is a natural not a juridical one (at least among those who follow Spinoza and Locke in the move away from Hobbes). Which is to say, it is binding only insofar as it is useful. So, the contract that gives rise to government is in a

sense the way in which a people understands and expresses its own utility, or the (often imperfect) way in which it represents its quest for rational self-determination to itself. A third feature of this contract, which really follows closely on the second, is that it is not and never can be total in the sense of signing away all individual rights. The individual always preserves some degree of power, and this power, as we know, takes the form of unalienable rights.

174 Although Rousseau is perhaps the author most famously associated with this distinction, his political philosophy, setting aside a number of idiosyncrasies, is much more a reflection of what came before than is widely understood.

175 *TP*, 7.25.

176 Ibid., 3.9.

177 Sidney, *Discourses*, ch. 3, sec. 41.

178 Trenchard and Gordon, *Cato's Letters*, no. 60, 1.413.

179 James Wilson, "Lectures on Law," in Hall, ed., *Collected Works of James Wilson*, 2.947.

180 *TTP*, 16.

181 *TP*, 7.2.

182 *TTP*, 16.

183 Etienne Balibar, *Spinoza and Politics* (Verso, 1998).

184 *TTP*, 16.

185 Sidney, *Discourses*, ch. 2, sec. 20.

186 "An Elector," *Pennsylvania Packet*, April 30, 1776.

187 *TTP*, 20.

188 Jefferson to John Taylor, May 28, 1816, in Peterson, ed., *Thomas Jefferson*, p. 1391.

189 *TTP*, 16.

190 *TP*, 6.3.

191 2TG, 11.134; also 11.141, 13.149, 13.153.

192 Ibid., 11.142.

193 Ibid., 11.135.

194 Jefferson, *Notes on the State of Virginia*, Query 13.

195 *TP*, 1.6; also 6.3; Locke of course is adamant that monarchs are often nasty: absolute power fails to "correct the baseness of human nature." (2TG, 7.92.)

196 Timothy Dwight, *The Nature and Danger of Infidel Philosophy* (Ft. Worth, privately published, 2001), p. 100.

197 Trenchard and Gordon, *Cato's Letters*, no. 33, 1.261; no. 12, 1.75.

198 Ibid., nos. 25, 62, 115.

199 Sidney, *Discourses*, ch. 2, sec. 25.

200 Paine, *Common Sense*, in Foner, ed., *Thomas Paine*.

201 See also Madison, *Federalist*, nos. 51, 53, and his convention notes for June

6, 1787; and also *Memorial and Remonstrance*, in Robert A. Rutland, ed., *The Papers of James Madison* (University of Chicago, 1973), 8.295.

202   Joel Barlow, *A Letter to the National Convention of France* (1792), pp. 16–17.

203   Thomas Young, "To the Inhabitants of Vermont," April 11, 1777, in Henry H. Edes, "Memoir of Dr. Thomas Young, 1731–1777," *Colonial Society of Massachusetts, Transactions 1906–7*, 11 (1910): 44.

204   Madison, *Federalist*, no. 37.

205   Sidney, *Discourses*, ch. 2, sec. 25. Shaftesbury, the virtue-intoxicated philosopher, borrows this argument for republican virtue from Spinoza and Sidney and shoves it in Hobbes's face. "There is no real love of virtue, without the knowledge of public good. And where absolute power is, there is no public," he says. "And thus morality and good government go together." (Anthony Ashley Cooper, Third Earl of Shaftesbury, *Characteristics of Men, Manners, Opinions, Times* (Cambridge University Press, 1999), p. 72.) With a Hobbesian dictator-sovereign, Shaftesbury means to suggest, there is no sense of partnership. "Thus in a civil state or public we see that a virtuous administration, and an equal and just distribution of rewards and punishments, is of the highest service, not only by restraining the vicious . . . but by making virtue to be apparently the interest of every one." (Ibid., p. 271.)

206   *TTP*, 16; see also Gassendi, *Three Discourses*, p. 229.

207   Trenchard and Gordon, *Cato's Letters*, no. 33, 1.236: "This shews that those magistrates that are at absolute defiance with a nation, either cannot subsist long, or will not suffer the nation to subsist long; and that mighty traitors, rather than fall themselves, will pull down their country."

208   The term "theocracy" has a distinct meaning in Spinoza's writings, and I am not using it in that sense here. With reference to the early Hebrew state, Spinoza calls it the rule of God. However, I agree with Balibar that Spinoza also makes theocracy into a theoretical concept for the first time and thus makes it available for us.

209   Lucretius, *De rerum natura* [hereafter *DRN*], 1.104.

210   *TTP*, preface.

211   Pope, *EM*, 3.246–49.

212   Locke, *Letter concerning Toleration*, p. 163.

213   Trenchard, *Independent Whig*, 2.271. "It is a Principle in Politicks, that a Happy People will never bear a Tyrannical Prince: He must therefore make his Subjects wretched, before he can make himself absolute. And this Principle holds equally true, in the Business of *Church Dominion*. The Laity must be Fools, before they can think the Priests to be Oracles; and they must be Slaves, before they can think the Priests to be Lords." (Ibid., 2.284.)

214   Ibid. Gordon, perhaps the most viscerally anticlerical of the group, explains: "Reason and liberty are the two greatest gifts which man has given us, and yet wherever a priestly authority prevails, they must either fly or suffer."

(Trenchard and Gordon, *The Character of an Independent Whig*, pp. 5–6, cited in Champion, *Republican Learning*, p. 159.) In Gordon's translation of Tacitus, the emperor Nero serves as the abject example of the theocratic tyrant: "To prevent the poor people, thus doomed to bondage and misery, from perceiving how inhumanly they were abused and betrayed by their professed guides and pensioners, and by these their paid protector, they were blinded and terrified by the witchery words and superstition, nay, threatened with damnation, if you would not be damned to be slave." (Thomas Gordon, *The Works of Tacitus* (London: J. Rivington, 1770), 5.9–10.)

215 Robert Molesworth, *An Account of Denmark as it was in the Year 1692* (London: Timothy Goodwin, 1694), p. 236.

216 David Hume in Dorothy Coleman, ed., *Dialogues concerning Natural Religion and Other Writings* (Cambridge University Press, 2007), p. 98.

217 Bernard Bailyn, ed., *Pamphlets of the American Revolution: 1750–1765* (Harvard University Press, 1965), p. 425.

218 John Adams, *A Dissertation on the Canon and Feudal Law*, 1765, in Taylor et al., ed., *Papers of John Adams* (1977), 1.115. Adams's explicit target here, of course, was the "Romish clergy." Though he thought the Puritans in America had established a much better civil and ecclesiastical model, his comments on the bigotry and zealotry of his fellow Protestants are often perfectly acidic, too.

219 Madison, *Memorial and Remonstrance*, 1785.

220 Philip Freneau, "Ode to the Americans," in Fred Lewis Pattee, ed., *The Poems of Philip Freneau: Poet of the American Revolution* (Princeton University Library, 1903), 3.203.

221 Hobbes, *Leviathan*, 1.15.

222 *TP*, 4.4.

223 *TTP*, 16.

224 Ibid.

225 *TP*, 4.4–6.

226 Ibid., 5.2; see Machiavelli, *Discourses*, III.29.

227 *TTP*, 7.30.

228 2TG, 13.149.

229 Ibid., 19.224; Locke, *Letter concerning Toleration*, p. 163.

230 2TG, 19.225.

231 Ibid., 13.155.

232 *TP*, 7.30.

233 2TG, 13.155; see also 131, 132, 221, 222, 240.

234 *TP*, 5.2, 7.30.

235 2TG, 3.20.

236 "Tho' every private man, singly taken, be subject to the commands of the magistrate, the whole body of the people is not so; for he is by and for the people, and people is neither by nor for him," Sidney asserts. "No private

person has the right to enforce these laws," he adds; but "the whole body therefore of a nation cannot be tied to any obedience that is inconsistent with the common good, according to their judgment." (*Discourses*, ch. 3, sec. 36.)

237 Blackstone's comments on Locke and the state of nature and social contract, for example, seem contemptuous: "This notion, of an actually existing unconnected state of nature, is too wild to be seriously admitted." William Blackstone, *Commentaries on the Laws of England* (Oxford: Clarendon Press, 1765), 1.47.

238 Jefferson to James Brown, October 27, 1808, in Paul Leicester Ford, ed., *Works of Thomas Jefferson* (Putnam, 1905), vol. 11.

239 Anonymous, *Four Letters on Interesting Subjects* (Philadelphia: Styner & Cist, 1776), pp. 18–19.

240 L. H. Butterfield, ed., *The Diary and Autobiography of John Adams* (Belknap Press, 1962), 3.335.

241 Thomas Young, "To the Inhabitants of Vermont," April 11, 1777, in Edes, "Memoir of Dr. Thomas Young," p. 45.

242 Hawke, "Dr. Thomas Young," pp. 184, 204.

243 Cited in ibid., p. 187.

244 James Madison, June 1, 1787, available in Jonathan Elliot, ed., *Debates on the Adoption of the Federal Constitution* (Philadelphia, 1836).

245 Mercy Otis Warren, *Observations on the New Constitution* (New York, 1788).

246 Adams perversely insisted that the president was nonetheless a monarch—but then lamented that a true monarch would have an absolute veto and complete control over appointments.

247 Madison, *Federalist*, no. 14.

248 James Wilson, October 6, 1787, in *Pennsylvania Packet*, October 10, 1787.

249 This is Wilson's roughly accurate transcription of a passage from Edmund Burke's, *Reflections on the Revolution in France* (London: J. Dodsley, 1790), pp. 88–89.

250 *A Circular Letter from His Excellency George Washington*, June 18, 1783 (Philadelphia: Robert Smith, 1783). To the relief of defenders of religion today, Washington went on to give credit to "the pure and benign light of revelation," along with the growing liberality of sentiment," the growth of commerce, and a number of other factors, as a "meliorating influence on mankind." This, however, was a characteristic gesture of Washington and the deistic Enlightenment—to give popular religion credit for pacifying the rebarbative masses—and is discussed in chapter 8 here.

251 Dorothy Twohig, ed., *The Papers of George Washington: Presidential Series*, vol. 2: *April–June 1789* (University Press of Virginia, 1987), p. 163.

252 Joel Barlow, "At the Meeting of the Connecticut Society of the Cincinnati" (1787), in William Bottorf, ed., *The Works of Joel Barlow* (Scholars Facsimiles, 1970), 1.19.

253 Jefferson to Roger C. Weightman, June 24, 1826, in Peterson, ed., *Thomas Jefferson*, p. 1517.

Chapter 8: The Religion of Freedom

1 Gertrude Himmelfarb, *Roads to Modernity* (Vintage, 2005).
2 Giordano Bruno, *The Ash Wednesday Supper*, Edward A. Gosselin and Lawrence S. Lerner, trans. (University of Toronto Press, 1995), p. 177.
3 Joshua 10:12–13.
4 Benedict de Spinoza, *Tractatus Theologico-Politicus* [hereafter *TTP*], 2. Hobbes makes the additional point that Joshua cannot have written Joshua, and Spinoza agrees. (Thomas Hobbes, *Leviathan*, Noel Malcolm, ed. (Oxford University Press, 2012), 3.33; *TTP*, 8.)
5 *TTP*, 5.
6 Ibid., 2.
7 Ibid., 13.
8 Ibid., 15.
9 Benedict de Spinoza, *Principles of the Cartesian Philosophy* [hereafter *PCP*], Ap.2.8.
10 *TTP*, 13, 15.
11 John Locke, *The Reasonableness of Christianity* (London, 1695), p. 265. Also: "But the instruction of the people were best still to be left to the precepts and principles of the gospel. The healing of the sick, the restoring sight to the blind by a word, the raising and being raised from the dead, are matters of fact, which they can without difficulty conceive." (Ibid., p. 146.) Even in his first *Vindication*, written in response to heated attacks from defenders of orthodoxy, Locke insisted that Christianity is "easie to be understood." (Locke, *A Vindication of the Reasonableness of Christianity, etc.*, in Victor Nuovo, ed., *John Locke: Writings on Religion* (Clarendon Press, 2002) p. 222.)
12 Locke, *Reasonableness of Christianity*, p. 2.
13 Ibid., p. 304.
14 Locke, *A Discourse on Miracles*, in Nuovo, ed., *John Locke: Writings on Religion*, p. 50.
15 Locke, *Reasonableness of Christianity*, p. 143.
16 Ibid., p. 154.
17 John Locke, *Two Treatises of Government*, Peter Laslett, ed. (Cambridge University Press, 1960) [hereafter 1TG or 2TG], 4.31. See Wim Klever, *Boerhaave 'sequax Spinozae'* (Capelle aan den Ijssel, 2006), for this and more.
18 *PCP*, Ap.2.8.
19 *TTP*, 14.
20 Ibid., 2.
21 See Lord Herbert of Cherbury's *De religione gentilium* (1663), Charles

Blount's *Great Diana of the Ephesians* (1680), John Trenchard's *Natural History of Superstition* (1709), Matthew Tindal's *Christianity as Old as the Creation* (1730), and, of course, Bolingbroke's writings.

22 Justin Champion, *Republican Learning: John Toland and the Crisis of Christian Culture, 1696–1722* (Manchester University Press, 2003), p. 149.

23 Anthony Ashley Cooper, Third Earl of Shaftesbury, *The Life, Unpublished Letters, and Philosophical Regimen of Anthony, Earl of Shaftesbury*, Benjamin Rand, ed. (Swan Sonnenschien, 1900), p. xxvii.

24 Cadwallader Colden, "Principles of Action in Matter," in Scott L. Pratt and John Ryder, eds., *The Philosophical Writings of Cadwallader Colden* (Humanity Books, 2002), p. 97.

25 Benjamin Franklin, "Doctrine to be Preached," in *Papers* (American Philosophical Society and Yale University, franklinpapers.org), 1.212.

26 Adams to Jefferson, April 19, 1817, in Lester J. Cappon, ed., *The Adams-Jefferson Letters* (University of North Carolina Press, 1959), p. 509.

27 Ethan Allen, *Reason the Only Oracle of Man* (Bennington, Vermont: Haswell & Russell, 1784), p.1 87.

28 *TTP*, 4.

29 Ibid., 1. See also Spinoza to Oldenburg, November 1675, in Benedict de Spinoza, *Letters* [hereafter just *Letters*], 73.

30 *TTP*, 1.

31 Ibid., 15.

32 Locke, *Reasonableness of Christianity*, p. 161.

33 *TTP*, 4.

34 Ibid., 11 and note 27.

35 Ibid., 4.

36 Ibid., preface.

37 Locke, *Reasonableness of Christianity*, p. 231.

38 Ibid., p. 261.

39 Ibid., p. 240.

40 Ibid., p. 18.

41 Ibid., p. 233. Matthew 6:14.

42 Locke, *Reasonableness of Christianity*, p. 213.

43 Ibid., p. 254.

44 Ibid., p. 231.

45 Ibid., p. 257.

46 Ibid., p. 264.

47 John Edwards, *Some Reflections on the Causes and Occasions of Atheism in the Present Age*, (London: J. Robinson & J. Wyat, 1695). See also John Edwards, *The Socinian Creed* (London: J. Robinson, 1697).

48 Consider the case of William Stephens's *Account of the Growth of Deism in England* (London, 1696). Though pitched as an attack on the "prejudices" of the deists, Stephens's pamphlet in fact serves as a sympathetic exposition

of their doctrines, and it makes the case through the use of Locke's *Reasonableness of Christianity*. In one passage, Stephens sustains the pretense that one of his friends, supposedly a recovering deist, has learned from Locke's treatise to appreciate anew "the reality of reveal'd Religion." It turns out, however, that what the "ex-" deist has learned from Locke is that revelation is essentially a load of bunkum required to teach the moral law to a people oppressed by priests. "There was need enough of Miracle" to make priests and a "priest-ridden people" pay attention to the moral teaching of the Bible, he explains. Twisting the knife, he adds that "our several Sects of Clergy" are so "bigotted" that no miracle would be enough to free them from their prejudices.

49 See John Leland, *A View of the Principal Deistical Writers* (London: Charles Daly, 1754), 1.387; and Henry St. John Lord Viscount Bolingbroke, *The Works of Lord Bolingbroke* (Cary & Hart, 1841), 4.295.

50 Wilson, Douglas L., ed., *Jefferson's Literary Commonplace Book* (Princeton University Press, 1989) [hereafter *Jefferson's LCB*], sec. 28.

51 Jefferson to Peter Carr, August 10, 1787, in Julian P. Boyd, ed., *The Papers of Thomas Jefferson* (Princeton University Press, 1955), 12.14.

52 Jefferson to Dr. Joseph Priestley, April 9, 1803, in Merrill D. Peterson, ed., *Thomas Jefferson: Writings* (Library of America, 1984), p. 1120.

53 Jefferson to Adams, August 22, 1813, in Cappon, ed., *Adams-Jefferson Letters*, p. 369.

54 Joseph Priestley, *The Theological and Miscellaneous Works* (Shallfield, 1831), pp. 4–5.

55 Jefferson to Dr. Benjamin Rush, April 21, 1803, in Peterson, ed., *Thomas Jefferson*, p. 1122.

56 Jefferson to Mrs. Samuel H. Smith, August 6, 1816, in ibid., p. 1403.

57 Jefferson to Dr. Benjamin Rush, April 21, 1803, in ibid., p. 1122.

58 Jefferson to Ezra Stiles, June 25, 1819, in Albert Ellery Bergh, ed., *The Writings of Thomas Jefferson* (Jefferson Memorial Association, 1907), 15.202.

59 Boyd, ed., *Papers* (1950), 1.549–50.

60 Jefferson to F. A. Van der Kemp, July 30, 1816, in Matt Misbach, ed., *The Van der Kemp Collection* (Misbach Enterprises, 2007), p. 29.

61 Jefferson to Adams, July 5, 1814, in Cappon, ed., *Adams-Jefferson Letters*, p. 433.

62 Jefferson to William Short, October 31, 1819, in Paul Leicester Ford, ed., *Works of Thomas Jefferson* (Putnam, 1905), 12.140.

63 Jefferson to Benjamin Rush, April 21, 1803, in Peterson, ed., *Thomas Jefferson*, p. 1122. See also Jefferson to Charles Thomson, 1816: "I am a *real* Christian." (Ibid., p. 1372.) Jefferson's understanding of Christianity and popular religion makes itself evident once again in his response to Adam Weishaupt, one of the more eccentric characters in intellectual life of the

time. A founder of the Order of the Illuminati, Weishaupt believed in the perfectibility of humankind and promoted a thoroughly rationalist interpretation of Jesus and primitive Christianity. He became a controversial figure, was denounced as a heretic, and was eventually arrested. In a letter to Bishop James Madison of January 31, 1800, however, Jefferson seems to find in the controversial Weishaupt nothing very surprising at all. He calls him "an enthusiastic philanthropist" and compares him with "the excellent Price and Priestley." According to Jefferson, Weishaupt merely takes the view that Jesus's "intention was simply to reinstate natural religion, & by diffusing the light of his morality, to teach us to govern ourselves." Weishaupt's view, in short, is hardly different from Jefferson's own, which is presumably why the president notes, rather casually, that had the professor simply come to America, he might have disseminated his ideas without the need for secret societies, since so many people openly share his views.

64 Jefferson to Dr. Joseph Priestley, January 29, 1804, in Peterson, ed., *Thomas Jefferson*, p. 1141.

65 Thomas Jefferson, *The Jefferson Bible*, Forrest Church, ed. (Beacon Press, 1989).

66 Hobbes, *Leviathan*, 4.47.

67 *TTP*, 19.

68 Ibid., 18, 19.

69 Benedict de Spinoza, *Treatise on Politics* [hereafter *TP*], 6.40.

70 John Locke, "Of the Conduct of the Human Understanding," in *Posthumous Works of Mr. John Locke* (Churchill, 1706), p. 66.

71 Some religious conservatives in America wish to hold religious institutions exempt from criticism or above civil law—often in the name of what they call "religious liberty." They sometimes propose, for example, that religiously minded employers should be allowed to violate laws designed to protect employees where those laws violate their religious principles; or that merchants should be excused from providing services to those whom they deem to be religiously bad; or that communities living within special religious enclaves should be governed under their own laws. But "religious liberty" in this sense amounts to an attempt to gain exemptions from the law, that is, to appropriate a part of the power of the sovereign for the purposes of one religious sect or another. It is an attempt to use the rhetoric of toleration as a defense of intolerance. It isn't part of liberalism as it was originally conceived, and it isn't in the U.S. Constitution for that matter.

72 *TTP*, 18.

73 Ibid.

74 Anthony Ashley Cooper, Third Earl of Shaftesbury, "Letter concerning Enthusiasm," in *Characteristics of Men, Manners, Opinions, Times* (Cambridge University Press, 1999), p. 9.

75 George Mason in Robert A. Kutland, ed., *The Papers of George Mason* (University of North Carolina Press, 1970), p. 1071.

76 Jefferson to Mrs. Samuel H. Smith, August 6, 1816, in Peterson, ed., *Thomas Jefferson*, p. 1403.

77 Jefferson to Meeting of the Visitors, University of Virginia, October 7, 1822, in Boyd, ed., *Papers* (1974), 19:414; see for more discussion Allen Jayne, *Jefferson's Declaration of Independence* (University Press of Kentucky, 1998), p. 57; and Gilbert Chinard, *Thomas Jefferson: Apostle of Americanism* (Library of Alexandria, 1943), p. 675.

78 Jefferson to Nehemiah Dodge et al., January 1, 1802, in Boyd, ed., *Papers* (2009), 36.258.

79 Thomas Young, "To Sir Aaron Davis," *Massachusetts Spy*, December 4, 1772.

80 Jefferson to Dr. Benjamin Waterhouse, June 26, 1822, in Peterson, ed., *Thomas Jefferson*, p. 1458.

81 Jefferson to Adams, April 11, 1823, in Cappon, ed., *Adams-Jefferson Letters*, p. 594.

82 Paine, *The Age of Reason*, in Eric Foner, ed., *Thomas Paine: Collected Writings* (Library of America, 1995), p. 667.

83 Allen, *Reason the Only Oracle of Man*, p. 456.

84 Jefferson to Dupont de Nemours, April 24, 1816, in Peterson, ed., *Thomas Jefferson*, p. 1384.

85 Jefferson to George Wythe, August 13, 1786, in Boyd, ed., *Papers* (1954), 10.243.

86 Jefferson to Charles Yancey, January 6, 1816, in Ford, ed., *Works*, vol. 11.

87 Alexis de Tocqueville, *Democracy in America*, vol. 2, part I, ch. 5, available in George Lawrence, trans., *Democracy in America* (Harper, 1966), p. 242.

88 See Rev. Fred. A. Ross, *Slavery Ordained of God* (Philadelphia: Lippincott, 1857). Those today who perpetuate the myth that religion freed the slaves should be compelled to read Ross's work, which offers a lucid, humorous, and horrifying expression of the white antebellum ideology according to which slavery not only is a boon to the slave but also ennobles the master and serves God's plan.

89 See Eugene D. Genovese, *Roll, Jordan, Roll: The World the Slaves Made* (Random House, 1972).

90 The ardent abolitionist William Lloyd Garrison, for example, appeared to lean to Unitarianism, expressed distinctly deist sentiments, and was formally associated with no orthodox religion or church at all. Lysander Spooner was an avowed deist. John Brown, on the other hand, was a hard-line Calvinist, and wielded his Bible against Garrison in favor of a violent approach to abolition. Many northern churches became central sources of support for the anti-slavery movement; and many opposed. What we know for sure is that every side of the struggle over slavery had God on its side.

91 A 2002 Pew Research Center says that 47 percent of Americans believe that morality is impossible without God, while the rest think it possible or don't know. Pew Center, "Americans Struggle with Religion's Role," March 20, 2002. See also Penny Edgell, Joseph Gerteis, and Douglas Hartmann, "Atheists as Other: Moral Boundaries and Cultural Membership in American Society," *American Sociological Review* 71 (April 2006): 211–34 "Atheists are less likely to be accepted, publicly and privately, than any others from a long list of . . . minority groups." See also Will Gervais et al., "Do You Believe in Atheists," *Journal of Personality and Social Psychology* 101(6) (December 2011): 1189–206. Phil Zuckerman, "Atheism, Secularity, and Well-Being," *Sociology Compass* 3(6) (2009): 949–71: "Atheism and secularism are positively correlated with societal well-being."

92 Cited in Bernard Bailyn, *The Ideological Origins of the American Revolution* (Harvard University Press, 1967), p. 230.

93 "The death of my little boy closely affected the tender passions of my soul," Ethan told brother Levi, feeling "the most sensible grief." Ethan to Levi, July 27, 1777, in John J. Duffy et al., eds., *Ethan Allen and His Kin: Correspondence, 1772–1819* (University Press of New England, 1998) [hereafter *EAK*],1.71.

94 Justus Sherwood, "Journal," *Vermont History* 24 (1956): 220.

95 Ethan Allen to Hector St. John de Crèvecoeur, April 14, 1787, in *EAK*, 1.231.

96 "Lord George Gordon," *Vermont Gazette*, May 16, 1786.

97 "For the Vermont Gazette," *Vermont Gazette*, June 26, 1786.

98 Ira Allen to Samuel Williams, June 6, 1795, in *EAK*, 2.444.

99 Charles A. Jellison, *Ethan Allen: Frontier Rebel* (Syracuse University Press, 1969), p. 331.

Index

Page numbers beginning with 439 refer to endnotes.

abolitionism, 34
Absurdity and Blasphemy of Depreciating Moral Virtue, The (Briant), 61
Absurdity and Blasphemy of Rev. Briant, The, 61
Account of Denmark (Molesworth), 378
Acts of the Apostles, 170
Adam, 53, 54, 300, 407
Adams, Abigail, 62, 408
   correspondence of John Adams and, 40, 330
Adams, John, 35, 82, 111–12, 203, 302, 317, 329–32, 409
   character and personality of, 17, 32, 235, 286
   childhood and adolescence of, 61, 207
   correspondence of Abigail Adams and, 40, 330
   diary of, 17–19, 111, 187–88
   education of, 47, 61
   extensive reading of, 32
   on Jefferson, 17
   Jefferson and, 36, 55, 99–100, 111,

188–89, 195–96, 221, 234–35, 239, 304, 404, 411, 421
   law career of, 62
   as "monarchical republican," 336
   on Paine, 32
   on Protestantism, 70
   religious beliefs of, 32, 61–62, 404
   resolution on new governments offered by, 363–67
   sources for, 441
   on spirit and matter, 235
   on Thomas Young, 21
Adams, Samuel, 18, 20, 32–33, 264–68, 302, 352
   arsenal gathered by, 266, 267
   patriotic militancy of, 134, 135, 264–66
   Thomas Young and, 332
Addison, Joseph, 301–2, 303
African Americans, 367
Age of Reason (Paine), 31–32, 127, 189, 247, 335, 421
Albany, N.Y., 18, 76, 133–34, 234, 331, 334

Allah, 209
Allen, Ethan, 1–2, 4, 9–16, 22, 31, 35,
    36, 112, 124, 127–28, 170, 353
    ambition and enterprise of, 9–13,
        47
    assault of Fort Ticonderoga by, 1,
        10, 11, 199–200, 316–21, 388,
        432
    atheism or deism of, 12, 14, 194–
        95
    authority defied by, 40–42, 132–33
    business pursuits of, 9
    character and personality of, 9–13,
        39–42, 47–48, 54, 74, 131–33,
        200, 203, 268–71, 318, 392–94,
        434
    childhood and adolescence of, 54,
        60, 201
    children of, 392
    condemnation of, 13–14, 435
    on conscience, 304
    controversial book of, 1–3, 11–16,
        23–24, 28, 31–32, 34, 47–48,
        54–55
    death and burial of, 423, 434–35
    drinking and blasphemy of, 39,
        40–42, 132–33
    first marriage of, 392–93
    God of Nature proclaimed by, 131,
        133, 138
    Green Mountain Boys led by, 1,
        9–11, 16, 131–33, 199–200, 316–
        21
    on human body, 238–39
    on human nature, 221
    later life of, 74
    on liberty, 270
    on miracles, 225
    on morality, 308
    mortality as preoccupation of,
        201–3
    pamphlets of, 132
    political aspirations of, 13
    popularity and fame of, 9, 13, 269
    as prisoner of war, 10, 13, 200, 202,
        321, 432, 433
    real estate of, 269
    religious and philosophical beliefs
        of, 12, 14, 54–55, 74, 194–95,
        201–3, 204, 217, 225, 308, 404,
        435, 489
    revolutionary militancy of, 1, 10,
        11, 199–200, 269–71
    scant formal education of, 9, 14,
        47–48, 54, 201
    second marriage of, 393–94, 432
    smallpox inoculation of, 39, 40–41,
        42, 74, 75, 239
    sources for, 441–42
    Thomas Young and, 23–24, 32, 39,
        40–42, 195, 197, 200, 205–6, 250,
        318, 431, 435
    trial and acquittal of, 43
    works of, 132, 202, 392
    see also Oracles of Reason (Allen)
Allen, Fanny Montresor, 392–94, 432
Allen, Ira, 20, 23, 54, 133, 317, 353,
    432
Allen, Joseph (Ethan's father), 60,
    201
Allen, Joseph (Ethan's son), 432
Allen, Mary Brownson, 392–93
Allen, Zimri, 133
Amenia, N.Y., 23, 39, 76
American Philosophical Society, 111,
    188
American Revolution, 1–7, 10, 77,
    104, 109, 111
    aftermath of, 12, 13, 24, 120, 200,
        385, 421–22
    alliance of infidels and enthusiasts
        in, 69–72, 73–74
    doctors in, 208
    emergence of modern world from,
        316
    heroes of, 389
    history of, 80
    leadership of, 319

lead-up to, 17, 20, 81, 127, 321, 378
message of, 390
philosophical and religious
  influences on, 2–7, 17–38, 68,
  79–80, 105, 138, 141, 144, 175,
  181, 322
political theory and, 327
principles of, 315
as struggle for independence, 314
unfinished business of, 431
Amsterdam, 140, 141
"Anatomie of the World, An"
  (Donne), 118–19
Anderson, George Pomeroy, 16,
  205–6
Anglo-Saxons, 26
animals:
  consciousness of, 211, 230
  dissection of, 206
  experiments with, 239
  propagation of, 102, 103, 212
anti-Federalism, 385–86
anti-transcendental social-contract
  theory, 327–28, 343–45
"Apple and Worm" (Klever), 2–4
Aristotle, 65, 78, 84, 85, 94, 97, 117–
  18, 295
Arminianism, 44, 58–61, 168
Arminius, Jacobus, 44
Arnold, Benedict, 321
  at Battle of Fort Ticonderoga,
    316–20, 388, 432
  character and personality of, 316–
    19, 388
"Articles of Belief" (Franklin), 115–16,
  185
asceticism, 291, 300
astronomy, 16, 67, 109–11, 118, 194,
  206
  plurality of worlds doctrine in,
    11–12
atheism, 3, 4–6, 14, 26, 28, 30, 35, 42,
  54, 59, 80, 85, 113, 118, 120, 124,
  131, 142, 313, 426

condemnation of, 85, 198, 229, 251
Enlightenment and, 5
forms of, 145, 146, 156, 168, 171,
  173, 174, 176, 194, 196
French, 196
gateway to, 327
medicine and, 206
pantheism vs., 194
promotion of, 83, 173
punishment for, 83–84
virtuous, 309–11, 427
Athens, 6, 80–81, 170
Atlantic Ocean, 43, 292
atomism, 94–95, 96–98, 100, 101, 106,
  119, 142, 219, 430, 466, 470–71
Augustine, Saint, 406
Augustinian order, 117
Autobiography (Franklin), 27, 186, 191,
  285, 308
Averroes (Ibn Rushd), 244, 478

Bacon, Lord Francis, 82, 84, 93–94,
  116, 513
Baker, Polly (fictional), 183–84, 186
Balibar, Etienne, 371
Baptist Church, 31, 361, 419–20
Barbé-Marbois, Marquis François de,
  187–88
Barlow, Joel, 7, 28, 138, 334, 375, 390
Bartlet, Phebe, 50–51, 52
Bartram, William, 138, 521
Bayle, Pierre, 78, 79, 84, 85, 140, 144,
  173, 279, 309–10
beauty, 302, 394
Becker, Carl, 141, 474
Beecher, Lyman, 28
"Belief and Unbelief" (Freneau), 218
believing, 216
  connection between willing and,
    217, 222
  evidence and, 217–18, 224
  involuntary, 217, 224
  in miracles, 222–23
  profession of, 218

Bellarmine, Cardinal Robert, 79, 117
Bennington, Vt., 13, 394
    Catamount Tavern in, 131–32
    First Church in, 199–200
Bennington Mob, *see* Green
    Mountain Boys
Bentley, Richard, 85, 168, 176
Berkeley, George, Bishop of Cloyne,
    173, 179, 181, 485
Bernier, François, 277
Beverley, Robert, 30
Bible, 14, 70, 117, 169, 224, 339–40,
    397–99
    as foundation of worship, 59, 145,
    226
    interpretation of, 206
    King James, 47
    moral actions directed by, 397
    New Testament, 29, 78, 409, 412
    Old Testament, 335
    parables of, 47, 398
    prophecies of, 398
    Protestant, 226
    see also specific Biblical books
big bang, 108
Blackmore, Richard, 85, 142, 173
Blount, Charles, 126, 127
    deism of, 402
    as Spinoza disciple, 142, 232
    works of, 15, 23, 28, 64, 86, 169
Boerhaave, Herman, 206–7, 237–39
Bolingbroke, Henry St. John,
    Viscount, 31, 65–67, 68, 121, 138,
    146, 153, 172–73, 310
    character and personality of,
    65–66
    on Christianity, 408–9
    deism of, 402
    influence of, 184
    on self-love, 282–83, 295
    sources for, 442
    on Stoicism, 302
    works of, 66–67, 100, 104, 109,
    139, 171, 233

Bolshevik Revolution of 1917, 365
Boston, Mass., 21, 29, 40, 56, 60, 61,
    64, 67, 77, 111, 125, 134–37,
    204–5, 250
    "Body" in, 263–65
    British driven from, 320
    British occupation of, 134–36,
    263–65
    Customs House in, 263
    deists in, 126–27
    educated population of, 30
    Faneuil Hall in, 264
    Harbor in, 264
    King Street in, 263–64
    newspapers of, 127, 136, 137–38,
    266
    Old South Church in, 17, 264–65
    radical faction in, 18–19, 20, 30,
    134–36
    town meetings in, 364, 449
Boston Committee of
    Correspondence, 18–20, 22, 30,
    134, 135, 204, 268, 355, 473
Boston Declaration of 1772, 352, 362,
    373, 449
Boston Evening Post, 127, 137–38
Boston Gazette, 127
"Boston Massacre," 136, 264
Boston Tea Party, 17, 30, 135, 264,
    265, 448
botany, 237
Boudinot, Elias, 32–33
Bowdoin, James, 266
Boyle, Robert, 166
Boyle Lectures, 27, 28, 85, 165–66,
    168, 176
Bracciolini, Poggio, 82
Bradley, Stephen, 393
brain, 221
    injuries of, 211
    as seat of sensation, 237, 239
    study of, 239
Braintree, Mass., 61
Briant, Lemuel, 61–62

British Army, 10, 263–64, 267, 269, 271
  Hessian and Hanoverian mercenaries in, 363
British Constitution, 138, 333, 335, 382–83
British Empire, 17, 18, 20, 334, 402
  see also England; Great Britain
British Parliament, 138
  colonial taxes imposed by, 133–34, 264
  House of Commons in, 333
  House of Lords in, 333
British Royal Navy, 363
Brooklyn, 1
Brown, Charles Walter, 14
Bruno, Giordano, 78–80, 82–84, 91, 93–95, 111, 115, 118, 120, 124, 128–29, 195
  on Bible, 397–98
  critique of miracles by, 222
  Epicureanism of, 79, 106
  fame of, 144
  on freedom, 253
  as "knight-errant of philosophy," 78, 117
  on nature of God, 150, 151, 349
  rediscovery of Lucretius by, 79–80, 82–83, 95, 108–9, 128–29, 166–67
  sources for, 442
  trial and execution of, 78–79, 117
  works of, 82–83, 86, 89, 183
Buddhism, 277
Bunker Hill, Battle of, 40, 208
Burke, Edmund, 387
Burlington, Vt., 432–35
Burr, Aaron, 43

Caesar, Gaius Julius, 301
Cain, 136–37, 186
Caldwell, Charles, 207
Caldwell, James, 263
Calvin, John, 55, 406, 434

Calvinism, 56, 62, 111, 168, 183, 300, 310, 312, 498, 513, 533
Cambridge, Mass., 317
Campanella, Tommaso, 156
Canada, 266, 320
  French Canadian and Indian army in, 321
Cannon, James, 331, 336, 337, 366, 384–85
Cape Cod, Mass., 46
capitalism, 429
Capitol, U.S., 25
Carr, Peter, 25, 198, 311–12, 409
Carroll, William, 146, 173, 477
Cato (Addison), 301–2, 303
Cato's Letters (Gordon and Trenchard), 64, 153, 163, 181, 232, 247, 282, 298, 302, 310, 351, 370, 501
Cato the Elder, 64, 301–2, 303
Catskill Mountains, 46
cause and effect, 101, 107, 154, 160
Causes and Occasions of Atheism in the Present Age, The (Edwards), 408
Characteristicks (Shaftesbury), 67, 152, 165
charity, 307, 308, 400, 417
Charles II, King of England, assassination plots against, 139–40, 347, 390
Chauncy, Charles, 60
Christianity, 5, 6, 31–33, 100–101, 138, 158, 170, 234, 298–99, 379, 405–16
  baptism and marriage in, 413, 415
  Biblical, 145, 397–99
  common law and, 26
  conversion to, 45, 50–52, 58–59, 62
  defense of, 145, 221
  deism vs., 137, 300–301
  democratization of church life in, 69

Christianity (*continued*)
disbelief in and opposition to,
11–12, 26, 28, 29, 30, 32, 37,
53–57, 59, 62, 66, 77–78, 136,
138, 145, 299–300, 402, 409,
414–15
doctrine of fall of man and original
sin in, 32, 53, 54, 61, 300–301,
411
doctrine of heaven and hell in, 45,
49–52, 110
doctrine of salvation through faith
in, 32, 54–55, 241, 300, 301
doctrine of the Eucharist in, 411
doctrine of the Trinity in, 61, 117,
312, 366, 406, 411
doctrine of transubstantiation in,
117
doctrines of election and
predestination in, 58
early, 192
emergence of, 81
Epicurean philosophy and, 82, 85
European culture infused with, 85
evangelical, 69
"fables" and "corruptions" of, 32,
101
founding of U.S. and, 28, 187,
423–25
morality and, 309
nationalist, 72, 444–46
priesthood in, 378–79, 408–9, 411,
413–14, 420–22
proliferation of sects in, 68–69
proselytizing in, 68–69
reward of virtue in, 299
rites of, 117, 413, 415
schism and controversy in, 60–63
stoicism and, 303
ultra-liberal, 145
versions of, 402
see also Jesus Christ; *specific sects*
Christianity Not Mysterious (Toland),
144, 408

Chubb, Thomas, 246, 248
Church of England, 402–3
deists in, 29
Cicero, Marcus Tullius, 81, 114,
350–51, 353
civilization, 209
liberal societies in, 210
civil state, 346–47, 350, 353–55
as Empire of Reason, 418–19
Clarke, Samuel, 165–66, 408, 487
Collins debate with, 165–66, 232–
34
Newton and, 165, 176, 178–81,
184
Clidophorus (Toland), 120
Colden, Cadwallader, 33, 194, 403
Collins, Anthony, 67, 68, 113, 140,
143, 149, 160, 165–66, 173,
177–79, 470
Clarke debate with, 165–66, 232–34
on liberty, 254–55
radical philosophy of, 212
works of, 153, 185
Columbia University, 29
Committee of War, 317
common law, 26
Common Sense (Paine), 19, 334–36,
375, 421
communism, 59
communitarianism, 313
community, 312–13
social values of, 293
"conatus" concept, 253, 255–56,
279–82, 285, 296
Concord, Battle of, 10, 270
Concord, Mass., 266
Congress, U.S., 79
Connecticut, 12, 23, 41, 59, 329, 390
Connecticut River, 43
conscience, 276, 304, 375
freedom of, 71–72, 73, 226, 363,
365, 420
moral judgment and, 297–98
sense of good and evil in, 305

consciousness, 101, 209, 283
  as action, 216
  of animals, 211, 230
  of children, 230, 231
  common, 211, 213, 215, 227, 235, 396–97, 430
  in form of ideas, 216
  picture-theory of, 210–11, 216, 222, 226–27, 235, 239–40
  radical view of, 213, 217, 227
  religious, 92, 98, 105, 106, 130–31, 174, 227, 309, 329, 397, 427
  self-, 230
  of thought, 212–13
conservatism, 19, 306
  religious, 6–7, 36, 40, 187, 532
Constitution, U.S., 28–29, 372, 385–88, 410
  Article III of, 386
  Bill of Rights of, 19, 386, 419
  contents of, 385–87
  defenders of, 386
  First Amendment to, 413
  foundations of, 370, 376
  Fourteenth Amendment to, 388
  institution of slavery embedded in, 387
  as part of revolutionary process, 386
  preamble of, 29, 367
  ratification of, 386, 388
  writing of, 28–29, 367, 419
Constitutional Convention of 1787, 187, 385
Continental Army, 21, 265, 389
Continental Congress, see Second Continental Congress
Copernican theory, 117, 119
Corinthians, First Epistle to, 77–78
corruption, 297, 300–301, 334, 376
cosmology, 106–12
cosmopolitanism, 294–95, 298
Cosway, Maria, 303
Counter-Enlightenment, 292
courage, 297

"CREED" (Young), 271–73
Crèvecoeur, John Hector St. John de, 10, 68, 433, 457–58
crime, 311
  avoidance of, 276
  punishment of, 355, 383
Cromwell, Oliver, 192
Cumberland, Richard, 343

D'Alembert, Jean-Baptiste le Rond, 28
Danbury, Conn., 361, 419–20
Darwin, Charles, 104–5, 427
Darwin, Erasmus, 104–5, 468
Darwinism, 106, 173, 342, 348–49
Darwin's Dangerous Idea (Dennett), 104
David, King, 137
Day of Judgment, 241
death, 235
  fear of, 87, 240
  life after, 31, 201–2, 204, 240–51, 389
  reality of, 202
Declaration of Independence, 290, 388
  case for rebellion in, 382–83
  final paragraph of, 191
  first draft of, 199, 262, 354
  forerunners of, 19
  Jefferson's writing of, 25, 138–39, 141, 199, 225, 262, 313, 314, 328–29, 354, 390–91
  opening sentence of, 129
  preamble to, 6, 328–29, 379–80
  religious references in, 6–7, 199
  revision of, 199
  revolutionary force of, 391
  second sentence of, 262
  signers of, 208, 329, 383
Defence of the Medical Profession against the Charge of Infidelity and Irreligion (Caldwell), 207
deism, 4–7, 14–15, 22–23, 27–34, 38, 47, 57, 142–43, 191

deism (*continued*)
  of American revolutionaries,
    33–34, 36, 37, 47, 53, 80, 93, 111,
    168, 188, 191, 197, 217, 247–48,
    284, 298, 301, 314, 403, 422–23
  "Christian," 73
  Christianity vs., 137, 300–301
  classical, 64, 175–77
  criticism of, 30–31, 85, 136–37, 186
  defense of, 137
  elements of, 5–7, 30, 176
  in England, 69, 196, 246, 254–55
  expression of, 71
  formal preaching of, 217–18
  history of, 145
  international character of, 33
  literature of, 25–26, 27, 29–30, 64,
    66, 79–83
  morality of, 412
  nature of, 126
  origins of, 5
  pantheism vs., 194–95
  philosophical, 401, 402
  popular, 401, 402, 404, 408, 410,
    418, 420, 422
  religion-friendly, 396, 402
  study of nature as core of, 197
  versions of, 73, 175, 181
  virtue and, 298–303
  see also God of Nature
Delaware, 336
democracy, 18, 19, 20, 26, 59, 63, 315,
    367, 370–73
  definition of, 370
  elections in, 372
  general principle of, 371–73
  liberal, 209, 423
  power of, 376
  representative, 334
  theocracy vs., 377
Democritus, 86, 95, 97, 155, 464–65
Dennett, Daniel, 104, 499
Descartes, René, 27, 84, 120, 206, 212–
    14, 227–29, 238, 255, 463, 471–72

  dead-animal laboratory of, 228
  disciples and influence of, 150,
    151, 160, 209, 228–29, 238
  dualism of, 227, 232, 500
  on human body, 235, 237
  on ideas, 216
  on imagination vs. understanding,
    213
  on immortality of soul, 240–41
  influence of, 150, 151, 160, 209
  insight and intuition of, 212–13
  "I think therefore I am"
    proposition of, 212
  materialism of, 287
  medicinal observations of, 236
  misinterpretation of, 212
  monism of, 228, 231, 241
  on senses, 219
  works of, 120, 168, 228
desire, 256–57, 285–86, 287–88
  control of, 291
  for virtue, 295–96
despair, 288
determinism, 480
  reductive, 155
Dewey, Jedediah, 199–200
de Witt, Cornelis, 36
D'Holbach, Paul-Henri Thiry, Baron,
    194, 196, 490
*Dialogue between A___ and B___ on a
    Subject of the Last Importance*, 29
Dialogue between my Head & my Heart
    (Jefferson), 303
*Dialogue concerning the Two Chief World
    Systems* (Galileo), 117–18, 167
Diary (Adams), 17–19, 111, 187–88
Dickinson, John, 141, 336, 337, 364,
    365
Dictionary (Rider), 193
Diderot, Denis, 56, 104, 194, 196, 491
Diogenes Laërtius, 81
Discourse on Miracles (Locke), 399
Discourses (Sidney), 63
Dissertation on Liberty and Necessity, A

(Franklin), 54, 184–85, 188, 207, 221, 242–43, 247, 285
Dissertation on Liberty and Necessity (Collins), 153
divine rights, 122
"Doctrine to be Preached" (Franklin), 403
Dominican order, 117
Donne, John, 118–19
doubting, 216, 221
dualism, 227, 232, 500
Dublin, 45
Dutchess County Courthouse, 56
Dutch language, 63
Dwight, Abigail, 308
Dwight, Timothy, 15, 41, 43, 66, 68, 328, 460
    sermons of, 40
    as Yale president, 13, 28, 453

East India Company, 17, 264
eating, 275, 276, 285
Edwards, Jonathan, 41, 56–63, 66, 68, 69, 158, 246, 408, 455
    character and personality of, 43–44
    death of, 63
    diary of, 43–44
    ministry and sermons of, 43–45, 48–52, 54, 56–62, 73, 74, 301, 430
    Princeton presidency of, 63
    sources for, 442
Edwards, Jonathan, Jr., 28, 34, 247
Edwards, Sarah, 51, 62
ego, 209, 212, 259–60
Einstein, Albert, 92, 174, 244–45
    relativity theory of, 401–2
Emerson, Ralph Waldo, 30
emotions, 288
    passive, 290, 297
Enfield, Conn., 49
England, 18–19, 45, 82, 97, 109, 111–12, 144–45, 168, 331

church and state alliance in, 26
deism in, 69
freethinking in, 54
Norman Conquest of, 26, 63
republican ideas in, 351
see also British Empire; Great Britain
English Civil War, 69, 84, 351
English Revolution of 1688, 351, 382, 452
Enlightenment, 73, 170, 200, 209, 266
    Anglo-American, 139
    atheism and, 5
    British, 281–82
    core religious sensibility of, 166–67
    critique of, 396
    Dutch, 4, 143, 206, 237, 490
    Epicureanism and, 286
    faith undermined in, 221
    French, 5, 33, 124, 144, 194
    hedonism and, 298
    heroes of, 55
    history of, 181
    moral philosophy of, 292–93
    philosophers of, 3–5, 130
    radical vs. moderate schools of, 147–48, 197, 293
    reason and, 394
    Scottish, 298–99
    theological drift of, 168
envy, 288
Epictetus, 409, 412
Epicurean philosophy, 79–80, 151, 179
    ascetic side of, 291
    Christianity and, 82, 85
    concept of evolution in, 102–4
    core guiding principles of, 79, 87–94, 96–97, 101, 107, 148–49, 297
    cosmology in, 106–12
    criticism of, 81, 82, 85, 142, 163, 298

Epicurean philosophy (*continued*)
  ethics and morality of, 275–77, 292
  four essential virtues of, 285
  hedonism of, 291
  historical impact of, 87–89, 105
  as lifestyle, 87
  philosophies influenced by, 80, 81,
    83–87, 89–90, 95–101, 126
  physical doctrines of, 88, 99–100,
    126
  pleasure doctrine in, 275–76, 278–
    79
  popular form of, 87
  promotion of, 82–83, 84, 86–87,
    96, 97
  pursuit of happiness in, 274–75
  revival of, 80, 82, 84–85, 106, 120,
    123, 291, 412–13
  spread and popularity of, 81, 84–86
  swerve (*clinamen*) doctrine in,
    155–56, 252
Epicurus, 79–90, 93–97, 99–108,
  118–20, 139, 142, 171, 212, 214,
  238, 323
  as "ancient master of the atheistic
    deists," 85
  birth of, 80, 105
  death of, 81
  dogmatism of, 94
  enemies of, 275
  friendship valued by, 275
  Greek predecessors of, 92, 95, 100
  on justice, 325–26
  letters and sayings of, 81, 93, 100,
    243
  philosophical garden commune of,
    80–81
  plain diet of, 275
  praise of, 83
  probity and honour of, 311
  Saint Paul vs., 125
  simple lifestyle of, 81
  sources for, 442
  "swerve" of the atoms doctrine of, 97

  virtue of, 310
Episcopal Church, 112
Eppes, Francis, 35
equality, 209, 315, 321–28
  independence and, 328
  moral imperative of, 322
  natural, 321, 323–26, 328
Erasmus, Desiderius, 82
Erasmus University, 4
Erastianism, 414
Erastus, Thomas, 414
esoteric writing, 121–23
*Essay concerning Human
  Understanding, An* (Locke), 141,
  146, 147, 148, 152, 157, 168,
  220–21, 224, 231, 278, 290, 479
"Essay on Government" (Locke),
  64
Essay on Man (Pope), 64–65, 67, 86,
  98, 126, 138, 145, 153, 181–83,
  301, 459–60
Ethan Allen furniture company, 11
ethics, 275–77, 283, 409
  radical, 346–47
Ethics (Spinoza), 153, 238, 292
Euripides, 67
Eve, 54
evolution:
  Darwin's theory of, 104, 105
  natural selection and, 102–5, 293
Expulsion of the Triumphant Beast, The
  (Bruno), 86
extraterrestrial life, 77–80, 83, 90,
  108–9, 110, 124, 126

Fable of the Bees, The (Mandeville),
  142, 207
faith, 125, 126, 226, 308, 398
  acts of, 92, 93, 261
  certainty and, 221
  definition of, 217–18
  good, 297, 373, 401
  leap of, 149, 209, 211
  reasoning and, 217, 224

religious, 221, 229, 309, 365
without works, 309
fatalism, 142, 151, 155, 168
fear:
of death, 87, 240
of deities, 87
exploitation of, 87
imagination and, 91
projection of, 126
Federalism, 311
Federalist essays (Madison), 385
Ferguson, James, 67, 110–11, 126, 189
feudal system, 395
Ficino, Marsilio, 82
Filmer, Robert, 122, 327–28, 516–17
fire, invention of, 103
First Great Awakening, 45, 60, 61, 62,
    332–33
Flourens, Jean Pierre, 239
*Folly of Atheism, or what is now called
    Deism, The* (Bentley), 85
Ford, Hezekiah, 187
fortitude, 285, 296
Fort Ticonderoga, 271
    assault of Allen and the Green
        Mountain Boys on, 1, 10, 11,
        199–200, 316–21, 388, 432
founders, American, 17–18, 71, 216,
        329, 430
    cult of, 37
    deism of, 33–34, 36–37, 47, 53, 80,
        93, 111, 168, 188, 191, 197, 217,
        247–48, 284, 298, 301, 314, 403,
        422–23
    diversity of, 34
    influence of books on, 24–31,
        63–68, 93–94
    religious and philosophical beliefs
        of, 2–7, 22–38, 93–94, 113, 130,
        225–26, 274, 284
    skepticism of, 94
    unique government set up by, 313
    virtue celebrated by, 274
    see also specific founders

Four Letters on Interesting Subjects,
    383–84
Fourth of July, 336
France, 5, 18, 66, 83, 120, 124, 147,
    196, 358–59, 366–67
    Enlightenment in, 5, 33, 124, 144,
        194
    religious practice in, 56
Franciscan order, 117
Francis of Assisi, Saint, 300
Franklin, Benjamin, 17, 19, 30, 33, 36,
        86, 104, 110–11, 170, 207, 217,
        329, 331
    as ambassador to France, 286,
        366–67
    business empire of, 403–4
    character and personality of, 28,
        32, 48, 93, 94, 285–86
    childhood and adolescence of, 27,
        32, 34, 35, 47, 48, 53–54, 67, 142,
        191, 251, 255
    deist beliefs of, 27–28, 29, 85, 138,
        168, 184–88, 197, 300
    on desire, 285–86
    education of, 47
    ethical stance of, 285
    extensive reading of, 27–28, 34,
        67
    fortune of, 403–4
    on happiness, 303
    humor of, 184, 285
    moral reform urged by, 286
    philosophical guides of, 67, 403
    on pleasure and pain, 285, 286
    religion rejected by, 27–28,
        53–54
    scientific interests of, 93
    on self-denial, 300
    sources for, 442
    vegetarianism of, 285
    writing and publishing of, 27, 48,
        54, 115–16, 121, 138, 184–86,
        188, 191, 207, 221, 242–43, 247,
        248, 285–86, 302, 303, 308

freedom, 108, 140, 153, 200, 252–62, 321
  bodily, 346
  common view of, 291
  of conscience, 71–72, 73, 226, 363, 365, 420
  definitions of, 252–53, 258
  loss of, 257
  natural, 324
  nature of, 209–10, 226
  radical idea of, 226, 252, 258, 291
  religious, 69–72, 225–26, 362, 411, 413, 459–60
  satisfaction of urges as, 291
  of thought, 258, 360–61
  understanding and, 316
freethinkers, 54, 55, 59, 121, 127, 206, 207, 238, 427, 462
free will, 153, 252–54, 257, 291
French and Indian War, 74
French language, 20, 26, 63, 79, 128, 393
French Revolution, 104, 111, 208, 409
  American support for, 28
Freneau, Philip, 47, 80, 99, 138, 251
  on death, 242
  education of, 93
  pantheism of, 193
  as "poet of the American Revolution," 28, 67
  on priesthood, 379
  sources for, 442
  works of, 191, 193, 218
Friendly Club, 30
friendship, 103, 275, 296, 299

Galen, 237
Galileo Galilei, 83, 117–18, 169, 177, 206, 212, 222, 427, 464–65
  on Bible, 397–98
  Copernican theory embraced by, 117
  Epicurean philosophy propagated by, 96

Inquisition trial of, 79, 117–18, 120, 167
  works of, 117–18, 167
gang of six, 331–33, 367, 384–85
Garasse, François, 168
Garden of Eden, 54
Gassendi, Pierre, 79, 84, 86, 118, 167, 168, 177, 231, 241, 277, 348, 462
  on human nature, 324
  on justice, 325
  materialist philosophy of, 175, 240
  sources for, 442
  on virtue, 275–76, 285
Gastrell, Francis, 146
General History of the Christian Church, A (Priestley), 410
general welfare, 370, 372–73
Genesis, Book of, 136–37
Geneva, 78
George I, King of England, 65–66
George III, King of England, 17, 23, 75, 271, 334, 379
German language, 63, 364
German Reformation, 73
Gifanius, Obertus, 128
Gildon, Charles, 169
God, 30, 37, 45, 49, 59, 110, 324–25, 403
  Allah as, 209
  belief in, 83, 130, 145, 149, 171, 174, 190, 273, 274, 308, 312, 365, 406, 425
  commandments of, 349
  concepts of, 5–7, 15, 36, 40, 51–55, 64, 83, 112, 156, 158–64, 167–84, 189–93, 197–200, 303, 307–8, 339, 341
  death of, 175, 307
  denial of, 12, 22
  dependence on, 227–28
  fear of, 56
  as first cause, 148, 150, 151
  grace of, 391
  judgment of, 339

kingdom of, 413
knowledge of, 307
Locke's proof of, 148–50, 152–54,
    156, 160–67
as love, 308–9
love of, 60, 172, 243, 245, 307–8,
    400
nature of, 130–31, 148–54, 160–63,
    170–72
obedience to, 307, 348–49, 400
power of, 150, 167, 177, 233, 322,
    342
praying to, 44, 50, 52–53, 57
revelations of, 127, 158, 172, 223,
    398
Spinoza on nature of, 149–54,
    160–63, 170–72, 174, 178, 179,
    243
spirit of, 169
as a "thinking thing," 159–64
will of, 328
word of, 58, 226, 335
worship of, 172, 184, 308, 361, 405
God is Back, 423
God of Nature, 160, 200, 298, 307
Allen's belief in, 131, 133, 138,
    195
genealogy of, 130–200
Young on, 138–39, 195
gods:
diversity of, 115
Epicurean, 113–16
fear of, 87
ideal existence reflected in, 114
relationships of humans and, 114
Golden Rule, 325, 348
Gordon, Lord George, 433–34
Gordon, Thomas "Cato," 63–64, 67,
    68, 109, 144, 255, 361, 374–75,
    377
sources for, 444
works of, 64, 153, 163, 181, 232,
    247, 282, 300
see also Cato's Letters

Gospels, 30, 44, 303, 412, 424
ridicule of, 31
gravity, 176–77, 401–2
Great Britain, 5, 15, 20, 55, 63, 124,
    328
colonists favoring reconciliation
    with, 19, 336–38
colonists favoring separation from,
    19, 363–67
corruption in, 334
democratic institutions of, 26
plague of 1640 in, 59–60
Reformation in, 73
Tory government in, 65
see also British Empire; England;
    Scotland
Greece, ancient, 6, 67, 79–81, 419
Greek language, 25, 95
Green, Ashbel, 31, 452
Green Mountain Boys, 435
assault on Fort Ticonderoga by,
    1, 10, 11, 199–200, 316–21, 388,
    432
Ethan Allen as leader of, 1, 9–11,
    16, 131–33, 199–200, 316–21
storming of Montreal by, 321
Green Mountains, 10, 13, 15, 20,
    25, 43, 75, 77, 112, 127, 131–33,
    189, 195, 200, 202, 248, 251, 266,
    316–20, 435
Grotius, Hugo, 327, 414
Gumley, Miss, 65

Hague, The, 402
Hale, Matthew, 341
hallucination, 218
Hamilton, Alexander, 17
Hamlet (Shakespeare), 82, 98, 100,
    118, 278
Hancock, John, 265
happiness, 92, 243, 250, 401, 410
freedom from pain as, 87
pleasure and, 79, 278–79
preservation of, 422

happiness (*continued*)
  private, 293
  pursuit of, 93, 263–313
  reason as key to, 125
  science and, 93
  source of, 88
  virtue and, 273, 274–78, 281, 283,
    285, 286–87, 289, 293, 302, 303,
    396
Harrington, James, 144, 378, 414, 453
Harvard College, 14, 61
  lampooning of, 48
hatred, 288, 299
  self, 301
Hawke, David Freeman, 21
Hawley, Joseph, 52
health, 302, 349, 356, 428
heart, 303
  beating of, 237, 238
Hebrews, ancient, 169, 417
hedonism, 275–77, 291, 298
heliocentrism, 117, 118
Henry, Patrick, 134, 141
  "Give me liberty, or give me
    death" slogan of, 301
hermeticism, 164
Herschel, William, 111–12
Hippocrates, 206, 237
*History of Early Opinions concerning
  Jesus Christ* (Priestley), 409, 410
History of the Corruptions of Christianity
  (Priestley), 409, 410
History of Virginia (Beverley), 30
Hobbes, Thomas, 59–60, 84, 85, 86,
  96–97, 142, 146–47, 162, 173,
  222, 341–50
  autobiographical poem of, 89–90
  on Christianity, 407, 413–15
  on civil state, 326
  "conatus" concept of, 253, 255–56,
    279–82
  as "the Devil's Secretary," 413
  Epicureanism reprised by, 212,
    277–78
  on equality, 323–24
  on freedom, 252–54, 346
  on good and evil, 277–78
  hedonism associated with, 298
  on human body, 255
  on immortality, 246–47
  influence of, 150, 225
  on laws of nature, 340–41
  materialism of, 287
  monistic parallelism of, 231
  as "monster of Malmsbury," 277,
    341
  "Natural Right" of, 341–44
  on origins of man, 327
  on power, 380
  social contract version of, 343
  on soul, 240
  sources for, 442
  on sovereignty, 370
  on spirit, 212
  split of Spinoza and, 343–46, 350
  on virtue and happiness, 289
  works of, 89–90, 347
Holland, 54, 82, 124, 140–43, 144,
  147, 168, 179, 197, 414
  Enlightenment in, 4, 143, 206, 237,
    490
  medicine in, 206–7, 237
  trading power of, 140
Holy Spirit, 365–66
honesty, 297
Hooker, Richard, 141
hope, 288
horticulture, 93
Hottentots, 239
Hudson River, 46, 333
Hughes, Hugh, 136
human beings, 97, 104, 208–10
  common nature of, 295
  conception of, 227
  cooperation of, 294
  corruption of, 297, 300–301
  empathy among, 322
  equality of, 209, 315

exceptionalism of, 209
human condition of, 100
ignorance of, 397
intelligence of, 101, 108, 218
natural, 29, 77–78, 125–28
origin of, 83
self-government of, 389
socialization of, 103, 294, 295, 296
understanding vs. wisdom in, 218
weakness of, 294, 301
human body, 101, 103, 125, 148,
    202–3, 235–39
affections of, 219, 238
appetite and physical state of, 229
circulatory system of, 237, 238
cultivation of, 300
death of, 235
definition of, 205, 235–36
as an enemy, 300
freedom of, 258
lump theory of, 240
nervous system of, 239
new philosophy of, 208
organs of, 206, 207, 220, 235
preservation of, 343
as process, 236
reflex actions of, 237
relationship of mind and, 229,
    237–38, 240, 241, 243, 249
scientific approach to, 206
vascular system of, 154
humanism, 81, 295, 427
Hume, David, 55, 69, 80, 104, 146,
    150, 188, 194, 225, 300, 414, 452,
    510
on Epicurus, 311
on Locke, 165, 224
on morality, 306
on reason as the slave of passions,
    279
on right and wrong, 281
on soul and body, 241
on thought processes, 213
works of, 233, 300

Hutcheson, Francis, 304, 306, 511–12
Hutchinson, Thomas, 18, 135, 264

ideas, 142, 210–27, 236
abstract, 216
as acts of understanding, 429–30
affirmation and negation of, 216
bad, 429
belief-like, 216
commerce of, 140
content vs. truth of, 222
false, 218
history of, 105, 117, 166, 209, 274,
    429
ideas about, 212–13, 215, 216, 221,
    225
internal measure of truth in, 214
miscommunication of, 210
nature of, 213–14, 227
radical theory of, 215–16, 218
reflexive, 213–14, 219
secrecy of, 210
senses and, 221
truth of, 22, 216
unconscious, 230
as words or signs, 210
imagination, 91, 106, 175, 240, 241
knowledge vs., 223–24
revelation and, 223–24
understanding vs., 213
immortality, 240–51
independence, 334, 336
equality and, 328
movement for, 336–38
Independent Reflector (Livingston), 217
Independent Whig, The (Gordon), 217
Indian widows, burning alive of, 305
inoculation, 39–43, 74, 330
Inquisition, 117, 119–20, 167
intelligence, cosmic, 164
intelligibility, 90–91, 92, 106
Ireland, 45–46
    Ulster County, 46
Isaiah, 158

Israel, Jonathan, 143
Italian language, 79
Italy, 124

Jacobins, 26
James, Saint, 308–9
James II, King of England, 139, 141
Jay, John, 32–33
Jefferson, Thomas, 35, 40, 73, 82, 121,
    248, 372
  character and personality of, 25–26
  childhood and adolescence of,
    24–25, 66–67, 412
  death of, 100
  diary of, 36
  education of, 24–29
  Epicureanism of, 252, 276, 284–85,
    306–7
  on Jesus, 409–11
  John Adams and, 36, 55, 99–100,
    111, 188–89, 195–96, 221, 234–
    35, 239, 304, 404, 411, 421
  John Adams on, 17
  on law, 373
  Lincoln on, 314
  on love, 304
  love affairs of, 303
  materialism of, 221
  "moral sense school" and, 306–7
  non-extinction theory of, 198
  political philosophy of, 105, 208
  presidency of, 93, 383, 410, 412
  Priestley and, 409, 410, 412
  primary education system
    proposed by, 422
  on property, 358–59
  reading and personal library of, 25,
    28–29, 30, 31, 35, 79–80, 84, 116,
    128, 144, 166, 171, 232, 239, 246,
    416, 431
  religious and philosophical beliefs
    of, 25–27, 35, 36–37, 55, 79–80, 94,
    99–101, 113, 190, 192, 194, 242,
    252, 276, 312, 409–12, 419–21, 425

  retirement of, 93, 412
  sources for, 443
  on state of nature, 352
  theocratic conspiracy seen by,
    26–27
  University of Virginia founded by,
    29, 112, 225, 422
  virtues listed by, 285
  Washington and, 321
  writing of, 25, 26, 55, 70–71,
    99–100, 104, 109–10, 113,
    138–39, 141, 173, 198–99, 225,
    233, 258, 262, 282, 284–85, 303,
    311–13, 314, 328–29, 362, 391,
    409, 450–51
Jefferson Memorial, 225, 226
Jerome, Saint, 81
Jesus Christ, 3, 26, 29, 51, 54, 56, 57,
    100, 124, 188, 299, 405–12, 414,
    424
  ascension of, 411
  belief in, 36, 37, 209, 309
  crucifixion and resurrection of, 32,
    177, 411
  divinity of, 61, 110, 365–66
  ethical system of, 409
  as Messiah, 406–7, 411, 486
  Second Coming of, 409
  Sermon on the Mount of, 406
  as Son of God, 110, 407
  teachings of, 406, 408, 411
  virgin birth of, 409
Jews, 3, 112, 142–43, 402, 421
John (evangelist), 159, 308–9
Johnson, Samuel, 55, 66, 146
Johnson, William, 134, 135
Joshua, 117, 397–98, 403
joy, 288
Judaism, 421
Judiciary Act of 1789, 386
justice, 285, 322, 325–26, 329, 400,
    417
  agrarian, 259
  God's, 339

Golden Rule and, 325, 348
natural history of, 103, 323, 377
rules of, 351
sources of, 348
theory of, 315, 316
utility and, 329
violations of, 326

Kames, Lord, 304
Kant, Immanuel, 65, 209, 259–60, 289
Kent, James, 30
Kepler, Johannes, 118
King's College (Columbia
    University), 29
Klever, Wim, 4, 147, 238
knowledge:
    determination of, 217
    experience and, 219
    of good and evil, 287, 304–5
    imagination vs., 223–24
    origin of, 214–15
    revealed, 221–25
    theory of, 211
    worldly, 219, 220, 230
Knox, Henry, 320
Knox, William, 246

La Grange, 128
Lake Champlain, 12, 269, 316, 318,
    321, 434
Lamb, John, 265, 268
La Mettrie, Julien Offray de, 238
Lao Tzu, 244
Latin language, 16, 23, 25, 63, 128,
    160
Lee, Jonathan, 41, 54
Leibniz, Gottfried Wilhelm, 3, 4, 102,
    103, 120, 146, 173, 178–79, 229,
    472
    "pre-established harmony"
        doctrine of, 238
    on soul, 241–42
Leiden, 207, 237, 238
Leland, John, 66, 142–43, 408, 484

Lenin, Vladimir, 365
Letter concerning Toleration (Locke),
    415
Letters to Serena (Toland), 179
Leucippus, 86
Leviathan (Hobbes), 90
Lexington, Battle of, 10, 270, 336
liberal arts, 431
liberalism, 248, 252, 260–62, 298,
    312–13, 315–16, 391
    common ideas of, 315
    modern, 429
    principles of, 315
    as theory of power, 316
liberty, 254–55, 349, 351, 355–56, 360
Library of Commerce, Jefferson
    Building of, 25
life:
    after death, 31, 201–2, 204, 240–51
    evolution of, 104–5
    great questions of, 224
*Life and Morals of Jesus of Nazareth,
    The* (Jefferson), 412
Lincoln, Abraham, 514
    on Jefferson, 314, 391
Litchfield, Conn., 60
literacy, spread of, 122
Literary Commonplace Book (Jefferson),
    25, 66–67, 104, 109–10, 173, 233,
    282
Livingston, Philip, 138, 311
Livingston, William, 217, 456
Locke, John, 3–4, 64, 67, 68, 73, 75,
    93–94, 100, 120, 122, 126, 127,
    159–70, 209, 348–52, 474–76
    on action at a distance, 157
    character and personality of, 139–
        40
    Christian belief of, 123, 145, 168,
        221, 224, 406–8
    conspiracies suspected of, 140
    death of, 146
    disciples of, 140, 143–45, 147,
        152–53, 165–66, 193, 232–33

Locke, John (*continued*)
on equality, 324
on eternal life, 241–42, 246
fame and influence of, 141, 143, 145, 197
on freedom, 290
on good and evil, 278, 279
on human body, 236–37, 258
on ideas, 220–21
on Jesus, 405, 407
on knowledge, 214–15
on laws of nature, 348–49
on legislative power, 373
on liberty, 254
as master of "ambiguity and circumlocation," 165, 223, 241, 254
medical practice of, 207
mentors of, 214, 220
on miracles, 223
monistic parallelism of, 231, 234–35
on morality, 305
"one incomprehensibilty" doctrine of, 234–35
on priesthood, 378
proof of God expounded by, 148–50, 152–54, 156, 160–67, 172, 173, 189, 231
on property, 356–58
on reason, 399
on rebellion, 381–83
on religion, 308, 415–16
on rights, 134, 355–56, 362, 381–83
sources for, 443
on thought, 217
on truth, 223
on virtue and happiness, 287
works of, 64, 139, 141, 146–48, 152, 157, 168–70, 220–21, 231, 278, 290, 399, 408, 415, 416, 499–505
London, 17, 54, 65, 67, 126, 142, 189, 286, 433
Batson's Coffee House in, 207
Cheapside Ale-House in, 207
Long Island, N.Y., 46
Long Island Sound, 43
love, 288, 304
of God, 60, 172, 243, 245, 307–8, 400
God as, 308–9
repaying hatred with, 299
self, 282–83, 291, 292–95, 301, 345
loyalty, 305, 435
Lucretius Carus, Titus, 79–80, 81–83, 87, 91–93, 95, 97–104, 106, 113, 122, 277, 493
exposition of physical doctrines of Epicurus by, 87–89, 99–100, 212, 214
on justice, 103, 323
rediscovery of, 79–80, 82–83, 95, 108–9, 128–29, 166–67
on senses, 214
sources for, 443
see also On the Nature of Things
Luther, Martin, 158, 309, 406, 434
Lutheran Church, 378
Lydius, John Henry, 74–75
Lyons, Dr., 207

Machiavelli, Niccolò, 82, 246–47, 300, 303, 344, 375, 376, 381
Madison, James, 17, 28, 47, 73, 141, 197, 199, 248, 291, 419
on Christianity, 379
on conscience, 375
on constitutions, 386
Jefferson and, 358–59
on religious freedom, 225–26, 459–60
sources for, 443
writing of, 138, 376, 385
Maier, Pauline, 208
Maistre, Joseph-Marie, Comte de, 146
Man a Machine (La Mettrie), 238

Mandeville, Bernard, 142, 207
Marat, Jean-Paul, 208
Marshall, Christopher, 332, 366
Martin, Benjamin, 67, 110–11, 189
Mary, Queen of England, 141
Maryland Gazette, 183
Mason, George, 419, 524
Masons, 109, 163
Massachusetts, 17, 18, 41, 43–46, 135,
    266–67, 329, 332
Massachusetts Committee of Safety,
    317
Massachusetts militia, 317, 322
Massachusetts Provincial Congress of
    1774–1775, 208
Massachusetts Spy, 52, 127
materialism, 3, 33, 54, 87, 89, 94,
    100–101, 106, 126, 165, 175, 180,
    221, 234, 240, 462
  criticism of, 195–96
  deterministic, 96
  first-order, 287
  second-order, 255, 287, 346, 481–82
mathematics, 217
Mather, Cotton, 35, 53–54, 191, 454
Matlack, Timothy, 129, 331–32, 336,
    366, 384–85
matter, 99, 162
  creation "ex nihilo" of, 164–66
  decay of, 101, 102
  infinity of, 179
  as mother of all natural things, 89
  organization of, 293
  spirit vs., 233, 235
  transformation of, 100, 101, 112
Maupertuis, Pierre-Louis, 104
Mayhew, Jonathan, 29, 60–62
medicine, 16, 22, 204–8, 210, 260
  clinical testing in, 237
  diagnosis in, 237
  in England, 207
  in Holland, 206–7, 237
  practice of inoculation in, 39–43,
    330
  reform in, 204–5, 208, 238
  surgical, 21, 57, 205
  treatments and cures in, 204, 205,
    207, 237
  in U.S., 21–22, 39–41, 46, 57, 63,
    203–5, 207–8
Meditations on First Philosophy
    (Descartes), 168, 228
Melville, Herman, 10, 14
memory, 235, 244, 361
mercy, 297
Mersenne, Marin, 83–84
metaphysics, 11, 84, 89, 101, 104, 120,
    206, 227, 233, 261
Meyer, Lodewijk, 206
midwifery, 62, 205
Milton, John, 73, 301
mind, 91, 98, 149, 216, 217, 219,
    226–29, 257
  as action, 227, 232
  basic questions of, 92
  conscious, 209
  freedom of, 259
  God as, 160
  matter vs., 72
  a mind within, 211
  nature of, 218
  philosophy of, 208, 210, 212, 213–
    14, 227, 234, 240, 259–60
  power of, 210
  radical theory of, 211–12, 225–26,
    232, 234, 240
  reason exercised in, 289–90
  relationship of body and, 229,
    237–38, 240, 241, 243, 249
  revolution of, 210
  self and, 240, 283
  self-ignorance of, 222
  speculative, 118
  strength of, 296
  tranquility of, 87, 275
  understanding and, 396
  weakness of, 291
mindfulness, 277, 296

miracles, 130, 149, 168–69, 192, 225, 240
  belief vs. disbelief in, 222–23, 399
  definition of, 222–23
"Mob, the," see Sons of Liberty of Albany
modernity, 73, 209–10, 295, 430
  liberal, 312
  theory of, 401
modesty, 297
Mohammed (Prophet), 124
Mohawk Indians, 17, 30, 265
Molesworth, Robert, 144, 378
Molineux, William, 30, 135
monism, 89–90, 152, 153, 227–29, 241–42
  radical, 228
  substance, 229, 430
  versions of, 229
monistic parallelism, 229, 231–33, 234–36, 242, 250
monotheism, 114, 406
Monroe, James, 31
Montaigne, Michel de, 82, 85, 93–94, 96, 300
Montepulciano, 143
Montesquieu, 120–21, 375, 472
Monticello, 79, 196, 412
Montreal, 321
moral agency, 72
morality, 245–46, 271–74, 279, 295–96, 304–12, 395, 534
  common conception of, 289, 290, 291, 293, 296
  conservatism and, 306
  "immanent" conception of, 274, 277, 283–84, 286
  intelligibility of, 284
  judgment and, 293, 395
  laws of, 400, 405–7, 414, 424
  "moral sense" school and, 304–7
  motives for, 284, 291
  precepts of, 429
  progress in, 313

radical conception of, 296
reform and, 286
"transcendental" conception of, 273–74, 309
  see also philosophy, moral
Moroni (angel), 423
Morris, Gouverneur, 28–29, 31, 36, 367
  education of, 47
Moses, 47, 124, 169, 192, 404
  laws of, 339
Mount Sinai, 339
"My Theology" (Allen), 392

Naples, 78
Narrative (Allen), 202
Native Americans, 30, 74
  decimation of, 185
  land deals of, 74–75
  missionary outreach to, 62
Natural Man, 29, 77–78, 125–28
nature, 6–7, 97, 126, 182, 183, 198
  absence of creation and destruction of matter in, 88, 89, 112
  change as transformational in, 88, 89, 112
  definitions of, 151
  forms in, 101
  as "goddess and creatress," 88–89, 90, 93
  homogeneity of, 89
  intelligibility of, 91
  laws of, 6, 88, 89–91, 97, 101, 112, 138, 139, 149, 155, 158, 171, 172, 202, 205, 291, 340–42
  limited knowledge of, 91
  nature of, 72, 90, 104
  order and coherence of, 155, 158
  outward aspect of, 88
  power of, 396
  self-explanation of, 91
  self-sufficiency of, 95
  state of, 347, 349–52

study of, 116, 120, 197
  as work of God, 325
  see also God of Nature
necessitarianism, 154–55, 156–57,
  190, 195, 234
Neo-Epicureanism, 298, 328
Neoplatonism, 82, 164, 167
neurosciences, 209
New England, 23, 34, 41, 44, 191,
  206, 251, 433
  churches of, 17, 25, 61
  crime and punishment in, 42,
    183–84
  frontier of, 9, 52, 62
  ruling class of, 316
  spiritual revival in, 44–45, 52, 56
New Hampshire, 10, 74, 131
New Hampshire Grants, 133, 271,
  353
New Jersey, 336
Newport, R.I., 267
Newton, Isaac, 85, 86, 98, 110, 112,
  165, 207, 462, 486
  Clarke and, 165, 176, 178–81,
    184
  criticism of, 178–82
  deism of, 194
  gravity theory of, 176–77, 401–2
  religious and philosophical
    pronouncements of, 123, 146,
    175–81, 184, 185, 188
  scientific achievements of, 67, 98,
    175–78, 194, 401–2
  works of, 178
new world order, 306
New York, 10, 23, 30, 33, 74, 136,
  271, 336, 423
  real estate industry in, 131
New York, N.Y., 47, 134, 267
New York Public Library, 19
Nietzsche, Friedrich, 244
nihilism, 171, 273, 274, 312, 313, 394,
  430
nobility, 297

Norman Conquest, 26, 63, 449
Northampton, Mass., 74
  religious and secular life in, 43–45,
    48–52, 56–58, 62
Notes on the State of Virginia
  (Jefferson), 70–71, 311

Ocellus, 194
Of the Conduct of the Human
  Understanding (Locke), 416
"Of the Immortality of the Soul"
  (Hume), 233
Oldenburg, Henry, 147, 154, 170, 236
"On the Constitution, or Frame of
  Nature" (Freneau), 193
On the Immense and Numberless
  (Bruno), 89
On the Nature of Things (De rerum
  natura) (Lucretius), 79–80, 81–83,
  86, 88, 89
  Einstein's preface to, 92
  memorization of, 102
On the Origin of the Species (Darwin),
  104
"On the Uniformity and Perfection
  of Nature" (Freneau), 191
On the Wonderful Secrets of Nature,
  the Queen and Goddess of Mortal
  Beings (Vanini), 83
Opticks (Newton), 178
Oracles of Reason, The (Blount), 15, 23,
  28, 64, 169, 447
  Lucretius Redivivus subtitle of, 86
Oracles of Reason (Allen), 1–2, 11–16,
  25, 31–32, 34, 47–48, 54–55,
  101, 112, 128, 251, 404, 421–22,
  432–34
  Appendix to, 194, 249–50
  criticism of, 13–16
  God of Nature explained in, 133,
    188
  intimations of mortality in, 202–3
  medical references in, 205, 238–
    39

Oracles of Reason (Allen) (*continued*)
  as possible plagiarism, 2–3, 15–16,
    23–24, 32, 34, 189–93, 195, 205–
    6, 248, 318
  praise of, 433–34
  preface to, 47–48, 432–33
  publication and printing of,
    433
Otis, James, 18, 134, 135, 141, 302,
    379, 449
Ovid, 81, 279
Oxford, 78, 236, 347
Oxford University, 140, 147

paganism, 5, 26, 85
pain, 98, 276
  evil of, 275
  expression of, 275
  freedom from, 97, 98
  pleasure and, 285, 287–88, 305
Paine, Thomas, 28–29, 34, 36, 93,
    120–21, 124, 126, 194, 291,
    384–85
  on agrarian justice, 359
  on American independence, 314
  on belief, 218
  childhood and adolescence of, 47,
    48, 53, 67
  Christian disbelief of, 53
  on cosmology, 110
  death of, 423
  deism of, 111, 335–36
  fame of, 331
  on immortality, 247
  on independence, 314
  Jefferson on, 35
  on morality, 304
  on natural philosophy, 197
  privateer adventure of, 48, 67
  restlessness of, 76
  on revelation, 225
  self-education of, 67
  on society, 375
  sources for, 443

  works of, 19, 31–32, 127, 189, 247,
    314, 332, 334, 359, 375, 421
Palmer, Elihu, 217–18
pantheism, 5, 15, 33, 166–71, 173–75,
    193, 427
  atheism vs., 194
  deism vs., 194–95
Pantheisticon (Toland), 109, 122, 169
Paradise Lost (Milton), 301
parallelism, monistic, 229, 231–36,
    242, 250
Paris, 19, 31, 56, 78, 83, 84, 118, 168,
    187, 286, 303, 366–67
  Academy of Arts & Sciences in,
    433
  Bastille in, 208
Parker, Henry, 414
Parker, James, 30
Parmenides, 213, 494
passion, 279, 326, 374, 396, 428
  natural history of, 301
  reason as slave of, 279
  self-destructive, 291
patriotism, 10, 134, 264
Paul, Saint, 22, 129, 158, 159, 170,
    339–40, 406
  life of "Spirit" professed by, 125–
    26, 128
  sin and redemption of, 125
Peale, Charles Willson, 389
Pemberton, Dr., 207
Penn, William, 331
Pennsylvania, 266, 329–32, 338
  efforts of Thomas Young to
    foment revolution in, 63
  pro-independence government of,
    19, 363–68
  Provincial Conference and
    Convention in, 365
Pennsylvania Constitution of 1776,
    19, 363, 366–68, 383–86, 387,
    517, 524
Pennsylvania Gazette, 286
Pennsylvania Packet, 337

Pentateuch, 169
Perkins, Nathan, 13, 30
Persian Empire, 404
Persians, ancient, 137
Philadelphia, Pa., 10, 19, 20, 30–31,
    32, 40, 77, 111, 138, 185, 188,
    203, 204, 217, 267, 383
  Continental Congress in, 320–21,
    329–32, 336–38, 363–65
  German immigrants in, 331, 337
  Liberty Bell in, 364
  newspapers in, 311, 330, 332
  population of, 331
  State House in, 337–38, 366
Philosophical Works (Bolingbroke),
    66–67
philosophy, 2–7, 24–25, 64–68, 94
  of the body, 208
  creation of modern world and, 78
  Greek, 92, 95
  guiding principle of, 178, 212, 253,
    260, 283–84
  history of, 82, 101, 106, 212, 213,
    299, 313
  jokes in, 150
  metaphysical, 11, 84, 89, 101
  of the mind, 208
  modern, 4, 56, 67–68, 72, 82, 87,
    93, 139, 170, 206, 215, 290
  moral, 25, 27–30, 31, 32, 79, 84,
    144, 232, 246, 271–74, 289, 292–
    93, 304–13, 409, 416, 431
  "moral sense" school of, 304–7
  natural, 197, 206
  political, 105, 148, 322, 344
  popular religion vs., 68
  radical, 6–7, 15–16, 23, 33, 64, 86,
    87, 92, 104, 124–25, 148, 159,
    164, 173–74, 195, 208, 209, 211–
    15, 235, 259, 274, 284, 304, 306,
    316, 396–97
  religion as branch of, 224, 306
  religion vs., 116–17
  science vs., 78

seventeenth-century revolution in,
    98
  as technical discipline, 24
  *see also specific philosophers and
    theories*
physics, 90
  Epicurean, 99
  laws of, 237
  modern, 96, 98
  seventeenth-century, 176
piety, 93, 113, 116, 147, 171–73, 183,
    198–99, 207, 224, 308, 406, 418,
    428
Plato, 7, 65, 85, 97, 100, 285
Platonism, 281
pleasure, 94, 275–76, 280–81
  definition of, 280
  of eating, 275, 276
  happiness and, 79, 278–79
  hope and, 288
  pain and, 285, 287–88, 305
  virtue and, 298
politics, 94
  conservative, 19
  moderation in, 6
  modern theory of, 82, 103
  propaganda and, 18–19
  radical, 18–19, 26, 329
  revolutionary, 33
polytheism, 115, 310
Pope, Alexander, 64–68, 98–100, 109,
    127, 190, 197, 283, 298, 481
  famous phrases of, 64
  on self-love, 294
  sources for, 443
  on Stoicism, 302
  works of, 64–65, 67, 86, 98, 126,
    138, 139, 145, 153, 157–58,
    181–83, 193, 291, 294, 301, 308,
    351–52, 377–78
poverty, 321, 324, 359
power, 293–94
  architecture of, 388
  democratic, 376

power (*continued*)
　of God, 150, 167, 177, 233, 322,
　　342
　growth of, 347
　legislative, 373
　liberalism as theory of, 316
　of nature, 396
　without right, 339
　in society, 368–69
　source of, 316
Prague, 78
prayer, 44, 50, 52–53, 57, 114, 115,
　116, 187
Presbyterian Church, 112
Price, Richard, 111
Priestley, Joseph, 28, 234, 311, 409–12
Princeton College, 28, 93
　Jonathan Edwards as president of,
　　63
Principles of Nature, The (Palmer),
　217–18
Principles of the Cartesian Philosophy
　(Spinoza), 147, 206, 213–14
printing press invention, 122
"Private Thoughts" (Paine), 247
property, 355–60
prophets, 106
Propositions in Scripture (Toland), 144
Protestantism, 11, 13, 37, 58, 70, 71,
　196, 363, 365, 435
　American Republic and, 72–73
　freedom of conscience in, 226
providence, 171, 175, 185, 186,
　191–92
prudence, 285
psychology, 260
Puritanism, 36, 43, 272
Pythagoras, 94

Quakers, 332
Quesnay, François, 120–21

Randolph, Edmund, 71, 385
Randolph, John, 31

reason, 11, 88, 235, 283, 285, 290,
　299, 305
　deductions of, 399
　enthusiasm and, 303
　faith and, 217, 224
　guidance of, 295
　as key to happiness, 125
　limits of, 396
　as only oracle, 25
　power of, 292
　religion and, 401
　as slave of passions, 279
　virtue of, 292
Reasonableness of Christianity, The
　(Locke), 399, 408, 529
rebellion, 380–83
redemption, 241
Redemption by the Death of the Son of
　God, 53
Reformation, 70, 73
　as symbol of modernity, 73
Regius, Henricus, 228–29, 231
Reid, Thomas, 234
religion, 4–7, 415–16
　afterlife concept in, 31, 201–2, 204
　belief in, 394–95
　as branch of philosophy, 224
　changing affiliation in, 425
　comparative, 402
　consciousness of, 92, 98, 105, 106,
　　130–31, 174, 227, 309, 329, 397,
　　427
　conservative, 6–7, 36, 40, 187, 532
　definitions of, 419, 427–28
　deism in, 29
　faith in, 221, 229, 309, 365
　fears exploited by, 87
　freedom of, 69–72, 225–26, 362,
　　410, 413, 459–60
　mainstream, 4, 62
　moderation in, 62
　monotheistic, 114
　morality and, 245–46, 395
　natural, 402, 404, 408, 422

opposition to, 11–12, 23, 26, 28, 29, 85, 109, 112
orthodox, 29, 32–33, 85, 145, 168, 240, 312
philosophy vs., 116–17
popular, 72, 79, 208, 379, 398, 399–404, 412, 420, 423–24
primitive, 106
private, 415–16
public, 403, 404, 417–18
radical, 85
reason and, 401
reform of, 70, 73, 423
revealed, 221–25, 239–40, 398
revivals of, 44–45, 52, 55, 56, 57–59, 61, 68–69, 72, 186, 365, 423, 457
science vs., 42, 55, 119
as set of practices, 395
as species of philosophy, 224, 306
supernatural, 104, 106, 126, 222, 224, 424, 431
superstitious, 42, 57, 69, 86, 87, 100, 110, 206, 430
theological, 85, 90
toleration of, 140, 361, 414, 416
traditional, 158, 159, 396
transformation of, 423–25
unknowable world as spur to, 158
utility of, 394–96, 403, 404
see also Christianity; *specific sects*
revelation, 221–25
definition of, 222
direct vs. indirect, 223
of God, 127, 158, 172, 223, 398
imagination and, 223–24
see also miracles
revenge, 305
Rhode Island, 267, 268, 330
right and wrong, 246
law as standard of, 325
rights, 10, 18, 19, 20, 72–73, 133, 138, 328, 341–44
civil, 353–54, 359–62, 394

divine, 327
God-given, 338, 339, 352
individual, 315, 385
Locke on, 134
natural, 331, 338, 342, 353, 355, 361
without power, 339
protection of, 312
of rebellion, 381–83
unalienable, 262, 329, 354–56, 360
voting, 20, 367, 371
Ripley, Ezra, 30
Rittenhouse, David, 111, 188, 469
Robinson, Moses, 393–94
Roman Catholic Church, 11, 56, 84, 139, 196, 362, 453
in England, 139, 141
priesthood of, 378
superstition in, 69
Roman Empire, 81, 101, 376–77, 419
corruption of, 301
fall of, 377
Romanticism, 166, 193
Rome, Campo dei Fiori in, 78
Rotterdam, 4
Rousseau, Jean-Jacques, 28, 65, 87, 103, 505, 525
Royal Society, 147
Rumbold, Richard, 390
Rush, Benjamin, 31, 208, 332, 334, 384–85, 411–12, 431, 449, 452
Russell, Bertrand, 150
Rye House Plot, 139, 347

sacrificial offerings, 100, 116, 137
Salisbury, Conn., 39–43, 54, 68, 74
Samos, 80, 105
Satan, 52, 59, 137
"Saxon Myth," 63
Saxony, ancient, 63–64, 333–34
scholasticism, 295
science, 101
ancient Greek, 95
definition of, 87

science (*continued*)
  happiness and, 93
  history of, 105
  of the human body, 206
  liberal, 112
  Newtonian, 67, 98
  philosophy vs., 78
  popular, 126
  pursuit of, 172
  religion vs., 42, 55, 119
  revolution in, 80, 96, 98, 116–17, 206
  spirit of, 93
scientific method, commitment to,
    92–93
Scotland, 18–19, 304
Second Continental Congress, 10,
    19, 203, 319, 320–21, 329–38,
    363–65, 380
  Massachusetts delegation to, 332
  Pennsylvanian delegation to, 336
Second Great Awakening, 68–69, 423
secularism, 423, 426–27, 430
self, 226–51
  authenticity of, 277
  consciousness of, 230
  control of, 297
  denial of, 300
  destruction of, 291, 297, 303
  determination of, 296, 313
  ego and, 209, 212, 259–60
  hatred of, 301
  interest in, 291, 428
  the "I" of, 211, 212, 213, 230
  loss of, 301
  love of, 282–83, 291, 292–95, 301,
    345
  mind and, 240, 283
  preservation of, 279, 302, 351, 353,
    356
  radical view of, 230–31
  realization of, 279, 280, 397
selfishness, 300, 301
Senate, U.S., 385
Seneca, 81, 167, 291–92, 376, 409

"sense qualia," 219
senses, 83, 95, 214, 219–21
  excesses of, 276
separation of church and state, 413,
    414, 417, 420
Sermon on Natural Religion ("Natural
    Man"), 29, 67, 77–78, 125–28
Sermon to Swine, A (Sherman), 13
Shaftesbury, Anthony Ashley Cooper,
    First Earl of, 140, 143, 207
Shaftesbury, Anthony Ashley Cooper,
    Third Earl of, 65, 126, 127,
    140, 143–44, 153, 163, 169, 173,
    182–83, 246
  on Christianity, 310
  church attendance of, 402
  on deism and atheism, 310
  on religion, 308
  sources for, 443–44
  Stoicism and, 301
  on virtue and vice, 281–82, 292,
    297, 298, 299, 304
  work of Spinoza disseminated by,
    294
  works of, 67, 152, 165, 251
Shakespeare, William, 82, 98
Shays, Daniel, 432
Sherman, Josiah, 13
Sherman, Roger, 29, 32–33
Short, William, 79
Sidney, Algernon, 63, 67, 68, 370, 371,
    375, 382, 453
  conspiracies against monarchy by,
    139
  on democracy, 376
  execution of, 140, 390
  sources for, 444
sin, 125, 241
Sinners in the Hands of an Angry God
    (Edwards), 49–50
skepticism, 218, 221
slavery, 34, 320, 324, 394, 424
  abolition of, 20, 315
  "three-fifths" compromise on, 387

smallpox, 432
  inoculation against, 40–42, 454–55
Smith, Adam, 86–87, 304, 462–63
  theory of knowledge expounded
    by, 86
Smith, William "Cato," 332, 335–36
social contract theory, 327–28, 343–
    45, 414
socialism, 361
Social Security, 359
society, 305, 375
  civil, 326
  corruption in, 297
  dissolution of, 297
  liberal, 316
  lower orders of, 397
  natural history of, 87
  pluralistic, 60, 69, 395
  power in, 368–69
  secular, 395
  unity in, 72
Society of the Cincinnati, 390
Socinianism, 60–61, 145, 146
Socrates, 6, 92, 213, 237, 252, 290
Socratic Method, 27
solar system, 115, 119, 177, 237
Some Friendly Remarks (Briant), 61
Some More Friendly Remarks (Briant), 61
Some Reflections on the Disputes between
    New-York, New-Hampshire, and
    Col. John Henry Lydius of Albany
    (Young), 74–75
Sons of Liberty, 240, 268
Sons of Liberty of Albany, 18, 133–34,
    473
soul, 100, 160, 176, 182, 202, 208–9,
    214, 221, 232, 248, 274, 361
  mortality vs. immortality of, 240–
    43, 245, 251, 259–60
  "naturalization" or "euthanasia" of,
    210
South Africa, 239
sovereign people, 368–71, 414,
    524–25

Sparks, Jared, 14
Spinosists, Hobbists, and most impious
    Freethinkers (Franklin), 121
Spinoza, Benedict de, 3–4, 124, 141–
    43, 146–47, 158, 195, 197
  on active vs. passive power, 257
  atheism of, 310
  on Bible, 399
  on civil state, 326, 346
  core philosophy of, 400
  on courage, 297
  deism of, 142–43, 145, 307
  on democracy, 371–73
  on desire, 256, 296
  emotions defined by, 288
  ethics of, 301
  on freedom, 254, 255, 258–59, 291
  funeral of, 402
  on good and evil, 278, 279, 280–81
  on human body, 235–37, 258
  on ideas, 213–14, 215, 216, 218–19
  on immortality, 244–45
  influence and disciples of, 142,
    144–45, 146, 180, 193, 220–21,
    225
  on Jesus, 405
  on knowledge, 220
  on love, 299
  materialism of, 287, 346
  on mind, 229–30, 256
  on miracles, 222–23
  on nature of God, 149–54, 160–63,
    170–72, 174, 178, 179, 243
  necessitarianism of, 154–55, 156–
    57, 189–90
  pantheism of, 169, 170–71, 173–
    74, 175
  parallelism of, 229, 231, 233
  on passion, 326, 374
  on peace, 346
  on pleasure and pain, 280–81,
    287–88
  on power, 293–94
  on priesthood, 413–34

Spinoza, Benedict de (*continued*)
  on reason, 290, 295, 299, 347
  on rebellion, 380–82
  on religion, 398–401, 415–17
  on rights, 360–61
  on senses, 219, 221
  sources for, 444
  split of Hobbes and, 343–46, 350
  on vice, 297
  on virtue, 283, 307–8
  works of, 142–43, 145, 147, 153,
    158, 169, 185, 189, 206, 213–14,
    238, 292, 344–45, 377, 399–400,
    416, 493, 495–97
  worm parable of, 154, 157
spirit:
  definition of, 212
  matter vs., 233, 235
spiritualism, 100, 239
Stamp Act of 1765, protests against,
  18, 133–34
Starry Messenger, The (Galileo), 118
Stephen, Leslie, 143, 145, 169
Stephen, Saint, 22
Stewart, Dugald, 100, 146
Stiles, Ezra, 28, 29, 35, 247, 410–11
  as president of Yale, 65, 67, 435
Stillingfleet, Lord Edward, bishop of
  Worcester, 144, 146, 221, 223,
  224, 232, 241, 499
Stoddard, John, 41, 62
Stoic philosophy, 81, 85, 150, 164,
  170, 252, 294, 298–99, 301–3,
  351
  criticism of, 302–3
  self-flagellation on, 303
Strauss, Leo, 146, 472, 478, 518
suicide, 52
  cult of, 302
*Summary View of the Rights of British
  Colonists* (Jefferson), 328
sun, 90, 102, 108, 177
  earth's orbit around, 117
  heat of, 216

standing still of, 397–98
worship of, 164
*Sun is my Father, the Earth my Mother,
  the World's my Country, and all
  Men are my Relations, The*, 163–64
superstition, 402
  religious, 42, 57, 69, 86, 87, 100,
    110, 206, 430
Supreme Court, U.S., 388
Syllabus of the Doctrines of Epicurus
  (Jefferson), 99, 113, 252, 284–
  85

Tacitus, 63
Tao Te Ching (Lao Tzu), 244
Tea Act, 264
telescopes, 117, 119, 177
temperance, 285
Theism, 196
theocracy, 377, 379
Thomas, Isaiah, 127
Thomas Aquinas, 155, 156, 190, 259,
  339
Thompson, Zadock, 16, 23–24
thought, 159–63, 212, 228
  consciousness of, 212–13
  freedom of, 258, 360–61
  mental conditions associated with,
    213
  modes of, 161–62, 229, 255
  power of, 217
  privacy of, 210, 211
  reflexive nature of, 213–14, 219
  thought against, 216
Tillich, Paul, 297
Tillotson, John, 408
Timaeus, 194
Timothy, Saint, 158
Tindal, Matthew, 402, 456, 461, 487
Tocqueville, Alexis de, 14, 69,
  423–25
Toland, John, 86, 111, 124, 140, 149,
  160, 163–64, 170, 178–79, 181,
  462, 480

character and personality of, 144
on Christianity, 408
deism of, 402
influence of, 144
Locke and, 144–45, 169, 224, 232
philosophical projects of, 144
protégés of, 153
works of, 109, 120, 122, 144, 169,
179, 408
Tory party, 22, 33, 267, 270
Toulouse, 78, 83–84
Townsend Acts of 1767, 134
Tractatus Theologico-Politicus (Spinoza),
142, 143, 145, 147, 158, 169, 189,
344–45, 377, 400
Tracy, Antoine Destutt de, 100
Treatise of the Three Imposters, 124
*Treatise on the Improvement of the
Understanding* (Spinoza), 416
Treaty of Tripoli (1797), 28
Trenchard, John, 63–64, 68, 109, 144,
160, 169, 179, 255, 361, 374–77
sources for, 444
works of, 64, 153, 163, 217, 232,
247, 282, 300
see also Cato's Letters
Triumph of Infidelity, The (Dwight),
68
truth, 120, 223–24
believing of, 217
certainty of, 214
coded, 122
evidence of, 217
explanations of, 217
of ideas, 216
as its own standard, 214
moral, 119
philosophical, 232
self-evident, 262, 388
uncovering of, 123
Turgot, Anne-Robert-Jacques, 120–21
Turkey, 80, 105
Two Treatises of Government (Locke),
141

un-Americanism, 59
Unitarianism, 29, 61, 111, 145, 234,
411, 420–21, 423, 425, 486
United States, 139
as Christian country, 28, 187,
423–25
as empire of reason, 7
exceptionalism of, 59
far reaching change and progress
in, 428
frontier of, 60, 69
government of, 28
as land of the free, 435
medical practice in, 21–22, 39–41,
46, 57, 63, 203–5, 207–8
as "one nation under God," 426
pluralism in, 60, 69
Protestant legacy in, 72–73
as republic, 15–16, 17, 38, 69–70,
72–73, 123, 148, 274, 329, 367–
68, 383, 412
rule of law in, 388
secularism in, 423, 426–27
slavery in, 20, 34, 315, 320, 324,
394, 424
understanding history of, 313
Universalism, 427
Universal Prayer (Pope), 193
universe, 97, 104, 175, 396
creation of, 102
future of, 96
as infinite and eternal, 106–13,
116–19, 123, 124, 126, 139, 149,
150, 156–57, 175–76, 185, 195,
207, 301, 430
intelligibility of, 92, 106
lawfulness of, 101
medieval concept of, 106
plurality of worlds in, 107–9,
112
Upanishads, 244
Updike, John, 186
utilitarianism, 280, 289, 306, 326
Utrecht, University of, 228

Valley Forge, Pa., 302
van den Enden, Franciscus, 206,
207–8
Vanini, Lucilio, 89, 142, 168, 173,
195, 222, 461
trial and execution of, 83–84, 120
works of, 167, 183
*Various Thoughts on the Occasion of a
Comet* (Bayle), 309–10
vegetarianism, 27, 137
Venice, 78
Vermont, 11, 23, 30, 132, 200, 317,
392–94, 423, 432–35
constitution of, 20
founding of, 9
naming of, 20
population of, 392
slavery banned in, 20
Vermont Gazette, 15, 433, 434
vice, 402
private, 297
self-destruction and, 297
virtue vs., 290, 291–92, 304, 400
Virgil, 81
Virginia, 31, 134, 226, 334, 358
plantations of, 34
Virginia, University of, 29, 112, 225,
422
Virginia Bill for Religious Freedom,
362, 411
Virginia Statute for Religious
Freedom, 225, 258
Virgin Mary, 56
virtue, 290–303, 309, 408
atheism and, 309–11, 427
common idea of, 375
definition of, 290
deism and, 298–303
desire for, 295–96
exaltation of, 299
happiness and, 273, 274–78, 281,
283, 285, 286–87, 289, 293, 302,
303, 396
individual utility and, 281–82

as its own reward, 298
pleasure of, 304
practice of, 307
private, 296–97
public, 293
science of, 286
Stoic concept of, 301–3
true, 396
as understanding, 291, 292
vice vs., 290, 291–92, 304, 400
Voetius, Gisbertus, 168
Volney, Constantin François de
Chasseboeuf, Comte de, 29
Voltaire, 28, 56, 65, 66, 182, 188,
198
voting rights, 20, 367, 371

Waller, Edmund, 97–98
Ward, Samuel, 330
Warren, Joseph, 135
as hero of Bunker Hill, 40
Washington, George, 194, 329
British driven from Boston by,
320
character of, 31
on Ethan Allen, 10
fables about, 37
Farewell Address of, 404–5, 422
first inaugural address of, 286–87,
389–90
Jefferson and, 321
Jefferson on, 36
military leadership of, 320, 334,
389
presidency of, 36, 422
religious beliefs of, 29, 31, 36, 37,
188, 191–92, 247–48, 452
revolutionary awakening of, 17
sources for, 444
at Valley Forge, 302
on virtue and happiness, 286–87
weapons technology, 103
Wentworth, Benning, 131
West Indies, 76, 93

Westminster, Vt., 269–70, 393
"Whether Christianity is part of
    the Common Law?" (Jefferson),
    26
Whigs, 86, 144, 333, 376, 378, 382,
    390
Whig Society, 389
Whitefield, George, 45, 52, 136–37,
    186, 404, 408
William III, King of England, 141
William & Mary, College of, 29
William of Orange, 141
Williams, Samuel, 435, 447
William the Conqueror, 63, 334
willing, 216
    connection between believing and,
        217, 222
Wills, Garry, 141
Wilson, James, 370, 386–88, 528
Winooski River, 432
wisdom, understanding vs., 218
witches, 59
Wittgenstein, Ludwig, 159, 244
World, The (Descartes), 120, 228
Wythe, George, 422

Yale College, 13, 43, 48, 201
    Dwight as president of, 13, 28,
        328, 453
    1778 class of, 28
    1793 class of, 28
    Stiles as president of, 13, 28, 65,
        67, 328, 435
yellow fever, 389
Young, John, 45–47
Young, Joseph, 46, 63, 76, 134
Young, Mary (mother of Thomas),
    45–47, 266–67
Young, Mary (wife of Thomas),
    266–67
Young, Thomas, 4, 18–24, 26, 30,
    36–38, 63–65, 68, 69, 141, 142,
    186, 329–36
    birth of, 46, 48, 333

blasphemy trial of, 56
Boston Tea Party instigated by, 17,
    264, 265, 448
character and personality of, 18,
    20–21, 22, 24, 41, 46–47, 48, 53,
    56–57, 63, 71–72, 75–76, 135,
    263–68, 271–73
childhood and adolescence of, 45,
    46, 48, 52–54, 66
critics and enemies of, 21, 22, 71,
    131, 136
deism of, 22–23, 29, 57, 67, 86,
    127, 131, 183, 190–91, 200, 239
education of, 46–47, 63
efforts to foment revolution in
    Pennsylvania by, 63
Ethan Allen and, 23–24, 32, 39,
    40–42, 195, 197, 200, 205–6, 239,
    250, 318, 431, 435
as "Forgotten Founding Father,"
    2–3, 21–22
God of Nature proclaimed by,
    138–39, 193, 239
illness and death of, 21, 22, 23,
    268, 388–89
on immortality, 250–51
liberty of conscience defended by,
    71–72
medical practice of, 21, 22, 39,
    40–41, 46, 57, 63, 203–5, 239,
    263, 268, 330, 388–89
moral theory of, 271–73
musical ability of, 63, 267
natural intelligence of, 46, 48
on natural right, 331
on peace, 359
plagiarism charged to, 142
on property and distribution of
    wealth, 359
radical gang of, 331–33, 367, 384–
    85
reading and personal library of, 23,
    25, 34, 47, 63–65, 66, 67, 86
real estate speculation of, 74–75

Young, Thomas (*continued*)
  on reason, 292
  religion rejected by, 53–57, 63, 66,
    71–72, 75, 134, 136, 203, 389
  restlessness of, 74, 76
  revolutionary leadership and
    political activism of, 17, 18–21,
    24, 26–27, 57, 63, 133–39, 183,
    203, 204, 205–6, 263–68, 367,
    371, 375–76, 383–86
  sources for, 439–41
  wife and children of, 23, 76, 266–
    67, 329–30, 389
  wounding of, 266
  writing of, 18–20, 22–24, 32, 35,
    52–53, 65, 71, 74–75, 127, 136,
    204–5, 271–73, 292, 308, 333–37,
    359

Zuckert, Michael, 146, 478, 522

11-20-2014